UMBERTO FRANZOI

PALACES AND CHURCHES
ON THE GRAND CANAL
IN VENICE

STORTI EDIZIONI

Text: Umberto Franzoi
Layout: Umberto Franzoi
Photos: Cameraphoto, Interstudio s.n.c.
Printed: March 1995

ISBN 88 - 7666 - 318-5
128 COLOUR ILLUSTRATIONS
8 BLACK AND WHITE ILLUSTRATIONS

STORTI EDIZIONI SRL
Casella Postale, 361
30170 MESTRE P.T.

Offices:
Via Tasso, 21
30170 MESTRE - VENEZIA

Via Miranese, 104
30035 LA FOSSA DI MIRANO (VE)
Tel. 045-431607 - Fax 041-432347

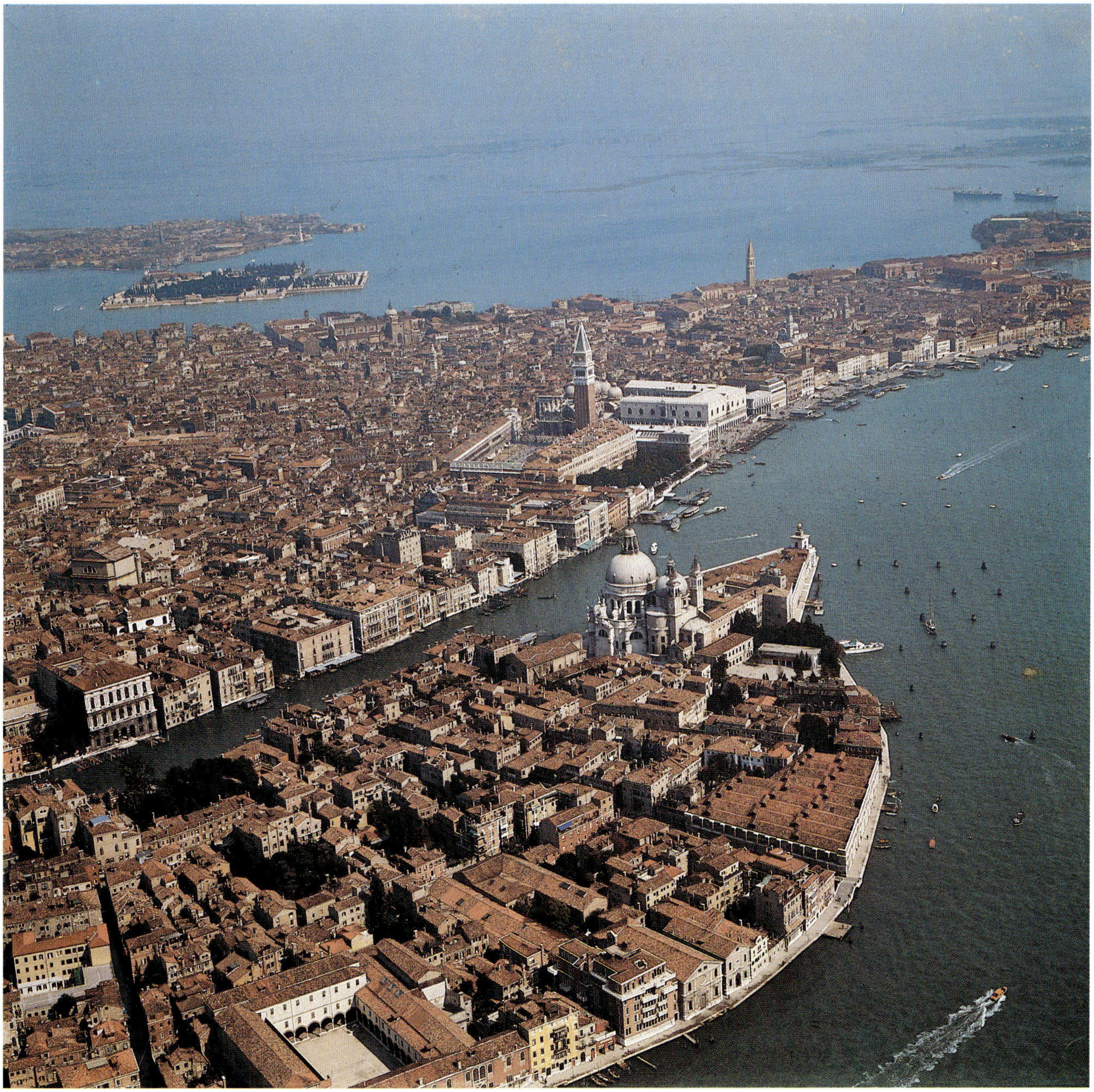

N° 1
St Mark's basin
The ancient customs house building stands on the wedge of land between the mouth of the Grand Canal, on the left, and that of the Giudecca canal, on the right. The dome of the Salute church soars above it, with the complex of St Mark's Square in the middle distance.

LEFT SIDE from no. 1 to no. 82

RIGHT SIDE from no. 1 to no. 90

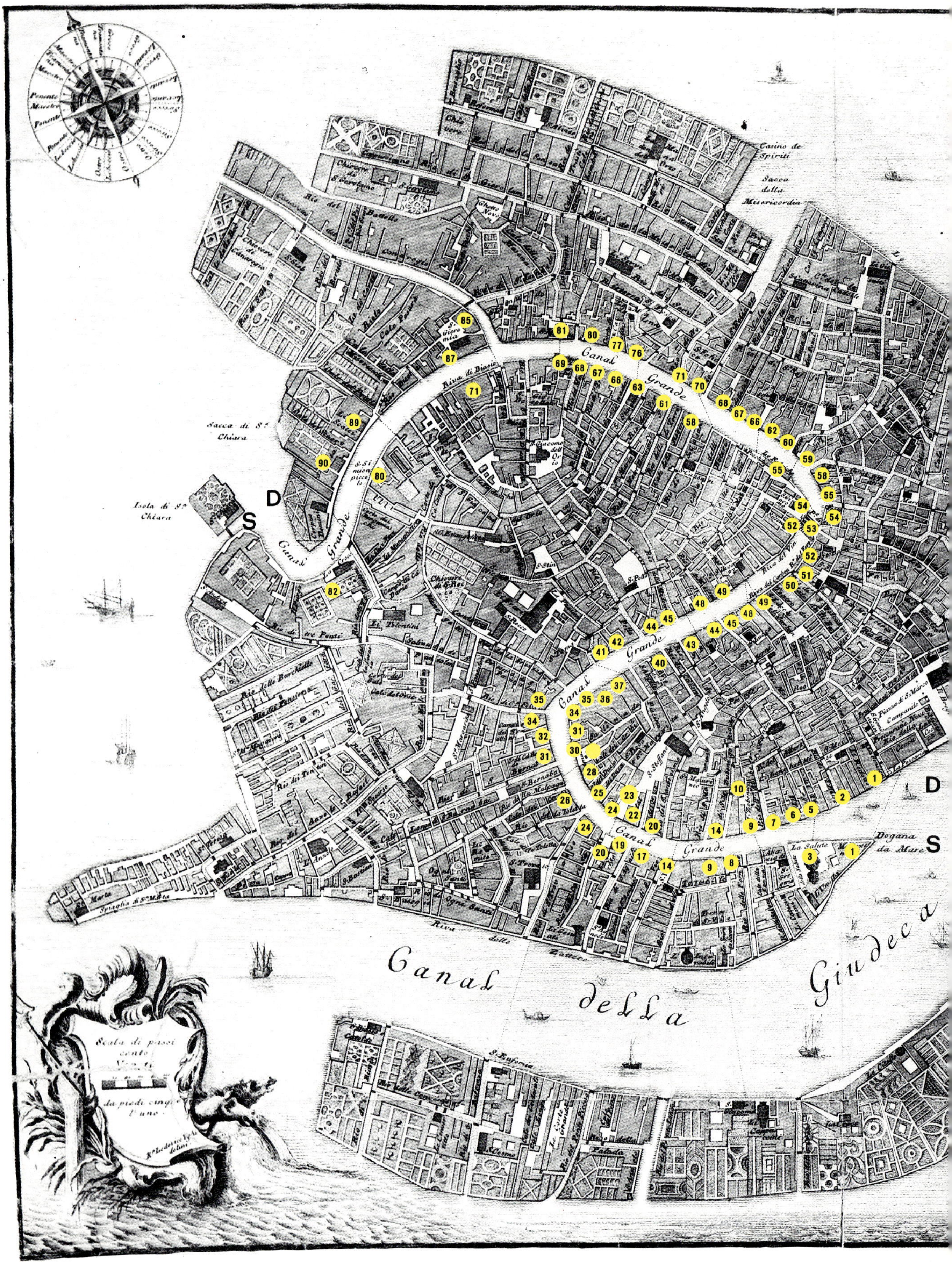

Canal Grande
Canal della Giudeca
Sacca di S.ta Chiara
Isola di S.ta Chiara
Casino de Spiriti
Sacca della Misericordia
Riva di Biasio
Dogana da Mare
La Salute
Scala di passi cento Venti da piedi cinque l'uno
D
S
D
S

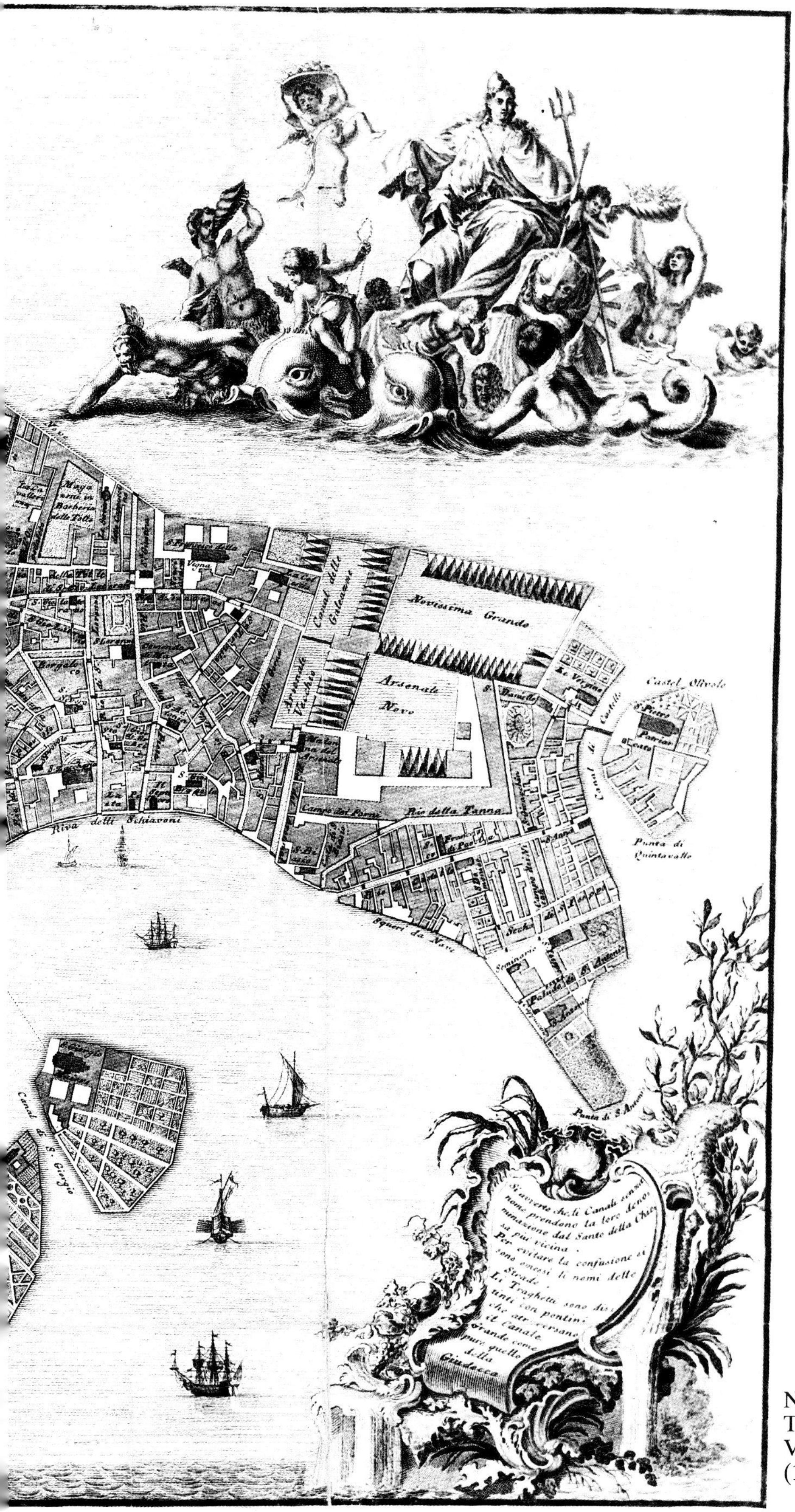

N° 2
Topographical map of the City of Venice, drawn up by Lodovico Ughi (1729).

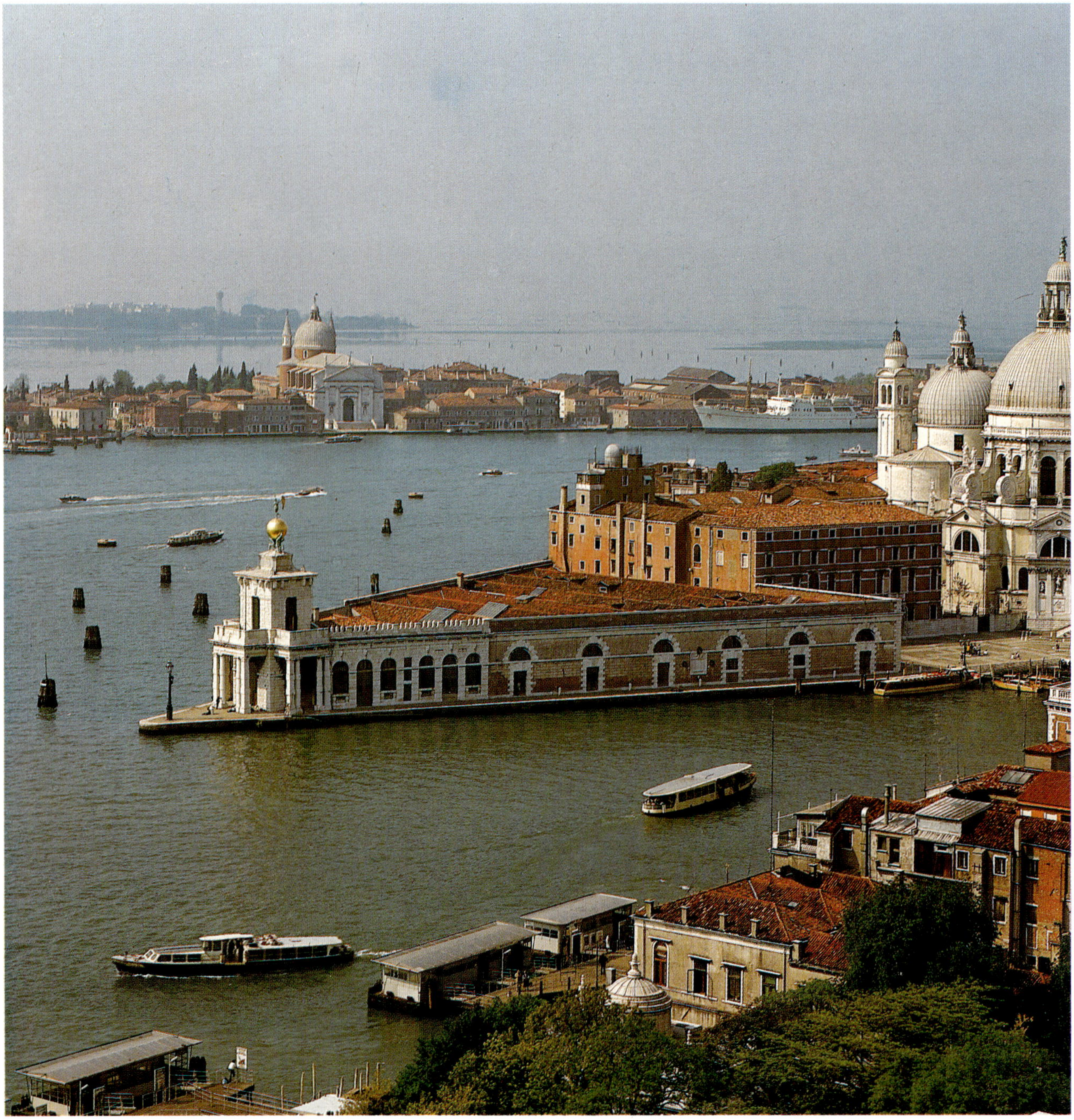

N° 3
The Punta della Dogana da Mar
In the background, beyond the Giudecca canal, the white façade of Andrea Palladio's Redentore, the votive church standing on Giudecca island.
(L. 1, page 10)

N° 4
Palazzo Giustinian
The shaft of walled-in apertures, left of centre, states the tie-up solution by means of which the interiors of two buildings intercommunicate.
(R. 1, p. 11)

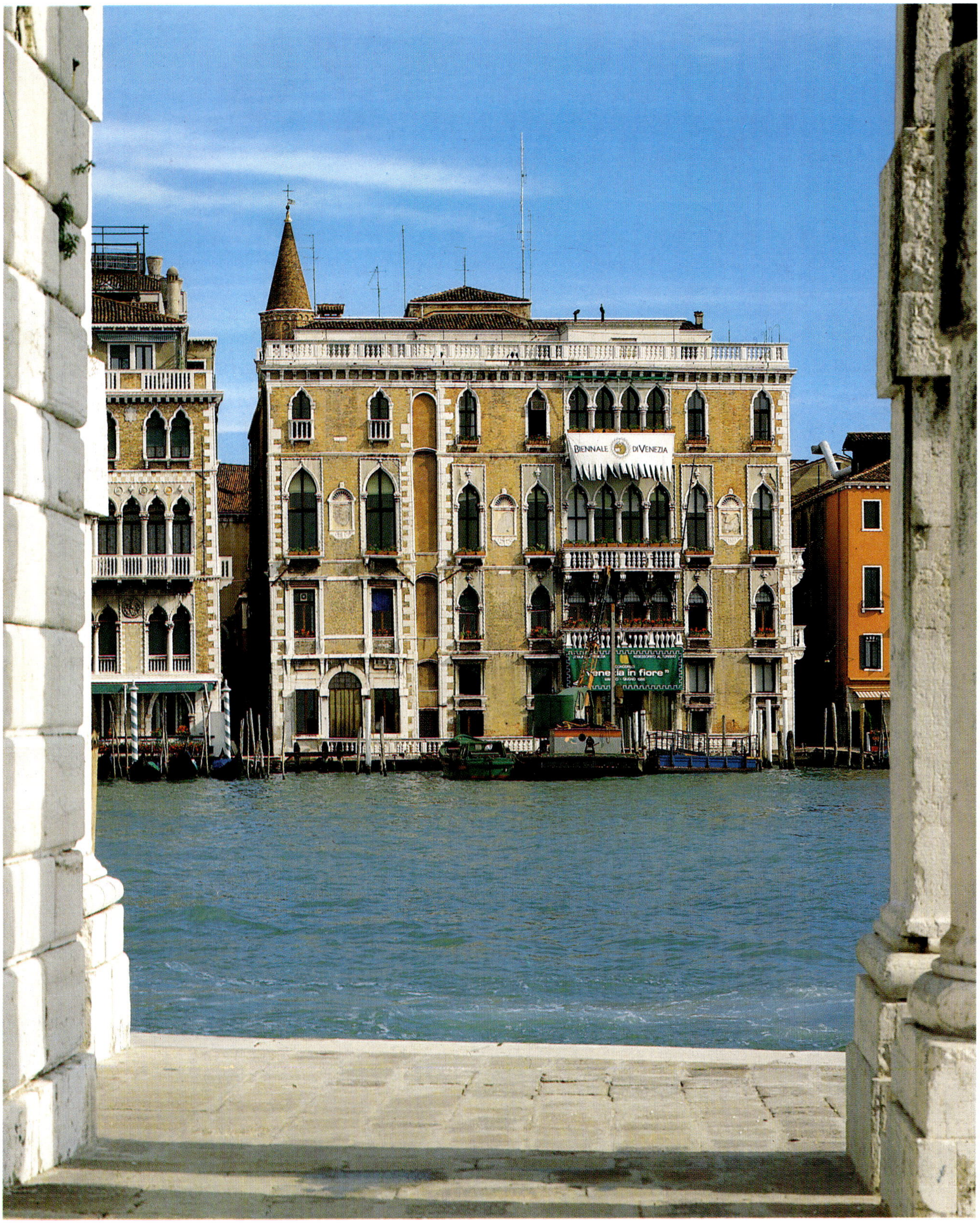
BIENNALE DI VENEZIA

L. 1
DOGANA DA MAR

It was called "da mar" (from the sea) because it was here that duty was levied on goods arriving by sea. In fact. there was also a land Customs which obviously dealt with all trade arriving or leaving via land. All goods in transit in Venice were put in the customs-sheds or they were unloaded here before being redistributed to the various shops or the Rialto market.
The first early Customs building stood at the end of the strip of land separating the Giudecca Canal from the Grand Canal, at the point where these both flow into St. Mark's Basin. It is clearly distinguishable in the foreground of the very fine city plan engraved by De' Barbari in 1500. This plan is often referred to as the only possible document which shows the exact appearance of buildings now completely destroyed. The layout of the building comprises lines of spacious, parallel rooms. They are more or less rectangular and their length gradually decreases as the triangle on which the building rests gets narrower with respect to the "fondamenta" along the sides overlooking the canal. The building's appearance was that of a construction fortified by tall battlemented walls and a tower at the vertex. It was built between 1315 and 1340 mainly to serve the salt warehouses (Punta della Dogana or "Punto del Sal").
The same functional room layout was maintained in 1677 when the Republic decided to reconstruct the old, by then decrepit building which certainly did not satisfy the artistic and formal taste of that time because of its defensive character. The work was considered to be of great importance and a public competition was announced which was entered by Cominelli, Sardi and Longhena himself as well as by Benoni (born in Trieste in 1618), an architect who was better known as a hydraulic engineer. The latter was the surprise winner, considering that better known and qualified artists had taken part. Benoni's aim was to experiment with an architectural element used to conclude the whole complex at the Basin end: the monumental tower in Istrian stone supported by a closely-spaced, strong, porticoed colonnade and surmounted by the large golden sphere which two strong Atlases support on their shoulders, together with the light, poised figure of Fortune.
The sculptures were the work of Bernardo Falcone, an artist from Lugano who came to Venice before 1659. Some of his other sculptures can still be seen in the churches of the Frari, of S. Maria di Nazareth and of the Scalzi, on the façade of the Scuola Grande di S. Teodoro, etc.
The parts of the sheds overlooking the canal, which had become unsafe and decrepit through old age and lack of upkeep, were partially modified in 1838 by Giovanni Alvise Pigezzi. He propped up the simple, bare surface with monumental portals surmounted by large, indented arches in Istrian stone, and he emphasized the building with an unbroken, rectilinear typanum, thus hiding the line of triangular roofs lying side by side.

L. 2
PATRIARCHAL SEMINARY

While the refulgent, golden Globe of Fortune on the Customs House may first draw the visitor's eye, the beauty of another building, the church of S. Maria della Salute, an architectural landmark with its spectacular play of volumes, soon commands attention.
Yet the Patriarchal Seminary, the large building preceding the church, linked to it by the perimetral wall of its spacious court, also merits consideration.
Designed by Baldassare Longhena, it was built in 1670, when the church was nearing completion, to house the Somasco order and, essentially, provide for adeguate teaching space.
With its deliberate simplicity of façade, rusticated up to the ground-floor window-sills, linked by white marble strips also on the upper storeys, the building's horizontal accent seems to offset the vertical thrust of the Salute dome. Regularity of window distribution relies on two axes, marked by the two depressed arch portals and the longer window apertures, enhanced by Istrian stone balconies on the first storey.
Within, the height of columns framing the spacious cloister and monumental central well, curbs the diameter of their ribbed arches. The great stairway is richly ornamented, with numerous statues on the balustrade and – work of the sculptor Giusto Le Court – in the niches of the precinct wall.
The ground-floor lapidarium contains cippi and ancient inscriptions from Venetia and Istria; the Manfrediniana Picture Gallery on the first floor is named for its dedicated collector, Federico Manfredini (1743-1829).

R. 1
PALAZZO GIUSTINIAN

Palazzo Giustinian is an imposing Gothic building erected in the second half of the 15th century around 1474. We find that several stone-masons were engaged in work on this building: Agostino da Bergamo, Paolo di Giacomo, Lorenzo di Alzano, Marino di Giovanni, Bartolomeo da Bergamo, and even others who also came from the area around Bergamo, traditionally rich in workers specialized in every aspect of working stone. The building has three floors as well as the ground floor and is crowned by a balustrade which also existed on the original building. The main part is flanked on the left by another building, also Gothic and an extension of the main residence. However, they are separated by a narrow passageway or rather a street, most of which is walled in order to form the internal passageway between the two buildings. The work we know was carried out at the beginning of the eighth decade of that century (1483), must refer to this extension rather than to an inexplicable restructuring-restoration of the main building erected only a short time previously.
The building's interior underwent important restructuring work in the 17th century when it became the property of the Morosini family. Further 19th century and contemporary restorations have hardened the line of the façade.
The first references to the Giustinian family living in San Moisè date back to 1310. Therefore, older Byzantine or early Gothic buildings once stood on the present-day site but in the second half of the 15th century it was decided to demolish them and rebuild. The large new building had to reflect the importance and wealth gained by the family which, according to geneologists, was supposed to descend from the Emperors Justinian and Justin II. They are said to have come from Constantinople to Venice, passing through Istria on the way and founding the city of Capodistria which was in fact called Justinopolis. The story also goes that this family would have become extinct, because all the male members were victims of the plague which broke out in the Venetian fleet, if the last remaining member Nicolò, a monk at San Nicolò, hadn't received the Pope's permission to marry the daughter of Doge Vitale II Michiel in order to continue the family. This legend has been proved untrue by notorial documents of that period which show the existence of various Giustinianis in Venice. Apart from their imperial origin and the saving of the family on the point of extinction, there can be no doubt that it was one of the most famous and long-standing Venetian noble families which belonged to the "old" group.
In particular a certain Lorenzo, born in 1381 and already Bishop of Castello, had the honour of being given the title of Patriarch of Grado and thus of uniting the two titles in the new religious figure of Patriarch of Venice, still with his See at S. Pietro di Castello. He was made a saint in recognition of his upright life and of his religious and humane acts and he was also the author of many spiritual and religious treatises. A portrait of him by M. Vecellio hangs in the Sala del Senato in the Doge's Palace. Before Palazzo Giustinian was built at San Moisè, it seems that Lorenzo Giustinian lived for a short time in the previous building during the years around 1432. He died in 1455. Lorenzo's two brothers were both eminent, educated statesmen: Bernardo, who died in 1489, was a member of the Council of Ten and in 1474 was elected Procurator of St. Mark, but he was also famous as a writer and his numerous works include an early history of Venice; Leonardo (1388-1466) is better known as a refined humanist and a scholar, the author of lyric poems in the vernacular which later formed a new, special literary genre called "justinian" or Venetian. He too was head of the Council of Ten and Procurator of St. Mark.

R. 2
PALAZZO EMO BAROZZI CORNER TREVES BONFILI

At the start of the 17th century an ancient Byzantine-Gothic building, owned in turn by the Barozzi, Corner and Emo families, was replaced by a new construction, its design attributed, not by hard fact but by tradition of "fairly ancient date", to Bartolomeo Monopola, the architect active in Venice between the end of the 16th century and the first two decades of the 17th. A volumetric presence, the palace conforms to the tripartite scheme; above ground-floor and mezzanine its façade exhibits a lofty first and second piano nobile, but no left wing. Hypothetically, the adjacent plot may not have been available for purchase as planned. The architectural fascia with the central Serliana section of the façade abuts on the left against a quite different building, minor in scale and inferior in quality.
Palazzo Emo occupies the corner site at the confluence of the Rio San Moisè and the Grand Canal. The project employs repetition of motifs to create unity of composition and accords equal exposure to both architecturally resolved flank and façade. Horizontal continuity is supplied by marble cornices for the full natural depth of the building, these dictating placement of window apertures, aligned to form a sequence of continuous vertical accents. Extensive restoration and interior structural alterations at the start of the 19th century also endowed the palace with important Neo-Classical decorations, largely the work of Sebastiano Santi (1789-1866) and Giovanni Demin (1786-1859), still preserved as significant evidence of the taste of the period.

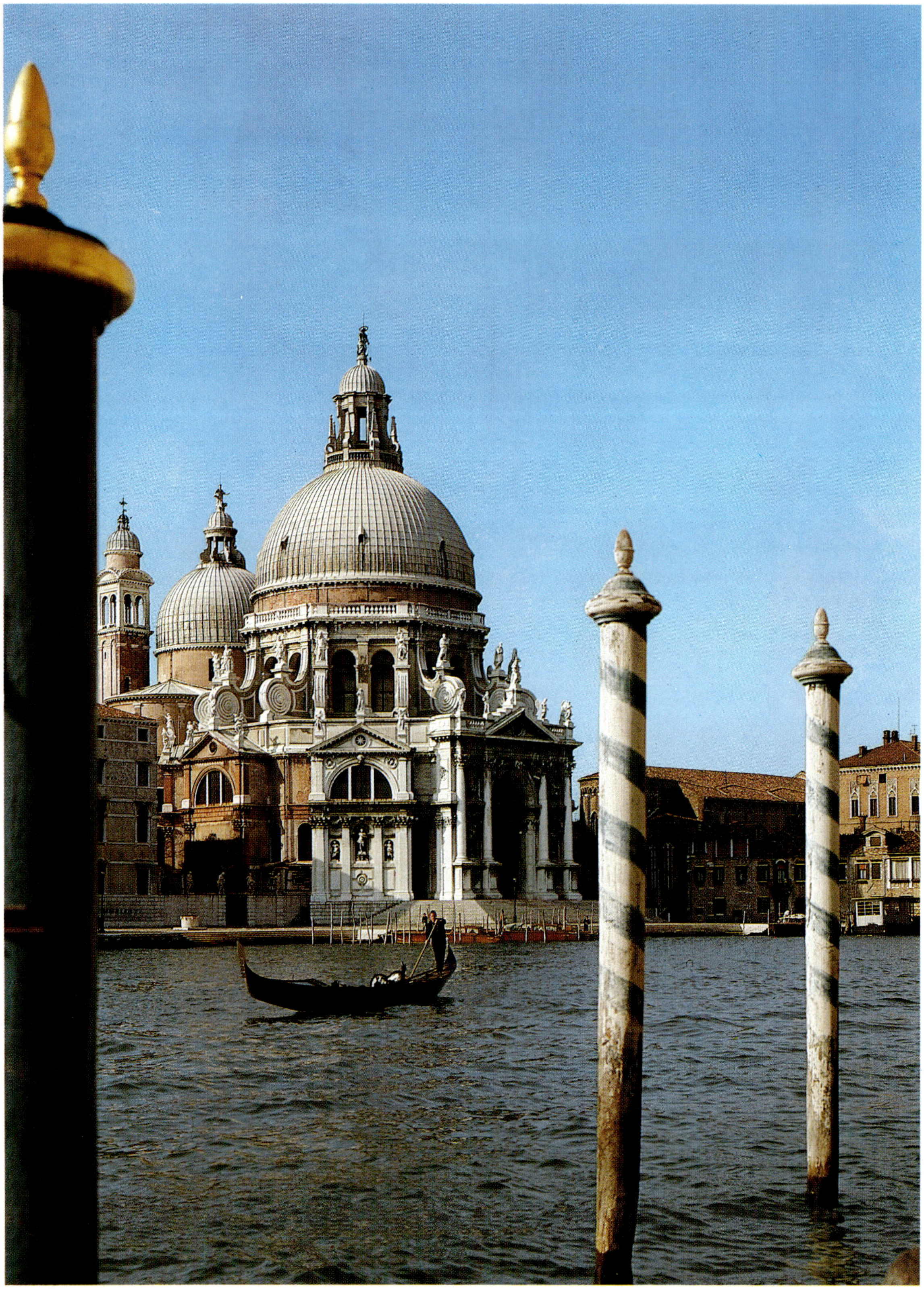

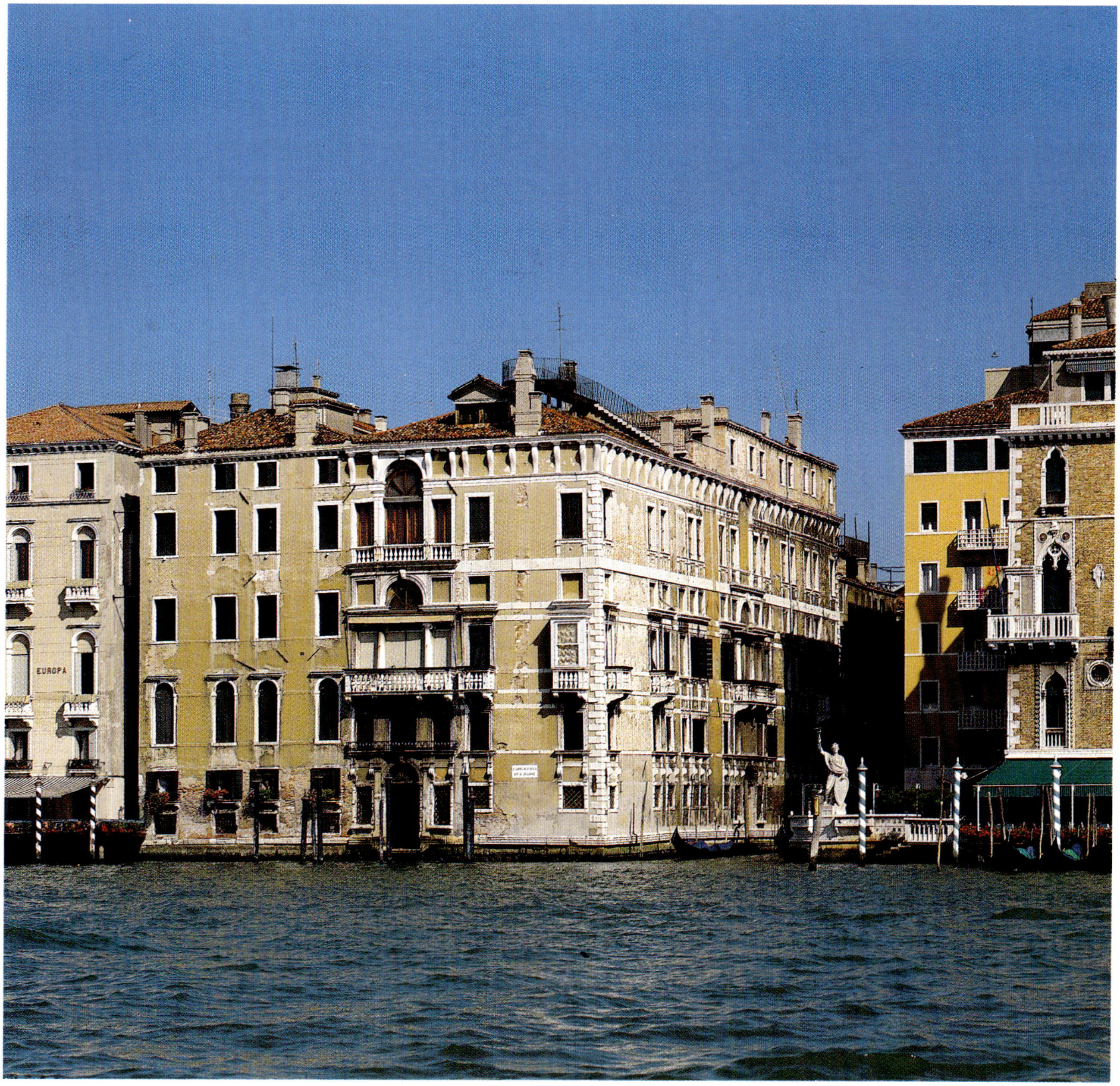

N° 5
Basilica of S. Maria della Salute, seen from St Mark's.
(L. 3, page 14)

N° 6
Palazzo Emo Treves dei Bonfili
Absence of the building's left wing clearly produces an incomplete statement.
(R. 2, page 11)

L. 3
THE SALUTE BASILICA

The Salute church is one of Venice's greatest religious constructions. However it is not only important for its urban and architectural worth; it is linked to an enormously tragic historical event, the plague which was brought to Venice by a galley from the East and which then spread all over Italy and over Europe, killing thousands and thousands of people.
This terrible plague decimated Venice's population until the latter was reduced by half. It also completely undermined the people's will and resistance.
Nowadays it is impossible to imagine and evaluate the dimensions of such a disaster in humane, psychological, material and economical terms, the terror of the people which for once saw the common people and the aristocracy on level terms, the rulers and ruled up against the impossible task of defending themselves in some way from the epidemic's raging in order to save their lives.
This is the frightful plague that Manzoni described with such accuracy and touching sensitivity in his "Promessi Sposi".
A large number of citizens, mostly nobles, fled to the country and shut themselves up in their villas thus avoiding contagion from people and things coming from other areas.
However, even if this measure seemed to be the best way of keeping the disease at bay, it often proved inadequate. Necessity or negligence would break through this hygienic barrier and the plague would attack other groups of people, thus widening its own circle of destruction.
It can be calculated that more than sixty thousand died in a city which saw nearly everything come to a standstill: all business and trade stopped, even political activity was reduced and likewise the number of meetings which very few attended either through death or because they voluntarily renounced going or because they were absent from the city.
We know the number of dead in one single day, on November 9: 595 people tragically died either alone or abandoned by all, between the walls of their then empty rooms or under the open sky of the lazarettos. In that same month more than 15,000 Venetians lost their lives.
The meetings of the Great Council, which were still held despite everything, where declared valid even if there was not a quorum of two hundred people. Another fact: the epidemic broke out at the beginning of June 1630 and spread with such virulence that it killed a quarter of the Venetian population in the first six months.
On October 22 a solemn ceremony in St. Mark's Basilica brought together the few nobles left in the city and the common people who were at the end of their strength through fear and the increasingly greater difficulty of finding food. Doge Nicolò Contarini made the solemn vow, already agreed on by the Senate, to build a church and to dedicate it to the Madonna in order to bring about an and to the terrible plague. In thanksgiving for the merciful help given to the people of Venice, the Doge, all the nobles and the entire population would go in devout pilgrimage to the church each year on the anniversary to lift up and renew their initial, dramatic and fervent vow.
However, after the winter when it seemed that the epidemic was abating, the beginning of spring 1631 saw it resume stronger than ever. The laying of the first stone of the new Basilica was postponed from March until April "because we are hoping that the Doge will recover from the plague which has also struck him down". But on April 2 Nicolò Contarini was already dead and buried. The plague continued to be rampant throughout the summer and autumn, increasingly worsening the general conditions of the city which had already been going through a period of serious difficulties, culminating in the downfall of Valeggio, before the plague started. Eleven designs were submitted for the building of this temple. The winning design was Baldassare Longhena's whose originality and magnificence made it superior to all the others. The building work lasted 50 years and the church was consecrated in 1687, after Longhena's death.
The building which stands at the top of a flight of steps, is devised on a centralized, octagonal plan and is covered by a mighty dome. The exterior is characterized by imposing, spiral counterforts called "orecchioni". The portal on the main façade has a pediment surmounted by statues which also adorn the intercolumns.
Still keeping to the octagonal plan, the exterior is divided by arches supported by grouped columns on which the cornice and the tambour of the dome run. The presbytery opens up opposite the main doorway and contains the high altar. On the latter stands the venerated image of the Greek-Byzantine Madonna which Francesco Morosini brought from Candia in 1672. The picture painted by Titian in 1512 depicting St. Mark among the Saints, is kept in the main vestry.

R. 3
PALAZZO TIEPOLO

Once owned by a branch of the Tiepolo family but today the Europa Hotel, this 17th century building post-dates Palazzo Emo by a few decades. As we see it today, the triple apertures of both piano nobile halls, together with the entrance portal, appear displaced to the left in respect of the original unabridged project in which they coincided with the central axis of the façade; absence of the left wing makes this another incomplete architectural statement. Over the centuries the inroads of time must have pulverized the series of neighbouring buildings clearly delineated in de' Barbari's 16th century townplan because at the start of the 19th century only a few, very mundane structures stand on this area, almost all of them – to judge by Quadri's image (1828) – empty or decaying, yet perhaps the ruins of the ancient and splendid Byzantine and Gothic palaces.
Tradition has it that a chain barrier would be stretched across the Grand Canal at the level of the Calle del Traghetto – a device forming part of the very ancient Venetian defence system against eventual pirate incursions way back in the 10th century.

R. 4
PALAZZO MICHELI GIUSTINIAN ALVISI

The name Micheli attaches to the 17th century house once belonging perhaps to the Giustinian family, owners in this parish of numerous plots and houses, most notable among them the great Gothic palace seen earlier. The family is also known to have owned the local theatre, where, to music by the illustrious Claudio Monteverdi, Ottavio Rinuccini's opera Arianna received its first performance in 1640.
Salient feature of the house is the central Serliana expressing the piano nobile hall on the façade, with a single side-window tied in by an important double string-course.

R. 5
PALAZZO CONTARINI

Adjacent to the Micheli house stands Palazzo Contarini, to the rear of which, also in this case, indication of local property ownership is supplied by loan of the family name to neighbouring sottoportico, calli and corte, where a coat of arms is visible, set into a wall. Moreover, Tassini reports existence of a 1502 legislation to clear the Corte Contarina of prostitutes.
The building, a Gothic construction dating from the second half of the 15th century, has a perfectly symmetrical façade with a second piano nobile, but the ground-floor portal is not of the period.
Arslan notes the "particularly harmonious distribution" of the building, "almost Renaissance in spirit" adding that he senses it to be, at the same time" not remote in spirit from the Cà Foscari".
In comparison with the doges' residence the scale is certainly minor, with less variety and quality of architectural detail; there is, for example, no quatrefoil. The four-light section on the Grand Canal is repeated on the rear frontage, but only on the first storey.

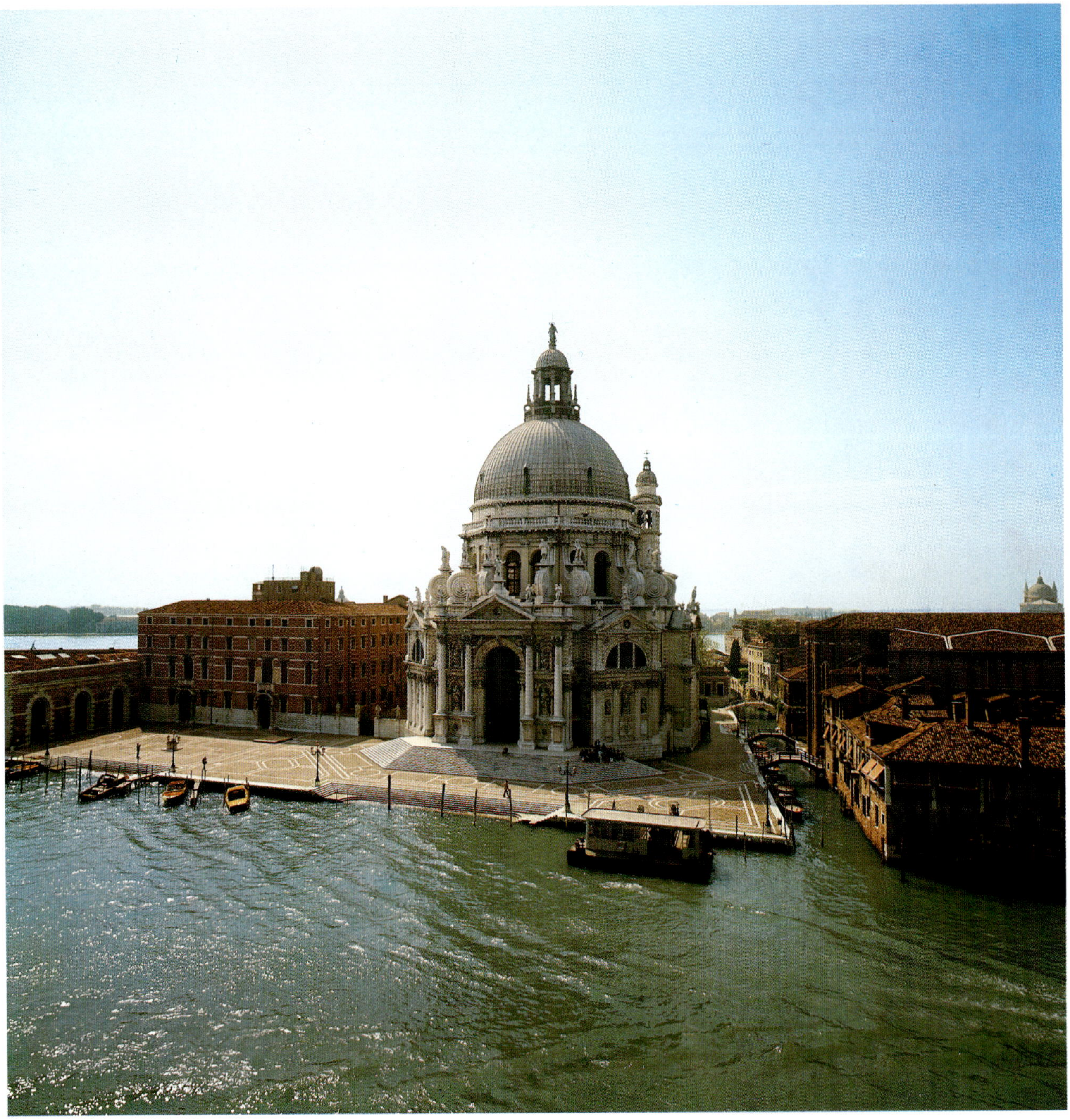

N° 7
Basilica of the Salute
The innovation for Venice of this architectural-urbanistic statement is strikingly evident.
(L. 3, page 14)

N° 8
From Jacopo de' Barbari's town-plan: the Maritime Customs House backed by the ancient Trinità church, demolished to further construction of the Salute votive temple.

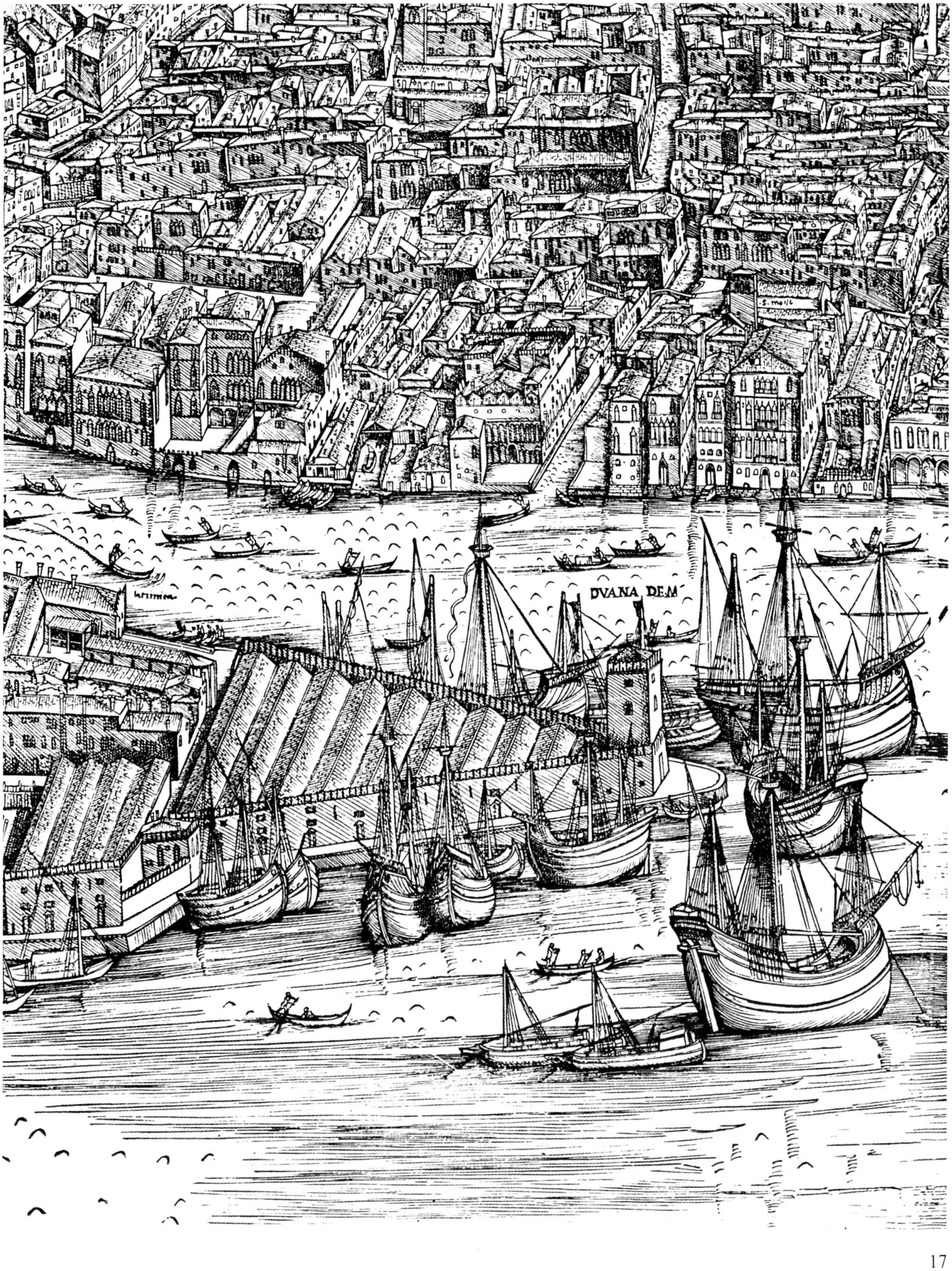
DVANA DE M

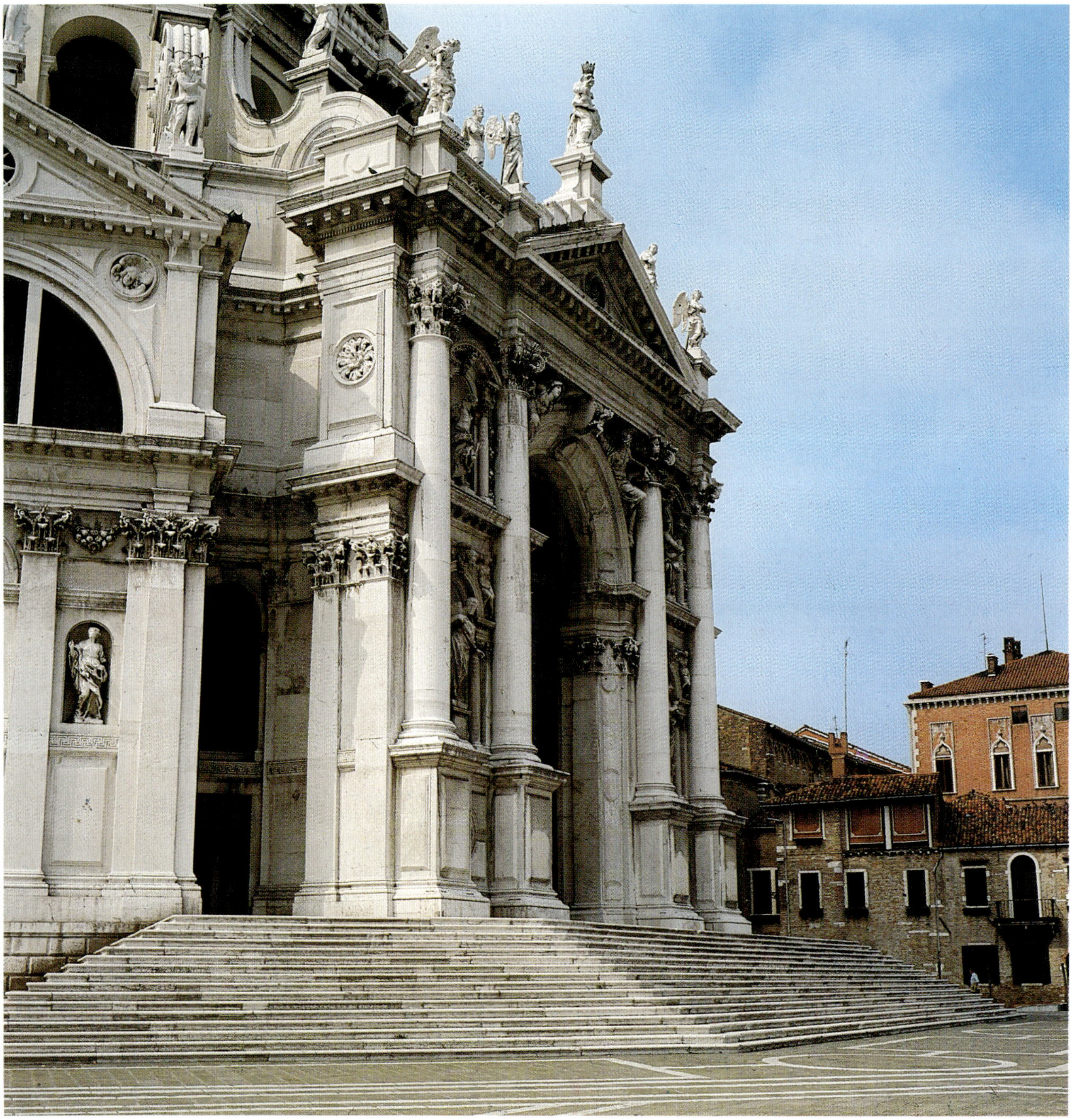

N° 9
Basilica of the Salute
The Great Doorway, entrance on the main façade.
(L. 3, page 14)

N° 10
Palazzo Contarini Fasan
Better known as the House of Desdemona. The balconies with their elaborate wheel motifs are of great architectural interest.
(R. 6, page 21)

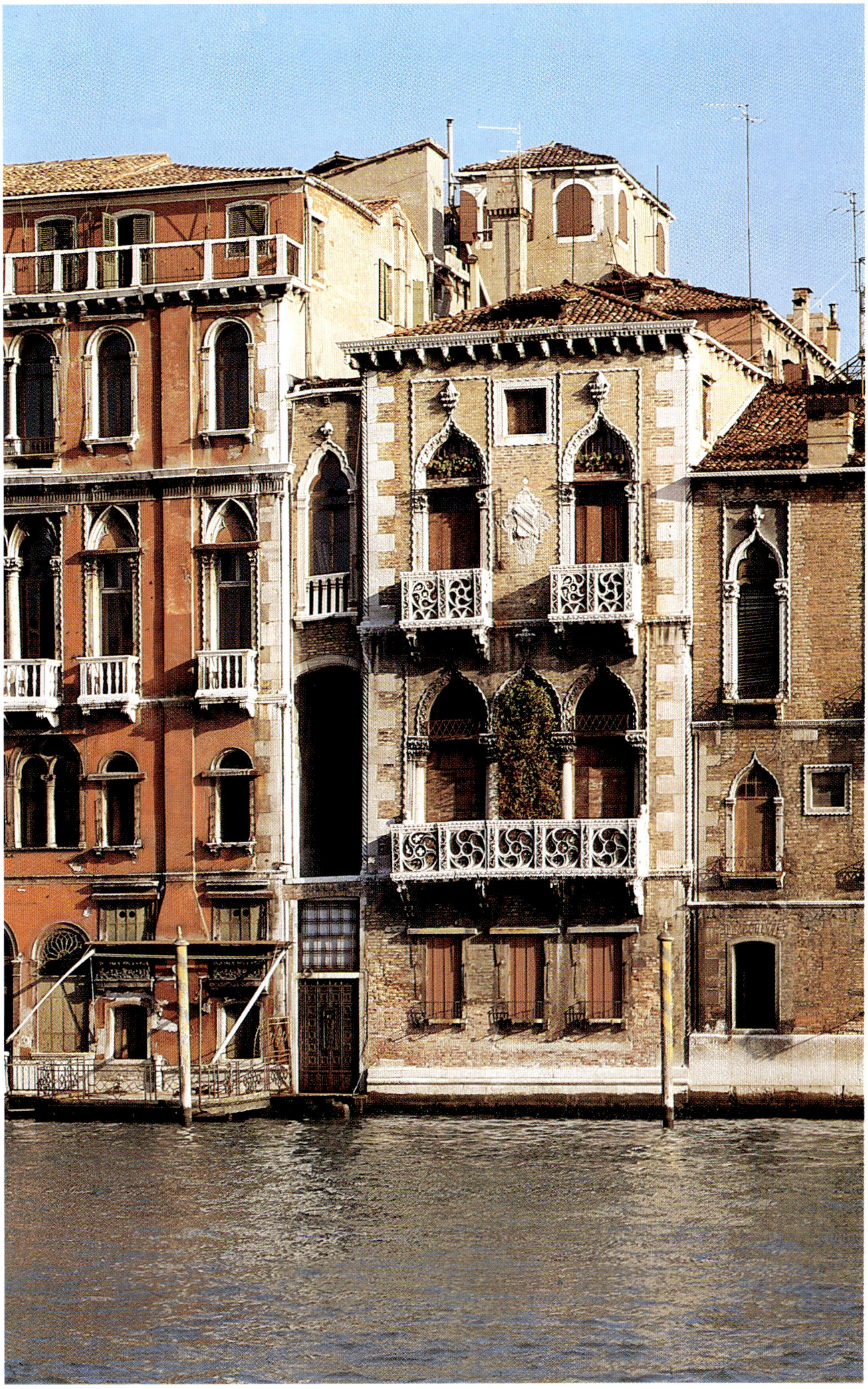

L. 4
ABBEY OF SAN GREGORIO

Changed political and territorial circumstances in the first half of the 13th century forced a group of Benedictine monks to leave S. Ilario, their mainland residence, for Venice and the ancient monastery of St. Gregory on the corner of Rio della Salute.

The monastery had always stood on the Grand Canal bank but its church, then Byzantine in style, lay to the rear, on an east-west axis.

The ancient buildings were subsequently demolished and, from the 14th century, the entire complex was rebuilt. Visible from the Grand Canal, the church apse, completed in c. 1461, has the typical twin-light Gothic windows with marble mullions and quatrefoils; a sequence of interlaced blind arches in fired brick runs below the eaves. Its façade, hidden from the Grand Canal, still features two great side windows, on two orders, with marble mullions. Insensitive intervention on its upper reaches, once similar to S. Maria della Carità, has reduced the three cusped ends with finials of marble foliage to a simple pitched roof.

At the end of the 19th century, unfortunate partial demolition of the monastery destroyed continuity of frontage between Rio della Salute and Calle del Traghetto. What survives is the part corresponding to the first cloister, its original 14th century Gothic forms with the architraved portico columns still intact. In 1775, the Republic abolished the title of Abbey and St. Gregory's became a parish church. In 1805 it was closed and the convent suppressed. Today, Monuments and Fine Arts uses it as a restoration centre.

L. 5
CASA GENOVESE

In 1892 the second Gothic cloister of the monastery of St Gregory was demolished to make room for this Neo-Gothic building by the architect Tricomi-Mattei, one of the most ill-advised townscaping interventions in Venice: a clear demonstration of 19th century indifference even to landmarks in the architectural heritage that allowed ancient buildings, whatever their artistic and historical importance, to be destroyed and replaced by structures devoid of originality, flaunting volumes so inflated as to obscure neighbouring fabric, in this specific case the church of S. Maria della Salute.

L. 6
PALAZZO ORIO SEMITECOLO

Notwithstanding the changes and structural alterations it has undergone, Palazzo Orio, later Semitecolo, still preserves original character and detail, notably the Gothic multi-light section and lateral single light, features of the façade that point to a second-half of the 14th century dating. In reality, the multi-light section – ostensibly a sequence of six light – consists of four lights linked by pilasters to the lateral single lights "in this way creating a measure of symmetry".

The canal entrance portal is also an original structure, while the practice of laying the upper string-course in contact with the apex of the reverse-curve arch further confirms the 14th century dating.

Although the name Orio has been made to derive by linguistic descent from "lupo" (wolf), a second interpretation by which it becomes a corruption of "del rio", seems more convincing by virtue of the mnemonic link between ancient family name and the fact of its property flanking the canal ("rio").

R. 6
PALAZZO CONTARINI FASAN

This building is one of the smaller palaces which overlook the Grand Canal but this fact certainly does not make it any the less notable then the others; the very ornate, late Gothic façade catches the observer's eye because of the richness of the decorations, especially of the balconies on the piano nobile with their circular motifs.
The building can be said to date from the second half of the 15th century, around 1470-1480: a florid Gothic full of imagination both in the general design and in the originality of the decorative architectural elements. Everything has been treated with the same elegance and delicacy as a piece of furniture but using inlaid marble instead of inlaid wood. Along the two edges of the façade, the Istrian stone ashlars with their indented design, forcefully finish the wall at the sides, while the wheel motif breaks up the severity of the edges as well as adding a further architectural motif.
The great three-mullioned window of the reception room on the first floor and the two lateral one-mullioned windows on the second floor are contained within this façade space.
All the windows are adorned by their original balconies. The one on the first floor goes right across the façade with the marble wheel motif repeating itself five times. This motif is also echoed in the balconies on the upper floor but on a reduced scale and resting on a second, curvilinear marble element.
"In Ramo Secondo Corte Contarina", the Contarini arms can be seen and it can be read in the chronicles that, since the 14th century, a certain Marin Contarini, the son of Nicolò, has been living in San Moisè", and again in Tassini "A law passed in 1502 prohibited prostitutes from entering Corte Contarina".
"Fasan", deriving from "fagiano" (pheasant), is the nickname given to one member of the Contarini family, the owner of this house, because of his great passion for shooting this bird.
This palace's fame comes from the legend according to which it was supposed to be the house of the beautiful Desdemona, Othello's innocent victim. They were the two tragic characters in the well-known play by Shakespeare.
It has not been possible to find out exactly why someone in the past pointed out this building as "Desdemona's home".

R. 7
PALAZZO MANOLESSO FERRO

A second-half of the 15th century dating for the building may be deduced from the first piano nobile on which the vertices of the simple trefoil arches on the central four-light section and flanking lights make contact with their tight denticular framing. This compositional device is redolent of methodologies and buildings as early even as the 14th century but the clearly Renaissance frieze, the unmistakably Late-Gothic succulent foliation on the capitals, and the twin colonnettes on the balconies confirm the building's second-half of the 15th century origin.
The first-storey mezzanine and the second storey exhibit fully-mature Renaissance idioms: echoes of Codussi in the window solution of broad arch span above the bifora with the oeil-de-boeuf space-filling device beneath the intrados; the round arch on the four-light section and flanking single light of the upper storey.
The terraced attic storey is a 19th addition. A calle separates this building from its neighbour but an overhead passageway featuring a balustraded Gothic window points to shared use of the two buildings.
Despite remodelling, the internal frontage of the palace also preserves many original Gothic features such as a four-light section, pateras, columns, pillars and single lights, all coeval with those on the façade.
The palace today, together with its neighbour, houses the main offices of the Regione Veneto.

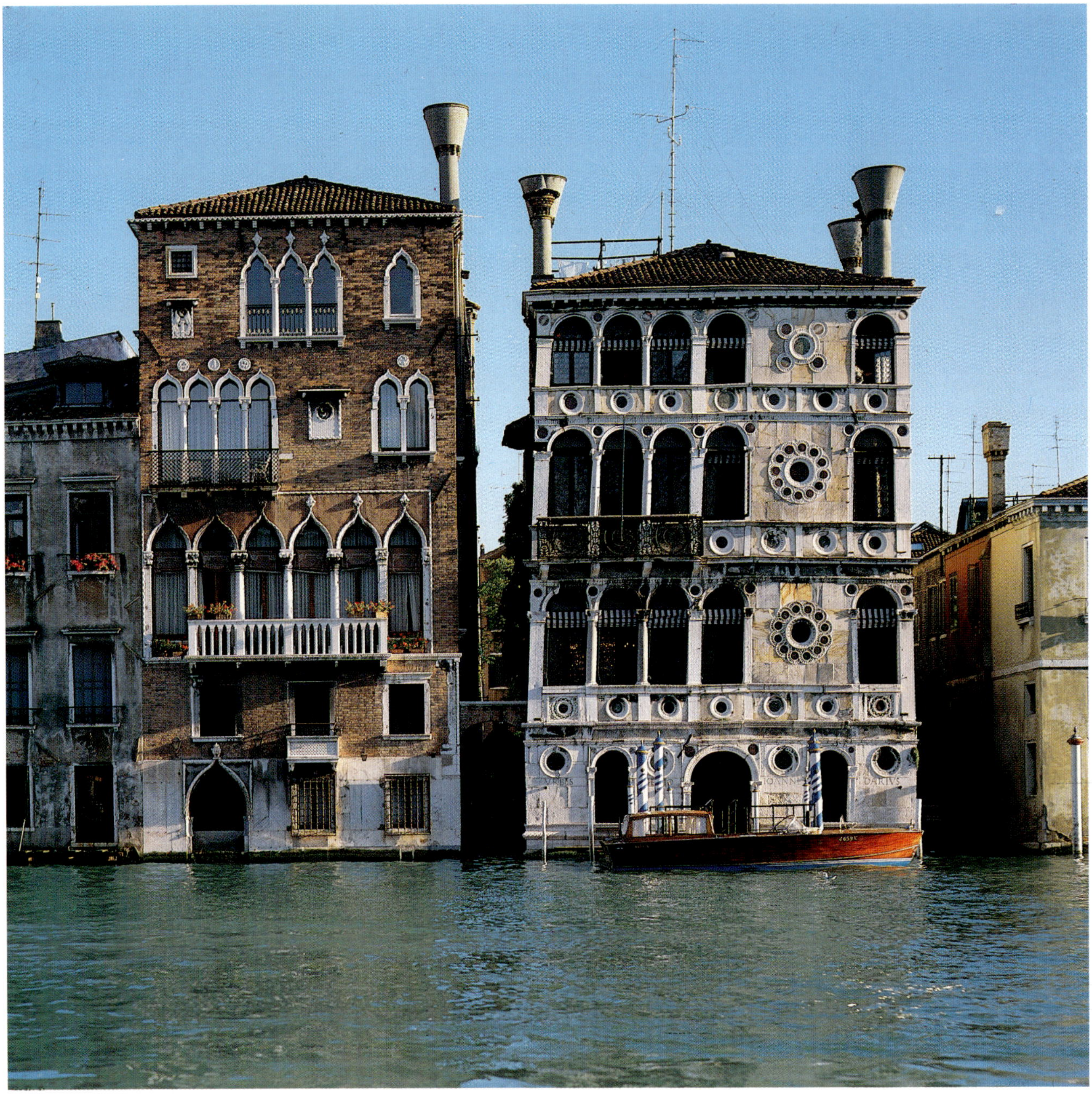

N° 11
Palazzo Dario
The façade with its polychrome inlay-work is a Renaissance contribution to the original Gothic building.
(L. 8, page 24)

N° 12
Palazzo Contarini Fasan
Detail of the façade illustrating balcony wheel-motifs.
(R. 6, page 21)

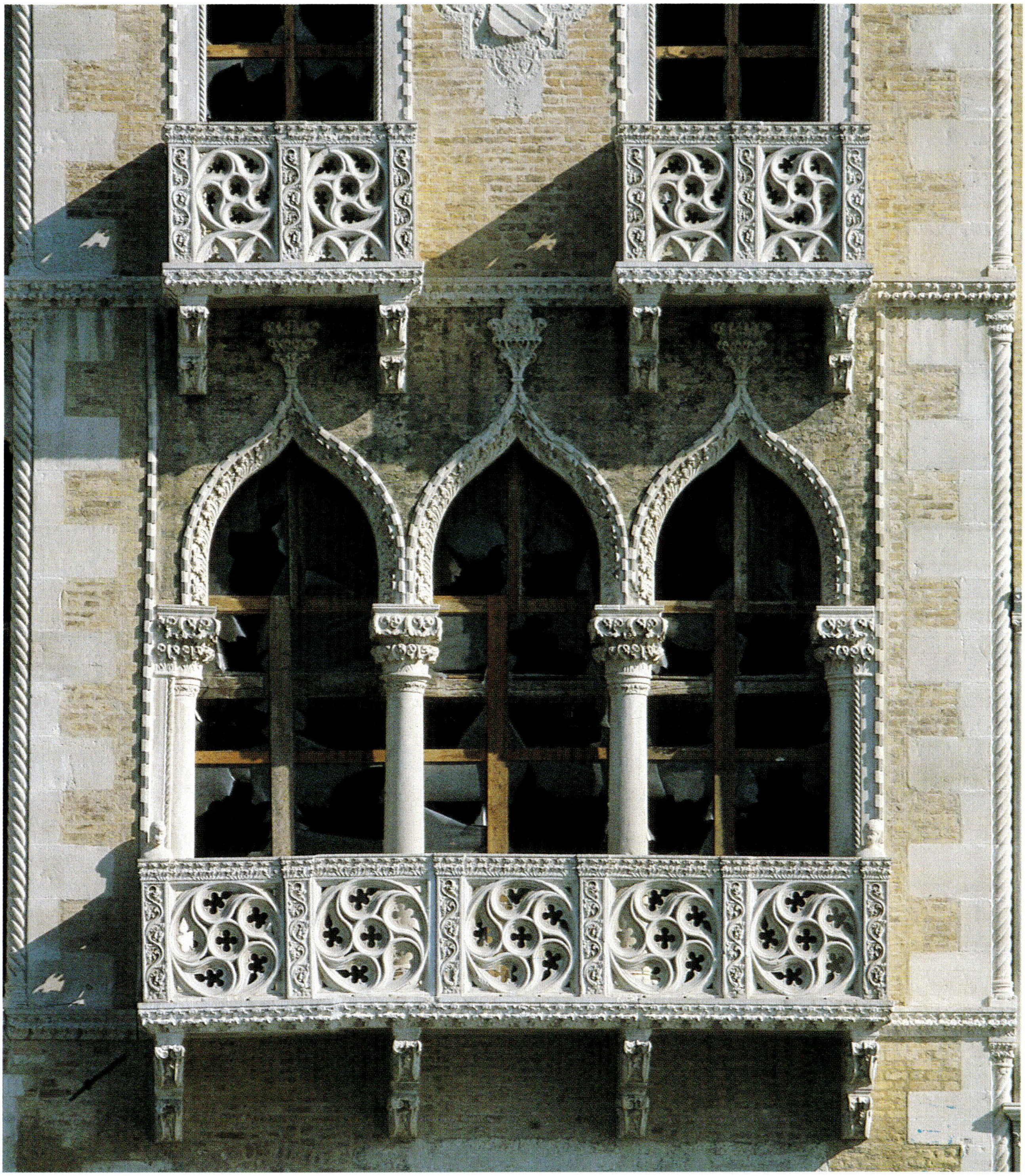

L. 7
PALAZZO BARBARO

Rio della Fornace was so-called for the presence on this site of a stone or brick kiln. Laws passed by the Republic established the size of bricks, blocks and tiles, and the time necessary for working clay which would take place in summer while baking would be done in winter.
Palazzo Barbaro rises beyond a small 18th century house, separated by a narrow lane from Palazzo Dario. This building, of modest dimensions like the previous one, was partially rebuilt and perhaps enlarged in relation to the original 15th century Gothic construction to which undoubtedly belongs the beautiful six-mullioned window on the first piano nobile. It repeats the design of the central four-mullioned columned window and the two one-mullioned side ones which follow in order but are differentiated by pilasters. The balcony communicates with the central windows while the dentil-cornice tightly encloses the whole which rests on a narrow string course.
The windows of the second floor (four-mullioned with two-mullioned balcony) of the Byzantine type with raised pointed arches on pilasters seem to be much older, but the general disarray of these windows to which are added those on the third floor (three-mullioned and one-mullioned) cut into the wall in trilobate arches with fleurons atop do not permit clear reading and lead one to suspect later modifications.
Of the ground floor and mezzanine only the square portal on the canal remains of the original building.

L. 8
PALAZZO DARIO

Palazzo Dario is the typical example of intervention on an existing building, in this particular case to modernise a Grand Canal façade, for which the new design wholly replaces its predecessor.
As architectural elements on the fronts overlooking the Rio delle Torreselle and the garden at the rear clearly denote, this is in fact a Gothic building of the 14th or, at most, of the early 15th century.
The main front, retaining its original proportions and spatial divisions, the play of solid against void of wall surfaces and window apertures, was conceived by Pietro Lombardo, working in the new Renaissance style. His vocabulary makes a feature of the sumptuous polychrome display of precious marbles, in fascias, string-course and corner roundels, to define and enhance vertical and horizontal spaces, window surrounds and balconies, etc., seemingly intent on depriving the building of structural meaning by transforming an architectural statement into a pictorial one.
Founder of a family of builders and architects all actively employed in the city on works of great beauty and originality, significant works for the history of Venetian architecture of their time, Pietro Lombardo commenced work on remodelling the Palazzo Dario façade when the building became the property of Giovanni Dario, the Republic's representative in Constantinople, in 1479, the year in which Dario's intercession in bringing about a peace treaty with the Turks had brought him the reward of lands in Noventa Padovana and a sum in gold.
The building, modest in scale, makes a compact, self-contained statement, prolonging the curtain of building fabric on the one side, flanked by the rio on the other. Claiming attention for the elegance of its design and the colouristic impact of its marble revetment, as an artistic and architectural achievement Palazzo Dario is a crucial presence on this first stretch of the Grand Canal.
The façade shows evident signs of early subsidence, probably due to an initial phase in adjustment to what are still, as has been noted earlier, the original foundations and external walls of Gothic times. Its impaired verticality – showing a pronounced tilt at the sides, with a number of structural elements well out of plumb especially on the left – is fortunately a phenomenon long ago halted and definitively stabilized by a series of restoration interventions.
The tree-lined campiello at the rear of the palace is extremely picturesque, the rio sweeping round to skirt one side of it before issuing into the Grand Canal. A high bridge with flaring access ramps lends another characteristic touch to the urban scene, while alternate use of brick and beaten earth in floorscaping, together with the boundary wall of the garden, further contribute to definition of the environment.

R. 8
PALAZZO FLANGINI FINI

A 1703 print from Carlevarijs's collection on Venetian palaces attributes the design and building of the Flangini residence, as well as of the landward façade of Palazzo Labia at San Geremia, to the architect Alessandro Tremignon. Many art and architecture scholars have expressed this opinion but we must consider the fact that in 1640, that is to say the year in which we can be sure that the ex-Contarini palace was completely restored, Tremignon could not possibly have been the designer and builder since he was born in 1635. From this comes the conviction that the design can be attributed to the architect Pietro Bettinelli. His name appears from 1628 onwards in the Flangini family's papers as being the foreman, and it appears again in 1645 when he is urged to make the final payments to a labourer who had been engaged in work on the house.
Tommaso Flangini, the son of Tommaso Apostolo da Corfù, was born in Venice in 1579 and became rich and famous as public prosecutor. In 1638 he bought the San Moisè palace on the Grand Canal, where he had lived as a tenant since 1620, from Giambattista Contarini. This Gothic building was by then decrepit and in need of extensive restoration which was paid for in part by the rent which Flangini had paid in advance to Contarini. Finally, when he also became the owner of the adjoining building on the right, Tommaso decided to completely restore the building. The size and spaciousness of the new building made it become far more important than the pre-existing building which De Barbari had portrayed so well.
The reconstruction took from 1638, the year the building was bought, to 1640. In little more than two years the Grand Canal saw a new, different palace rise up with surprising speed: "The Contarini house was demolished and then rebuilt and the testator declares that fifty thousand ducats were spent on it". November 30 1640 is the date on the new will in which Tommaso Flangini writes: "... and to my daughter Marietina I leave my new house which cost me so much money, effort, hard work and expenditure, together with the house next to it, Cà da Ponte, which became part of the former after I bought it".
After Tommaso's death and the death of his daughter, the latter's husband Benedetto Soranzo rented the house to the Fini family. This family too came from Cyprus and, in the same way as the Flangini family had done, they bought the building after about ten years as tenants.
The design of the façade is simple and linear. On it we can note the decorative elements of the heads on the window keystones whose shadow emphasizes the marble facings of the extrados.
Another interesting point is that the traditional planimetry of the central and side rooms is only partially respected here: starting from the canal we find two one-mullioned windows followed by the three-mullioned window of the portico, then another two one-mullioned windows and at the end an exact repetition of the three-mullioned window which means a central reception room with portico on the upper floors and a second canal entrance on the ground floor. The balconies of the three-mullioned windows, either joined to those of the one-mullioned windows or separated by varied spaces, create a modular movement of openings and wall while the facings above the arch forcefully block any remaining architectural motif and other wall spaces with the strips of Istrian stone inserted into the plaster.

R. 9
PALAZZO PISANI GRITTI

This building can be said to date from the middle of the 15th century but the simplicity of certain design ideas and of the ornaments, in particular the use of simple trefoil arches on the first floor windows, makes us put forward the construction date by some decades. However, if these are 14th century features, then others, such as the corner columns at the edges of the building, belong to the 15th century.
The restorations carried out at various times have harshened the building's layout and structure and made them far from clear. In the 16th century the wide spaces on the façade overlooking the Grand Canal were decorated with frescoes later attributed to Veronese (and now completely lost). The façade overlooking the square was completely restructured between the 16th and 17th century; at the end of the 18th century the interior decorations were entirely redone by Borsato and Landi. Today the building is one of the best known and most comfortable hotels in the city.
To the main branch of the Gritti family belonged the Doge Andrea, elected in 1523 and whose palace may be seen in the San Francesco della Vigna parish.
It was Gritti himself who ordered this palace built in 1525. Later it was acquired by the Republic and donated to Pope Sixtus V who made it a residence for his ambassadors.

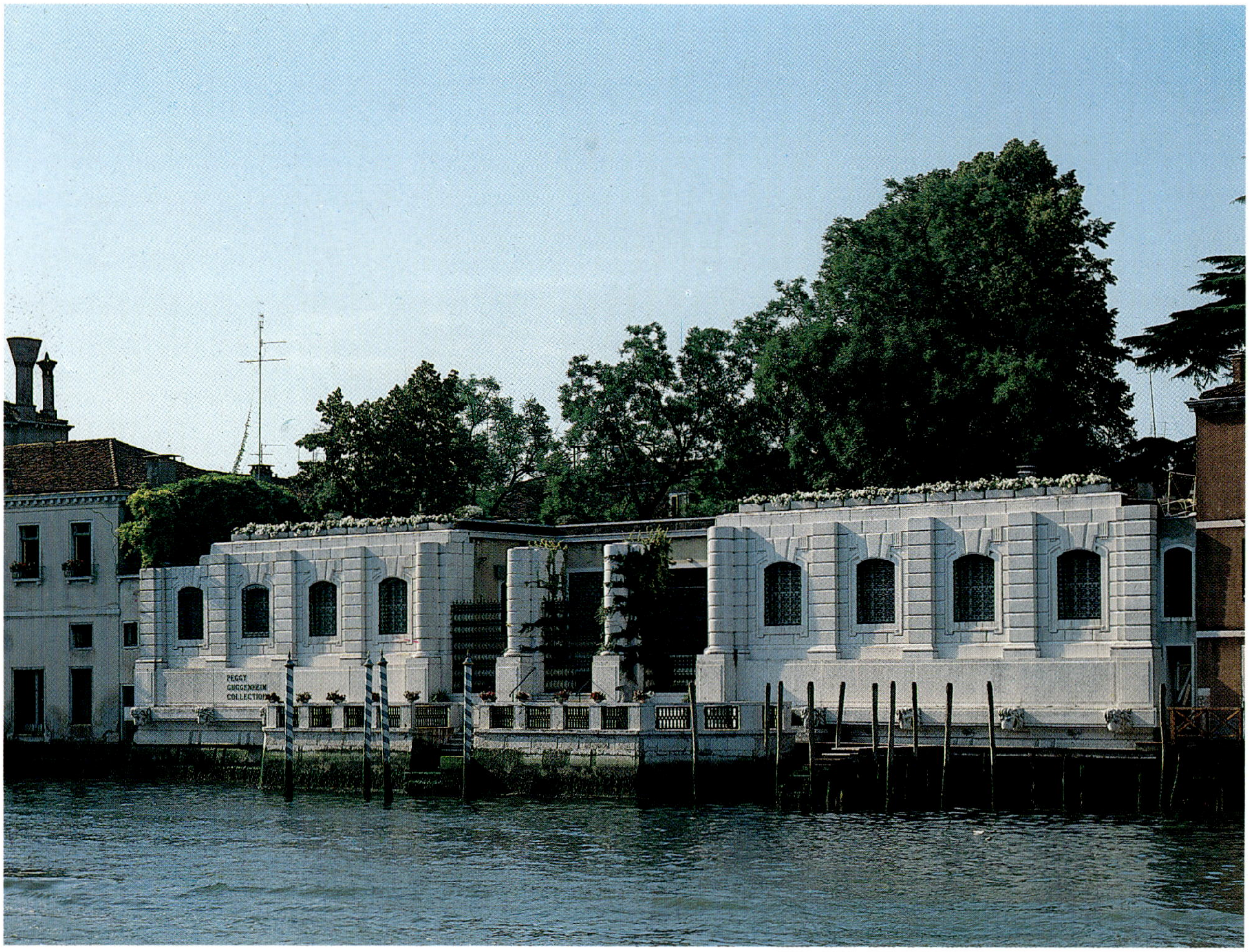

N° 13
Palazzo Venier dei Leoni
The ground floor of the palace, all that was built, today housing the important Guggenheim Museum of Contemporary Art.
(L. 9, page 28)

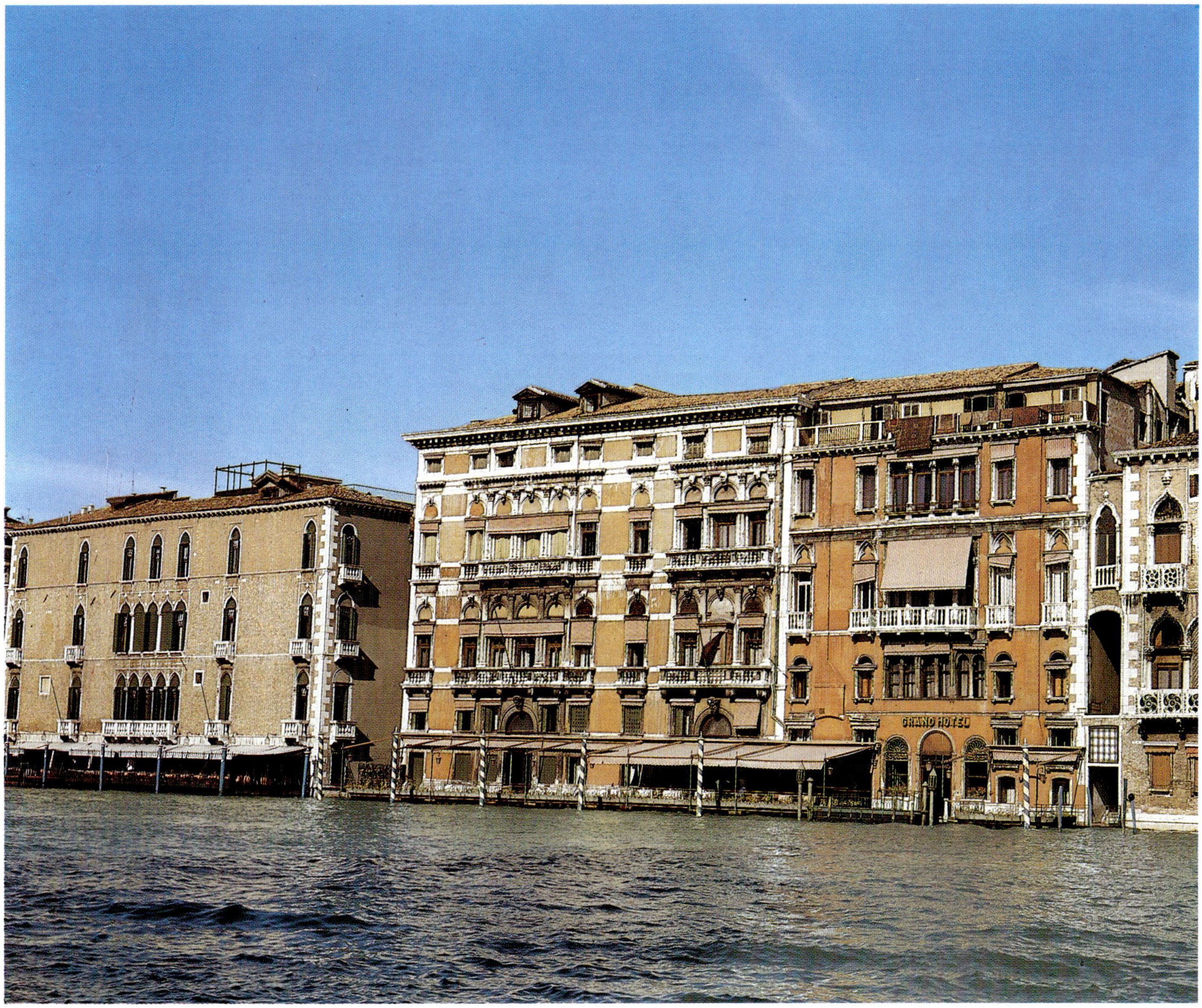

N° 14
From right to left, adjoining palaces: Manolesso Ferro (R. 7, page 21), Flangini Fini (R. 8, page 25), Pisani Gritti (R. 9, page 25). The first two house Regione Veneto offices; the third, one of the city's most prestigious hotels.

L. 9
PALAZZO VENIER DEI LEONI

There are countless Venier houses in Venice. They belonged to the various branches into which the old original family had been dividing itself right from the early centuries.
However, this building overlooking the Grand Canal was built in the middle of the 18th century: the Venier family which owned the site, commissioned the architect Lorenzo Boschetti in 1749 to carry out the plan. He designed a grandiose palace spread over a very vast area from the Grand Canal as far as the fondamenta at the back. The main parts of the building which are opposite one another, are linked together at the sides by two narrower wings. The four sides enclose a large, rectangular courtyard with an oval peristyle which in the model was then built as a square in tribute to works by Sansovino. This wooden model, which is kept in the Correr Museum, together with prints of that time by Fossati, gives the idea of the magnificence of the building, at least as it was intended in the original design because in fact only the ground floor of the part overlooking the Grand Canal was ever completed.
The Veniers were reduced to living in this modest part which was finished first while the remaining area became a garden where it seems that one or more lions were kept in large cages; hence the building's nickname "dei leoni" (of the lions).
Boschetti collected motifs used by Sansovino and Longhena and re-rendered them in the planimetrical and architectural design and also in the use of special decorative structures. Everything remained unfinished, perhaps because of a sudden lack of money. More or less adjacent to Palazzo Venier dei Leoni stood another palazzo Venier which was called "della Toresela" after the look-out tower which rose above the roofs. It was built in Gothic times as it is still possible to see from some elements still in place. In the 15th century the building was divided up between some members of the Venier family before passing into the hands of the Scuola di San Rocco which in turn sold it to the Donà family. In the end, probably because of its structural conditions, it was completely demolished except for some boundary walls containing the above-mentioned Gothic elements. Palazzo Venier was supposed to have been completely covered with Istrian stone as can be seen in that part of the ground floor already built; in front of the façade there is a wide landing place which gives onto the central loggia through three large arches. It then became the property of the American art collector Peggy Guggenheim and is now the home of one of the most comprehensive modern art collections. In fact, works by Pollock, Max Ernst, etc. are among the countless others to the found here.

L. 10
CASA BIONDETTI

This building has no noticeable architectural claims but it is famous because it was the home of the very well-known Venetian painter Rosalba Carriera who was born here in 1675 and died here at the age of 81. She began her professional training with the painter G. Diamantini, then at school where she studied under A. Balestra while her works clearly show the influence of Pellegrini. There can be no doubt about her success in Italy and also abroad, especially as regards her portrait painting, the genre which suited her best and which constituted the main bulk of her work. Her portraits are done in coloured pastels, a medium with which she knew how to express herself with great simplicity and with softness: a careful pictorial expression and great technique accompanied by an unusually fresh psychological insight into the personality. Her fame as we have already said often took the artist away from Venice to paint portraits of important people, and we must not forget that Rosalba, the painter-artist-woman, was an unique combination for those days; she was in Paris around the twenties where her meeting with Watteau meant a further step forward in perfecting her art; after her stay in Paris she went to the Este court in Modena and then in 1730 to the Emperor's court in Vienna.
As well as being a pastel portrait painter, she was also a very capable miniaturist.
Countless are her portraits of well-known and less-known ladies, young girls and gentlemen: we can remember the portrait of the Duke of Wharton, of Caterina Barbarigo, of Anne Charlotte Genthier de Loiserolle, the four portraits of the Leblonde family, especially the splendid blue-eyed boy (these latter paintings together with her self-portrait are in the Accademia Galleries). More, equally interesting portraits are on display in the rooms of Cà Rezzonico museum (Venetian 18th century).

R. 10
CHURCH AND CAMPO S. MARIA DEL GIGLIO

Looking down the long, rectangular Campo S. Maria del Giglio from its short side on the Grand Canal, the church façade is visible, in abrupt foreshortening, at the far end. Of extremely ancient origin (9th century), the church was rebuilt by the architect Giuseppe Benoni after numerous structural interventions and much restoration between 1670 and 1680. The façade, terminated in 1683, was designed by Sardi in the Baroque style, profusely ornamented with relief work and statuary.
Antonio Barbaro, governor general of Dalmatia, left a bequest of 30,000 ducats to pay for the façade, on condition that precise historical reference to his family and person should make a celebratory monument of it. Effigies of his four brothers thus stand in deep niches between the columns of the first order, while that of Antonio appears in the central section of the second order.
The great family coat of arms is displayed above, while carved on the column bases below are such episodes in his life as battle scenes, together with relief maps of Italian and Dalmatian cities where he held important political and military office for the Republic: Zara, Candia, Padua, Rome, Corfù and Spalato (Split).

R. 11
PALAZZO VENIER CONTARINI

Campo S. Maria del Giglio terminates on the left-hand side in a nameless palace, period 16th century, designed in the usual symmetrical tripartite scheme. The two storeys above ground floor and mezzanine exhibit central three-light windows emphasized by projecting balconies. A simplified version of this design also appears on the campo façade.
The next building also heads a long block, contained by the narrow Calle Gritti, otherwise Campanile (commemorating the unstable bell-tower demolished in 1775) and the Rio S. Maria del Giglio, otherwise Furlani, on which its left frontage stands. The palace was built by the Venier family in the Gothic period, towards the mid 15th century; Contarini refers to its later owners. From this period it preserves the fenestration on the piano nobile and the second storey, with the four-light section displaced to the right of the façade to form, together with the two single-lights on the left, an incomplete tripartite scheme. Taller round-arch windows in respect of the originals are a legacy of alteration to the first storey in the classical period, but their placement to form an aligned four-light section remains unchanged.

R. 12-13
THE BARBARIGO GIUSTINIAN AND MINOTTO PALACES

With adjacent frontage on the Grand Canal, Campiello Feltrina to the rear, the 17th century Palazzo Barbarigo and the 15th century Gothic Palazzo Minotto stand between Rio S. Maria del Giglio and Rio S. Maurizio. Both façades exhibit asymmetrical structural elements, with the multi-light section of the portego reception room carried to the extreme edge of the composition.
To account for these undeveloped façades it may be conjectured that either scant canal frontage prompted recourse to the bipartite scheme at the planning stage or that, as elsewhere, some motive such as budget, prevented purchase of adjacent land necessary to complete the façades as planned.
The large Serlianas on the same axis as the portal, flanked by the mezzanine windows, create a continuous sequence of voids to offset the adjacent stretch of solid wall, its sweep adequate to take in the single-lights, thereby setting up a surface contrast of void against solid, dark against light, re-entrant against salient features.
A wall-tablet on the Barbarigo façade commemorates the birth here in 1655 of the Blessed Gregory Barbarigo.
The building known as Palazzo Minotto is of Byzantine origin and notwithstanding total restructuring in the Gothic period, towards the mid 15th century, it still preserves such period features as the 12th-13th century cornice of reversed acanthus leaves.

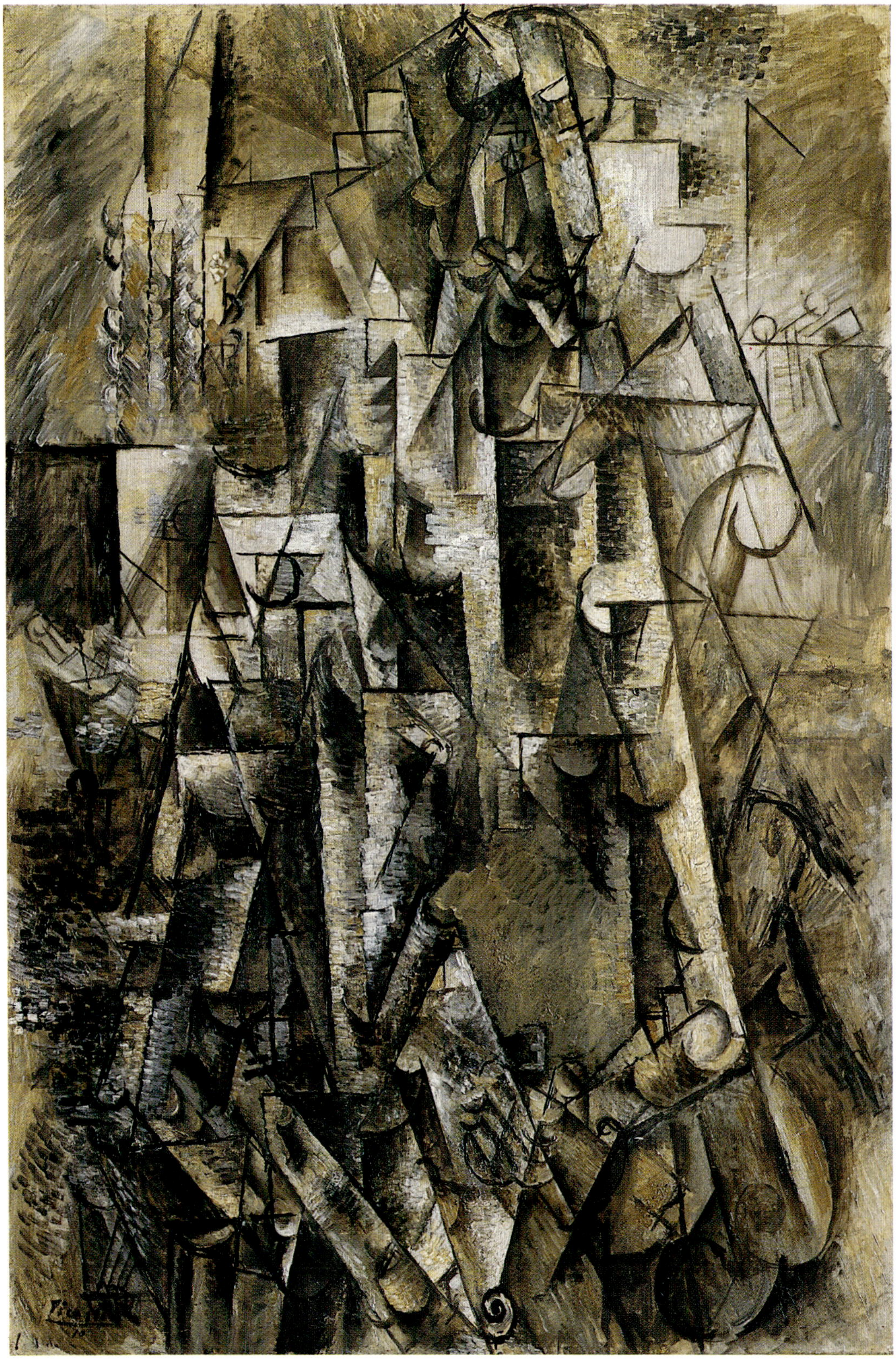

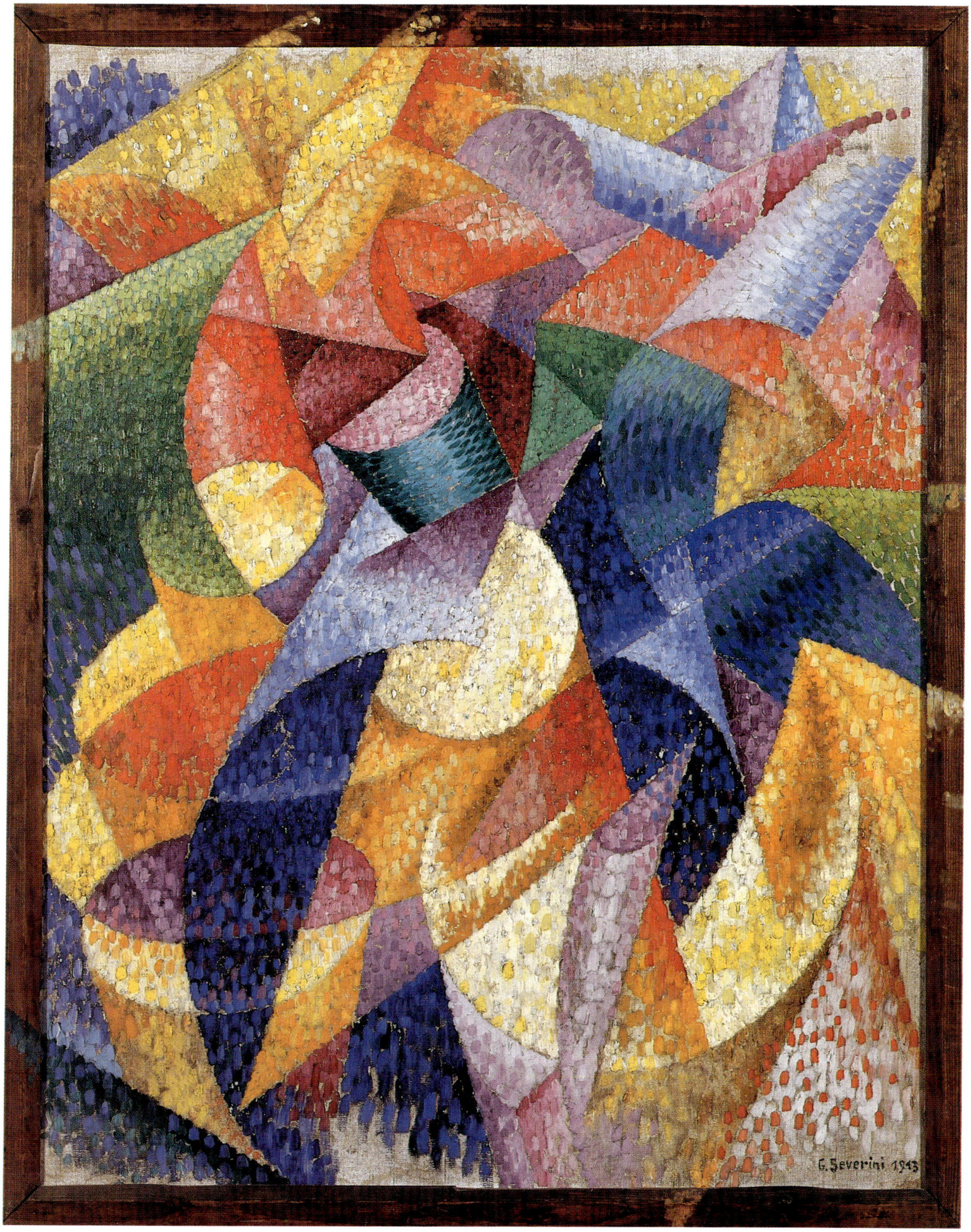
G. Severini 1913

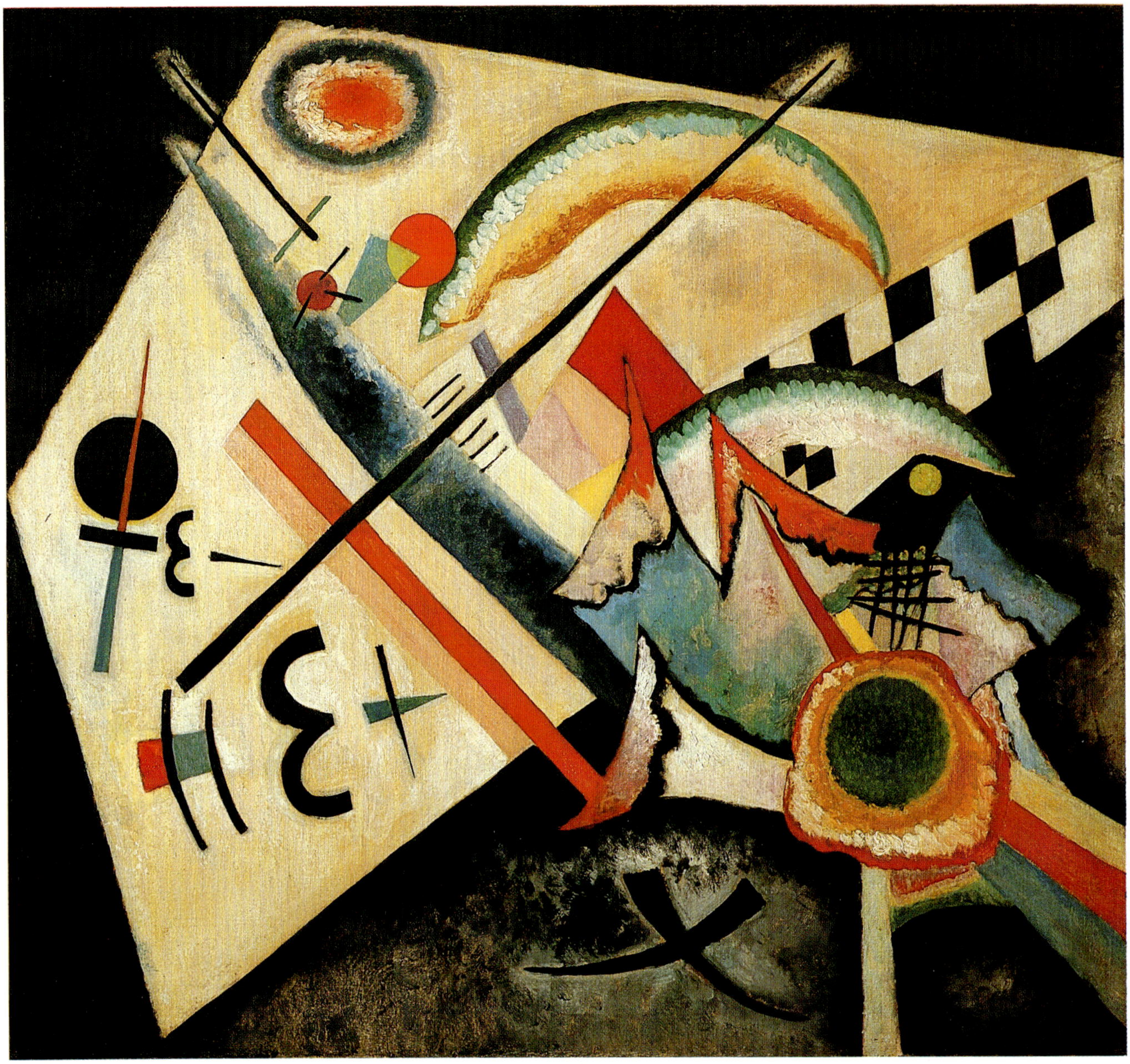

N° 15
The Guggenheim Museum at Palazzo Venier dei Leoni:
"Le Poète" by Paolo Picasso (1911).
(L. 9, page 28)

N° 16
The Guggenheim Museum at Palazzo Venier dei Leoni:
"Mare-Ballerina" by Gino Severini (1914).
(L. 9, page 28)

N° 17
The Guggenheim Museum at Palazzo Venier dei Leoni:
"White Cross" by Wassily Kandinsky (1922).
(L. 9, page 28)

N° 18
The Guggenheim Museum at Palazzo Venier dei Leoni:
"Dressing the Bride" by Max Ernst (1940).
(L. 9, page 28)

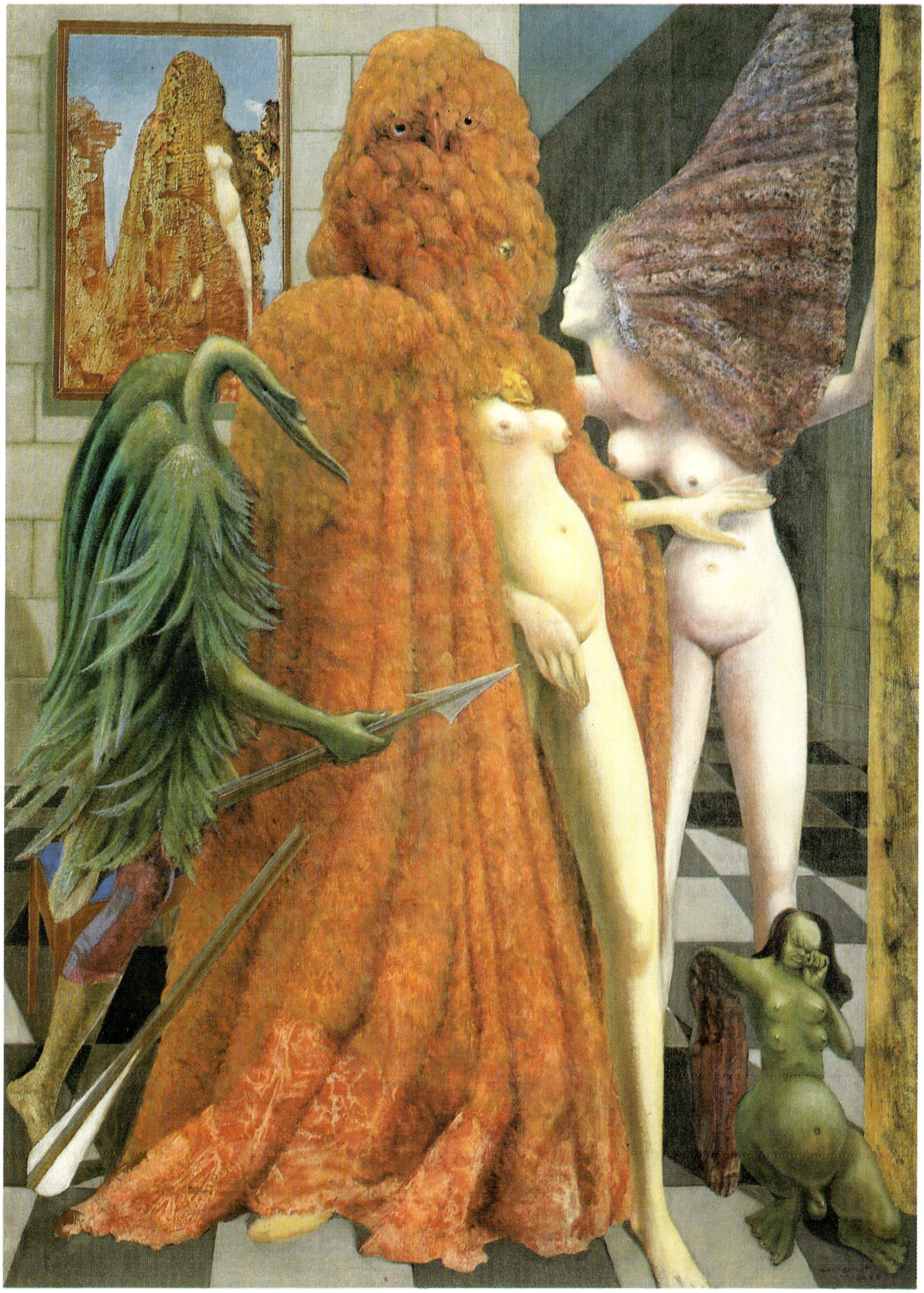

L. 11
PALAZZO CENTANI

The senior branch of the Centani family resided in the palace best known as the birthplace of Carlo Goldoni, in the San Tomà district. From the 14th century a cadet branch was established in one of the buildings overlooking the Grand Canal in the San Vio parish. Although the original fabric of the area has gone, through-ways such as the "sottoportico" and "corte" still bear the family name and there is one survivor in a humble 18th century house, its narrow, anonymous façade overlooking the Grand Canal.
Tassini mentions a certain Lorenzo Centani, whose testament, dated 1603, bequeaths part of his property to the "Incurabili" hospital where he was head administrator.

L. 12
PALAZZO DA MULA

Palazzo Da Mula an interesting, large Gothic building dating from the early 15th century, even through more archaic antecedents are suggested by certain features of the four-light section on the first piano nobile, such as the sturdiness of its columns, pilasters and arches, these latter, low and only slightly curved. Instead, a pronounced vertical accent marks the four-light section and other windows on the second storey, where the fleuron-crowned trefoil arches have slim supporting columns and the capitals are of the rosette-motif 14th century type. The balcony is 16th century, as is the moulding beneath the eaves of large modillions resting on a narrow marble fascia, its line broken by the cusps of the arches on the small four-light section and single lights aligned to the axes of the windows below.
The presence of the Da Mula family in Venice seems to date from the city's early days, with residence in the parish of S. Vio from the 15th century. Numerous members of the family distinguished themselves in the service of the Republic of this and the following century, chiefly as military commanders and administrators.

L. 13
PALAZZO BARBARIGO

The large 16th century building on the corner of the Grand Canal and Campo San Vio makes a plain statement, straightforward layout of elements on the ground floor and each piano nobile with, as was Gothic practice, the central three-light section in close proximity to the two lateral single lights – so close as to suggest a five-light section were it not for the projecting balcony underlining the central three lights. Parallel fascias running the full breadth of the façade tie the whole together and create geometric areas of solid wall. In the 19th century Giulio Carlini painted cartoons for the mosaics, still decorating these areas on the palace front today and detracting from its original, dignified architectural presence.

R. 14
PALAZZO CORNER DELLA CÀ GRANDE

On August 16 1532 a fierce fire destroyed the old building which stood on this site, the Gothic-Byzantine palace which had been built by the Malombra family. The founder of this family, Bartolomeo Malombra, a very wealthy Venetian citizen, had been nicknamed "dalla bella casa" (of the beautiful house) to indicate the spaciousness and quality of the building. The old building was bought for 22 thousand ducats by Giorgio Corner, the brother of the Queen of Cyprus. His intention was to rebuild it in order to increase his family's prestige and fame, but his death in 1527 prevented this from being carried out and everything was left in his son Jacopo's hands. In 1533 the foundations of the new edifice had already been laid, but it had been the serious fire in 1532 rather than the wishes of the executors, which had determined the course of events. Marin Sanudo, who witnessed the disastrous event, wrote that "once the flames had been extinguished, only the columns of the façade overlooking the canal were left standing while all the rest was destroyed". Jacopo Corner, the nephew of the famous Queen of Cyprus, was a very wealthy and highly educated man. He wanted to rebuild his residence immediately and use its vastness and architectural richness to make it a palace on that side of the Grand Canal worthy of the personal and family pre-eminence which the Corners enjoyed in Venice. It is clear that Jacopo wanted to pursue a real commemorative policy by building this enormous palace. The architect Jacopo Sansovino, commissioned for the work, erected the new building on the Grand Canal near St. Mark's Square, completely satisfying his client's wishes. In designing this new building, the architect did not break much with the Venetian cultural tradition but modernized it though in line with new requirements and new tastes. In fact the layout remains linked to that of the old private buildings while features which are stylistically close to the maturer Renaissance concepts deriving from the artist's experiences in Tuscany, are included and developed.

The Corner family remained the owners of the palace until the beginning of the 19th century when they sold it to the Austrian government to be used as the official headquarters of the Imperial Lieutenancy.

As we have already said, the Corner family had been one of the most distinguished in Venice since early times, one of the four Evangelist families. In 1365 Marco, who that same year had already turned eighty, was the first member of the family to be elected Doge. He had enjoyed, and continued to enjoy, a very important position in Venetian public life. However, besides trading and taking part in politics, he also dedicated himself to studies and his reputation as an educated man is linked to the fact that he possessed an extensive library in his house at SS. Apostoli. It is well known that, during Bajamonte Tiepolo's plot, he "ruled the Republic as vice-Doge and commanded the armed garrison in St. Mark's Square". Another Corner, Giovanni, became Doge in 1625. This branch of the family lived in San Polo in the large palace which they had had built at the beginning of the 16th century according to the design by the architect Sanmicheli. Seven cardinals, four bishops, four Procurators of St. Mark, commendatori, chancellors plus four Doges: a net result so gratifying that the very Corners considered themselves superior to almost all the other Venetian noble families.

This excessive power caused long, relentless conflicts inside Venetian politics and struggles between opposing power groups with the Corner family on one side supported by the wealthiest patricians and on the other the party consisting of the less important and poorer nobles led by Renier Zen who made public the misuses and abuses practised by the Corners as well as the tolerance shown by the Council of Ten in their regard.

Francesco, the son of Doge Giovanni I, also became Doge in 1656 but he died only a few days later. The last of the Corner Doges was Giovanni II elected at the first round of voting on May 22 1709.

It has been said that the layout of the palace follows in every detail the traditional Venetian one but there is no lack of variations to bring the building in line with the times. The façade maintains its role as a status symbol on the Grand Canal but this design idea in a certain way conceals the tripartition of the internal plan which is really maintained in its entirety: the large central portico and the side rooms. In fact, the plan of the windows with the intervening supporting structures and twin columns, create the spatial and expressive continuity without modifying the elevational relationship between the openings and the wall which conceals or rather does not betray the internal tripartition, as happens in Gothic and Renaissance architecture.

As regards the ground floor plan, if we follow the central axial line starting from the Grand Canal, we find the vestibule, reached through three central arches, followed by the portico and finally the inner courtyard around which there are no boundary walls but buildings wide enough to be used.

All construction work was completed around 1560.

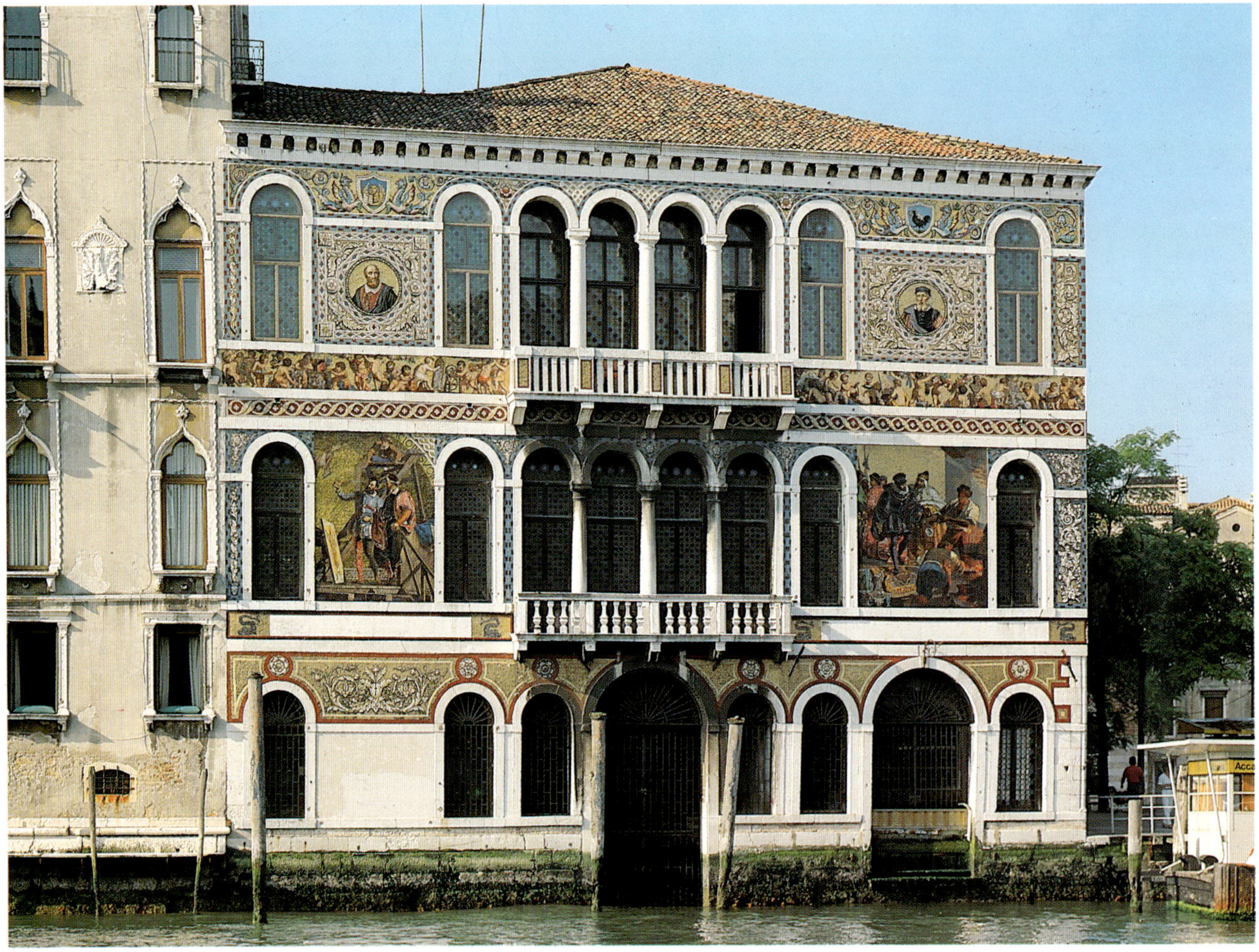

N° 19
Palazzo Barbarigo
The mosaics on the façade are 19th century work, based on cartoons by Giulio Carlini.
(L. 13, page 34)

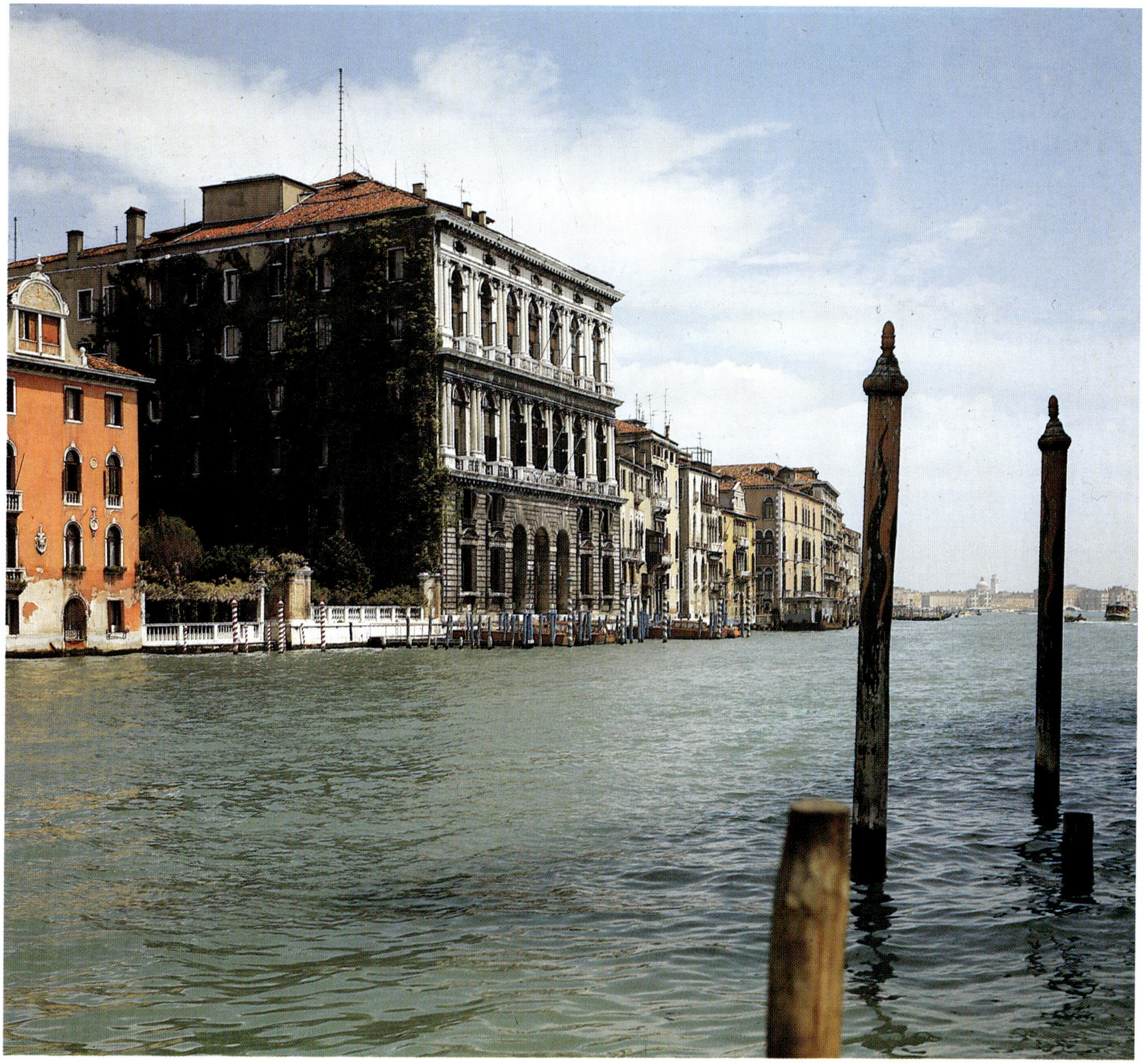

N° 20
Palazzo Corner della Cà Grande
A graceful building, the work of Jacopo Sansovino.
(R. 14, page 35)

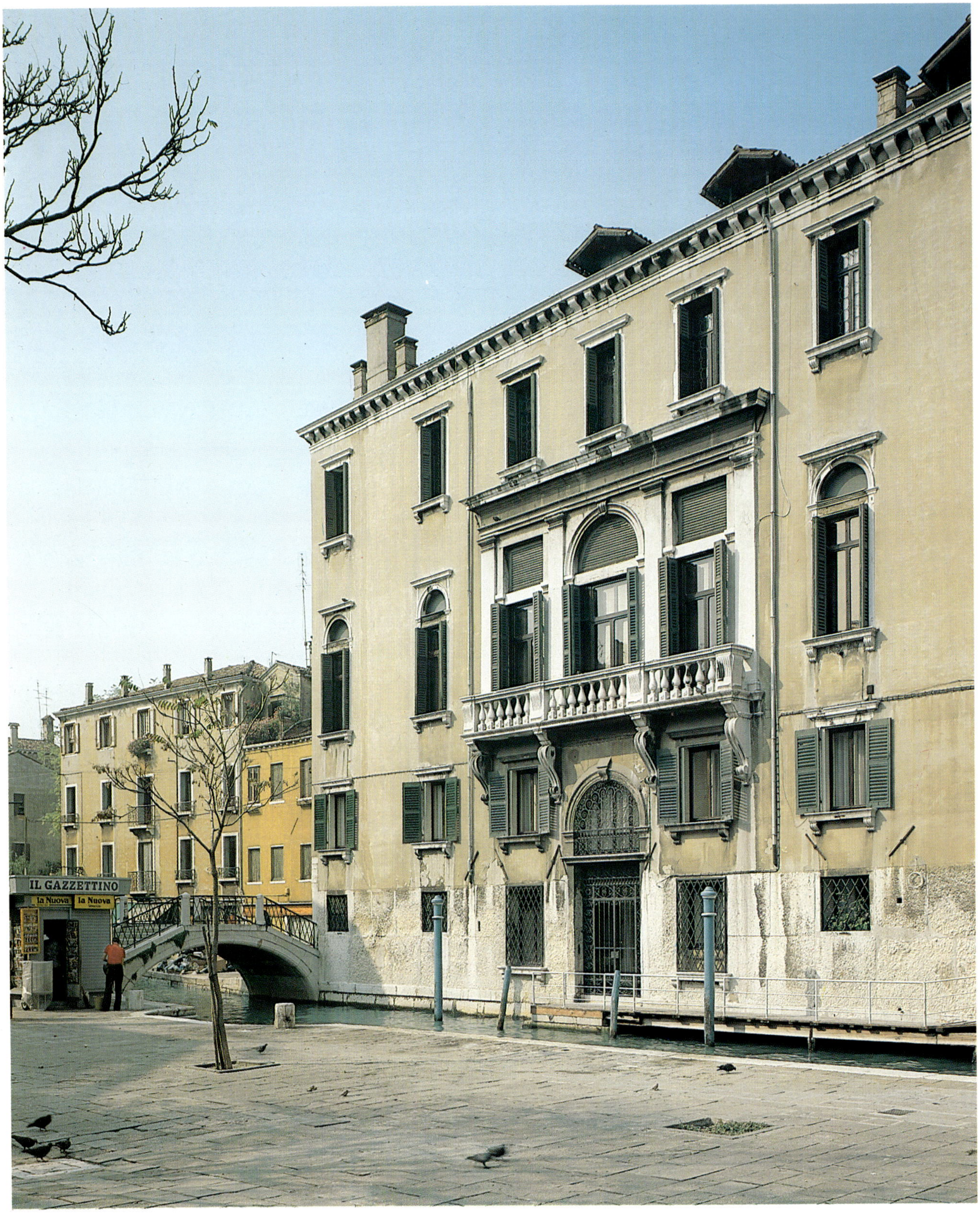
IL GAZZETTINO
la Nuova
la Nuova

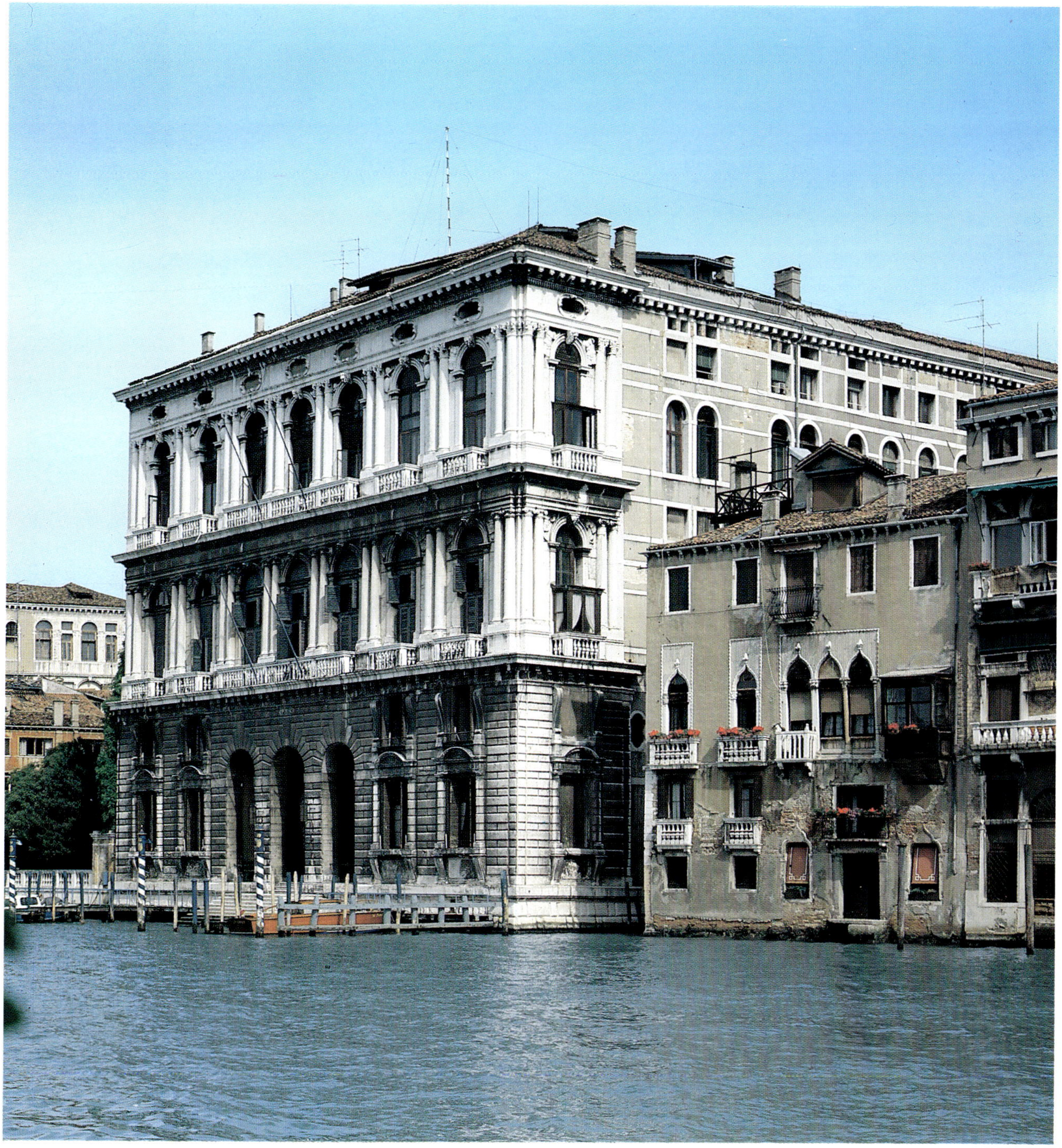

N° 21
Campo San Vio with Palazzo Loredan Cini.
(L. 14 and L. 15, page 40)

N° 22
Palazzo Corner della Cà Grande
Architectural conception and volumetric presence made this the most important city building of its age.
(R. 14, page 35)

L. 14
CAMPO SAN VIO

Campo San Vio results from demolition of the ancient houses once occupying the area, an intervention post-dating 1310, enacted by the Republic to facilitate disembarkation of the doge and retinue proceeding to the church of S. Vio (no longer extant) where, on the Saint's Day, 15 June 1310, safeguarding of the city's institutions by defeat of the Baiamonte Tiepolo plot was solemnly celebrated.

The short side heading the long rectangular concourse opens onto the Grand Canal, one long side is flanked by the S. Vio canal, with access from the concourse to the S. Maria della Carità zone via the bridge on the right.

The calle on the opposite side to this bridge led to the church, an extremely ancient building, Byzantine in style, with three aisles and bell-tower adjoining the apsidal area, a presence graphically attested to by the de' Barberi townplan.

L. 15
PALAZZO LOREDAN CINI

Palazzo Loredan is a typical exemplar of 16th century building in the classical style, displaying all the relevant architectural features the slow but sure wind of change introduced in those years. Frontages of the vast building flank the Grand Canal and the Piscina del Forner at the rear, adjoining the S. Vio bridge.

The left side-front rising from the canal reveals the commanding sweep of the building facing Campo S. Vio, in the south-eastern corner of which the very ancient church of S. Vio once stood.

At the turn of the last century this palace was the residence of Don Carlos of Bourbon, Pretender to the Spanish Throne.

There were various branches of the rich and powerful Loredan family, one of the most ancient in Venice, its arrival there dating from the early 11th century. Besides the S. Vio palace, many others bear its name: Loredan degli Ambasciatori on the Grand Canal, others variously sited in Campo Santo Stefano, at San Luca, in the S. Marcuola zone and, later owned by the Condulmer family, one at the Tolentini, facing the homonymous church.

L. 16
PALAZZO MOLIN BALBI-VALIER DELLA TREZZA

The building adjacent to Palazzo Loredan, Palazzo Molin, later became Balbi-Valier after a branch of the Venetian family known as "della trezza" by reason of an unusual decorated band, resembling a braid (treccia), on its coat of arms. One of its better known members was Gerolamo Maria Balbi, whose many political offices included that of Governor of Dalmatia.

Formerly a Gothic building, the palace was demolished and rebuilt in the 17th century. Structural alterations at later times brought change to both interior and exterior. In the course of these it acquired the ground-floor extension preceding the façade.

The vast garden alongside the palace was planted after demolition of the Paradiso family residence.

R. 15
CASINA DELLE ROSE

This is a small, modern construction preceded by a small garden where grows the pomegranate, covered by scarlet flowers in spring. This house's fame derives from the people who have temporarily lived there.

First of all Canova used these rooms as his studio where he modelled his famous "Daedalus and Icarus" before leaving for Rome. This work was commissioned by the Pisani family and can now be admired in one of the first rooms of the Correr Museum.

The second person of renown who lived in the Casina was Gabriele D'Annunzio during the 1915-18 war.

R. 16-17
PALACES ON FONDAMENTA SAN MAURIZIO

Beyond Campo San Maurizio, the short fondamenta at the far end of Calle del Doge leads to two buildings, the second of which exceeds the first by the full width of the fondamenta. Both are 17th century in period, but the singularity of the first is that with storeys all of the same height, emphasis on breadth, rectangular fenestration alternating single and double lights, it conveys the impression of a building designed for rental, the plan repeating a scheme of identical apartments throughout. The second, notwithstanding its simplicity, indeed, poverty of concept, is recognizably a small-scale, single-proprietor palace, its piano nobile accentuated by greater height and central Serliana.

Reverting to the Calle del Doge: its ancient name stems from the presence of a house or palace, property of the Da Ponte family. The doge Nicolò (1578-1585) is said to have used it as his residence in 1578, after "a quarter of the Doge's Palace" had been destroyed by fire. Tassini has a reference to the disastrous 1577 fire at the Palace, when the Scrutinio chamber and that of the Maggior Consiglio were destroyed.

R. 18
PALAZZO PISANI

Monumental scale, importance, and family prestige withal, the architectural history of the imposing Palazzo Pisani in Campo S. Stefano is by no means clearly charted. Existing documents date the building to 1614-15, when the senior family member was Alvise. Absence of an architect's name lends support to the hypothesis that the owners themselves superintended building, aided perhaps by some technical adviser. Stylistically, Palazzo Pisani may be likened to Palazzo Ruzzini in Campo S. Maria Formosa, and as Bartolomeo Monopola is known to have designed the latter, he is also attributed with the former. Monopola, at the time, was the leading artist in the city and the Republic itself had engaged him for the difficult task of replacing the 14th century groundfloor wall of the Doge's Palace courtyard, with the portico we see today on the south and west sides.

A wing of Palazzo Pisani, destroyed by the 1634 earthquake, was rebuilt unchanged. The family purchased lands and buildings adjacent to its property towards the end of the century and further purchases were made in 1716. In 1728 it engaged Girolamo Frigimelica to undertake extension of the original building and alterations to include a second piano nobile and a new courtyard communicating with the existing one by means of a portico of broad-span arches on slim columns. But behind this continuous, costly building activity and accumulation of property, the Pisanis' ultimate goal was to gain access to frontage on the Grand Canal, and they finally achieved this in 1751.

L. 17
PALAZZO CONTARINI DAL ZAFFO

This Palazzo Contarini is a very interesting building dating from the early Venetian Renaissance. It stands not far from the Accademia near to the bridge of the same name which spans the Grand Canal and was built by the Austrians during the first half of the 19th century with a linear, iron structure and then replaced by the present wooden one. As regards the building, Lorenzetti defines it as being "Venetian Lombardesque architecture". It is the result of the restructuring and transformation of an older Gothic-Byzantine building. Its architectural and stylistic expressiveness, both in the general design and in the decorative details, has caused the work to be attributed to Mauro Codussi, one of the most capable and important early Renaissance architects. The marble decorations are simple, restrained and above all seem a part of the structure which emphasizes rather than breaks up the pattern. It is precisely their quality that has made this building, that is to say the design of the façade, without forgetting the existence of the earlier building, attributable to Codussi rather than to Pietro Lombardo, though we can not entirely exclude a possible intervention by the latter. In fact, there is a slight tendency towards an over-emphasis of decoration which could make us think of a more restrained Lombardo or at the same time of a Codussi inclined to give the architectural pattern some underlinings of colour. Moreover, we must remember that Giovanni Antonio Buora also had a hand in this reconstruction work as a stone-mason. His artistic personality was certainly sufficient to dictate personal design ideas to the client and make them accepted.
The palace changed hands several times: in 1783 it passed from the Contarini family of the "dal Zaffo" branch to a very wealthy family of silk merchants, the Manzoni family, related to the Venetian Angaran family, before passing to the Montecuccoli Counts and then to Duke Decazes. In the 18th century, probably after the building had changed hands again, its interior was decorated with paintings by Giandomenico Tiepolo, some parts of which are still visible today.

L. 18
PALAZZO BRANDOLIN ROTA

In 1878, the English poet Robert Browning (b. London 1812, d. Venice 1889) lived in this next palace, a 17th century building bearing the name of Brandolin Rota, it too the result of restructuring and trasformation of an earlier building. The palace was the property of the Rota (or Rotta) family, very probably responsible for the building as we see it today. The family gained the right to attend Maggior Consiglio sessions in 1685, signifying that the Serenissima had accorded it patrician status. This prompts the thought that the family may have taken steps to establish itself in a comfortable residence, fittingly sited on the Grand Canal, a symbol of new social prestige. Francesco Rota had acquired his wealth in the legal profession in Venice, practising "the art of advocacy".
In the collection of engravings of Venetian palaces, Coronelli reproduces the building, attributing ownership specifically to this family, whose coat of arms was carved on the well in the interior courtyard. Ownership passed to Girolamo Brandolin in 1750, on his marriage to Francesco Rota's daughter.

R. 19
PALAZZO BENZON FOSCOLO

Palazzo Benzon Foscolo was built in the 17th century, on the site of an ancient Byzantine-Gothic building.
The Venetian bent for restructuring and rebuilding, so prevalent in certain periods, was obviously impelled by the extreme age and disrepair of the older buildings. But its underlying cause was the urge for cultural and aesthetic renewal: to contemporary eyes the modernity of one's home, however modest, was a source of satisfaction and prestige.
With its accent on breadth rather than height, the Palazzo Benzon façade displays a simple three-light section, surround true to Gothic tradition and, albeit well spaced out, lateral single lights, all emphasized by projecting balconies.
A Giorgio Benzon, seigneur of Agnadello and Crema, his birthplace, was accorded Venetian patrician status in 1407.
Having lost all his lands he came to Venice, where the Republic nominated him freelance condottiere with the land militia.

R. 20-21
PALAZZI BARBARO

The Barbaros were one of the most distinguished Venetian families but they were never able to reach the heights of nobility even though they took part in several of the Republic's important historical-political events in various capacities.
The design of their coat-of-arms, a red circle on a white ground, derives from a legendary act of bravery which saw one member of the family use his own arm, cut off by a stroke from an enemy sword during a naval battle against the Turks, to trace that new symbol with his blood.
There are two Barbaro buildings overlooking the Grand Canal and standing next to each other; the first one we see dates from the end of the 17th century. It was restored between 1694 and the end of that same century to a design by Antonio Gaspari who had the interior decorated with lavish if not elegant stuccoes created by the same artists who put their hand to those in Palazzo Zenobio at the Carmini.
The next palazzo Barbaro is in Gothic style with architectural structures and a stylistic design which assign it to the first half of the 15th century. The Bon workshop was directly or indirectly involved in most of the Venetian buildings constructed during those decades because it had known how to create a definite trend of good taste which others used as a model. This style is present in palazzo Barbaro in such a definite and marked way that the building's design and construction can be considered to be by the Bons themselves, in particular by Giovanni to whom reference is made in a document mentioned by Paoletti in his work on Venetian architecture during that century.
This document specifically mentions a sum of 5 ducats which Marino Contarini includes in his expenses in the summer of 1425 in order to pay the builder and stone-mason Giovanni Bon who was busy working on the Barbaro's house together with his helpers Zane and Rosso who were due to receive a payment of 10 ducats.
The traditional façade design does not change at all with the Bons while their work is characterized by the use of a taller module for the shafts of the columns especially on the second floor. In this way the windows become more slender, in contrast to the use of the still "obsolete" architectural elements such as the rosette capitals and the ogee non-trefoil arches. These elements can be added to others typical of the evolution of Gothic architecture in the 15th century, such as the large-leafed capitals, the semi-quatrefoils on the lower four-mullioned window and the use of the fleuron at the top of every arch. The top floor which can be seen intact in Carlevariis's 1703 engraving, was later transformed, thus altering its previous meaning and proportions. According to what Tassini asserts, it was the nobleman Zaccaria Barbaro, a knight and Procurator of St. Mark, who bought the building from Lucia Coppo, the widow of Nicolò Aldioni. From 1499 it housed the French ambassador and in 1514 the Hungarian ambassador. For some time in 1524 it was the residence of Isabella d'Este, the widow of the Marquis of Mantua and daughter of Duke Ercole of Ferrara and Eleonora of Aragon. At the age of sixteen she was married to Francesco Gonzaga and actively helped him in governing public affairs with wisdom and intelligence. Her fame is particularly linked to culture which she persistently patronized by inviting, supporting and protecting every kind of artist. In this way she contributed to raising the importance and reknown of her small marquisate, making the court of Mantua one of the most fruitful, active and elegant of the Renaissance. Indeed Mantua under her was a centre of true "culture". She was also a skilled diplomat as seen when she negotiated with Venice the release of her husband Francesco Gonzaga, a condottiere imprisoned in the Doge's Palace in the famous "Toresella".

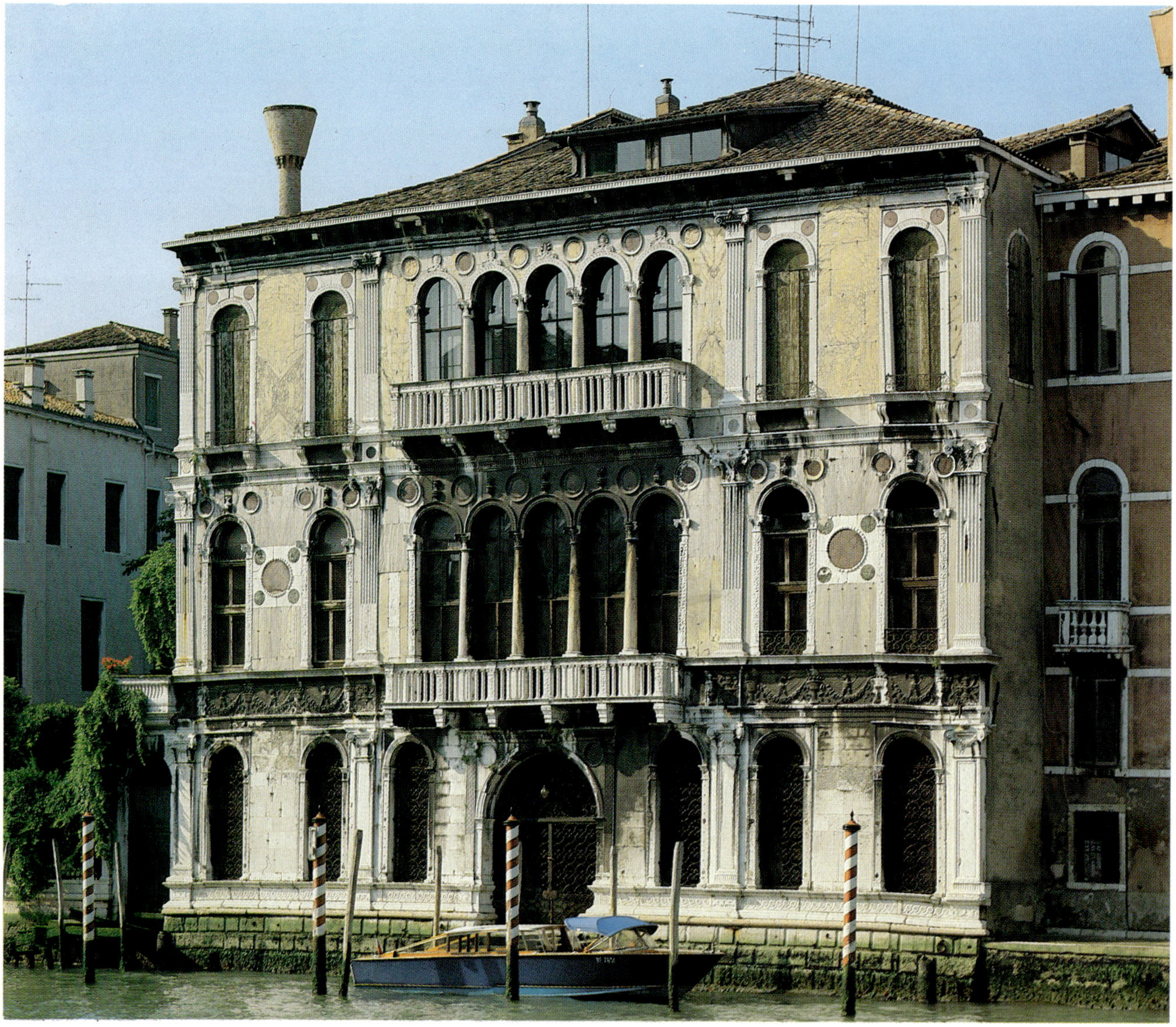

N° 23
Palazzo Contarini dal Zaffo
The façade of the building employs the characteristic idioms of Renaissance architecture.
(L. 17, page 42)

N° 24
The Barbaro palaces
The first on the right dates from the end of the 17th century, the second exhibits Gothic architectural structures of the first half of the 15th century.
(R. 20-21, page 43)

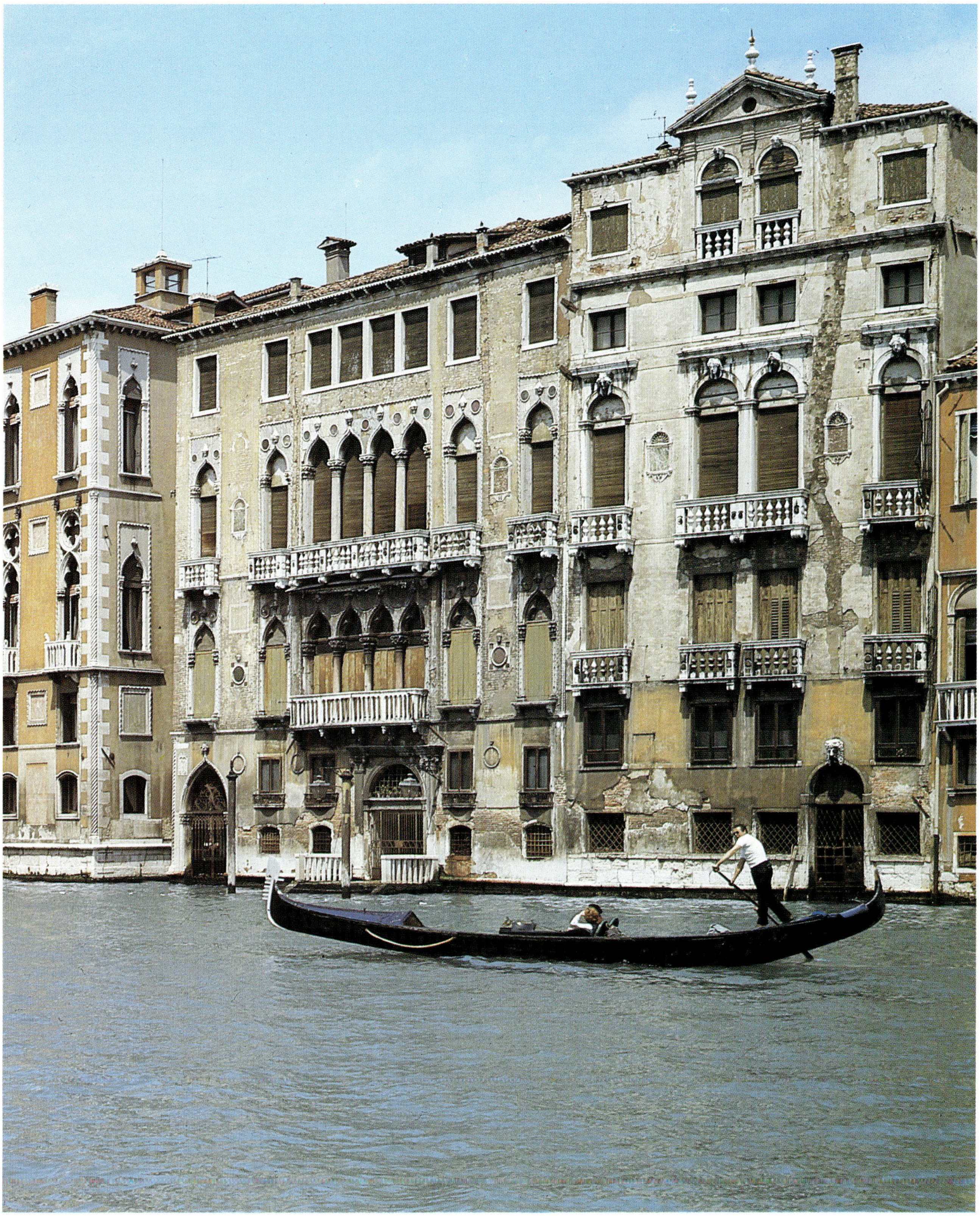

L. 19-20
CHURCH AND SCUOLA S. MARIA DELLA CARITÀ
THE ACCADEMIA PICTURE GALLERIES

The building complex at the Accademia, partially modified in respect of its original appearance, comprises the former church of S. Maria della Carità, the adjoining monastery of the Lateran Canons and the Scuola, also dedicated to S. Maria della Carità. The church, deconsecrated in 1807, height of nave today cut by an attic floor and façade stripped of the original marble ornament, was built between 1441 and 1452 in the Gothic style, in plan, a single nave without transept, terminating in three polygonal apsidal chapels.

The façade, tripartite, with cusps bearing characteristic ornament of rampant foliage, aedicules framing statues, would seem to have been designed and built by Bartolomeo Bon. The bell-tower of the apsidal area, capped by a conical brick spire, collapsed without warning in 1741, without damaging the church.

At an angle to the façade, the portal decorated with second-half of the 14th century reliefs (1377), gave access to the monastery, where the first cloister is typically Gothic, with columns supporting timber framework. The second cloister was designed in 1552 by Palladio, to enlarge the first; only one wing was built, facing Rio S. Agnese, today Rio Terrà. The monastery is flanked by the Scuola, also built in the Gothic period, but with its façade on the campo remodelled to a design by Giorgio Massari in Neo-Classical times. Today it forms the entrance to the Accademia Picture Galleries.

The Carità Scuola was one of the six Scuole Grandi in Venice. They were run by lay confraternities dedicated to piety and charitable works to benefit the needy, and hence known as "dei Battuti".

At the start of the 19th century the architect Selva commenced remodelling of a first group of rooms, others were to follow, to house the very important collection of paintings whose basic nucleus came from bequests; the most conspicuous being those of Ascanio Molin (1815), Felicita Renier (1850), and, above all, Gerolamo Contarini (1838). Additional works came from suppressed churches and scuole.

Prestigious names of Venetian artists and masterpieces of singular beauty offer a complete panorama of the evolution of Venetian painting from the early gold-ground altarpieces of the primitives to 18th century canvases. The collection comprises works by Paolo Veneziano, Lorenzo Veneziano, Nicolò di Pietro, Jacobello del Fiore, Alvise and Bartolomeo Vivarini, Michele Giambono, Jacopo Bellini, Gentile Bellini, Gentile da Fabriano, Antonio Pisanello, Giovanni Bellini, Cima da Conegliano, Vittore Carpaccio, Andrea Mantegna, Piero della Francesca, Cosmè Tura, Giorgione, Lorenzo Lotto, Paris Bordone, Bonifacio Pitati, Titian, Palma Vecchio, Palma Giovane, Paolo Veronese, Jacopo Tintoretto, Sebastiano del Piombo, the Bassano dynasty, Andrea Schiavone, Domenico Tintoretto, Domenico Fetti, Johann Lys, Bernardo Strozzi, G.B. Pittoni, Jacopo Amigoni, G.B. Tiepolo, Marco Ricci, Francesco Zuccarelli, Giuseppe Zais, Alessandro Magnasco, G.B. Piazzetta, Pietro and Alessandro Longhi, Canaletto, Guardi.

L. 21
THE ACCADEMIA BRIDGE

Under the Republic, the only bridge spanning the Grand Canal was that of the Rialto. As far back as the 15th century the proposal was made – but never implemented by the Venetians – to put up a bridge in the S. Maria della Carità area.

Only on Austrian initiative was a new bridge erected, a rectilinear, iron structure spanning the Canal horizontally from stone-based steps on either bank; it survived until 1933. In that year a competition for a new stone bridge was published and while demolition of the Austrian bridge proceeded, the "provisional" timber structure we see today was erected alongside.

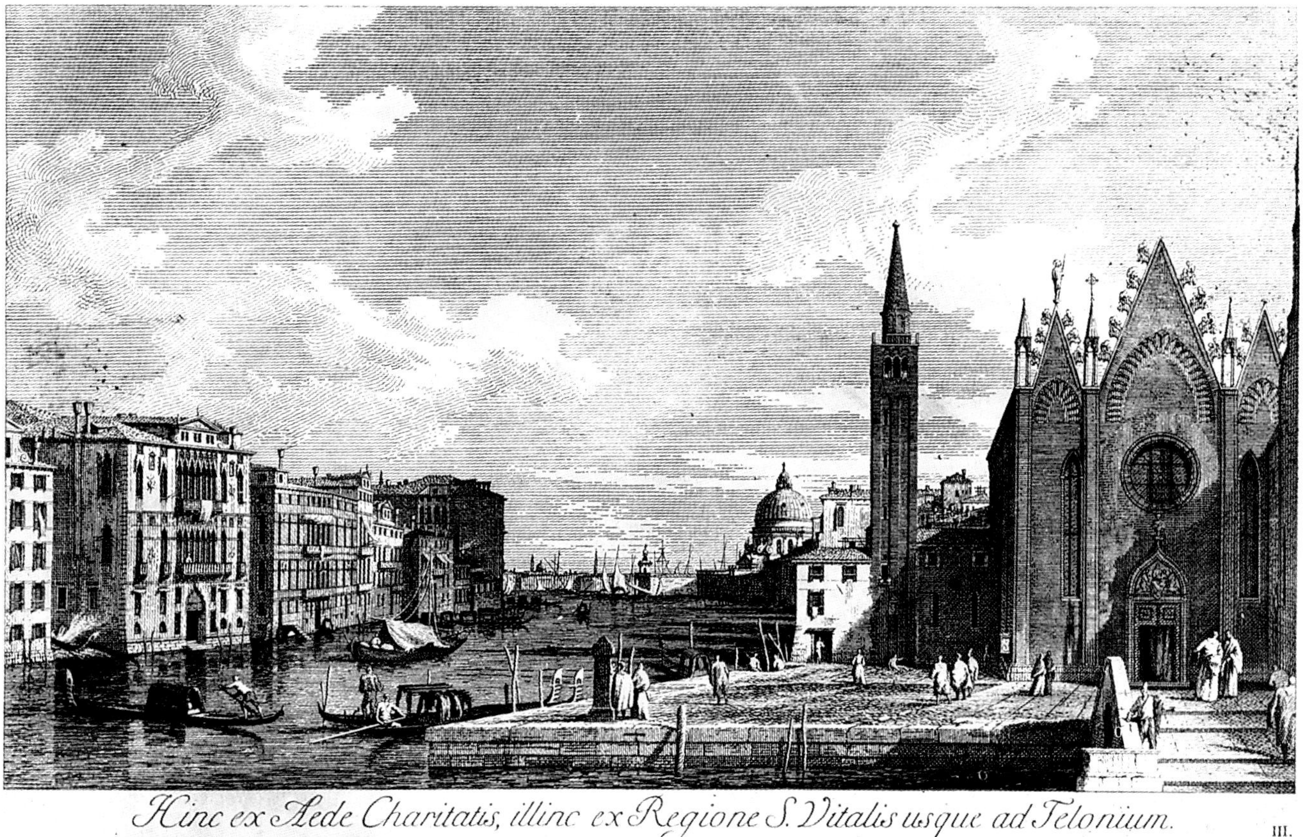

N° 25
The Grand Canal at the Accademia
Engraving by Antonio Visentini.
The church façade still preserves its pristine architectural aspect, complete with marble ornament on the cusps.

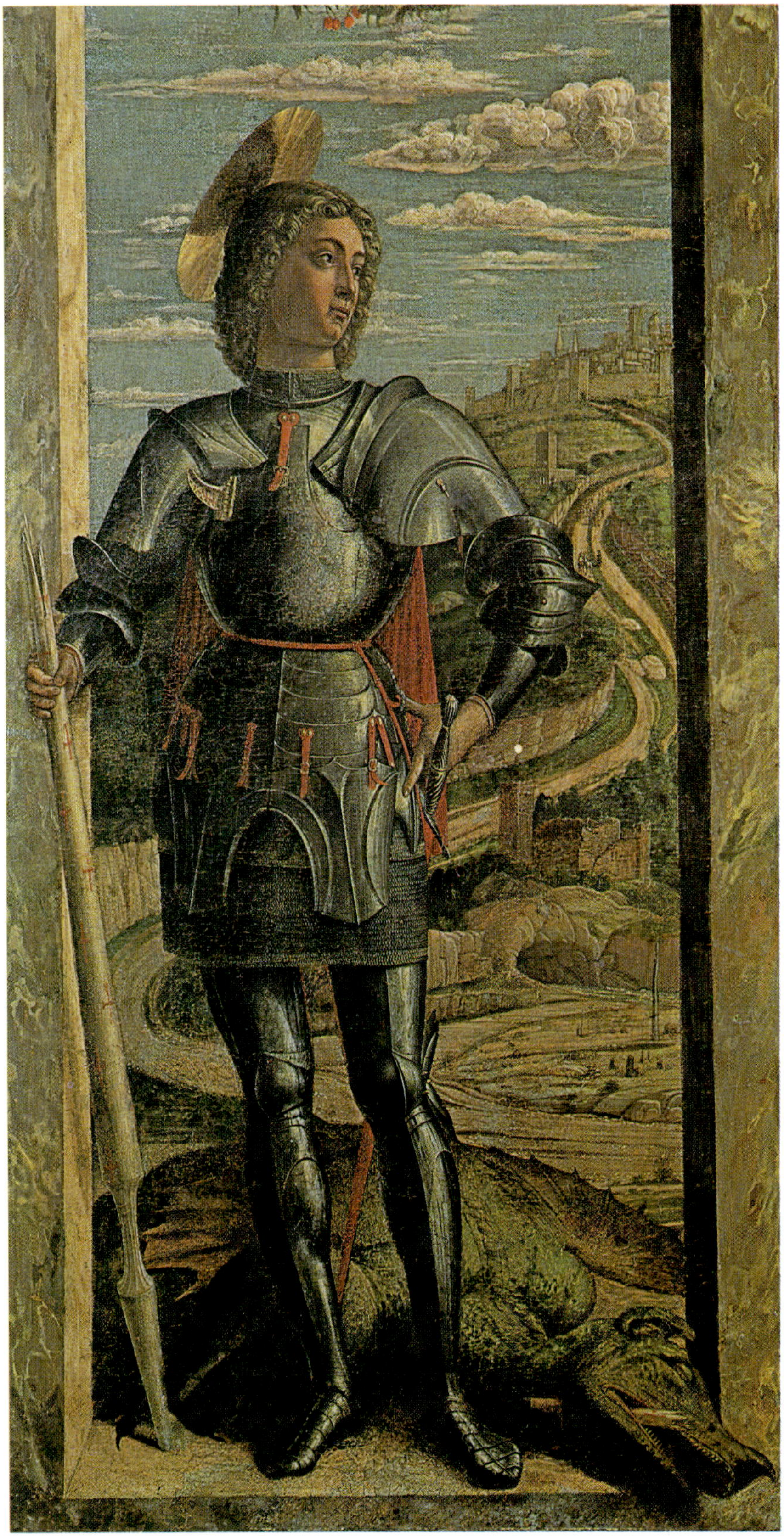

N° 26
Accademia Picture Galleries
"St George" by Andrea Mantegna.
(L. 19-20, page 46)

N° 27
Accademia Picture Galleries
"Portrait of a Young Man" by Hans Memlinc.
(L. 19-20, page 46)

N° 28
Accademia Picture Galleries
San Giobbe Altarpiece; *"Madonna Enthroned and Saints"* by Giovanni Bellini.
(L. 19-20, page 46)

N° 29
Accademia Picture Galleries
"The Madonna and Child between St Catherine and St Mary Magdalen" by Giovanni Bellini (detail).
(L. 19-20, page 46)

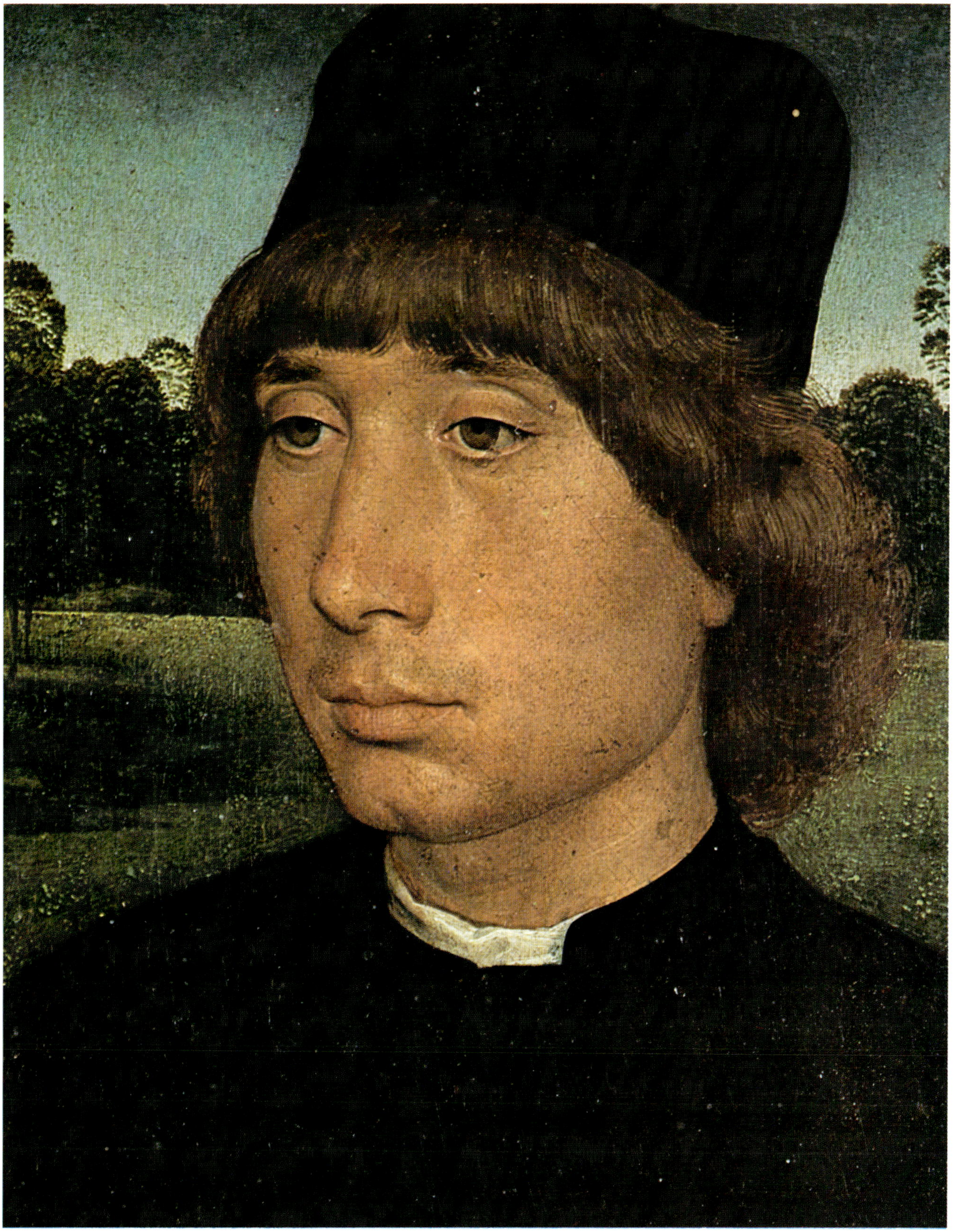

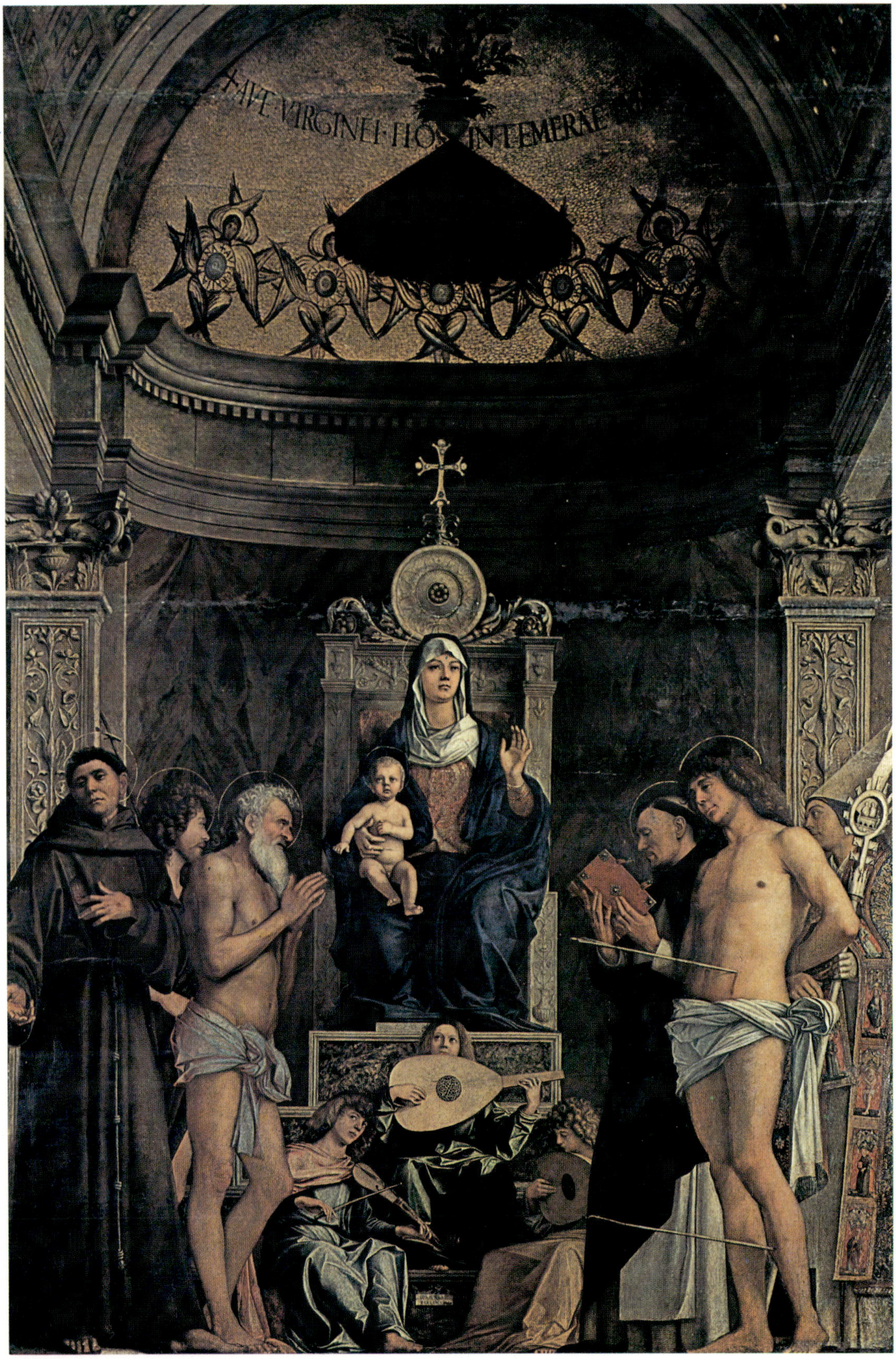

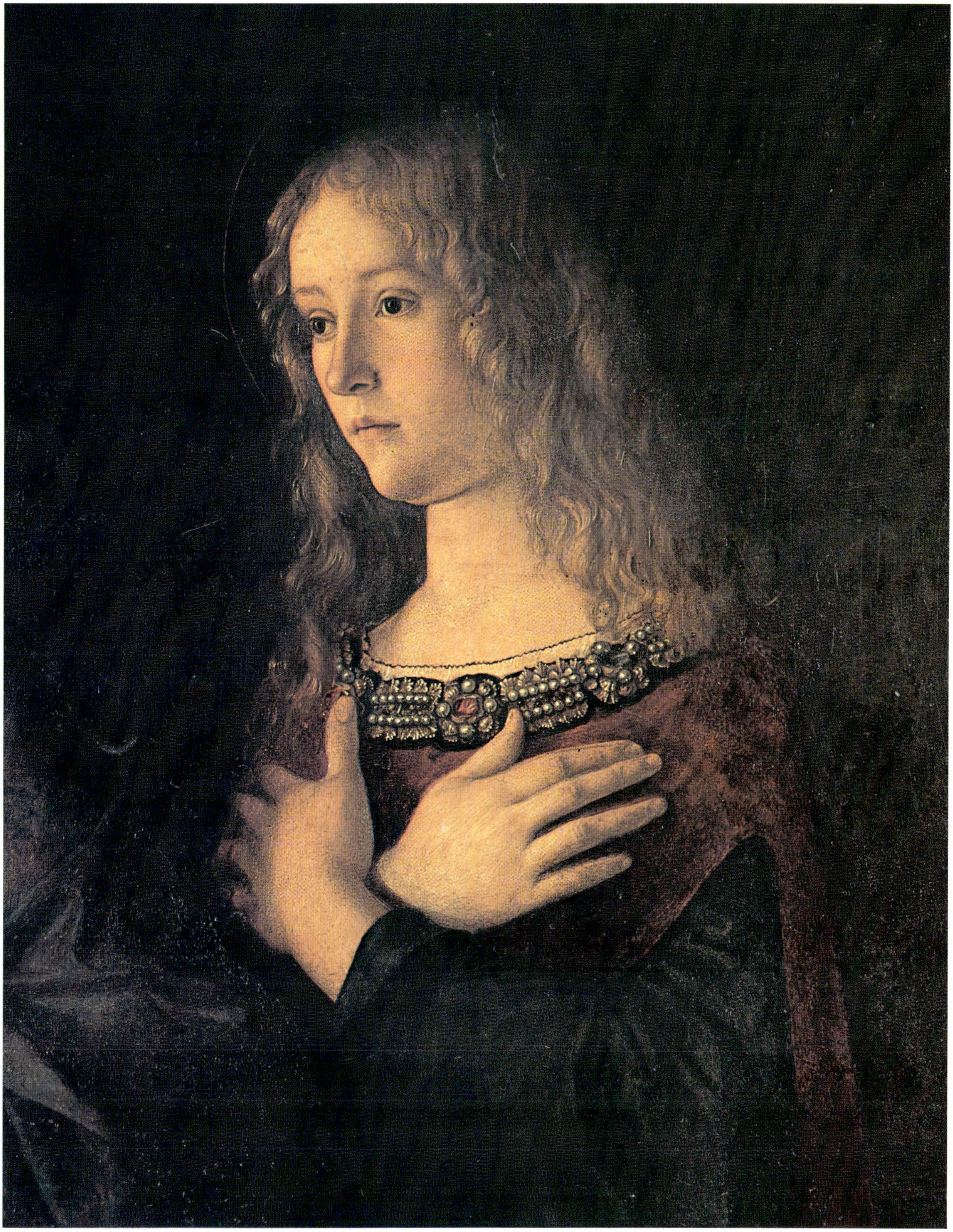

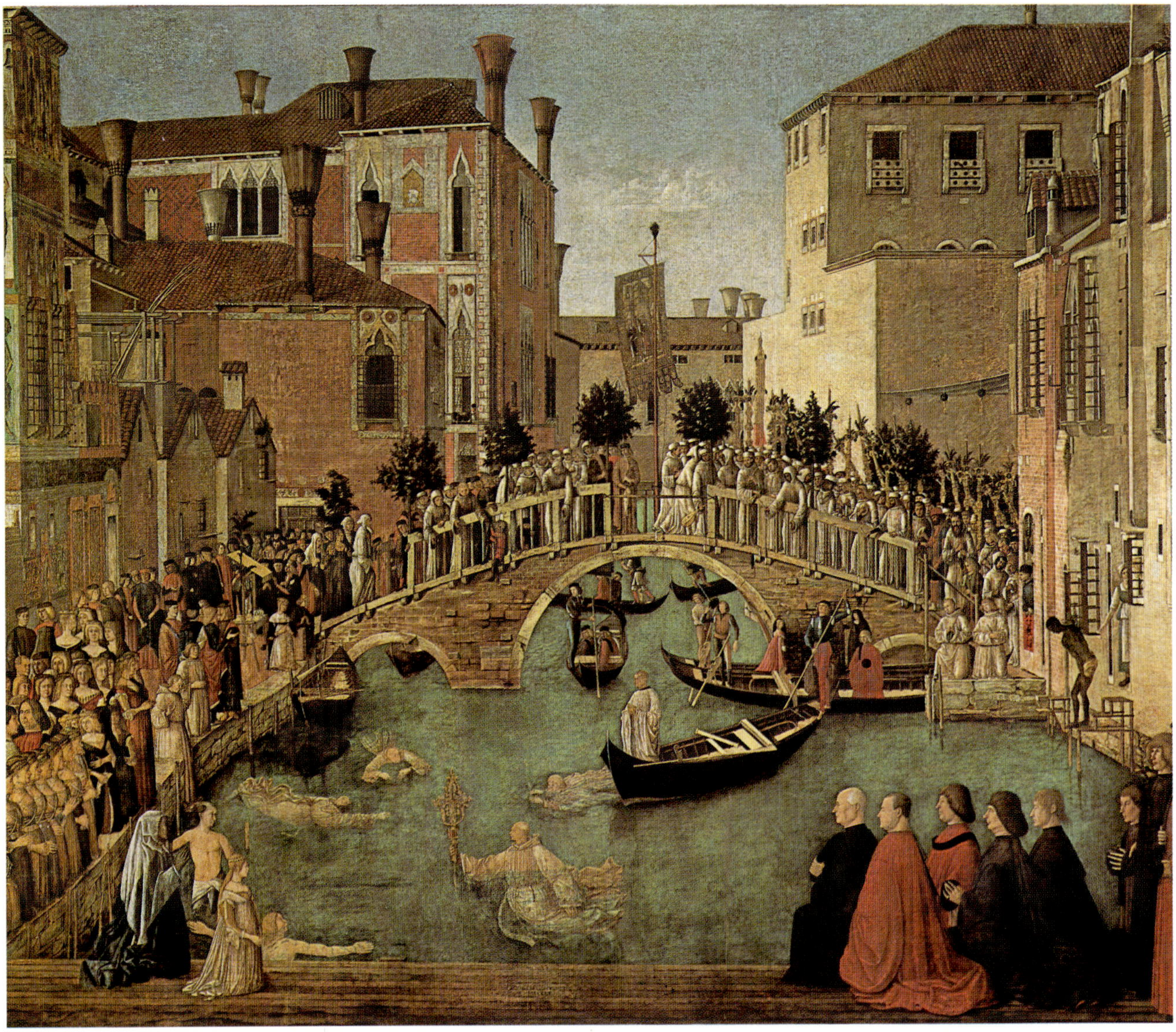

N° 30
Accademia Picture Galleries
"The Miracle of the Cross" by Gentile Bellini.
(L. 19-20, page 46)

N° 31
Accademia Picture Galleries
"The Madonna of the Orange" by G.B. Cima da Conegliano.
(L. 19-20, page 46)

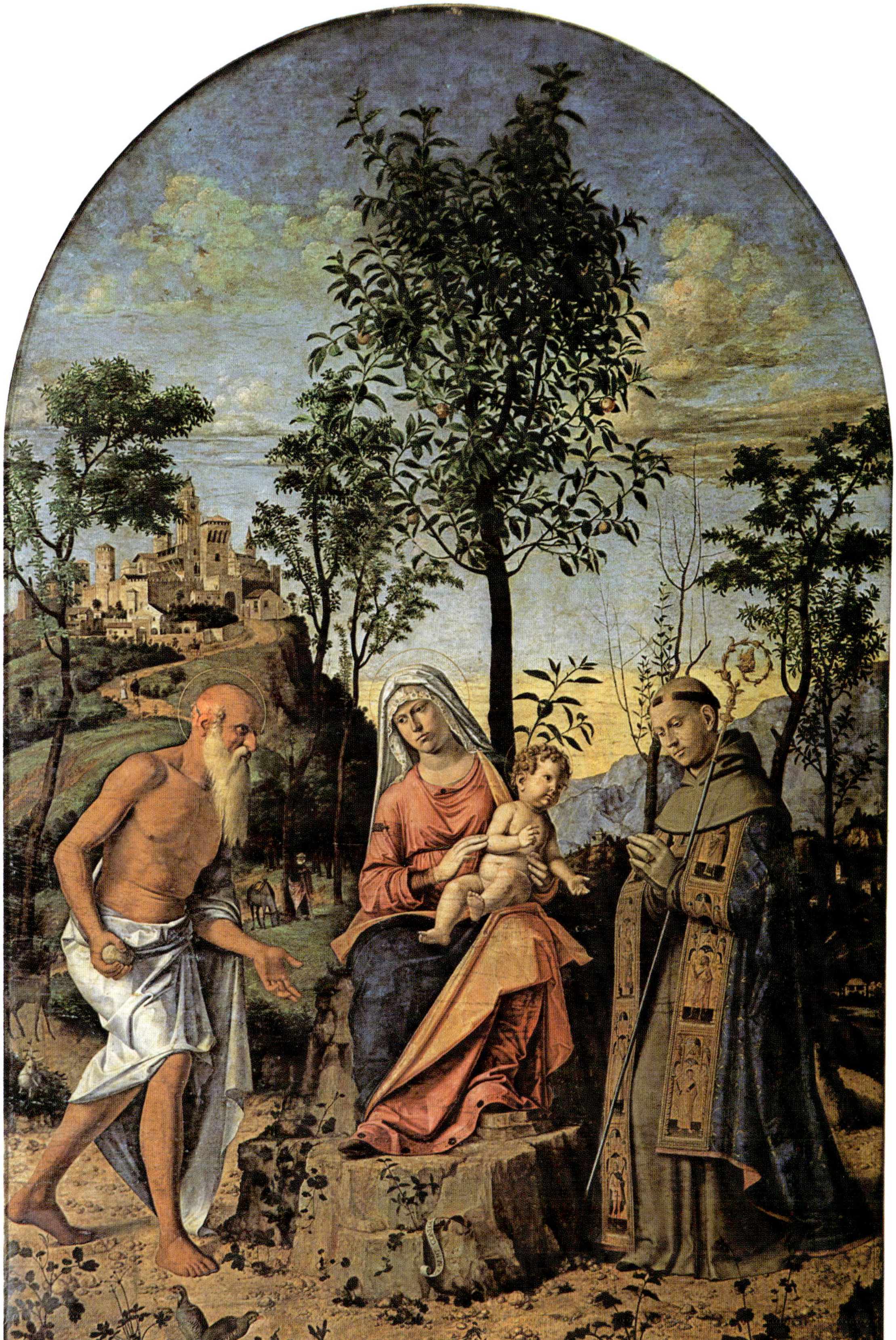

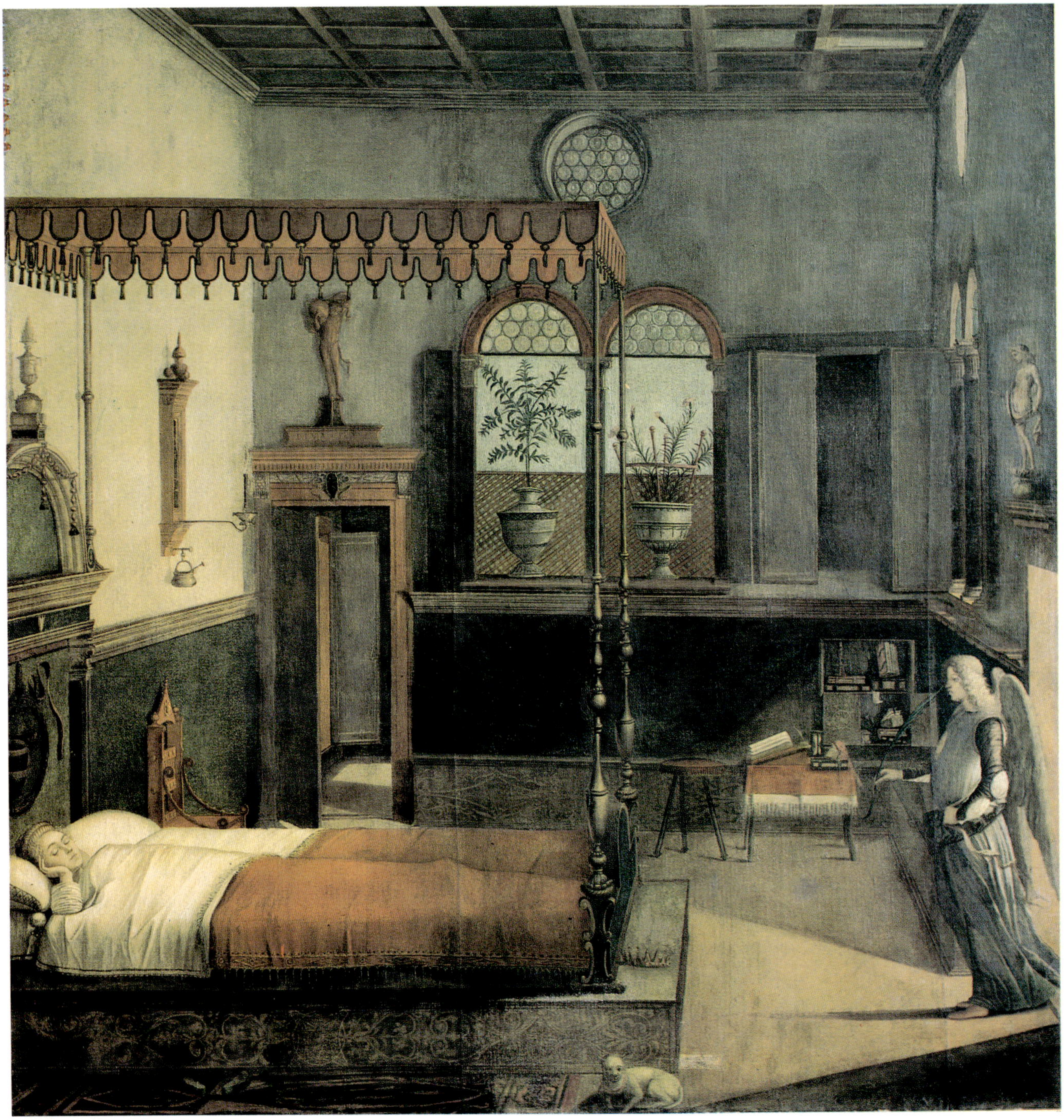

N° 32
Accademia Picture Galleries
"The Dream of St Ursula" by Vittore
Carpaccio.
(L. 19-20, page 46)

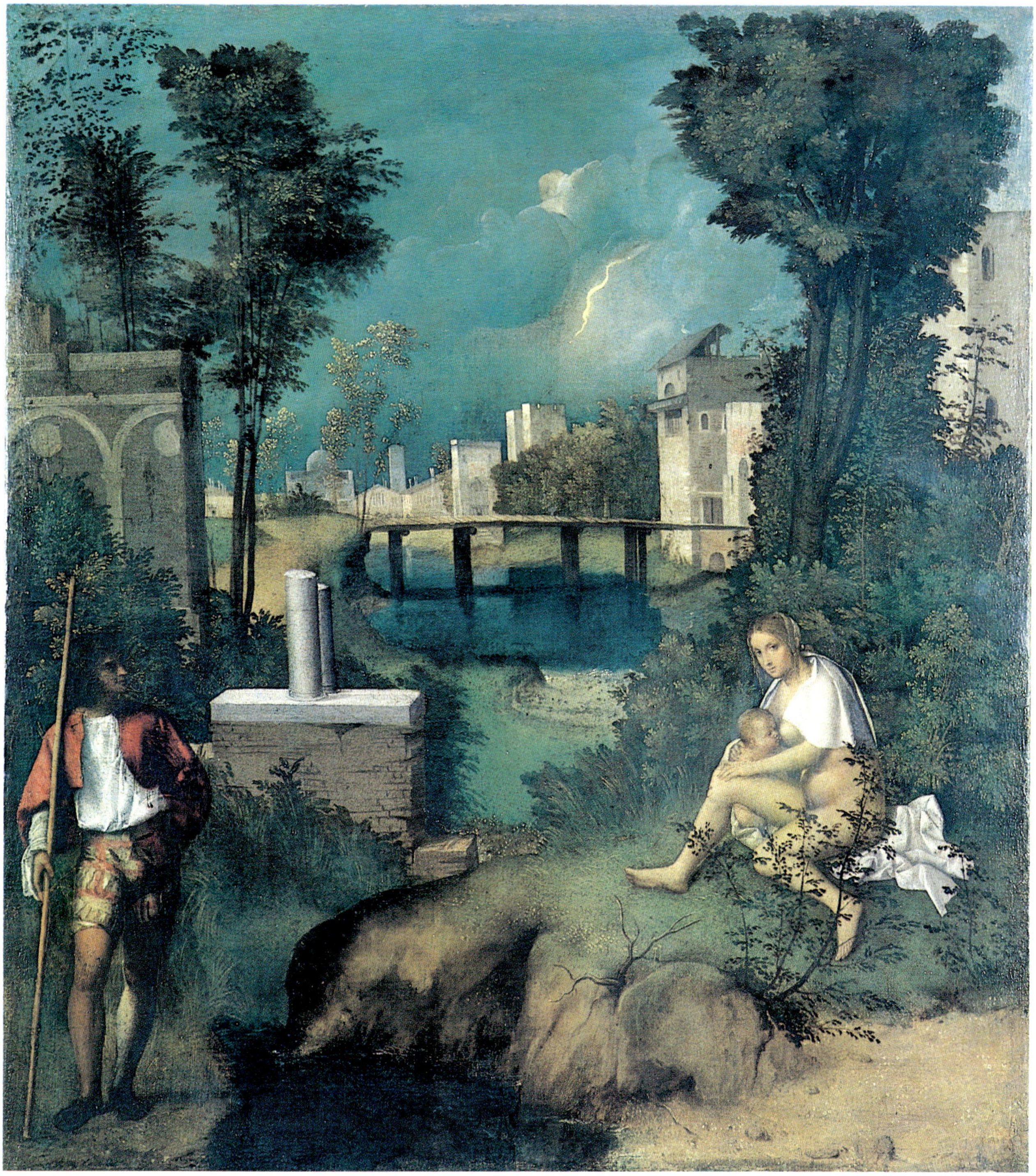

N° 33
Accademia Picture Galleries
"The Tempest" by Giorgione.
(L. 19-20, page 46)

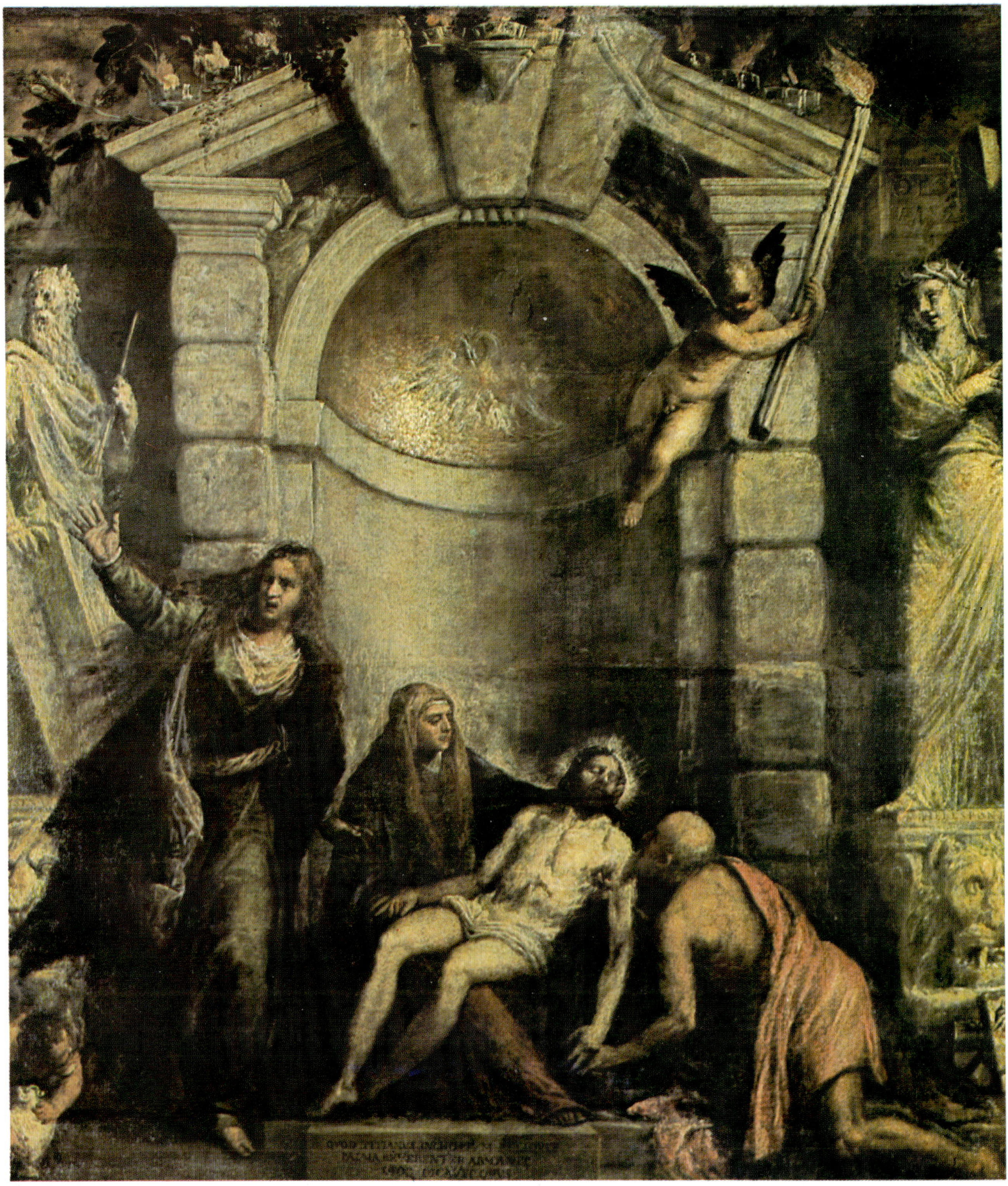

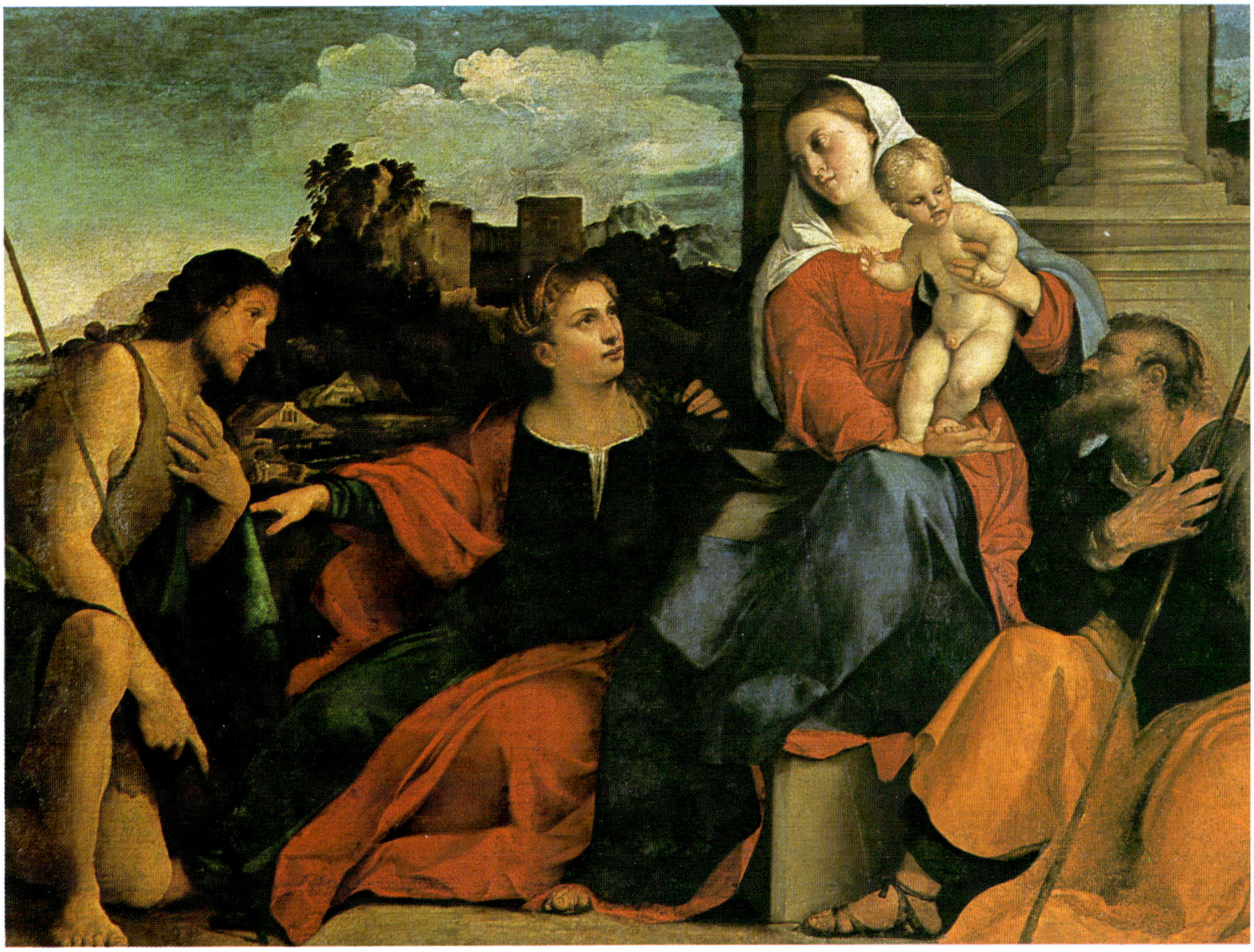

N° 34
Accademia Picture Galleries
"La Pietà" by Titian.
(L. 19-20, page 46)

N° 35
Accademia Picture Galleries
"Sacra conversazione" by Jacopo Palma Vecchio.
(L. 19-20, page 46)

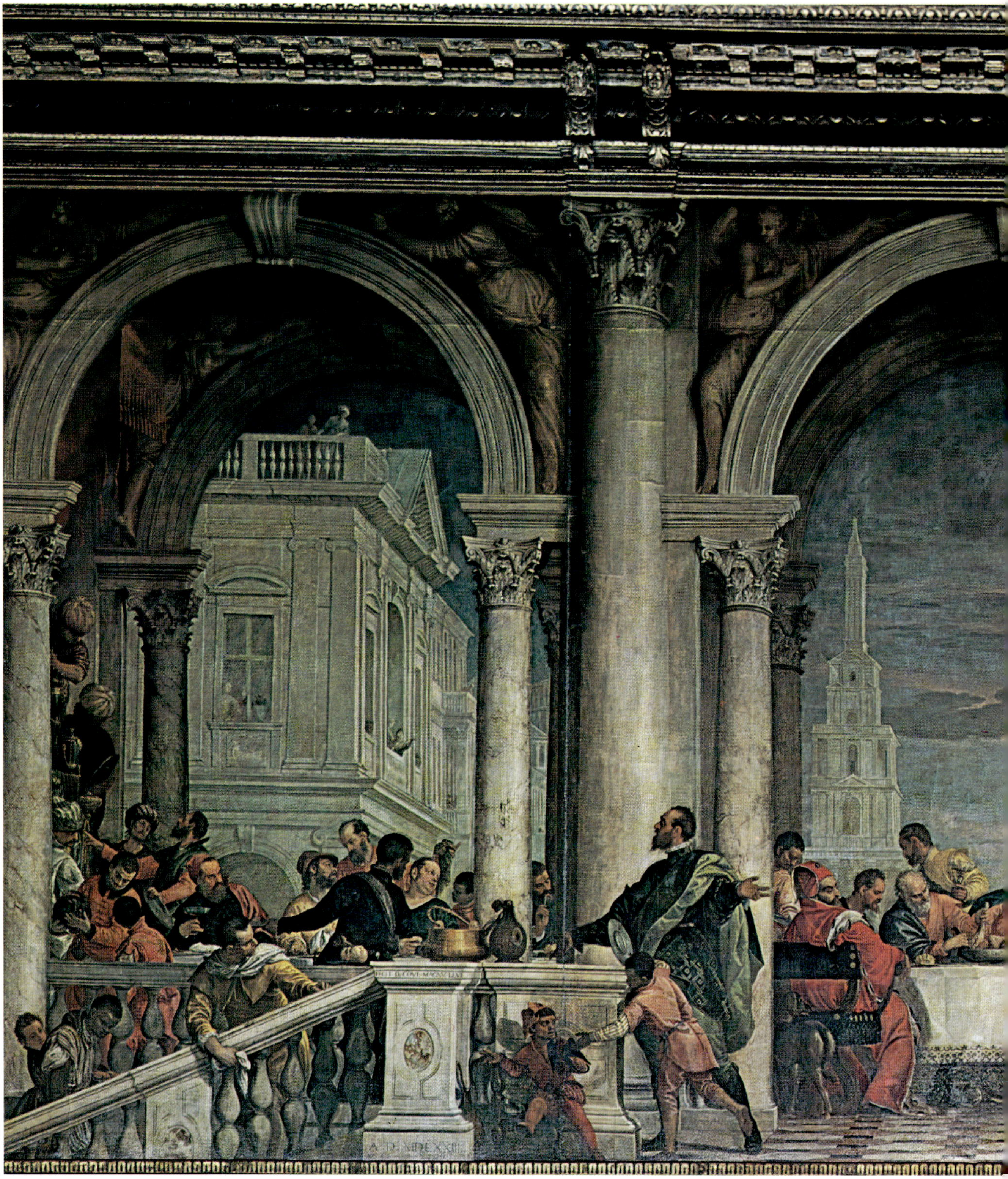

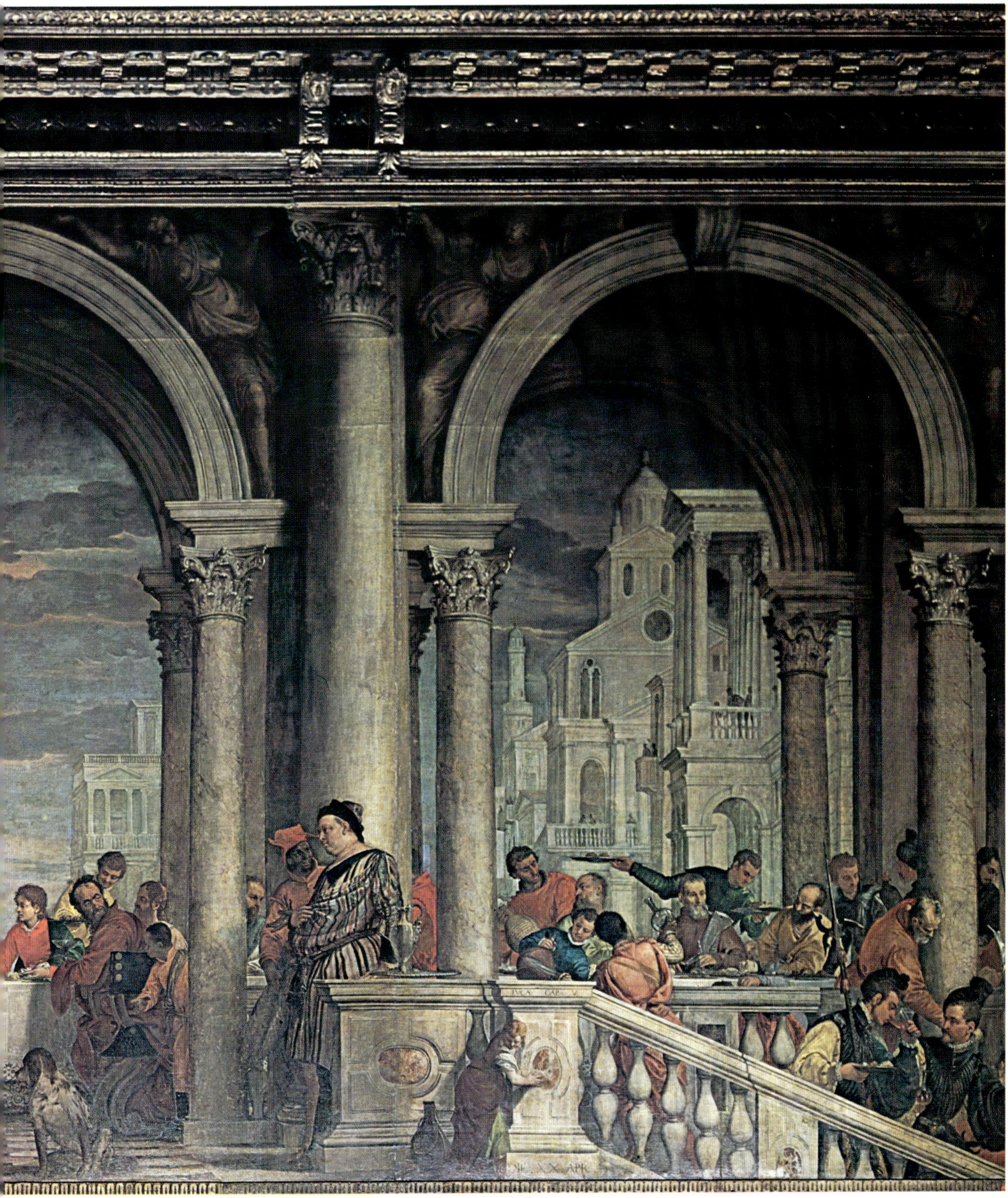

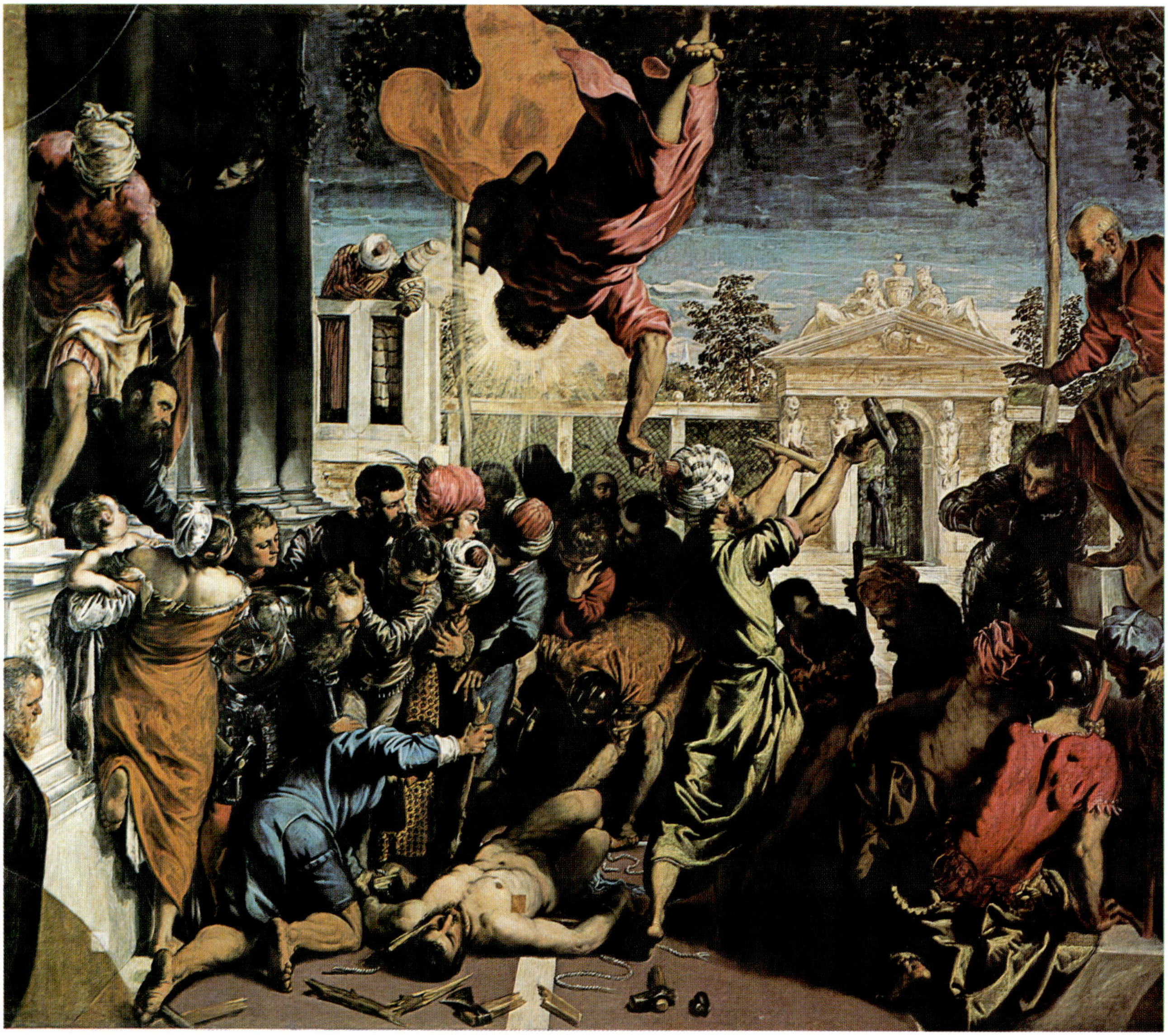

N° 36
Accademia Picture Galleries
"Supper in the House of Levi" by Paolo Veronese.
(L. 19-20, page 46)

N° 37
Accademia Picture Galleries
"St Mark frees a Slave" by Jacopo Tintoretto.
(L. 19-20, page 46)

N° 38
Accademia Picture Galleries
"The Fortune-teller" by Giambattista Piazzetta.
(L. 19-20, page 46)

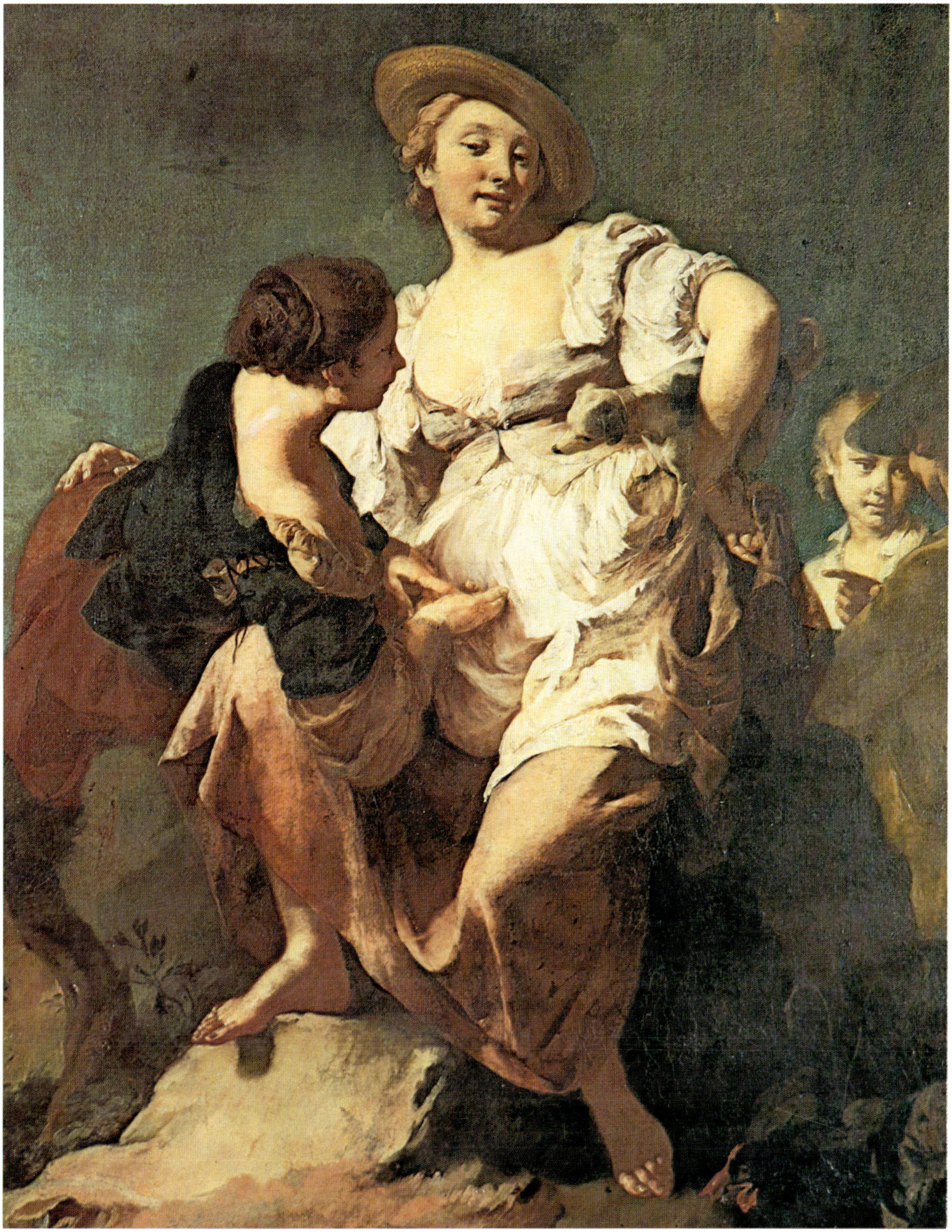

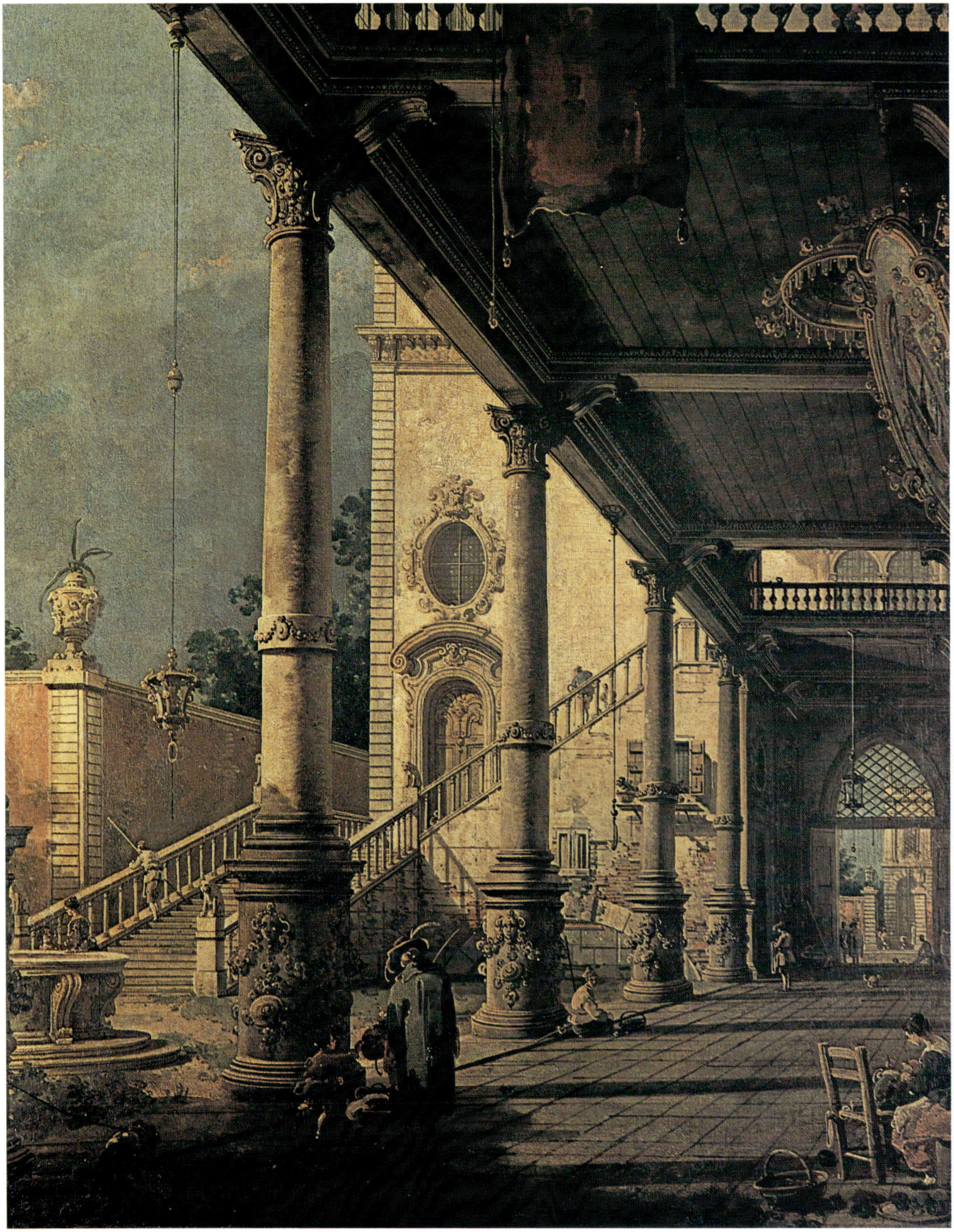

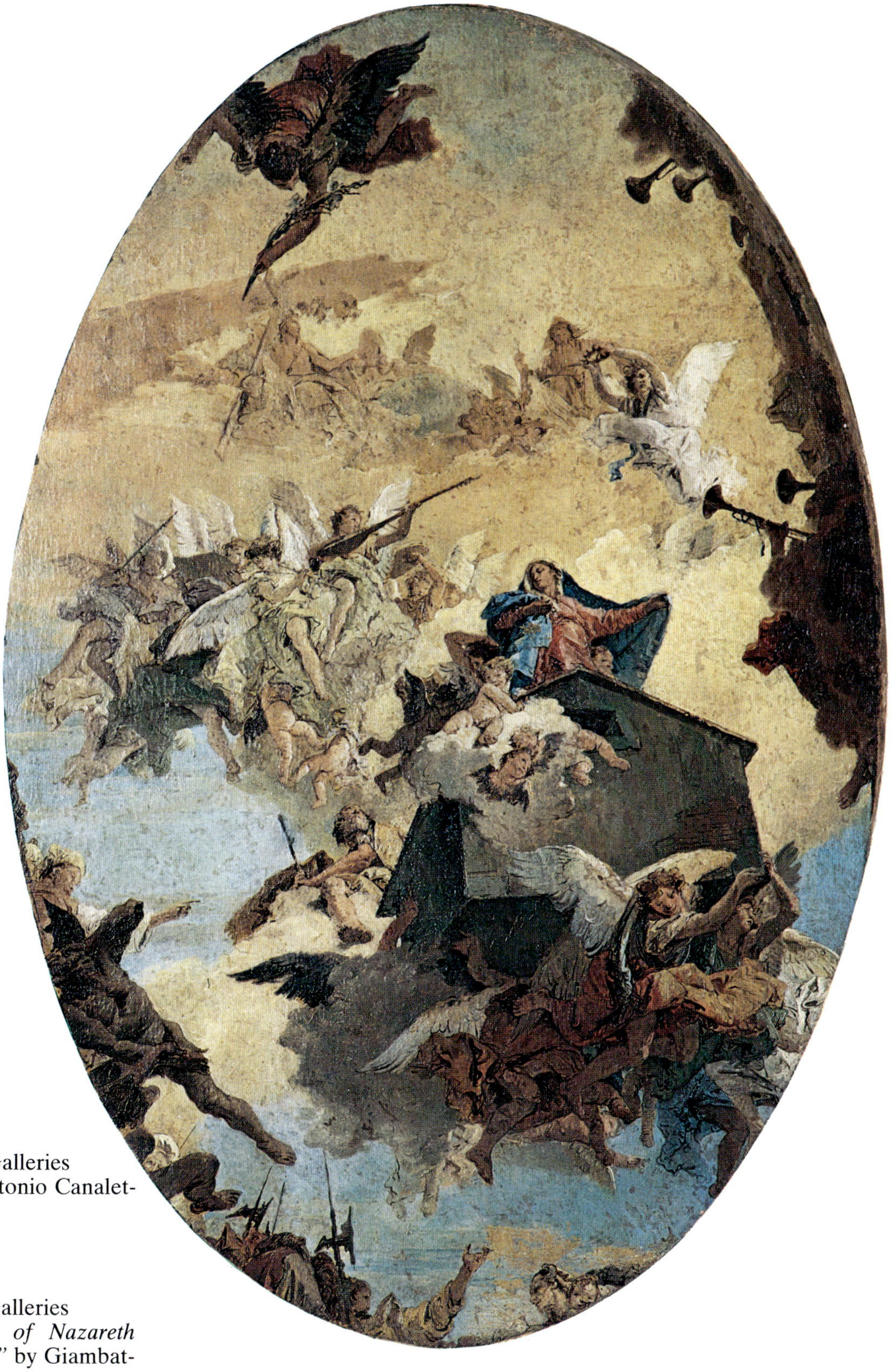

N° 39
Accademia Picture Galleries
"The Portico" by Antonio Canaletto.
(L. 19-20, page 46)

N° 40
Accademia Picture Galleries
"The Sacred House of Nazareth transported to Loreto" by Giambattista Tiepolo.
(L. 19-20, page 46)

L. 22
PALAZZO QUERINI

Immediately after Campo della Carità, just beyond the brief stretch of inland-bound canal cut short by 19th century earthing-in, stands the palace of one of the numerous branches of the Venetian patrician family Querini, in this case a rather minor branch. Palazzo Querini a simple, straightforward, 18th century construction stands on the site of an earlier building, which may have been of the Gothic period.

L. 23
PALAZZO MOCENIGO GAMBARA

Palazzo Mocenigo was built in the latter half of the 17th century. The façade, consisting of a tall mezzanine storey, a first piano nobile of unexceptional height and a second storey, is marked by shift of its characterizing Serliana and triangular pediment to the right, leaving articulation of the space on the left to a series of pedimented single lights. Taken as a whole, general proportions and architectural solutions add up to a modest building.

The campiello to the rear of the building, like the palace itself, bears the name of the Gambara family, which came into possession of the building when Eleonora Gambara married Francesco Mocenigo of the Carità branch in 1678.

Boschini draws attention to this palace as the birthplace of "that memorable and glorious sea-captain, Lazzaro Mocenigo" and also by reason of the Pordenone frescoes of historical and allegorical scenes on the interior court frontage.

The Gambara family was accorded patrician status only in 1653 but had already made its mark in the political and military spheres on several occasions. Moreover, it numbered among its forbears, four cardinals and, to quote Tassini "Veronica, that distinguished female poet and bride of the seigneur of Correggio".

Veronica, well versed in letters and the humanities, was born at Pralboino di Brescia in 1485. On the death of her husband, Gilberto X, seigneur of Correggio, she administered his tiny state with wisdom and energy.

Widely famed in her time, major literary figures such as Bembo, Ariosto, Tasso and Aretino, enjoyed her friendship. Her own literary output includes the "Rime", measured and elegant in the Petrarchian manner, and, rich in human insight, the lively and spontaneous "Lettere".

A final note on Lazzaro Mocenigo, a capable commander, resolute and valiant, born in Venice in 1624, who repeatedly defeated the Turks in the field of action at Candia, causing them great loss of men and materials. He held office as Procuratore di San Marco before nomination as captain general, and died fighting in 1657 in the course of one of the numerous battles to blockade the Dardanelles.

R. 22
PALAZZO FRANCHETTI CAVALLI GUSSONI

At the end of the 19th century, the palace, formerly Gussoni, later, Cavalli, was restored by its new owner, Baron Franchetti, who enlarged the rear block and the great stairway to conform to an arbitrary project by the architect Camillo Boito.
Notwithstanding, it remains one of the most interesting Gothic buildings of the latter half of the 15th century. The multi-light section with its quatrefoils, clearly inspired by the loggia on the Doge's Palace, is of especial interest.
Famous tenants have included the Archduke Ferdinand of Austria, who died here in 1836, and the Comte de Chambord, who created the garden on the adjacent site of a small house and boatyard.
The building rises from ground floor through a relatively low mezzanine to a first and second piano nobile.
The central five-light section stating reception rooms on both first and second piano nobile offers dazzling architectural solutions. The first piano nobile displays full quatrefoils on the concavity of the reverse-curve arch, enclosed by a rectilinear denticled surround. The multi-light section of the second storey claims attention for the enhanced verticality resulting from taller columns, colonnetted parapet flush with the façade, and an upper fascia of semi-quatrefoils. The luxuriant foliage on the capitals is even more eloquent of the period.
A by no means minor factor contributing to the geometrical scheme of the façade, beyond the clarity and precision of alignment and distribution of detail is the closure solution supplied by a counter-change pattern of ashlar blocks laid either side of the corner, embellished with carved spiral colonnettes running the full height of the building.

R. 23
CAMPO S. VIDAL AND ITS CHURCH

Campo S. Vidal, sited between the Palazzo Franchetti gardens and the homonymous canal, with access to the left bank via the Accademia Bridge on its short side, is linked by spatial continuity to the vast concourse of Campo S. Stefano. Closure element in articulation of the area is the S. Vitale church, its nave running parallel to the Grand Canal, from which its left flank is visible in a building aggregate comprising church, ancient cuspated bell-tower and a three-storey house.
Founded in 1084, the church was restored – perhaps rebuilt – towards the end of the 12th century, together with its bell-tower, which still preserves the structures of those times.
At the end of the 17th century, renewal was urged and S. Vitale, like many other city churches, was totally rebuilt. The Byzantine-Gothic edifice with three aisles and tripartite brick façade, was replaced by a new church on a single-nave plan, with apsidal chapels and altars lining the side walls. Taken as a whole, the project respects essentially 17th century Venetian tradition in religious building.
The architect Antonio Gaspari, in fact, had to shelve his initial fanciful proposals, judged to be "excessively complicated in architectural composition". The new building was originally intended to be an imposing funerary monument celebrating Francesco Morosini, doge from 1688-1694, and his exploits as the last great Venetian sea captain. His victorious sea campaigns against the Turks had restored to the Republic, albeit briefly, a number of former possessions in the Near East, among them, the Peleponnese.
That Gaspari had been master-builder to the Pisani family may explain how he came to be chosen to carry out this project, but the executive plan finally accepted by the commissioning body differed greatly from the first solutions he had submitted, as may be seen from drawings in our possession.
In 1700, the church was completed in all but the façade, for which Morosini's heirs were reluctant to provide further funds, thereby withdrawing from the programme in celebration of their predecessor.
The façade was finally built by the architect Andrea Tirali, between 1734 and 1737, on the initiative of the Contarini family.

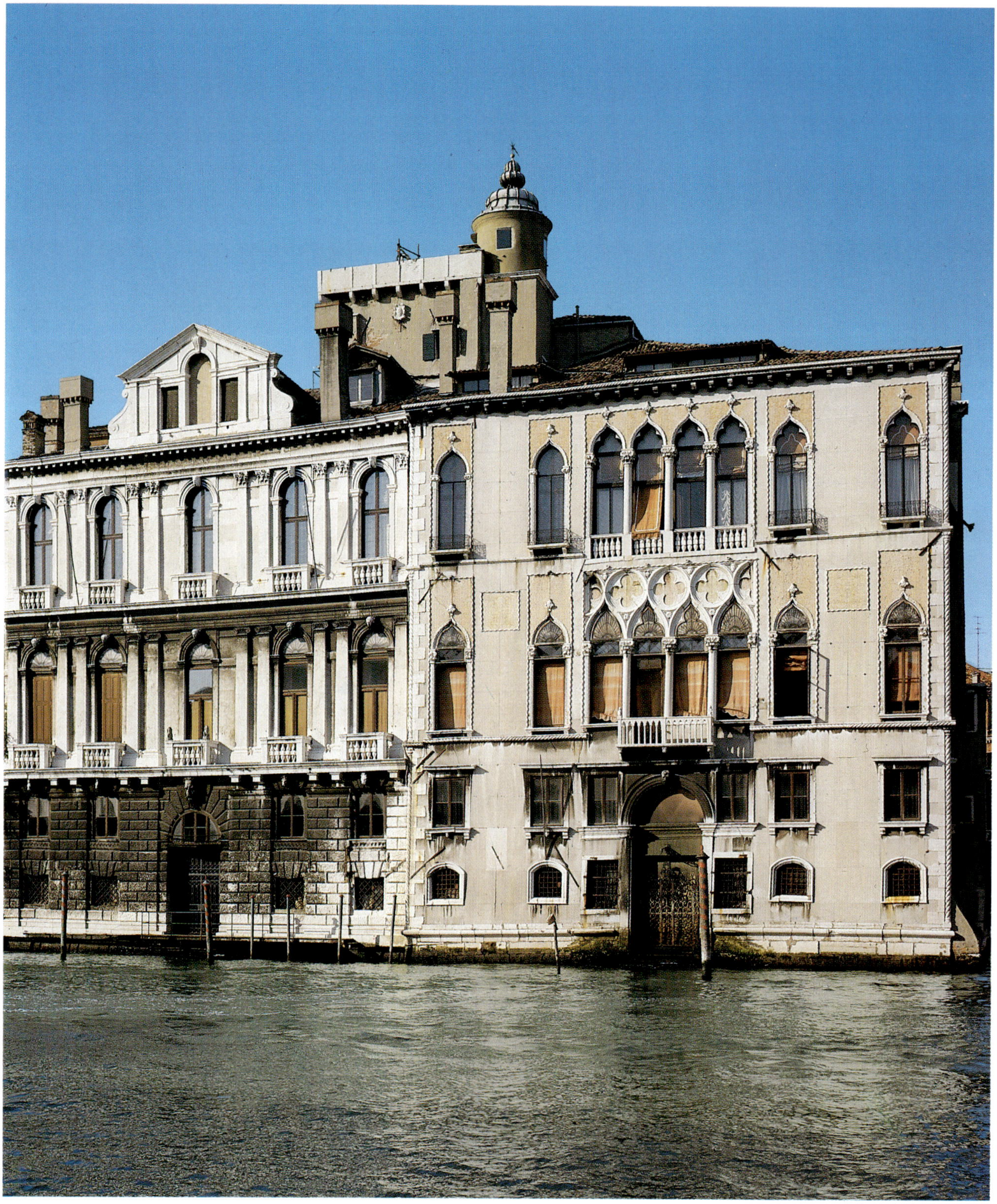

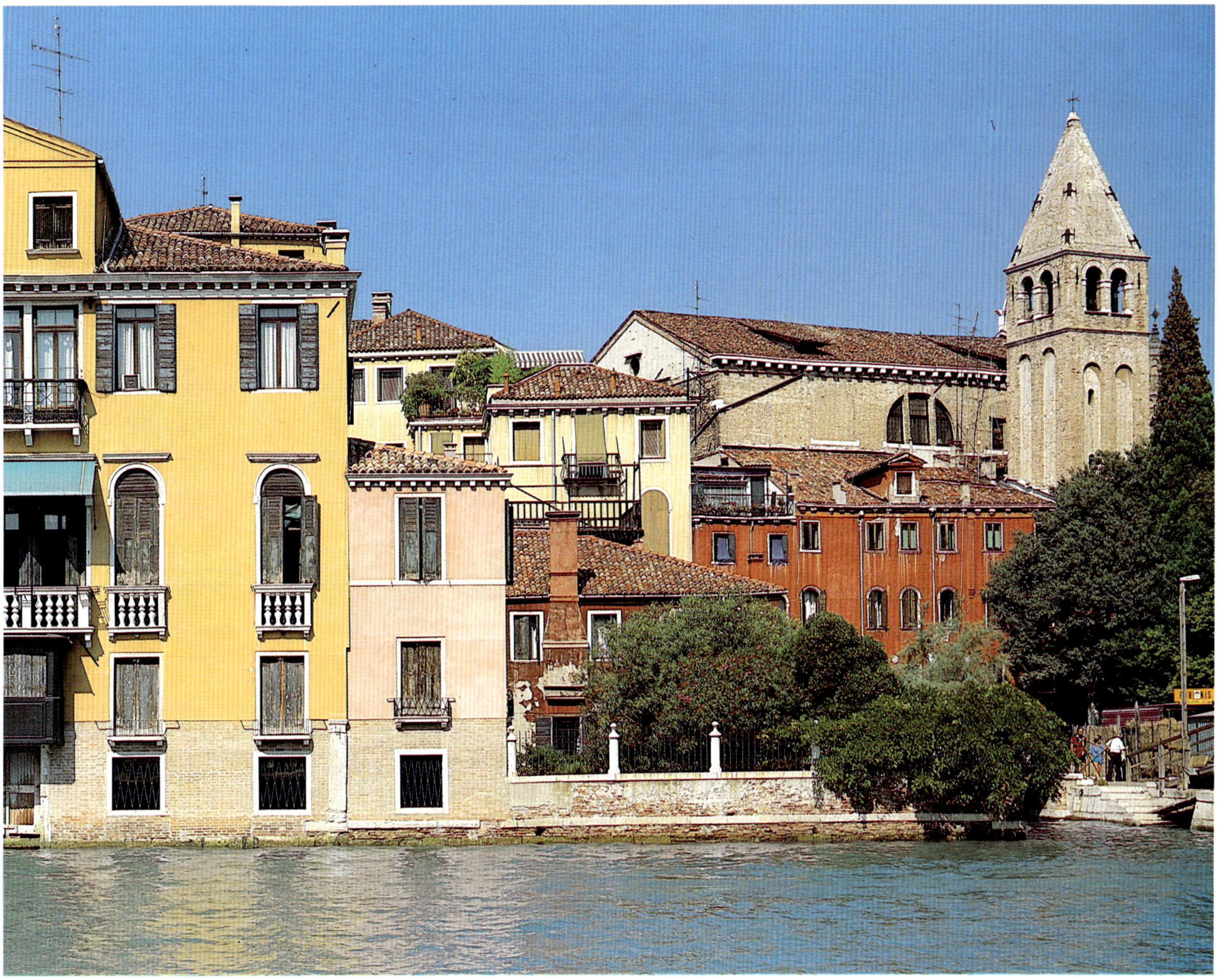

N° 41
The Contarini dagli Scrigni palaces
Girolamo Contarini bequeathed his exceptional collection of paintings to the City of Venice in 1838, thereby providing the collections of the Accademia Picture Galleries with their most significant nucleus of works.
(L. 24-25, page 70)

N° 42
Campo S. Vidal
In the background the homonymous church, its side frontage masked by a private house. Only the bell-tower preserves its original structures today.
(R. 23, page 65)

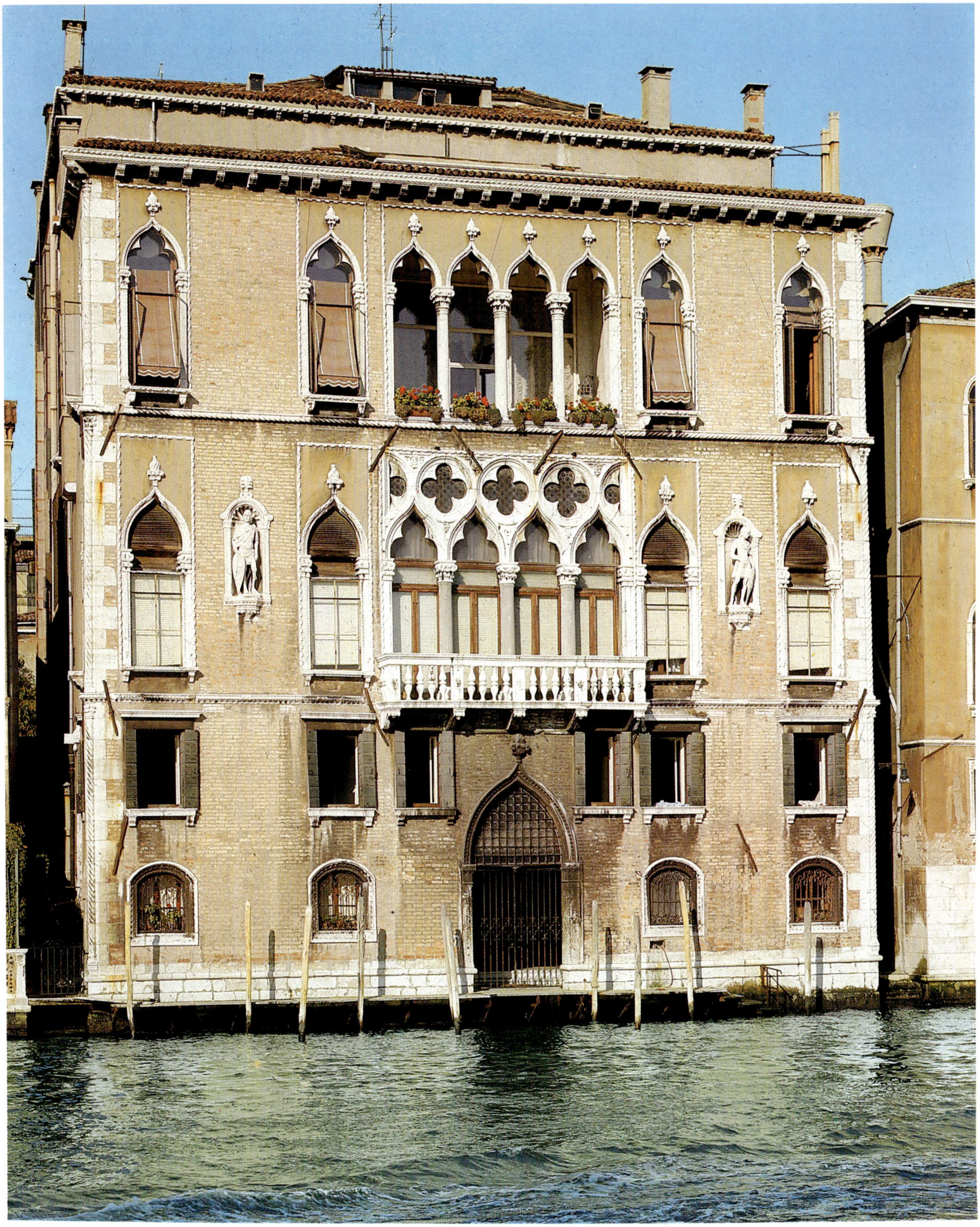

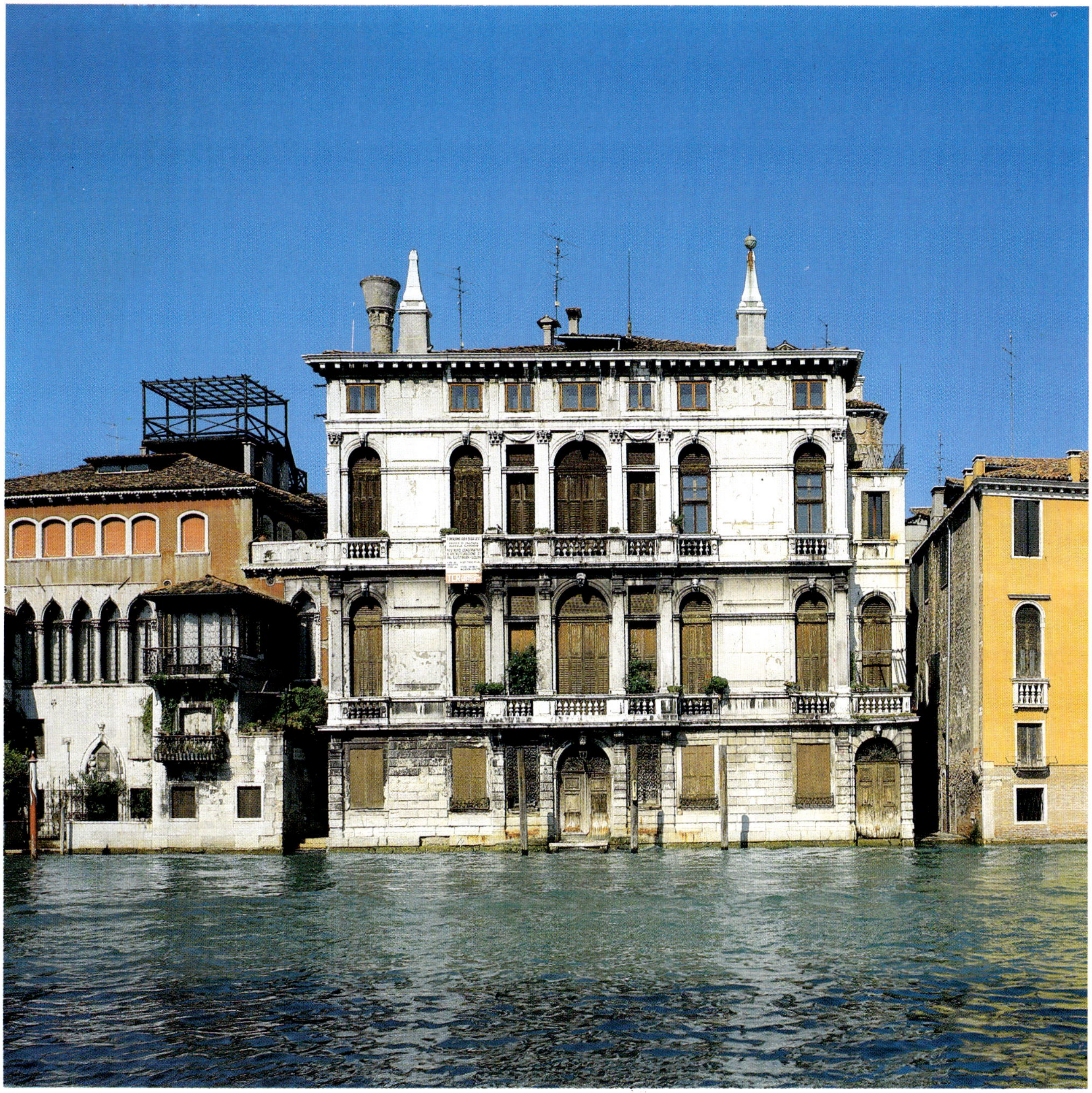

N° 43
Palazzo Loredan dell'Ambasciatore
Residence of the imperial ambassador from 1574, the Gothic building dates from the latter half of the 15th century.
(L. 26, page 70)

N° 44
Palazzo Giustinian Lolin
The building is the product of structural interventions in c. 1639, by Baldassare Longhena.
(R. 25, page 71)

L. 24-25
PALAZZO CONTARINI DAGLI SCRIGNI

The Contarini dagli Scrigni Corfù branch is one of the many important ones into which the family had gone on dividing itself over centuries of growth and history. Right from early times it was a wealthy, powerful family which produced no less than eight Doges as well as countless politicians who held all the highest positions in the State.
Starting with Domenico I Contarini who was Doge in 1043, over the various centuries we find the continuity of this social position emphasized by Jacopo in 1275, Andrea from 1368 to 1382, Francesco for a very short dogeship in 1623 equal to Nicolò's equally short one in 1630 and then by Carlo in 1655.
Domenico II Contarini was elected Doge in 1659 and then Alvise a few years later in 1676.
The nickname "dagli Scrigni" (of the caskets) given to this branch of the Contarini family at SS. Gervasio e Protasio, had come from the large number of caskets which, according to Fontana, the family possessed in the Piazzola villa. This property came into the hands of the Contarinis as part of the dowry for Maria, the daughter of Giacomo da Genova who was the gentleman owner of those lands and the villages built there, when in 1414 she married Nicolò Contarini from San Cassiano.
Society chronicles then recount that in 1524 the marriage of Doge Andrea Gritti's grandaughter to Paolo Contarini was celebrated with great pomp: "after the church service in St. Mark's Basilica and after the solemn banquet in the Doge's Palace, the newly-weds, accompanied by numerous parties of ladies and gentlemen, boarded the "bucintoro" where they gaily danced and amid the sound of music and artillery shots, they arrived at the Palazzo degli Scrigni at SS. Gervasio e Protasio, decorated from top to bottom with hangings and tapestries, and inside the rooms bright with many lights, a magnificent ball was begun". The property really extended over two communicating buildings standing next to each other. First comes the one designed by the architect Vincenzo Scamozzi as an enlargement of the one in Gothic style standing on the neighbouring site.
The limitations imposed by the pre-existing building, not least having to keep the floors of the two buildings on the same level, were very binding and forced the architect Scamozzi to accept sizes and proportions which certainly did not suit the artist's freedom of expression. This building can be easily recognized by its characteristic turret plus terrace above the roof. This is at the top of the very beautiful, internal, ovoid spiral staircase which runs from top to bottom of the building.
As we have already said, the second palace is in Gothic style with a bipartite façade characterized by the splendid central multi-mullioned windows containing the design idea of the quatrefoil, while the tiers of very slender trefoil arches remind us of other Venetian buildings such as Palazzo Bernardo which also stands on the Grand Canal. Such buildings can be said to date from the middle of the 15th century or better still from the first half of the century.
This building has maintained almost intact its external architectural characteristics but the interior was extensively restored around the 17th century by the architect Francesco Smeraldi called Fracà, a follower of Palladio, who had worked on the reconstruction and completion of the Church of S. Pietro in Castello.
The wealth and opulence of the furnishings and interior decorations were renowned as was the collection of paintings which Girolamo Contarini bequeathed to the city of Venice in 1838 and which made up the most important and impressive nucleus of the collections in the Accademia Galleries.

L. 26
PALAZZO LOREDAN DELL'AMBASCIATORE

This Gothic building was most probably erected around 1470 as suggested by the use of quatrefoils to adorn the multi-mullioned window contained within a square-like geometric figure, and by the use of the spiral motif at the edges and so on.
What characterizes this building, or rather the façade, is the great severity of the architecture, the conciseness of style which emphasizes the very thin plain surfaces lacking in light and colour contrasts, rather than its dimension so near to that of a square which somehow makes it less noticeable as a whole with respect to other buildings of that time.
It has two piani nobili with corresponding multi-mullioned windows.
The middle of the 15th century had passed (1470) and althrough the architecture is still clearly Gothic, a new era was approaching in which the general idea which characterized the whole was no longer that of other times even though each element taken singularly derived from the past.
A characteristic feature is the two niches with shield-bearing pages, situated in the empty wall spaces which, together with the two one-mullioned windows, make up the side settings: as regards these new architectural and sculptural motifs, Arslan emphasizes the contribution of "Renaissance" artists, but cannot "date them to before Pietro Lombardo's arrival in Venice".
The Loredans, who owned the building, were one of the most distinguished families of the so called "new houses". In 1501 the family gained dogal dignity with Leonardo Loredan and a second time with Francesco in 1572. The latter's wealth was very sizeable as we can gather from reading his tax returns but the expenses he bore during his important political-military assignments before and during his dogeship considerably reduced his resources.
Palazzo Loredan was called "dell'

R. 24
PALAZZO CIVRAN BADOER BAROZZI

On the opposite bank of Rio S. Vidal, preceded by a garden of oleanders, stands Palazzo Civran Badoer, 16th century in period, with the later addition of a second storey. The three-light central section and round-arch on its piano nobile conform to the familiar tripartite scheme.

R. 25
PALAZZO GIUSTINIAN LOLIN

This building is the result of one of the first restorations carried out by the architect Baldassare Longhena while he was still young. This can be clearly seen from the numerous façade elements including the most evident which is the considerable, perhaps excessive, height of the windows which denote and emphasize their Gothic origin, as well as the lack of the ground floor mezzanine. In fact, the Giustinian building was originally Gothic and was then transformed but many of the already existing structures were kept. The most conspicuous part, that is to say the façade overlooking the Grand Canal, was given a modern touch in line with the times without having to demolish and rebuild (thus avoiding greater expense).

This period of restructuring and restoration can be said to date from 1639, the year in which Giovanni Lolin named his son-in-law Giovanni Giustinian as heir to the palace. On that occasion the latter added his father-in-law's surname to his own. Moreover Lolin generously left a considerable sum to pay for the building work.

All the architectural and stylistic elements used here by Longhena appear to respect the tradition of local architecture, likewise the use of the rustic work on the lower order, of the superimposed pillars to accentuate the middle of the façade with its central three-mullioned window emphasized by the Serliana.

R. 26
PALAZZO FALIER CANOSSA

Palazzo Falier Canossa, an unusual Gothic construction with numerous details and factors of style pointing to a first-half of the 15th century dating, looks to the "liago" of Venetian tradition for the salient feature of its façade: two projecting side loggias built up to the water's edge. In consequence, the central section of the "true" façade, its portal leading directly into the portego, or reception hall, stands back from the canal. Relevant to the Falier family, Tassini, drawing on documents reporting its presence in the S. Vidal neighbourhood in ancient times, quotes: "Giacomo Falier, popularly known as 'el grando', was from S. Vitale". The Faliers had probably lived in the area since 1084; Vitale Falier was elected doge, built the church dedicated to S. Vitale, and died within that same year.

In 1102, the family again produced a doge, Ordelafo, and in 1354, another, the notorious Marino, whose conspiracy to gain absolute power, revealed before it could take effect, led to his execution, together with that of his accomplices, in 1355.

Ambasciatore" (of the Ambassador) because it was the seat of the Imperial Ambassador in Venice after General Von der Schulenburg had stayed there.
The first ambassador from the Court of Vienna to live in the palace was Count Filippo Rosenburg-Orsini from 1574 onwards. We know about the offer made by Doge Francesco Loredan himself to "make over this palace to the Imperial ambassadors for a period of time not inferior to twenty-nine years, on the condition that the rent should be paid in one lump sum and that the ambassadors themselves should pay for its restoration".

L. 27
PALAZZO MORO

This Renaissance palace, dating from the first decades of the 16th century, occupies the corner site on the left bank of the Rio di Malpaga, a name recording an attribute of the Michiel family, whose residence formerly stood facing it on the opposite bank. The round-arch windows of Palazzo Moro, floral motifs on the extrados keystone, are set against a plastered façade unrelieved by any other decorative feature. As composition places the accent on breadth as opposed to height, the perfectly symmetrical multi-light section of its piano nobile makes a generous horizontal statement and all other windows are set uncompromisingly in axis to it.
There are two very different trends in architectural treatment in this period of the Renaissance – from the end of the 15th century to the early decades of the 16th – where the first fully exploits the decorative contribution of polychrome marble inserts on the façade in addition to its structural elements, the second observes the maximum restraint, indulging only in some ornamental motif on the extrados keystone, offset by a simple coat of plaster, in the Gothic manner, covering the remainder of the wall surface.

L. 28-29-30
PALAZZETTO STERN AND THE CONTARINI MICHIEL PALACES

The Michiel Malpaga palace, almost wholly demolished in the 19th century, occupied the corner site on the right bank of the Malpaga canal. It was replaced at the beginning of the 20th century by what is known as the "Palazzetto di Madame Stern", a mock Byzantine-Gothic building designed by the architect Berti and, in respect of its predecessor, standing back from the canal. According to the genealogist Barbaro it was in 1425 that the Malpaga nickname was first attributed to Fantino Michiel, who built "the Castle of Malpaga... near Ragusa, in a single night. He engaged oars-men, and on reaching Venice convinced the Signoria that payment of the tenth part of all man-of-war hand wages for dismantling the fleet should not be observed". Now, when the oars-men "pass by the castle they always imprecate against him and throw sticks and stones".
Beyond the calle of the S. Barnaba ferry, two adjacent buildings form the frontage of the building block separating it from the homonymous canal. Both date from the first half of the 16th century and, as may be seen, are incomplete – one devoid of its right wing, the other of the left – inasmuch as the multilight section corresponding to the reception hall on the piano nobile of both buildings is set adjacent to the border line between the two. The successive proprietors in both cases were the Contarini and Michiel families.

R. 27
CÀ DEL DUCA

Immediately after the canal we find some marble remains such as a very thick corner column, rhomb-shaped rustic work as a base and on the façade overlooking the canal some Istrian stone structures denoting the presence of large portals and windows. These remains are proof of work on a large building left unfinished. Marco Corner, the father of the Queen of Cyprus Caterina, together with his brother Andrea had begun to have it built as their own home around the middle of the 15th century (1453), commissioning the architect and stone-mason Bartolomeo Bon to carry out the design. The historical accounts then relate how shortly afterwards the Republic "gave Francesco Sforza, the Duke of Milan, the palace in campo San Polo previously owned by General Gattamelata". Sforza made it over to the Corner family receiving in exchange in 1461 the site and the palace being built on the Grand Canal at San Samuele. However, the work which had been temporarily interrupted, did not proceed due to the hostility which arose between the Republic of Venice and the Duchy of Milan. This hostility which became increasingly more fierce and deeprooted, prevented Sforza from carrying on building the palace until the Serenissima confiscated "for itself the beginnings of the planned palace upon which a more modest building was later erected". Previously on this site there had been a brick building, then the existing buildings were bought by Bon and later a large shed was set up which Titian turned into a studio where he prepared and painted the large canvases commissioned at that time by the Republic to be used to decorate the rooms in the Doge's Palace; these works were completely destroyed in the 1574 and 1577 fires in the Palace. In 1525 the Cà del Duca was sold to the Este family and during Sansovino's time it belonged to the Grimani family.

R. 28-29
PALAZZO CAPPELLO MALIPIERO AND CHURCH OF SAN SAMUELE

A garden and then Palazzo Malipiero; this was once a Gothic building of which some elements remain, such as windows and portals on the façade overlooking the square. In 1662 it took on its present appearance in a somewhat classical style with the insertion of by then Baroque motifs which have seemed to indicate an early work by the architect Longhena, where Alessandro Vittoria's influence is still clearly present. The coat-of-arms between the two twin portals of the main entrance is characteristic. The palace stands on the corner area of campo San Samuele where only the 12th century Veneto-Byzantine bell-tower remains of the very early church. Unfortunately a house built in 1915 by the painter Augusto Cezanne now adjoins the bell-tower. Tradition has it that the church was founded around 1000 and then completely rebuilt in 1683. It is now deconsecrated, has lost the works which were kept there and is of no interest at all to the visitor.
The historical accounts in our possession tell how the San Samuele quarter was famous for grim stories of adultery and illicit love affairs. At the end of the 14th century the church's parish priest was having a good time with the married women who "ran away from their own homes to the parish priest with whom they committed adultery". In 1468 a law forbade "such prostitutes, under the penalty of ten lire and twenty-five lashes, to live or even stop together or with a man in the area from the end of the narrow street which leads to the church of S. Samuele, as far as the grocer's shop in San Stephano". However this quarter was also famous for being the birthplace or home or workplacc of many very talented artists, from Bartolomeo Bon to Titian, from the sculptors Tullio and Antonio Lombardo to Sante Lombardo who died there. Girolamo Campagna and Paolo Veronese lived there in relatively modest houses; the latter also died there in 1588 of a "high temperature after attending the solemn procession of the second feast-day of Easter". Benedetto Caliari, Veronese's brother, and his sons Carlo and Gabriele also lived in this quarter as did Pietro Libera in the nearby Palazzo Moro-Lin. San Samuele was also the birthplace of Giacomo Casanova, the adventurer, lover and writer of memoirs which were famous throughout the world thanks to the great charm he could exert.

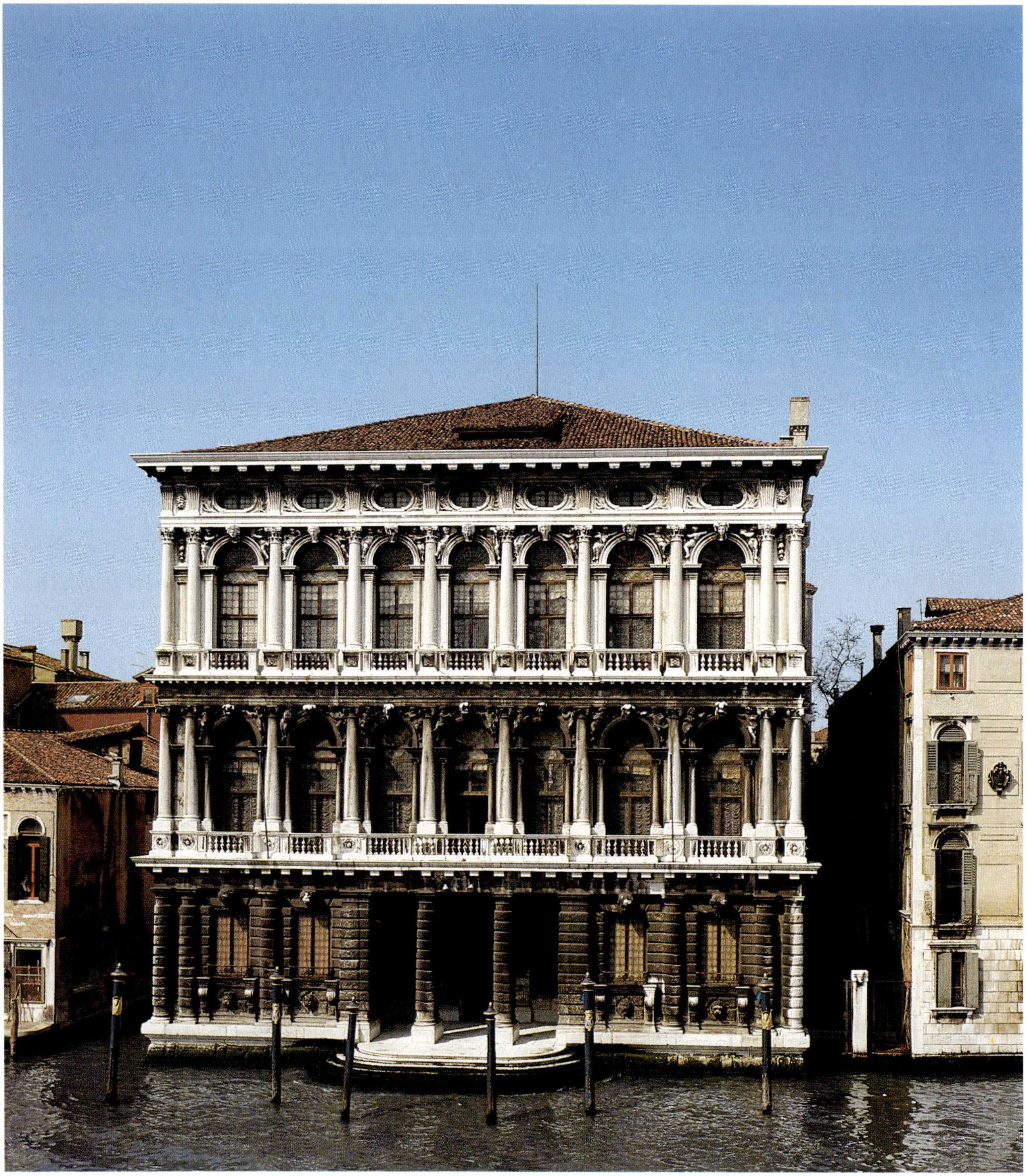

N° 45
Palazzo Rezzonico
This building is one of Baldassare Longhena's most significant works.
(L. 31, page 76)

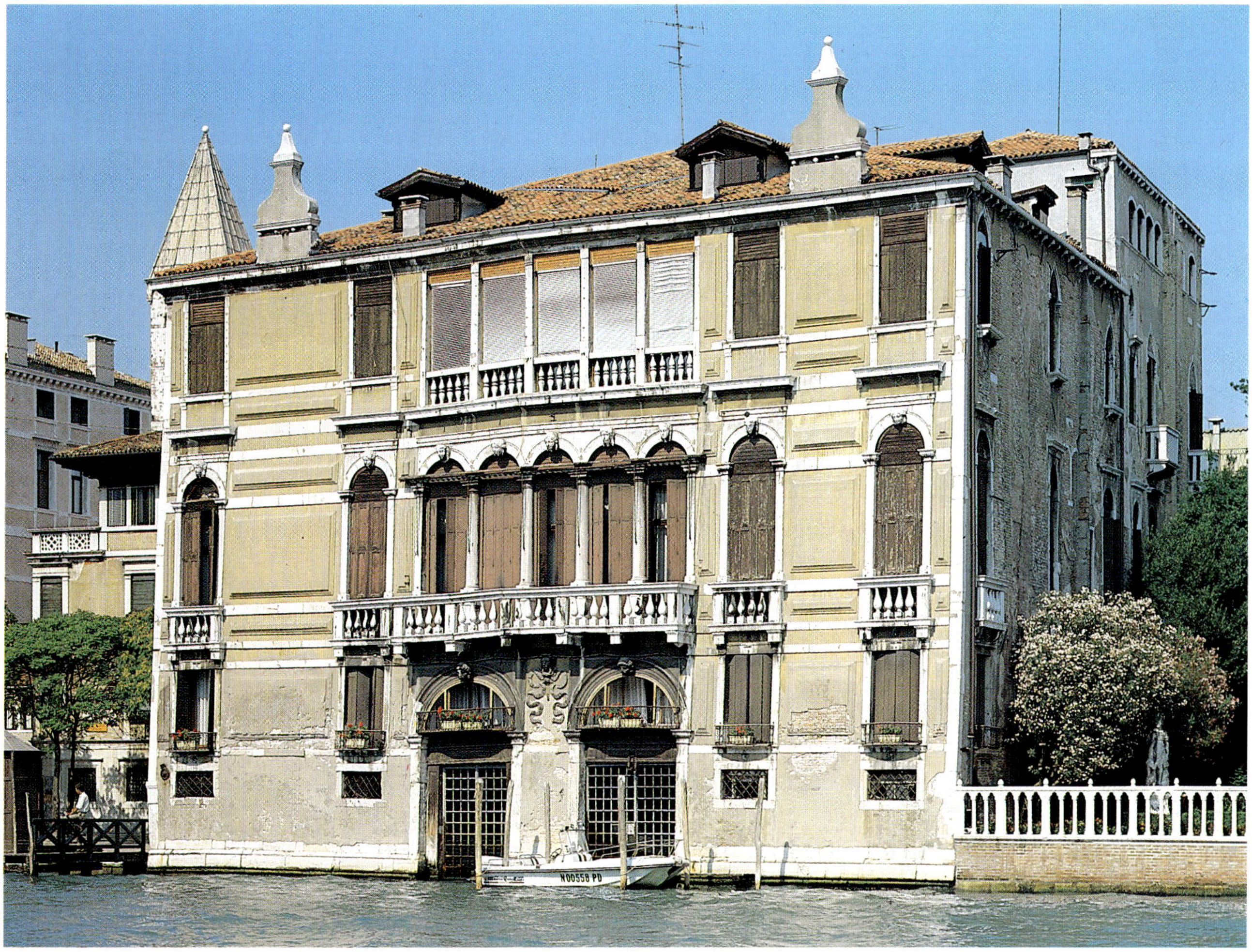

N° 46
Palazzo Cappello Malipiero
The threshold of Campo S. Samuele may be seen on the left.
(L. 28-29, page 73)

N° 47
Palazzo Rezzonico
The ballroom, dating from Giorgio Massari's intervention in the 18th century, when the building was completed by the addition of its second storey.
(L. 31, page 76)

L. 31
PALAZZO REZZONICO

The Rezzonico "fondamenta" was previously called "Fondamenta de Cà Bon" after the Bon family which owned the buildings overlooking the Grand Canal on the corner with the San Barnaba canal; they were very old buildings in Byzantine and Gothic style. The fragmentary nature of the buildings and their structural condition, as well as their modest size, made Filippo Bon decide to turn them into a new, magnificent palace. The design was entrusted to Baldassare Longhena who began building work in 1667.
However, more than a century was to pass before this magnificent house belonging to the Bons was completed (the same was to happen with Palazzo Pesaro). When Longhena died in 1682, the ground and first floors had been built and all the rooms ran alongside the internal canal so that the building could be lived in even during construction. Some prints dating from the beginning of the 18th century by Coronelli and by Lovisa on drawings by Canaletto, show the palace with just the first floor. When Bon died in 1712, work came to a standstill for more than two decades, also because the client's financial difficulties had prevented further work from being carried out after the very substantial initial outlay. Here too Longhena keeps to the traditional Venetian planimetry and (on the façade) he uses the innovations made by Sansovino and also the courtyard overlooked by the building's central and lateral façades. If a comparison is to be made with Longhena's other large, important palace on the Grand Canal, Cà Pesaro, it can be said that the latter shows a certain vividness of architecture and new decorative features, while the former at San Barnaba is more uniform and monotonous as regards details, structures and also the use of the ground floor architraves over the main central portico. Since they were unable to complete the building and to pay for its upkeep, the Bons were already thinking about selling it in 1745. Five years later they found a buyer in the very wealthy Rezzonico family from Lombardy. The members of this family settled in the city towards the middle of the 17th century and by paying the sum of 100,000 ducats, they entered the ranks of the aristocracy. After this the Rezzonicos went on to gain continuing importance (perhaps more so in the church than in Venetian politics) until they reached their greatest moment of glory when Carlo Rezzonico was nominated Pope in 1758 under the name of Clement XIII. Once the property was in the hands of the Rezzonico family, work to finish the building began again under the architect Giorgio Massari. By 1752 the second floor, as foreseen in Longhena's original design, had been built and the entrance stairway from the canal was completed in 1756. For this part Massari followed the plans left by Longhena, except for some minor alterations; on the other hand, for the part not included in the original design, that is to say the area between the courtyard and the back garden, Massari used his own style and expressiveness.
He brought character and intimacy to the "fondamenta" entrance with the romantic wall fountain built on the left as you enter; opposite we find the wide staircase which starts from a portico adjoining the spacious vestibule. In this way, together with the following, pre-existing courtyard on one side and the narrow space of the fountain which acts as a backdrop on the other side, it constitutes a series of different spaces; this spatial continuity also reaches the portico of the palace which, from its wide, architraved doorways, allows us to catch a glimpse of the Grand Canal and the movement of the water.
The staircase with its two wide flights of steps leads to the enormous ballroom which transversely closes the whole width of the building and blocks the two wings, the courtyard remaining enclosed in the centre. In this room Massari "played at creating illusions" (Bassi) with a series of false perspectives in the ceiling fresco painted by G. Battista Crosato. The fresco depicts allegories of the four parts of the world through which Phoebus' bright chariot passes.
Massari summoned other painters, the most famous of whom was G. Battista Tiepolo, to fresco other rooms in the building. On July 29 1758 Carlo Rezzonico's elderly mother died; for the stately funeral a pontoon bridge was built across the Grand Canal so that the coffin could be taken to the tomb in the Church of the Mendicanti. Just as famous for its splendour and great pomp and magnificence was the marriage of Ludovico Rezzonico to a Savorgnan; this event was remembered in a ceiling by Tiepolo who frescoed there one of his most delightful pictures on the theme of the allegory of marriage. In 1769 the Republic chose Palazzo Rezzonico as the venue for a sumptuous reception in honour of the Austrian Emperor Joseph II who was visiting Venice.
The palace was bought by the English poet Robert Browning who lived and worked there before he died in Venice in 1889. It then became the property of the Town Hall and an important museum was set up inside. This museum comprises 18th century furnishings, works of art and furniture, as well as an excellent collection of porcelain and clothes also from that period.

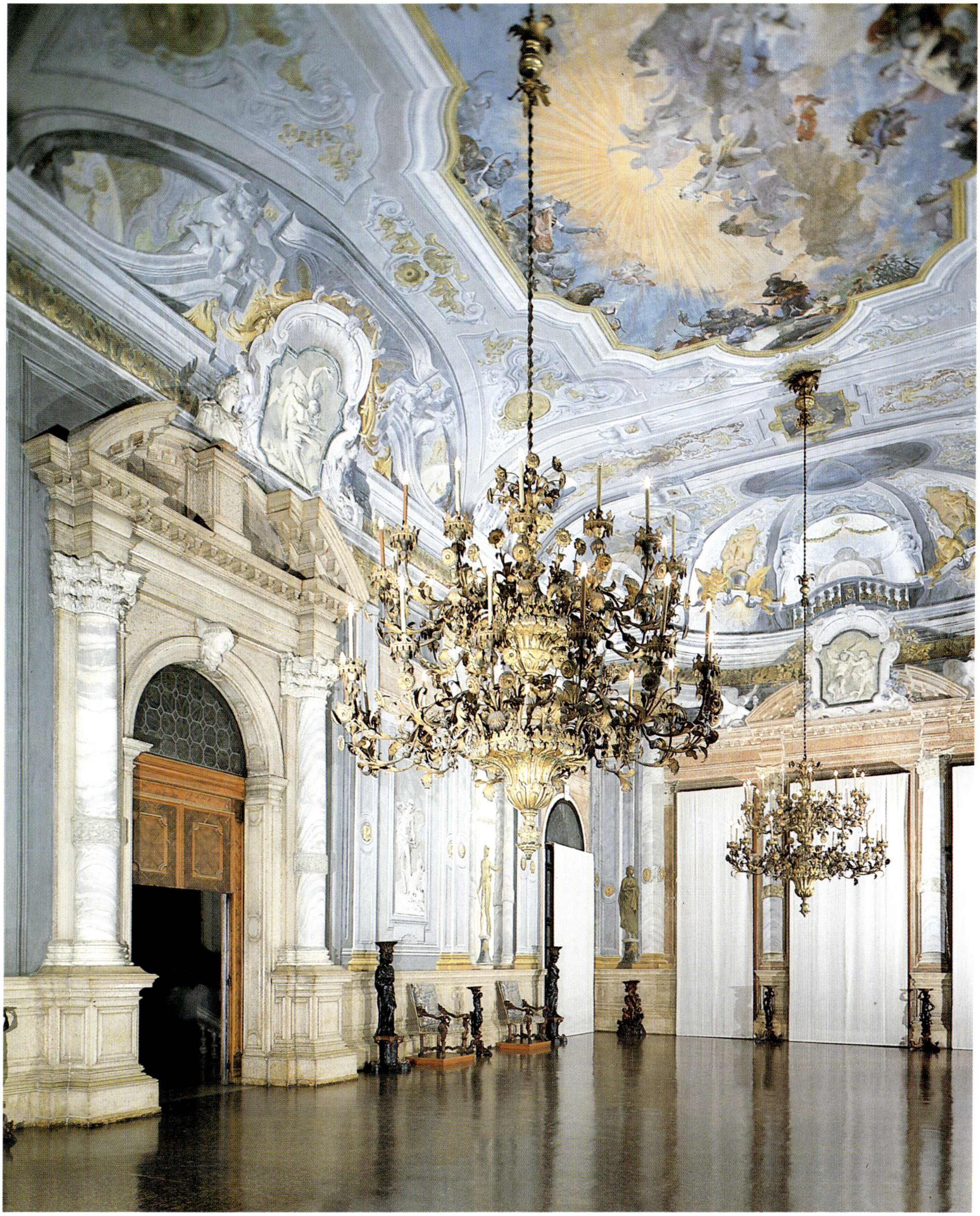

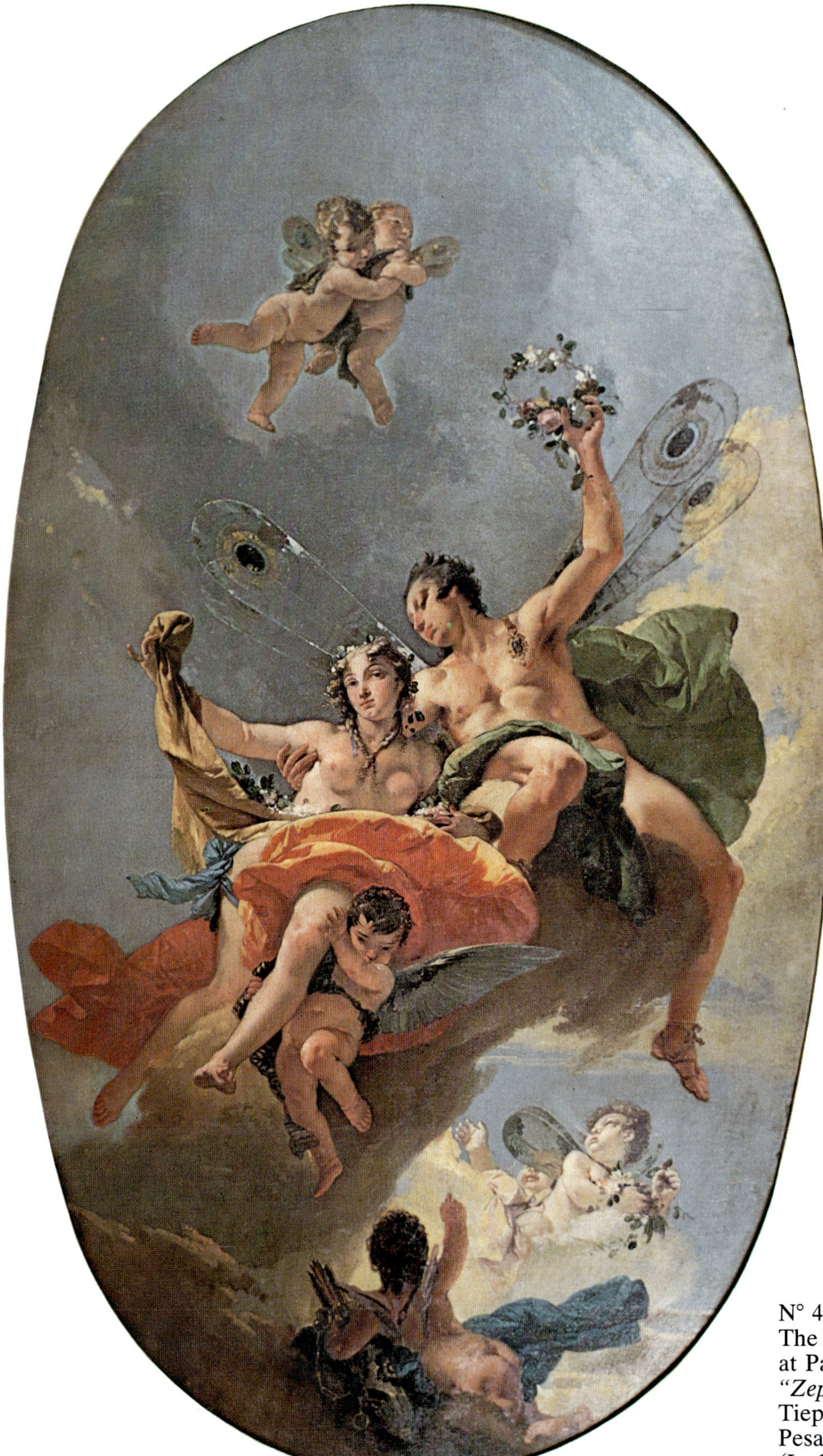

N° 48
The Museum of 18th century Venice at Palazzo Rezzonico
"Zephyr and Flora" by Giambattista Tiepolo (transferred from Palazzo Pesaro).
(L. 31, page 76)

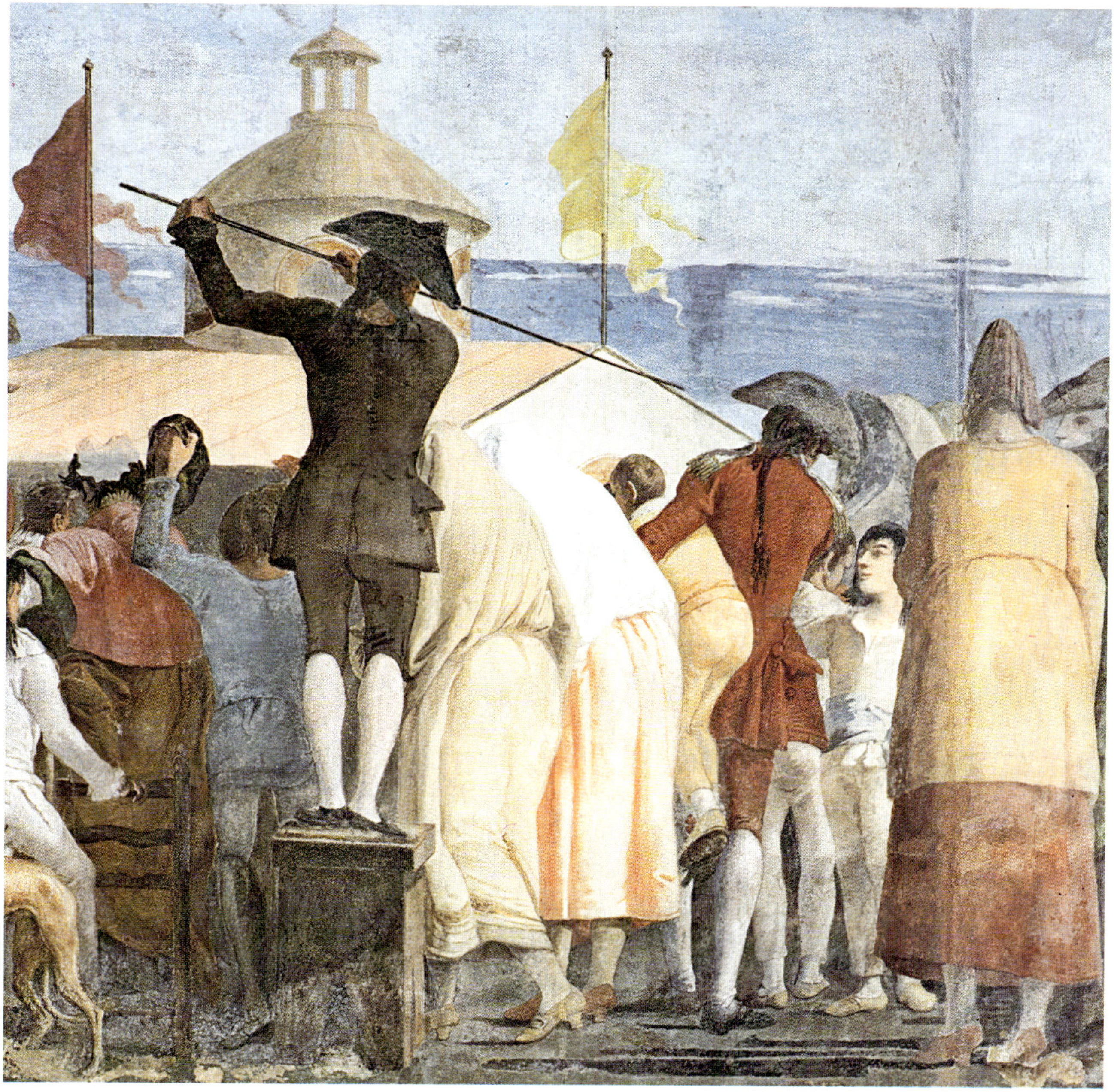

N° 49
The Museum of 18th century Venice at Palazzo Rezzonico
"The New World" (detail) by Giandomenico Tiepolo (fresco, provenance Villa Zianigo, the artist's home).
(L. 31, page 76)

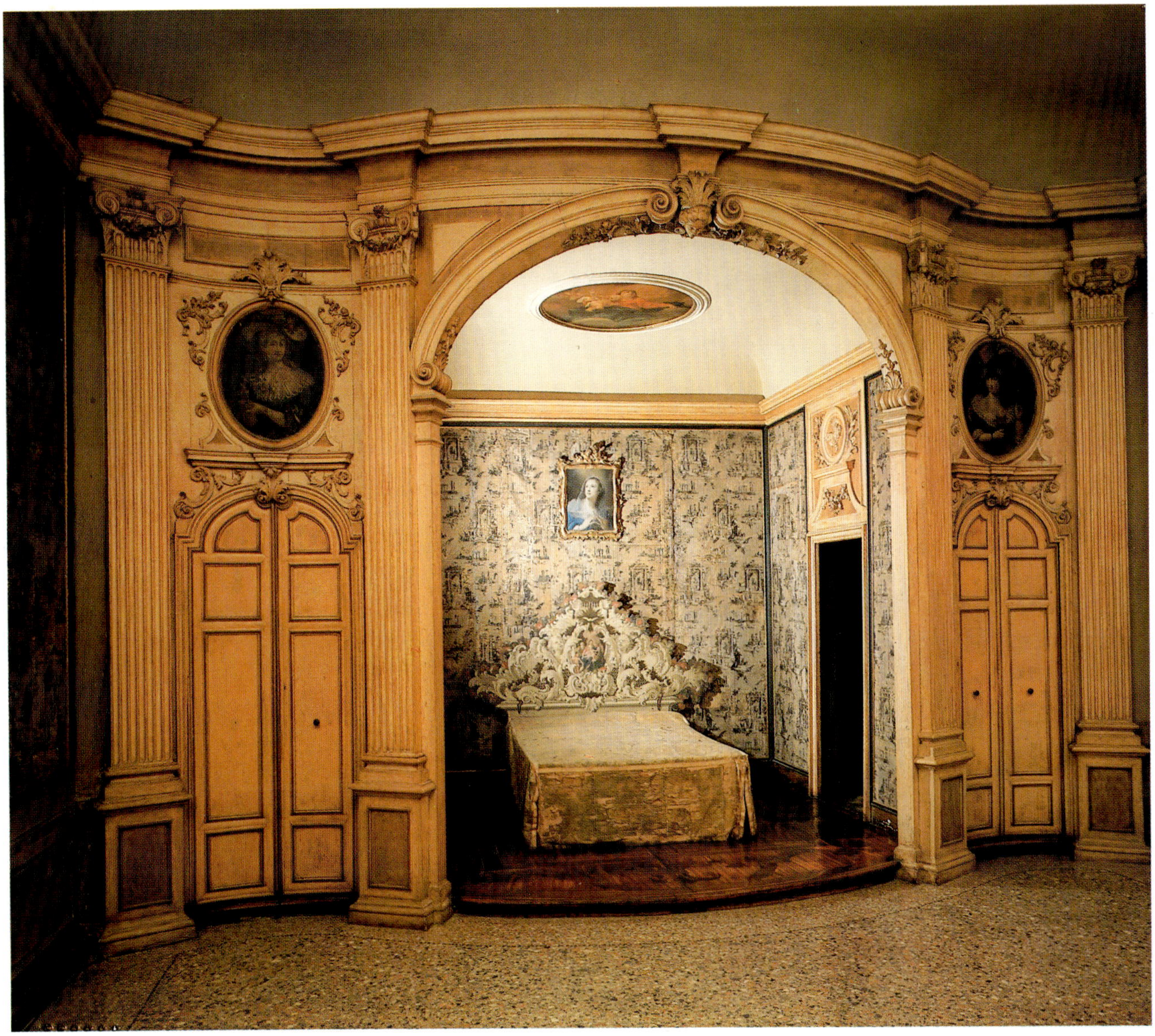

N° 50
The Museum of 18th century Venice at Palazzo Rezzonico
The Alcove. The small picture above the bed is a pastel by R. Carriera, depicting the Madonna.
(L. 31, page 76)

N° 51
The Museum of 18th century Venice at Palazzo Rezzonico
"La Toilette" by Pietro Longhi.
(L. 31, page 76)

N° 52
The Museum of 18th century Venice at Palazzo Rezzonico
"The Fried-foods Seller" by Pietro Longhi.
(L. 31, page 76)

N° 53
The Museum of 18th century Venice at Palazzo Rezzonico
"Exhibition of the Rhinoceros" by Pietro Longhi.
(L. 31, page 76)

N° 54
The Museum of 18th century Venice at Palazzo Rezzonico
"Portrait of a Patrician Family" by Pietro Longhi.
(L. 31, page 76)

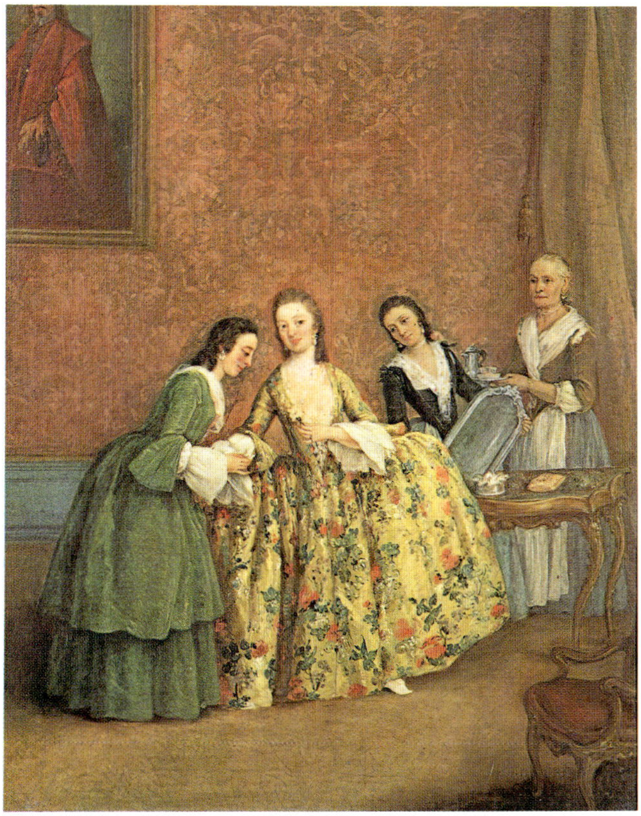

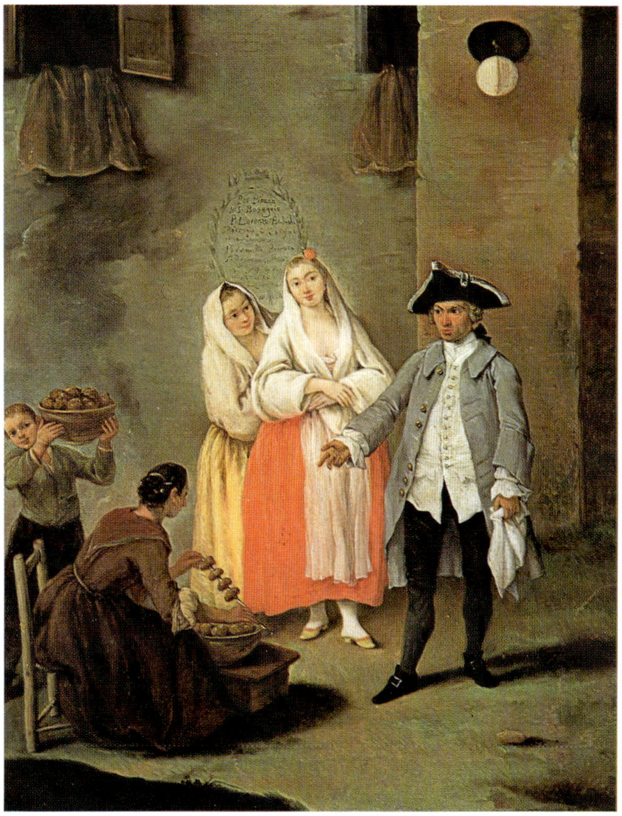

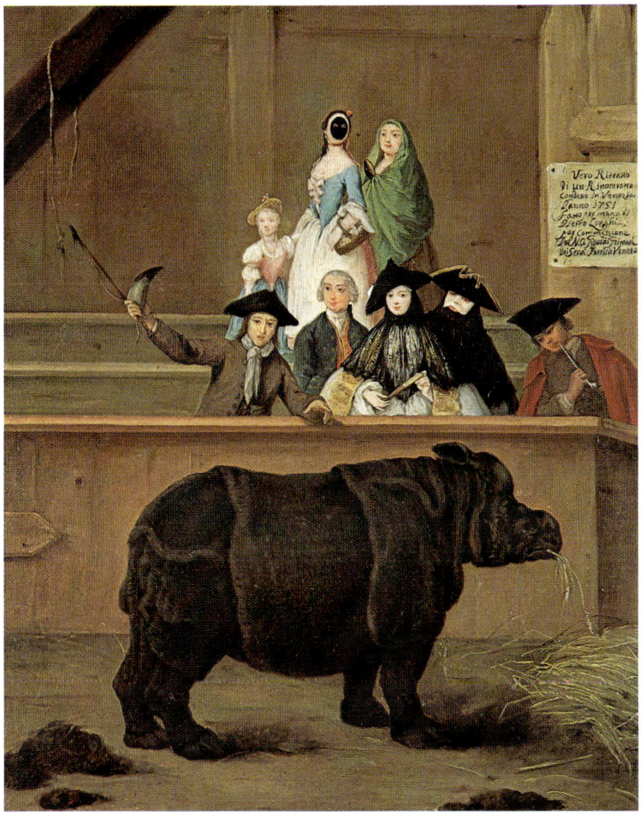
Vero Ritratto
condotto in Venezia
l'anno 1751
fatto per mano di
Pietro Longhi
per commissione

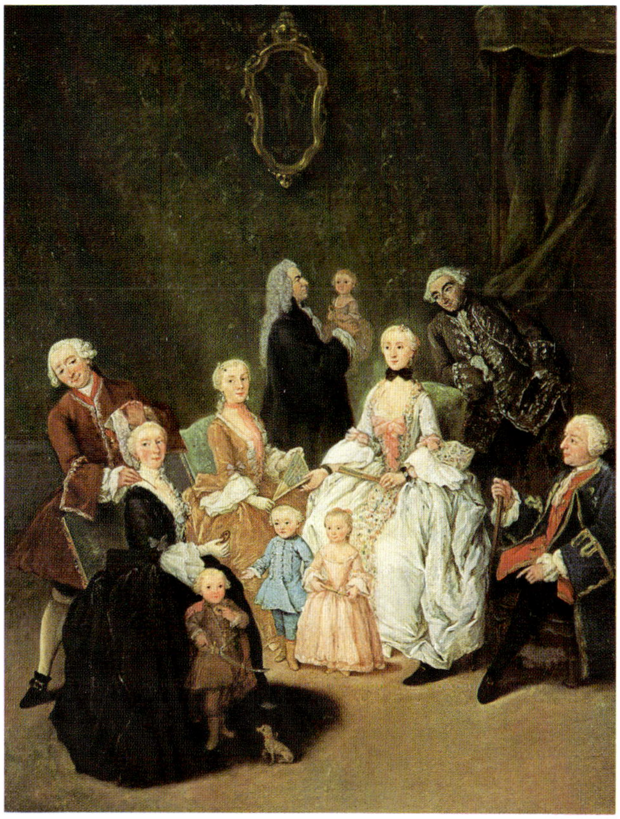

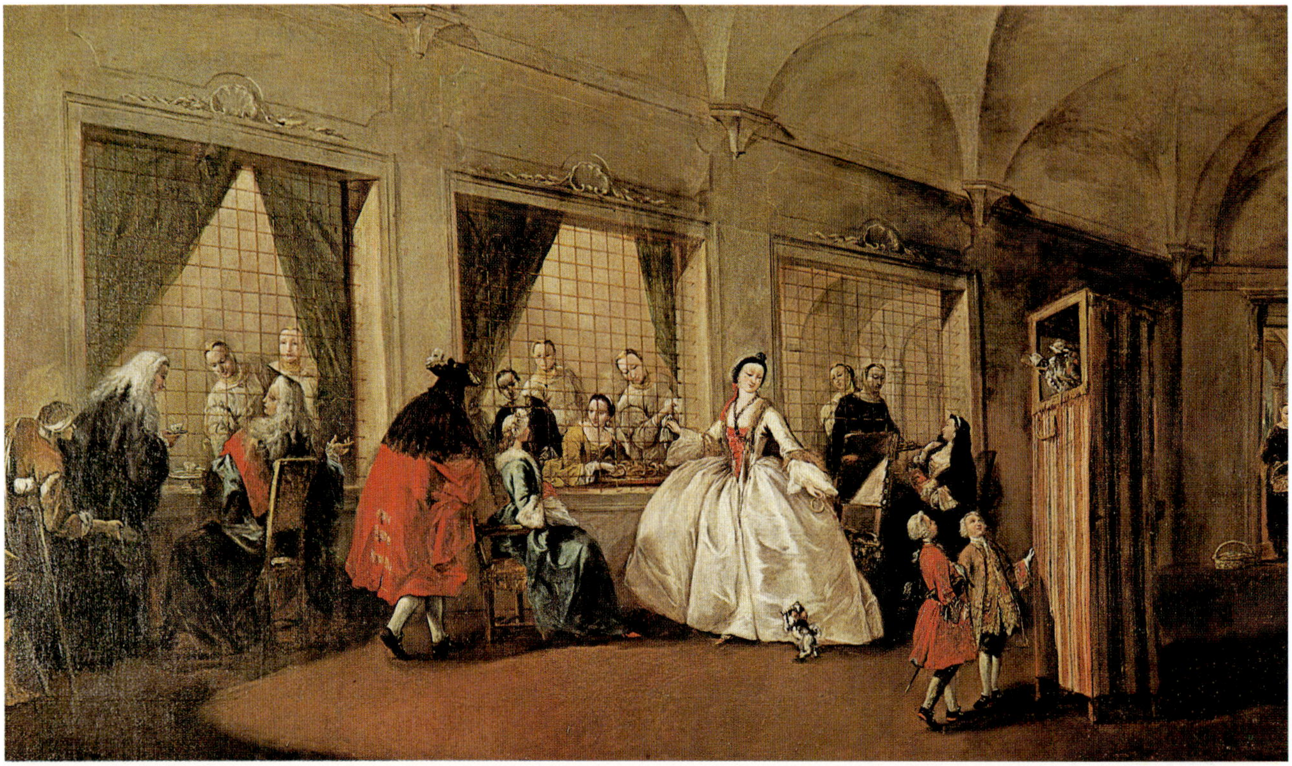

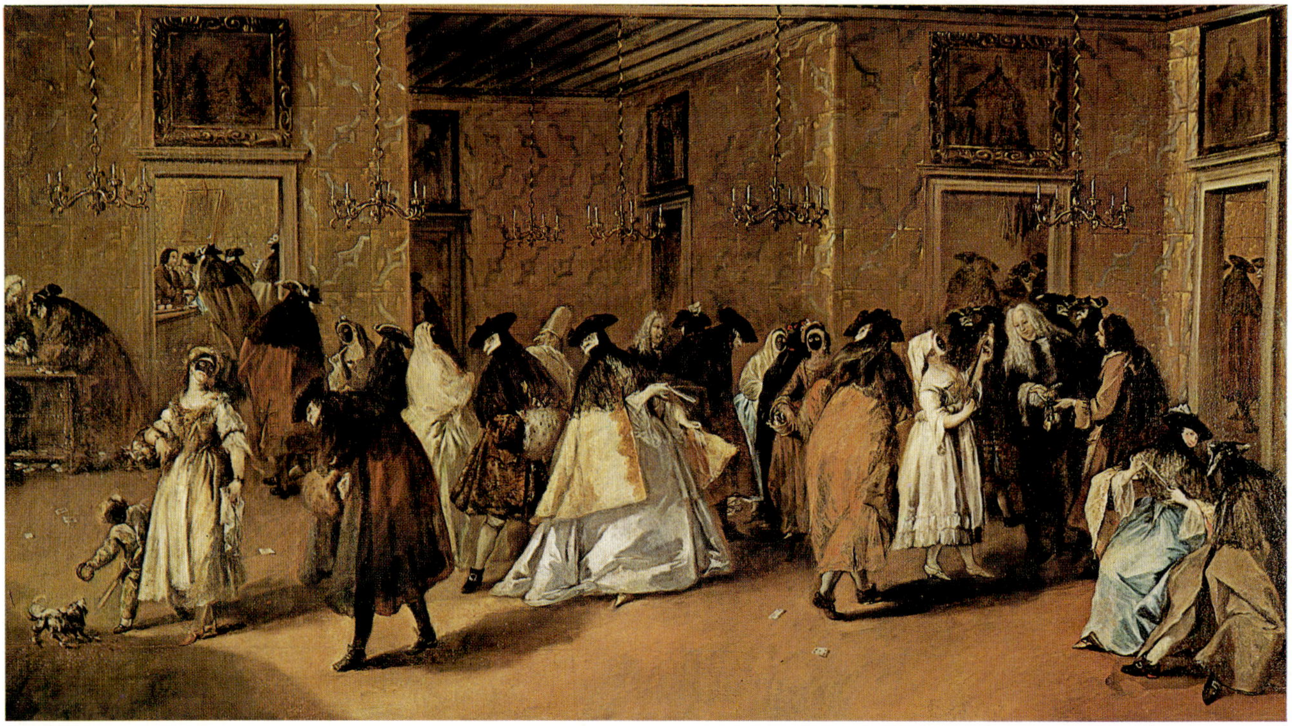

N° 55
The Museum of 18th century Venice at Palazzo Rezzonico
"The Nuns' Parlour" by Francesco Guardi.
(L. 31, page 76)

N° 56
The Museum of 18th century Venice at Palazzo Rezzonico
"The Foyer" by Francesco Guardi.
(L. 31, page 76)

N° 57
The Museum of 18th century Venice at Palazzo Rezzonico
"Portrait of a Lady" by Rosalba Carriera.
(L. 31, page 76)

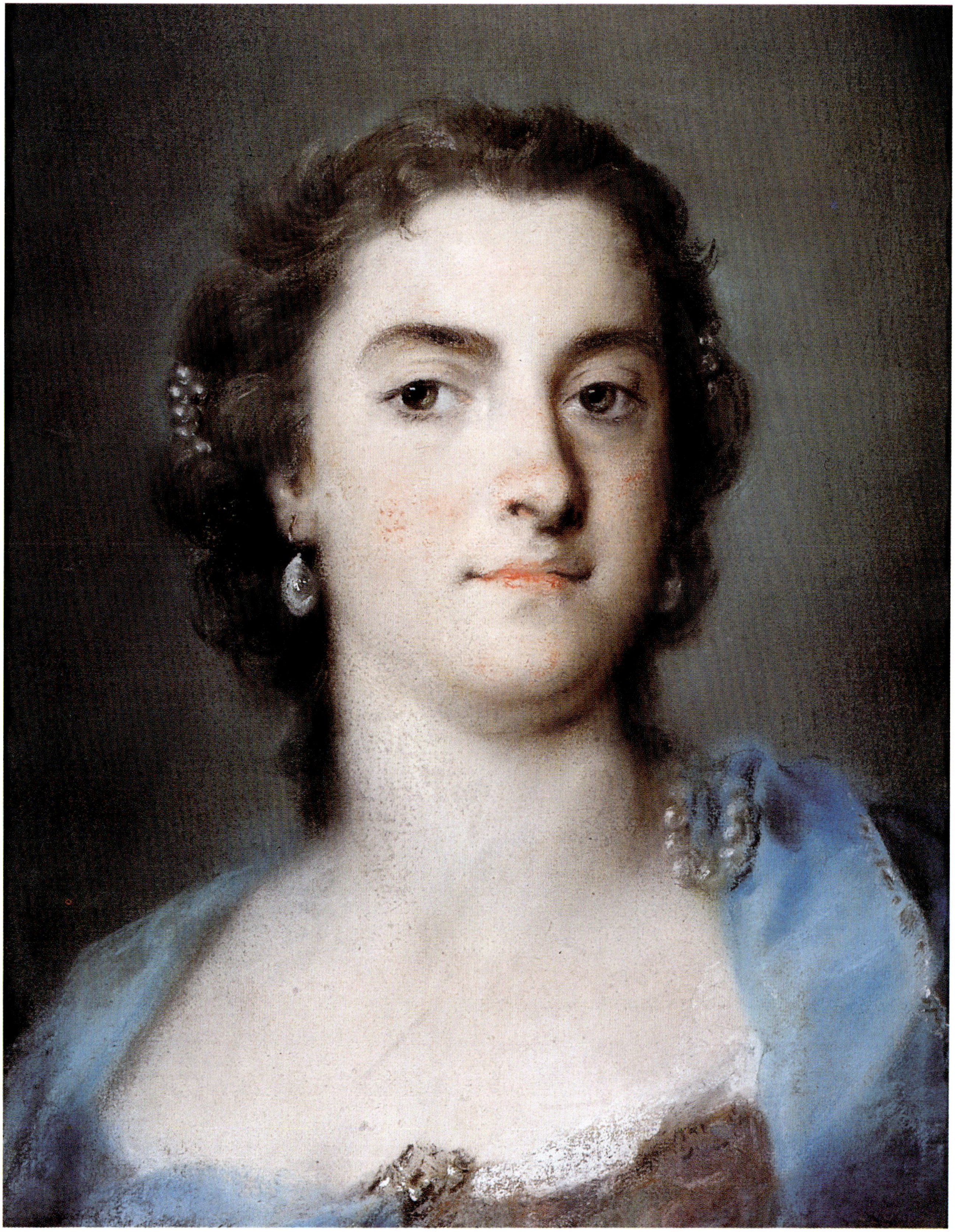

L. 32-33
PALAZZI GIUSTINIAN

In the 12th century the Giustinian family was on the verge of extinction since all its male members had died in battle during the war against the Eastern Emperor Manuel Comnenus.
There was only one survivor, Nicolò, who was a monk on the Lido. Papal dispensation gave him permission to leave monastic life, to marry the daughter of Doge Vitale II Michiel and to father children. Once this was done Nicolò wanted to return to monastic life while his wife also took the veil in the convent of S. Adriano on Costanziaca, an island in the eastern lagoon no longer existing today.
As regards the Giustinian family, let us remember once again the Patriarch of Venice, San Lorenzo, canonized in 1690 by Pope Alexander VIII, and Marcantonio who was elected doge in 1683.
Palazzo Giustinian is a magnificent Gothic building erected in the middle of the 15th century. Its general design and stylistic details are very similar to those of the Bon workshop under Giovanni and Bartolomeo. Documents seem to support those who maintain that the Bons worked on the building.
The single and multi-mullioned windows on the piano nobile are characteristic with their ogee arch whose tracery gives rise to the openings of the quatrefoils which are very similar in concept to the 14th century ones on the Doge's Palace.
According to Tassini, the palace, or rather the Giustinian palaces, were begun after 1451. They represent one of the finest examples of Venetian Gothic architecture: a lavish wall which unfolds with its succession of multi-mullioned windows so that, together with Cà Foscari, it becomes an incomparable backdrop in "volta da canal" for everyone coming from Rialto towards San Marco.
If we study the façade carefully, the double pattern of its design is soon individualized; in fact, there are two buildings, placed one after the other on two central axial lines along which the canal entrance and the upper floor six-mullioned windows are traditionally arranged. In line with a third axis running between the two buildings, the façade presents two one-mullioned windows which are much wider than the others and also architecturally more decorative with their four-sided openings similar to those on the Porta della Carta and with small hanging arches as on the Cà D'Oro.
The use of sculpted heads in the centre of the capitals further confirms and underlines the presence of Bartolomeo Bon.
Although as we have already said, they are two adjacent buildings, the close positioning of the windows, of the multi-mullioned windows, suggest that the designer intended to create a uniformity of design across the whole façade despite the need to keep the two houses separate.
This is why the two multi-mullioned windows on the second piano nobile, which is the most important and highest one, are arranged along a different axial line moved towards the centre to create the illusion of a closer tie between one sector and the other. This results in a more compact and continuous positioning of the architectural elements which is undoubtedly greatly helped by the quatrefoils over the ogee arches of the six-mullioned windows and by the difference in size of the other windows.
The whole surface of the façade is enclosed and blocked at the edges by Istrian stone quoins and at the top and bottom by the cornice and wainscot respectively. Planimetrically speaking, the houses are tripartite with a spacious, long, L-shaped reception room. The two houses are divided by an inner passage-way marked and emphasized on the outside by the portal in the centre of the façade.
At the back there are two large courtyards each surrounded by high walls which on the inside were the continuation of the passageway and on which the elegant outer three ramp staircase rested. Only the staircase belonging to the right hand palace still remains today. A second, much smaller, inner courtyard exists in the space between the side rooms and the outer staircase while the back staircase served the second piano nobile at the far back end of the portico. The mezzanine and top floor were served by wooden, internal staircases.
It is clear that the importance of the Giustinian palaces, together with Palazzo Foscari, is above all environmental (although we must not neglect and forget its architectural and stylistic worth) because they characterize in a very special way that part of the Grand Canal which is so important urbanistically speaking. This is even more so if we consider them in the building context of that time when the townscaping as a whole along that part of the Grand Canal was far more modest. It was only from the middle of the 15th century onwards that it gained greater prestige with the building of particularly important and rich palaces, not only because of their size but also because of their figurative motifs. Such palaces ended up by dominating the scene with their emergent, massive structures along the unbroken and previously far more uniform banks of the Grand Canal.

R. 30
PALAZZO GRASSI

In 1718 the very wealthy Grassi family of Bolognese origin, bought its way into Venetian patrician circles for the sum of 60,000 ducats. Angelo Grassi commissioned the design of this monumental palace on Campo S. Samuele from Giorgio Massari towards the mid-18th century when the architect was building the second floor of Palazzo Rezzonico on the opposite bank of the Grand Canal facing the Grassi palace site. Massari turned his attention to the Grassi project in 1748 when, as reported by Gradenigo, the foundations were being dug and laid.
The initial building phase was interrupted, or, more precisely, we know that efforts "to enlarge internal structures of the magnificent modern palace" were still being made in 1766.
Massari died in September of that year.
Layout of the building is clearly indebted to schemes Sansovino introduces to Venice back in the 16th century: an atrium and arcaded portico preceding a square court, also arcaded and in axis with the monumental three-flight staircase, articulated as a central first flight from which two side ramps lead up to the internal loggia on the piano nobile. Alessandro Longhi frescoed the front wall of the staircase with a series of courtly figures in masks and dominoes looking down from trompe-l'œil windows and balustrades. The piano nobile rooms still retain their rococo decoration and other frescoes by Jacopo Guarana and Fabio Canal.
For all its novelty as a spatial solution the generous, arcaded square court effectively impoverishes interiors flanking it, their utility confined to obligatory transit between front and rear areas of the building. Above the architraved portico a colonnaded balustrade states continuity of piano nobile fenestration on all four sides of the court, coupled pillars coinciding with court columns. Depth of the ground-floor portico allows for two facing terraces on the second floor. Whereas the originally roofless court left many interior spaces exposed to the rigours of winter, the "open" interior structure around the court, salient planning feature of the entire building, made life in the palace far more comfortable in the summer.
Before Giorgio Massari designed the grand triple-ramp stairway leading up from the court, the vertical axes of two minor side staircases provided for intercommunication from ground level to top floor. Massari also appears to have been the author of extension in depth of the building during resumption of work in c. 1766, twenty years after the initial phase, work that continued after his death.
Grand Canal frontage makes a horizontal statement; both rusticated ground floor and mezzanine and the first storey with multi-light central section and single lights, differentiated by coupled pillars, closely resemble the solutions adopted by Sansovino on Palazzo Corner. Detail contributing to façade design includes round-arch windows with ornamental keystones, repetition of single balconies also on the second storey, alternation of triangular and curvilinear pediments above the windows.
Prominent string-course and eaves introduce a discreet note of shade underlining the whole.

R. 31
PALAZZO MORO-LIN

This building, nicknamed for obvious reasons "dalle tredici finestre" (of the thirteen windows), is the result of two adjacent pre-existing Gothic buildings being restructured, at the same time incorporating the passageway which divided the two. Therefore we have a building whose façade has a portico all along the ground floor and on the two upper floors a series of windows linked together by balconies. The windows are of equal size except for the wider central one which corresponds to the above-mentioned passageway.
The building in its restructured form belonged to the painter Pietro Liberi who also seems to have been its designer. A second hypothesis makes Sebastiano Mazzoni the designer. He too was a painter who came from Florence but who had always worked in Venice.
Liberi died in this house in 1686.
The present name of the palace derives from the name of the owners after Liberi, the Lins, a family from Bergamo who joined the Venetian aristocracy in 1686, and then in 1788 the Moros who inherited the building (which by then had been raised by a second floor) after the marriage between Gaspare Moro and Isabella Lin.
In the first half of the 19th century, these rooms were occupied and used as a studio by another two painters, Francesco Hayez and Ludovico Lippanini, while Bellucci, Molinari, Lazzarini, Simonini, Luca Carlevariis in 1700, Bevilacqua and Moro in the 19th century decorated the interiors and carried out in successive stages frescoes and paintings which have now completely disappeared.

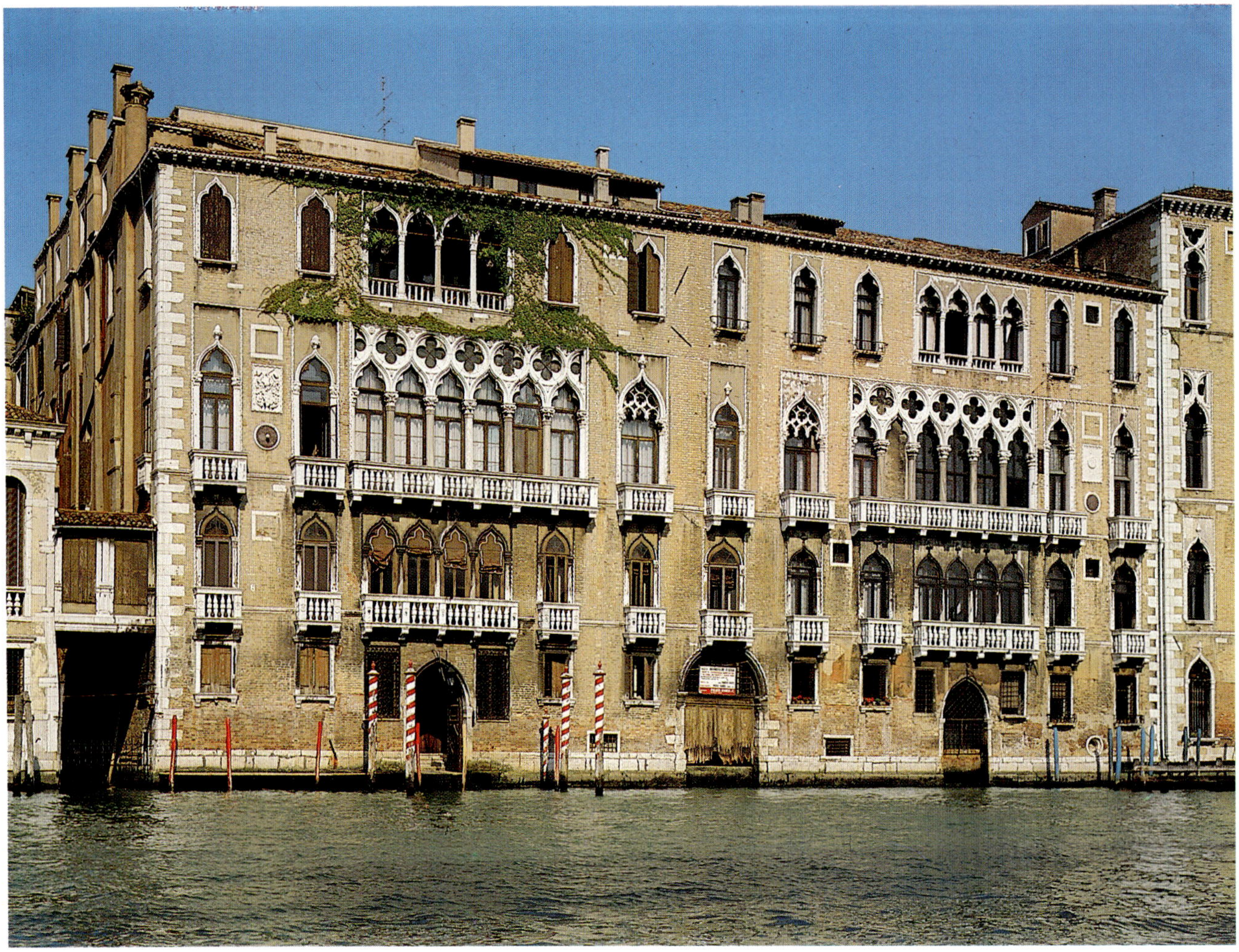

N° 58
The Giustinian Palaces
On either side of the central calle dividing the palace interiors identical distribution of architectural elements produces a single, long façade overlooking the Grand Canal.
(L. 32-33 , pag. 84)

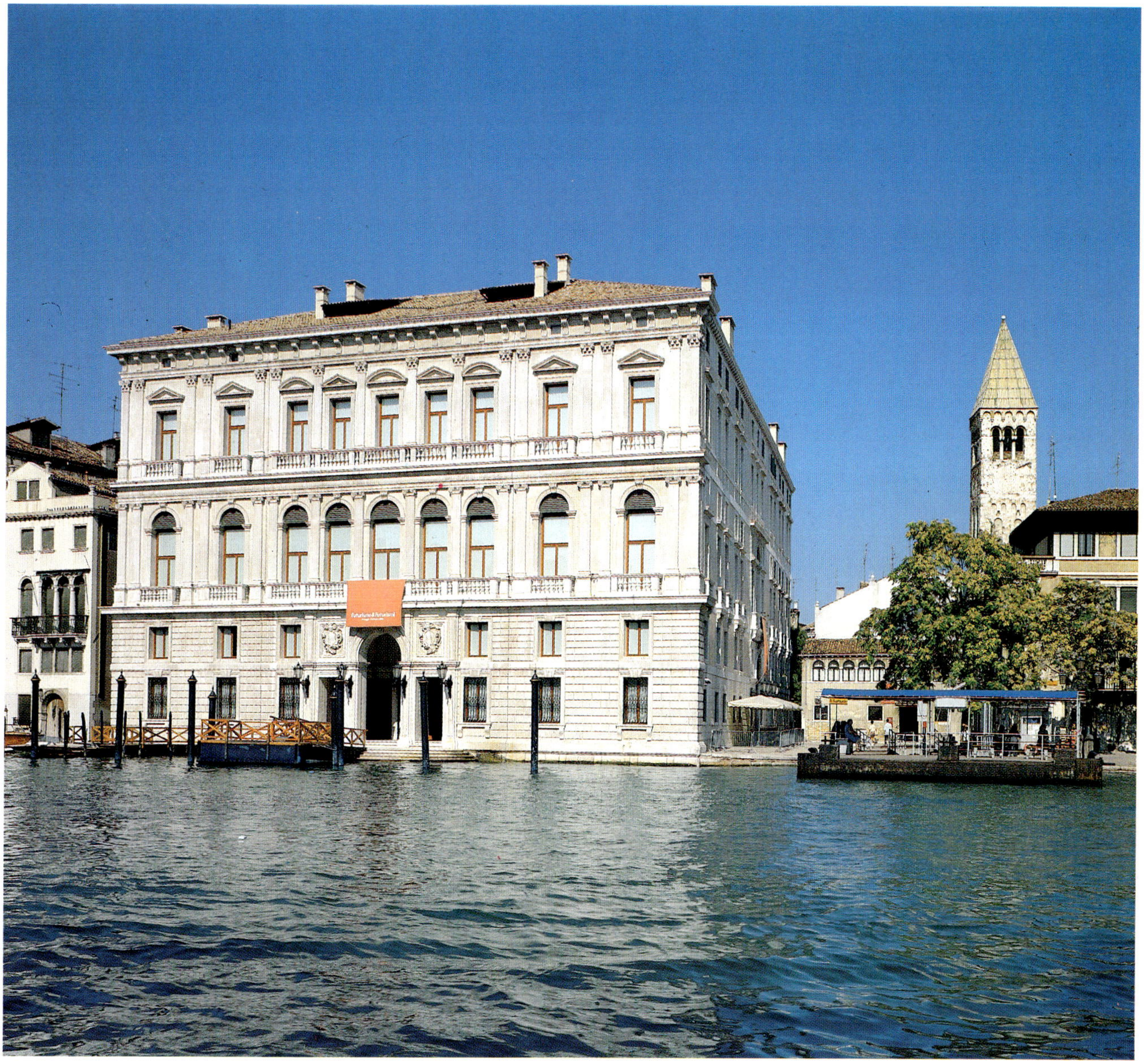

N° 59
Palazzo Grassi
The building represents one of the last significant 18th century contributions to architecture on the Grand Canal.
(R. 30, page 85)

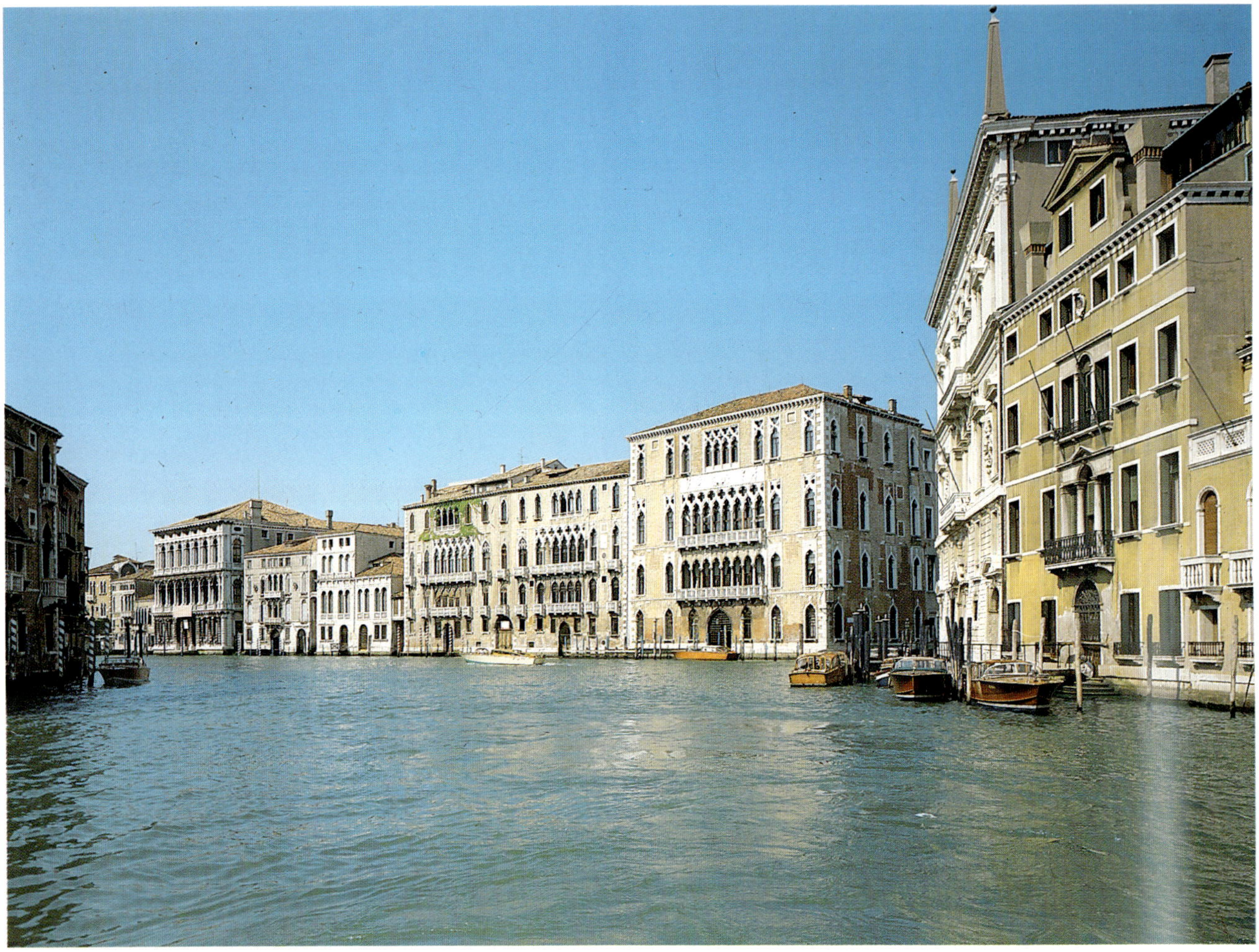

N° 60
The Balbi, Foscari, Giustinian and Rezzonico palaces, lining the bend in the Grand Canal.

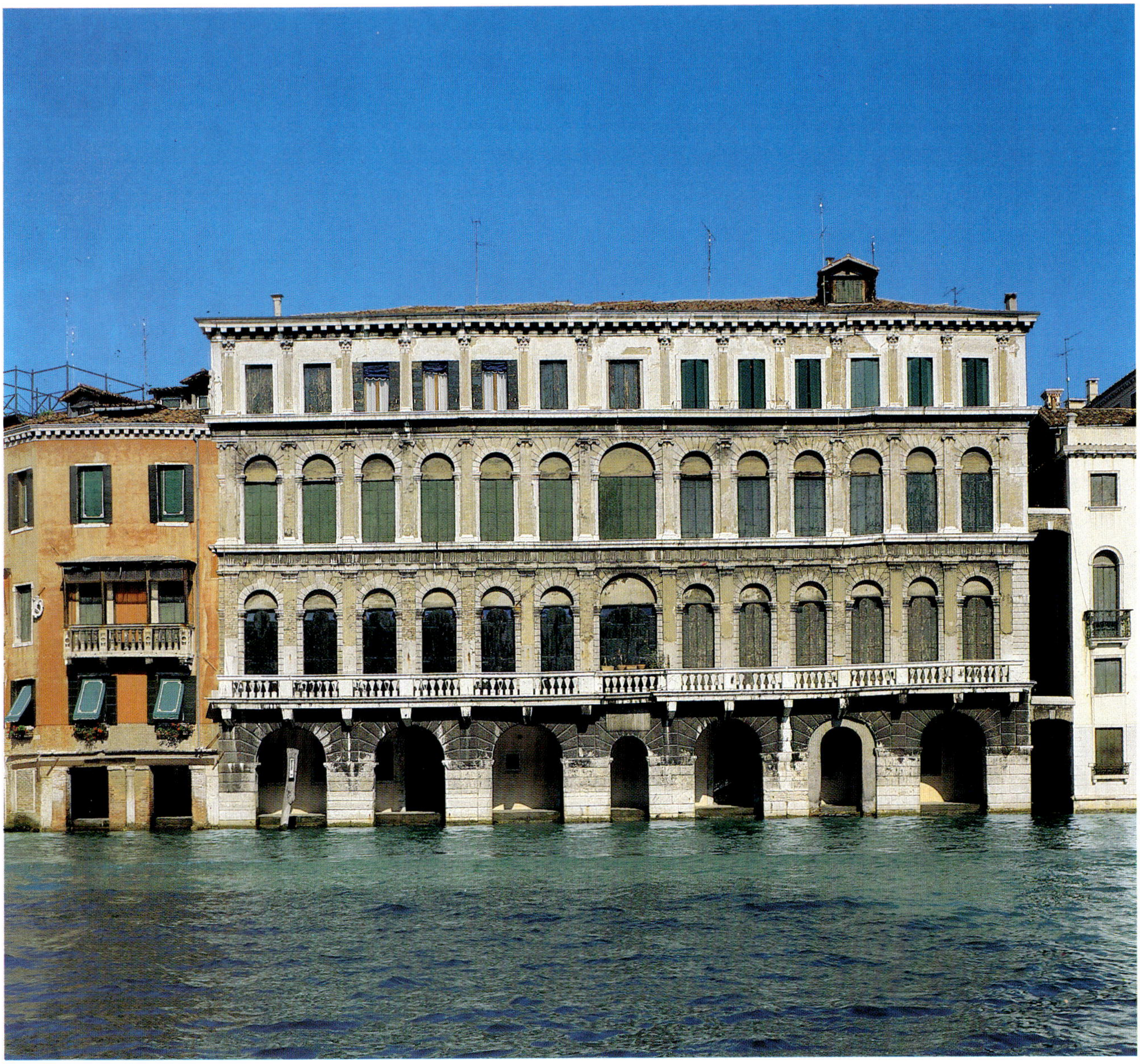

N° 61
Palazzo Moro Lin
Also known as "the palace with thirteen windows", its design is attributed to the painter Liberi, who lived and died here.
(R. 31, page 85)

L. 34
PALAZZO FOSCARI

The Giustinian family which was responsible for building the two above-described adjacent palaces, also owned the building which stood on the corner of the Grand Canal and the rio di San Pantalon. It was very probably an old Byzantine fondaco-house called "delle due torri" (of the two towers) after the two towers at the sides of the façade. The Venetians erected such towers on many buildings of that period, most probably following an earlier defensive custom. Towards 1428 the house was sold by the Giustinians to the Marquis of Mantua who at that time was serving the Republic as a commander of Venetian land forces. In 1439 the palace changed hands again because the Republic had confiscated it from the Marquis and offered it to Francesco Sforza; finally in 1452 it was put up for sale again and was bought by Francesco Foscari "who rebuilt it more magnificently and, according to the geneologist Girolamo Priuli, moved it from the place which is now the courtyard on the corner of the canal which goes to S. Pantalon, to where it now stands, leaving room for the courtyard behind where the house once was". Francesco Foscari was a very eminent person; he was born in 1374 in Egypt where his father Nicolò from S. Simeon Piccolo had been exiled following disagreements which had arisen between the Republic and his family, in particular with Paolo, the Bishop of Castello and his father's brother. After returning to Venice, Francesco Foscari very soon made such a name for himself in public life that he was elected member of the Quarantia (bench of forty magistrates) when he was only 27, that is to say before reaching the minimum age laid down by the law. At the age of 31 he was the State lawyer, then ambassador at the Italian and Imperial courts and at the court of the Sultan Mohammed II. At forty he wore the purple gown of the Procuratore de Citra. He stood at the head of the party of those nobles who sustained that it was necessary to expand on the mainland, not so much for economic reasons but rather to give Venice a buffer state in "physical" opposition to the Italian states which had or were being formed, in particular the Duchy of Milan. It was feared that since the city's territory was limited to the lagoon on whose edges probable enemies were lined up, then this was no longer a political-military position sufficient to ensure the independence and continuance of the Republic as it had been in the past. The state boundaries would have to be greatly moved back at any cost: in this way the boundary reached Ghiera d'Adda to the west and the Trentino to the north. Foscari played a decisive role in carrying this out. When Doge Tommaso Mocenigo died, Foscari was elected as his successor at the age of only 49: it was April 15 1423. The voting saw Pietro Loredan come out as the defeated party and, together with the other members of his powerful family, he became an unyielding adversary. An attempt at reconciliation through the marriage of one of the Doge's daughters to Loredan's second son, failed and this only worsened the situation. This conflict led to murmurings that the doge himself had been behind the "suspect" deaths by poisoning of Pietro Loredan and his brother Marco. The death of the latter was attributed to Foscari because it occurred immediately after an inquest conducted by Loredan in his capacity as lawyer against the doge's son-in-law Andrea Trevisan for abuses committed while he was governor of Legnano. However, as the years went by, this bitterness abated considerably but the fierceness of the wars, the resulting cost of conquering the mainland and the struggles against the Duke of Milan, Filippo Maria Visconti, and his successor Francesco Sforza did not diminish. Despite the economic collapse, during this period the city of Venice went through a time of great building development whose first main incentive once again came from the doge. It was his wish that the wing of the Doge's Palace overlooking the Piazzetta should be erected, thus completing the building. He then had his own palace on the Grand Canal built with such magnificence that it became the largest building on the Grand Canal and in the whole city at that time. At the age of 83 Foscari was obliged to accept the decision of the Council of Ten which had officially decreed his abdication. However, he remained in the Doge's Palace for a few more days because his house at S. Pantalon was not ready; it still lacked windows and doors. On October 27 1457 he was settled in Cà Foscari; on November 1 of that same year he died. Information left by Francesco Sansovino was badly interpreted by many scholars who had mistakenly fixed the building's construction in the first half of the 15th century until Tassini, basing himself on evidence given by the geneologist Girolamo Priuli, placed the beginning of construction work in 1452 which corresponds to the very year the building passed from the Giustinians to the Foscari.

The façade of the building was built in line with those of the Giustinian palaces, thus forming a single, very rich row of palaces in that part of the Grand Canal called "volta de canal", that is to say on the bend. This position means that the building can be seen from a very wide angle and the width of the San Pantalon canal allows its spaciousness to be evaluated. The façade is richly and singularly characterized by the two eight-mullioned windows, one over the other on the first and second main floors, with their effective tracery and quatrefoils as well as the Istrian stone facing sculpted in low relief with the coat-of-arms of the Foscari family and held up at the sides by four cherubs. The high base wall and the quoin finish maintain and confirm the same architectural approach which, together with the other elements, point to the presence of the Bons and their work-

R. 32
PALAZZO DA LEZZE

It may be seen that Palazzo Da Lezze still preserves its original 15th century Gothic layout. Although the window apertures on the low-level ground floor betray 18th century intervention, every element and the overall design itself on both first and second piano nobile points to a mid-15th century dating. The central four-light section and balcony (today in iron) exhibits on both storeys elongation of form, with slender columns and fleurons crowning the reverse-curve arches.
The Lezze or Da Lezze family name would seem to derive from their submission to the government of a proposal for "legislation of general utility". The mansion was built by the Lezze family in 1654, to a design by the architect Longhena; it stands beside the Scuola Grande Misericordia on the fondamenta of that name.

R. 33
PALAZZO ERIZZO NANI MOCENIGO

This palace, Erizzo, later Nani Mocenigo, also in the Gothic style, seems to date from around 1470-1480 – slightly later than Palazzo Da Lezze – which lends it closer affinities with Palazzo Foscari facing it. The remodelled ground-floor windows, of the architraved type, classical in design, are out of keeping with the rest of the building. The four-light section of the first piano nobile – on the central axis of the façade – is characterized by the original balcony with twinned colonnettes, a foretaste of Renaissance idioms, and very elaborate lion-headed corbels, an essentially Gothic motif, as much as the seated lions on the corners of the balcony itself. The denticled surround of the four-light section and later single-lights concedes generous space to the large rosace of the arch cusps. Capitals bear two rows of carved acanthus leaf ornament.
The second storey, of greater simplicity and lesser height, terminates beneath the diamond-pointed rustication in Istrian stone at the eaves. The corners are finished with stone blocks, alternating in width and fashioned to form colonnettes, allowing a break in continuity between storeys.
The Nani family, which succeeded the Erizzo as owners of this palace, were apparently also owners of Palazzo Nani at S. Trovaso. Documents state that in 1537 Francesco owned "six houses in S. Samuel, in Corte Cà Nani", and the name is still in current use.

R. 34
PALAZZO CONTARINI DALLE FIGURE

This name derives from two figures in low relief, like two caryatids, placed over the doorway almost as if to support the balcony on the first piano nobile. The façade of this building was restored during the Renaissance following the restructuring of the pre-existing Gothic-Byzantine building. This façade, completely covered in Istrian stone slabs, maintains the traditional tripartition with an emphasis towards absolute symmetry and a regular window distribution.
It has a very low ground floor with a mezzanine which on the other hand is higher than usual, both being contained within a fixed height. They support the two piani nobili which are both emphasized by the architectural continuity of the window-sill which becomes a balcony in front of the reception room's four-mullioned windows. The first of these windows is surmounted by a triangular tympanum just like the side one-mullioned windows, while all the windows on the second floor are arched and contained within rectangular spacings created by small pillars similar to the far more evident ones which emphasize and seem to support the various floors and which denote the longitudinal walls of the building. A leaning towards over-decoration led the designer to fill the wall spaces at the sides with decorative low reliefs which are repeated on all three floors. It seems that the building was constructed during the early years of the 16th century: as regards the architect, the name of Antonio Abbondi, called Scarpagnino, has been mentioned.
In the 16th century it was the home of Jacopo Contarini, a widely educated man who was famous for his library and picture gallery which, when he was dying, he left to the Republic to enrich the collections in the Marciana Library and the Doge's Palace. He was a protector and friend of artists and a deep friendship bound him to the famous architect Andrea Palladio.

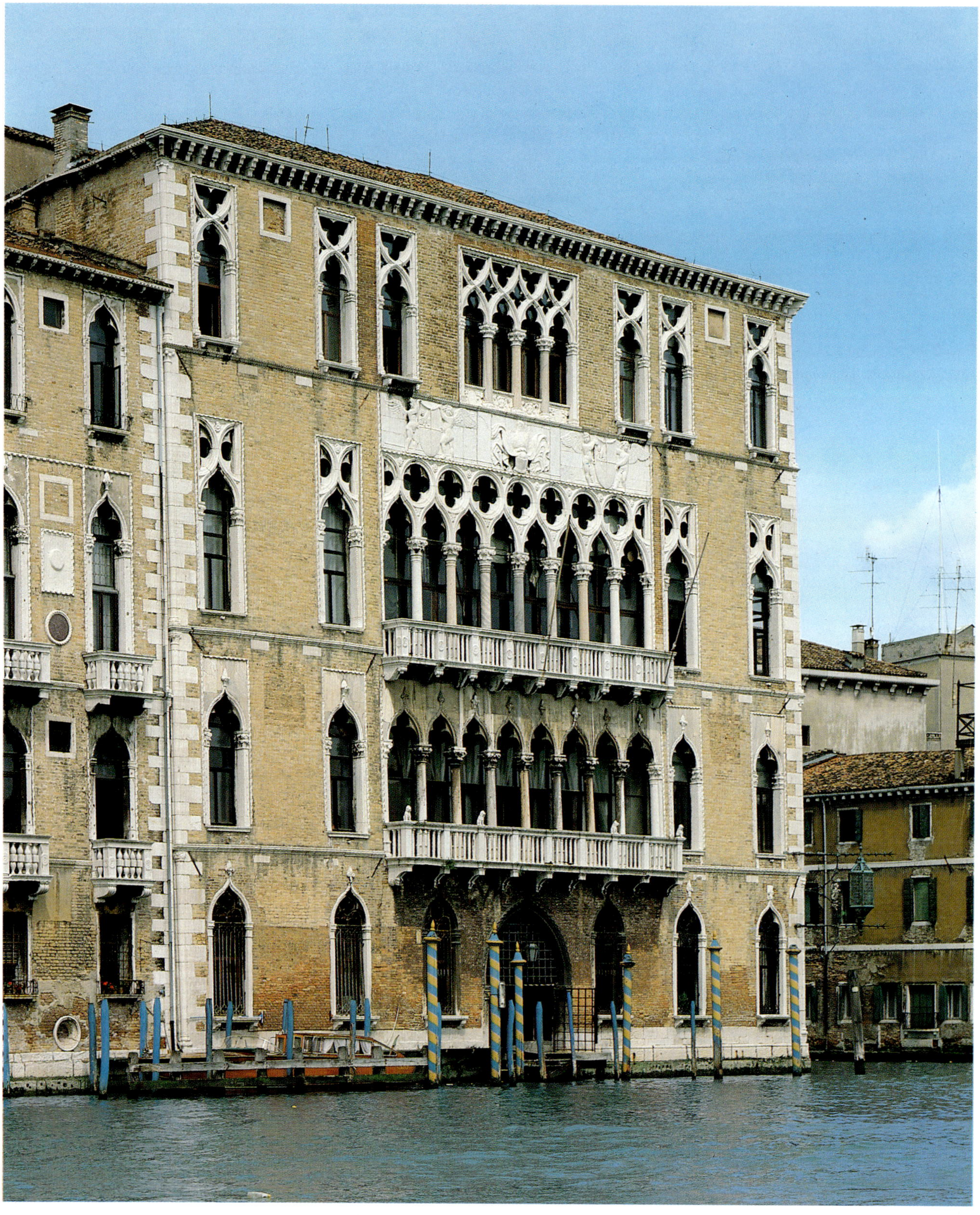

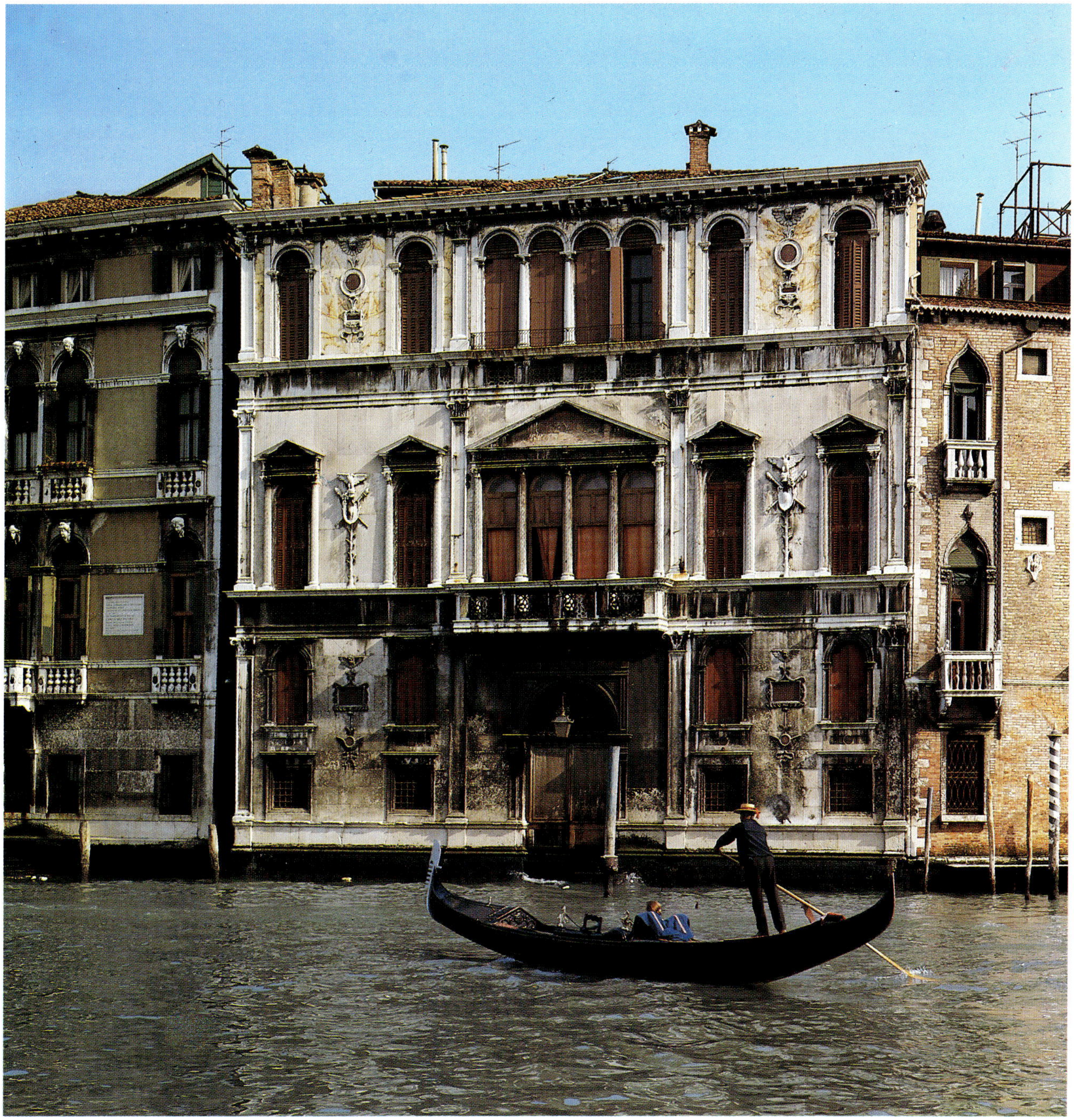

N° 62
Palazzo Foscari
The building was commissioned by the great and famous doge, Francesco, but due to enforced removal from dogal office by the Serenissima, he resided here only a few days.
(L. 34, page 90)

N° 63
Palazzo Contarini dalle Figure
Clearly Renaissance in design, the sumptuous marble revetment of the façade highlights the tympanum of the central four-light section.
(R. 34, page 91)

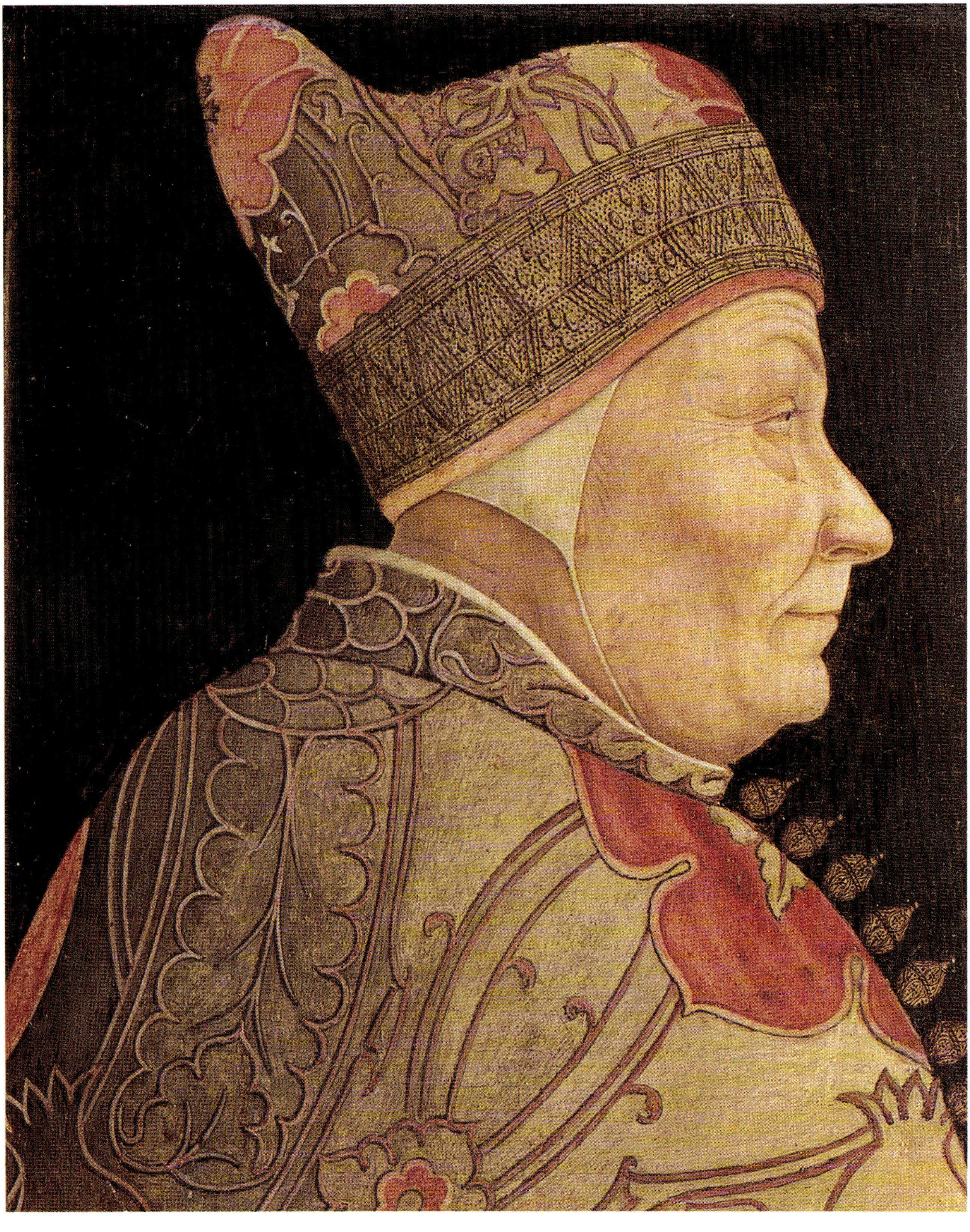

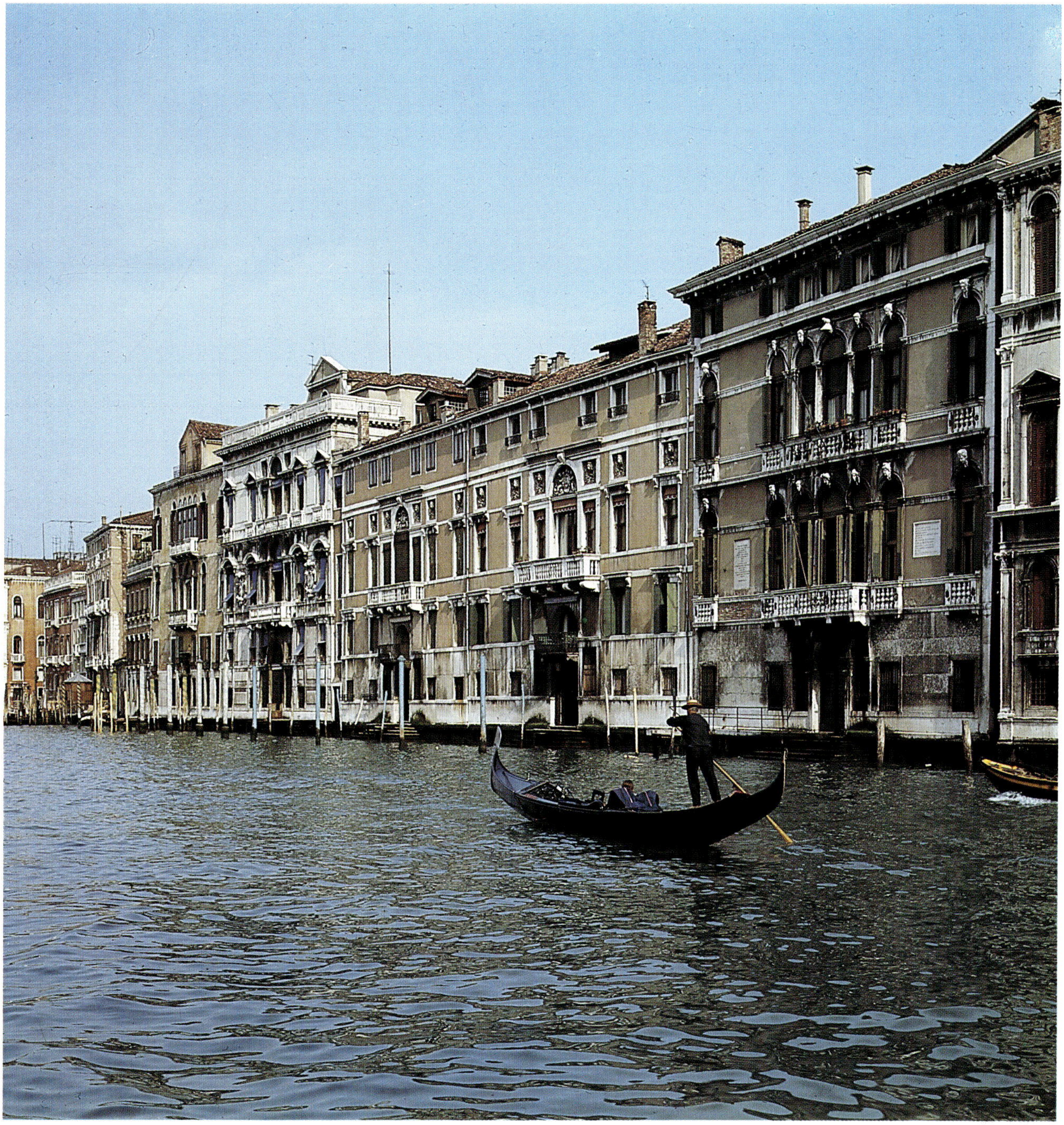

N° 64
Portrait of Doge Francesco Foscari
Correr Museum, Venice.
(L. 34, page 90)

N° 65
The Mocenigo Palaces
These are three adjacent buildings: Casa Vecchia and Casa Nuova at the two extremities, linked by a building with double frontage.
(R. 35-36-37, page 97)

shop, on the lines of the design ideas carried out a century before in the Doge's Palace and thirty years previously still in the Cà D'Oro. For various reasons work went on for several years as can also be seen from design ideas which in their turn point to the Renaissance, such as the design of the balconies and the style of the low reliefs. The plan is tripartite with an L-shaped portico partially overlooking the Canal. The internal staircase on the left is illuminated by large windows which open onto an inner courtyard. Originally the main staircase, which climbed to the piano nobile, was outside in the courtyard as was customary at that time. The staircase was partially built against the boundary wall and partially against the back façade and led to a wide balcony at the head of the reception room. It underwent a first restoration between the end of the 17th and the beginning of the 18th century. In the 19th century it underwent its biggest and most disastrous restructuring which, besides demolishing the magnificent external staircase, totally changed the architecture with a complete transformation of the windows on the back façade and on the side one overlooking the canal. The courtyard with the old staircase is illustrated in one of Coronelli's engravings, a valuable piece of evidence of this structure which the 19th century destroyed. In 1699 Maria Casimira, the Queen of Poland, was a temporary resident in this beautiful palace, in the rooms on the piano nobile. Previously in 1574 Henry III of France stayed here as the distinguished guest of the Serenissima on his way from Poland to Paris to be crowned King of France. Henry received such a triumphal welcome in Venice that he postponed his departure for some time, attracted by the festivities and entertainments which the Republic continually invented and organized for his pleasure and which were recorded in writings, paintings and engravings.

L. 35
PALAZZO BALBI

The design and building of this palace can be attributed to Alessandro Vittoria. He was not only a sculptor and architect but also an artist and educated man who had a considerable influence on Venetian culture during the second half of the 16th century, both directly through his works and indirectly through the effect of his writing and contributions in the field of art. He was born in Trent in 1525 where he began his artistic career. Then, while still young, he moved to Venice to frequent Jacopo Sansovino's workshop. He was a particularly gifted and intelligent man who was able to merge the many needs of that time into an extremely original style. By following the most lively and imaginative form of mannerism, Vittoria achieved a style which had "a great formal elegance ringing with a vividness in the Venetian tradition". He used various techniques and different materials but he was interested in and devoted himself to sculptural stucco-work more than anything else, managing to make it an integral part of architecture and painting. However, he covered the whole range of sculptural design, from large marble sculptures in full relief to small and large bronzes, to coins, to designing altars and buildings. Returning to Palazzo Balbi, the façade clearly shows the classic mannerist approach, both in the overall design and in the architectural and stylistic details. It is completely covered with Istrian stone and ensures that the Grand Canal maintains its great magnificence and expressive character.
Construction dates can only be determined indirectly from some surviving papers dealing with the Balbi family's administration and taxes. In 1581 the palace had not yet been built because the family's declaration to the Dieci Savi alla Decima not only does not include it but describes as family property a barren piece of land at San Pantalon on the Grand Canal. The Balbis began building their own home on this piece of land perhaps a year later. Legend has it that all the family had found a temporary place to live in a large boat moored in front of the future palace until they were able to move into their new rooms, even though building work was not yet finished.
In 1591, eight or nine years after building work began, Nicolò Balbi, sensing that a serious illness which prevented him from even writing, was about to send him to his grave, drew up his will which mentions the new palace complete with first and second floors.
The building stands in "volta de canal", on the opposite side to Cà Foscari, where the San Pantalon canal flows into the Grand Canal.
The layout is still tripartite as can be clearly seen from the position of the central three-mullioned windows and the side one-mullioned windows. However, we must point out the extreme freedom with which architectural elements are used to emphasize a greater sculptural quality: the strong cornices, the balconies, the broken arches over the windows, the difference in height of the central windows with arches supported by twin columns, the very low relief pilaster strips, the coats-of-arms on the side spaces of the first piano nobile.

R. 35-36-37
PALAZZI MOCENIGO

The building complex which the Mocenigo family owned along this part of the Grand Canal, is one of the largest along the whole length of the Canal. It includes two palaces, one at each end, the first called the "casa vecchia" (old house) and the last called the "casa nuova" (new house). They are linked together by a long building on whose façade the same pattern is repeated twice.
"Vecchia e Nuova" (Old and New) correspond to the division of the two branches of the family: the former was clearly the owner of the oldest house whose inner courtyard still contains the remains of the pre-existing 15th century Gothic building, before it was completely restructured in the 17th century, as can be clearly seen from the façade; the latter branch took on the title of "Casa Nuova" and took possession of the building on the left, built at a later date, seemingly after 1454. This new house was also restructured around 1579 according to a design attributed to Alessandro Vittoria in view of the architectural similarities with the façade of Palazzo Balbi. In Vittoria's work, the two main floors are emphasized by the balconies of the side one-mullioned windows and by those of the central Serliana. They are balconies which are designed in an unbroken line of contours and profiles. The windows are surmounted by triangular and circular tympanums. A marble parapet crowns the building on top of the cornice. Completely covered in Istrian stone, the façade is striking because of the richness of the architectural elements and the richness of the covering material whose whiteness clearly stands out against the plaster of the adjacent buildings.
Giovanni Mocenigo's will is dated 1579 and from it we learn that the large building between the old and new houses did not then exist. This situation did not last many years. Indeed, it can be thought that as a continuation of the restructuring work, the Mocenigos of the Casa Nuova also set about this second building whose peculiarity consisted in bringing together two identical buildings as regards the planimetry, the overall design and the architectural ideas for the façades. The axial lines of the façades can be individualized from the main entrance and the Serlianas above on the piano nobile. The windows on this floor are surmounted by a series of marble compartments, like square windows, enclosed by marble slabs on which the lion of St. Mark (which the Venetians call "in moleca") has been sculpted in relief.
Many famous guests stayed in the rooms of Palazzo Mocenigo. Emanuele Filiberto, the Prince of Savoy called Ironhead (1528-1530) was a guest for some time in the Old House in 1574. He moved the centre of gravity of the State of Savoy to the Piedmont, making Turin the capital. The small fleet that he had put together, took part in the battle of Lepanto.
Giovanni Mocenigo had invited the philosopher Giordano Bruno to the the Old House but in 1592 he had him arrested, yielding to the entreaties of the Holy Office or rather to the decision taken by the Republic to get rid of an element who compromised relations with the Church of Rome. On the other hand, another version tells how it was Mocenigo himself who denounced the heretic monk. The Roman inquisitors kept him in prison in Rome for seven long years, trying in vain to make him retract and abjure his heretic dogma. In the end he was burnt alive.
Another tragic event linked to the presence of guests in the Mocenigo palaces, had as protagonists Anne of Shrewsbury, the wife of Thomas, Duke of Arundel and Marshal of England, and the Venetian nobleman Antonio Foscarini who was accused of treason by the Republic for having disclosed state secrets during his many visits to the English lady, who also received various personalities including ministers and foreign diplomats. We know how severely the courts of the Serenissima punished meetings between Venetians and foreigners and how much caution was used by law when such meetings were made necessary. Foscarini was found guilty and condemned to death in 1622. It was only some time afterwards that he was proclaimed innocent and his name was publicly reinstated.
Whether Foscarini was innocent or guilty, this story of love and interests remained in the history of the Republic on one hand as a warning not to break the laws concerning foreigners, and on the other to acknowledge that the Venetian government was also ready to admit its own mistakes publicly or even ready to pretend to have been wrong.
Other guests, this time from the world of art, were the poets Thomas Moore and Lord Byron. In 1818 the latter wrote many works here including Don Juan, Marino Faliero, the Sardanapalus and the Visions of Judgement. During this period Byron, who was famous in Venice for his love affairs, had as his lover a very beautiful baker's wife.

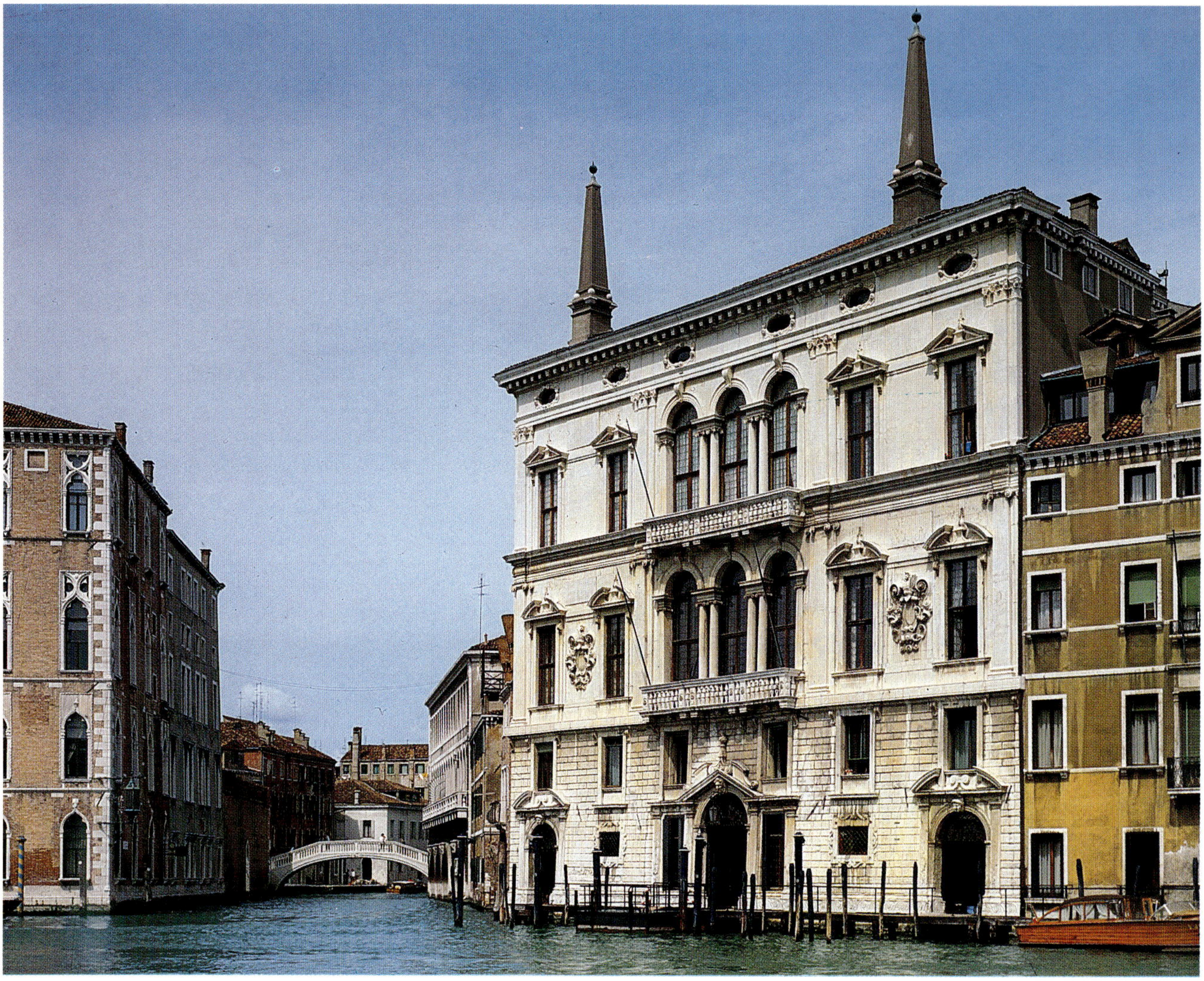

N° 66
Palazzo Balbi
Design of the building is attributed to Alessandro Vittoria.
Foundation work began in 1583.
(L. 35, page 96)

N° 67
The Mocenigo Palaces: Casa Nuova
Clearly inspired by Alessandro Vittoria's design, if not actually built by him.
(R. 37, page 97)

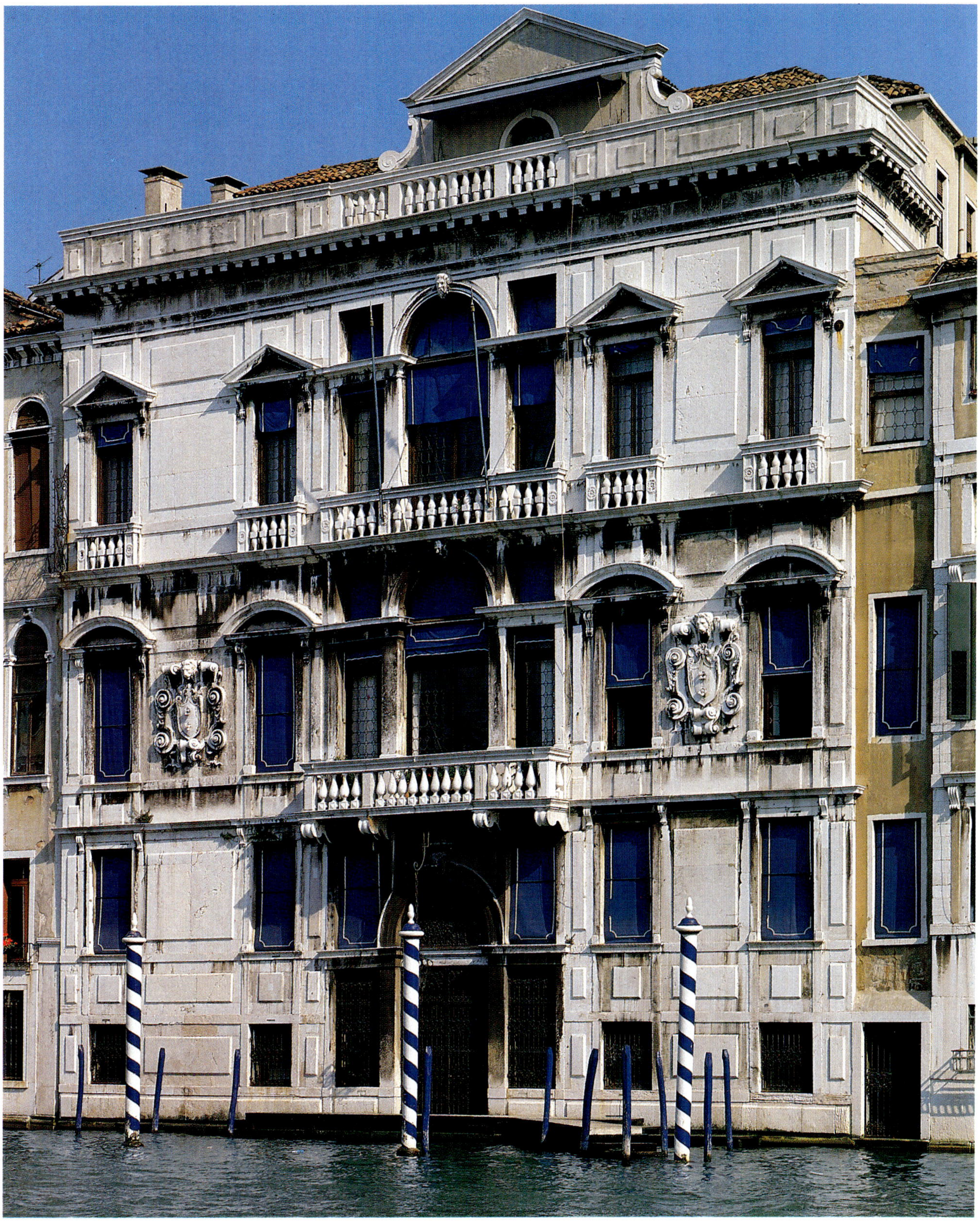

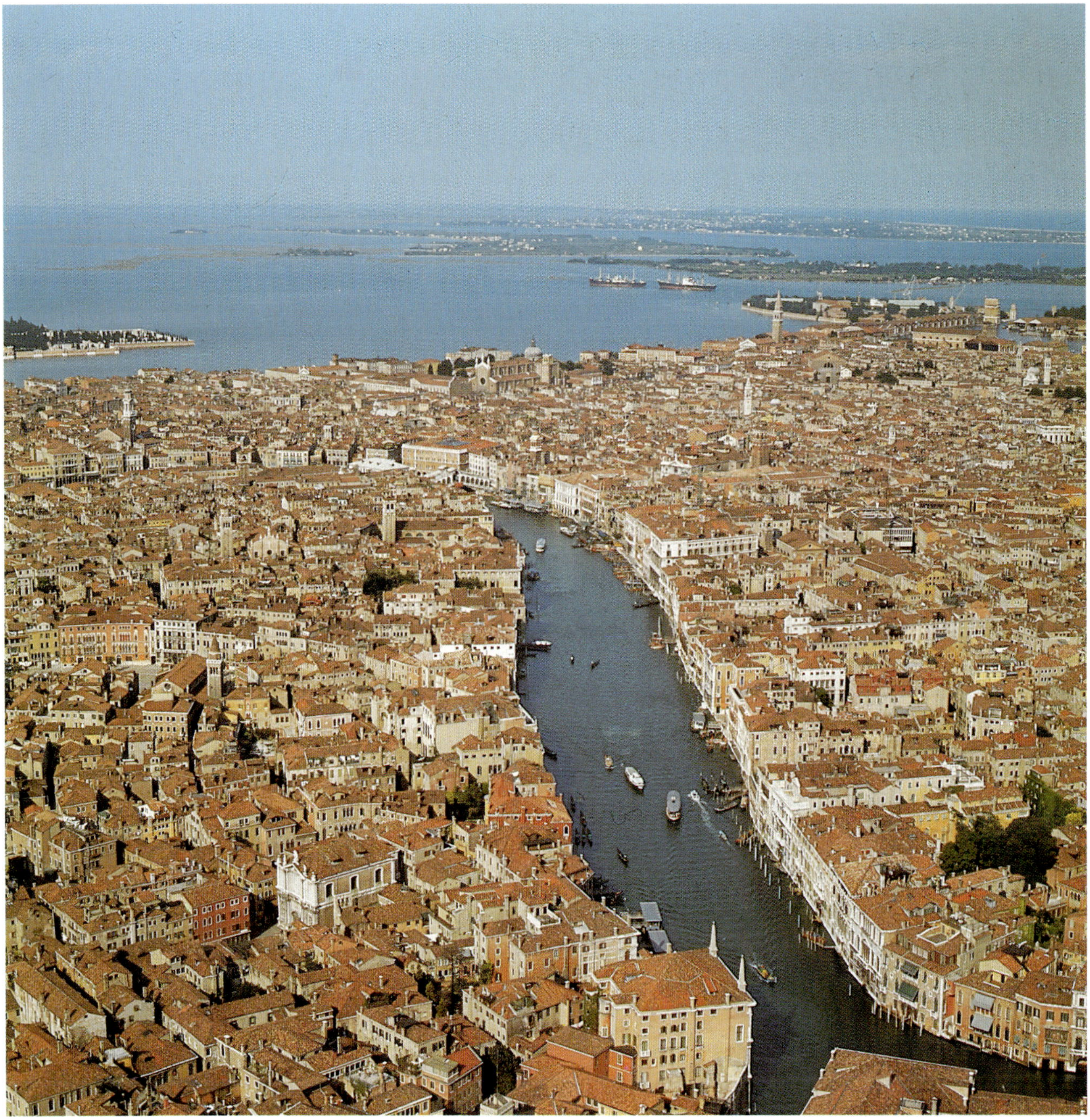

N° 68
An aerial view of the stretch of the Grand Canal between Palazzo Foscari and the Rialto.

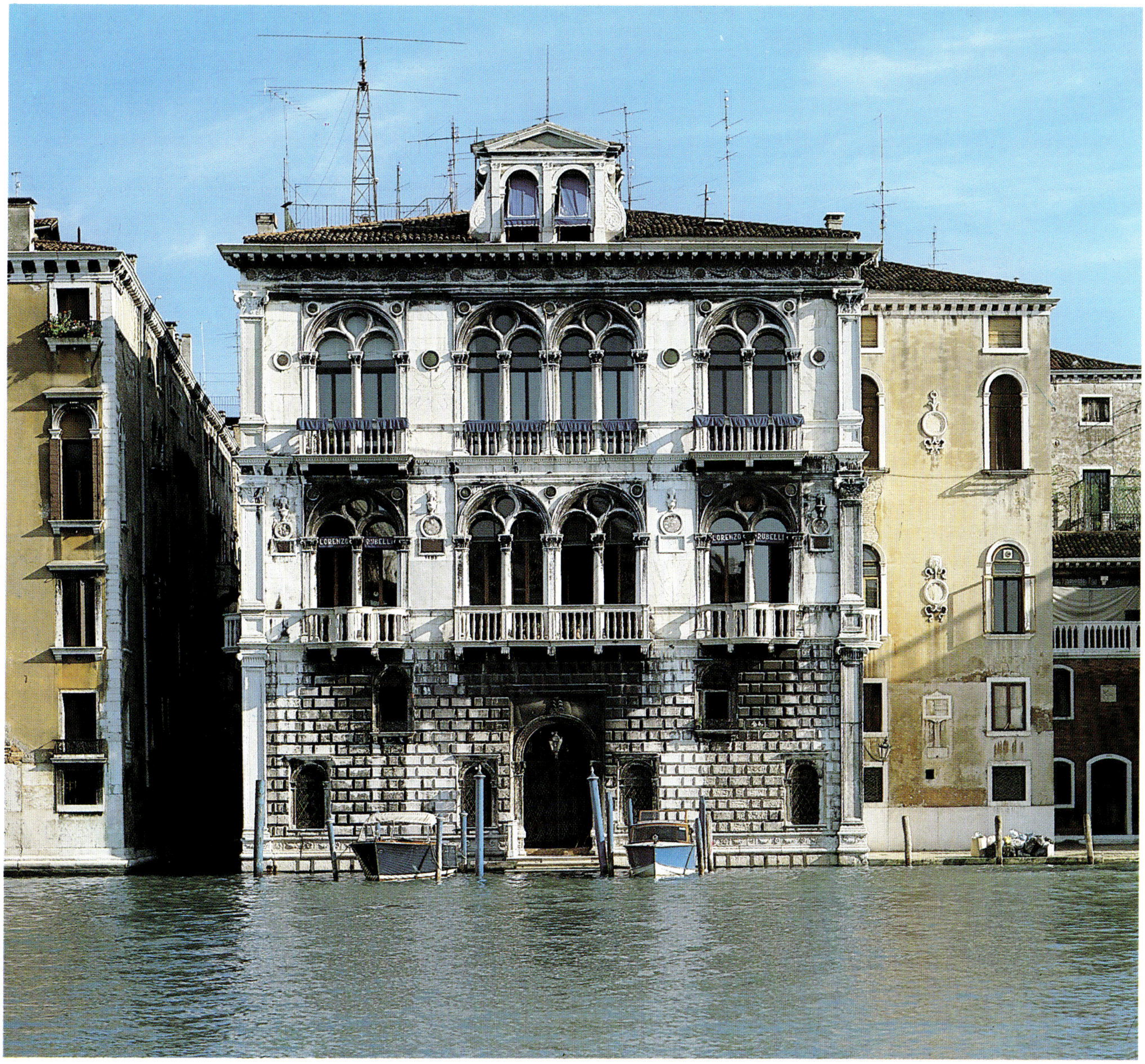

N° 69
Palazzo Corner Spinelli
Design of the façade, especially of the windows, suggests an attribution to Mauro Codussi.
(R. 40, page 103)

L. 36-37
THE CIVRAN GRIMANI AND DANDOLO PALACES

The Rio della Frescada flows into the Grand Canal shortly after the bridge sharing its name. On the right stands the large Palazzo Civran, later Grimani, built not long before, or shortly after, the turn of the 16th century.

Design of its façade clearly draws on the classicising idioms of post-Palladian architecture, it represents a revivalist statement of the great master's taste and artistic tradition, coming at a moment in those latter years of the century when the culture of the time had already set its sights on other formal ideals.

There is a stiff, cut-and-dried look about this façade, also to be detected in its handling of architectural elements and their spatial relationships. At the rear of the palace the presence of a garden may be sensed behind its tall perimetral wall.

The next palace is the 17th century Palazzo Dandolo, originally a lower building than it now appears after general restoration at a much later period endowed it with an additional storey. There is evidence that the patrician Fantino Dandolo had a mansion at S. Tomà in 1740. That a branch of this famous family, its most illustrious member Doge Enrico, unrivalled protagonist of the Fourth Crusade in the Republic's heyday, should have been resident at S. Tomà for centuries, is confirmed by its purchase of a tomb in the church there, from the Morosini family.

L. 38
PALAZZO GIUSTINIAN

Before entering the Grand Canal, Rio S. Tomà winds round to the left, describing a curve that also lends movement to the façade of an interesting 15th century Gothic building, Palazzo Centani, better known as Casa Goldoni, where Carlo, the famous playwright was born in 1707. A building sited at some distance from the canal however, and only partially visible in the background. Instead, Palazzo Giustinian, a Renaissance building of the first decades of the 16th century, occupies the right-hand corner site at the juncture of the Rio with the Grand Canal. Its unknown author is true to all the architectural elements and stylistic tenets of the Lombardo dynastic tradition, albeit eschewing marble revetment of the façade. In the tripartite distribution of the façade it is such features as the cornices, profiling of arches, delicate mouldings and elegance of proportions that, notwithstanding the overall impression of an unassuming statement, evoke the Lombardo contribution to architectural culture.

L. 39-40
THE TIEPOLO PALACES

The two buildings following on Palazzo Giustinian both bear the name Tiepolo; the first, a Gothic edifice, preserves something of its original character notwithstanding changes introduced by structural interventions in later periods; the second derives from an ancient building formerly standing on the site and was rebuilt in the classical style, which dated it to the second half of the 16th century. As was customary in those times its façade was decorated with frescoes, work attributed to Andrea Meldolla, otherwise known as "lo Schiavone", a native of Zara but long active in Venice, where he died in 1563.

R. 38
PALAZZO CORNER GHELTOFF

The Mocenigo Palaces are followed by the late 16th-century Palazzo Corner, built, in all probability, towards the tail end of the century. Flanked by lateral single-lights with framed arches, the central three-light section on the first piano nobile is of the Serliana type. The width of this Serliana section is respected in the interesting four-light section stating the central reception hall on the second storey. All the architectural elements are perfectly in axis. The palace is reached from the inland Piscina S. Samuele via a long calle which, together with the court following it, still bears the Corner family name today.
Surviving remodelling interventions over the centuries, a number of architectural features on the rear frontage testify to the Gothic origin of the palace. The courtyard is, in Lorenzetti's words, "picturesque, with an open staircase and a Gothic-style façade".
At the centre it still preserves its ancient, 10th century Byzantine-Gothic well-head.
Calle Corner's designation "del Magazen" probably harks back to a certain period in the 18th century when there was a wine cellar here, a deposit with premises for wine-tasting run by its owners, the Corner family. From the architectural standpoint the modern reconstructions immediately following the palace are of no artistic merit. Today, all documentary evidence of what were probably ancient buildings once standing on this site has been lost. Quadri's illustration of this part of the Grand Canal is, however, of interest for a building that might have been one of the Republic's granaries, its gable-and frontage featuring a series of only very tiny square windows at the extremities and at the centre.

R. 39
PALAZZO GARZONI

This building, which rises between the street of the same name and the Sant'Angelo canal, stands out because of its considerable size, flanked as it is by low, anonymous buildings. The design of the Gothic façade with its two piani nobili, the mezzanines and the ground floor, is characterized by the regular distribution of the windows which creates a perfectly symmetrical composition. Stylistic elements which can be dated to after the middle of the 15th century, are a feature of the building.
It seems that the palace became the property of the family which gave it its name, only towards the middle of the 17th century.
The calle Garzoni ferry which links San Samuele to campo San Tomà on the opposite bank of the Grand Canal, is one of the oldest ferries in Venice. Even today it is one of the last still in use in view of the recognized need to be able to cross quickly from the San Marco quarter to the Santa Croce one on course for Piazzale Roma and the railway station.

R. 40
PALAZZO CORNER SPINELLI

The old Gothic building was demolished and in its place the present-day palace was built between the end of the 15th and the early years of the 16th century. It is one of the most noteworthy and original Renaissance buildings in Venice. Its architectural characteristics make it very similar to the style of the architect Mauro Codussi who in this palace "created the model for the larger scale Palazzo Vendramin Calergi", also on the Grand Canal. Today Palazzo Corner Spinelli still has a courtyard called "dell'Albero" (of the tree), probably because a large centuries-old tree once grew there.
Vasari in his "Vite", when referring to Palazzo Corner, says that in 1542 it must have been "reorganized inside for the Cornaro family at S.Benedetto all'Arbora (he confuses it with S. Angelo) by Sanmicheli who was a very good friend of Giovanni Corner".
Whether Sanmicheli carried out restoration or restructuring work, he only dealt with the interior because the façade maintained its original form and hence its imaginativeness in its entirety: completely covered in Istrian stone, it has an extraordinary richness despite its modest size. The ground floor up to the bottom of the first floor windows is characterized by carefully regular rustic work which contains the ground floor and mezzanine small windows as well as the squared doorway; there are corner pilasters on each floor, a common feature at that time, the wall spaces are decorated by polychrome marble facings and medallions and the tripartite division is maintained.
However the reduced width has made the architect choose a central two-mullioned window and a lateral one-mullioned window which is positioned in the centre of the wall space: single and double windows are really two-mullioned and four-mullioned windows contained within a large round arch resting on columns which are more prominent

L. 41
PALAZZO PISANI MORETTA

This magnificent building dating from the second half of the 15th century deserves a special mention because of its perfectly symmetrical façade. The very beautiful six-mullioned windows open up along the central axial line and are adorned by a series of quatrefoils which, on the first floor, originate directly from the pointed trefoil arches. However, on the second floor, they originate from the round arch tracery where each arch is supported by two columns: another trefoil window motif is found between the extrados of two simple trefoil arches and the curve of two quatrefoils.
The motif of round arch tracery which gives rise to pointed arches and also the quatrefoil on the top of that same arch, is frequently used in Italian Gothic architecture in the 13th and 14th centuries.
These motifs also appear in Venice in the 14th century but they can only be seen together in three palaces (Pisani Moretta, Giovannelli, Franchetti). The motif of the multi-mullioned window on the first floor with the quatrefoil inserted into the space between the two arches because it originates from the inflected part of the arch itself, is the same motif which appears on the loggia of the Doge's Palace.
The two doorways are characteristic. The building is crowned by the Istrian stone balustrade of a terrace belonging to a later addition of a floor.
The corner pilasters of the building are Renaissance elements which indirectly confirm the age of the palace.
The double name Pisani Moretta seems to derive from the fact that the founder of this branch of the Pisani family was a certain Almorò (1420) "whose name was corrupted to Almoretto, hence Moretto o Moretta".
In 1742 the interior of the palace was restored and the greatest artists of that period were called to carry out the decorations. They included G.B. Tiepolo and G.B. Piazzetta who painted the large canvas depicting "The Death of Darius". A famous work by Paolo Veronese "The family of Darius at the feet of Alexander the Great", was kept in the reception room until 1857 when it was transferred to the National Gallery in London.

L. 42
PALAZZO BARBARIGO DELLA TERRAZZA

Next to Palazzo Pisani Moretta stands a part, that is to say the left wing, of an imposing building which was then left unfinished. It is crowned by the marble parapet of a large terrace which gave the building its name.
It was built around 1568 and was probably designed by Bernardino Contin: its lines are very simple and unadorned and it has no noteworthy feature except perhaps its size with the two very high piani nobili.
In the 19th century the Barbarigo family was famous for the very important art collection it kept in the palace. This collection had a nucleus of many paintings by Titian which were sold to the Czar of Russia for the Hermitage Museum in Leningrad.

than the central column supporting the inner arches. The space between the latter and the underneath of the larger arch is occupied by a marble medallion which is the Renaissance answer to the Gothic quatrefoil. Generally speaking, this new layout of the windows, characteristic of Codussi's architecture, seems nothing more than a modern classical interpretation of Gothic designs. The different sizes and shapes of the balconies give light and shadow contrasts over the whole façade; the more imaginative ones are based on a trefoil motif with curvilinear parapets. The building is finished at the top by a prominent cornice on the festoon-decorated architrave and by a delightful garret in the centre with a triangular tympanum over two windows.

R. 41
PALAZZO BENZON

Modest in proportions, façade design regular and true to scale, stone pediments above the windows, Palazzo Benzon was rebuilt in the first half of the 18th century by a branch of the Querini family requiring a more modern and functional residence than its predecessor. It follows a late 17th or early 18th building taking the name Curti Valmarana.

Palazzo Benzon claims attention not as architecture but as the one-time residence of Countess Marina Querini Benzon, the leading light of social and literary gatherings noted for their vivacity and attended by such celebrated artists and writers as Canova, Ippolito Pindemonte, Moore, Foscolo and, enamoured of the lady, the ubiquitous lord Byron. Countess Benzon was also remarked by Stendhal. Her intelligence and beauty inspired one of the most popular Venetian songs "La biondina in gondoleta", words by A.M. Lamberti set to music by J.S. Mayr.

R. 42
PALAZZO VIARO MARTINENGO

Dating from roughly the first half of the 16th century and classicizing in manner, the building exhibits the typical architectural idioms of a period well-launched on the path to maturity, rallied by the earlier contributions of Codussi and the Lombardo family. On the one hand courtly solemnity of language, bespeaking splendour and opulence, on the other a schematic approach to design that, notwithstanding recourse to common stylistic motifs, engenders simplified statements and, generally speaking, inflexible handling. What played a determinant role in enriching the Palazzo Viaro façade were the frescoes, no longer visible but once covering all plane surfaces and extending beneath the windows. The work was carried out by G. Antonio Sacchiense, better known by the name of Pordenone, after his birthplace, a painter active in Venice for long spells between commitments in other Italian cities, who died in Florence in 1593.

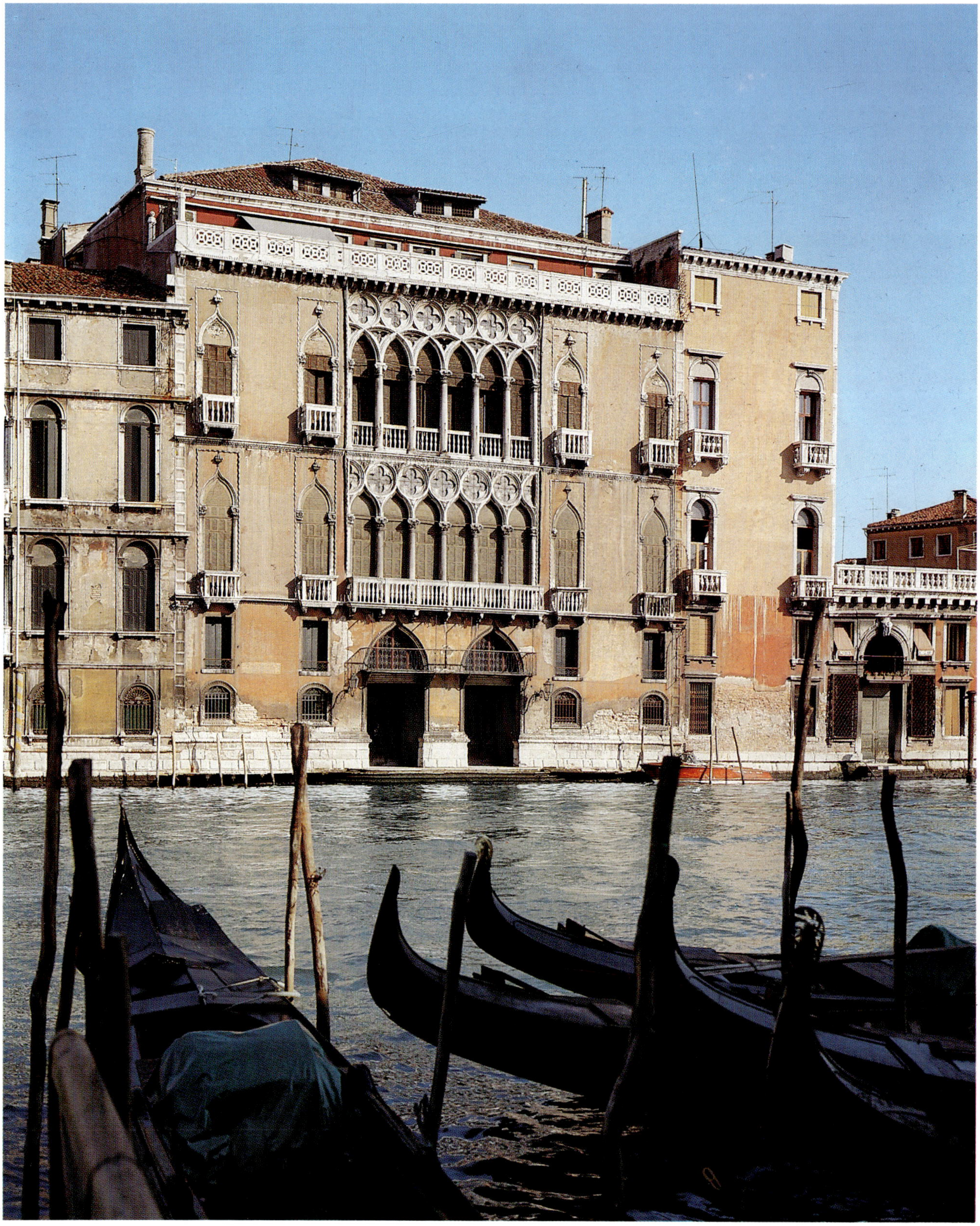

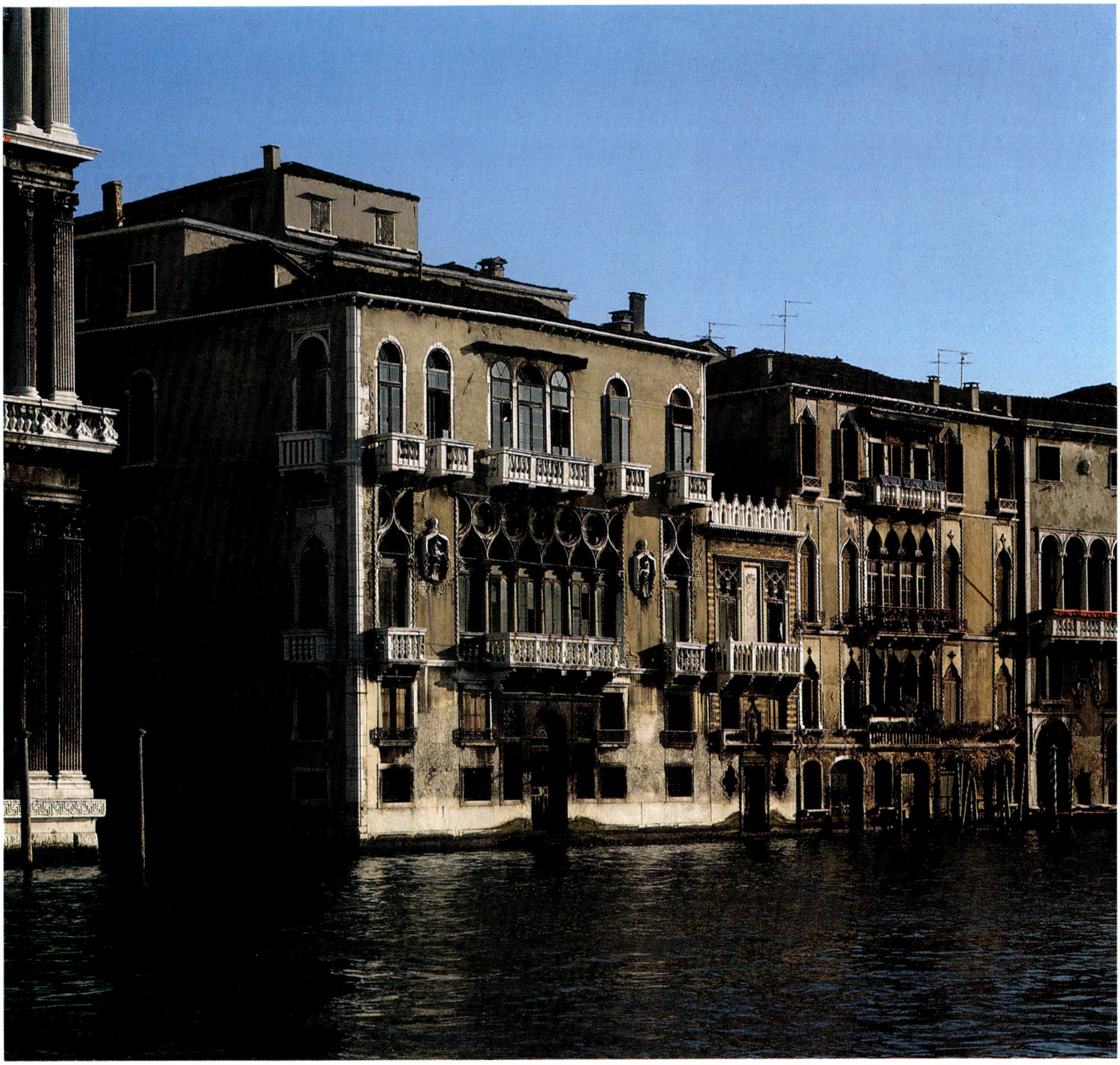

N° 70
Palazzo Pisani Moretta
The canal portals suggest that the building was shared by two distinct family units. On the right, the incomplete Palazzo Barbarigo della Terrazza.
(L. 41, page 104)

N° 71
Palazzo Corner Contarini dei Cavalli
Horses carved on the family coat of arms give this palace its name.
(R. 44, page 111)

N° 72
Palazzo Grimani Marcello
A Renaissance building dating from the beginning of the 16th century.
(L. 44, page 110)

N° 73
Palazzo Grimani
Acclaimed by John Ruskin in "*The Stones of Venice*": "Of all Venetian buildings, the most noble is the Grimani palace", the building was designed by the architect Michele Sanmicheli.
(R. 45, page 111)

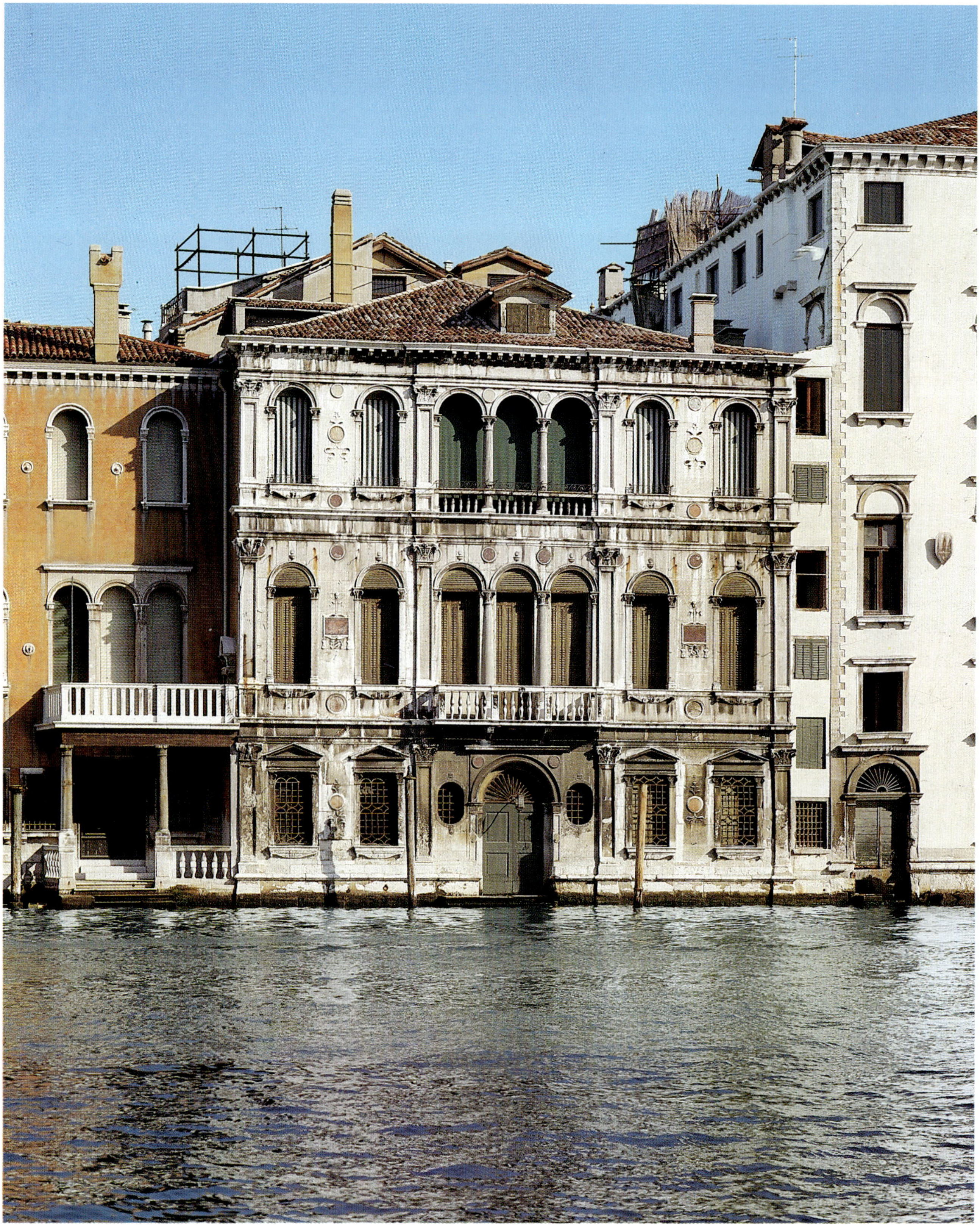

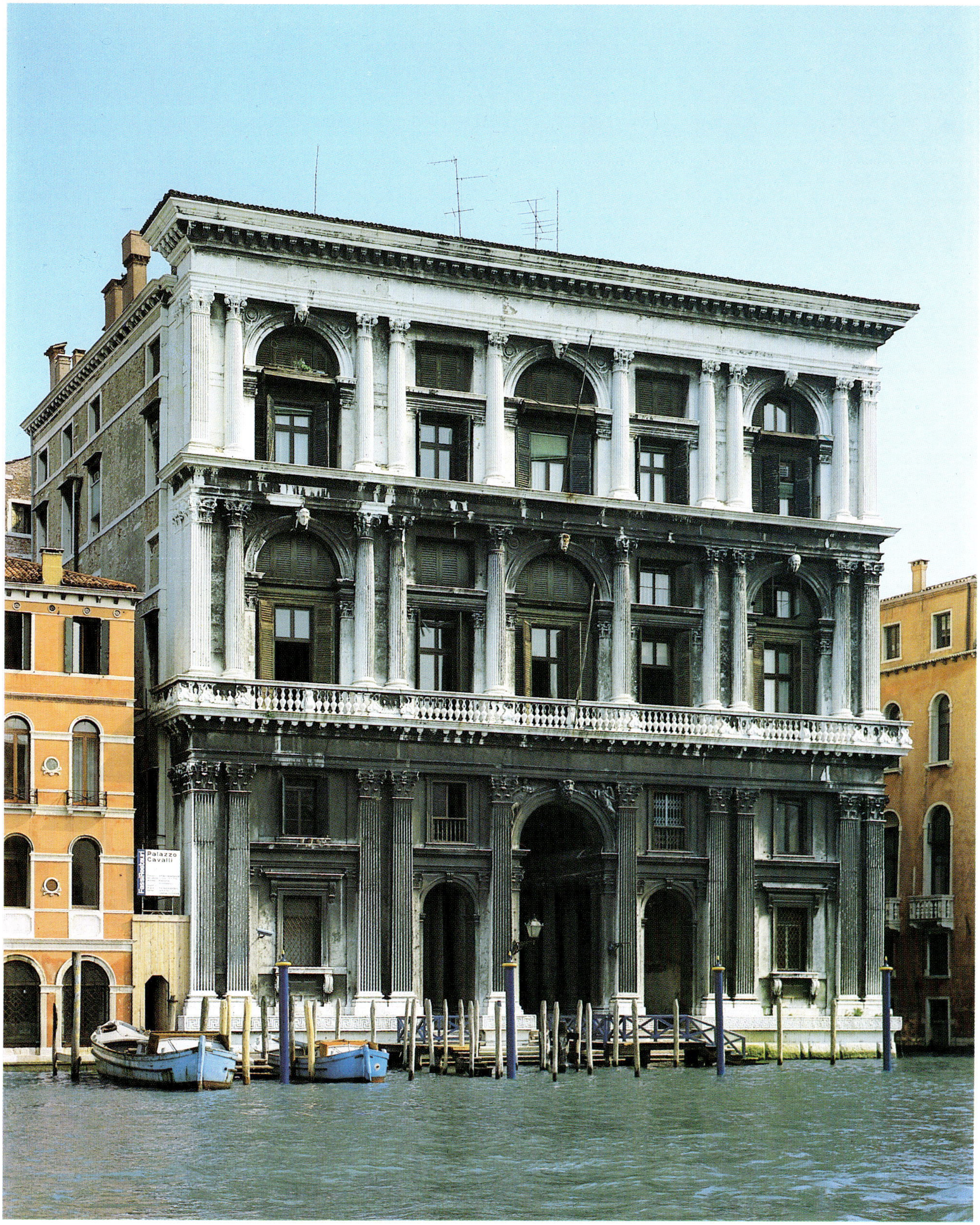
Palazzo
Cavalli

L. 43
PALAZZO CAPPELLO

It is also called Layard after its owner Sir Henry Austen whose famous, important collection of paintings went to the National Gallery in London after his death in 1915.
The building, in Renaissance style, dates from the 16th century. Originally the façade was frescoed with works by Veronese and Zelotti which no longer exist today.
The designer is unknown but he seems to have lost the sense of Lombardesque decorative quality. The polychrome marble encrustations have disappeared, the wall has reverted to its traditional appearance of coloured plaster, and in the same way the windows have been reproposed in the "old fashion".
The building is characterized by its double façade since it stands on the corner where the Grand Canal and the rio di San Polo meet.

L. 44
PALAZZO GIUSTINIAN GRIMANI MARCELLO

This building was erected by one of the many branches of the Giustinian family. Other sources say that it was initially owned by the Vendramins who perhaps had some of their property here.
This is another Renaissance building, constructed during the early years of the 16th century. It has maintained all the architectural and structural characteristics which have been seen in some of the other countless buildings which rose up over the years between the end of the 15th and the first two decades of the following century. The approach is the same one the Lombardos had always used when designing their buildings which had become stylistic models for contemporary and successive artists.
The size of the façade is very restrained though the heights of the piani nobili are well proportioned: but this is not the case with the ground floor which has been inexplicably kept low. The tripartite plan is maintained and emphasized in the Classical style by small pillars on the unbroken trabeation at the corners and at the sides of the reception room's three-mullioned window in the centre. While the windows on the main floors have round arches, those on the ground floor are surmounted by a triangular tympanum. The use of tablets and polychrome marble rounds on the wall spaces is conserved.
The building has an optimum size and spaciousness for a house to be lived in, so different from the other palazzo Grimani which we shall soon see on the other side of the canal.

L. 45
PALAZZO BERNARDO

This building has all the architectural and stylistic characteristics of the Gothic buildings of the middle of the 15th century. In fact it seems that the building was begun in 1442 for the Bernardo family.
On the ground floor the portals of the two canal entrances lie on the same axial lines as the wall spaces which constitute the pauses between the lateral one-mullioned windows and the central multi-mullioned ones; the one on the first floor has pointed arches with a fleuron on top and is contained within the narrow space created by the contour facings and by the bottom line of the unbroken balcony.
The importance of the second floor, the piano nobile par excellence, is emphasized by various elements such as the wider side windows with elaborate tracery. Here the six-mullioned window, moved to the left with respect to a hypothetical central axial line, is embellished by ogee quatrefoil arches as in the Doge's Palace, and only has a balcony at the two far windows while the other ones are protected by low balustrades in line with the columns.
In the back courtyard there is the typically Gothic external staircase, a fine example of this type of structure dating from the middle of the century.
Francesco Sforza, the Duke of Milan, together with his wife Bianca Visconti, was a guest in Palazzo Bernardo towards the middle of the 15th century.
The building preceding Palazzo Bernardo belongs to the 17th century and was the property of a branch of the Querini family.

R. 43
THE TRON PALACES

A curtain of buildings in the 15th century Venetian Gothic style extends from this point to the Rio S. Luca. The façades of those belonging to the Tron family, however, have lost much of their pristine character due to restoration over the centuries. In Arslans's opinion the first of the Tron palaces (its ground floor totally remodelled, first and third storeys partially modified) still preserves archaic accents: "With their sturdy build and diversity of hue" Arslan writes, "the tall columns of the four-light section are in contrast to the trefoil arches, whose presence is also almost emasculated by proximity to very bulky capitals", suggesting that the building should be antedated to the first half of the 15th century.

Tron Memmo, the small adjacent palace, is instead, a "19th century counterfeit", as Quadri's drawing of what appears to be an entirely different building would confirm.

R. 44
PALAZZO CORNER CONTARINI DEI CAVALLI

After some small classical palaces, the 16th century Viero Martenigo palace and the 15th century Tron palace, both partially altered by later work, we find palazzo Corner Contarini dei Cavalli (of the horses) on the corner of the rio di San Luca. It is so named after these animals on the crest of the coat-of-arms.

It seems that work began around 1445 and this is confirmed by the richness and maturity of the architectural and stylistic elements. The addition and transformation of the second floor is immediately evident; the ground floor too has been extensively restructured both as regards the windows and the main Serliana. The windows and multi-mullioned windows on the first piano nobile remain unaltered. They are decorated with quatrefoils which in the one-mullioned windows become two halves in harmony with the inflection of the arch. The considerably projecting balconies constitute a strong element which, together with the supporting brackets, emphasize the base of the floor.

Wall space here is practically non-existent as it is completely broken up by windows, architectural elements, contours, columns, pillars, arches, quatrefoils as well as the two coats-of-arms which interrupt the only wall spaces left on an axial line with the two side rooms.

Despite its richness of expression, the building keeps its own restrained spatial dimension with respect to other buildings of the same period along the Grand Canal and in other places in the city. This dimension is compensated by the quality of the architecture and style despite the successive transformations which have been carried out in the 17th century, also on the façade overlooking the rio di San Luca.

R. 45
PALAZZO GRIMANI

"Of all the buildings in Venice, the noblest is the Casa Grimani. It is composed of three stories of the Corinthinian order, at once simple, delicate and sublime; but on so colossal a scale that the three-storied palaces on its right and left only reach to the cornice which marks the level of its first floor. There is not an erring line, nor a mistaken proportion; and the exceeding fineness of the chiselling gives an appearance of lightness to the vast blocks of stone out of whose perfect union that front is composed". This is what John Ruskin wrote in his book "The Stones of Venice" when mentioning the grandiose Palazzo Grimani. It was built on the corner of the San Luca canal towards the middle of the 16th century by the architect Michele Sanmicheli and to be exact in 1556, the year we know the land was bought for 9,000 ducats. When the architect died in 1559, the building was still incomplete but was soon to be finished.

It was Girolamo Grimani, a nobleman and Procurator of St. Mark, who commissioned the building of the palace. He was the father of the future doge Marino, elected in 1595 after a long, eventful conclave with no less than 71 rounds of voting while the people, who had been helped by his generosity during a famine, loudly clamoured for his election.

This branch of the family was called "of San Luca" after its place of residence. 2840 ducats were spent on just the first floor of the palace; even so the entrance was still without "the Veronese stone floor and ten rhomb-shaped iron gratings over the windows on the first floor overlooking rio Menudo". It is clear the client wished his own home to have a grandiose appearance which the designer knew how to create both as regards the size and the architecture with the powerful arches on each floor, with the wide columned vestibule on the ground floor and with the heavily projecting string-courses.

The great main entrance is flanked

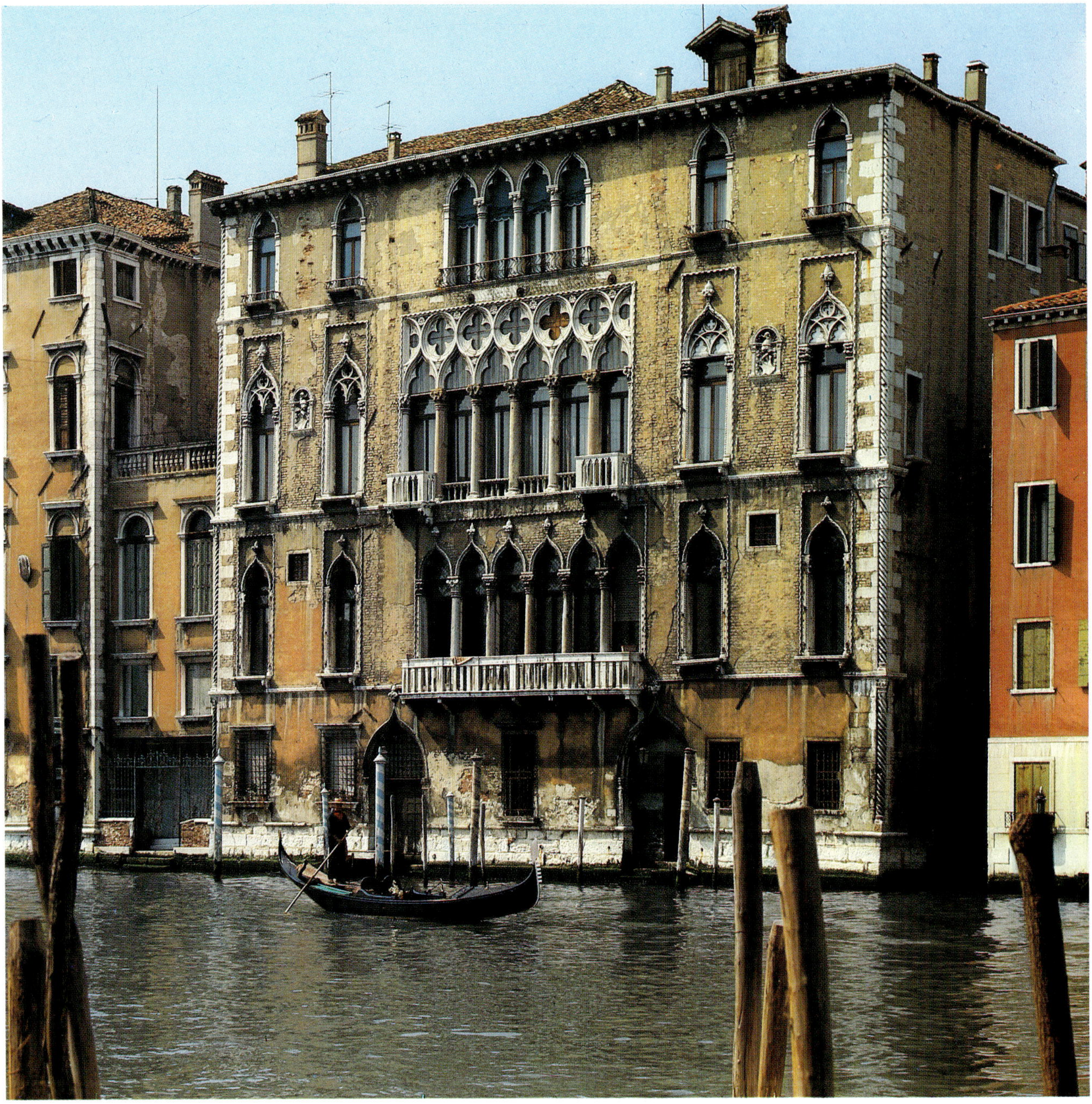

N° 74
Palazzo Bernardo
Architecturally, the more structured statement is the six-light section with its series of quatrefoils on the second piano nobile.
(L. 45, page 110)

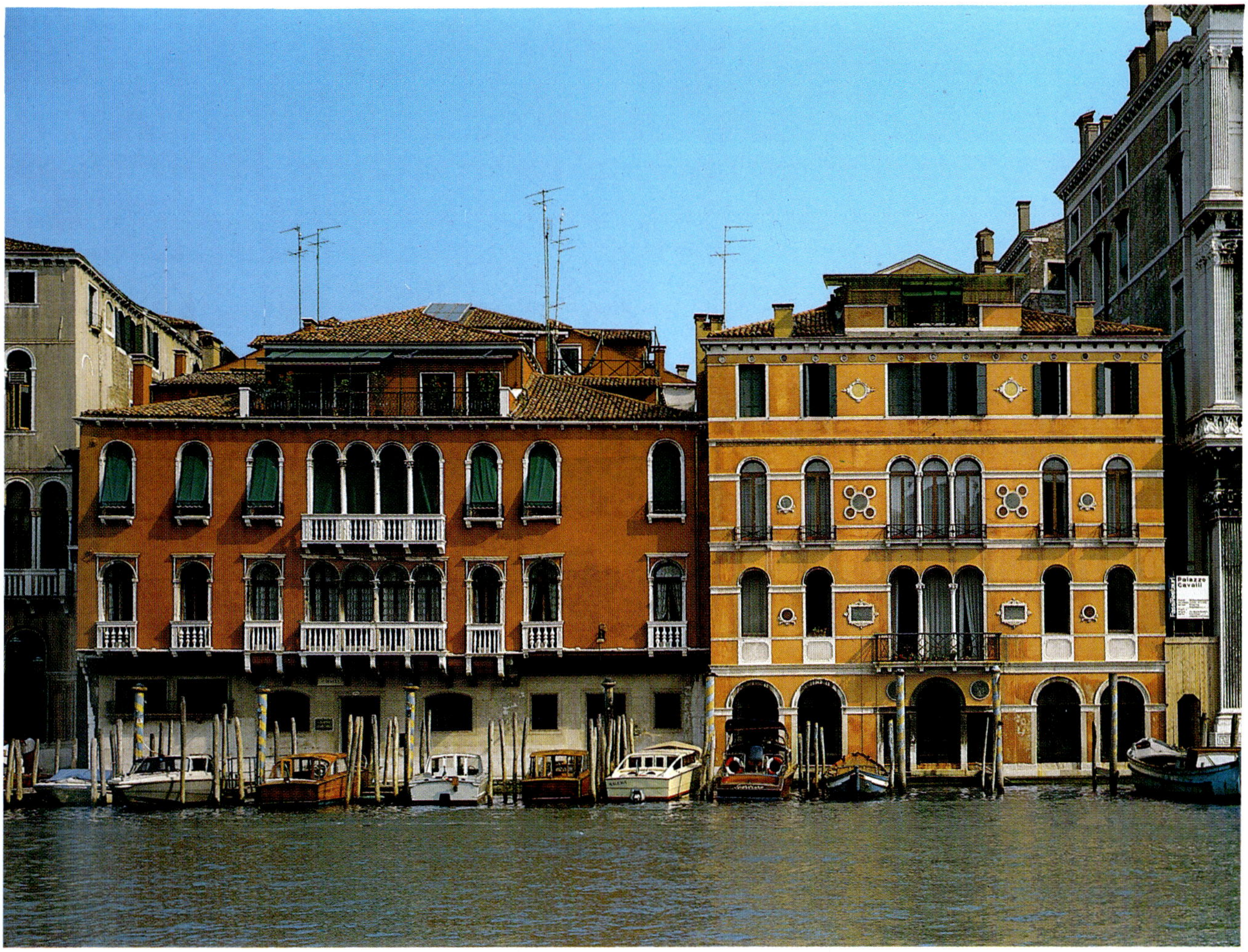

N° 75
The Corner Valmarana and Corner Martinengo palaces.
Both palaces are Renaissance building of the first half of the 16th century.
(R. 46-47, page 115)

L. 46-47
PALAZZI DONÀ

After the rio della Madonnetta we find some parts of a Byzantine house dating from the 12th-13th century which was extensively restructured over the following centuries. The raised arches of the main multi-mullioned windows and the highly interesting and fascinating capitals with their very ornate motifs are typical features; on the wall there are the characteristic, decorative paterae.
The Rialto area where these and other similar buildings stand, is the one which was urbanized earliest of all because it was the site of the market which more or less originated at the same time as Venice itself.
This is why the oldest buildings in the city, or some parts of them incorporated into more recent buildings, are to be found here: arches and columns which form multi-mullioned windows, and closed vault porticos incorporated directly into the masonry, or freed and returned to their old splendour after careful, recent restoration. These buildings ought to belong to the period between the 11th and the 13th century, preference being given to the middle one, the 12th century, but it certainly is not easy to specify this with any exactness.
These architectural remains are very valuable evidence of the first Venetian construction work and also of the special appearance of the fondaco-house with its open portico on the ground floor and on the piano nobile the use of the continuous line of windows which often occupied the whole length of the façade.

L. 48
PALAZZO COCCINA TIEPOLO

The Coccinas originally came from Bergamo but settled in Venice to personally supervise their many commercial interests which they had developed in the city. They owned an area overlooking the Grand Canal near Sant'Aponal and, after deciding to completely rebuild their house, they commissioned the architect Gian Giacomo dei Grigi with its design and building towards the middle of the 16th century. He was the son of the more famous Guglielmo dei Grigi who worked in Venice between 1515, the year the first mention of his work is made, and 1539, the year he died.
Gian Giacomo had carried on his father's work and in 1554 he had entered the competition to become Proto al Sal della Repubblica, considered a position of great responsibility, which shows the seriousness and continuity of the artist's work during the previous years.
The fact that both the family and the architect came from Bergamo can be thought to be a decisive factor in commissioning this large undertaking. The architect lost no time in supervising the work to everyone's satisfaction and the building appears to have been completed around 1560.
The classical approach is evident within the usual Venetian plan. There is a sense of well-proportioned spaces on a façade which had very wide rows of windows. The side ones are surmounted by triangular or semi-circular tympanums while the middle ones are taller and reach the cornice above. Finally, the central part of the façade, in line with the portico, creates a vertical strip of clear elevational contrasts between the openings and the wall.
All these elements including columns, balconies, capitals, tympanums, mouldings, seem to want to express themselves in such a way that the spatial unity of the façade keeps to a plan without creating important, noteworthy chiaroscuro effects other than those which denote the horizontal and vertical inner subdivisions.
The unbroken and elaborate architectural motif on the ground floor and mezzanino becomes more relaxed on the two piani nobili with just one still prominent section on the balcony of the first floor, while on the second floor light reigns in its entirety. Above the upper floor cornice, there is a row of oval openings before the slightly projecting marble eaves finish the building. The Coccinas attached great importance to interior decorations and furnishings. This is why they summoned countless artists, decorators and painters, but the most important one was certainly Paolo Veronese who painted four great works which were to adorn the reception room on the piano nobile.
The canvases, which went to Dresden where they can still be seen today, depict sacred subject-matter animated by numerous figures including the portraits of members of the family.
The Coccinas sold the palace to the Tiepolo family who lived here until the beginning of the 19th century during which time they acquired important valuable collections of coins, books and historical curios. There were several owners from the beginning of the century until 1864 when it passed into the hands of the Papadopoli Counts who carried out important restoration work but above all built the side wing against the oldest building in the garden area. This wing stands back from and parallel to the Grand Canal and overlooks the internal canal (1874-75).
Nicolò Papadopoli was also an educated man and his collection of Venetian coins remained famous. On his death it passed to the Correr Museum where it can still be seen today.
Palazzo Coccina, as we have already seen, was always famous ever since it was built because of the art collections which the various owners over the centuries had been able to build up and maintain.

by two smaller portals in order to leave room for the windows of the mezzanine floor. In the centre the two single pilasters differ from the twin pilasters on the sides. The choice of single and twin pilasters is repeated on the two upper floors: the first floor is emphasized by the balustrade of an unbroken balcony resting on the architrave.
The second floor has lower windows where the sill is included in the second, projecting string-course.
Finally, the strong crowning element and the prominent cornice provide the unexpectedly heavy finish to the top of the building if compared to Venetian buildings which traditionally keep such cornices much lighter to allow a closer relationship with the light and colour of the sky.
The room layout used in Palazzo Grimani is the traditional one; the use of the vestibule is a classical element already introduced into the city by Sansovino. However, what is striking about this building is its magnificence, not only in its enormity but rather in the use of the architectural elements for their size and mutual relationships, the strong contrast of light and shade, the depth of the openings.
The courtyard occupies the space behind the building; one side overlooks the San Luca canal while the others are enclosed by a wall.
Historical accounts tell how the palace was at the centre of magnificent celebrations which were remembered by historians and diarists for their lavishness and individuality.
In 1576, on behalf of the Republic, the Grimani family organized a wonderful reception to honour the Duke and Duchess of Mantua who were visiting Venice. One hundred ladies were present "dressed in white and among the most beautiful in the city and they were all arrayed in gold and jewels whose likes had never been seen before".
However, even more lavish were the celebrations for the coronation of Morosina Morosini, the wife of Doge Marino Grimani. The latter had asked and was granted permission by the Serenissima to celebrate with all the pomp which writings and pictures leave to our imagination. Only the older senators showed their opposition. They saw it not only as an immense waste of money for the grandiose mise-en-scène and for the building of sumptuous apparatus including a large round machine "which seemed to rise up out of the water" representing a large theatre with beautiful dancing women, but also as a demonstration of political power and the glorification of a name and family.
On that day, 4 May 1597, the Bucintoro, the dogal boat used for the wedding with the sea, also sailed along the Grand Canal as far as Palazzo Grimani to fetch Morosina and take her to the Doge's Palace. It was followed by countless dogal "peate" (Venetian barges) carrying the Councillors and other nobles and the Chief Chancellor "who, at the sound of the trumpets and the firing of the guns, all ascended the stairs and entered the room. Then the Doge's Cavaliere fetched the princess who immediately came before them all and made the same oath as before the Dogal Commission, giving a golden bag to each of the Councillors containing a gold medal with her effigy. After this ceremony (which took place in the reception room on the first floor of Palazzo Grimani) the Dogaressa went aboard the Bucintoro to go to San Marco where she alighted in Piazzetta".

R. 46-47 THE CORNER VALMARANA AND CORNER MARTINENGO PALACES

Both palaces formerly belonged to branches of the wealthy Venetian family Corner. The first, later owned by the Valmarana family, is a sixteenth century building still informed with the idioms of Renaissance times.
No significant differences, especially in height, mark the three storeys above the ground floor but placing of balconies lends diversity to the regular, symmetrical distribution of the window openings in the tripartite scheme, its central three-light section emphasizing the "portego". First and second storey piano nobile read as a single entity, isolated from ground floor and third storey by two understated string-courses. Wall space between apertures is inset with roundels and other decorative motifs in marble.
The short fondamenta and adjacent calle leading into Campo San Luca take the name Cavalli from the family at a certain moment become owners of Palazzo Corner Martinengo. This is a 16th century building with a two-storey overhang above the ground floor to enhance breadth of what was judged to be an overly narrow fondamenta on the Grand Canal. Like the previous palace this building too is overshadowed both volumetrically and as an architectural statement by proximity to Palazzo Grimani.
Undifferentiated height and detail on both piano nobile storeys suggests design for shared occupancy or property to be rented out, a single-scale module corresponding to identity of commercial and social standing.

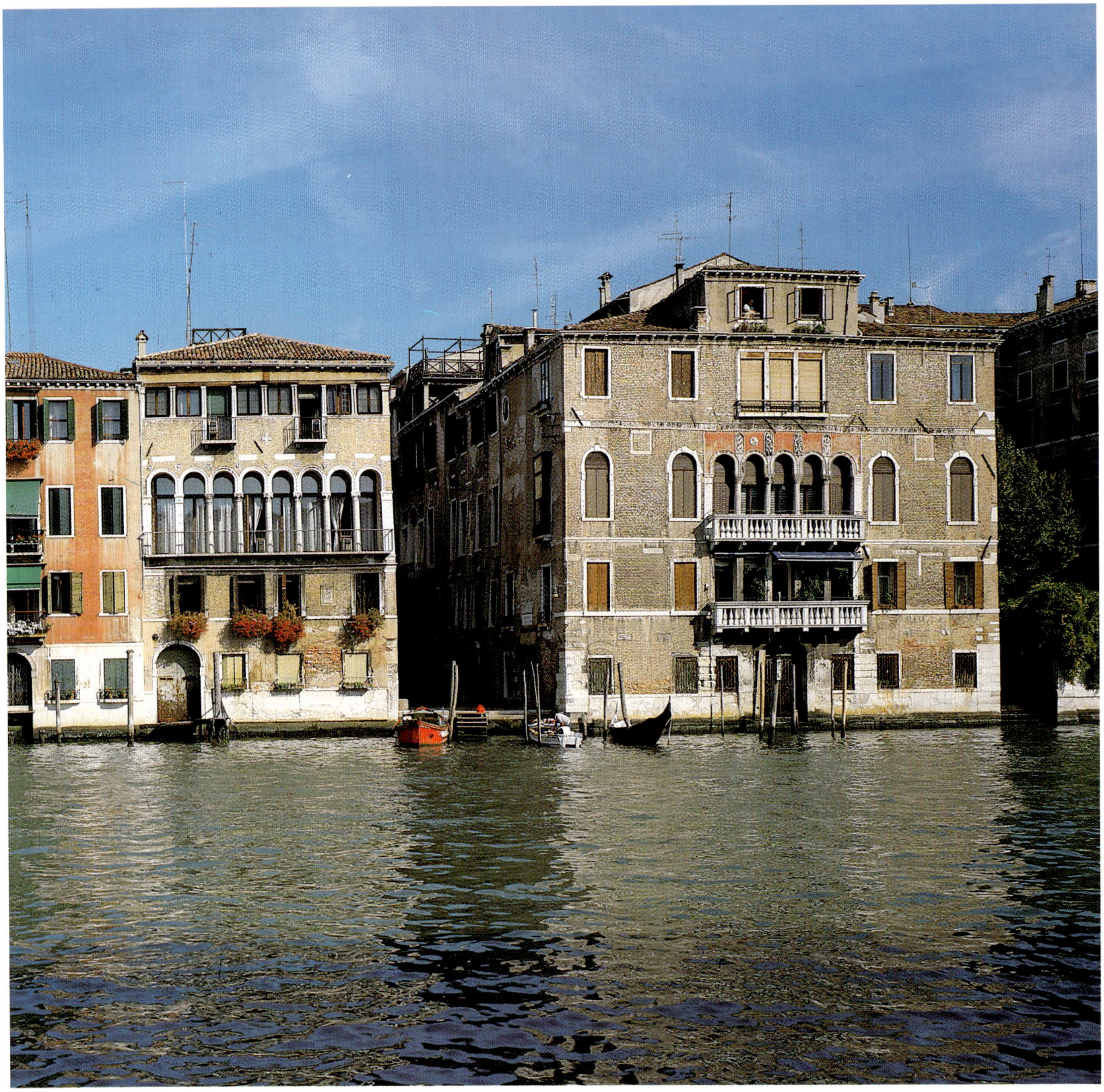

N° 76
The Donà della Madonnetta palaces
Evidence of Byzantine architectural ancestry is visible on both palaces.
(L. 46-47, page 114)

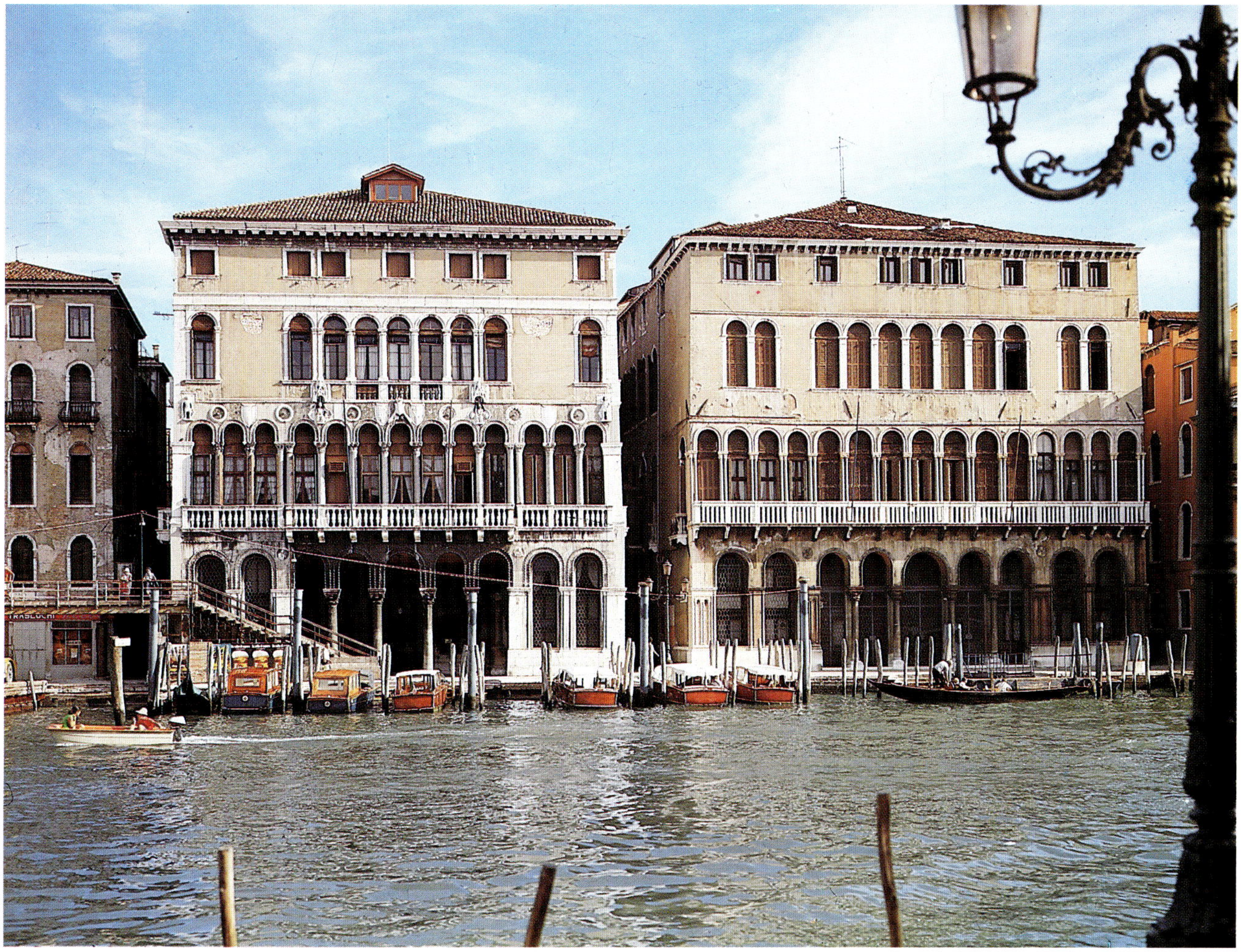

N° 77
The Dandolo Farsetti and Corner Loredan palaces
The earliest part, Byzantine in style, is the arcading spanning the full breadth of the façade on the ground floor and first storey.
(R. 48-49, page 119)

L. 49-50
THE BUSINELLO AND BARZIZZA PALACES

The Businello palace, previously owned by a branch of the Giustinian family, is the product of 17th century structural intervention to remodel a formerly Byzantine building. Its ancestry is clearly denoted by surviving features on the façade, especially those of the ground-floor portico, albeit walled-in, the columns, capitals and arches raised on a piedroit, central entrance arch broader in span than those at the sides, features dating from between the end of the 12th century and the beginning of the 13th. More elaborate but of the same period, the Byzantine structures on the ground floor and first piano nobile of the neighbouring Barzizza palace, a building restructured at a much later date.
A district known as Businello or Bisinello, after a resident family of that name, formerly existed in Venice close by the present-day Campo della Lana. The family subsequently moved to the Sant'Aponal district (San Silvestro), where it bought the palace owned by the Giustinians.
Belonging to the "Venetian-origin citizen class" but never patrician, the Businello family distinguished itself in the sphere of public administration, on two occasions – with Marcantonio in 1646, Pietro in 1698 – holding the highest office of Grand Chancellor. The former is of note for the episode of his imprisonment by the Imperialists at Mantua in 1630 as a reprisal for his having swallowed the secret cipher of the Republic to prevent its discovery by the enemy, a gesture interpreted as an excessive display of Republican loyalty.

L. 51
CASA RAVÀ

A large Neo-Gothic house preceded by a small garden, Casa Ravà was built at the beginning of the 20th century by the architect Giovanni Sardi.
The site was once occupied by the residence of the Patriarch of Grado, exiled from his own institutional seat initially for reasons of security, later due to the decline of the island after the first half of the 12th century. Numerous clashes over territorial jurisdiction took place in later centuries between the Patriarch of Grado and the Bishop of Olivolo, whose own seat was at San Pietro di Castello.
This difficult situation, at times causing the Serenissima authorities the displeasure of papal intervention, was resolved in 1451 when the Republic succeeded in unifying the two seats under the single title of Patriarch of Venice.

L. 52
PALAZZO DEI X SAVI

Trade was thriving and the market was more prosperous than ever when, in 1513, a very bad fire broke out and rapidly spread to the whole area causing incalculable damage to buildings and goods. The Republic was quick to act. It sent in soldiers to safeguard what could be recuperated and it immediately began rebuilding work since the welfare of the entire city depended on the normal functioning of the market and business. The rows of long, tall houses, separated by narrow streets and still existing today, were built on the lines of the previous ones. The ground floor was used as a warehouse or a shop and the upper floors as offices or flats. The Church of San Giovanni Elimosinario was rebuilt and the Fabbriche Vecchie were reconstructed. The typical campo San Giacometto was rebuilt to a design by the architect Scarpagnino and was characterized by the arched portico along each façade. In this square the rich Venetian nobles, either personally or through their agents, opened up pawnshops and carried on a wide-ranging activity side by side with the real market. It was here that the galleys leaving for the East were let out on contract. In the square there is a famous column, supported by a caryatid, which the Venetians call the "Gobbo" and from which the new laws and sentences were proclaimed. The side façade of these buildings along the Fondamenta del Vin overlooks the Grand Canal beside the Rialto Bridge whose central and final external ramps rest directly against the buildings. The buildings called Palazzo dei X Savi, so named after an old magistrature which superintended the deciding and payment of tithes, was built, as we have already seen, by Scarpagnino between 1520 and 1522. The architecture is extremely simple and the aim by those concerned to get the building erected and functioning in the shortest time possible appears quite clear.

R. 48-49
PALAZZO DANDOLO FARSETTI AND PALAZZO CORNER LOREDAN

These two neighbouring palaces, divided by a narrow street, both date from the end of the 12th or beginning of the 13th century. Here we find the traditional motifs of the Byzantine "fondaco" house developed in a dignified way with the wide portico on the ground floor and the unbroken loggia on the first floor running right across the façade.
Both buildings have undergone many restorations and during the 16th century two floors were added and the interior was enlarged and altered. They now house the offices of Venice Town Hall. The patina of time which the building had without doubt assumed, was altered or rather cancelled by the last 19th century restorations which replaced the external marbles and introduced some uncalled for new ideas. Nevertheless, if we use our imagination to cancel out the two upper floors, thus reducing the building to just the ground and first floors, we have in these two neighbouring buildings the most substantial examples of the "fondaco" house. They were owned by two of the richest and most powerful families of that time. The first is Palazzo Dandolo. Enrico, elected doge in 1192, belonged to this family and his name is linked to the very famous IV Crusade and the conquest of Byzantium in 1202. It was on that occasion that Venice reached her greatest political, military and commercial power in the Orient. This exploit was prepared long in advance and its aim was to liberate the Holy Land of the infidels. However, owing to a series of internal vicissitudes, its initial aims were soon distorted to such an extent that the army of crusaders carried by the Venetian fleet ended up by defeating an Empire which, although Greek Orthodox, was certainly Christian. The old Byzantine Empire fell with the conquest of Constantinople and a new dynasty was installed in the person of the Emperor Baldwin, while Enrico Dandolo, on behalf of Venice, took possession of naval and commercial bases and fortresses in the most strategic positions and set up a series of ports of call along the whole stretch of coast-line from the lower Adriatic, the Aegean to the Mediterranean and also on the islands. An inner district of the city of Constantinople became Venetian. It had all it needed to live independently and had a "basilio" as its leader, almost like a Vice-Doge to deal with and defend the interests of the Republic. Palazzo Dandolo overlooks the Grand Canal on the "Fondamenta del Carbon", so called after the boats carrying coal which moored here to unload and after the shops selling it. By tradition the building is known as Enrico Dandolo's house but the family also owned the neighbouring houses along the "fondamenta" and also on the landward side towards campo San Luca. The famous Pietro Aretino, Titian's friend, lived until his death in 1556 in one of these houses belonging to Leonardo Dandolo. In 1669 the palace was bought by the wealthy Farsetti family which set about carrying out important restorations and which much later founded the famous "Accademia Farsetti" attended by many young artists including Antonio Canova. In 1826 it passed into the hands of the Public Administration which made it the offices of the Town Council which until then had used the Doge's Palace. Like the nearby Palazzo Dandolo, the ground and first floors of this palace are also in the 13th century Veneto-Byzantine style while the floors above are the result of a 16th century addition. Tradition has it that the Boccasi family from Parma had it built while later the Venetian Ziani family seems to have been the owner. The latter was one of the oldest families in the city and it produced Doge Sebastiano who was famous for having mediated between the Emperor Frederick Barbarossa and Pope Alexander III in 1177 in order to find an agreement, after long years of conflict, on the problem of the investitures on which the supremacy of one over the other rested. In the 14th century the building was inhabited by a branch of the famous Corner family which, after the IV Crusade, had become enormously wealthy through trading and property owning, especially in Cyprus. In 1365 Federico Corner received Peter de Lusignan, the King of Cyprus, as a guest in this palace. The latter showed his gratitude for the gift of 70,000 ducats by making Corner a Knight. As a result Corner put the Lusignan coat-of-arms on the façade together with the emblems to which the knights were entitled: helmet, sword and motto. Corner was also given the feud of Piscopia, a castle in Cyprus which had extensive adjoining lands and the name was added to his surname. The palace passed to the Loredan family only in 1703 following the marriage of the last of the Corner-Piscopia, Lucrezia, to G. Battista Loredan. In 1867 it became the property of Venice Town Hall. If we observe the loggias of the two reception rooms on the first piano nobile, two completely different concepts stand out despite their similarity: the first, on palazzo Dandolo, has a series of arches supported by identical twin columns right across the façade, theoretically presupposing an unbroken line of architecture even if the palace had been longer; the second, on Palazzo Loredan, has a central seven-mullioned window and lateral three-mullioned ones which denote the internal room distribution and which will be taken up and repeated over the following centuries with greater or lesser emphasis; furthermore, the two corner pilasters block the building at the outside corners, something which does not happen on Palazzo Dandolo where the two twin columns, identical to the inner ones, constitute only a temporary end to the façade. It would have been possible to add more arches on either side without altering the architectural design.

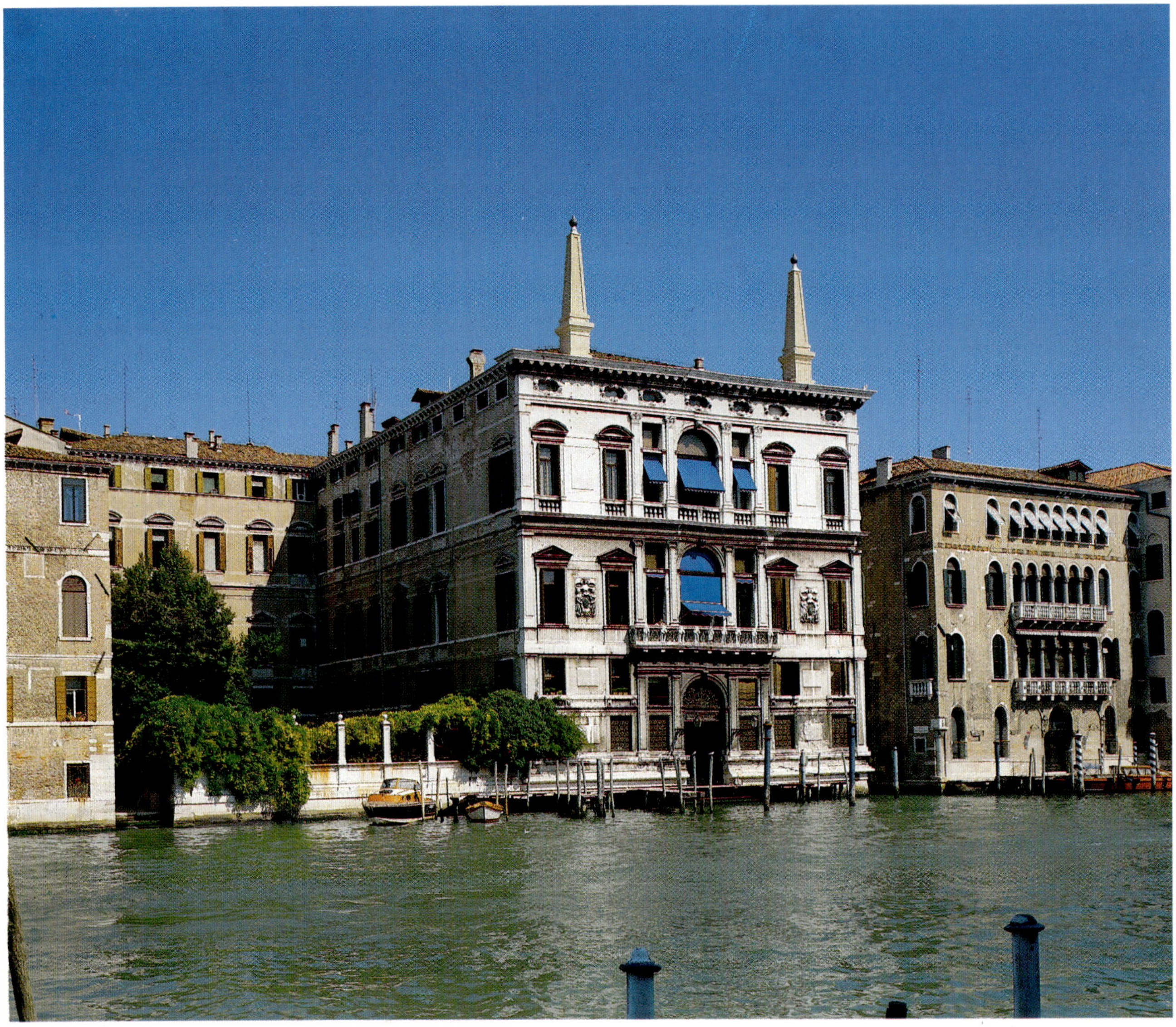

N° 78
Palazzo Coccina Tiepolo
In these rooms the Tiepolo family, owners of the building until the beginning of the 19th century, displayed their valuable art collections, a patrimony wholly dispersed today.
(L. 48, page 114)

N° 79
Palazzo Bembo
The birthplace in 1470 of Cardinal Pietro Bembo, noted by his contemporaries for his erudition and author of, among other works, "Gli Asolani".
(R. 50, page 123)

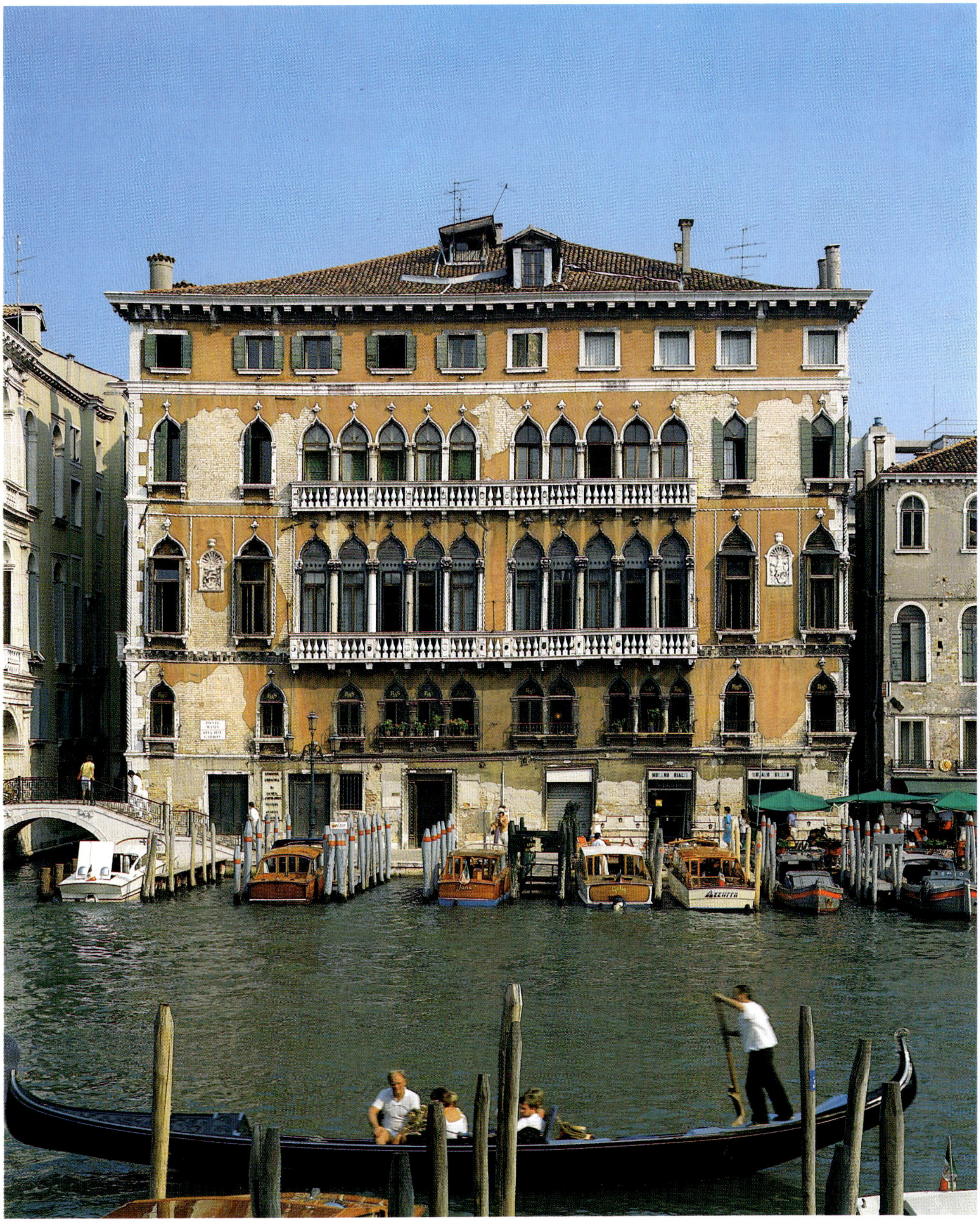

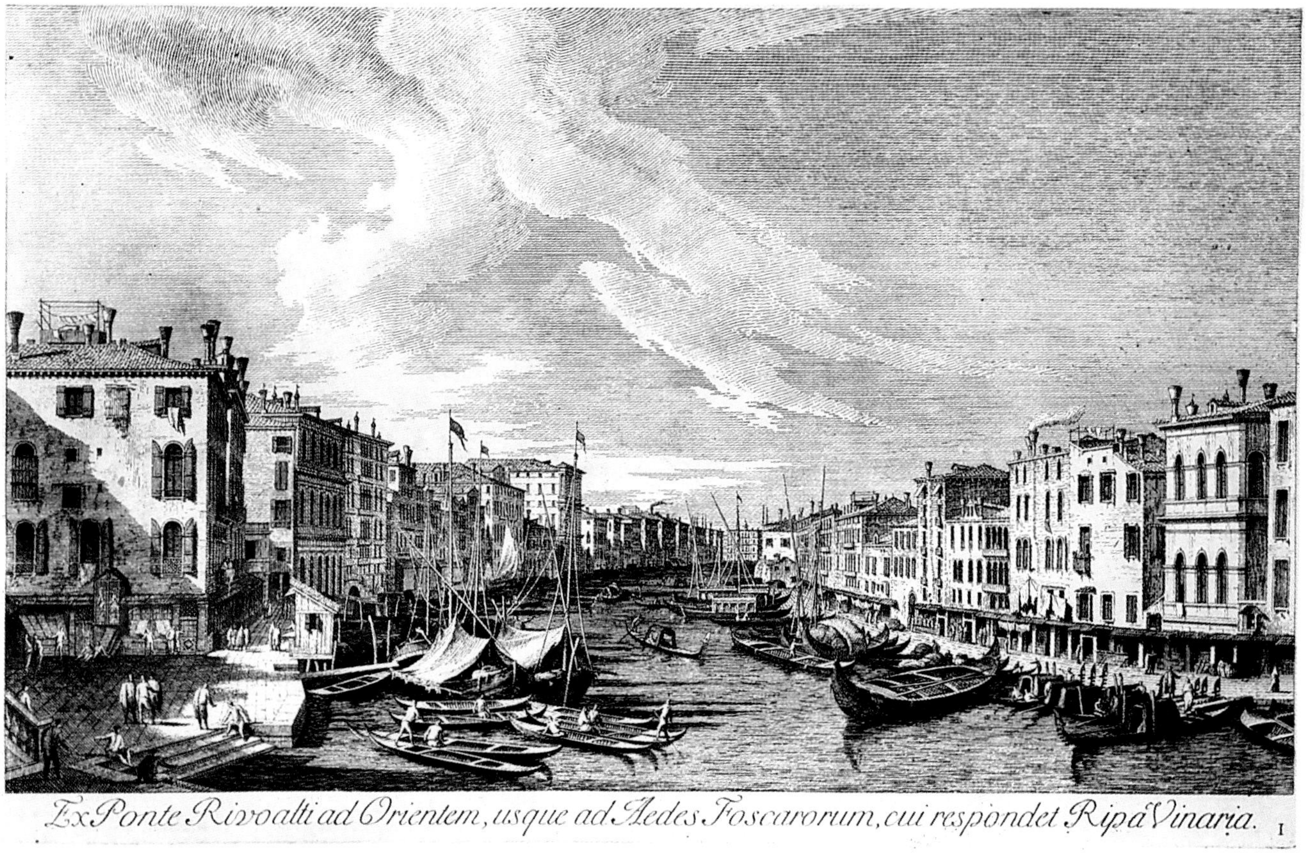

N° 80
Seen from the Rialto bridge, the Grand Canal with the "fondamenta del Vin" on one side, "fondamenta del Carbon" on the other. Engraving by Antonio Visentini.

R. 50
PALAZZO BEMBO

This is a large 15th century Gothic building very probably built on the remains of a Byzantine building of which some parts are still visible: the closing element in stone on the right hand corner of the ground floor and the moulding with its large acanthus leaves in Romanesque style dating from the 12th century.
In contrast to many other Venetian palaces, the façade of this building has two axial lines denoted by the two five-mullioned windows separated by a short stretch of wall yet united by the unbroken balcony.
The first piano nobile is taller, the window spaces are outlined by dentil facings while those on the second floor are undecorated and the ogee arch of the windows is crowned by an open rosette in the wall space. The general impression is that the building has been erected over several successive epochs up to the top floor which has completely different architectural characteristics from those underneath.
Pietro Bembo was born in this house in 1470. He was made Cardinal in 1539 by Pope Paul III and was well-known universally for his learning. His father Bernardo had already been a learned humanist and also a shrewd politician. He had introduced his son into the main Italian cultural circles, including the court of Lorenzo the Magnificent, the courts at Ferrara and Este as well as the one at Urbino.
From 1512 to 1520 Pietro Bembo was in Rome as Secretary to Pope Leo X. After returning to Venice, he took an active and brilliant part in social life and erudite and literary activities. In 1530 the Republic appointed him director of the Marciana Library and official historian. After being made a Cardinal in 1539 as we have already seen, he lived mostly in Rome. He was a poet and a great Latin and Greek scholar and he himself wrote in Latin and in the vernacular. He was one of the initiators of "Petrarchism and of treatise writing on being a Platonist".
He wrote the three books of the "Asolani" dedicated to Lucretia Borgia, and "Le Prose del volgar lingua", a sort of grammar of the vernacular which gave rise to a long debate on this question. These books number among his well-known works. His stories of Venice of which we still have "book XII Rerum Venetorum", written between 1487 and 1513, have the single purpose of glorifying the Serenissima's exploits.
Giovanni Bembo was elected Doge in 1615 and governed for three short years; he distinguished himself as a naval commander in the conflicts against the Uskok pirates in the Adriatic.

R. 51
PALAZZO DOLFIN MANIN

The Manin family, which originally came from Udine, was very wealthy and owned houses, villas and land in Friuli, in the Veneto and in Venice, including the famous Villa di Passariano, the Villa Barbaro di Maser and, in the city Palazzo Dolfin at San Salvador. Lodovico Manin was born in 1725; after entering public life "he immediately did well for himself thanks to his honesty and generosity, to the kind ways and dignified appearance and most of all because of his noble birth".
However, Manin's name is linked to the fact that, during his dogeship, the Republic of Venice came to an end with the arrival of the French army under Napoleon.
The words the doge pronounced before decreeing the end of the Republic before the Great Council, have remained famous: "Tonight we shan't feel safe even in our own beds".
The building of the palace on the Grand Canal was begun in the San Salvador parish in 1538 for Giovanni Dolfin. He owned a row of small houses in that area and he wanted to merge them into one single building which was to look directly onto the Grand Canal while a portico constituted the unbroken line of the fondamenta.
Two years later this façade was already finished. Dolfin had summoned the great architect Jacopo Sansovino to design the palace. After being superintendent of the Serenissima, Sansovino was using those years to carry out the most important Venetian works of his career in this lagoon city.
The building's plan differs in that it has the uncommon inner courtyard which was later to be used by other designers in numerous houses.
In the centre we have the four-mullioned window of the reception room on the two main floors, at the sides the one-mullioned windows denoting the side rooms with the characteristic attached column in the middle of the wall space. The use of the orders is closely linked to the

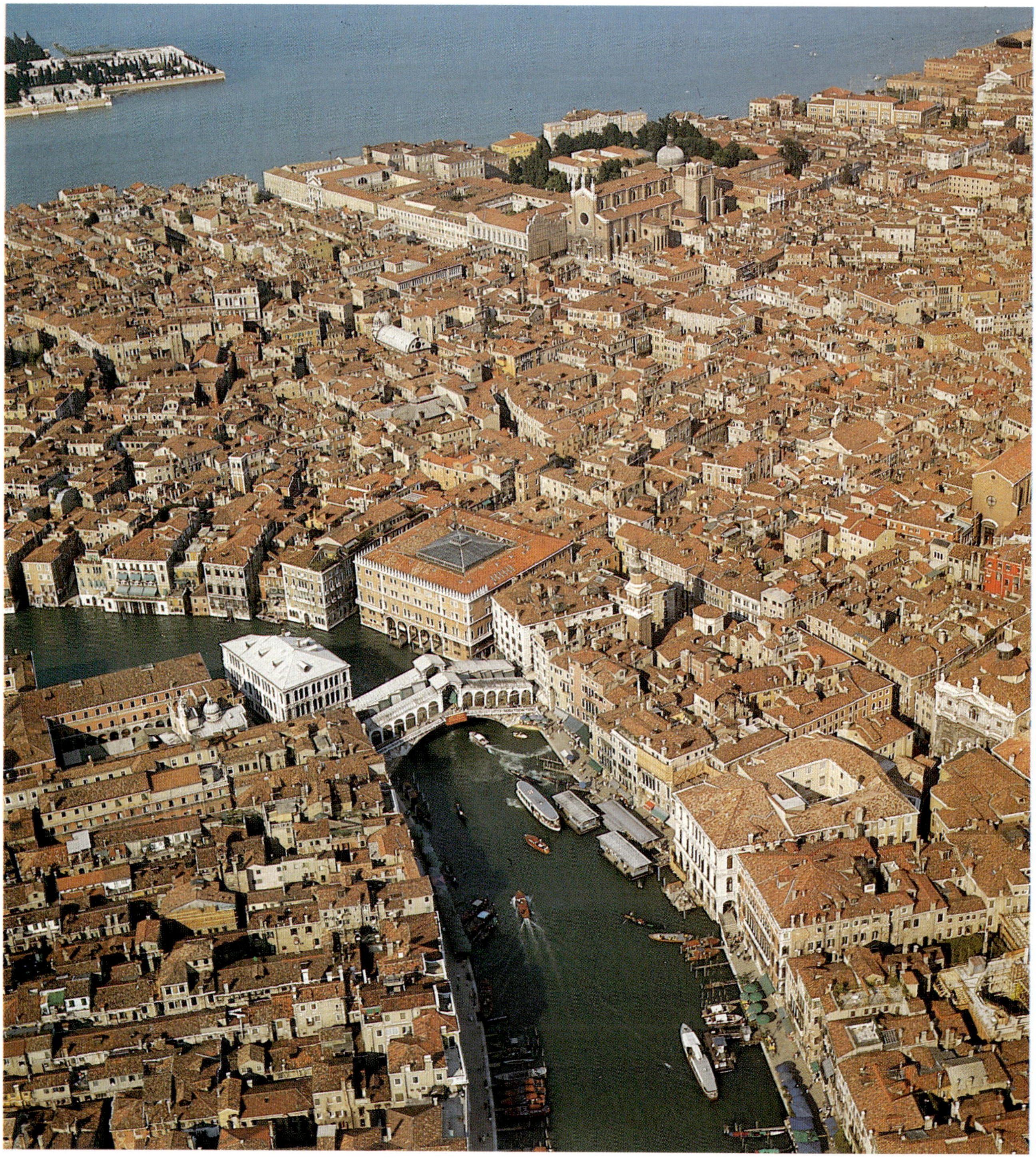

N° 81
The Grand Canal in the Rialto zone, with the bridge and the Fondaco dei Tedeschi. Visible on the left, the upper storeys of the imposing, white Camerlenghi palace.

N° 82
Palazzo Dolfin Manin
Residence of the last doge of Venice, Lodovico Manin, building was begun in 1538 by the Dolfin family. (R. 51, page 123)

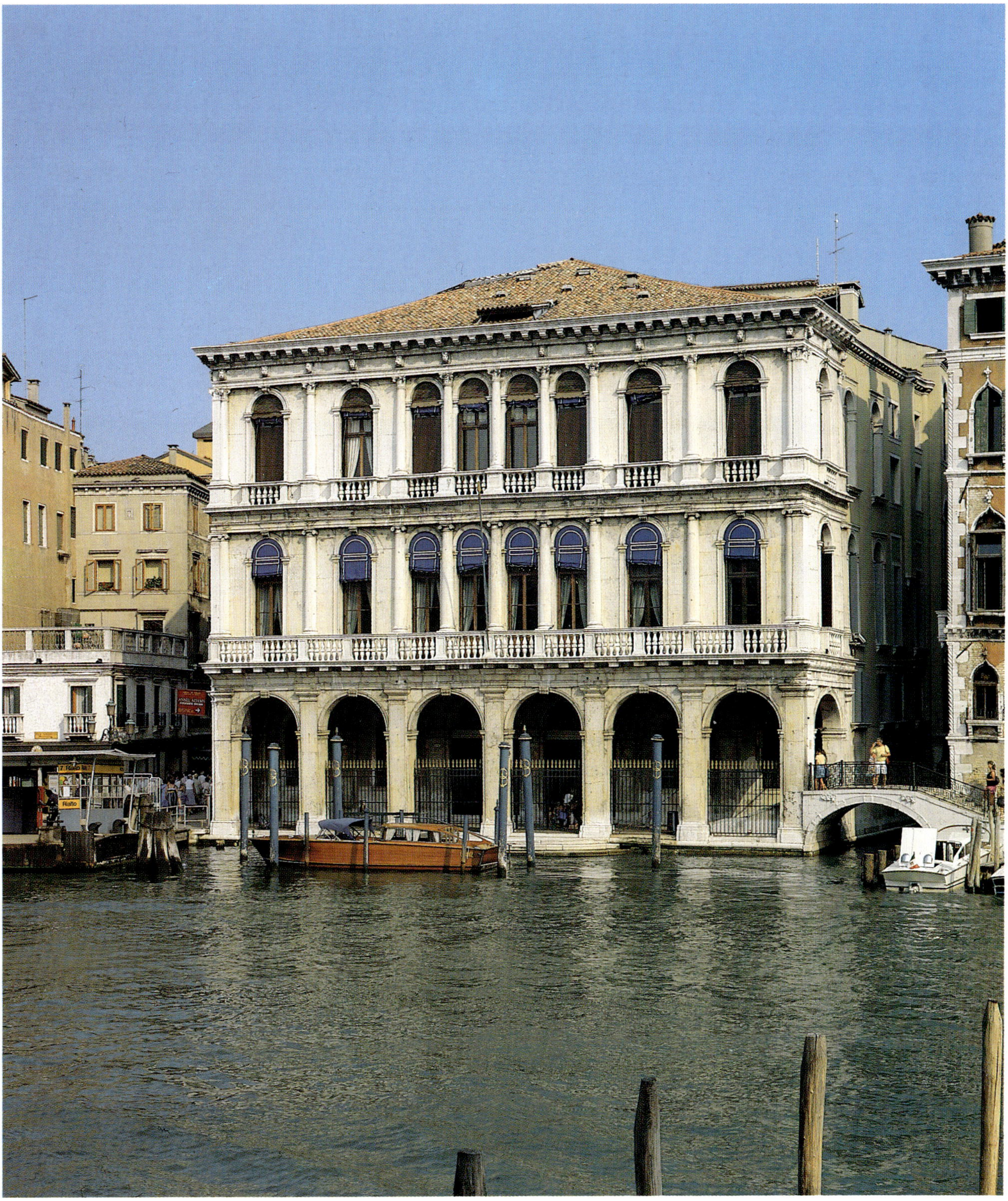

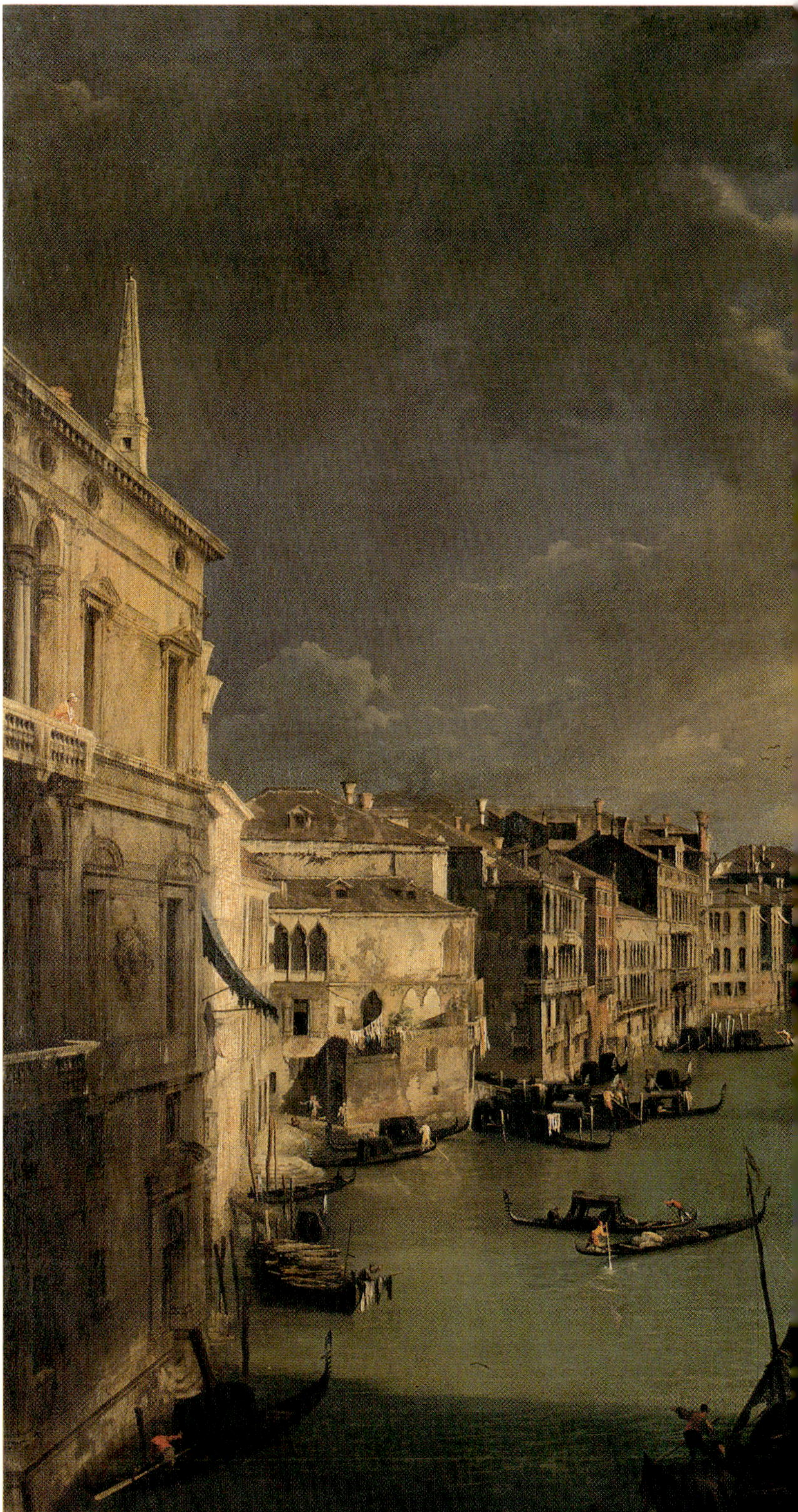

N° 83
"*The Grand Canal towards the Rialto*" by Antonio Canaletto.
Correr Museum, Venice.

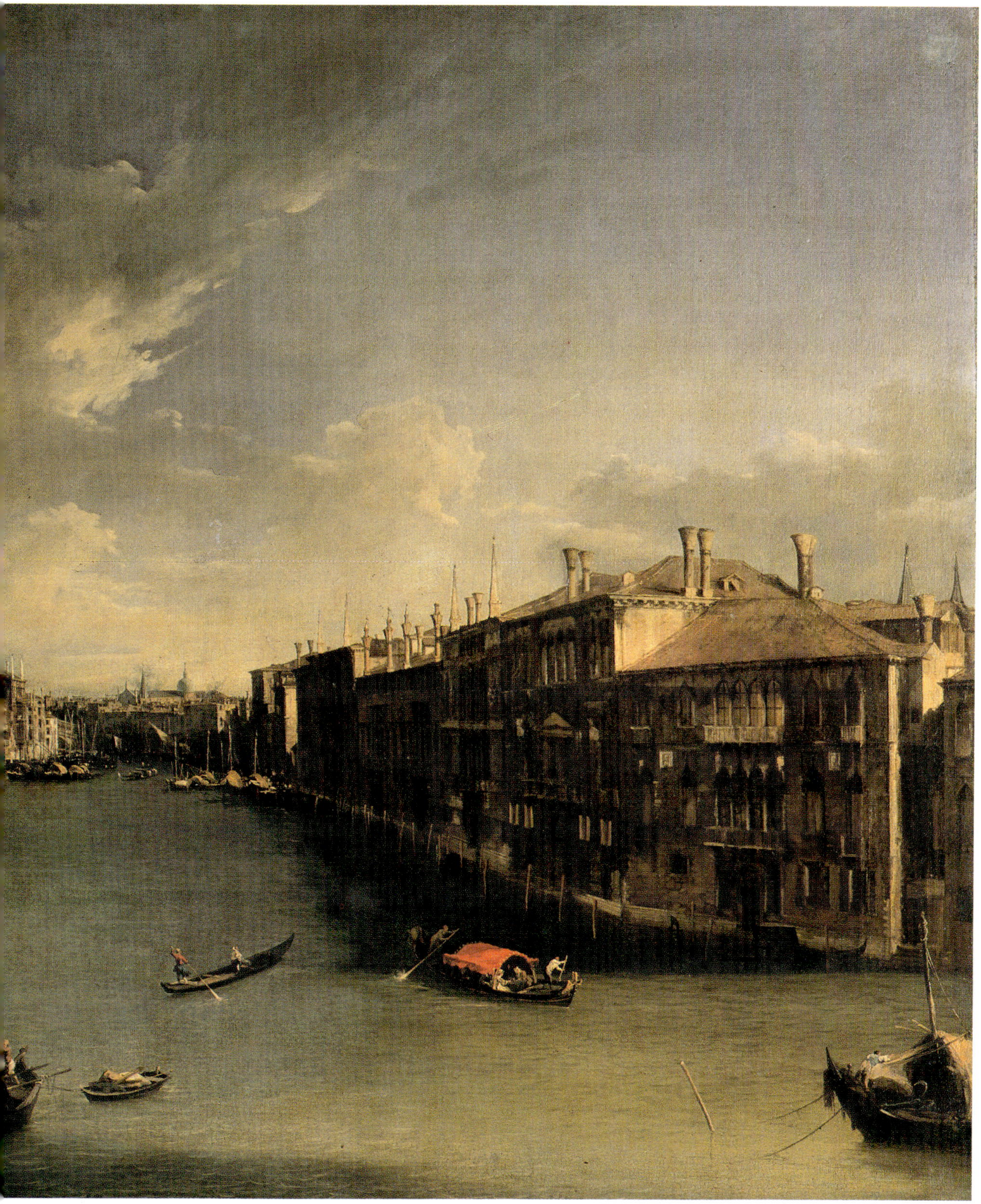

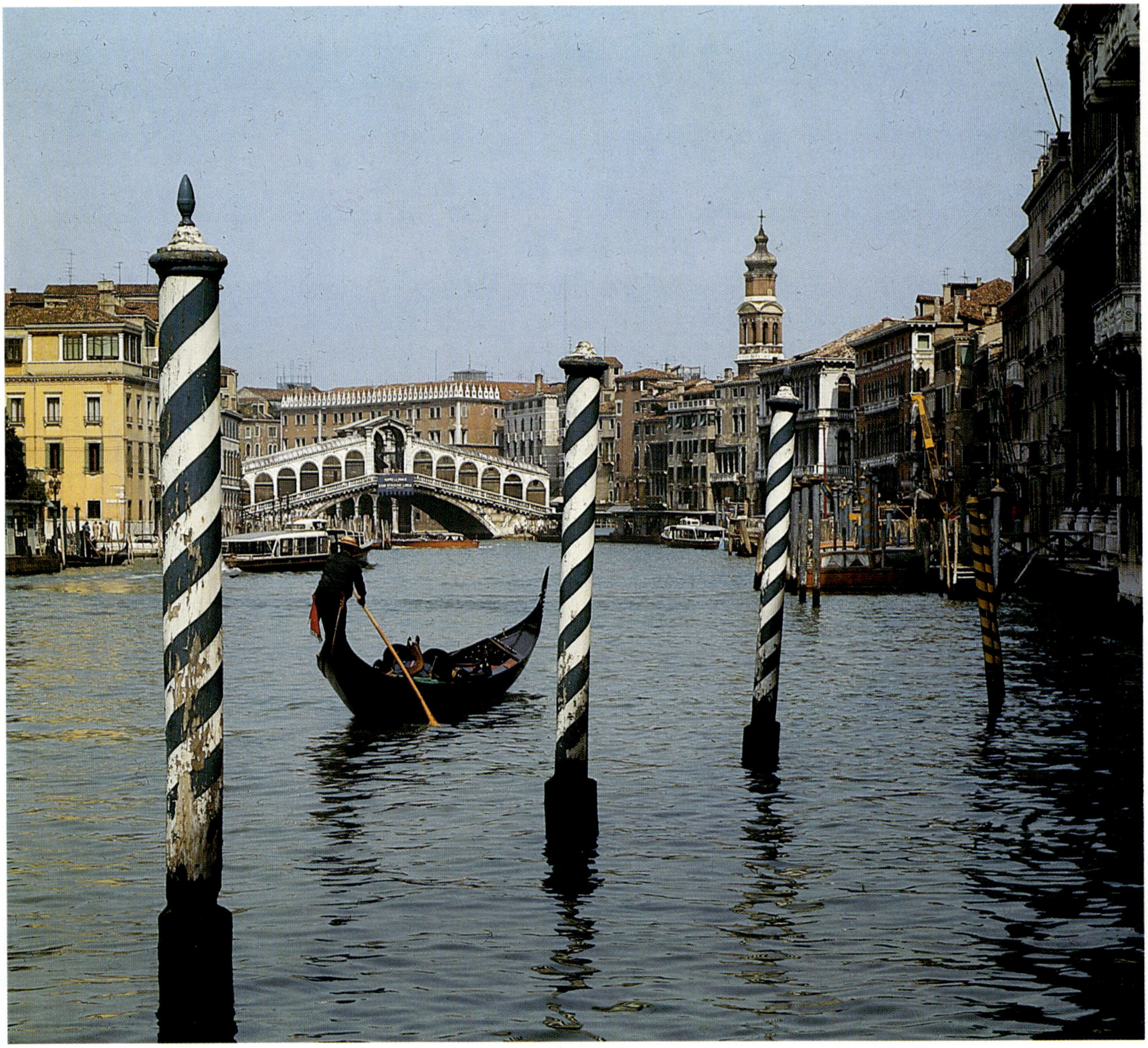

N° 84
The Rialto Bridge
On the right, in foreshortening, a number of structures of the Grimani palace followed by the Bembo and Manin palaces. The bell-tower belongs to the San Bartolomeo church. Beyond the bridge, the Fontego dei Tedeschi.
(L. 53, and R. 53, page 130, 131, 133)

N° 85
The Accademia Picture Galleries
"*Healing of a Man possessed of the Devil*" by Vittore Carpaccio. The iconographic importance of the painting is evident inasmuch as it shows the ancient Rialto bridge, a wooden structure with central drawbridge consenting to passage of galleys.

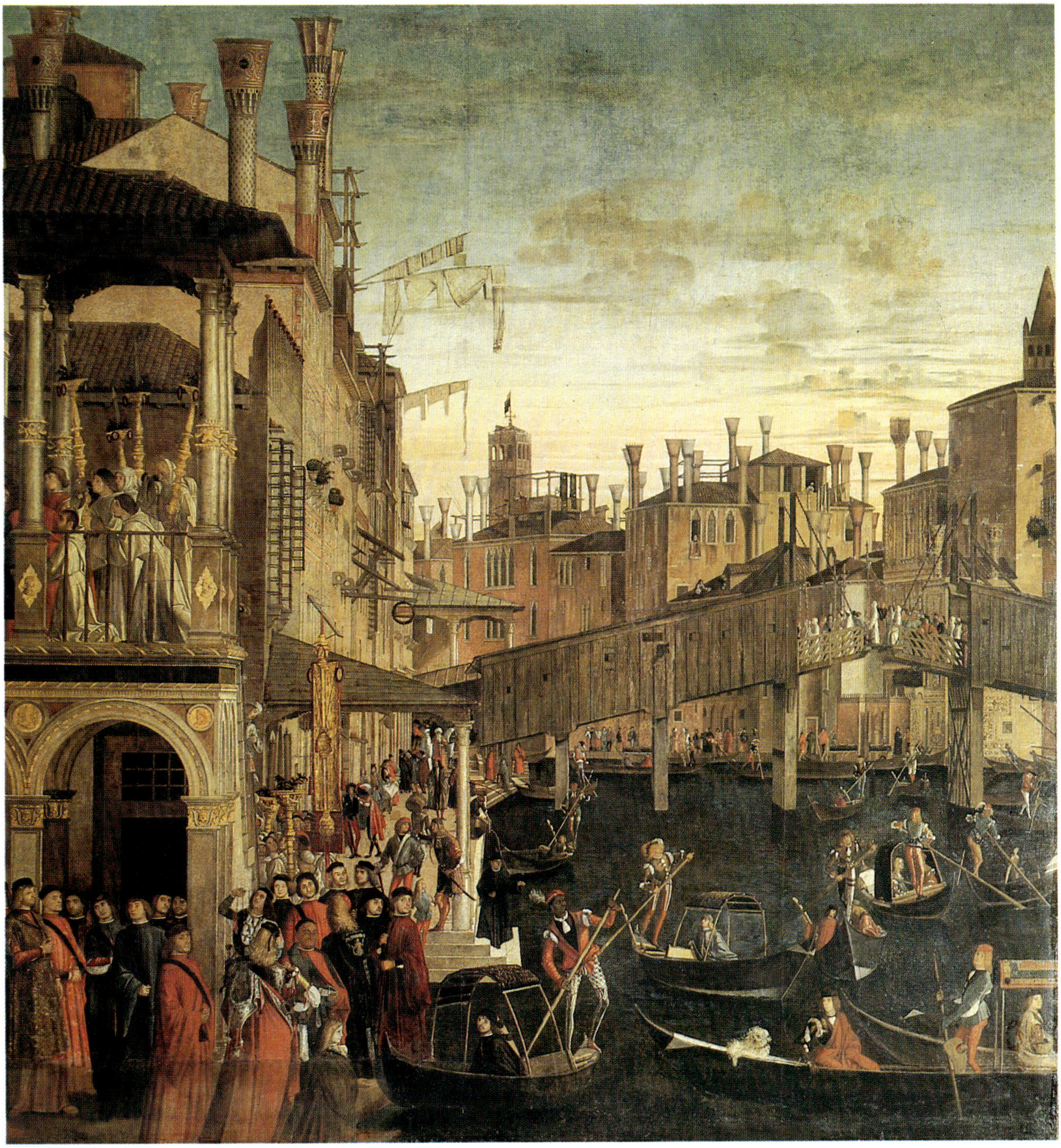

L. 53
RIALTO BRIDGE

Originally this was the only bridge which linked the two banks of the Grand Canal, right in the area where most Venetian trading was carried out. It seems that in the 12th century it was a pontoon bridge, the work of L. Barattieri. It was later replaced by a wooden bridge which, at the time of the Bajamonte plot (1310), was destroyed by the fleeing rebels to stop their pursuers. Even after being restored, it was in a very bad condition in the 15th century when it actually collapsed under the weight of the crowd rushing to see the Marchesa of Ferrara on a visit to Venice.

Carpaccio's painting "The relic of the Cross" shows us the bridge as it was after its reconstruction: still in wood but wider with many shops and a central drawbridge. About a century later, it was again in a very bad condition and it was decided to rebuild it, this time in stone. All the most famous architects submitted designs: Michelangelo, Sansovino, Palladio, Scamozzi and Da Ponte who was eventually the winner. The construction of the bridge was brought to completion between 1588 and 1591 during the dogeship of Pasquale Cicogna. The bridge has a single arch span of 28 metres which supports two rows of shops linked in the centre by two large arches which bear the whole structure. There are sculptures by A. Rubini and T. Aspetti on the tympanums of the arches.

L. 54
PALAZZO DEI CAMERLENGHI

A covered loggia had existed on this site since 1525, standing adjacent to some rooms used by the magistracies which looked after State finances and commerce, while the external area was used by the merchants for their meetings and bargaining. There were three Camerlenghi and they also stayed in office for a year; many people, clerks and secretaries, were in their service.

In 1525 the old building which no longer satisfied the State's increasing financial and commercial requirements, was demolished and in its place an elegant building was built. This building can still be seen today standing next to Rialto Bridge and at the beginning of the enormous area set aside for trading and the market. It is clearly a Renaissance building linked to the general trend of the Lombardesque and Codussi style, built to a plan which follows the bend in the Grand Canal at that point. Therefore it has five façades completely covered in Istrian stone with sculpted stringcourses and contours in slight relief; various sized multi-mullioned windows and one-mullioned windows alternate; pillars are continually used for the windows and to outline the spaces; there are two main floors, a ground floor over a basement and part of the latter was used as a prison.

The design of the palace is attributed to Guglielmo dei Grigi, an architect from Bergamo whom we have already mentioned in reference to another building along the Grand Canal. It was begun in 1525 and after three years it was nearing completion and being used inside for the state business mentioned earlier. Most probably the sculpted parts of the wall covering were being put in place. However we must make this observation about its position within the urban framework: we have already seen that its position was a decisive factor in its design. It occupies an isolated position between the canal, the bridge and the landward space behind and therefore its façades are visible from many directions, giving it a prominent place within the surrounding urban network. Furthermore, the lead roofing, as in the Doge's Palace, seems to emphasize the use of such a material in public buildings.

classical tradition starting with the ground floor: Doric, Ionic and Corinthian. The upper frieze under the cornice, low and insignificant, is decorated with lion heads.
In his biography of Sansovino, Vasari writes that Palazzo Dolfin cost its owner 30,000 ducats. In 1789 the building was bought by the Manins after passing from one heir to another after the extinction of the Dolfin branch in 1602.

R. 52
THE FONDAMENTA DEL CARBON AND FONDAMENTA DEL VIN

The "fondamente" face one another on either side of the Grand Canal, each terminating in a flight of steps leading up to the Rialto bridge. Strictly speaking, only the first stretch of the right bank is the "fondamenta del Carbon", its continuation being the "fondamenta del Ferro", while "fondamenta del Vin" applies to the left bank.
The first name derives from the presence of coal barges on the "Riva del Carbon" stretch where a permit allowed only two barges at a time to pull in and sell their load. Fuel stores also existed on this bank, two of them property of the Bembo family, a third owned by the Donà. From a dogal deed of sale relating to Ordelafo Falier we may deduce that the second stretch of fondamenta gains its name "del Ferro" or "della Moneta" from a building used as a mint. In the early days of the Republic both wine und iron goods were sold on either bank, hence the confusion over site names associated with one or other product until 16th century legislation established precise anchorage and sale points. The "fondamenta del Vin" in fact was long known as "fondamenta del Ferro".
Coal merchants and vintners formed recognized trade corporations; the former with its own "scuola" for devotions in the church of San Salvador, the latter, comprising porters and "decanters of wine" in the church of San Silvestro, with a private altar.
On the left bank the façades of houses and sometimes the entire building were all demolished and rebuilt between the 19th and early 20th century; those on the right bank however, still preserve some original features dating from the late 16th or the 17th century.

R. 53
THE RIALTO BRIDGE

Described in March 1400 as "devastated and rotting away", the bridge called for total rebuilding. But for almost two hundred years this was not to be: a little at a time as was Venetian practice, first the load-bearing structures of the wooden bridge, then its cladding, were progressively restored and repaired.
At a cost of 2327 ducats, by 1431 it had been almost entirely rebuilt and thenceforward, notwithstanding growing signs of deterioration, there is no further mention of on-going restoration work. In 1458 building of shops on the bridge commenced, to cover at least part of maintenance costs from rents.
At the start of the 16th century a number of structural interventions took place, initially at the hands of Giorgio Spavento, later under Scarpagnino.
Transit beneath the bridge became so difficult and dangerous that the Bucintoro could no longer pass without disembarking and reembarking its passengers.
On several occasions between 1514 and 1524 the Senate discussed proposals to rebuild the bridge entirely, in stone and with a single span, just as it was to be designed – at least, according to Vasari – by Fra Giocondo in 1544.
On 14 August part of the bridge suddenly collapsed, together with the shops above it; a disaster mitigated by the fact that it took place on a Sunday and victims were few. A few days before this event the Fondaco dei Tedeschi had been arrayed to receive the Duke of Urbino, nominated commander-in-chief of the army. After the customary exchange of courtesies, we are told, the duke had been accompanied on foot across the bridge – at grave risk to all involved – to the landing-stage prepared for the occasion on the opposite bank.
The Senate passed a resolution that the bridge should be rebuilt and three superintendents nominated on 25 September 1525, but despite growing support for this radical solu-

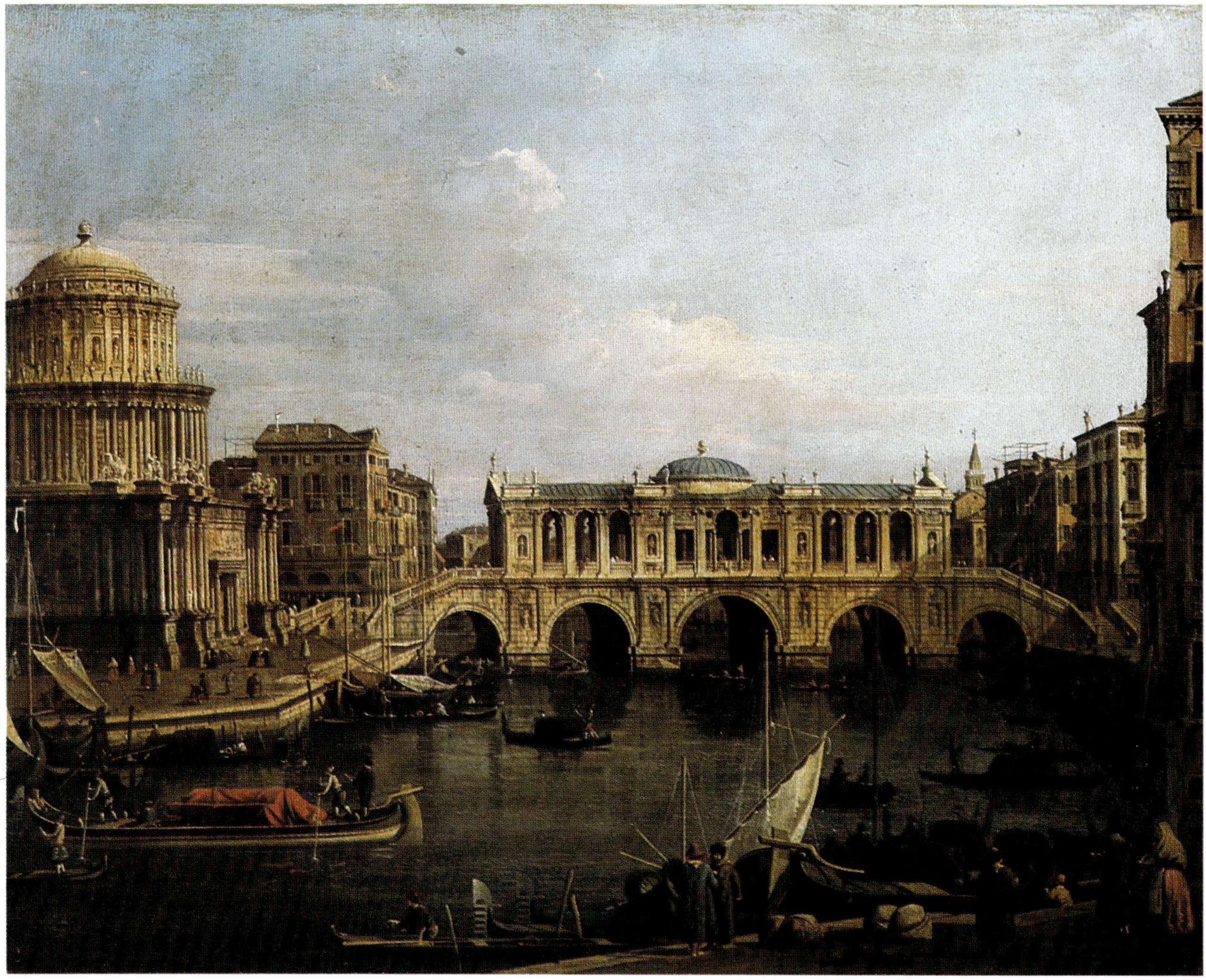

N° 86
"*Capriccio with the Rialto Bridge*"
attributed to Antonio Canaletto.
National Picture Gallery, Parma.
The bridge depicted visualizes the project drawn up by Andrea Palladio when 16th century Venice decided to build a new stone bridge.

tion it was put off once more and the policy of piecemeal restoration continued for several decades.
A start was made on drawing up the first projects towards the mid-16th century; one may have been by Michelangelo Buonarroti, produced during a stay in Venice, another, by Andrea Palladio, is certain because images of his design for a great structure of five spans are known to us. In the same period projects were probably submitted by Vignola and Sansovino, but only word of these survives. The specially nominated commission failed to examine these proposals in 1554 and also in 1569 when outbreak of war interrupted work almost immediately.
In 1587 the problem of the bridge seemed to be definitively laid aside, also because the Council of Ten, arrogating the matter, had adopted a non-intervention solution. Curtailment of this magistrature's excessive power consented to raising the matter in the Senato once more and the three superintendents elected were thus able to forward request for suitable projects to the master-builders of the sectors concerned.
Projects were submitted by Tiberio Zorzi, Antonio da Ponte, Giacomo de' Guberni, Guglielmo dei Grandi and Bonaiuto Lorino.
Subsequent discussion of these while not producing an effective project, did elicit a series of fundamental indications for the new work, the most important being that the bridge should be built of stone, its foot on the side facing San Bartolomeo re-sited to allow right of way alongside the church, skirting the bell-tower. Moreover, the central passageway over the bridge was to be flanked by two rows of shops, behind them, allowing uninterrupted view of the canal, the side passageways and relative access ramps, in the interests of greater enhancement of the canal prospect endowed with balconies and colonetted balustrades.
The question of a single or double span for the bridge was held over due to differences of opinion.
Having initially submitted a three-span project, Antonio da Ponte changed his mind and joined the single-span lobby "in promise, a more handsome and astounding" solution, moveover costing less and responding better to static pressure.
With general criteria established, authorization granted for costs – covering expropriation of shops on the ancient structure and of houses in the San Bartolomeo zone where the foot of the new bridge was to be laid – the decision was reached to go ahead with demolition of the precarious wooden structure and erection of a temporary cat-walk. Thus the operation was finally launched, lacking only a plan and a definitive final project.
Da Ponte the master-builder took charge of procedure, laying the pilework support for the single-span structure. A support described as "serrated, with three levels of 10 foot elm piles driven in to varying depths, firmly wedged together and each embedded in larch-pile casing and bridgework, transversally and longitudinally. Layers of newly-hewn stone were inserted between each section of pilework", this agglomerate providing the base on which the true foundations in stone would be laid, inclusive of the sloping stress zone of the arch. In the city unanimous support for this technique was lacking and further interruptions ensued, but by this time the problem was nearing solution. The Scamozzi project was reproposed but discarded on the grounds of excessive monumentality; Da Ponte was called in to enlarge on the technical criterion behind his serrated pilework and also to revise the entire preliminary project which, on the whole, met with approval, on the one hand for the impression of sturdiness it conveyed, on the other for its architectural simplicity of statement and fitness for purpose.
By the beginning of September 1590 it was possible to walk over the new bridge, the shops were to be built the following year, together with whatever else remained to be done and all at a total cost of 250.000 ducats.
The building was completed at last.

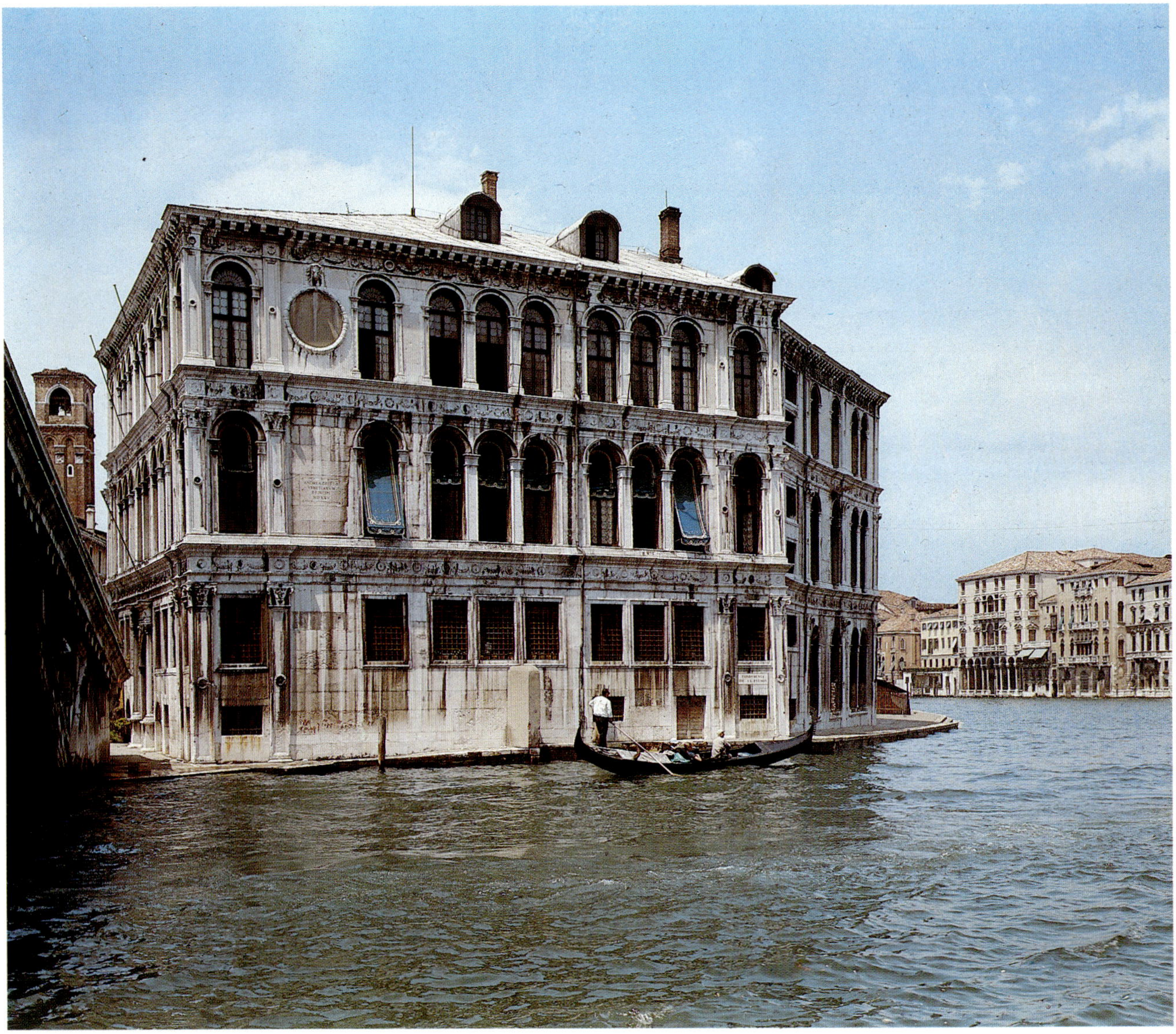

N° 87
Palazzo dei Camerlenghi
Seat of the Venetian magistrature holding jurisdiction over State expenditure, especially in commerce.
(L. 54, page 130)

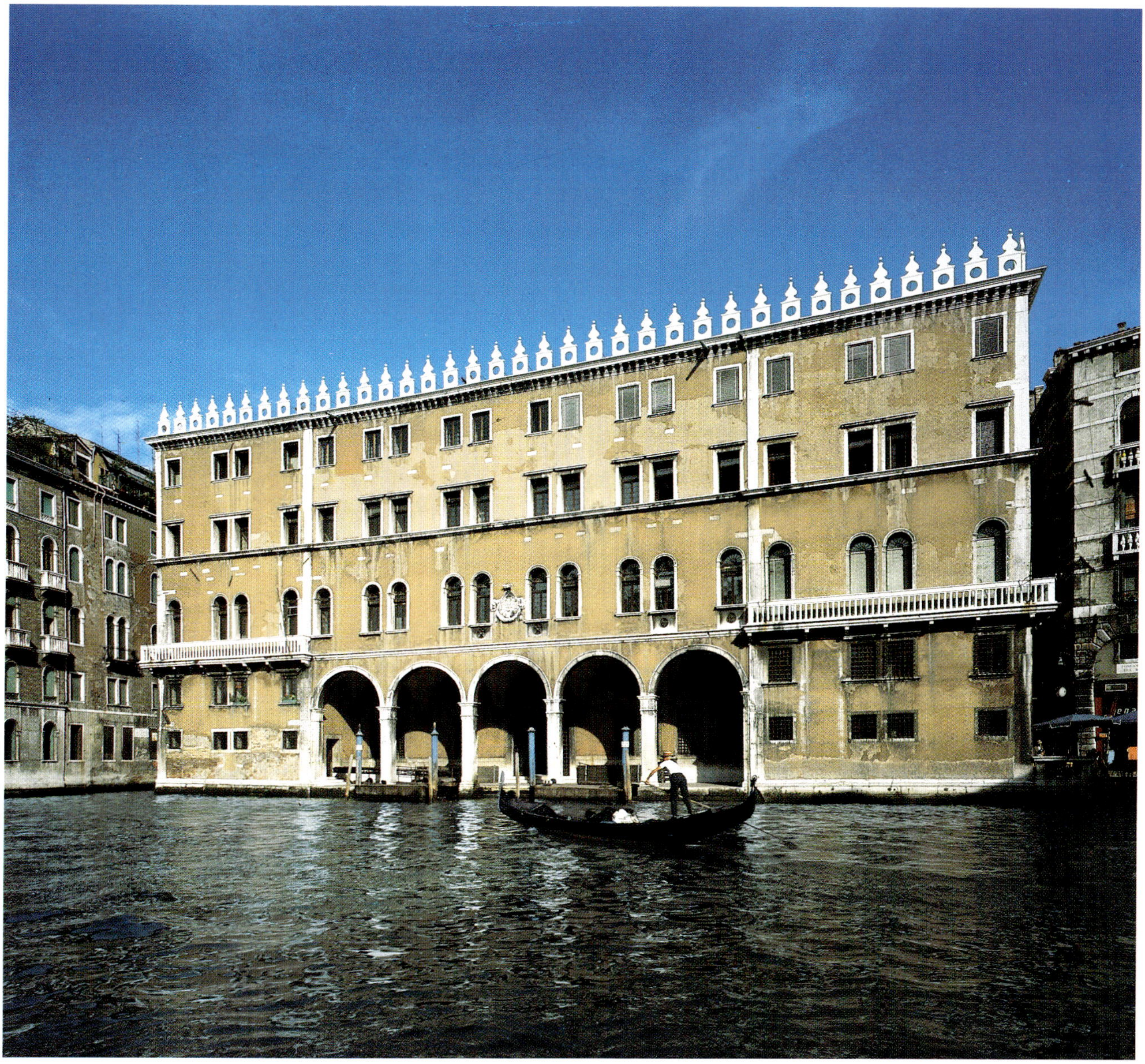

N° 88
Fontego dei Tedeschi
There was always a populous German community in Venice, where trade in a wide variety of products offered a substantial turnover.
(R. 54, page 137)

L. 55
FABBRICHE NUOVE DI RIALTO AND THE MARKET

Ever since the city was founded, the economic centre of Rialto developed parallel to the political-religious centre of St. Mark's Square. Vast areas of sand-banks and pools were gradually reclaimed, and buildings were erected suitable for housing the goods which changed hands at Rialto, the offices for the merchants and agents and for all relative administration. The fish market, the fruit and vegetable market, the goldsmiths and the merchants selling materials, spices, and basic essentials in general, each found its own place here.
Every kind of ship and boat, loaded with goods, moored alongside the Riva del Carbon or the Riva del Vin amid an endless excitement of bargaining and trade.
The houses which today go from Ruga degli Orefici to the Church of San Silvestro, were often owned by the various communities (Germans, Tuscans, Milanese, etc.), who sold goods from their own regions at the market.
The "Beccheria" (meat market) and the "Pescheria" (fish market) were among the first buildings to be erected on the high ground.
At the same time the Church of San Giovanni Elimosinario and the Church of San Giacomo di Rialto were rebuilt. The former was rebuilt several times and its last restructuring dates from the period between 1527 and 1539 and followed a design by Scarpagnino. The latter, in the square of the same name, still conserves today its 12th century interior.
So much for the Fabbriche Vecchie. The construction of the Fabbriche Nuove at Rialto, whose design is attributed to Sansovino, was carried out between 1552 and 1555.
In fact, the Republic had thought that the market was by then in need of more buildings which could also be used for public and private commercial business and as offices for the magistracies.
The Fabbriche Nuove, so named to distinguish them from Scarpagnino's Fabbriche Vecchie, were the result and, as we have already seen, the architect Jacopo Sansovino was perhaps commissioned for the design.
These buildings have a long, porticoed façade which runs entirely alongside the Grand Canal. Behind, it has a "C" plan which creates a vast open space for public use, a square adjacent to campo San Giacometto.
The cubic magnitude of the Fabbriche Nuove with respect to the Fabbriche Vecchie is far more prominent and cumbersome and has traces of the taste or rather of the concept of the new mid 16th century grandiosity.
The old names of the streets and squares are full of meaning and self-explanatory:
NARANZERIA
(orange/fruit market)
RUGA DEGLI OREFICI
(goldsmiths row)
PORTICATO DI BANCO GIRO
(credit bank arcade)
ERBARIA
(vegetable market)
CAMPO DELLA PESCARIA
(fish market)
PANETTERIA
(bread market)
CAMPO DELLE BECCARIE
(meat market)
RIVA DELL'OLIO
(oil embankment)
CASARIA
(dairy market)
RIVA DEL VIN
(wine embankment)
RIVA DEL CARBON
(coal embankment)

L. 56-57
PALAZZO BRANDOLIN AND CASA FAVRETTO

This building was originally owned by the Morosini family from San Cassiano which had had it built in Gothic style in the 15th century. Considerable alterations were made later, including the demolition of the second floor perhaps because of the building's stability. It later became the property of the Brandolin family whose name it kept.
A false Gothic building erected in the 20th century, separates Palazzo Brandolin from the palace formerly owned by the Bragadin family, better known as Casa Favretto because the famous painter Giacomo had lived there. He was born in Venice in 1849 (d. 1887) and in his paintings he reintroduced the colours of Venetian 18th century painting which he used to depict scenes of Venetian life, rich in shrewd observations of customs and in pictorial effects which brought him great public success. His portraits and his paintings of interiors showed greater simplicity and reality.
Casa Favretto is also in Gothic style but is older than Palazzo Brandolin. It probably dates from the 14th century and is the result of restructuring an even older Byzantine building of which only a moulding remains, dating from the end of the 11th or beginning of the 12th century.

R. 54
FONTEGO DEI TEDESCHI

The German community in Venice was always numerous and had its greatest importance in trading with Central Europe.
This economic importance led the Republic to set aside a grandiose building near Rialto market big enough to provide adequate accommodation and sufficient warehouses to hold the goods on arrival or awaiting dispatch.
In 1505 a fire had destroyed the old building which stood on that site. A far more important one was erected but still in keeping with the traditional layout of the Venetian "fondaco" which expected the inner courtyard to be protected, that is to say enclosed on all four sides by parts of the building.
The side with the main façade differed in that it was broader with a portico in the middle and at the sides it had higher, architecturally distinct wings which recalled the old defence towers of the much older public or private Byzantine "fondaco". In fact, the two side wings of the present-day building were higher than the central part but were brought to the same level during restoration in 1836. The wide portico with its high arches, gives onto the central section thus creating a functional covered area to load or unload goods from the boats.
The new Renaissance building was designed by the architect Giorgio Spavento who had already held the office of Proto of the Procurators of St. Mark and who had made an excellent name for himself in his field. He died in 1509 but he had already been helped previously in this work by the architect Antonio Abbondi, called Scarpagnino. The earliest information we have about this second artist dates precisely from 1505 on the occasion of this commission. Three years later in 1508 the building must have been finished, showing the Republic's great care over this reconstruction work. The Republic was most probably under pressure from the German community and it had every interest in seeing to it that the building's functioning had a favourable effect on business. 1508 is also the year when Giorgione was presumably commissioned to begin frescoing the façades. These decorations were later continued and completed by Titian.
Using a new concept of painting, Giorgione arranged a series of nudes and imaginative figures in the spaces between one window and another. The chromatic presence of these figures, both allegorical and symbolic, seemed to adorn the plain façade of the "fondaco", broken up by a symmetrical elevational relationship between openings and wall, which is emphasized by inconsequential string-courses. The present-day unbroken line of the crowning element, originally taller at the sides because of the towers, is embellished and emphasized by a series of patterned Istrian stone pinnacles. All that is left today of the paintings is the figure of a female nude seen from behind and a series of decorative fragments.

R. 55
PALAZZO CIVRAN

Standing neighbour to a partially remodelled 15th century Gothic house, Palazzo Civran was built in the early 18th century on classicizing lines. Bassi finds in its design, attributed to Massari, many of the idioms employed by this architect on Villa Negri at Istrana, terminated in 1715. In this case Massari's brief was to modernize an existing Byzantine building also referred to in Martinoni in connection with structural renewal. "It is probable that Massari concluded an interrupted intervention at some later date and the palace certainly uses the vocabulary of his early work" remarks Bassi.
The considerable height of ground floor and mezzanine is clad in blocks of Istrian stone with recessed joins; a balcony runs the full length of the first piano nobile where the characterizing feature, a tall, central window with an ornamental marble head on the keystone of its round arch, reaches up to the second storey string-course. The triangular pediments above the four single lights at the sides – two close-set to the central window, two at the extremities of the façade – are tied in to the capitals of the central arch by a fascia of smooth stone.
Identical triangular pediments crown the spaced-out single lights set in flat frames on the second storey.
Istrian stone at the corners lends definition to the building and at the same time supplies closure. Treatment of the side fronts, leaving the first part plain, borrows architectural elements and motifs from the façade, using the same window apertures to make a feature of vertical accents.

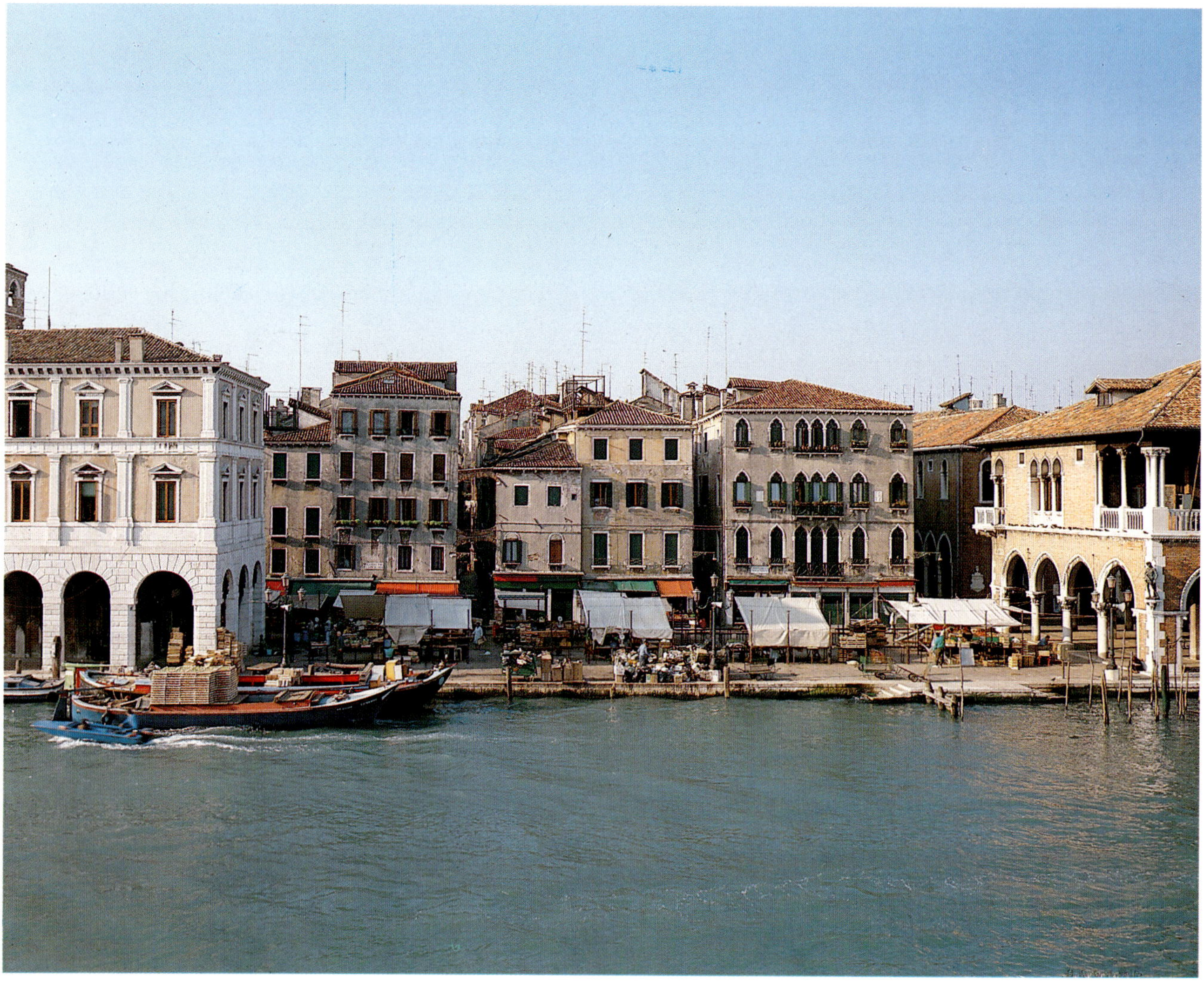

N° 89
The fruit and fish market at the Rialto
Today it is hard to imagine this site as the hub of activity and commerce it must once have been; especially in the early days of the Republic.

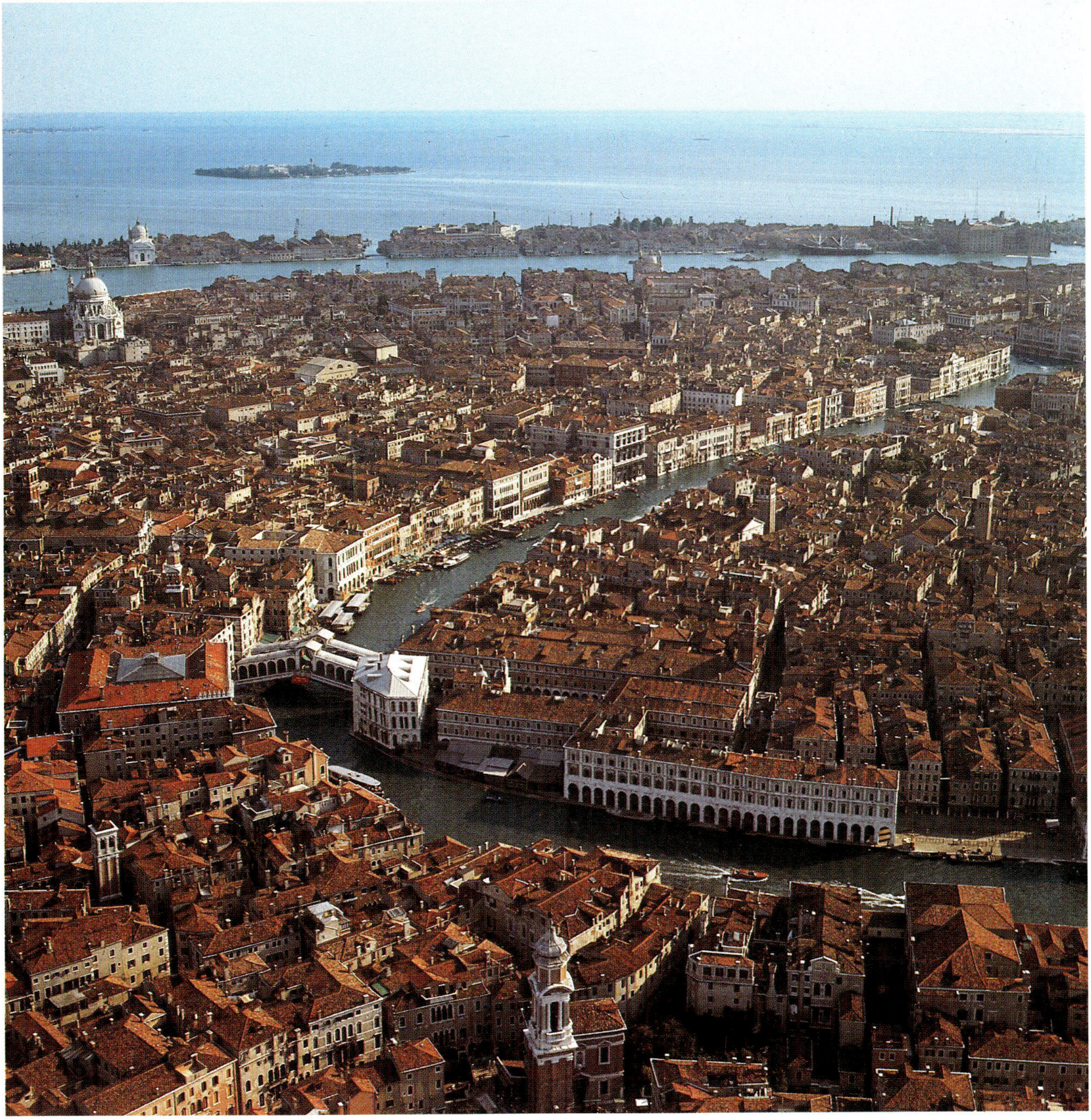

N° 90
The Grand Canal beyond the Rialto bridge
Attention is claimed by the "Fabbriche Nuove" designed by Sansovino to house state and privately-owned business offices, together with warehouses and shops on the ground floor.

L. 58
PALAZZO CORNER DELLA REGINA

This is another of the grandiose palaces which the Corner family owned along the banks of the Grand Canal.
Caterina Cornaro who in fact was born in 1454 in the parish of San Cassiano, descended from this branch of the Corner family. She married James II de Lusignan and became Queen of Cyprus, the large island in the east Mediterranean occupying one of the most important strategic positions. After the death of her husband, she handed over the island to the Republic following much insistence by the latter. When her husband died in 1473, Caterina had tried to govern the island with independent aspirations in the name of her young son who died the following year. However the difficulties were too great: internal opposition, the struggle by pretenders to the throne and pressure from Venice itself to cede the island.
When she returned to Venice, she was bestowed with great honour and gratitude. She received Asolo Castle as a gift and went to live there surrounding herself by a small but intellectually brilliant court, including some prominent persons such as Pietro Bembo who in his "Asolani" described life at the court of the former Queen.
As a result of the war which the Republic had to wage against the Italian and European states allied together against Venice in the League of Cambrai and during which Venice lost nearly all its own lands on the mainland, Caterina Cornaro was forced to leave Asolo and take refuge in Venice in the then Gothic palace at San Cassiano where she died a short time later in 1510.
This Gothic palace where Caterina was born and lived out the last moments of her life, no longer exists today because it was demolished to make room for another building designed by the architect Domenico Rossi who began work towards 1724. In fact, in the archives we read that "the old building was knocked down and the new one was built from foundations". Building work was begun and quickly brought to completion: we know that in 1726 the façade had already been built and that the interiors were being decorated during the following year.
Domenico Rossi was born in 1657 at Lake Lugano: his father Francesco had married one of Giuseppe Sardi's sisters. He was sent to Venice as a boy to learn architecture from his uncle Giuseppe who, unable to get the boy to study, placed him as a stone-mason in Alessandro Tremignon's workshop and later in Longhena's.
Perhaps because of this theoretical and practical training, Rossi does not always show structural and stylistic uniformity in his works. He gives far more attention to sculptural and architectural details than to layouts which are sometimes confused and not always well defined.
Temanza wrote of him: "an uneducated man but well versed in the practical side of building, who had little or no good taste in art". His life was not one of the quietest and he kept bad company and squandered money. He was everybody's friend, he gave frequent banquets and during Carnival many high-ranking ladies and gentlemen were his guests.
However, later on he learnt to behave better and "he made a lot of money by dealing in Carrara marble".
The façade of Palazzo Corner della Regina has a very high ground floor also including a mezzanine; it is covered by a layer of rustic work whose sense of monotony and dullness is neither relieved by the window and door openings nor by the mascarons on the keystones or on the architraves.
The main piano nobile shows the architectural re-use of 16th century models. The sense of wall surface is lost and the structure seems to consist of a series of single or twin columns and of the unbroken line of window openings; on the second floor the spaces between the semi-columns and the pilasters are filled by squared windows surmounted by triangular tympanums. The level of each floor is marked in the old-fashioned way by continuous balconies.
At the top, on the upper mezzanine, the double architrave is broken up by small square windows.

R. 56
PALAZZO LION MOROSINI

Preceded by a mid-19th century building featuring a projecting ground-floor block clad in slabs of smooth-finish Istrian stone, the secluded little Campiello del Remer, offering occasional glimpses of surviving elements of ancient Byzantine and Gothic buildings, is the site of Palazzo Lion, later Morosini (13th century). The open stairway on the rear front accentuates the archaic character of the building "destined for demolition in 1542 after an act of treason by Matteo Lion but saved because joint ownership allotted part to Lion, part to his wife by pledge of dowry and part to his brother Lodovico" (Tassini). The name of the square, "Remer", derives from production of oars (It. remi) in a local workshop of the time.
Elsewhere in his book "Curiosità Veneziane", Tassini relates that a Maffeo Lion, son of Lodovico, "Avogadore di Comun" and in 1540 "Savio di Terraferma" was put on trial and found "guilty of receiving commission from the French king to reveal the Republic's secrets". Condemned to exile from Venetian territories and with a price of a thousand scudi on his head, Lion's only recourse was to take refuge at the French court. Here, however, neither support nor financial aid appear to have been forthcoming and he was reduced to giving grammar lessons to survive.

R. 57
PALAZZO BOLLANI ERIZZO

The late 16th century Bollani palace, later owned by the Erizzo family, stands on the corner between Rio San Giovanni Grisostomo and the Grand Canal. Here too we see the product of structural alteration to an earlier building. The palace façade, with first and second piano nobile, features three-light sections of round-arch windows with continuous fascias of Istrian stone marking the string-course and the level of the capitals. The top storey is a much later addition. The palace would seem to have been the home for a certain period of Pietro Aretino. His lover, Angela Serena, an amateur poet who died, as Aretino's letters tell us, in 1540, herself lived not far away in the same parish.
Precisely when the Bollani family was elevated to the Venetian nobility is uncertain. Some historians date its patrician status to the earliest times, with presence on the Maggior Consiglio during the Serrata epoch. Others post-date the event to 1381, justified by merit shown during the Chioggian War against the Genoese.

R. 58
PALAZZO DOLFIN

Gothic in style, the architectural distribution of piano nobile windows on both first and second storey of "Casa Dolfin" reverts to use of the continuous fenestration motif, running across the entire façade: a simulated six-light section on the first storey in reality disguises subdivision of interior layout, on the second storey, a seven-light section. Plans and elevations in this period – end of the 14th to beginning of the 15th century – foster a more regular and organic statement with strong definition to well-built arches, the solid-void transition between window apertures attenuated by the rotundity of columns where, formerly, the pillar pointed up contrast with the flat surface, albeit supplying continuity by repetition.

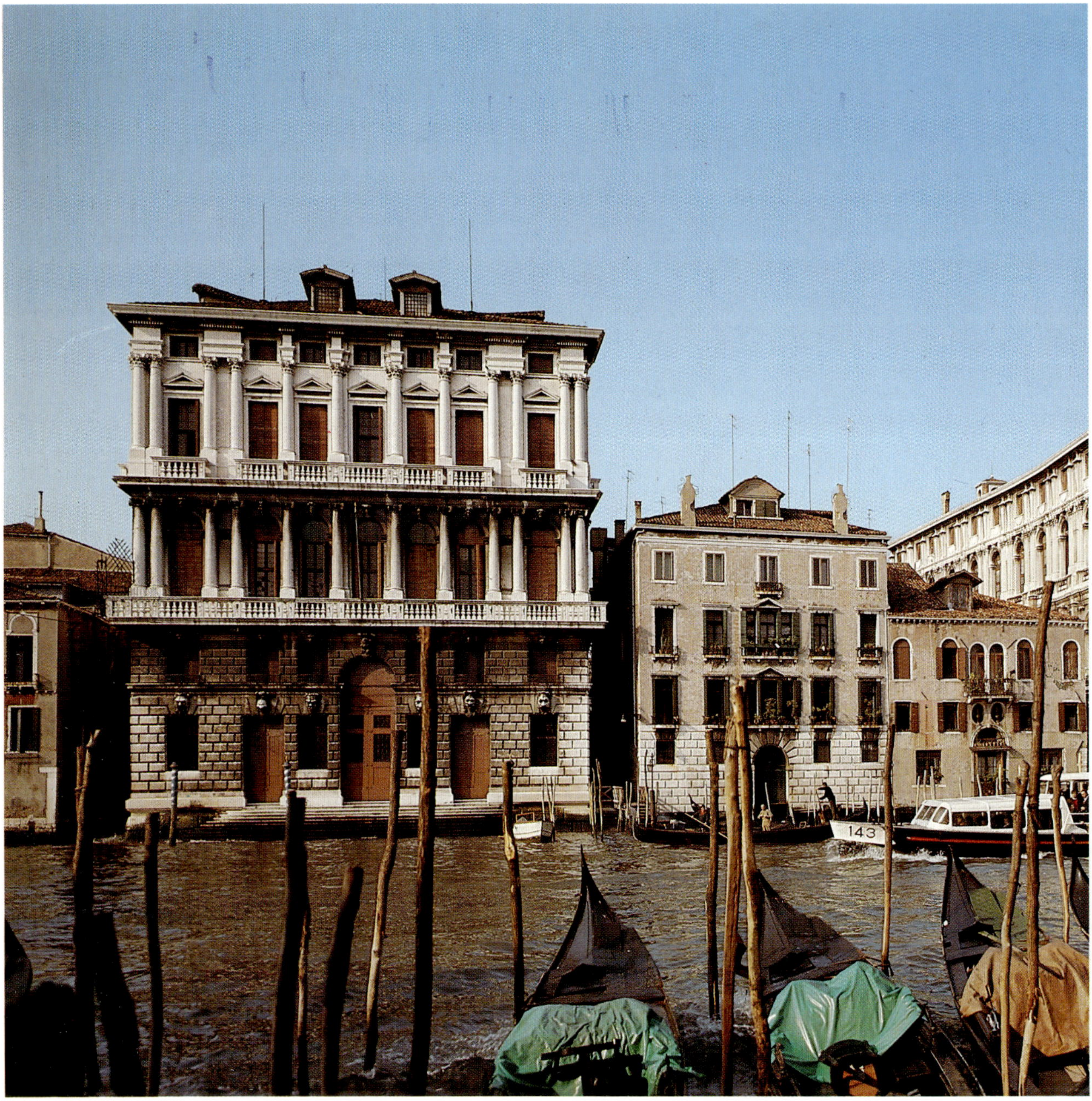

N° 91
Palazzo Corner della Regina
This is the branch of the very wealthy Corner family from which Caterina Queen of Cyprus descended. After the death of her husband she ceded the island to the Venetian Republic, under which it became one of the most important strategic bases in the Mediterranean.
(L. 58, page 140)

N° 92
Cà da Mosto
The ancient Byzantine building consists solely of the ground floor and first storey (the second storey is a 17th century intervention).
This was the birthplace of Alvise da Mosto, the famous seafarer.
In far more recent times the building became a hotel with the name of "Leon Bianco".
(R. 59, page 145)

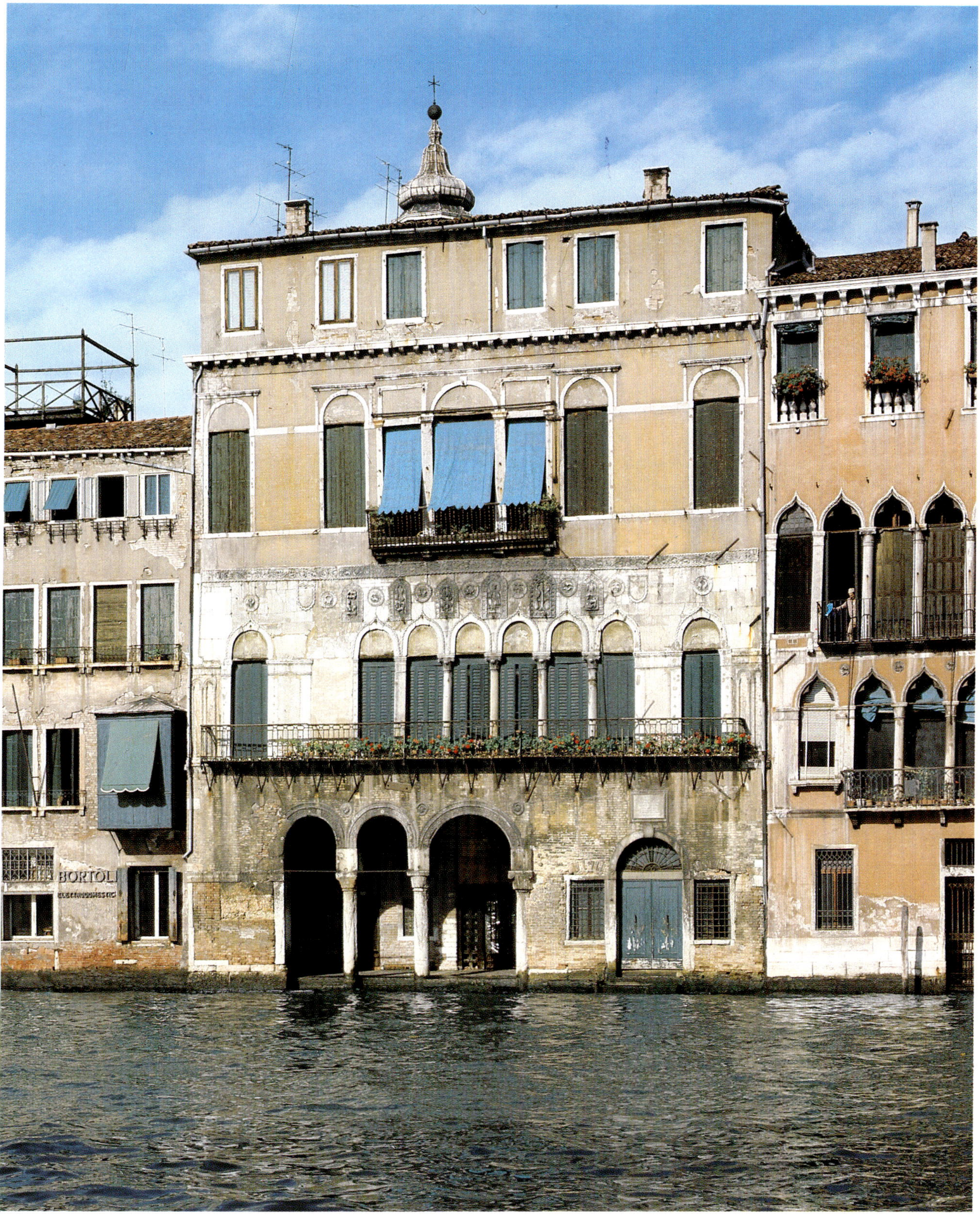
BORTOLI

L. 59-60
THE CORREGGIO AND DONÀ SANGIANTOFFETTI PALACES

The two buildings together provide Grand Canal frontage for the building block bounded by Calle della Regina and Rio Pesaro, lying within an area of urban fabric dominated by the monumental palaces Corner della Regina on one side, and Cà Pesaro on the other. Palazzo Correggio and Palazzo Donà, by comparison more modest in scale, are both products of 18th century rebuilding on more ancient Byzantine-Gothic structures.
The façades of both buildings, three storey the first, two-storey the second, are defined with extreme simplicity of line, string-course expressed by a fascia of Istrian stone. Windows of the Correggio house are uniformly rectangular, a small triangular pediment placed over the central aperture of the three-light section; instead, the Donà façade employs a round-arch motif, but comparison of scale and spacing between structural elements and architectural motifs reveals a discrepancy in overall design.

L. 61
PALAZZO PESARO

The work of Baldassare Longhena, Palazzo Pesaro stands on the site of three Gothic buildings whose existence is known to us from such visual documents as Botari's plan or from vestigial structures incorporated into the later building, one of the most monumental architectural statements on the Grand Canal.
The architect began work at the rear of the court, gradually moving forwards to the canal to conclude with the façade, terminated by him at the height of the first piano nobile. Work was in fact interrupted at the time of his death in 1682 and only resumed in 1710. Two prints by Coronelli and Carlevarijs offer interesting graphic documentation of this moment of stasis, clearly indicating the provisional nature of the steeply pitched "tympanum" roofing above the façade and also that, albeit incomplete, the building had been in use for some time.
Tassini deduces that the Pesaro family also owned the buildings formerly occupying this site "inasmuch as records state that in his childhood the doge Giovanni Pesaro, born in 1590, fell from his family's palace in the S. Stae parish".
While not ranking among Venetian patricians of early date – it moved from Pesaro to Venice only in 1225 – the family was among the most conspicuous and, above all, wealthiest. Over the centuries after its arrival in Venice, besides the aforementioned Giovanni, elected doge in 1658, its members held high office in public life as well as in the political, military and ecclesiastic spheres.
Relevant to real estate, a house at S. Stae owned by the family since 1558 was known as the "house of the two towers" due to these characterizing features at each end of the façade, which also date the building to Byzantine times. In 1569 the family acquired another house in the area between the Rio della Pergola and the rio taking its name from the tower feature of their first residence, the Rio delle Due Torri. In 1625 their third acquisition here completed the area that was to offer Longhena the site for his new project. Work commenced in 1652 and dragged on for over a century, suspension and resumption of activity providing a clue to the wavering finances of the Pesaro family at that time.
By 1658, when Giovanni Pesaro was elected doge, work was already under way. His will entrusts his grandson and heir, Leonardo, with the task of enlarging and completing the building; whether this legacy covered the means to do so is not known. In 1663 reports state that Palazzo Pesaro "is entirely rebuilt in the modern way on the land side, with arcading and a stately court framed by graceful loggias and passageways". The façade becomes a building event in 1676 and three years pass before news of completion of its Istrian-stone cladding up to the first piano nobile, a fact confirmed by the date "1679" inscribed in Roman and Arabic numerals on two cherubs on the corner windows. Three more years elapse before completion is reported of Nicolò Bambini's ceiling decorations for the corner hall overlooking the Grand Canal.
The year 1682 is marked by the near-contemporaneous deaths of Longhena and Leonardo Pesaro, halting work until the dawn of the new century when the architect Antonio Gaspari completed the building, following Longhena's original plans for the second piano nobile and introducing a new project of his own for the slightly curving frontage following the course of the side canal.
Gaspari completed the rear staircase, the new layout of frontage on the court and perhaps the rooms beyond it, all work presumably carried out during the early years of the 18th century; a cherub on the second storey bears the date 1709 and Coronelli's print, showing the palace terminated on the second storey, dates from 1710.
Today the building houses the Museum of Modern Art, a collection of works of art that may be

R. 59
CA' DA MOSTO

This building can be dated between the 11th and 13th century or rather some elements of the ground floor portico, such as the arches, seem to be attributable to the year 1000 while the multi-mullioned window on the piano nobile with its arches showing a more advanced stage of development can be dated between the end of the 12th and the beginning of the 13th century, and then the capitals belong to the next century again.
Despite the variety of architectural elements and leaving aside completely the 17th century additions which have totally distorted its original form, it conserves the appearance of the Veneto-Byzantine houses. A "fondaco-house" with an open ground floor portico to allow direct contact with the canal, and an inhabitable first floor very well lighted by an unbroken multi-mullioned window across the whole façade. An interesting collection of paterae can still be admired on the façade of this palace. They are on the piano nobile at whose ends there are marble facings sculpted to represent blind arches.
Together with Palazzo Loredan, this building shows the Venetian custom in Byzantine times to cover the façades of their house with marble facings. This use was completely abandoned during the centuries of Gothic architecture and then reintroduced during the Renaissance from the second half of the 15th century. In Byzantine times facings were attached to the brick, structurally load-bearing walls underneath in contrast to the classical use where the facings were themselves partially load-bearing.
In the centre there is the six-mullioned window and at the sides the two separate one-mullioned windows: in fact, in the internal room distribution, the reception room only corresponds to the four-mullioned window. The depth of the building today is far greater than it was originally since further additions at the back have been made.
The name of the building derives from the name of the family owning it. The members of the Da Mosto family were famous seafarers and were remembered for their seafaring exploits. From the 16th to the 18th century the Da Mosto palace was turned into the "Albergo del Leon Bianco" (White Lion Inn), one of the most elegant and famous inns in the city, where illustrous persons including the Counts of the North in 1782 and Emperor Joseph II took lodging.
In their honour the Republic put on exceptional festivities and entertainment along the Grand Canal where it ordered everything to be set up for the Historical Regatta with eight-oared gondolas and decorated boats. Likewise in St. Mark's Square and in the Piazzetta complicated and costly stands and platforms were built from which they could watch very lavish processions of floats and the traditional bull-chase.
The Da Mosto family came to Venice from Padua in very early times and was admitted to the ranks of the aristocracy in 1292. The most famous member was Alvise born in 1432, a skilled navigator who explored the Atlantic coasts in two memorable journeys. He wrote accounts of these journeys and they were printed in 1507 and entitled "New-Found countries and New World". The Canaries, the Cape Verde islands, the mouth of the Rio Grande were some of the lands he explored. After returning to Venice in 1463, he continued to deal in commerce.
In 1474 he was appointed to defend the port of Cattaro and in 1481 took command of the fleet on the trade route to Alexandria in Egypt. He died in 1488.

R. 60
PALAZZO MANGILLI VALMARANA

This palace is famous above all because it was the residence of the English Consul Joseph Smith whose name was inseparable from that of Canaletto and Venetian 18th century painting.
The artistic background and love of art of George III's diplomatic representative in the lagoon city, played an all-important role in building up the very rich art collections belonging to the English Crown and museums. In fact, it is in England that you can admire the best examples of Venetian 18th century painting and in particular of the great view painter of that time, Antonio Canal, called Canaletto.
The old Gothic-Byzantine building which stood on the corner where the rio di Santissimi Apostoli flows into the Grand Canal, belonged to a branch of the noble Venetian Soranzo family when it became the English Embassy and home of Smith. It was Smith who had it restored according to the style of that time. In fact, in 1743 he summoned the architect, painter and engraver Antonio Visentini who designed the new façade and supervised the work which lasted for several years until 1751. The façade only went as far as the first piano nobile: the other floors were added later when, in 1784, the palace passed into the hands of Count Giuseppe Mangilli. The latter also wanted to have the interior redecorated and he commissioned Antonio Selva who created one of the most lavish and uniform Neoclassical environments in the city, still perfectly preserved today.
During those years Smith's name soon became famous as patron of the arts and artists and as an art collector and dealer.
Not only was he interested in works by Visentini and Canaletto but also in works by numerous other artists such as Rosalba Carriera and the Riccis: he commissioned and bought for his own collections or on behalf of other English collectors these artists' most significant works.
In 1760 Smith resigned as Consul

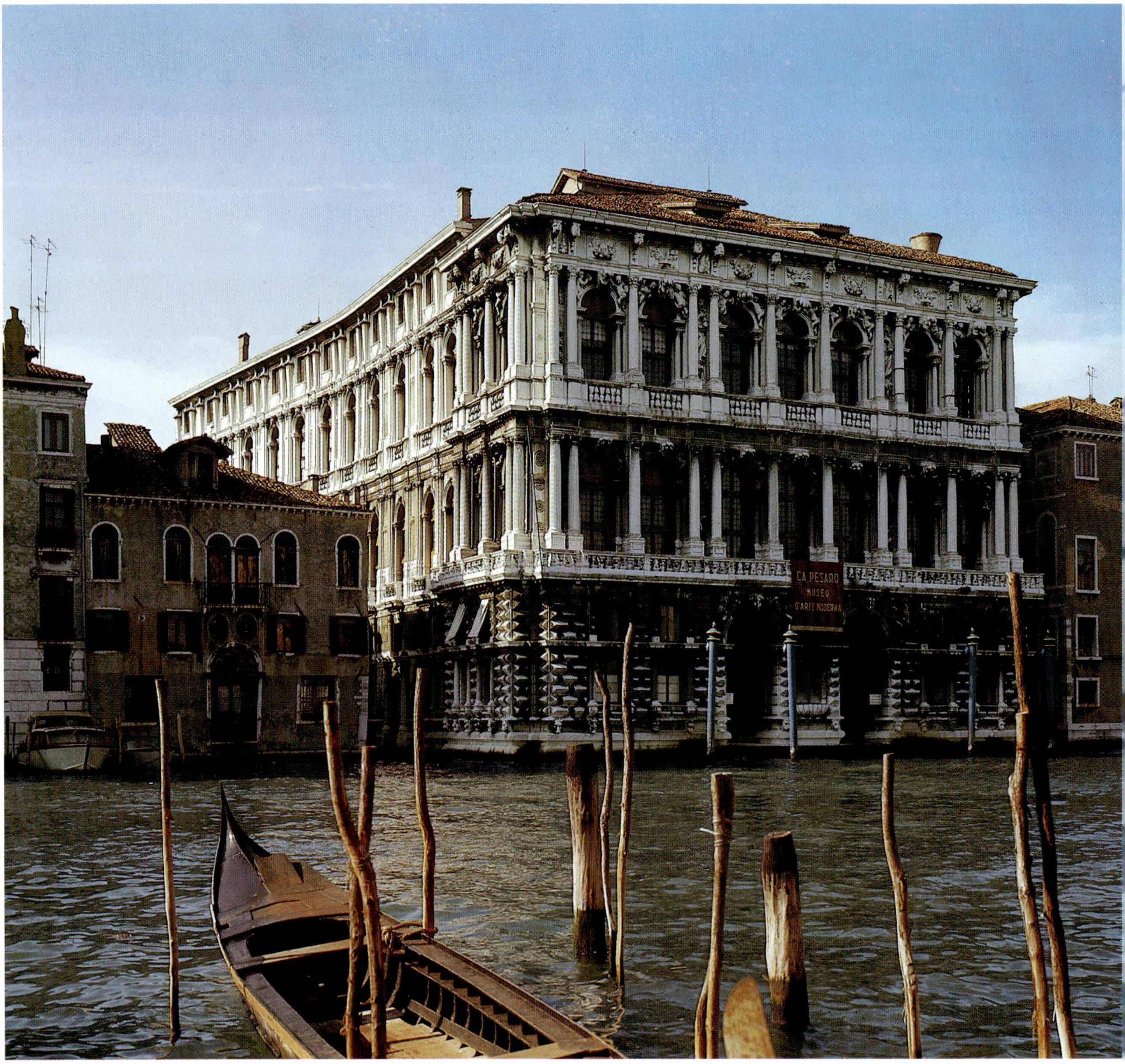

N° 93
Palazzo Pesaro
Sited on an area formerly occupied by three Gothic buildings and designed by Longhena who commenced work on this magnificent palace in 1652; after interruption work was resumed by Gaspari in 1682 and the first piano nobile was completed in c. 1710.
(L. 61, page 144)

N° 94
Palazzo Mangilli
Formerly the residence of Joseph Smith, the British consul in Venice, noted chiefly as an art-lover, especially of painting, and for his contribution to building up the art collections of the royal family and national museums in Britain.
(R. 60, page 145)

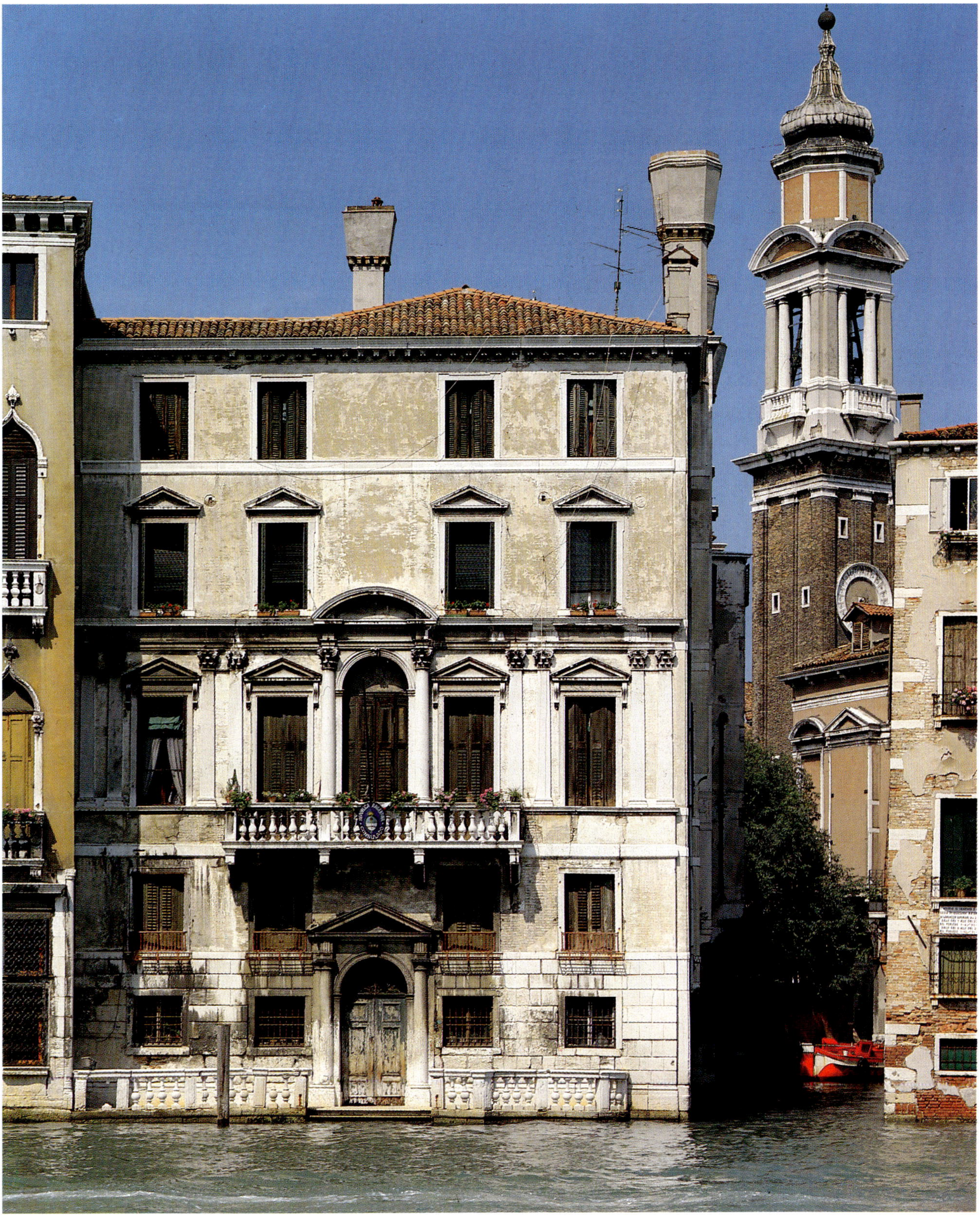

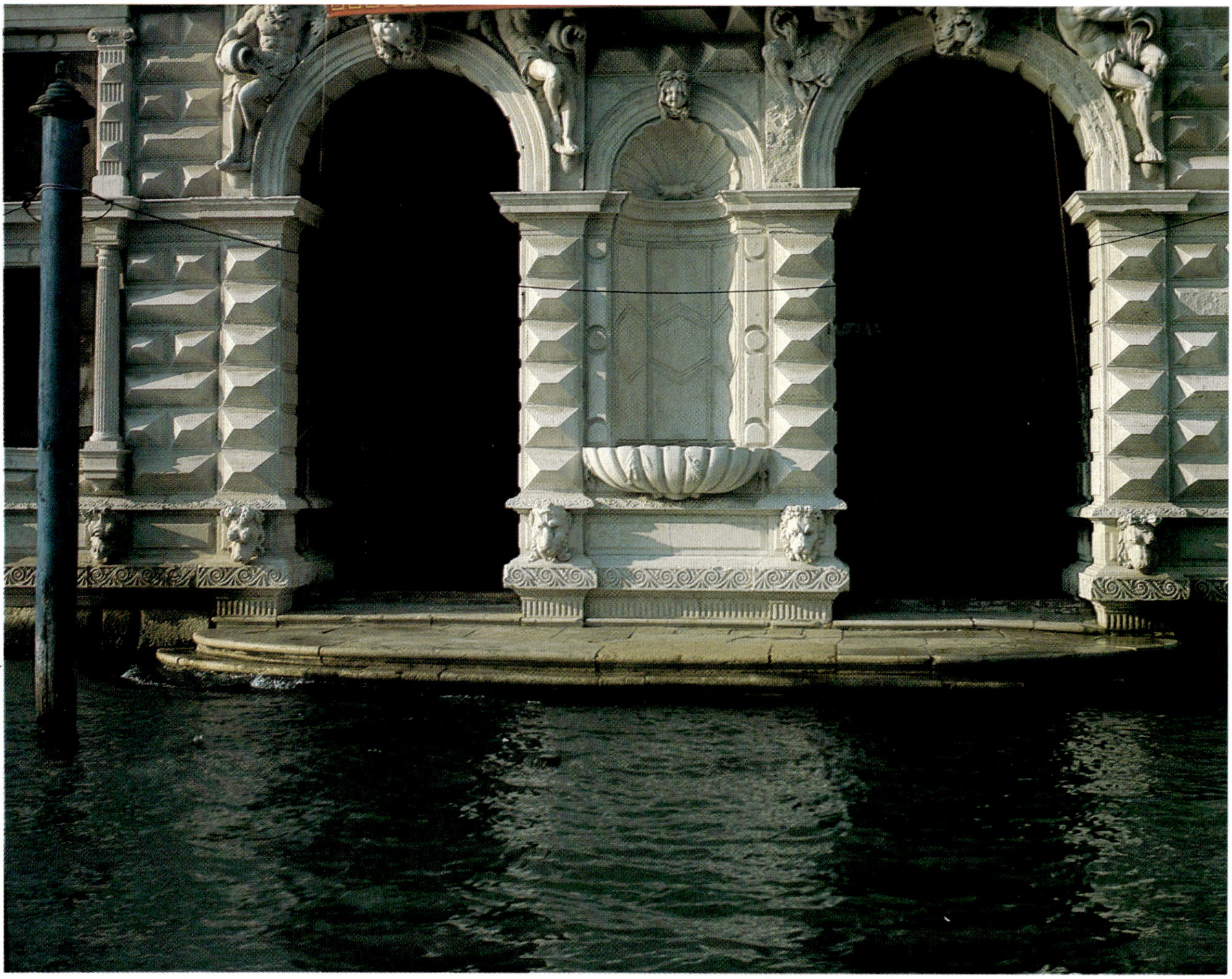

N° 95
Palazzo Pesaro
Detail of the entrance portal on the Grand Canal.
(L. 61, page 144)

N° 96
Museum of Modern Art at the Cà Pesaro
"*Head of a boy*" by Medardo Rosso
(L. 61, page 144)

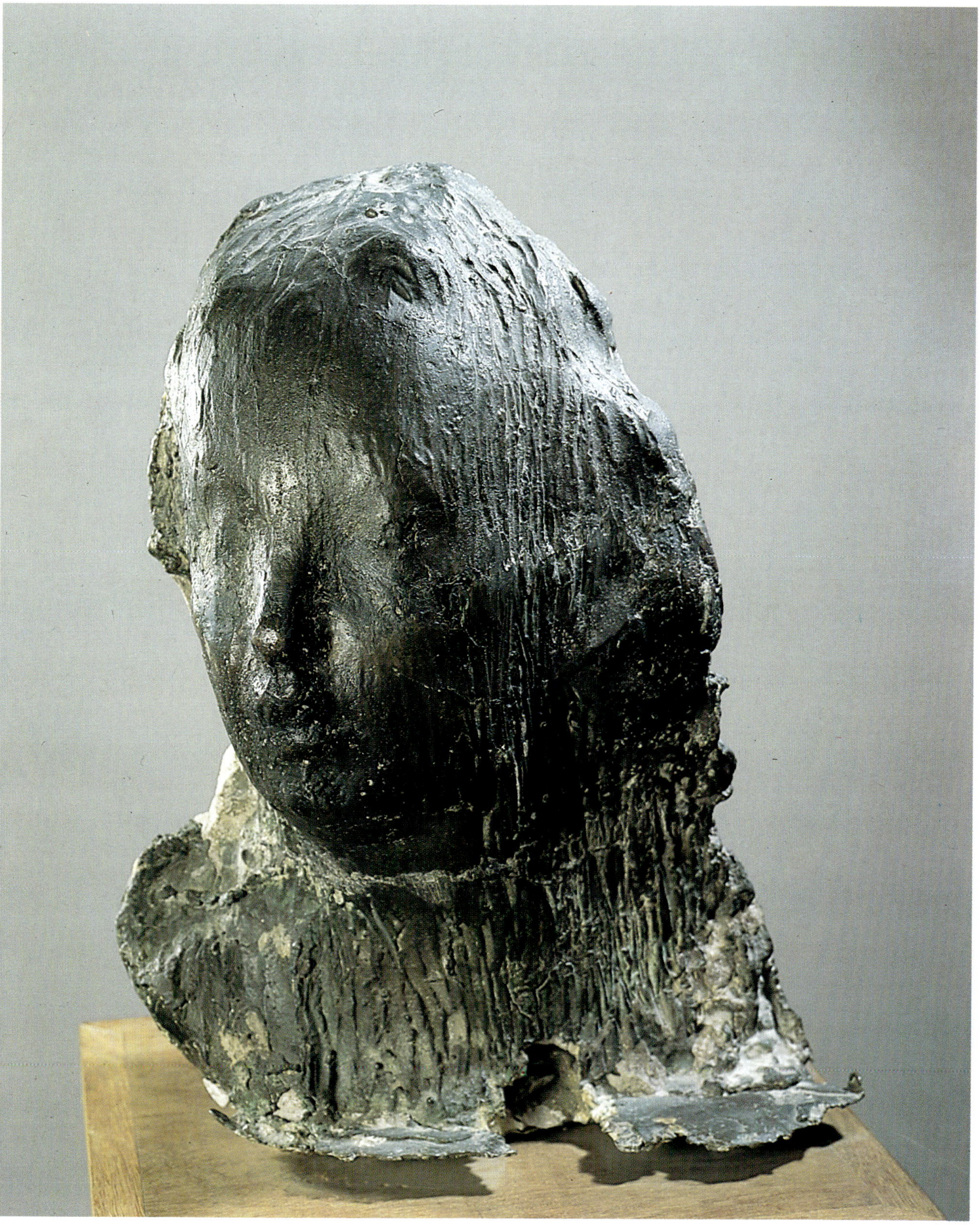

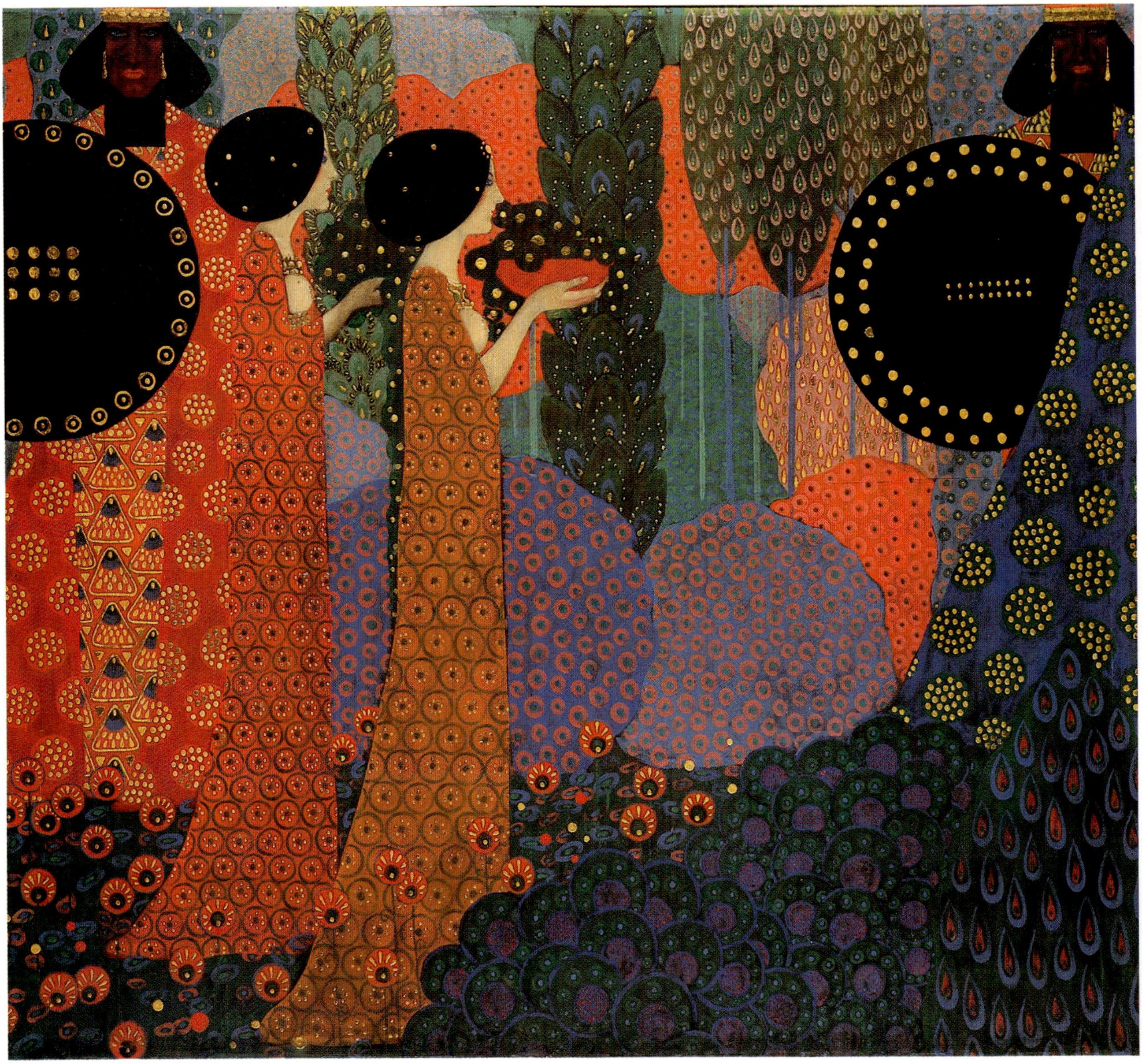

N° 97
Museum of Modern Art at the Cà Pesaro
"*The Thousand and One Nights*" by Vittorio Zecchin.
(L. 61, page 144)

N° 98
Museum of Modern Art at the Cà Pesaro
"*The Rabbi*" by Marc Chagall.
(L. 61, page 144)

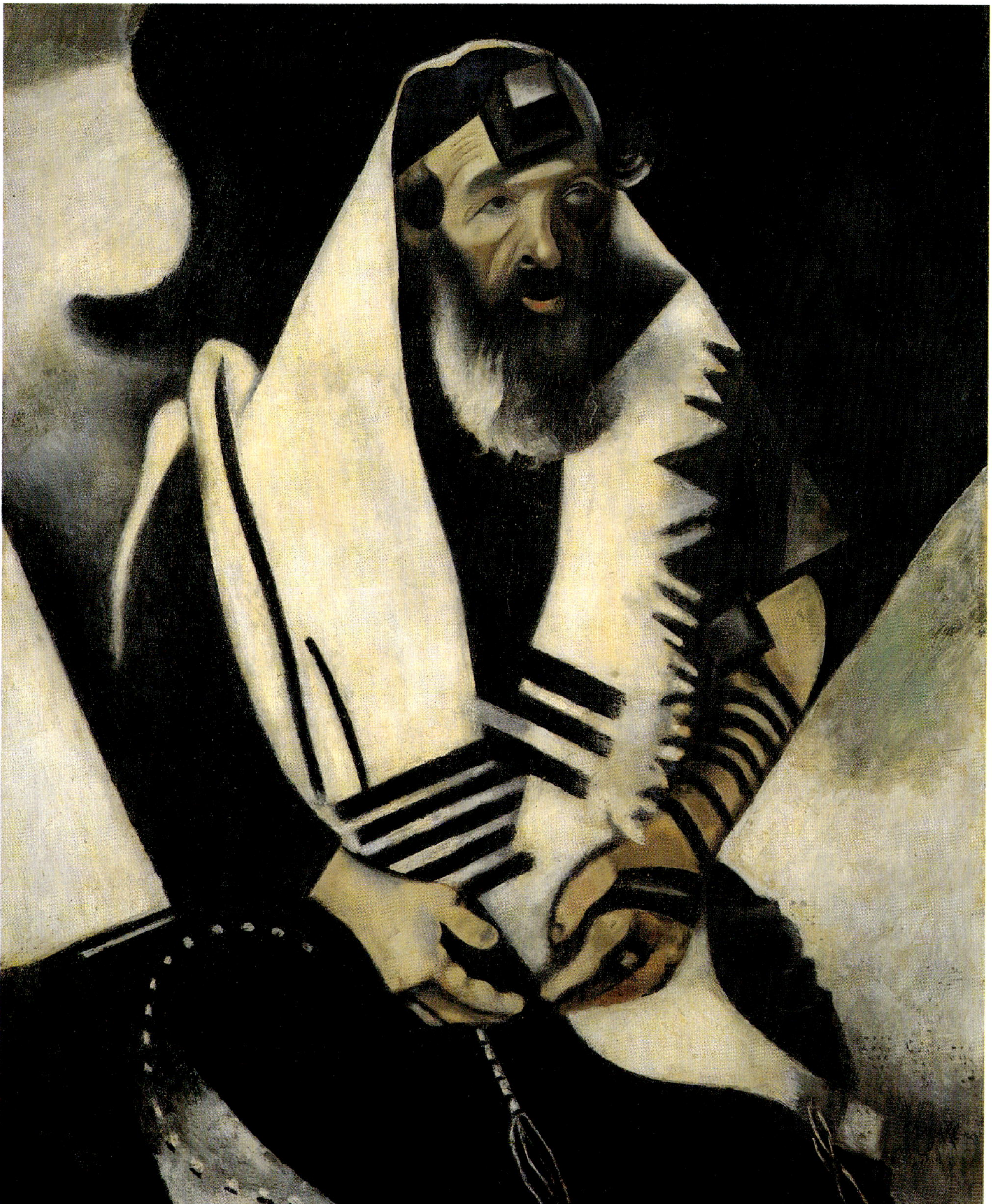

broadly classified as comprising 19th century Italian works and 20th century works by Italian and foreign artists. The former places the accent on artists native of or working in Venice, or else works handling themes of local interest.
The museum was founded in 1897; its definitive layout was achieved in 1902. A summary of the more important artists represented includes: Teodoro Matteini, Francesco Hayez, Ludovico Lipparini, Ippolito Caffi, Tranquillo Cremona and Federico Zandomeneghi; Guglielmo Ciardi, Giacomo Favretto, Luigi Nono and Alessandro Milesi; Pietro Fragiacomo and Ettore Tito; Giovanni Fattori, Telemaco Signorini, Giuseppe de Nittis, Antonio Mancini.
Besides an interesting collection of sculpture by Medardo Rosso, the 20th century offers works by: Umberto Boccioni, Gino Rossi, Arturo Martini, Felice Casorati, Pio Meneghini, Luigi Cadorini, Giorgio de Chirico, Carlo Carrà, Giorgio Morandi, Mario Sironi, Filippo de Pisis, Massimo Campigli, Felice Carena, Virgilio Guidi, Bruno Saetti, Antonio Music, Mario de Luigi, Marco Novati, Fioravante Seibezzi. Among the sculptors: Francesco Messina, Giacomo Manzù, Alberto Viani, Emilio Greco, Claudio Trevi. Among the best-known foreign artists: Rodin, Liebermann, Klinger, Marquet, Derain, Bonnard, Chagall, Matisse, Rouault, Klimt, Kandinsky, Klee, Grosz, Ernst.

L. 62 PALAZZO COCCINA FOSCARINI

Beyond the rio della Pergola, named after an aristocratic family from Santa Maria Mater Domini, and next to a rather anonymous building, rises Palazzo Coccina Foscarini. The building was in fact constructed on an older edifice by the Coccina family who later sold it to the Giuntas, famous printers and publishers who Sansovino recalls in his "Venezia città nobilissima".
Two daughters of a Giunta later married two Foscarini brothers who settled here until 1751 when they moved to Palazzo Foscarini at the Carmini, inherited from another branch of their family.
Thus the palace was rented to the Giovanelli family whose name is still often linked to this building. Construction was begun around the mid 16th century in reference to the external frescoes by the painter Zelotti who died in 1578. Other Venetian palaces built during the same period show very similar construction elements such as the Serlianas placed one above the other, the modillions running the length of the windows and the projecting cornices above them, thus enclosing them in a rectangular geometric figure.
On the rio della Rioda front appear a series of double mullioned windows corresponding to the internal staircase while the Grand Canal front is characterized by an asymmetrical façade owing to an addition on the left side. If it were not for this, the front would be perfectly square with the Serlianas one above the other along the central axis, set just slightly to the left due to the larger size of the corner room.
Only the frescoes on the internal façade of the courtyard seem to have been done by Zelotti according to a brief description by Antonio Maria Zanetti.

L. 63 THE CHURCH OF SAN STAE

S. Stae is the dialect version of Sant' Eustachio. The Savinia chronicle dates the church's foundation to the middle of the 10th century but the earliest documents which explicitly mention it by name carry the date 1127. However, it is permissible to suppose that by then the church had already existed for quite some time since it was already called a parish church. Whatever the date of its foundation may be, the building which stands on the bank of the Grand Canal had the architectural characteristics of Veneto-Byzantine art which were retained until the second half of the 17th century when the old building was demolished and completely rebuilt according to a design by Giovanni Grassi. The axial line of the church, which previously ran parallel to the Canal, was turned 180 degrees so that the façade overlooked the Canal. The one-naved interior reflects the general tastes at that time which were still under the influence of Palladio.
The church was still without its façade and the interior without altars when, in 1709, a substantial amount of money left by Doge Alvise Mocenigo on his death, enabled the missing works to be carried out. A public competition was announced and won by the architect Domenico Rossi and by 1710 the façade was already finished.
On the left hand side of the church, at the foot of the iron bridge rises a little building with a curious 18th century façade used by the goldsheet makers' scuola.

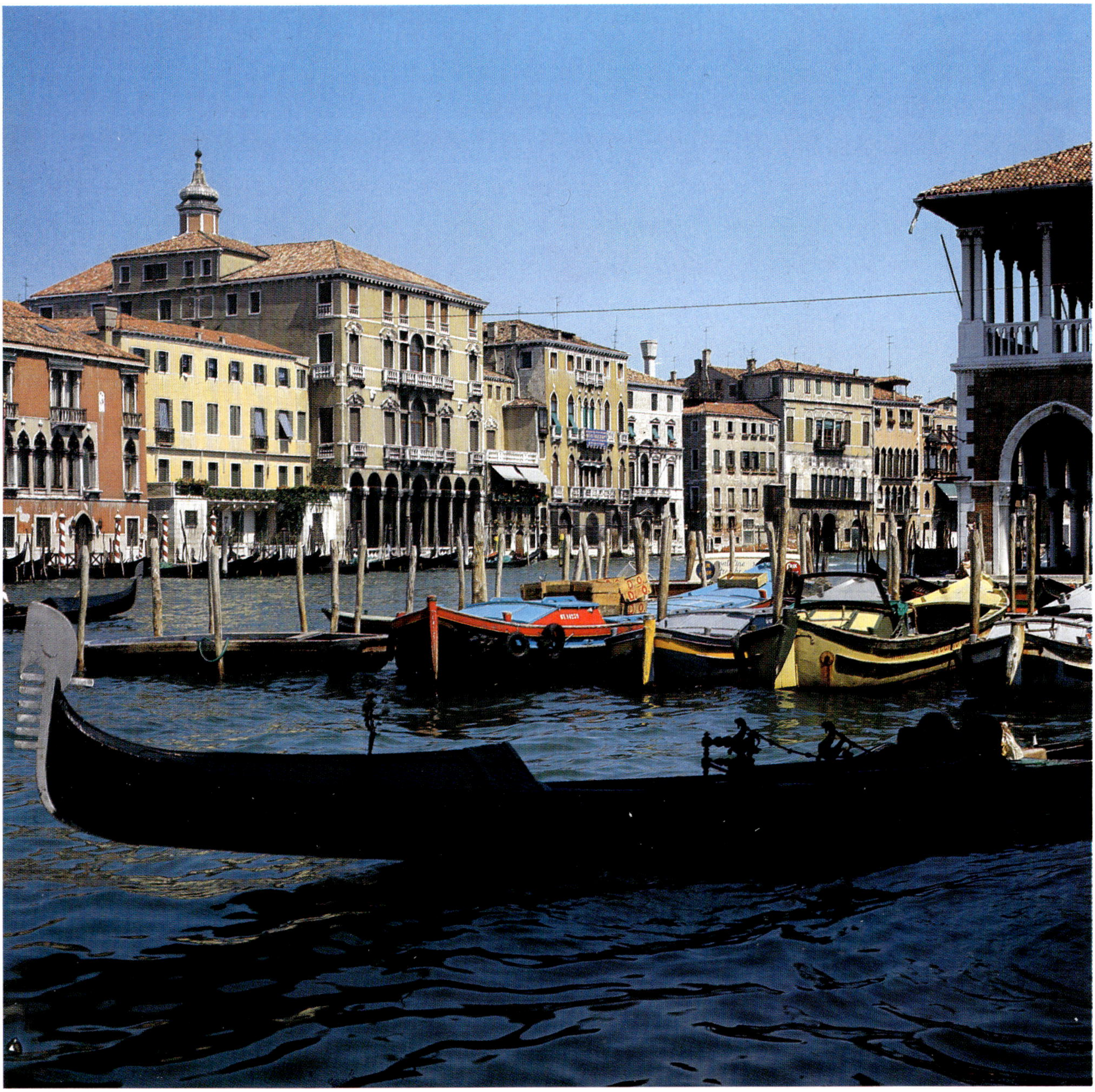

N° 99
The sequence of buildings on the right bank, facing the Rialto market. The pronounced volumes of the Michiel del Brusà and Michiel delle Colonne palaces may be remarked. (R. 61 and R. 62, page 155)

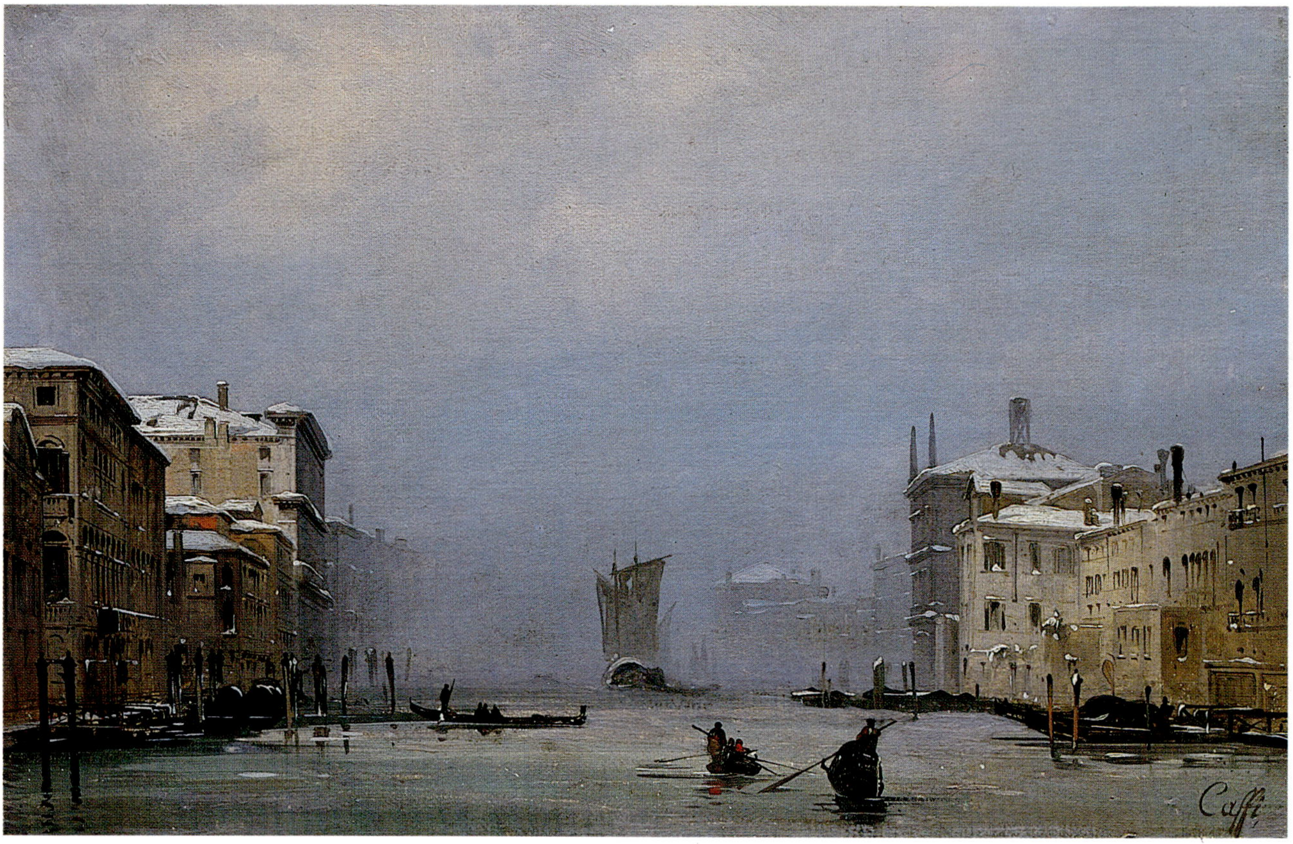

N° 100
Museum of Modern Art at the Cà Pesaro
"*The Grand Canal*" by Ippolito Caffi.
(L. 61, page 144)

and during that same year he began to sell parts of his collection for financial reasons. The largest part was sold to representatives of the English king, something like fifty paintings and 140 drawings by Canaletto and by other artists such as Zuccarelli. The extensive, specialistic library was also sold by Smith to the English monarch and it became the nucleus of the King's Library in the British Museum. His great love of books had led Smith to finance publishers and printers such as Pasquali in the reprinting of the "Four Books of Architecture" by Palladio. This was instrumental in the rediscovery of the great 16th century architect and in leading to a renewed influence on future architecture, especially in England.
Smith died in 1770 and was buried in the Protestant cemetery in Venice.

R. 61
PALAZZO MICHIEL DEL BRUSA'

Its nickname (of the fire) clearly derives from the terrible fire which destroyed the palace in 1774.
The building was rebuilt about three years later in 1777 with financial help from the Republic. A memorial tablet in the vestibule recalls the event: "Quos Ignis Consumpsit Patria Mementa Majorum Nepotibus Patrios Lares Restituit S.E. VI Idis Januarii 1777".
The pointed arched windows are very tall and the side ones larger compared with those of the central salon, all decorated with fleurons atop the arches. The general aspect of the façade is very rigid owing to its perfect symmetry.
It was a Gothic building belonging to the old Michiel family which had given Venice three doges way back in the 11th and 12th centuries: Vitale I in 1096, Domenico in 1118 and Vitale II in 1156. The family's importance then declined and was never recovered.
The first of the Michiel doges was slaughtered during a city revolt after holding office for only a few years; the second one, Domenico, is remembered because, during the siege of Tyre, he made the ships belonging to the Venetian fleet disarm and had the sails and rudders taken ashore to assure the crusader allies that he would not abandon them until the city was conquered, as in fact happened. The third, Vitale II, perished like his great-grandfather at the hands of plotters while leaving the church of S. Zaccaria to which he had made his annual visit.

R. 62
PALAZZO MICHIEL DELLE COLONNE

An architectural feature surviving from its Byzantine predecessor – the tall, arcaded porch stretching across the façade on the ground floor – gives Palazzo Michiel "delle colonne" its allusive name, distinguishing it from the previous palace dealt with, the property of the same family. Reconstruction was carried out in the last decade of the 17th century by Antonio Gaspari who, here as elsewhere, as drawings confirm, restored the Byzantine structure, supplying it with such new architectural detail as curvilinear pediments and large balconies of varied design, also modifying window and central Serliana-section surrounds.
Originally owned by the Grimani family but rebuilt by its successor, the Zeno family, the palace was acquired by the last Duke of Mantua, Ferdinando Carlo Gonzaga who, during his brief tenancy in 1707, brought with him valuable furnishings, paintings, sculpture and other works of art. In 1715 it became the property of the Michiel family who, a year later played host to the Elector of Saxony, Frederick II, later King of Poland, and subsequently to Charles Albert, Elector of Bavaria, for whom the Republic organized the customary receptions and such entertainments as the "Labours of Hercules", documented in prints by Lovisa with the Michiel palace in the background.

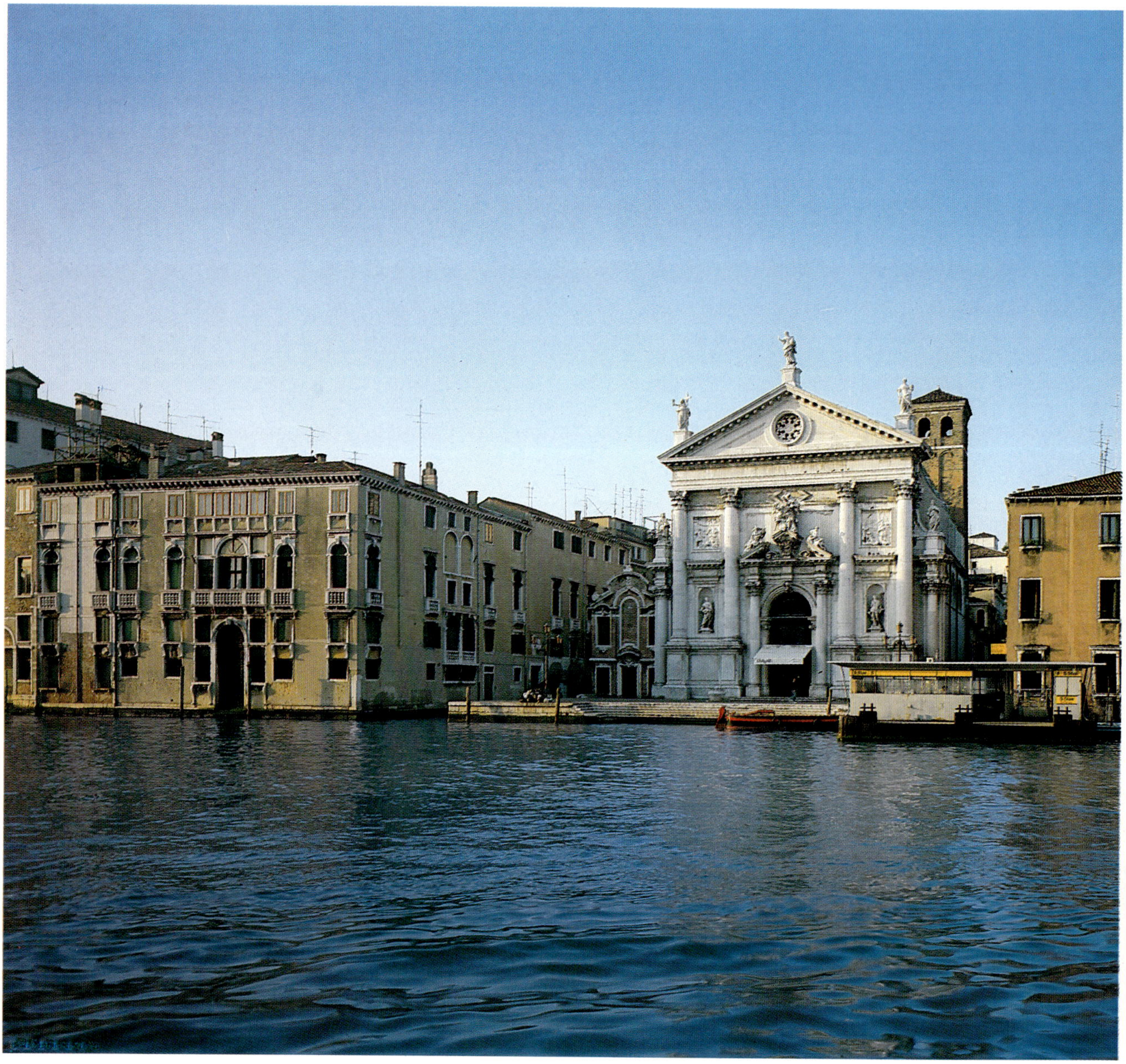

N° 101
The Church of San Stae and the adjacent gold-sheet makers' scuola. Palazzo Coccina Foscarini, attributed to the architect Giuseppe Sardi, stands to the left of the narrow canal flanking the campo.
(L. 63, page 152)

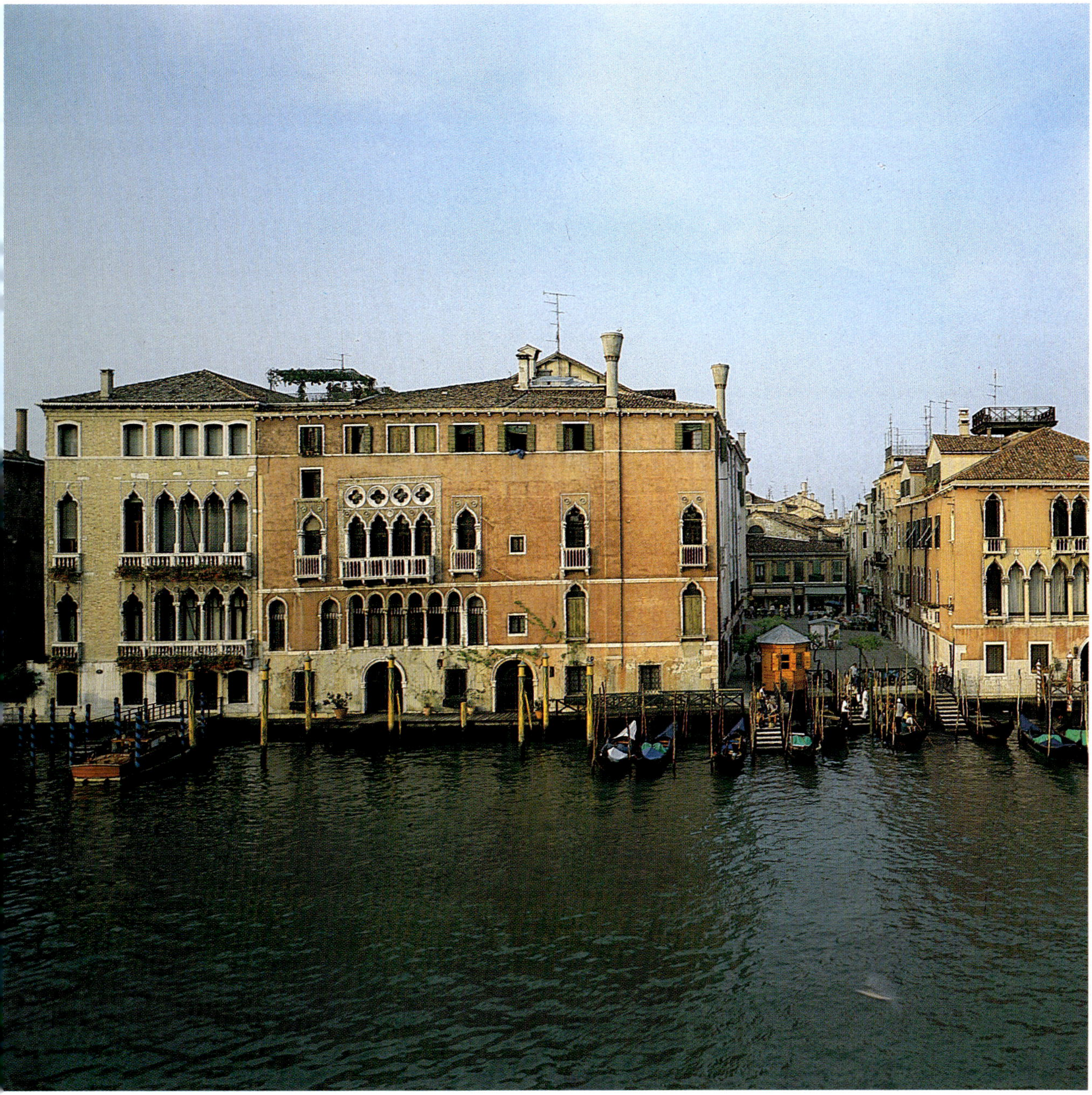

N° 102
Palazzo Sagredo
The façade of the building is an aggregate of Byzantine and Gothic elements resulting from a series of enlargement and remodelling interventions.
(R. 64, page 159)

L. 64
PALAZZO PRIULI BON

This building dates from the end of the 13th century or the beginning of the following one with additions and modifications carried out in later periods. From a stylistic point of view the building clearly shows the periods of transition and evolution of Venetian architecture from the Byzantine to the Gothic style.
The traces of the early structures with elements of the Veneto-Byzantine period are on the ground floor: the typical portico structures, now walled up, with round arches raised on high columns. The arches of the central multi-mullioned window on the first piano nobile are clearly early Gothic since they are pointed, deriving directly from the Byzantine arch and later evolving into the ogee arch. The building is very interesting precisely because of its architectural and stylistic appearance which spans Byzantine and high Gothic building techniques.
To the right of the palace today, you can see a garden where an old palace once stood. It was altered many times over the centuries until the 19th century when it was destroyed by a fire and totally demolished.
In Coronelli's engraving "Singolarità di Venezia", the building is engraved under the name of Palazzo Giustinian at San Eustachio on the Grand Canal. It is also known as Palazzo Contarini who were its owners after the Giustinian family.
According to historical accounts, this palace was the home of Count Francesco Carmagnola, a captain in command of the Republic's land forces. He was suspected of having betrayed the Venetians to the Duke of Milan against whom Venice was waging war. He was tricked into coming into the city with the excuse of agreeing on the next military campaign against Milan, imprisoned, tried and quickly sentenced to death. He was beheaded in the Piazzetta between the two columns of Mark and Theodore on May 5 1432. It was a public "ceremony" to warn all future captains enlisted by the Republic to command the armies in the mainland war.
It is a shame that the building no longer exists today because it was rich in history: it originally belonged to the Lion family and then later to the Veniers; it was bought by the Republic and given to Prince Pandolfo Malatesta who inherited the title of Lord of Rimini from his brother in 1432. He was a splendid lord, a protector of the arts, but he was also a man of uncontrollable passions and avid for triumphs and money. He aroused enmity and implacable hatred until he was excommunicated and sentenced to be burnt at the stake in 1461 by Pope Pius II. He fled to Venice where he was given protection and hospitality in the palace on the Grand Canal.

L. 65
PALAZZO DUODO

Dating from the end of the 14th century the Gothic Palazzo Duodo stands immediately after the garden of the no-longer extant Contarini palace.
Stylistically, this period is marked by a blend of more archaic idioms and motifs heralding an innovative trend in Gothic taste that was to come to full maturity in the 15th century.
Palazzo Duodo, otherwise known as Balbi Valier, has a single piano nobile with a four-light central section of reverse-curve arches and projecting balcony, identical architectural features carrying over to the lateral single lights, the whole underlined by a finely-drawn stringcourse in Istrian stone. Ground floor and mezzanine are the product of remodelling in later epochs. The modest scale of the building should not be allowed to detract from its importance as a significant exemplar of transition and evolution of Venetian Gothic between the 14th and 15th century. The main branch of the Duodo family – its senior branch – owned houses in the S. Maria del Giglio parish, certainly from 1265 when, as a resident there, Leonardo Duodo sat on the Maggior Consiglio. The original building was rebuilt by the architect Scamozzi after 1588.

R. 63
PALAZZO FOSCARI

Employing Gothic idioms of the second half of the 16th century this small but well-proportioned building displays a command of asymmetry in handling distribution of window apertures around the square surround of the central six-light section on the piano nobile. It stands on the corner of Campo Santa Sofia, the squat little bell-tower of the homonymous church visible at the far end.

Owned by a junior branch of the Foscari family, bearing its crest in marble on the façade, in 1520, according to Tassini's "Curiosità", the palace became the residence of the Mantuan ambassador.

R. 64
PALAZZO SAGREDO

A 13th century Byzantine palace in origin, bearing clear signs of the structural alterations of later periods, Palazzo Sagredo stands on the opposite side of the same campo. The first floor still preserves a series of windows framed by cusped Byzantine arches springing from slender columns. While the bases are plain, the corner capitals exhibit lush foliation with prominent caulicoles. In this six-light sequence flanked by single lights, window distribution follows the familiar tripartite scheme of Venetian palaces.

Extensive enlargement of the palace increased its volumetric presence both vertically and horizontally by the addition of a tall piano nobile and a new wing on the campo. This intervention, probably dating from between the end of the 14th and the beginning of the 15th century is characterized on the new Gothic storey by an ornately carved fascia defining the surround of the central four-light section with disengaged quatrefoils – a solution unique of its kind – and generous single lights at the sides.

Prior to purchase by the Sagredo family, Morosini ownership of the palace had lasted up to the start of the 18th century.

Roberto Strozzi was a palace guest in 1582 and over two centuries later the former Grand Duke of Tuscany, become Emperor Leopold II, observed the 1791 Historical Regatta from its windows.

R. 65
PALAZZO PESARO

Owned by a branch of the Pesaro family, the mid-15th century Gothic palace, whose façade adjoins that of the Sagredo palace, formerly belonged to the Giustinian family. Flanked on the left by a calle once known as "Ca' Zustinian", the spatial interval between the palace and the Ca' d'Oro is enhanced by a small enclosed garden, once perhaps public domain.

The façade is characterized by asymmetrical design, with the fourlight sections holding the right, offset by an unbroken stretch of wall before closure on the extreme left by a vertical strip of single lights. The top storey is a 19th century addition.

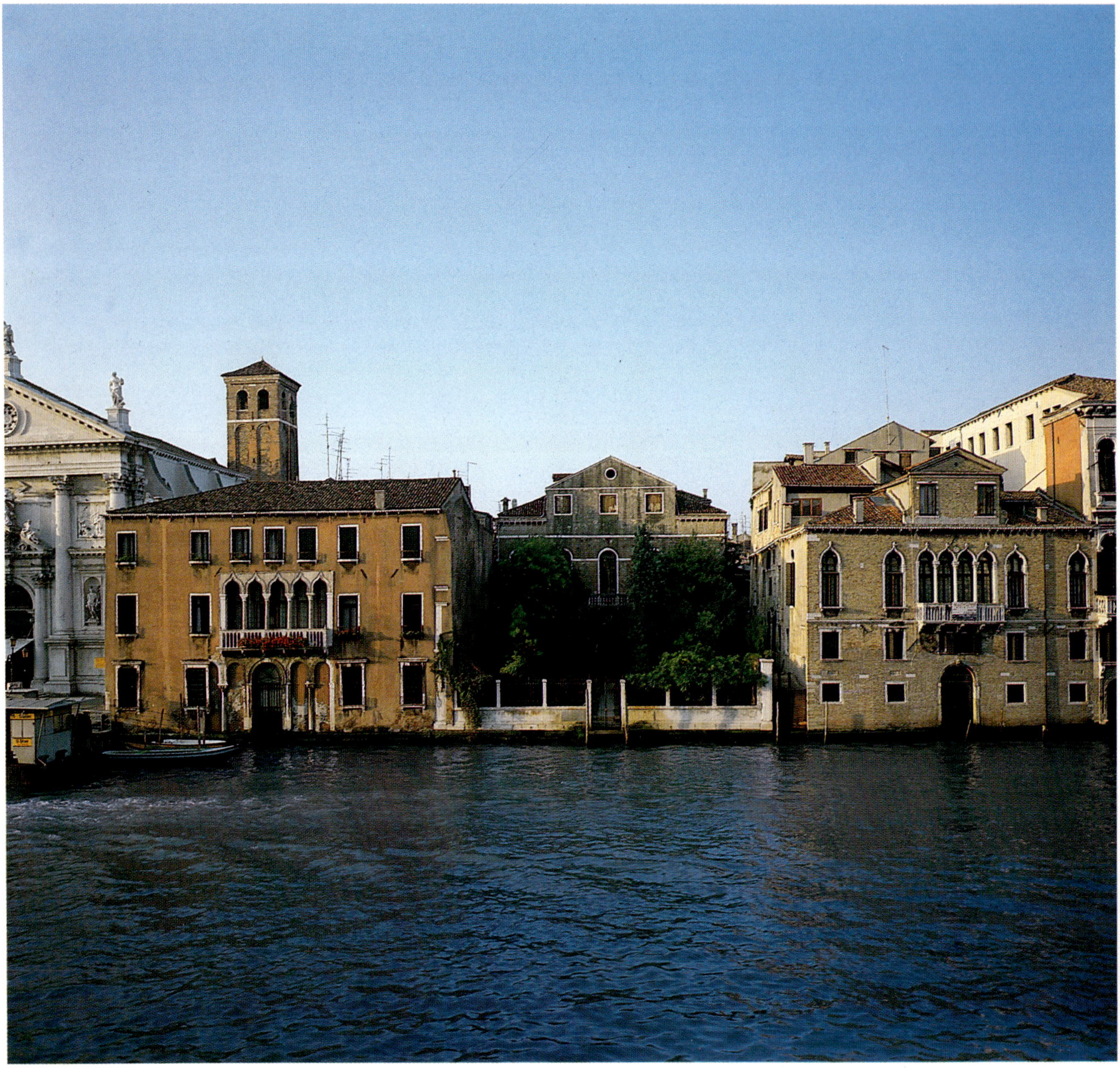

N° 103
The Priuli Bon and Duodo palaces
The garden separating the two palaces was formerly the site of what may have been the residence of Francesco Carmagnola, famed Captain General of the Serenissima land forces, condemned to death and decapitated for high treason.
(L. 64 and L. 65, page 158)

N° 104
Cà d'Oro
Commissioned by Marino Contarini and one of the most important testimonies to Venetian Flamboyant Gothic architecture, the palace was built between 1421 and 1440 by the architects G. and B. Bon in collaboration with Matteo Raverti. Its name alludes to the wealth of architectural detail, use of polychrome marbles and – no longer visible today – extensive recourse to gilding.
(R. 66, page 163)

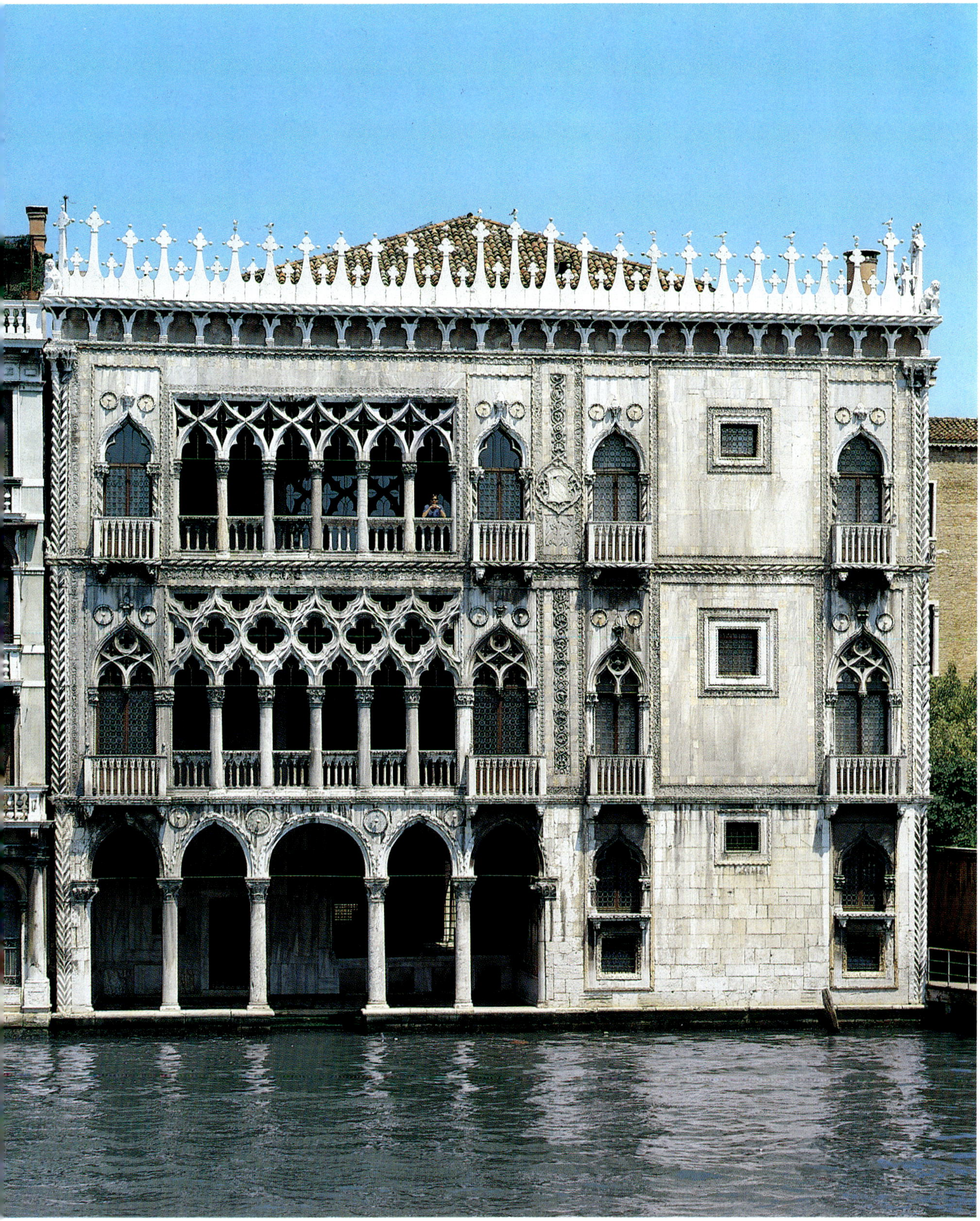

L. 66
PALAZZO TRON

The Tron family had this building erected towards the end of the 16th century on the site of a pre-existing, by then decrepit Gothic building. The style is high Classical and the usual Venetian tripartite layout with the large central room is retained.
The Trons were a rich, powerful, Venetian aristocratic family with very old origins. In fact, they are mentioned with regard to the foundation of the Church of San Stae in 966 together with other aristocratic families living in the area. Therefore it is probable that this palace was in fact also built in far earlier times, a link with the family's permanence in the area since early years. Later on, during the following centuries, the same building was restructured or rebuilt several times: it went from the Byzantine "fondaco" to the Gothic palace and then finally became the finished 16th century building which has remained unaltered until the present day. In the 18th century the rooms were magnificently decorated and painted by Jacopo Guarana. In 1775 a splendid ball was given in the ballroom by the Republic and by Andrea Tron and it remained famous for its lavishness and the magnificent entertainments in honour of Emperor Joseph II of Austria.
The same Andrea Tron, a distinguished man in cultural and state affairs and senator of the Republic, was held in high esteem by the heir apparent to the Russian throne who wanted Tron always by his side during the visit he and his wife made to Venice in 1782. This also provided the opportunity for the Republic to give splendid parties and entertainments which remained for a long time in the memory of the admiring Venetians who watched or took part. The open-air, nocturnal festivities, the bull-chases and the regattas on the Grand Canal in honour of their Russian majesties, called the Dukes of the North, are recorded in many paintings and prints.

L. 67
PALAZZO BELLONI BATTAGIA

This building is one of the most beautiful and interesting Venetian civil constructions of the 17th century. Towards the middle of the century the architect Baldassare Longhena designed it for the Belloni family who wanted a new modern residence on the Grand Canal in the San Cassiano parish.
The building was designed and erected by Longhena between 1645 and 1649. In this case too, it was a restructuring and modernization of a pre-existing, certainly Gothic building. No definite record exists proving that the building can be attributed to this artist: the only proof is the work itself and the architectural and stylistic elements which Longhena often used in the works which he definitely designed during that period.
As regards the Belloni family, we know that it became part of the Venetian aristocracy in 1647 and that is was probably Bortolo Belloni who, on that occasion, wanted the palace rebuilt. In the documents on "L'origine delle famiglie aggregate", we read that "Belloni was the son of a criminal lawyer on the Veneto Law List... who earned a fortune which he left to this son Bortolo and which the latter spent on magnificent buildings and precious furnishings". and these riches did not last long; they were squandered so quickly that, a few years after the palace was built, it was rented to Count Umberto Czernin, the Austrian ambassador, while the Belloni family ended up in another, certainly more modest building.
The architectural elements of Palazzo Belloni can easily be seen as similar to those of Longhena's early restructuring of Palazzo Giustinian Lolin, near the Accademia bridge, which we have already looked at. In particular we must note the lengthened module of the doors and windows which derive directly from the 14th century Gothic structure. The string-course contours are in high relief and even more so the architectural elements made up of the tympanums with the unbroken line of the buttresses and the double architrave.
The centrally interrupted tympanums of the windows, the two large marble coats-of-arms which decorate the side wall spaces on the first piano nobile, the wall panels, the care taken over details and finally the sculptured heads at water level are all elements which were often used by the master in his buildings. Taking all this into consideration, Palazzo Belloni Battagia can be said to be a work by Longhena dating from around 1650.
As regards the second name Battagia, Tassini comments that this family, which came from Milan, "became a part of Venetian aristocracy in 1500 because Pietro Antonio Battagia, the keeper of Cremona castle, ceded that fortress to the Republic. Further-more, he received the gift of a house on the Grand Canal, a villa near Verona and twenty-six thousand ducats in cash".
In 1667 another member of the family, Girolamo, was elected Governor General on the island of Candia: "he behaved courageously and was wounded by bombs but, after the surrender and returning to Venice, he was accused of bad conduct and put in prison. However, his innocence soon came to light and he was acquitted and promoted to new honours".

R. 66
THE CA' D'ORO

The name of this building derives from its wealth of architectural detail and the ornament decorating the façade.
On purchase from the Zeno family of the ancient building formerly occupying the site, Marino Contarini decided to demolish it to build a magnificent new residence. Work on this building between 1421 and c. 1440 produced one of the finest exemplars of Venetian Gothic architecture. The commission was placed in the hands of Giovanni and Bartolomeo Bon who, together with Matteo Raverti, supervised structural work on the multi-light sections of the first and second piano nobile and the marble tracery of the single lights. Vestiges of the former Byzantine building may have been reemployed on the deep loggia on the ground floor. The architectural solution that devised rich marble tracery of reverse-curve arches inset with quatrefoils for the multi-light sections is stupendous. Partial gilding of long stretches must be imagined, gleaming against the natural hues of the polychrome marble surround.
In concept the building is still faithful to the traditional portego plan, stated by the multi-light apertures on the façade and possibly intended to be flanked by other rooms.
In this sense the Ca' d'Oro is incomplete, inasmuch as circumstances prevented building of the left wing. But a careful reading of the overall façade as it stands effectively shows balance in the ratio of height to breadth to be enhanced, eliciting a more intriguing set of spatial dynamics from the play of solid against void. While the gradual evolution of flamboyant Gothic between the end of the 14th and the first half of the 15th century does not substantially affect structure here, it does extraordinarily enrich decorative treatment. In advance of its times the Ca' d'Oro is the most complete exemplar of this architectural style.
Building began in 1424. Documents dated 1426 report Matteo Raverti's commitment to handle carving of much of the stone detail on the façade for Marino Contarini, inclusive of arches, balconies and capitals. Less elaborate in detail but equally mature as an architectural statement, the sequence of apertures on the court flanking the calle at the rear of the building lends light to the central portego on both storeys. An external staircase leads up to the first piano nobile.
One most striking feature, evoking a similar solution on the Doge's Palace, is the series of Istrian stone finials crowning the cornice on the Grand Canal façade.
The building houses an important museum of works bequeathed to the State in 1916 by Baron Giorgio Franchetti. The collection comprises Gothic and Renaissance period furniture, Persian carpets and Flemish tapestries, sculpture and numerous important paintings; of outstanding beauty and importance in a rich collection of medals and numerous plaquettes, are those by Pisanello and Matteo de' Pasti (Pietro Morosini Bequest).
Besides works of the Italian schools of painting – Venetian (Giovanni Bellini, Alvise Vivarini), Ferrarese, Florentine, Lombard, Sienese (Pietro Lorenzetti) – the presence will be noted of such celebrated Venetian, Italian and foreign artists as Michele Giambono, Antonio Vivarini, Andrea Mantegna, Jacopo de' Barbari, Vittore Carpaccio, Filippo Lippi, Luca Signorelli, Cima da Conegliano, Titian, Paris Bordone, Bernardino Licinio, Jacopo and Domenico Tintoretto, Anthony Van Dyck, Francesco Guardi and Alessandro Longhi. Among the sculptors mention must be made of Andrea Riccio, Vittore Gambello, Pietro and Tullio Lombardo, Jacopo Sansovino and Alessandro Vittoria.

R. 67
PALAZZO MIANI COLETTI GIUSTI

This building stands next to the Ca' d'Oro to which it creates such a sharp contrast as regards architecture and style, a natural comparison between architecture so different in style and period. We can also draw conclusions about the social-economical level of the two building periods and of the families which had the palaces built.
The architect was Antonio Visentini, a painter, engraver and architect, born in Venice in 1688, the same man who designed Consul Smith's house.
The date of construction, 1766, is sculpted on the façade of the building. The almost eighty year old artist expressed all his architectural and stylistic concepts in this work which can be considered a recapitulation of his career with "the disposition of the openings which respect the Venetian tradition, thus returning to the tripartite division, while it just as clearly reveals Palladio's influence in distributing light and shadow contrasts on the first piano nobile, and the alternating of arches, columns and niches".
The Correr Museum has a watercolour of the façade which was later to be realized with a few changes. If we look at the drawing as a whole, we can note how the floors are accurately outlined by the contour lines and balconies which become lighter the higher they get and are finally enclosed by the terrace parapets on a level with the cornice.

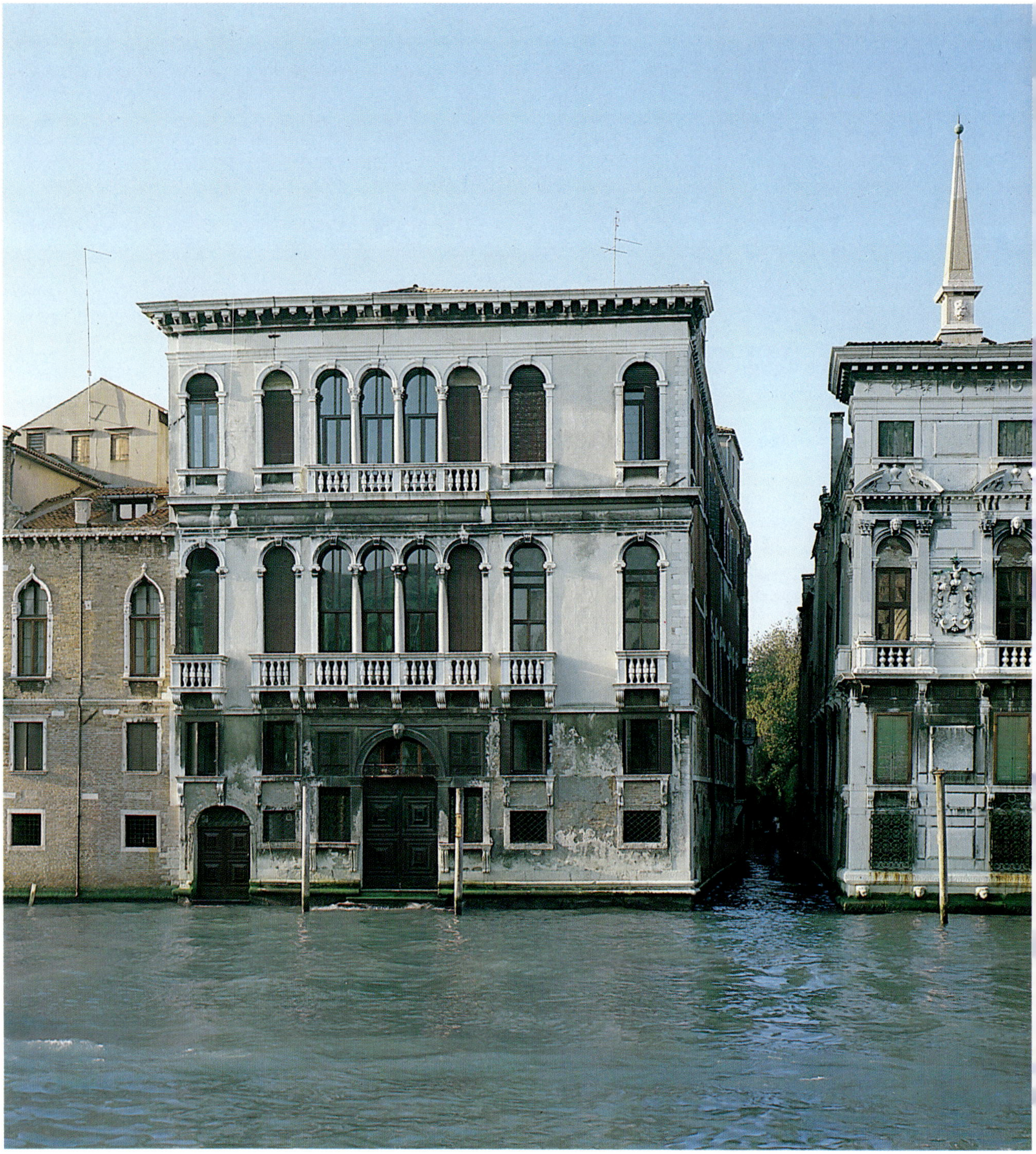

N° 105
Palazzo Tron
A 16th century building. A reception in honour of Joseph II, Emperor of Austria, was held in the piano nobile hall in 1775.
(L. 66, page 162)

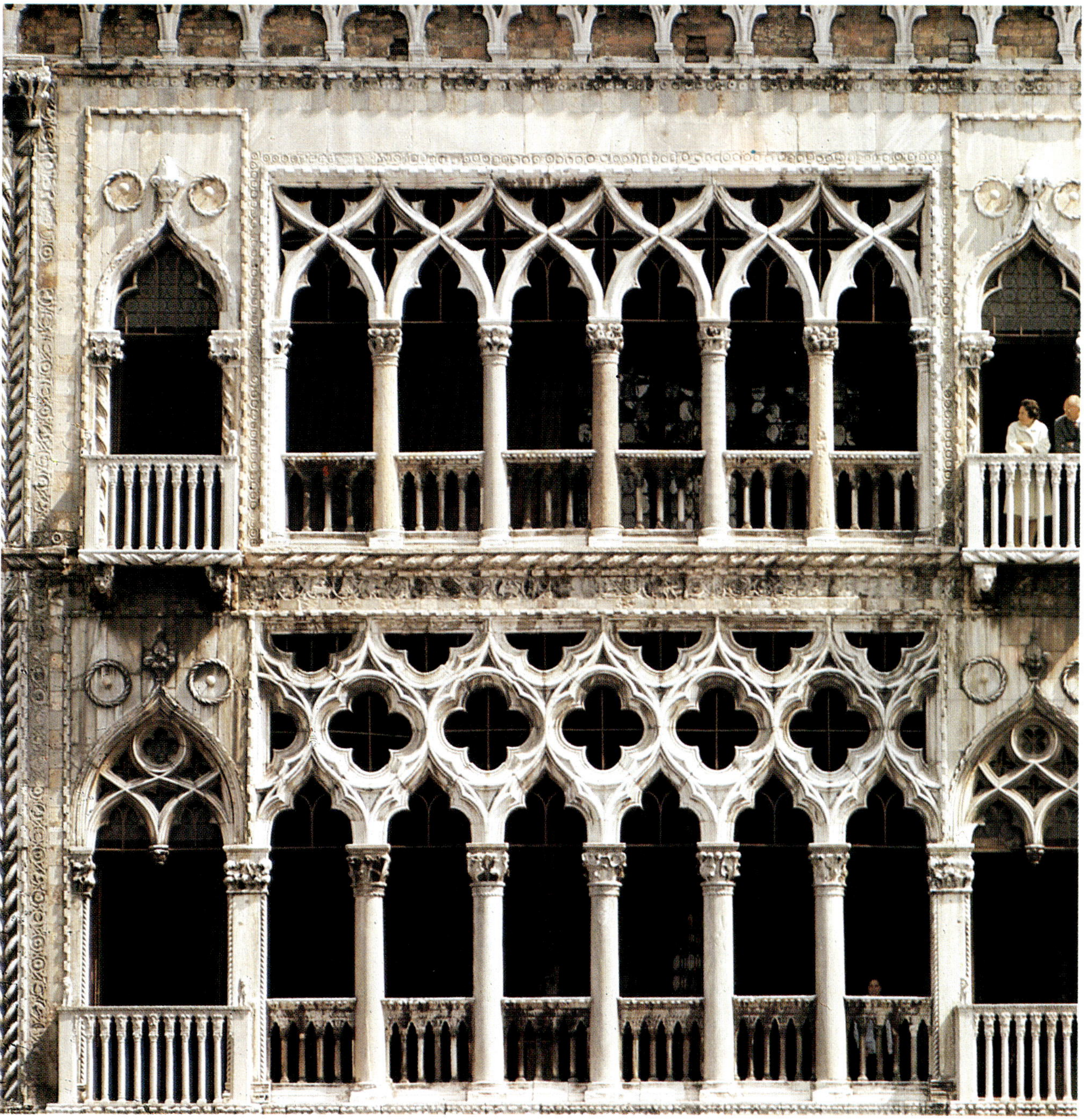

N° 106
Cà d'Oro
In close-up, the unusual wealth of architectural and sculptural detail on the multi-light section of the piano nobile.
(R. 66, page 163)

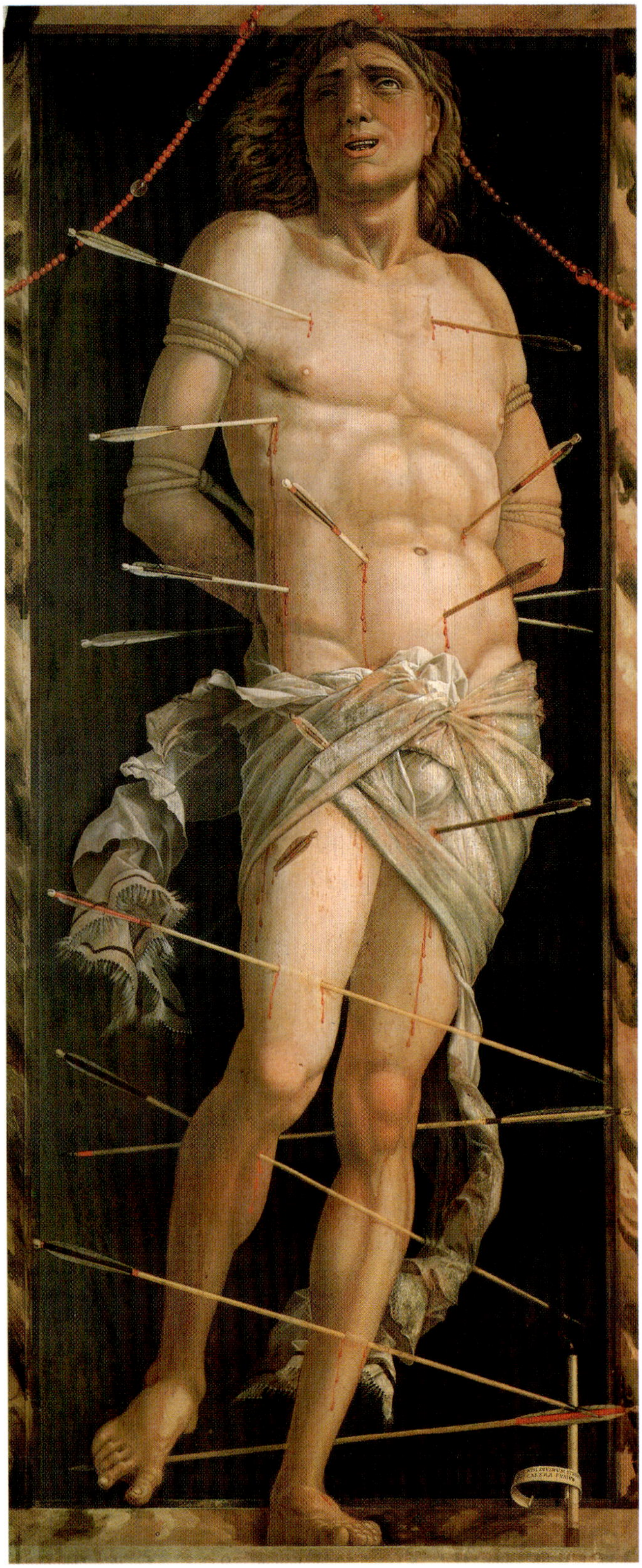

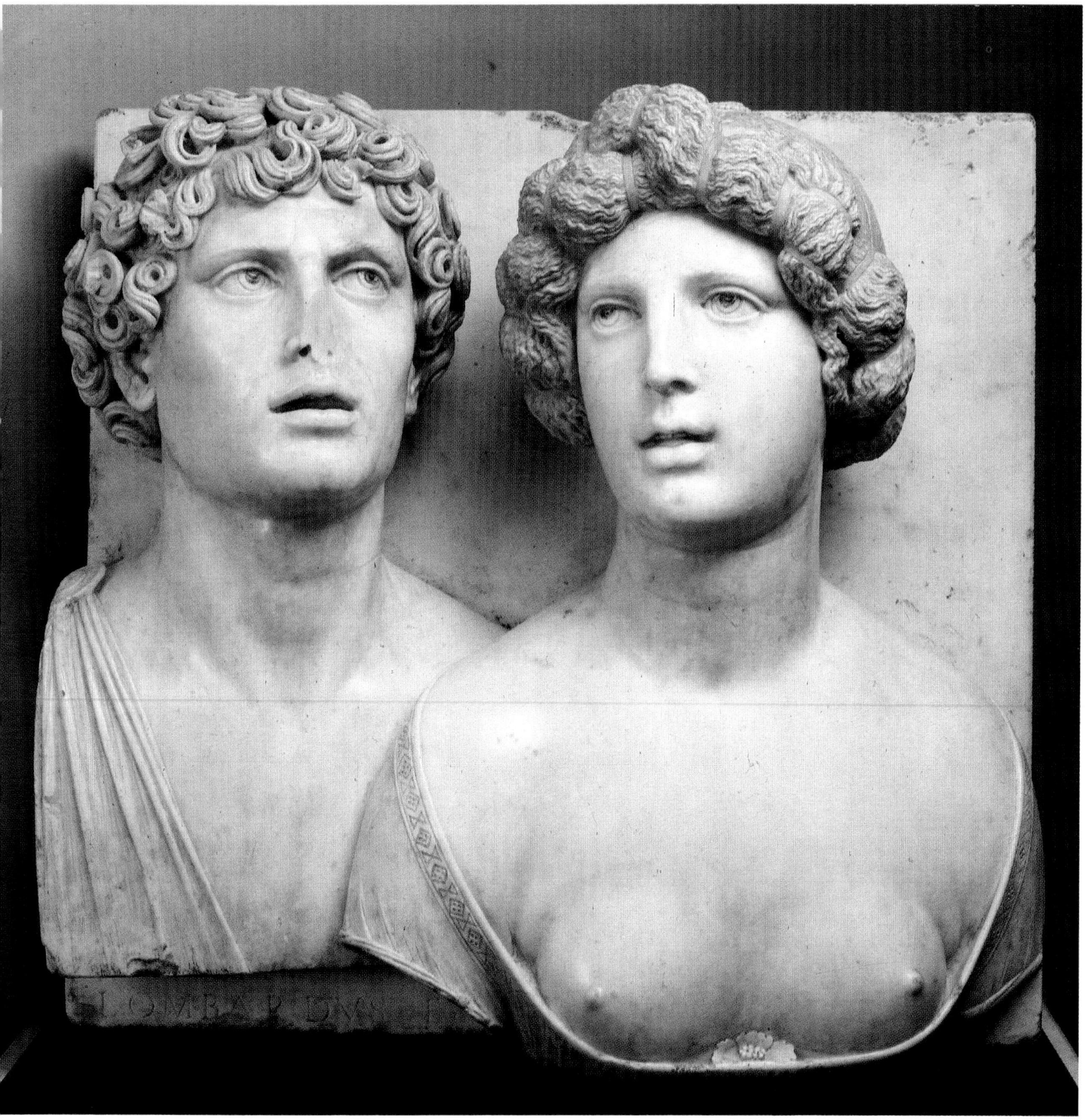

N° 107
The Franchetti Picture Gallery at the Cà d'Oro
"*St Sebastian*" by Andrea Mantegna.
(R. 66, page 163)

N° 108
The Franchetti Picture Gallery at the Cà d'Oro
"*Young Couple*" by Tullio Lombardo.
(R. 66, page 163)

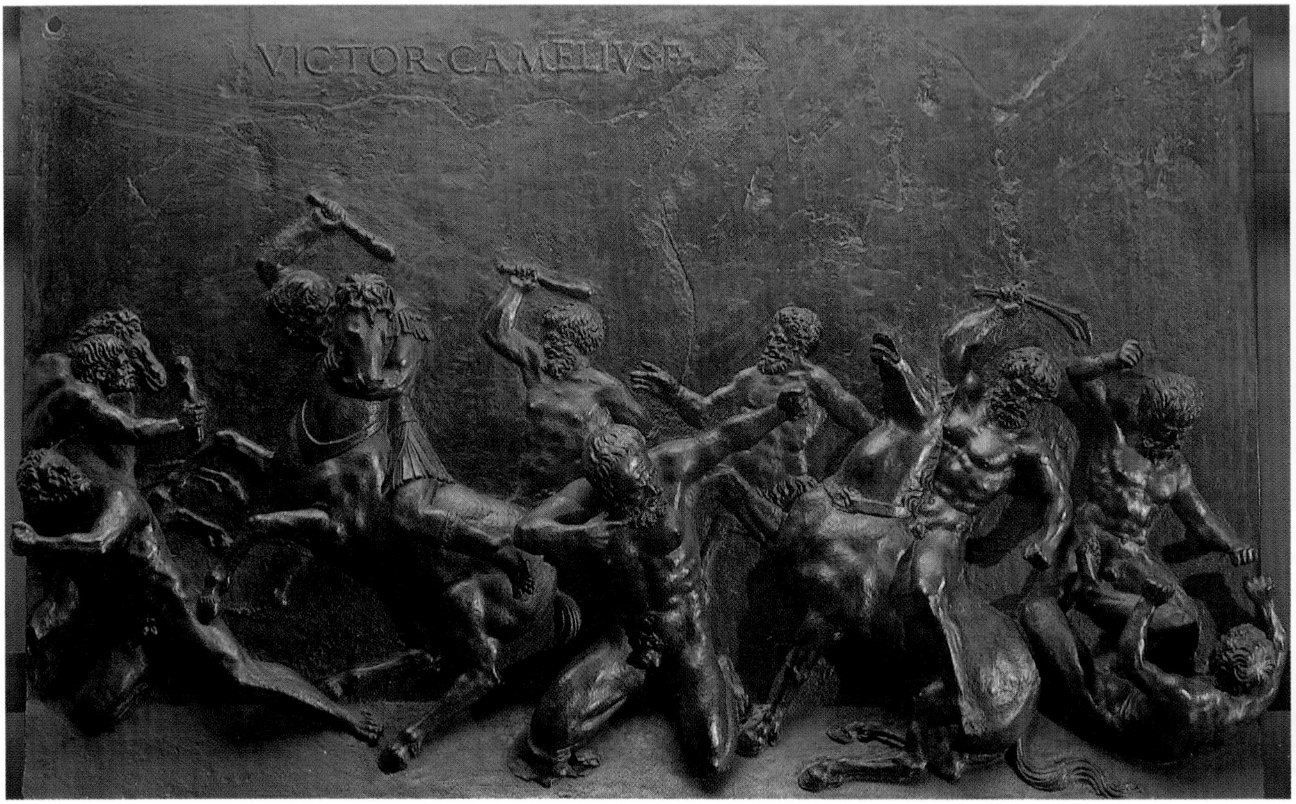

N° 109
The Franchetti Picture Gallery at the Cà d'Oro
"*Battle between Satyrs and Giants*"
by Vittore Gambello.
(R. 66, page 163)

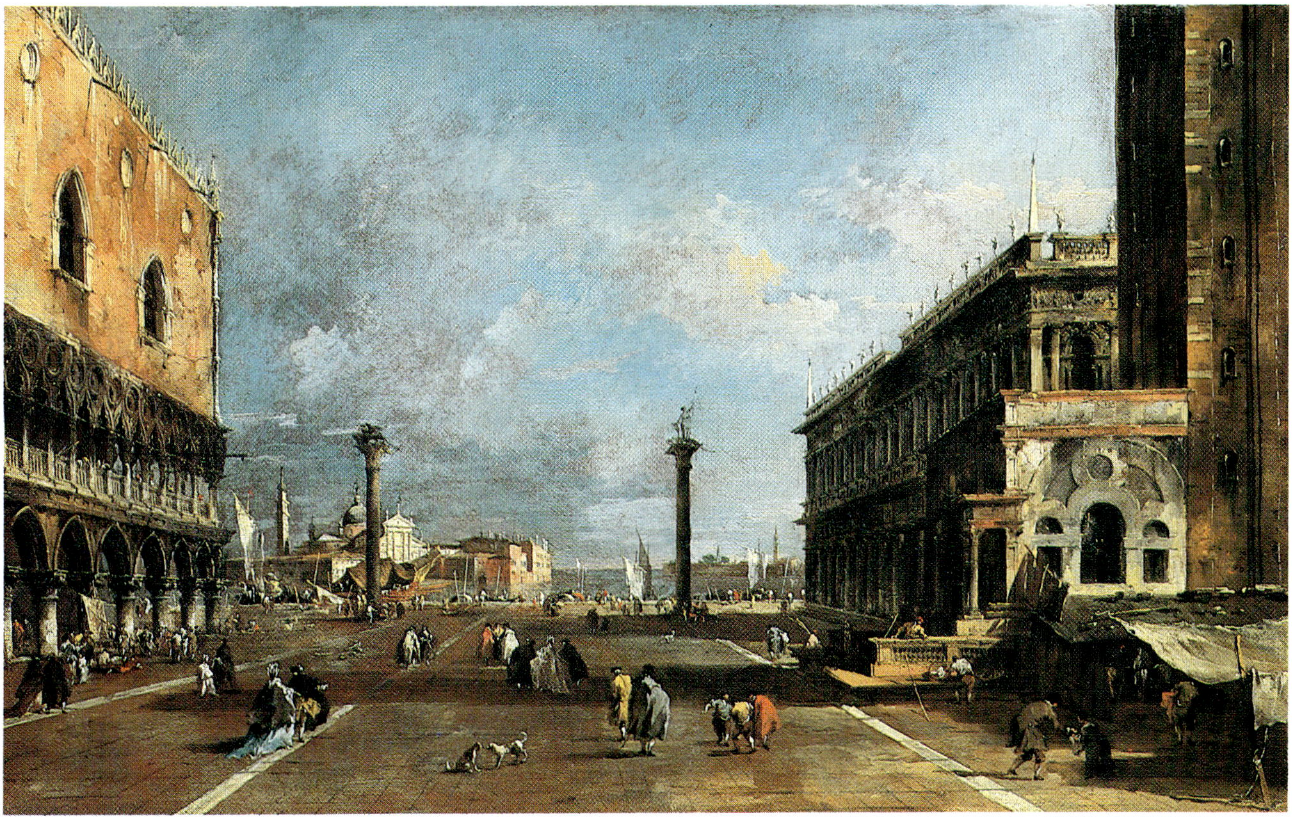

N° 110
The Franchetti Picture Gallery at the Cà d'Oro
"*La Piazzetta*" by Francesco Guardi.
(R. 66, page 163)

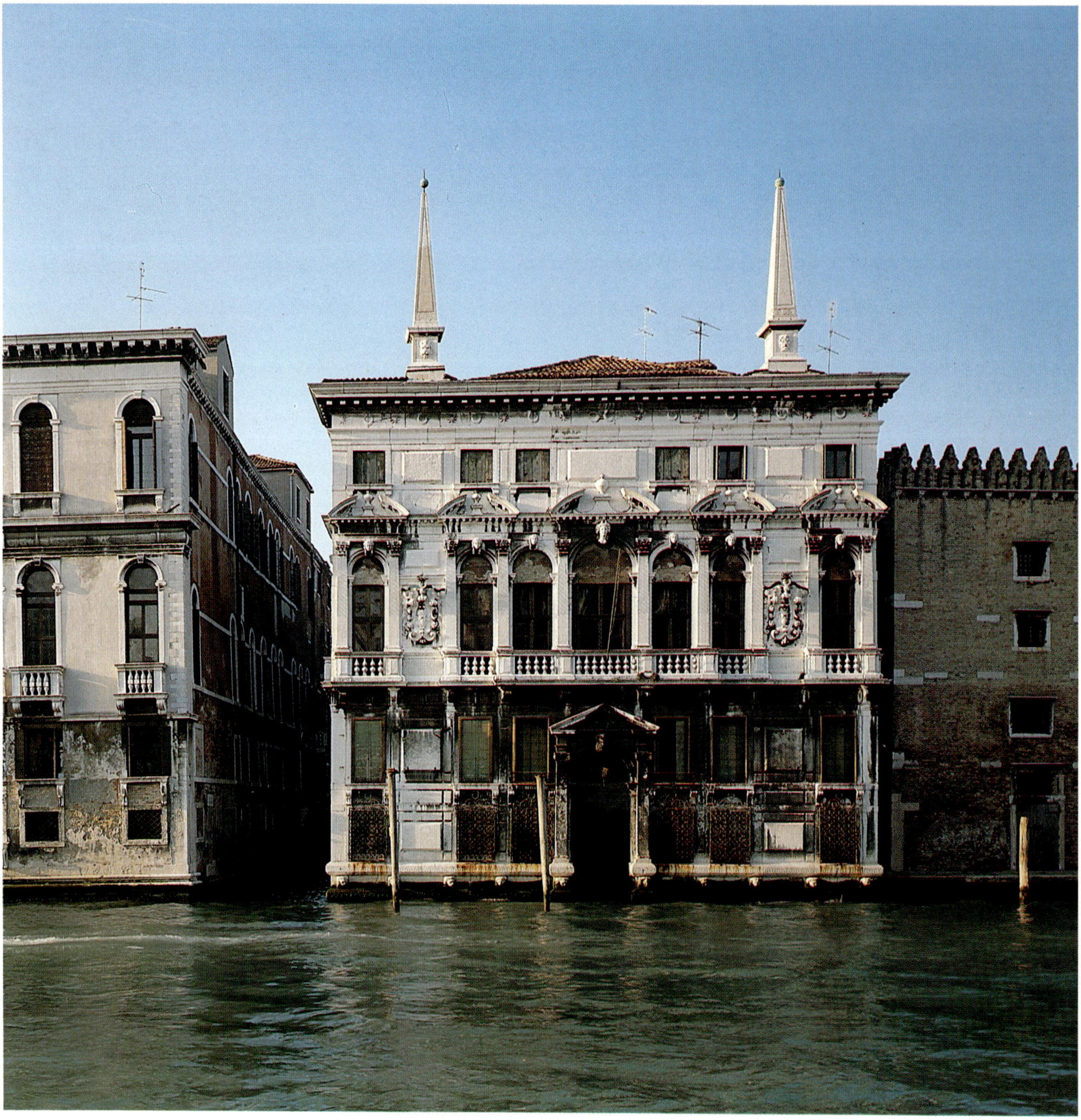

N° 111
Palazzo Belloni Battagia
Another building designed by Longhena and built between 1645 and 1649. Working on a confined scale elicits a more considered handling of proportion and detail from the architect, either by choice or force of circumstance.
(L. 67, page 162)

N° 112
Palazzo Miani Coletti Giusti
The 18th century idioms of the palace contrast sharply with the adjacent Cà d'Oro.
(R. 67, page 163)

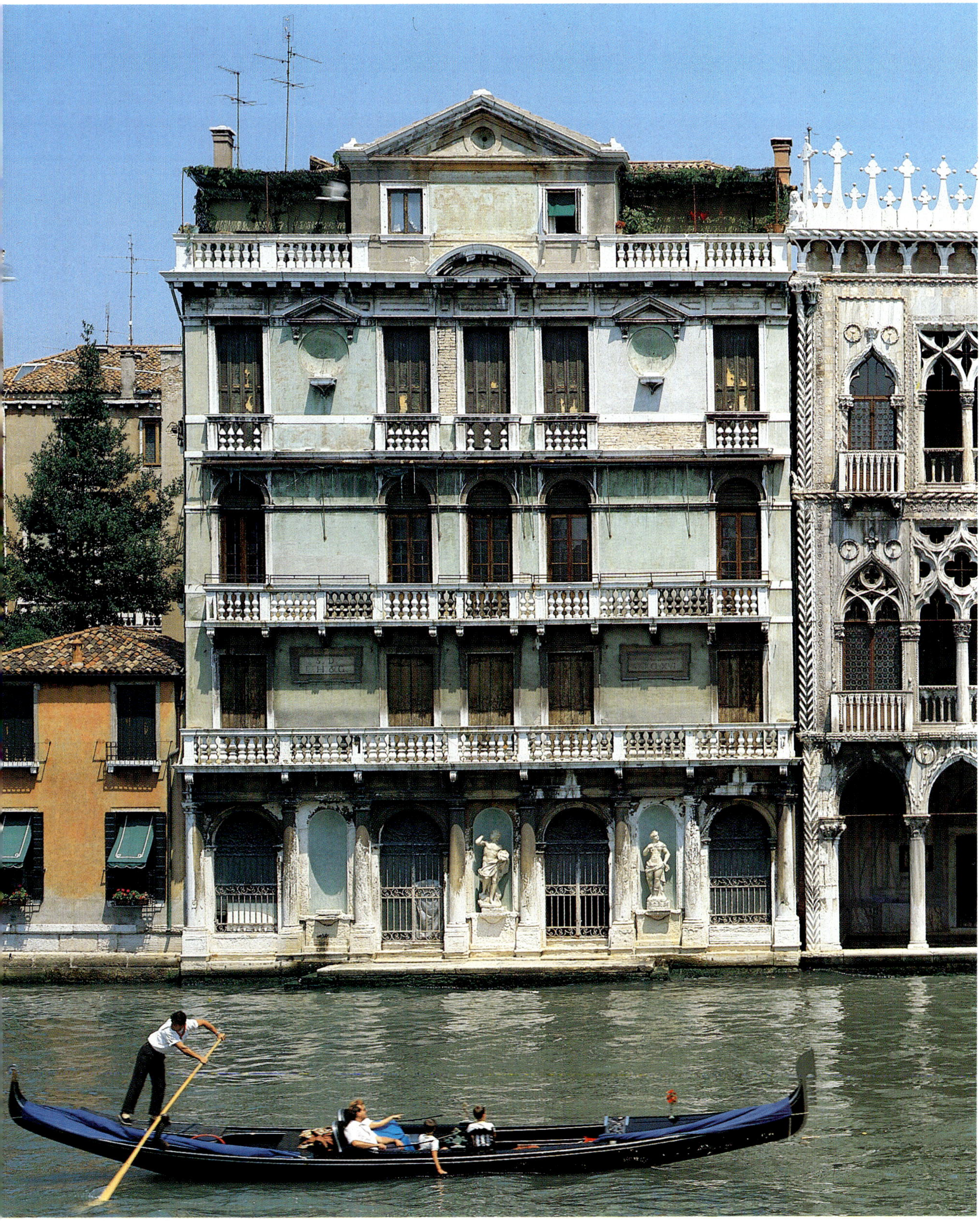

L. 68
FONDACO DEL MEGIO

This building was owned by the Republic and used as a public granary storing millet and grain in general. At that time millet was used to make the bread which was sold in the shops for the common people. The Republic had always seen to it that the warehouses were kept full for the times of famine which often occurred during those years when bread was the basic foodstuff of the less well-off: "Millet made into flour to make the bread for the common people" (Tassini). In fact, many people would have died in the 1346 famine... "nisi fuisset milium quad erat tunc Venetiis, et fuerat bene per XX, XXI et XXII annos". Likewise in 1559 "a great part of the people would have died if the providence of the Senate had not opened the warehouses containing millet kept for this purpose". The present-day building has a characteristic brick façade with three large doorways giving onto the short "fondamenta" and a triple row of windows on the upper floors. It was built by the Republic in the 15th century, perhaps to replace or to enlarge an older building used for the same purpose. Another architectural characteristic is the crowning crenellations often used in public buildings.
Inside, the plan consists of a large courtyard enclosed by high walls and parts of the buildings. Modern alterations on this façade have totally obliterated the original structure.

L. 69
FONDACO DEI TURCHI

The original building was erected in the 13th century by the wealthy merchant G. Palmieri according to the concept of the fondaco-house of that time. Unfortunately this characteristic was lost after the disastrous restoration carried out during the last century which completely distorted its original appearance.
The Republic often used this palace to accomodate high-ranking visitors including the Emperor of Constantinople, John Palaeologus, and Alfonso d'Este and his wife Eleonora. In the 17th century it was owned by the Pesaro family who sold it to the State to be used for the Turkish community living in Venice. The Turks kept it until the middle of the last century as the base for all their commercial activities. It now houses the Natural History Museum.

L. 70
PALAZZO GIOVANNELLI

A building very probably dating from the mid-15th century, Gothic in style, Palazzo Giovannelli originally belonged to the Foscarini family, who leased it to the Giovannelli in 1755.
A merchant family, native of Bergamo, the Giovannelli settled in Venice, acquiring patrician status in 1668; illustrious members include three procurators and a patriarch. The building frequently offered "commodious lodging for kings and persons of rank", most notable among them Frederick Christian IV, King of Denmark, in 1709.
The neighbouring garden, together with the area of an adjacent modern building, was formerly the site of the Bembo palace, a sumptuous residence, its few remaining vestiges unfortunately wholly demolished in the 19th century.
In fact, these vestiges are shown in a print by Quadri to be confined to a continuous stretch of ground-floor portico, four spans of archways so placed as to leave a solid expanse of corner wall on the left and to adjoin the area of a much later building on the right. Albeit incomplete or partially transformed and walled up, this could be a structural solution pointing to an important Byzantine building with the characteristic feature of a waterfront entrance portico such as has been seen on other buildings along the Grand Canal.

R. 68
PALAZZO FONTANA

The Fontanas belonged to a wealthy family of merchants from Piacenza. Since their best clients were in Venice, they decided to settle in the lagoon city where they arrived in 1548. They bought a piece of land and an old house in the San Felice parish along the Grand Canal and they built a large house whose architectural and stylistic features are clearly classical. The vertical line of multi-mullioned windows is moved slightly to the left and closely flanked by the lateral one-mullioned windows. On the right, planimetrically speaking, there is another room denoted at each end by two windows (the one on the right, already mentioned, is almost a two-mullioned window). The balconies above and below, the capitals of the arched windows, the architraves of the mezzanine's rectangular windows and the columns are kept in line by horizontal and vertical marble strips along the wall spacings. A regular geometrical subdivision is thus created where wall spaces and openings are interwoven and closely linked together as part of the general pattern.
It seems that it was Giovanni Fontana's idea to build the palace which became the property of the Rezzonico family but we do not know whether this family inherited or bought it. In fact in 1693 it was the birthplace of Carlo Rezzonico who was later to become Pope Clement XIII in 1769.

R. 69
PALAZZO CONTARINI PISANI

Palazzo Contarini Pisani is the product of 17th century reconstruction on the area of a building of an earlier period that must have been an elaborate and prestigious Gothic statement of imposing volumetric presence, judging by the scale, especially in circumference, of a possible surviving element, the massive Istrian-stone corner-column and Gothic capital on the Calle del Traghetto San Felice.
The porticoed ground floor echoes the structural rhythms of the piano nobile three-light section with pillars supporting the apertures.

R. 70
PALAZZO BOLDÙ GHISI CONTARINI

The building stands level with the preceding Contarini palace at the eaves but allocation of storey heights differs: the rusticated ground floor and first mezzanine are jointly of greater height, while the second mezzanine between the two piano nobile storeys is lower. With axes of entrance portal and triple apertures of the hall set right of centre, balance of the façade is asymmetrical.
Round-arch windows and balconies with tight lateral and overhead framing are a legacy in taste from 16th century tradition.
The original Boldù palace was later acquired by the Ghisi family and rebuilt in the 17th century, as stylistic reading of the building today confirms. By a second change of hands it became the property of the Contarini Pisani, owners of the adjacent palace of this name, an acquisition that enabled them to enlarge their premises by transforming both properties into a single dwelling unit.

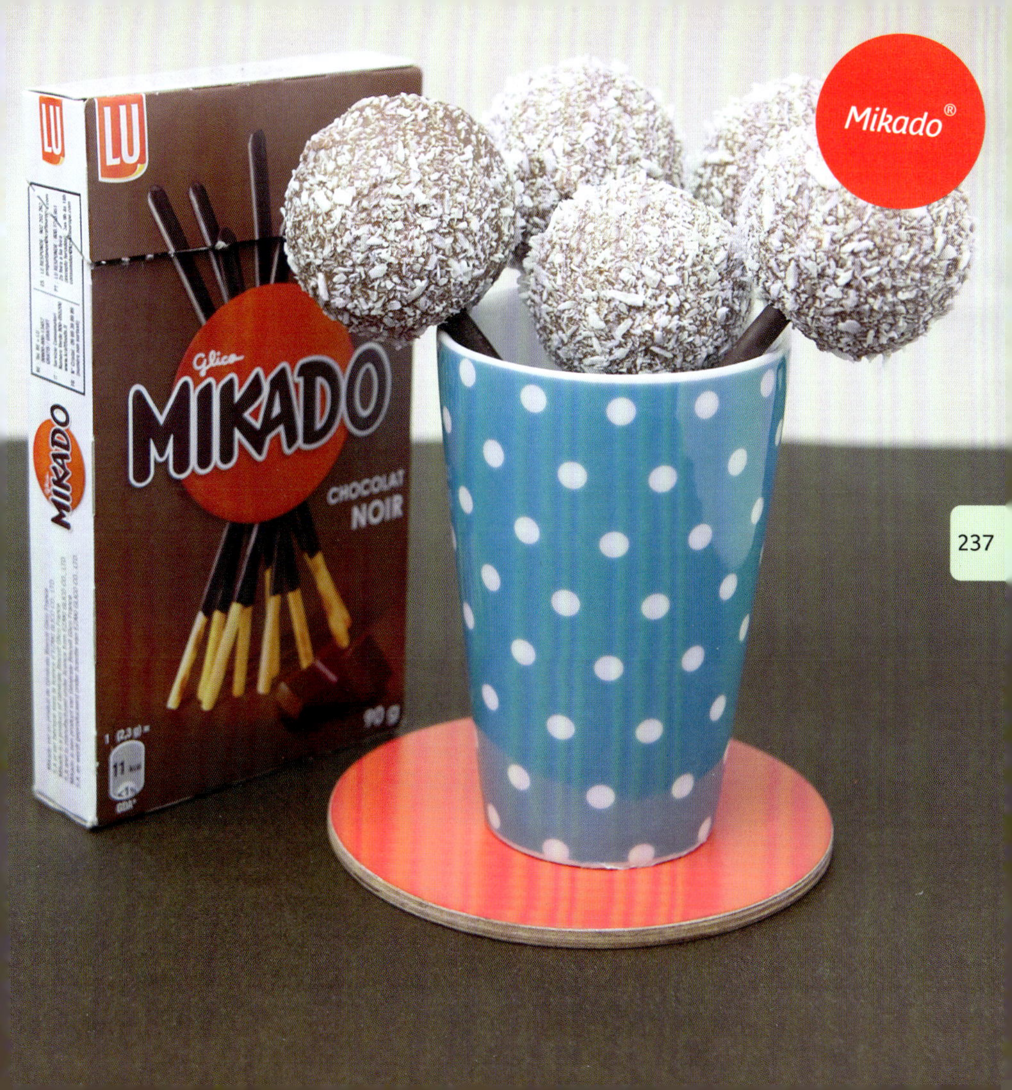

Mikado®

Aubergines farcies aux anchois
Remplacez les lardons par 8 filets d'anchois à l'huile, que vous ajouterez hachés dans le saladier sans les faire cuire.

Aubergines farcies aux deux tomates
Remplacez les lardons par 150 g de tomates séchées à l'huile taillées en lamelles et le coulis de tomate par 4 tomates pelées et concassées.

Aubergines farcies au boulgour
Remplacez les lardons par 250 g de boulgour cuit dans 2,5 fois son volume d'eau bouillante salée.

Courgettes farcies
Remplacez les aubergines par 4 courgettes moyennes et les lardons par 200 g de bœuf haché. Remplacez le basilic par du persil.

Mozzarella Galbani®

AUBERGINES FARCIES À LA MOZZARELLA

Préparation : 15 min • **Cuisson :** 50 min • **Pour 4 personnes**

*1 boule de mozzarella Galbani® • 2 échalotes • 4 c. à s. d'huile d'olive
4 petites aubergines • 200 g de lardons fumés • 20 cl de coulis de tomates
quelques feuilles de basilic • sel et poivre*

- Préchauffez le four à 210 °C.
- Coupez la mozzarella Galbani® en petits dés. Épluchez les échalotes et émincez-les.
- Faites chauffer 2 c. à s. d'huile d'olive dans une poêle et faites-y revenir les échalotes.
- Lavez les aubergines, coupez-les en deux dans l'épaisseur aux 3/4 de la hauteur. Prélevez la chair, puis coupez-la en dés. Ajoutez-les dans la poêle et faites revenir pendant 5 min. Réservez les aubergines évidées.
- Dans une autre poêle, faites revenir les lardons.
- Versez le tout dans un saladier et ajoutez le coulis de tomates, la moitié de la mozzarella Galbani® et le reste d'huile d'olive. Salez et poivrez.
- Garnissez les aubergines évidées de ce mélange, puis parsemez-les du reste de mozzarella Galbani®.
- Faites cuire au four pendant 40 min.
- Rincez le basilic, puis essuyez-le avec du papier absorbant, et ciselez-le. Servez les aubergines farcies parsemées de basilic.

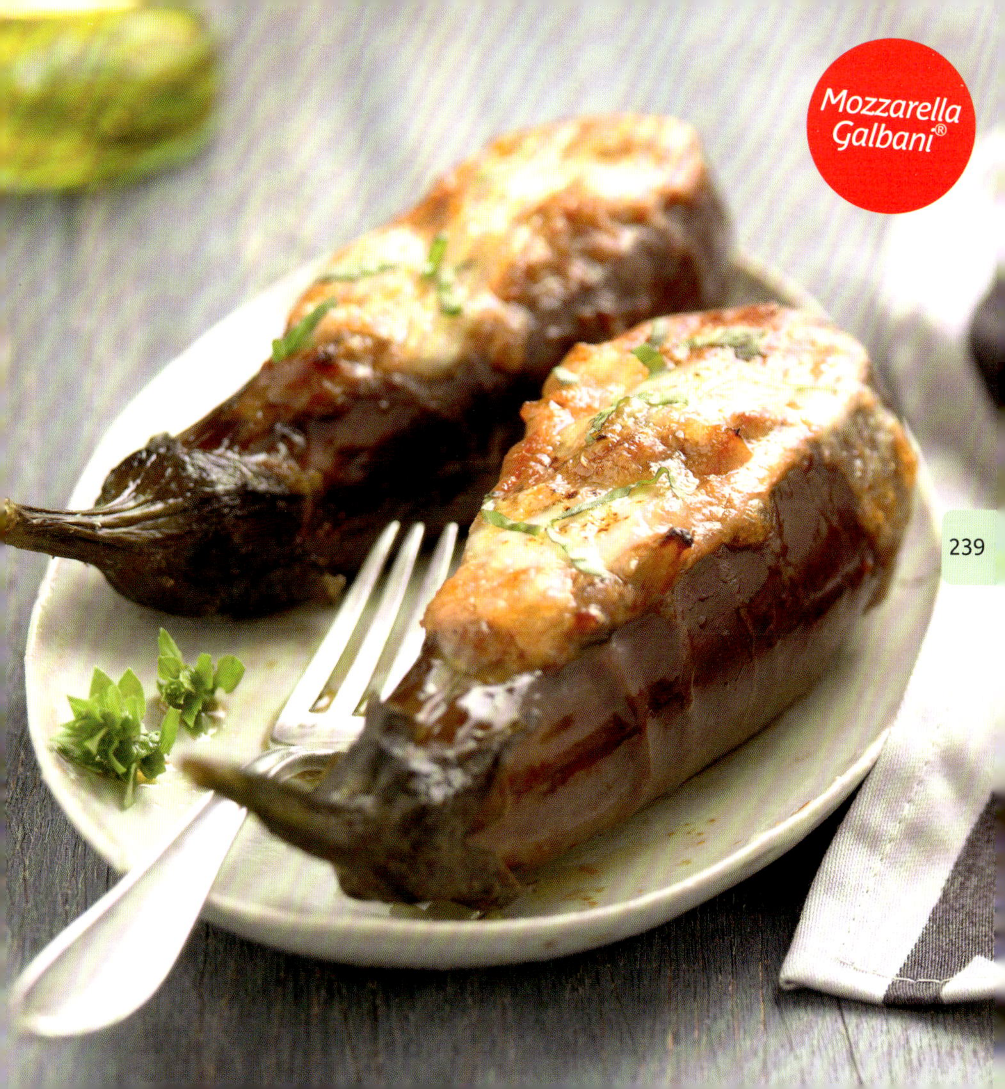
Mozzarella Galbani®

Mozzarella Galbani®

BOUCHÉES CHIC À LA MOZZARELLA

Préparation : 15 min • **Cuisson :** aucune • **Pour 32 bouchées**

250 g de mozzarella Galbani® • 8 tranches de jambon de Parme
32 feuilles de basilic violet • 16 tomates séchées

- Coupez la mozzarella Galbani® en dés.
- Taillez chaque tranche jambon de Parme en 4 lamelles.
- Rincez le basilic, puis essuyez-le avec du papier absorbant.
- Coupez les tomates séchées en deux.
- Enroulez chaque dé de mozzarella Galbani® dans 1 lamelle de jambon de Parme, enfilez chacun sur une pique à cocktail avec 1 feuille de basilic et 1 demi-tomate séchée. Répétez l'opération jusqu'à épuisement des ingrédients.
- Servez à l'apéritif.

Bouchées chic à la mozzarella et à la figue

Remplacez les morceaux de tomate séchée par des figues coupées en quatre.

Bouchées chic à la mozzarella panée

Passez les dés de mozzarella dans l'œuf battu, puis dans de la chapelure, puis faites-les dorer à la poêle avec de l'huile d'olive.

Bouchées à la mozzarella et au raisin

Reprenez la recette ci-dessus, puis enfilez 1 morceau de mozzarella panée et 1 grain de raisin rouge sur chaque pique.

Minisandwiches roulés à la mozzarella et au poivron

Aplatissez au rouleau à pâtisserie 8 tranches de pain de mie, puis coupez-les en quatre. Déposez sur chaque morceau 1 lamelle de mozzarella, 1 lamelle de jambon de Parme, 1 feuille de basilic et 1 lamelle de poivron grillé. Roulez et maintenez avec des piques.

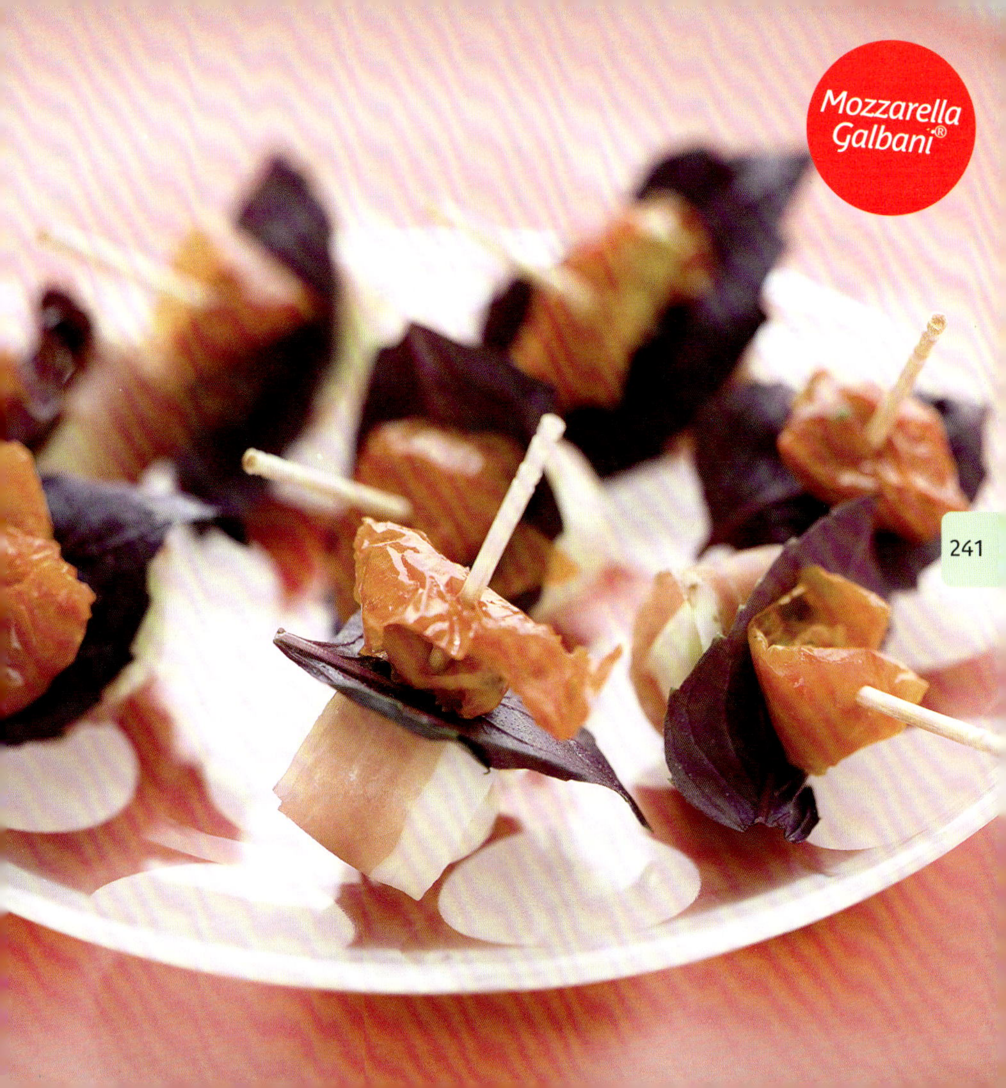
Mozzarella Galbani®

Pommes de terre à l'agneau et aux pruneaux
Supprimez la carotte, le céleri et l'avocat. Remplacez le bœuf haché par de l'agneau émincé et les haricots rouges par 250 g de pruneaux dénoyautés.

Pommes de terre à la ratatouille
Remplacez la garniture au bœuf et aux légumes par de la ratatouille, préparée en faisant revenir 1 oignon, 1 poivron rouge, 2 petites courgettes et 4 tomates dans une sauteuse. Supprimez l'avocat.

Pommes de terre au poulet et aux champignons
Remplacez le bœuf par des dés de poulet, les haricots rouges par 300 g de champignons de Paris émincés. Supprimez le concentré de tomate. Ajoutez un peu de béchamel en fin de cuisson.

Mozzarella Galbani®

POMMES DE TERRE GARNIES AUX HARICOTS ROUGES

Préparation : 10 min • **Cuisson :** 30 min • **Pour 4 personnes**

4 grosses pommes de terre • 1 gros oignon • 1 carotte
2 branches de céleri • 2 piments rouges • 250 g de mozzarella Galbani®
1 c. à s. d'huile d'olive • 300 g de bœuf haché
2 c. à s. de concentré de tomate • 1 boîte de haricots rouges en conserve
1 avocat bien mûr • 1 c. à s. de jus de citron • sel et poivre

- Pelez les pommes de terre et faites-les cuire dans de l'eau bouillante salée.

- Pendant ce temps, épluchez l'oignon et émincez-le. Pelez la carotte et râpez-la. Rincez le céleri et taillez-le en lamelles. Lavez les piments et émincez-les finement. Râpez la mozzarella Galbani®.

- Faites revenir l'oignon, la carotte et le céleri dans l'huile, jusqu'à ce qu'ils commencent à se colorer. Ajoutez la viande et le piment, et faites revenir jusqu'à ce que la viande soit bien dorée. Salez et poivrez. Ajoutez le concentré de tomate, les haricots égouttés et un peu d'eau, puis laissez mijoter pendant 20 min environ.

- Une fois les pommes de terre cuites, égouttez-les, pratiquez une incision en forme de croix dans chacune, puis ouvrez-les. Ajoutez la moitié de la mozzarella à la farce, mélangez, puis répartissez la préparation dans chaque pomme de terre.

- Retirez la peau de l'avocat. Taillez la chair en lamelles et arrosez-la de jus de citron. Salez et poivrez. Ajoutez-les sur la garniture, puis parsemez du reste de mozzarella râpée. Servez sans attendre.

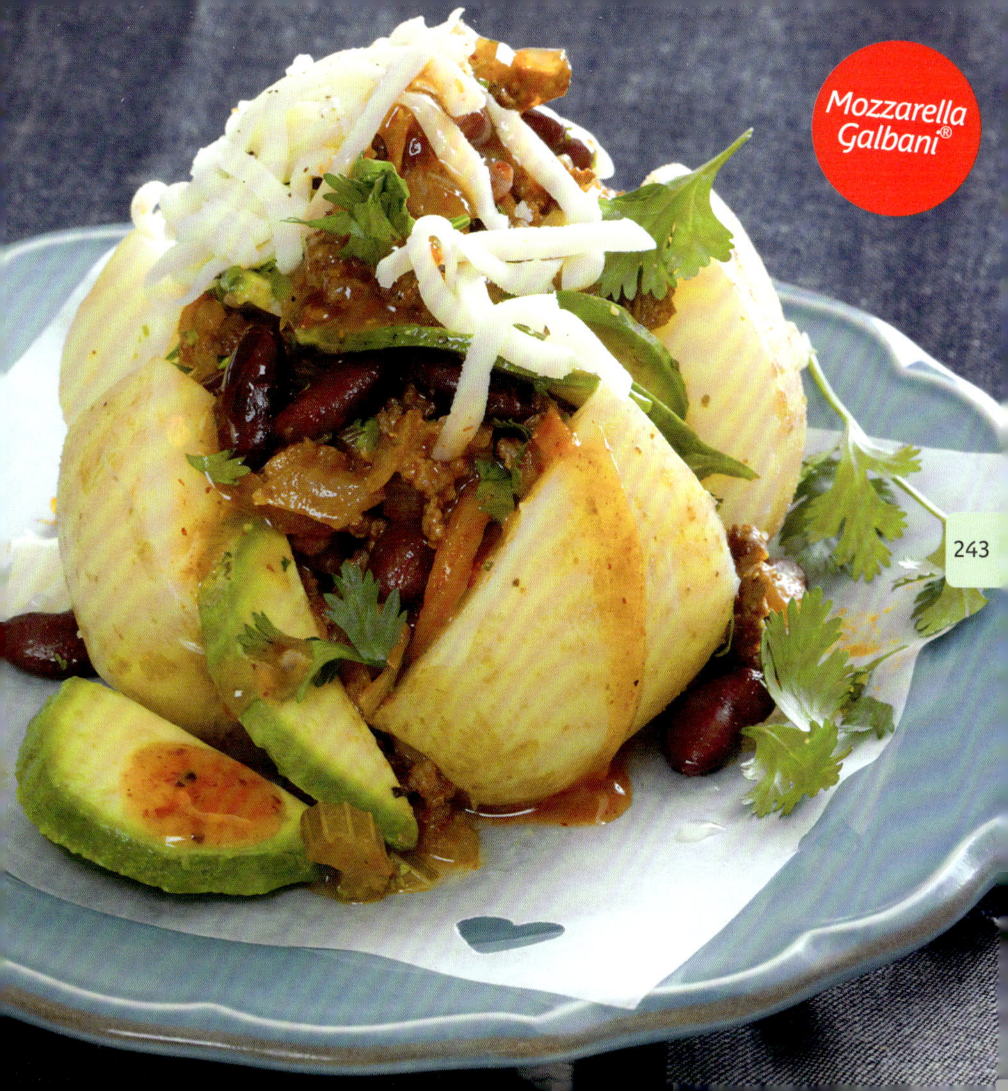
Mozzarella Galbani®

Mozzarella Galbani®

ROULÉS DE LÉGUMES GRILLÉS À LA MOZZARELLA

Préparation : 15 min • **Cuisson :** 8 min • **Pour 18 roulés**

1 grosse aubergine • 2 c. à s. d'huile d'olive • 5 tranches de jambon cru
275 g de poivrons marinés • 18 grandes feuilles de basilic
9 billes de mozzarella Galbani® • sel et poivre

- Préchauffez le gril du four ou le barbecue.
- Lavez l'aubergine, puis coupez-la en 9 tranches. Coupez celles-ci en deux, dans le sens de la longueur.
- Huilez chaque face des tranches, salez et poivrez.
- Faites griller de 3 à 4 min sur chaque face, puis laissez refroidir.
- Coupez le jambon en quatre, puis placez 1 lamelle sur chaque morceau d'aubergine.
- Égouttez les poivrons marinés sur du papier absorbant. Coupez-les en morceaux et déposez-en sur chaque lamelle de jambon.
- Rincez le basilic, puis essuyez-le sur du papier absorbant. Ajoutez 1 feuille sur chaque morceau de poivron.
- Coupez les billes de mozzarella Galbani® mini en deux, puis ajoutez-les par-dessus.
- Roulez, puis maintenez le tout avec des piques en bois.
- Servez à l'apéritif.

Roulés au pesto

Mixez les feuilles de 1/2 bouquet de basilic avec 25 g de pignons de pin, 50 g de parmesan et 1/2 c. à c. de gros sel. Robot toujours en marche, incorporez 7 cl d'huile d'olive. Supprimez le poivron et le basilic. Nappez le jambon de pesto.

Roulés au pesto rosso

Reprenez la recette ci-dessus en remplaçant le basilic par 80 g de tomates séchées. Supprimez le poivron. Nappez le jambon de pesto rosso.

Roulés au poulet et aux asperges

Remplacez l'aubergine par des lamelles très fines de poulet, et le poivron et le basilic par des pointes d'asperges vertes.

Roulés à la courgette et au saumon

Remplacez l'aubergine par 1 grosse courgette, le jambon par du saumon fumé, et le basilic par de l'aneth.

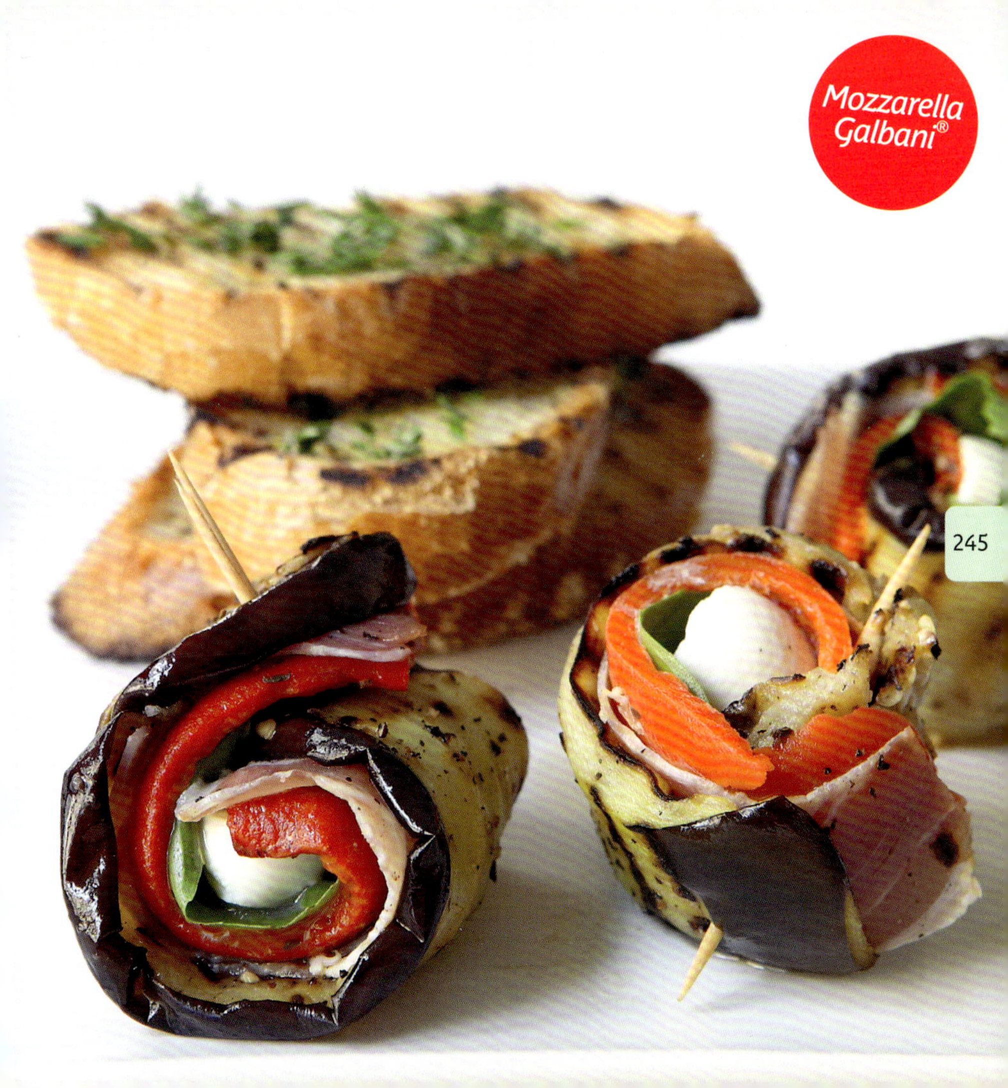
Mozzarella
Galbani®

Tatin de tomates parfumées

Ajoutez 1 gousse d'ail hachée et les feuilles de 1 branche de romarin sur les tomates avant de les faire cuire au four.

Tatin de tomates à la moutarde

Badigeonnez la pâte à tarte de moutarde avant de la retourner et de la déposer sur les tomates confites.

Tatin de tomates et d'échalotes

Remplacez la moitié des tomates par 400 g d'échalotes épluchées et émincées.

Tatin de tomates aux lardons

Faites revenir 200 g de lardons fumés à la poêle sans matière grasse. Répartissez-les sur les tomates confites avant de déposer la pâte par-dessus.

Mozzarella Galbani®

TARTE TATIN DE TOMATES

Préparation : 15 min • **Cuisson :** 50 min • **Réfrigération :** 30 min

Pour 1 tarte

pour la pâte : *200 g de farine + un peu pour le plan de travail*
170 g de beurre ramolli • 1 œuf • 5 g de sucre • sel
pour la garniture : *10 cl d'huile d'olive • 40 g de cassonade*
800 g de tomates • 250 g de mozzarella Galbani® • thym frais

- Préparez la pâte : mélangez la farine, le beurre coupé en parcelles, 10 g de sel, l'œuf et le sucre. Formez une boule de pâte, recouvrez-la de film alimentaire, et laissez reposer au réfrigérateur pendant 30 min.

- Préchauffez le four à 150 °C. Pour la garniture, versez l'huile d'olive dans un plat à four rond pouvant aller sur la table de cuisson. Parsemez de cassonade. Faites chauffer à feu doux sur la table de cuisson, jusqu'à l'obtention d'un caramel blond.

- Lavez les tomates, coupez-les en deux, puis épépinez-les. Hors du feu, déposez les demi-tomates dans le plat, chair vers le bas. Faites cuire au four pendant 25 min. Laissez tiédir. Coupez la mozzarella Galbani® en tranches et disposez-les sur les tomates.

- Étalez la pâte au rouleau sur le plan de travail fariné, puis placez-la sur les tomates, en rentrant les bords de la pâte entre les tomates et le bord du moule.

- Augmentez la température du four à 180 °C. Faites cuire la tarte pendant 25 min. Retournez la tarte encore chaude sur un plat de service. Parsemez de thym frais.

- Servez chaud ou froid.

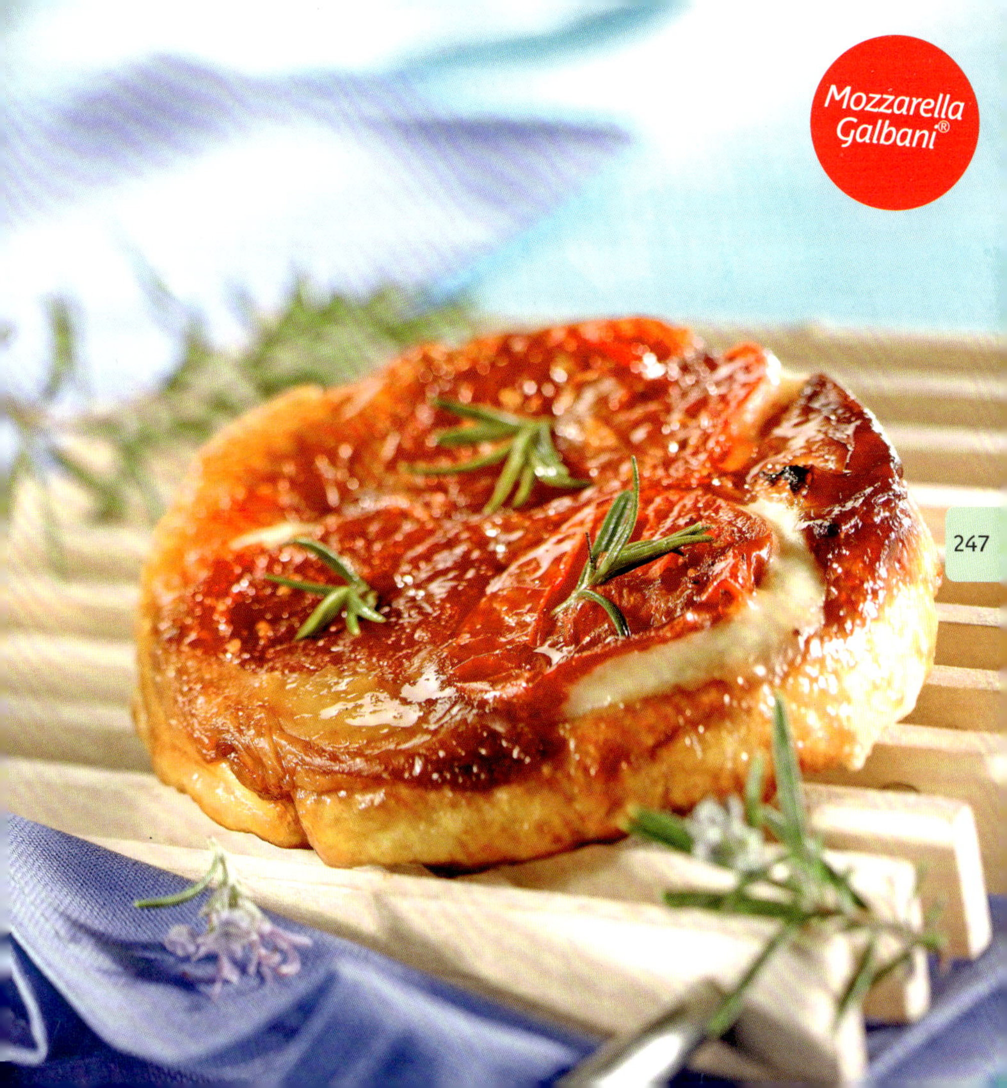
Mozzarella Galbani®

Mozzarella Galbani®

TARTINES À L'ITALIENNE

Préparation : 10 min • **Cuisson** : 12 min • **Pour 4 personnes**

1 gros pain focaccia (ou 2 petits) • 1 gousse d'ail • huile d'olive
2 tomates • 2 boules de mozzarella Galbani® • 4 tranches de jambon de Parme • 8 feuilles de basilic

- Préchauffez le gril du four.
- Coupez le pain focaccia en deux dans l'épaisseur, puis dans la largeur, de façon à obtenir 4 morceaux.
- Faites-les griller au grille-pain.
- Déposez-les sur une plaque à pâtisserie recouverte de papier sulfurisé, mie vers le haut, et frottez-les avec la gousse d'ail.
- Arrosez chacun d'un petit filet d'huile d'olive.
- Coupez les tomates et la mozzarella Galbani® en rondelles.
- Déposez, sur chaque morceau de focaccia, 2 ou 3 rondelles de tomate, 1 tranche de jambon de Parme et 2 ou 3 rondelles de mozzarella Galbani®.
- Passez sous le gril du four de 8 à 12 min. Surveillez la cuisson : les croques sont cuits lorsque le fromage commence à fondre et à dorer.
- Servez sans attendre, après avoir déposé 2 feuilles de basilic sur chaque tartine.

Tartines au caviar d'aubergine
Nappez le pain grillé de caviar d'aubergine avant d'ajouter les autres ingrédients.

Tartines végétariennes
Remplacez le jambon par 1 courgette taillée en rondelles très fines. Ajoutez 50 g d'olives noires coupées en deux. Remplacez le basilic par de la coriandre.

Tartines aux champignons
Remplacez les tomates par 300 g de champignons de Paris frais taillés en lamelles et revenus à la poêle pendant 15 min avec de l'ail haché et du persil. Remplacez le jambon par des lardons fumés revenus à la poêle.

Croque-monsieur à l'italienne
Remplacez le pain focaccia par 8 tranches de pain de mie grillées. Répartissez les tomates, le jambon, la mozzarella et le basilic sur 4 tranches, puis recouvrez des tranches restantes. Déposez 2 rondelles de mozzarella sur chaque croque et faites dorer sous le gril.

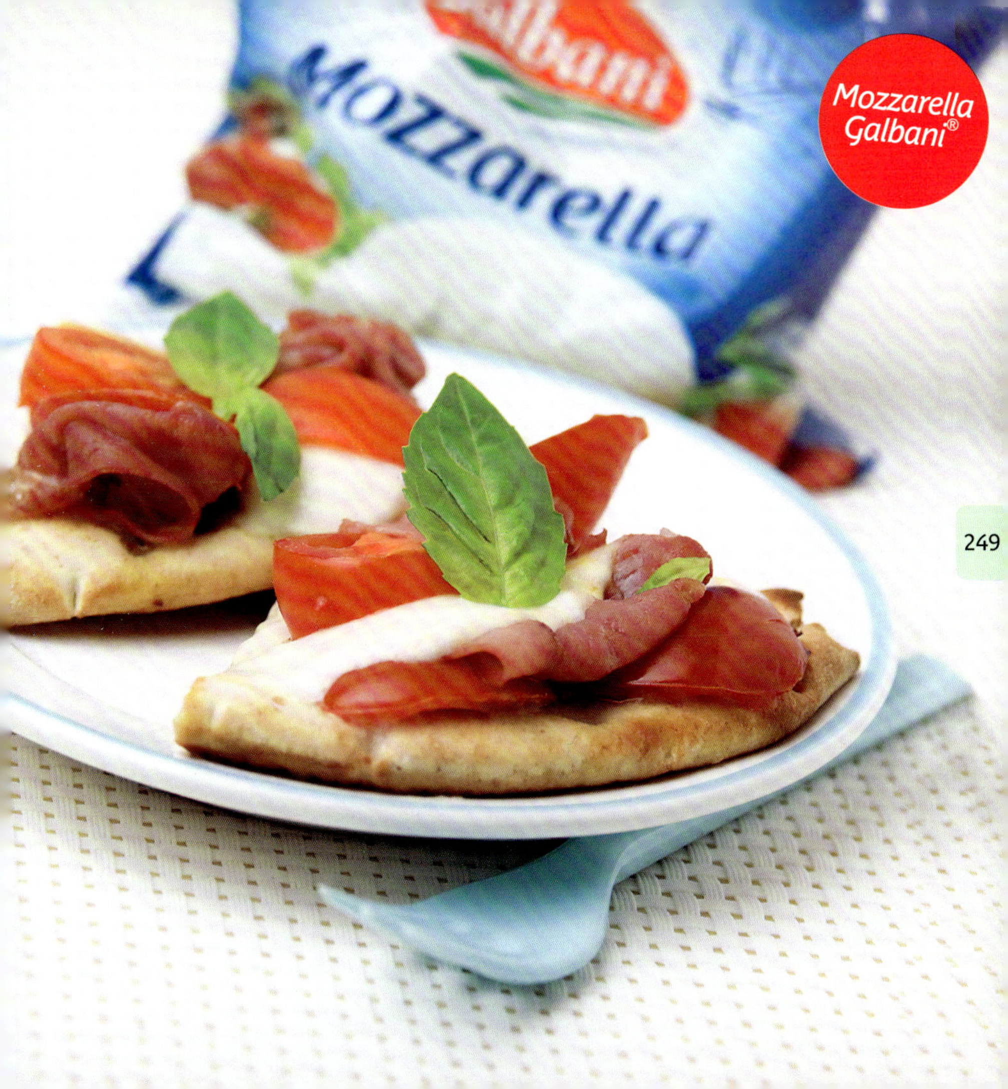

Mozzarella Galbani®

CARAMELS MOUS AU NUTELLA®

Préparation : 15 min • **Cuisson :** 10 min • **Pour 10 personnes**

165 g de crème fleurette • 125 g de sucre • 125 g de glucose
125 g de Nutella® • 5 g de beurre doux

- Mettez la crème fleurette, le sucre et le glucose dans une casserole. Faites cuire à feu doux en remuant de temps en temps, et utilisez un thermomètre à sucre pour vérifier la température : vous devez atteindre exactement 118 °C. Retirez la casserole du feu.
- Ajoutez le Nutella® et le beurre. Versez le mélange sur une feuille de papier sulfurisé, puis lissez la surface à l'aide d'une spatule, de façon à obtenir un caramel de 1,5 cm d'épaisseur.
- Laissez refroidir complètement, puis détaillez en carrés.
- Consommez rapidement.

Caramels aux amandes

Parsemez le caramel étalé sur le papier sulfurisé de 40 g d'amandes effilées tant qu'il est encore chaud.

Caramels en résille de chocolat blanc

Faites fondre 100 g de chocolat blanc, puis faites-le couler sur les caramels refroidis le long d'une cuillère à café, de façon à former des résilles de chocolat.

Caramels au café

Ajoutez 60 g de grains de café broyés et 2 c. à s. de café soluble dilué dans 1 c. à s. d'eau à la préparation, en même temps que le Nutella®.

Caramels à la fève tonka

Ajoutez 1 fève tonka broyée à la préparation, en même temps que le Nutella®.

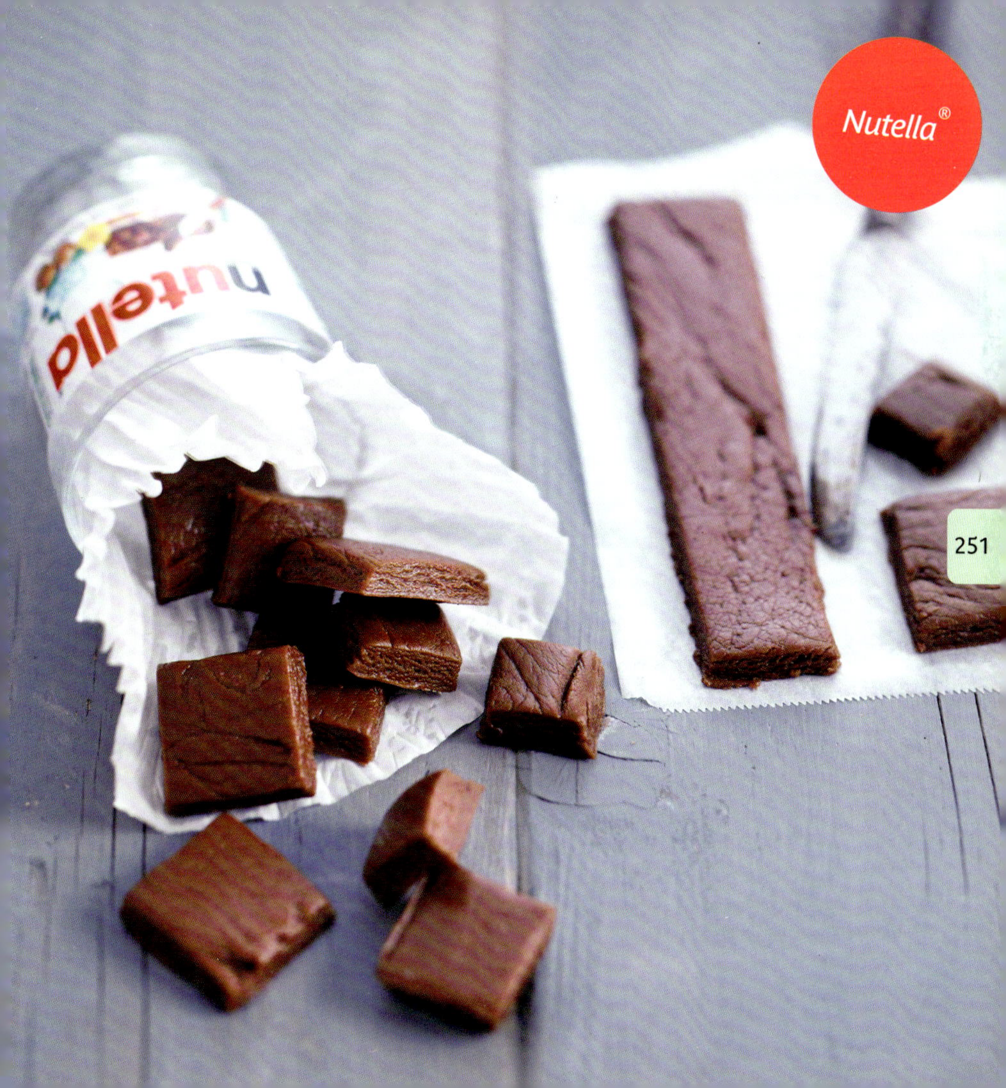
nutella

CUPCAKES AU NUTELLA®

Préparation : 10 min • **Cuisson :** 10 min • **Pour 6 personnes**

100 g de beurre ramolli • 100 g de sucre • 2 œufs • 100 g de farine
1/2 sachet de levure • 150 g de Nutella®

- Préchauffez le four à 180 °C.
- Détaillez le beurre en parcelles et mettez-le dans un saladier avec le sucre. Battez au fouet électrique, jusqu'à ce que le mélange blanchisse.
- Cassez 2 œufs dans un bol et battez-les légèrement. Versez-les et incorporez-les petit à petit à la préparation précédente. Ajoutez la farine et la levure. Mélangez.
- Déposez 8 caissettes en papier dans un moule à muffin et remplissez-les aux 2/3 de la préparation.
- Faites cuire au four pendant 10 min ou jusqu'à ce que les petits gâteaux soient dorés. Laissez refroidir.
- Remplissez une poche à douille de Nutella® et utilisez-le pour décorer la surface des cupcakes.

Cupcakes aux agrumes

Ajoutez le zeste et le jus de 2 citrons non traités dans la pâte à cupcakes. Vous pouvez également utiliser 1 orange ou 2 clémentines non traitées.

Cupcakes cœur Nutella®

Garnissez les caissettes en papier de pâte à moitié, déposez 1 c. à c. de Nutella® par-dessus, puis couvrez de pâte pour remplir les caissettes aux 2/3.

Cupcakes à la banane

Ajoutez la chair de 1 banane écrasée et 1/2 c. à c. de cannelle à la préparation.

Cupcakes meringués au Nutella®

Portez à ébullition 4 c. à s. d'eau avec 120 g de sucre en poudre, puis faites cuire à frémissements pendant 1 min. Montez 2 blancs d'œufs en neige, puis incorporez-y le sirop en filet, en fouettant sans cesse. Incorporez très délicatement 2 c. à s. de Nutella®. Ornez les cupcakes de meringue et passez rapidement sous le gril du four.

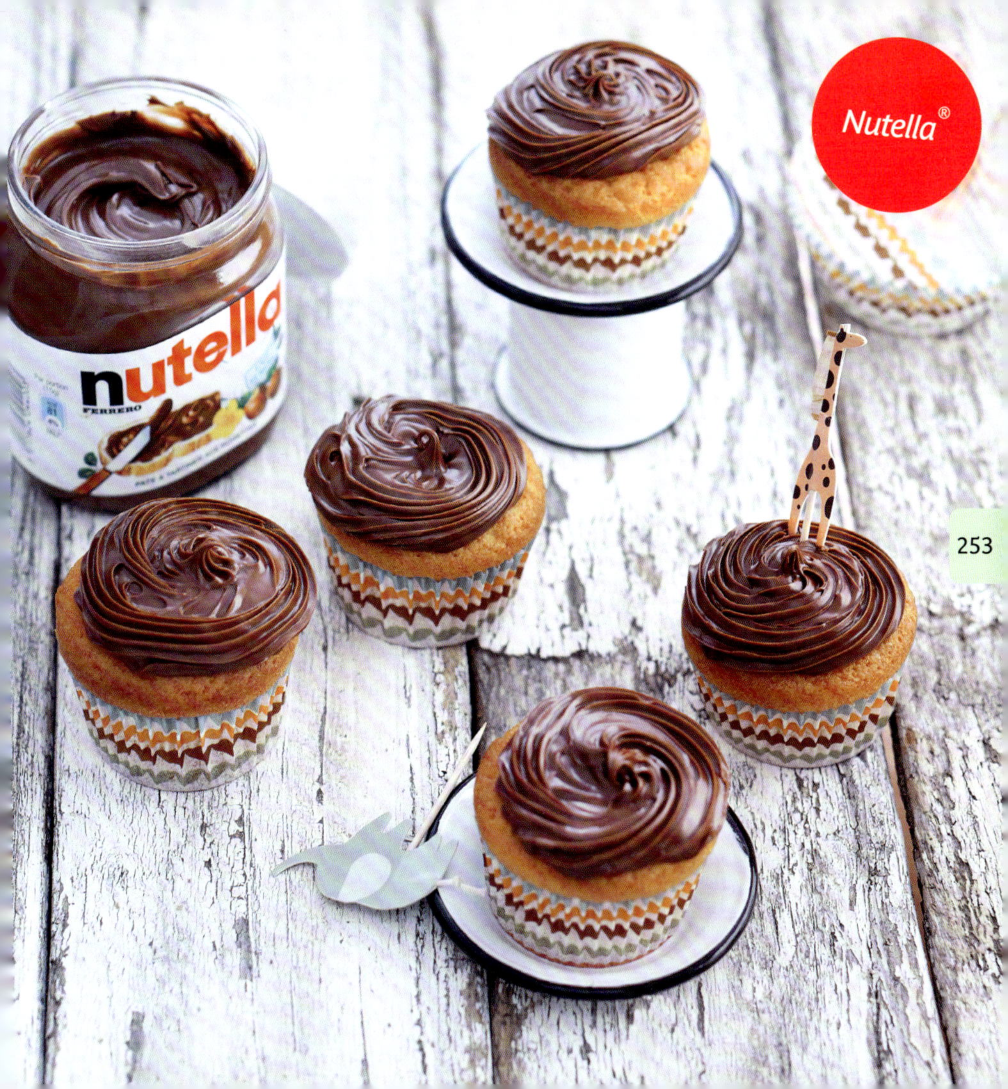
nutella
FERRERO

SMILEYS AU NUTELLA®

Préparation : 50 min • **Cuisson** : 10 min • **Réfrigération** : 2 h
Pour 10 personnes

150 g de beurre ramolli • 90 g de sucre glace • 1 gousse de vanille 1 œuf • 30 g de poudre d'amandes • 250 g de farine + un peu pour le plan de travail • 100 g de Nutella® • sel

- Préchauffez le four à 180 °C. Détaillez le beurre en parcelles. Mettez-le dans le bol d'un robot avec le sucre glace, 1 pincée de sel, la gousse de vanille et ses graines, l'œuf et la poudre d'amandes. Incorporez la farine, et mixez, jusqu'à l'obtention d'une pâte bien lisse.
- Formez une boule avec la pâte et enveloppez-la dans du film alimentaire. Aplatissez-la légèrement et réservez-la au réfrigérateur pendant 2 h.
- Farinez le plan de travail, déroulez la pâte au rouleau sur une épaisseur de 4 mm. Découpez-y des cercles de 5 cm environ de diamètre : la moitié avec un moule à smileys et l'autre moitié avec un cercle de dimension équivalente (ou découpez tout avec un emporte-pièce rond si vous n'avez pas de moule à smileys).
- Déposez tous les disques de pâte sur une plaque à pâtisserie recouverte de papier sulfurisé. Faites cuire au four pendant 10 min environ : les gâteaux doivent être très légèrement dorés.
- Tant que les biscuits sont encore chauds, déposez une noisette de Nutella® sur les disques pleins, et étalez-la légèrement, puis recouvrez avec les disques smileys. Appuyez délicatement pour que le Nutella® se répartisse bien. Laissez refroidir avant de servir.

Smileys au safran et au Nutella®
Ajoutez dans le bol du robot 1 dosette de safran en filaments préalablement réhydratés dans de l'eau chaude pendant 15 min.

Biscuits aux épices douces et au Nutella®
Ajoutez dans le bol du robot 1 c. à c. de clous de girofle en poudre, 1 c. à c. de cardamome en poudre, 1 c. à c. de gingembre en poudre et 1 c. à c. de cannelle en poudre.

Biscuits à la cassonade
Pour un goût plus prononcé, remplacez le sucre glace par de la cassonade.

Café aux épices
Portez à ébullition 50 cl d'eau avec 4 c. à s. de café moulu, 1 capsule de cardamome fendue en deux, 1 bâton de cannelle et 1 pincée de noix muscade. Laissez décanter, filtrez puis servez avec les smileys.

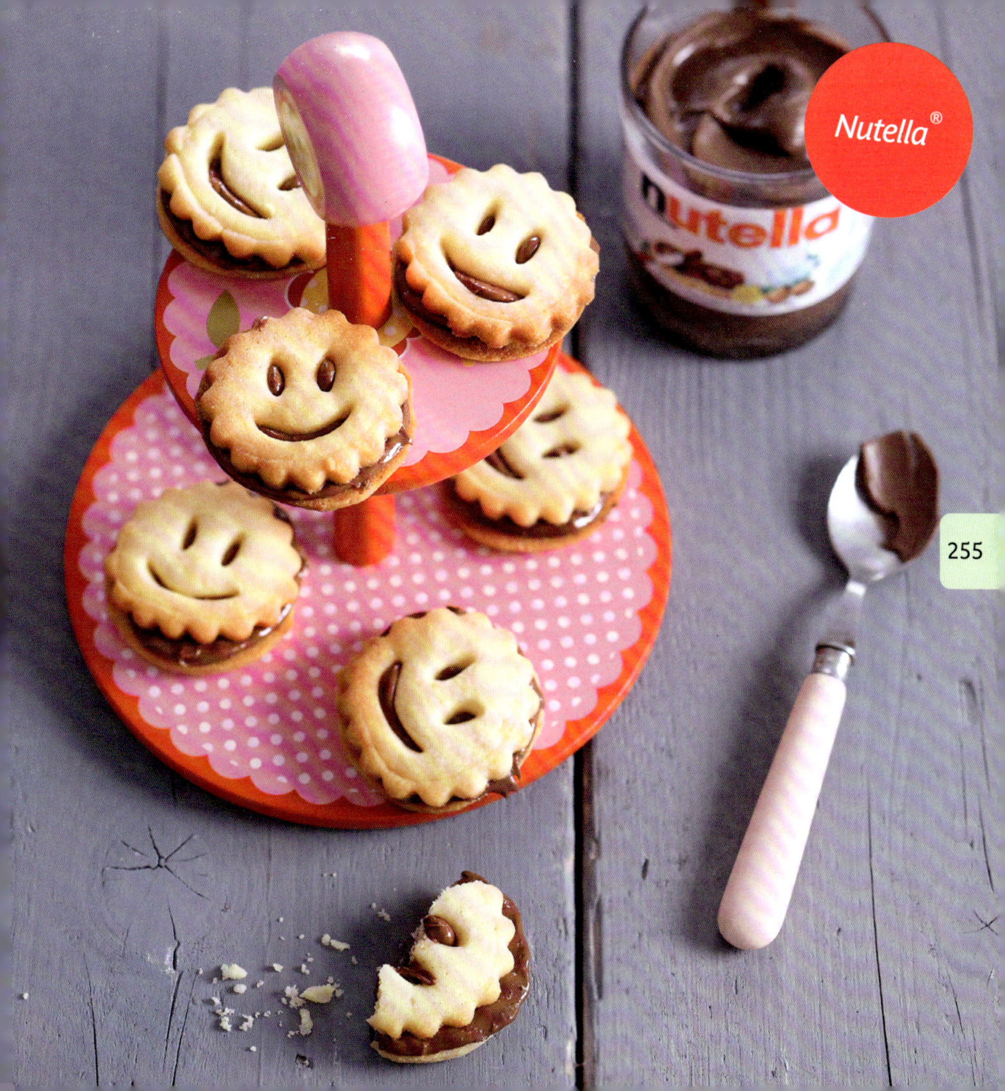
Nutella®
nutella

SOUFFLÉS AU NUTELLA®

Préparation : 10 min • **Cuisson** : 10 min • **Pour 4 personnes**

2 jaunes d'œufs • 70 g de sucre en poudre + un peu pour les moules
15 g de fécule de pomme de terre • 100 g de Nutella® • 15 cl de lait
4 blancs d'œufs • 5 g de beurre pour les ramequins

- Dans un saladier, mélangez les jaunes d'œufs et 10 g de sucre. Incorporez ensuite la fécule de pomme de terre et le Nutella®.
- Faites bouillir le lait dans une casserole, puis versez-le sur la préparation précédente. Reversez le tout dans la casserole et portez à ébullition sans cesser de remuer, de manière à obtenir la consistance d'une crème pâtissière. Laissez refroidir.
- Préchauffez le four à 180 °C.
- Montez les blancs d'œufs en neige ferme, puis ajoutez progressivement le reste du sucre. Prélevez 1 c. à s. des blancs en neige et incorporez-la à la crème pour la détendre. Versez cette préparation sur le reste des blancs, et incorporez-les très délicatement à l'aide d'une spatule.
- Beurrez les ramequins et sucrez-les, puis retournez-les pour ôter l'excédent. Garnissez-les aux 3/4 de la préparation.
- Faites cuire au four pendant 10 min environ.
- Servez dès la sortie du four, car les soufflés retombent assez vite.

Soufflés au Nutella® et à la noix de coco

Ajoutez 20 g de noix de coco râpée à la préparation. Parsemez les soufflés de noix de coco râpée juste avant de servir.

Soufflés au Nutella® au Grand Marnier

Ajoutez 15 cl de Grand Marnier à la préparation, en même temps que les jaunes d'œufs.

Coulis de framboises

Préparez un sirop avec 200 g de sucre et 20 cl d'eau. Mixez 500 g de framboises avec ce sirop. Passez au tamis, laissez refroidir et servez avec les soufflés.

Granité au café

Mélangez 20 cl de café fort avec 2 c. à c. de sucre roux, 2 c. à c. de crème liquide et 1 c. à c. d'armagnac. Versez dans un récipient supportant le froid et mettez au congélateur pour 6 h. Grattez toutes les 2 h avec les dents d'une fourchette. Servez avec les soufflés.

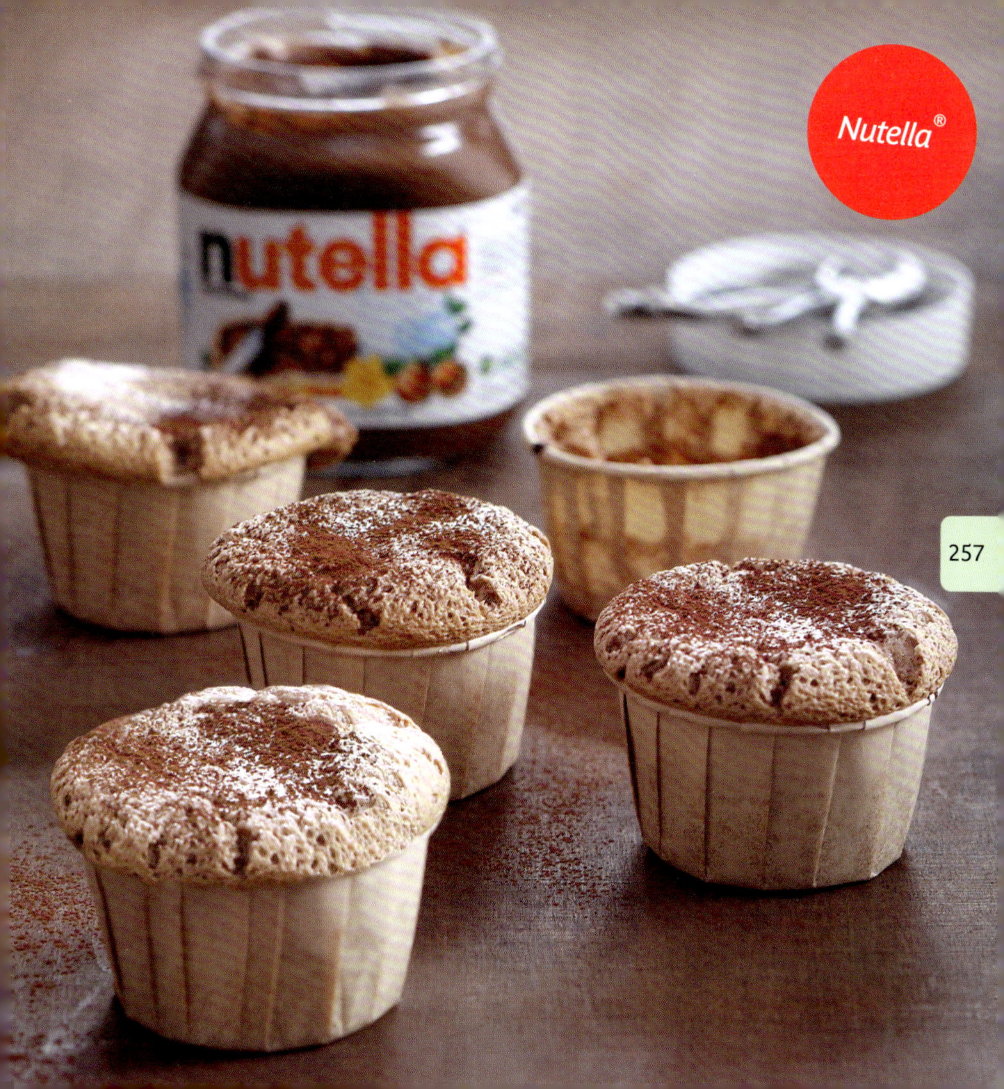

Nutella®

CAFÉ FRAPPÉ AUX OREO®

Préparation : 10 min • **Cuisson :** aucune • **Pour 2 personnes**

café • 2 morceaux de sucre • 6 boules de glace à la vanille • 6 glaçons
6 Oreo® • chantilly • cacao amer

- Préparez 2 tasses de café noir.
- Ajoutez le sucre, remuez, puis laissez refroidir.
- Mettez le café sucré dans un blender avec la glace et les glaçons.
- Mixez jusqu'à ce que les glaçons soient pilés.
- Répartissez le mélange dans 2 grands verres.
- Cassez grossièrement les Oreo®, puis ajoutez les morceaux dans les verres.
- Nappez rapidement de chantilly et saupoudrez de cacao amer.
- Servez sans attendre.

Chicorée frappée
Remplacez le café par de la chicorée nature ou au chocolat. Vous pouvez également préparer une boisson en utilisant du café et de la chicorée à parts égales.

Café frappé au caramel
Remplacez la glace à la vanille par de la glace au caramel au beurre salé. Parsemez les cafés frappés d'éclats de caramel (en épicerie fine).

Café frappé aromatisé
Ajoutez 5 cl de cognac à la préparation. Vous pouvez également utiliser de l'amaretto.

Thé frappé aux Oreo®
Remplacez le café noir par 2 tasses de thé à la bergamote.

Oreo®

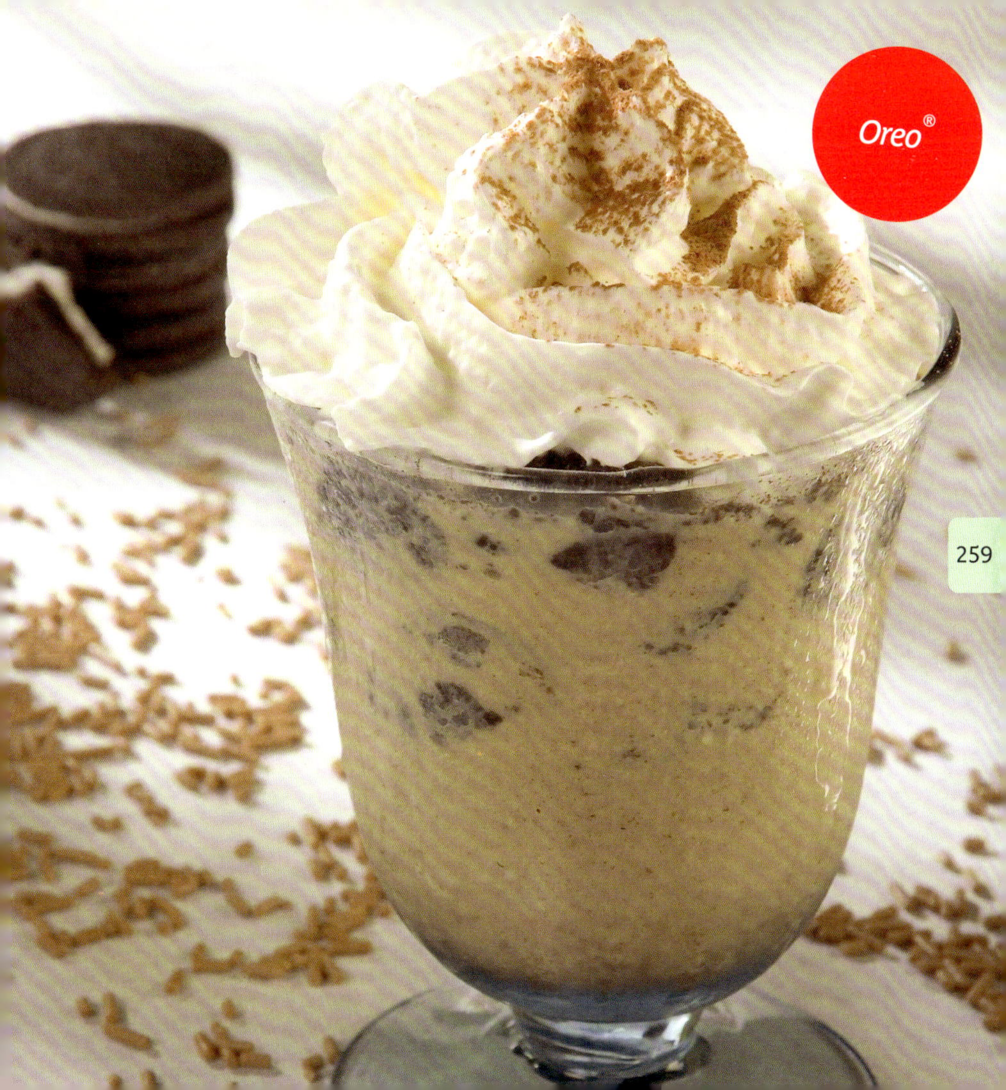

CUPCAKES AUX OREO®

Préparation : 25 min • **Cuisson** : 20 min • **Pour 9 cupcakes**

pour les cupcakes : *110 g de beurre ramolli • 70 g de sucre en poudre*
1 sachet de sucre vanillé • 2 œufs • 100 g de farine
1 sachet de levure chimique • 18 miniOreo® • 150 g de chocolat noir
1 c. à c. de cacao amer
pour le glaçage : *100 g de beurre ramolli • 2 c. à s. de lait*
150 g de sucre glace

- Préchauffez le four à 180 °C. Pour les cupcakes, battez au fouet le beurre, le sucre et le sucre vanillé, jusqu'à ce que le mélange blanchisse. Incorporez les œufs et battez de nouveau avant d'incorporer la farine et la levure.
- Mettez 9 miniOreo® dans un sac à congélation et fermez-le. Écrasez-les grossièrement à l'aide d'un rouleau à pâtisserie. Incorporez le tout à la préparation et mélangez.
- Cassez le chocolat en morceaux, puis faites-les fondre à feu doux au bain-marie. Ajoutez-les à la préparation et mélangez bien.
- Déposez 9 caissettes en papier dans les alvéoles d'un moule à muffin, puis garnissez-les aux 2/3 du mélange. Faites cuire au four pendant 20 min.
- Pour le glaçage, travaillez le beurre à l'aide d'une cuillère en bois jusqu'à ce qu'il blanchisse, puis ajoutez le lait petit à petit. Incorporez le sucre glace progressivement. Battez au fouet.
- Sortez les cupcakes du four et laissez-les refroidir complètement avant de les décorer avec le glaçage, que vous déposerez à l'aide d'une poche à douille. Déposez 1 miniOreo® sur chaque cupcake, parsemez de cacao amer, et servez.

Cupcakes blancs à la ricotta
Remplacez le beurre par 150 g de ricotta, et le chocolat noir par du chocolat blanc.

Cupcakes aux abricots et aux Oreo®
Ajoutez 6 abricots secs coupés en dés à la préparation. Vous pouvez aussi utiliser des figues séchées.

Glaçage au mascarpone et aux Oreo®
Mélangez 200 g de mascarpone avec 2 c. à s. de sucre glace et 2 Oreo® réduits en poudre. Glacez les cupcakes cuits et refroidis avec ce mélange.

Glaçage à la noix de coco
Mélangez 100 g de sucre glace avec 2 c. à s. de crème fraîche et 3 c. à s. de noix de coco râpée. Glacez les cupcakes cuits et refroidis avec ce mélange.

Oreo®

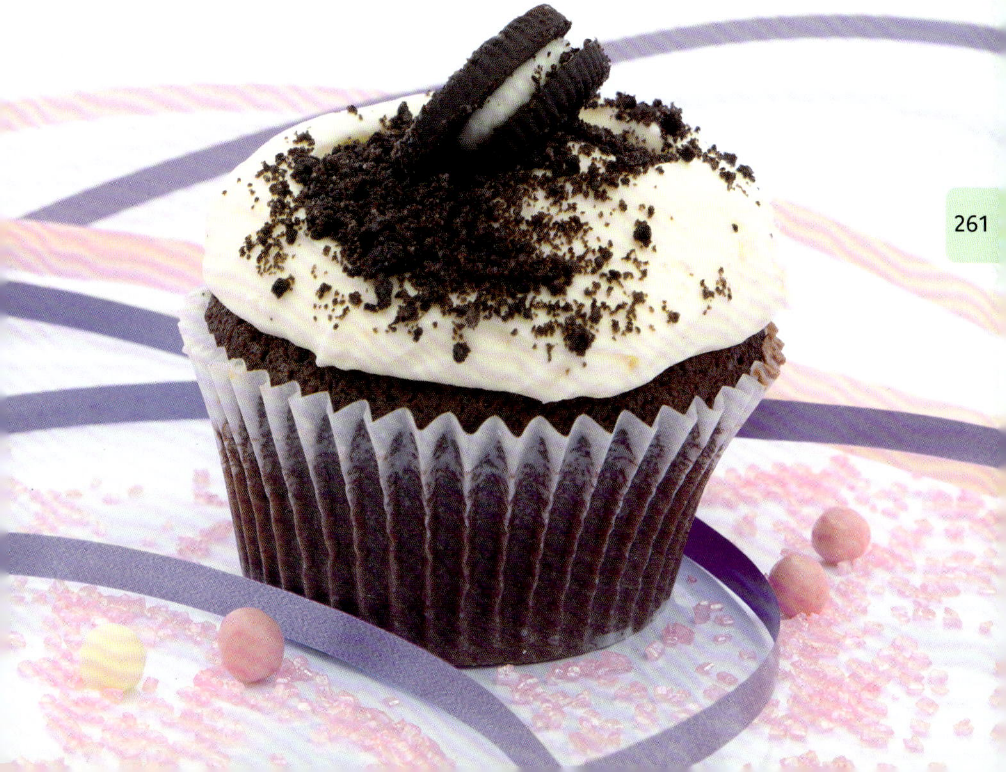

GÂTEAU AU YAOURT ET AUX OREO®

Préparation : 10 min • **Cuisson :** 35 min • **Pour 1 gâteau**

4 œufs • 1 yaourt brassé nature • 1 c. à s. d'huile de tournesol
240 g de sucre en poudre • le jus de 1/2 citron • 360 g de farine
1/2 sachet de levure chimique • beurre pour le moule
8 à 10 Oreo® • sel

- Préchauffez le four à 180 °C.
- Dans un saladier, battez les œufs au fouet.
- Ajoutez le yaourt et fouettez, puis versez l'huile et fouettez de nouveau.
- Incorporez le sucre, sans cesser de fouetter, puis le jus de citron. Ajoutez enfin la farine, la levure et 1 pincée de sel. Mélangez bien.
- Versez la moitié de la préparation dans un moule à manqué beurré. Déposez les Oreo® par-dessus, en les plaçant côte à côte de façon à couvrir la surface, puis couvrez du reste de pâte.
- Faites cuire au four pendant 35 min.
- Laissez refroidir sur une grille avant de déguster.

Gâteau au yaourt aux trois farines

Utilisez 120 g de farine de châtaigne, 120 g de farine complète et 120 g de farine de riz ou de blé.

Gâteau aux pommes et au fromage blanc

Remplacez le yaourt par 120 g de fromage blanc. Ajoutez 2 pommes pelées, épépinées et râpées à la préparation.

Gâteau aux carottes et au yaourt

Remplacez la moitié de la farine par 200 g de carottes râpées. Remplacez le sucre par de la cassonade, et ajoutez 2 c. à c. de gingembre en poudre.

Glaçage au fromage frais

Battez au fouet 150 g de fromage frais et 100 g de mascarpone. Incorporez au fouet 3 gouttes d'extrait de vanille liquide et 400 g de sucre en poudre. Nappez le gâteau refroidi de ce glaçage.

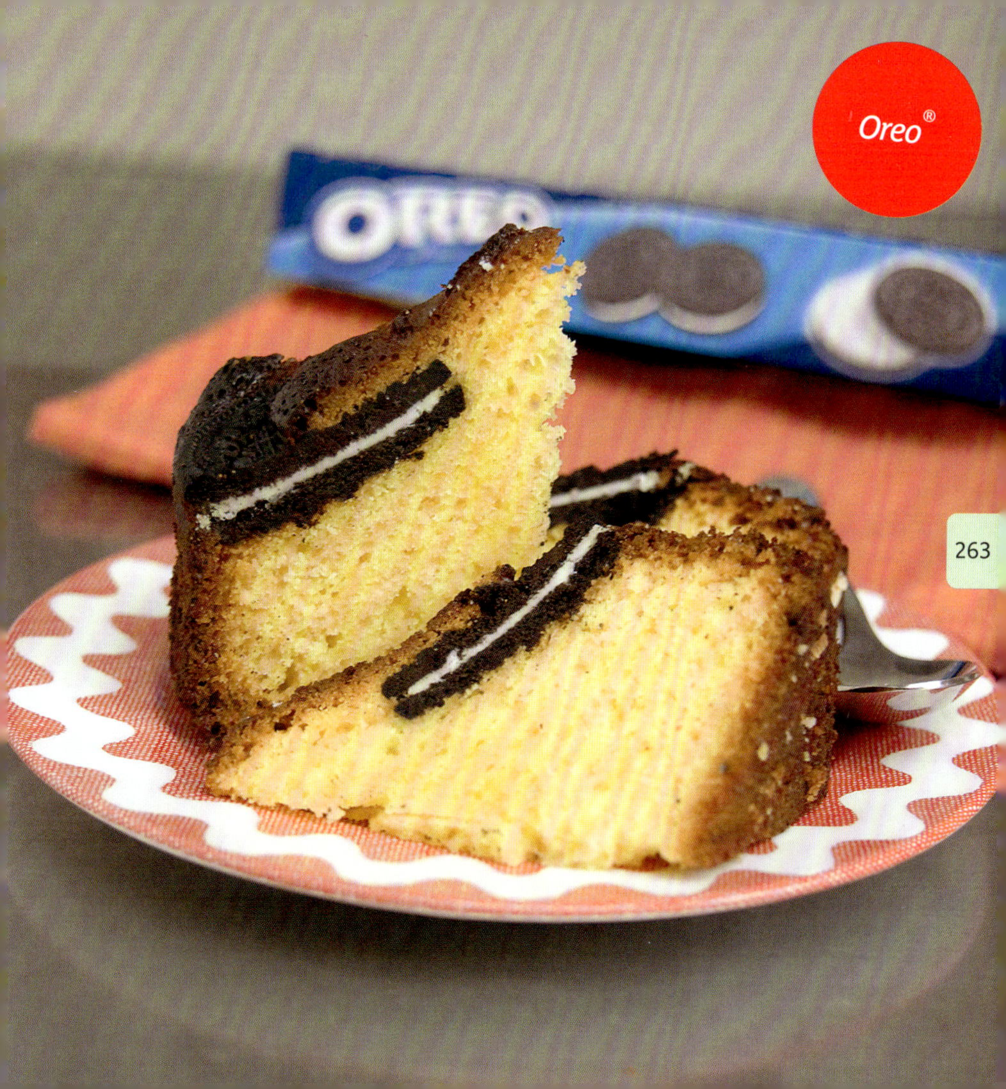
OREO

Penne Barilla®

GRATIN DE PENNE À LA FETA ET AU POTIRON

Préparation : 15 min • **Cuisson** : 55 min • **Pour 6 personnes**

500 g de potiron • 6 gousses d'ail • 250 g de lardons fumés
2 c. à s. d'huile • 400 g de penne Barilla® • 100 g de feta
40 g de persil • 50 g de mozzarella • sel

- Préchauffez le four à 180 °C.
- Coupez la chair du potiron en dés. Épluchez les gousses d'ail.
- Mettez les dés de potiron dans une sauteuse avec les lardons, les gousses d'ail entières et 1 c. à s. d'huile. Remuez bien, puis faites cuire à feu doux de 30 à 40 min, jusqu'à ce que le potiron soit tendre. Écrasez ensuite les gousses d'ail.
- Faites cuire les penne Barilla® al dente dans une casserole d'eau bouillante salée.
- Pendant ce temps, émiettez grossièrement la feta. Rincez le persil, essuyez-le sur du papier absorbant, puis ciselez-le. Râpez la mozzarella.
- Égouttez les pâtes, en réservant 25 cl d'eau de cuisson. Mélangez-les avec la préparation au potiron, la feta, et mettez le tout dans un plat à gratin. Versez l'eau de cuisson et la mozzarella râpée.
- Faites cuire au four pendant 25 min, puis parsemez de persil ciselé.
- Servez chaud.

Gratin de penne à la courge musquée
Remplacez le potiron par de la courge musquée. Vous pouvez aussi utiliser du potimarron.

Gratin de penne aux légumes d'été
Remplacez le potiron par 1 poivron, 1 aubergine et 2 courgettes lavés et taillés en dés, revenus à la sauteuse. Ajoutez 20 cl de coulis de tomates et 1 c. à s. d'herbes de Provence.

Gratin de penne au poireau et au chèvre
Remplacez le potiron par 500 g de blancs de poireau finement émincés, que vous ferez cuire à la sauteuse avec 2 échalotes hachées. Remplacez la feta par 2 crottins de Chavignol émiettés. Ajoutez, éventuellement, 1 c. à s. de pignons de pin grillés. Supprimez les lardons et le persil.

Gratin de penne au brocoli
Remplacez la préparation à base de potiron par 600 g de brocolis cuits à la vapeur. Remplacez la feta et la mozzarella par 1 brique de béchamel, et parsemez de parmesan râpé avant d'enfourner.

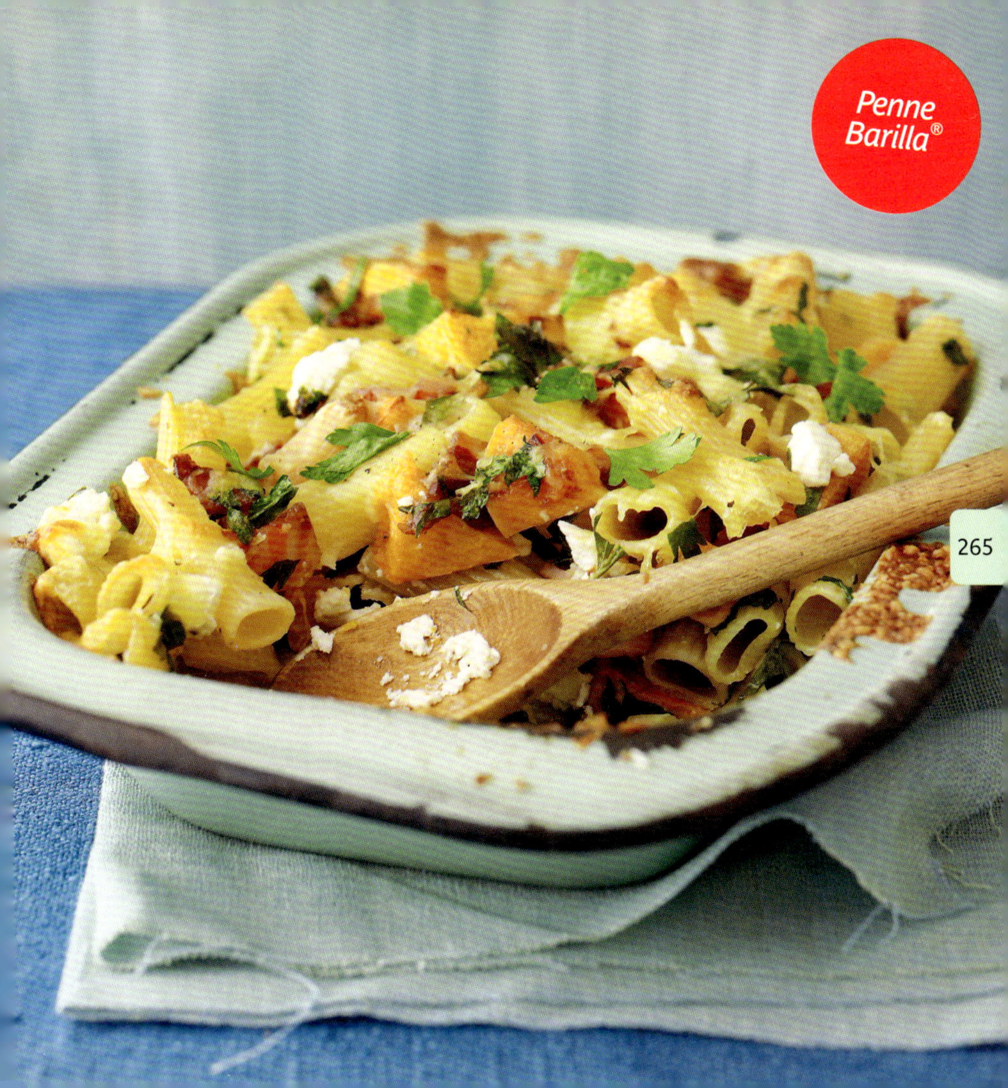
Penne
Barilla®

PENNE AU CHORIZO ET À LA MIMOLETTE

Préparation : 15 min • **Cuisson** : 20 min • **Pour 4 personnes**

1 gros oignon • 1 gousse d'ail • 2 c. à s. d'huile d'olive • 2 tomates 100 g de chorizo • 400 g de penne Barilla® • 100 g de mimolette jeune 200 g de crème fraîche épaisse • sel

- Épluchez l'oignon et l'ail. Émincez l'oignon et hachez l'ail.
- Faites-les revenir à la poêle avec l'huile d'olive jusqu'à ce qu'ils soient translucides.
- Pendant ce temps, lavez les tomates, épépinez-les et taillez-les en petits dés.
- Pelez le chorizo et coupez-le en rondelles.
- Ajoutez-les dans la poêle et faites cuire en remuant de 7 à 8 min.
- En parallèle, faites cuire les penne Barilla® dans une grande quantité d'eau bouillante salée.
- Détaillez la mimolette en copeaux.
- Juste avant de servir, ajoutez la crème fraîche dans la poêle. Laissez chauffer pendant 2 min, sans laisser bouillir.
- Égouttez les penne Barilla®, puis répartissez-les dans des assiettes creuses. Versez la sauce au chorizo par-dessus. Parsemez de copeaux de mimolette.
- Servez sans attendre.

Penne au chorizo et aux poivrons

Faites revenir 2 poivrons rouges taillés en dés à la poêle avec de l'huile d'olive. Ajoutez-les à la préparation. Remplacez la crème fraîche par 1 boîte de tomates concassées.

Penne à la pancetta et aux tomates séchées

Remplacez le chorizo par de la pancetta taillée en lamelles, et les tomates fraîches par 150 g de tomates séchées taillées en dés. Doublez la quantité de crème fraîche.

Penne au thon et au maïs

Remplacez le chorizo par 1 boîte de thon au naturel. Ajoutez 100 g de maïs doux en boîte égoutté, en même temps que la crème fraîche.

Penne au thon et aux câpres

Reprenez la recette ci-dessus en remplaçant le maïs par 2 c. à s. de câpres en saumure. Remplacez la crème fraîche par du coulis de tomates.

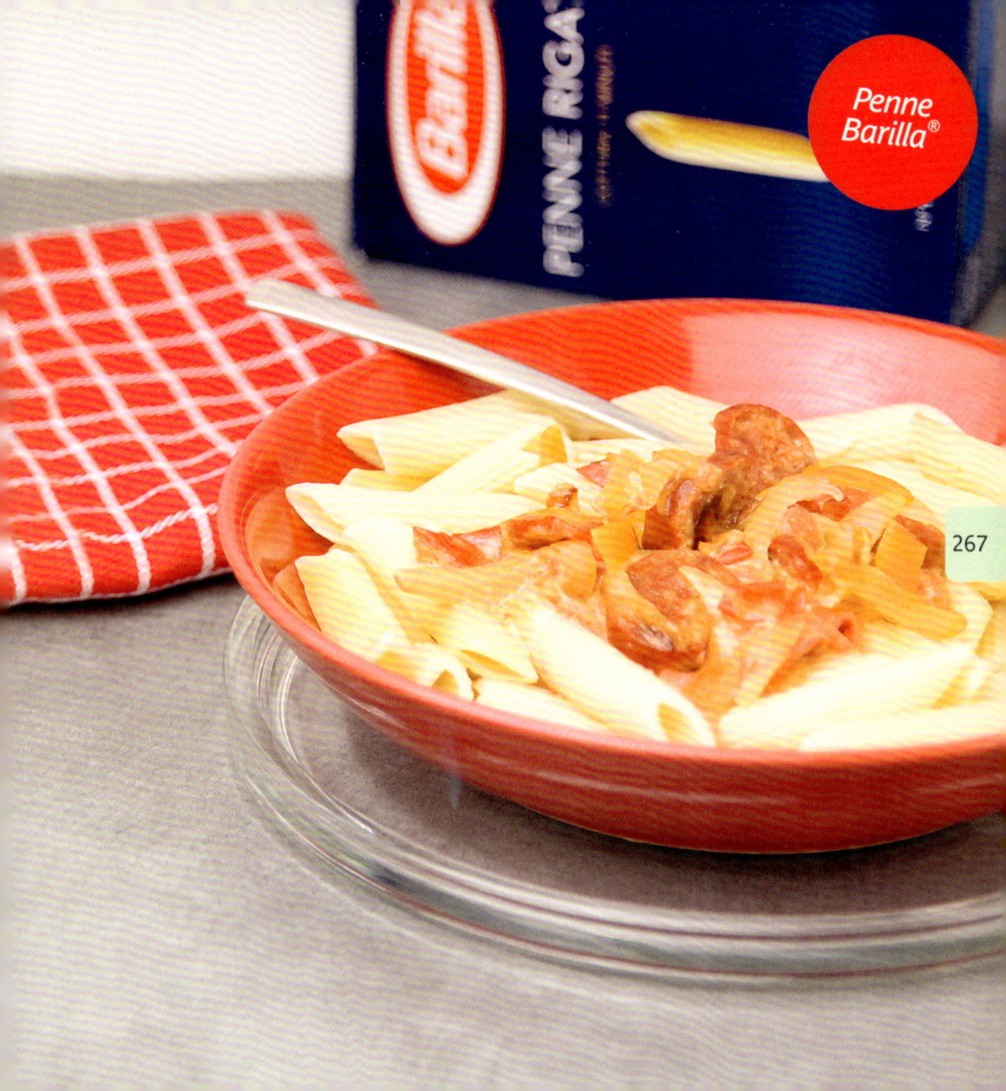
Penne
Barilla®

PENNE AU SAUMON ET AUX ASPERGES

Préparation : 15 min • **Cuisson** : 8 min • **Pour 2 personnes**

200 g de penne Barilla® • 100 g d'asperges • 200 g de filet de saumon sans la peau • le jus et le zeste de 1/2 citron non traité • 2 c. à s. de sauce hollandaise • parmesan râpé, pour accompagner • sel et poivre

- Faites cuire les penne Barilla® al dente dans une grande casserole d'eau bouillante salée.
- Pendant ce temps, rincez les asperges, puis coupez-les en tronçons de 2,5 cm. Détaillez le saumon en dés.
- Faites-les pocher dans de l'eau bouillante salée pendant 4 min.
- Mélangez le jus et le zeste de citron avec la sauce hollandaise dans un saladier. Poivrez.
- Égouttez les pâtes, puis mélangez-les avec la sauce hollandaise, le saumon et les asperges. Salez et poivrez.
- Parsemez de parmesan râpé et servez sans attendre.

Penne au saumon et au mascarpone

Remplacez la sauce hollandaise par 100 g de mascarpone mélangé avec 25 cl de crème fleurette et 10 brins de ciboulette ciselés.

Penne à la truite et aux épinards

Remplacez le filet de saumon par des filets de truite et les asperges par 4 grosses poignées d'épinards frais bien nettoyés. Faites-les pocher pendant 2 min.

Penne au saumon fumé et à l'orange

Remplacez le saumon frais par du saumon fumé, et les asperges par 2 oranges séparées en quartiers, le tout cru. Supprimez la sauce hollandaise et arrosez de vinaigrette. Parsemez de baies roses.

Penne au poulet et aux petits pois

Remplacez le saumon par du poulet taillé en lamelles et revenu à l'huile d'olive à la poêle. Remplacez les asperges par 100 g de petits pois cuits à l'eau. Utilisez de la crème fraîche épaisse à la place de la sauce hollandaise.

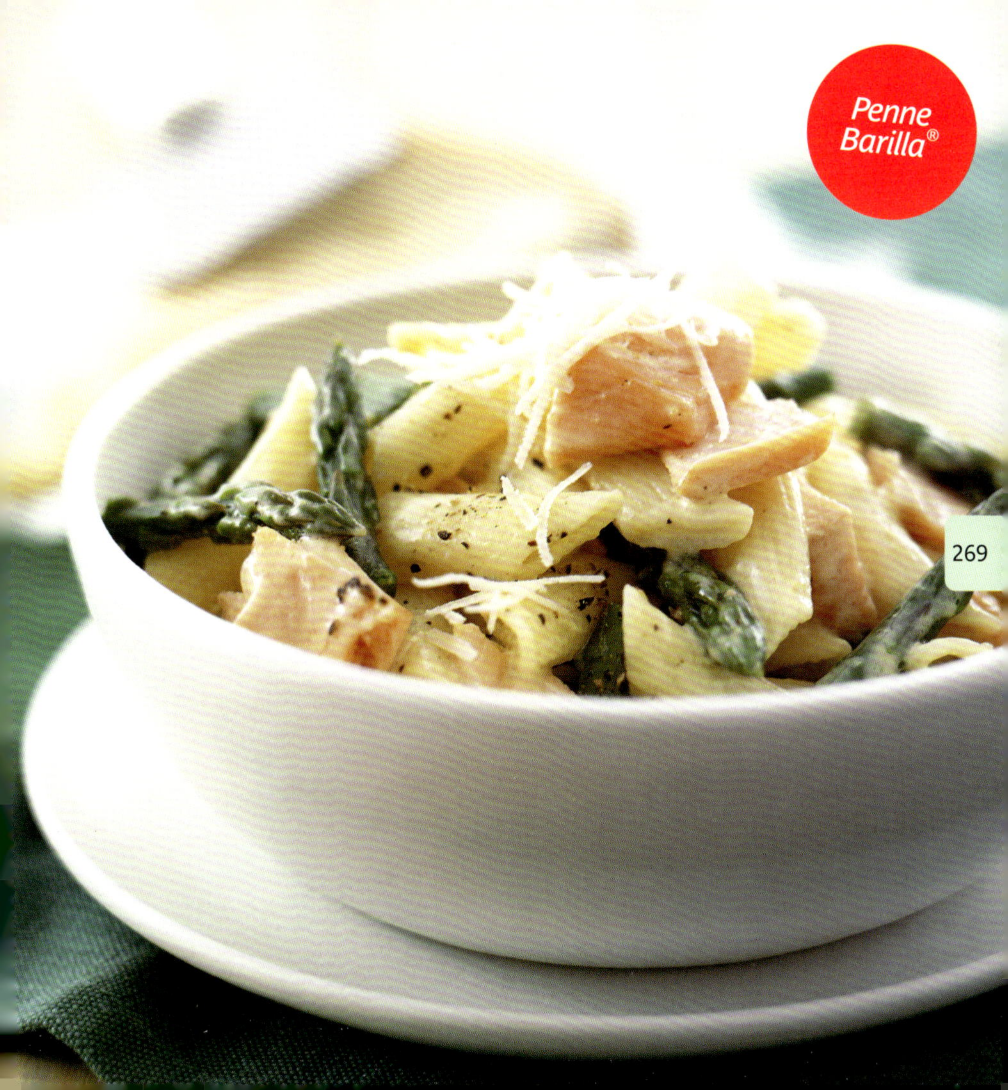
Penne Barilla®

PENNE AUX ÉPINARDS ET AU BACON

Préparation : 10 min • **Cuisson** : 15 min • **Pour 4 personnes**

400 g de penne Barilla® • 5 tranches de bacon • 4 gousses d'ail
2 piments oiseaux • 100 g de jeunes pousses d'épinards
2 c. à s. d'huile • le zeste et le jus de 1 petit citron non traité
parmesan râpé • sel

- Faites cuire les penne Barilla® dans une grande casserole d'eau bouillante.
- Pendant ce temps, taillez le bacon en morceaux. Épluchez les gousses d'ail et hachez-les. Rincez les piments, puis émincez-les. Rincez les jeunes pousses d'épinards.
- Faites chauffer 1 c. à s. d'huile dans une poêle à feu moyen. Faites-y cuire le bacon pendant 3 min environ, jusqu'à ce qu'il soit bien doré et croustillant.
- Ajoutez l'ail et le piment, et poursuivez la cuisson pendant 1 min environ. Ajoutez le zeste et le jus du citron, et laissez mijoter pendant encore 1 min.
- Égouttez les pâtes en réservant 12 cl d'eau de cuisson.
- Mettez les penne Barilla® dans la poêle. Ajoutez le jus de cuisson, le reste d'huile et les épinards. Mélangez bien. Laissez mijoter jusqu'à ce que les jeunes pousses d'épinards soient bien tendres.
- Salez, puis répartissez dans des assiettes. Servez parsemé de parmesan râpé.

Penne aux tomates cerises et au basilic

Remplacez le bacon par 150 g de tomates cerises coupées en deux, et les pousses d'épinards par des feuilles de basilic fraîches.

Penne aux tomates séchées et à la roquette

Remplacez les piments oiseaux par 50 g de tomates séchées, le citron par 1 c. à s. d'origan séché. Supprimez les pousses d'épinards. Parsemez les pâtes de feuilles de roquette fraîches.

Penne au bacon et au chèvre

Supprimez l'ail et le piment. Ajoutez 100 g de bûche de chèvre émiettée dans la poêle en même temps que les épinards.

Penne au bacon et au persil frit

Plongez 1 bouquet de persil frisé dans de l'eau bouillante pendant 15 s, puis égouttez-le et placez-le dans un bol avec des glaçons. Essuyez-le, puis ciselez-le. Faites-le frire à l'huile pendant quelques secondes. Parsemez les pâtes de persil frit.

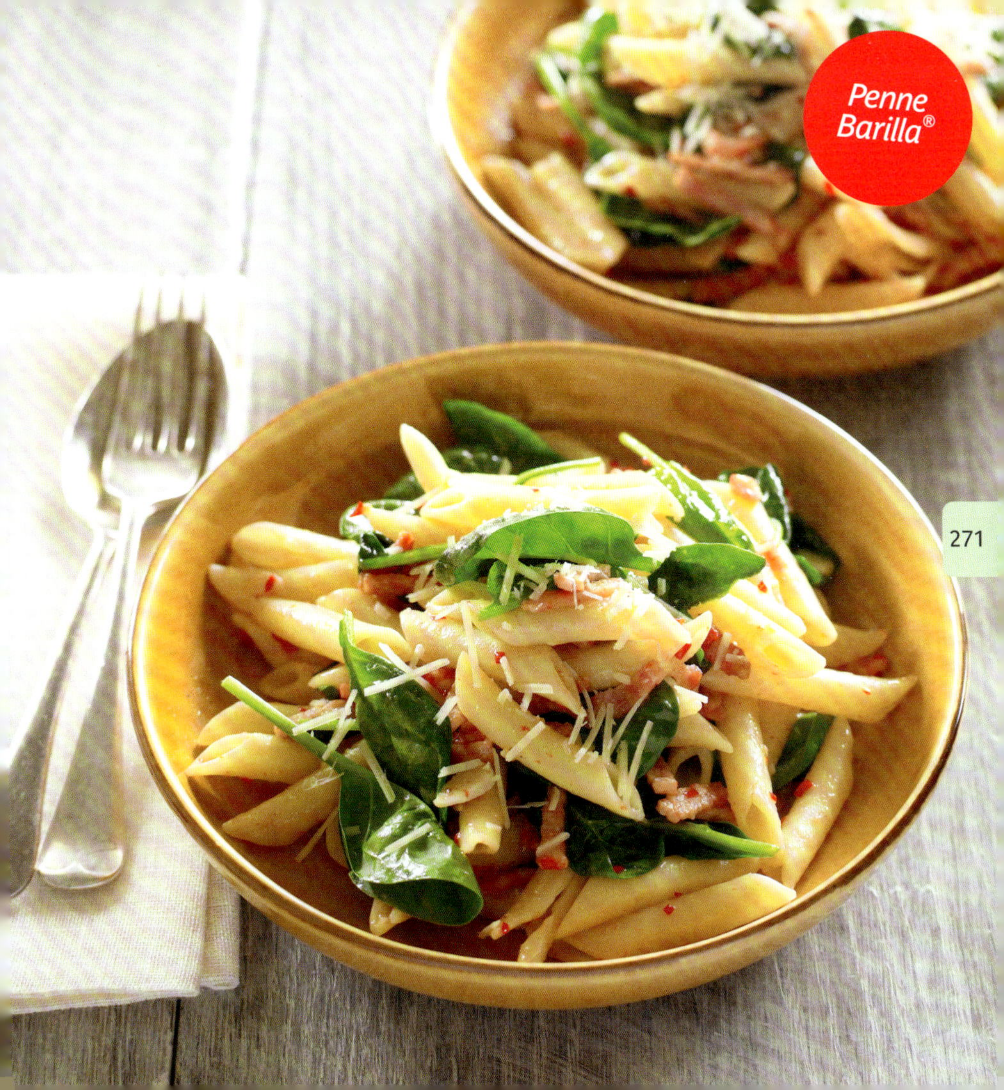
Penne
Barilla®

Salade de penne aux langoustines et au mesclun
Remplacez les crevettes par des langoustines, et les jeunes pousses d'épinards par du mesclun.

Salade de penne aux crevettes et au gorgonzola
Remplacez les jeunes pousses d'épinards par 125 g de gorgonzola taillé en morceaux. À défaut, vous pouvez utiliser de la fourme d'Ambert.

Salade de penne aux légumes grillés
Remplacez les tomates fraîches et les jeunes pousses d'épinards par 60 g d'aubergine grillée et 60 g de courgette grillée taillées en dés.

Salade de penne aux crevettes panées
Passez les crevettes dans de l'œuf battu, puis dans de la chapelure croustillante, avant de les faire revenir à la poêle. Vous pouvez aussi utiliser des lamelles de poulet.

SALADE DE PENNE AUX CREVETTES

Préparation : 15 min • **Cuisson :** 13 min • **Pour 4 personnes**

400 g de penne Barilla® • 3 c. à s. d'huile d'olive • 400 g de crevettes cuites • 1 échalote • 2 poignées de jeunes pousses d'épinards • 2 tomates • 50 g de pignons de pin • 1 c. à s. de vinaigre balsamique • sel et poivre

- Faites cuire les penne Barilla® dans une grande casserole d'eau bouillante salée. Égouttez-les, puis mettez-les dans un saladier. Arrosez-les de 1 c. à s. d'huile d'olive et remuez bien. Laissez refroidir complètement.
- Décortiquez les crevettes. Épluchez l'échalote et hachez-la finement. Rincez les jeunes pousses d'épinards, puis essorez-les. Lavez les tomates, puis taillez-les en petits dés. Faites griller les pignons de pin à sec dans une poêle.
- Faites revenir l'échalote dans une poêle avec 1 c. à s. d'huile d'olive. Au bout de 3 minutes, ajoutez les crevettes et faites chauffer en remuant pendant 2 min.
- Ajoutez ce mélange aux pâtes refroidies. Incorporez les dés de tomate, les jeunes pousses d'épinards et les pignons grillés. Salez et poivrez.
- Mélangez le vinaigre balsamique et l'huile d'olive restante. Arrosez la salade de vinaigrette, et mélangez bien avant de servir.

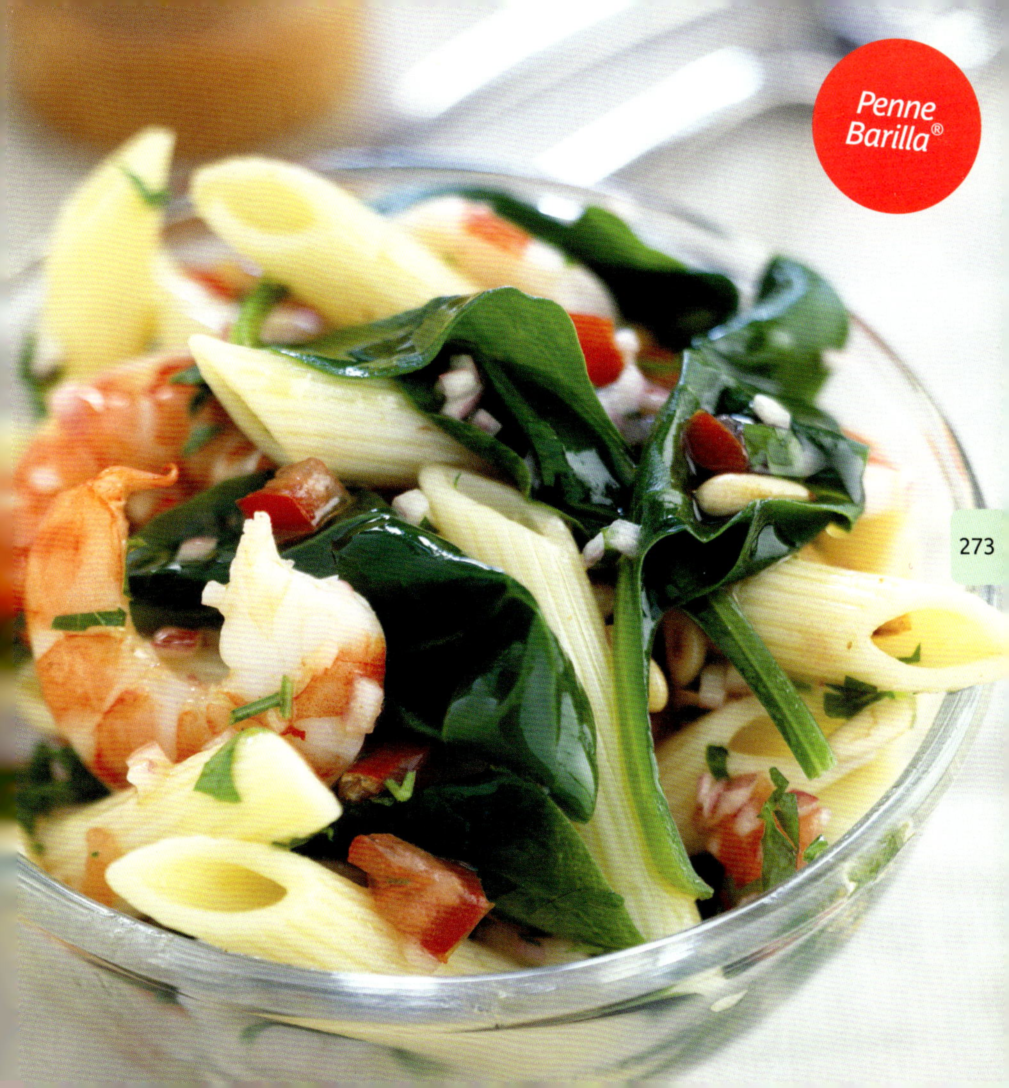
Penne Barilla®

GRATIN DE PÊCHES AUX PETITS BEURRE

Préparation : 10 min • **Cuisson :** 25 min • **Pour 4 personnes**

6 à 8 pêches (selon leur taille) • 150 g de petits beurre Lu® 40 g de poudre d'amandes • 80 g de beurre ramolli 40 g de sucre roux en poudre • 1 sachet de sucre vanillé

- Préchauffez le four à 180 °C.
- Pelez les pêches, dénoyautez-les et coupez-les en morceaux. Répartissez-les dans 4 moules à crème brûlée.
- Mettez les petits beurre Lu® dans un grand sac à congélation et fermez-le.
- Écrasez-les grossièrement à l'aide d'un rouleau à pâtisserie.
- Mettez les miettes dans un saladier, puis ajoutez la poudre d'amandes, le beurre et les sucres. Mélangez bien.
- Répartissez la préparation sur les pêches.
- Faites cuire au four de 20 à 25 min.
- Servez sans attendre.

Gratin de pêches au caramel
Faites un caramel avec 50 g de sucre en poudre et 1 c. à s. d'eau dans une poêle. Arrosez les pêches de caramel avant d'ajouter la préparation à base de petits beurre.

Gratin de fruits rouges aux petits beurre
Remplacez les pêches par 600 g de fruits rouges mélangés surgelés. Ajoutez 1 œuf à la préparation à base de petits beurre.

Gratin de pêches aux noisettes
Remplacez la poudre d'amandes par de la poudre de noisettes, et ajoutez 50 g de noisettes grossièrement concassées aux pêches.

Gratin de pêches au miel au romarin
Faites chauffer 4 c. à s. de miel liquide avec 2 brins de romarin. Arrosez les pêches de miel au romarin avant d'ajouter la préparation à base de petits beurre.

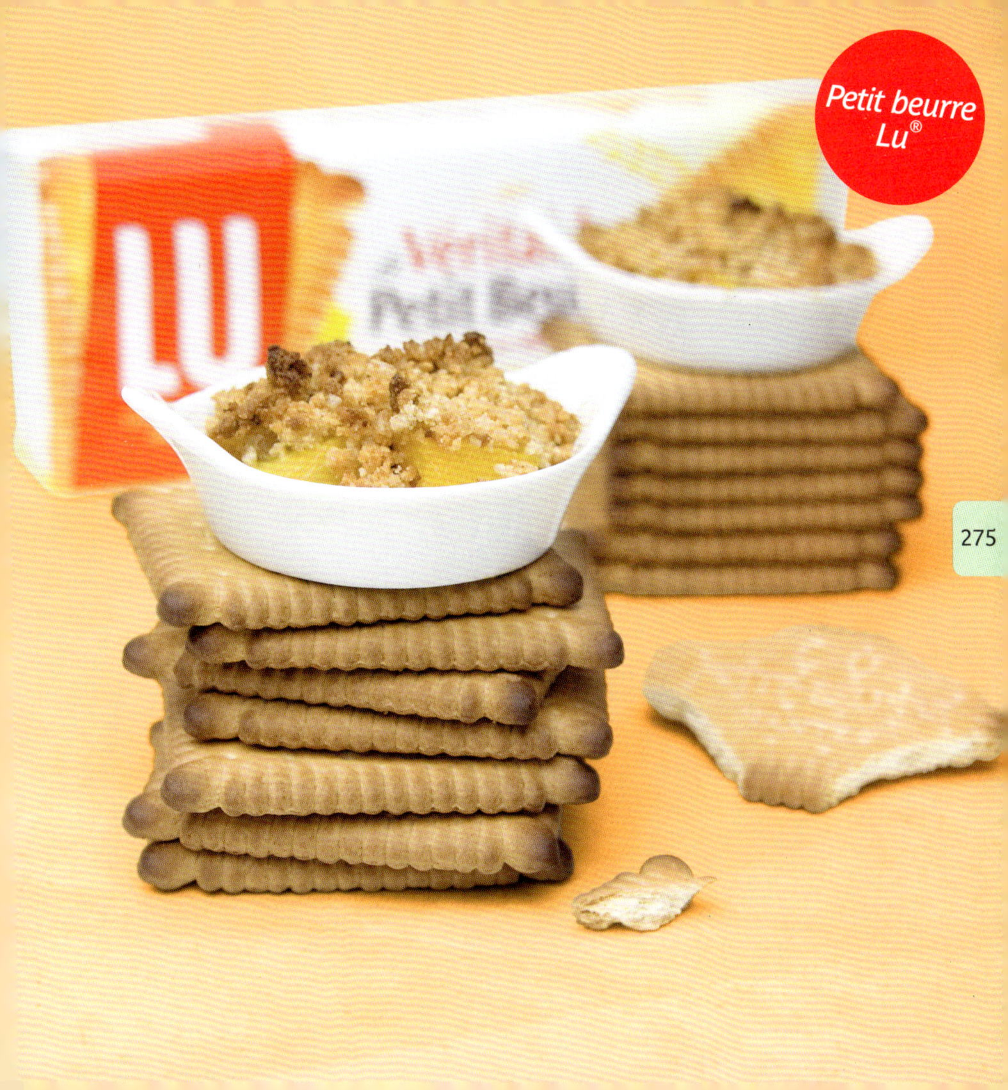
Petit beurre Lu®

SANDWICHES GLACÉS AUX PETITS BEURRE

Préparation : 5 min • **Cuisson :** aucune • **Réfrigération :** 1 h
Pour 6 personnes

24 petits beurre Lu® • 50 cl de sorbet à la fraise
50 cl de sorbet au citron

- Nappez 6 petits beurre Lu® d'une belle épaisseur de sorbet à la fraise. Recouvrez avec 6 autres petits beurre Lu®. Appuyez légèrement, puis lissez les bords de la glace à l'aide d'une spatule ou d'une petite cuillère.
- Faites de même avec les 12 petits beurre Lu® et le sorbet au citron.
- Déposez tous les sandwiches sur une plaque et placez au congélateur pour 1 h.
- Servez très froid.

Sandwiches glacés au chocolat

Choisissez des petits beurre Lu® aux pépites de chocolat, et remplacez les sorbets par de la glace au chocolat.

Sandwiches au lemon curd

Remplacez le sorbet par du lemon curd. Vous pouvez aussi utiliser de l'orange curd.

Sandwiches glacés à la pomme et au cidre

Remplacez les sorbets par du sorbet à la pomme verte. Portez à ébullition 125 g de sucre en poudre, 1 c. à s. d'eau et 25 cl de cidre doux. Laissez frémir pendant 5 min, puis incorporez 50 g de beurre ramolli. Servez chaud, avec les sandwiches.

Coulis d'abricots

Faites chauffer 50 g de sucre avec 2 gouttes d'extrait de vanille liquide et 20 cl d'eau. Ajoutez 500 g d'abricots dénoyautés et coupés en deux, et faites chauffer pendant 10 min. Mixez. Laissez refroidir. Servez avec les sandwiches.

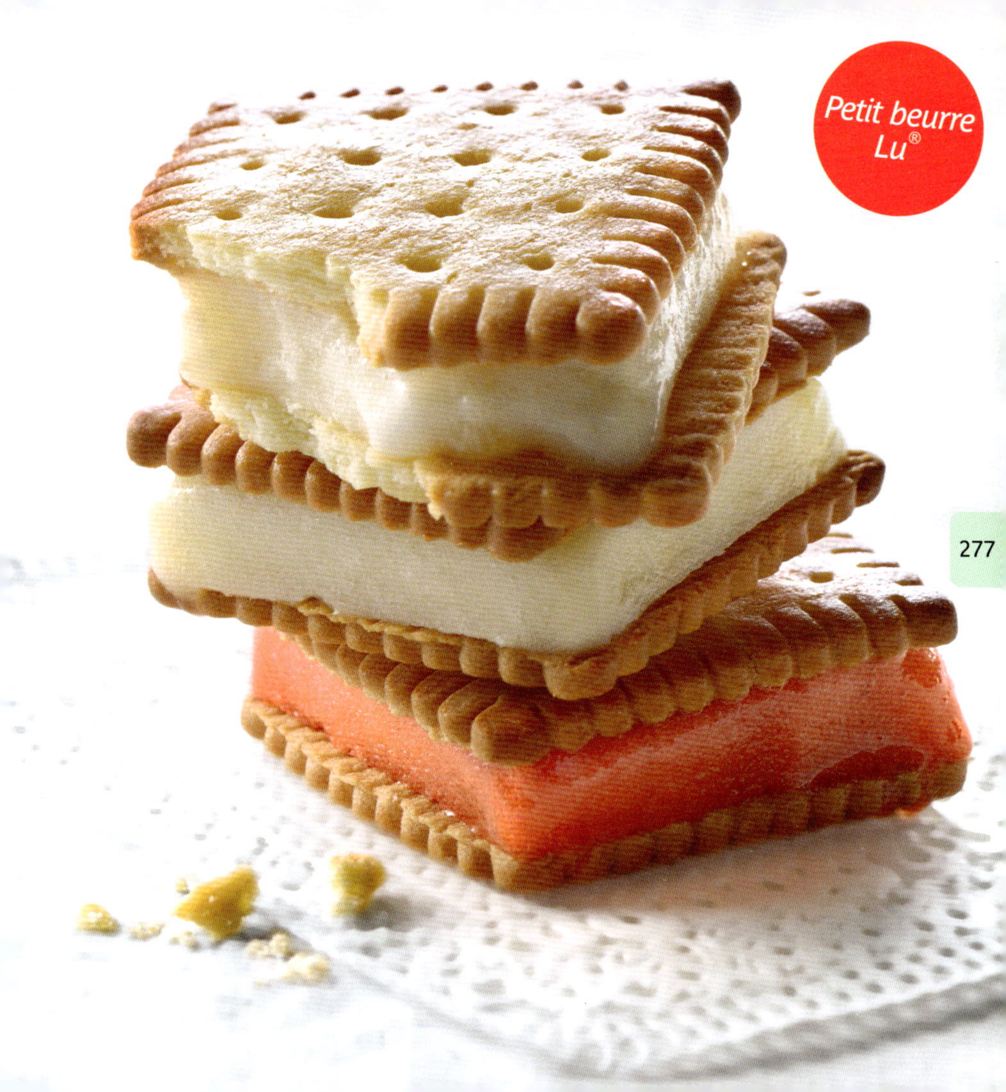

Petit beurre
Lu®

Verrines à la rhubarbe et à la vanille
Remplacez les oranges par 400 g de compote de rhubarbe, et le pavot par les graines grattées d'une gousse de vanille.

Verrines au melon et à la framboise
Remplacez les oranges par la chair de 2 petits melons détaillée en billes. Remplacez les graines de pavot par 50 g de framboises.

Verrines à la mangue et au fromage blanc
Remplacez les oranges par la chair de 2 mangues détaillée en lamelles. Remplacez le mascarpone par du fromage blanc.

Verrines au chocolat et au thé vert
Préparez un sirop avec 20 cl d'eau et 90 g de sucre. Hors du feu, ajoutez 1 c. à c. de thé vert matcha. Incorporez au mélange au mascarpone. Supprimez les graines de pavot. Remplacez les oranges par de la mousse au chocolat.

Petit beurre Lu®

VERRINE À L'ORANGE ET AU PAVOT

Préparation : 20 min • **Cuisson :** aucune • **Réfrigération :** 1 h
Pour 4 personnes

4 grosses oranges • 12 petits beurre Lu® • 4 œufs • 50 g de sucre
250 g de mascarpone • 1 c. à s. de graines de pavot

- Pelez les oranges à vif et détaillez-les en quartiers. Broyez grossièrement les petits beurre Lu®.
- Séparez les blancs des jaunes d'œufs. Dans un saladier, battez les jaunes et le sucre jusqu'à ce que le mélange blanchisse.
- Ajoutez le mascarpone et les graines de pavot, tout en continuant à mélanger jusqu'à l'obtention d'une préparation homogène.
- Battez les blancs en neige et incorporez-les au mélange.
- Répartissez les miettes de petits beurre Lu® dans 4 verrines. Ajoutez une couche de crème, répartissez les quartiers d'orange, et terminez avec la crème restante.
- Réservez pendant 1 h au réfrigérateur avant de servir.

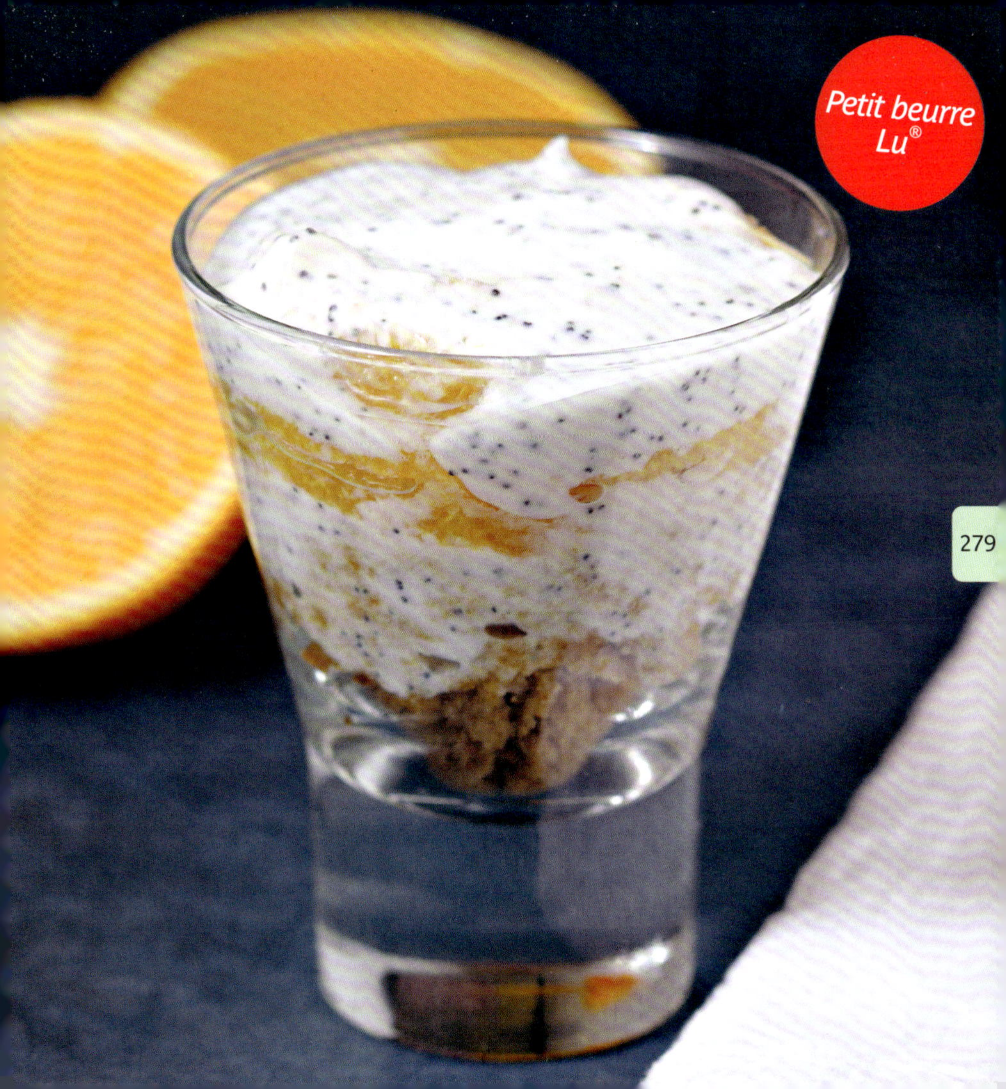
Petit beurre
Lu®

BÂTONNETS GLACÉS AUX FRUITS ROUGES

Préparation : 15 min • **Cuisson** : aucune • **Réfrigération** : 2 h
Pour 6 glaces

4 petits-suisses Gervais® nature • 500 g de fruits rouges
4 c. à s. de sucre de canne liquide • 6 bâtonnets en bois

- Retirez les petits-suisses Gervais® des pots. Réservez-en 2 pour une autre recette et mettez les autres dans un saladier. Conservez les pots.
- Lavez les fruits rouges. Coupez les plus gros en deux ou en quatre. Réservez-en 100 g.
- Mixez le reste, puis versez-le dans le saladier.
- Ajoutez le sirop de sucre de canne et les fruits réservés, puis mélangez.
- Faites turbiner en sorbetière.
- Répartissez la glace dans les pots réservés. Plantez un bâtonnet dans chaque pot.
- Laissez prendre au congélateur de 1 à 2 h avant de démouler, en passant la base des pots sous l'eau chaude.

Bâtonnets glacés à la grenadine
Aromatisez la préparation avec 2 c. à s. de sirop de grenadine.

Bâtonnets glacés aux fruits jaunes
Remplacez les fruits rouges par la chair mixée de 2 pêches et de 6 abricots.

Bâtonnets glacés à la fleur d'oranger
Reprenez la recette ci-dessus en ajoutant 1 c. à s. d'eau de fleur d'oranger à la préparation.

Bâtonnets glacés à la menthe et au basilic
Remplacez les fruits rouges par les feuilles de 1/2 bouquet de menthe et de 1/2 bouquet de basilic.

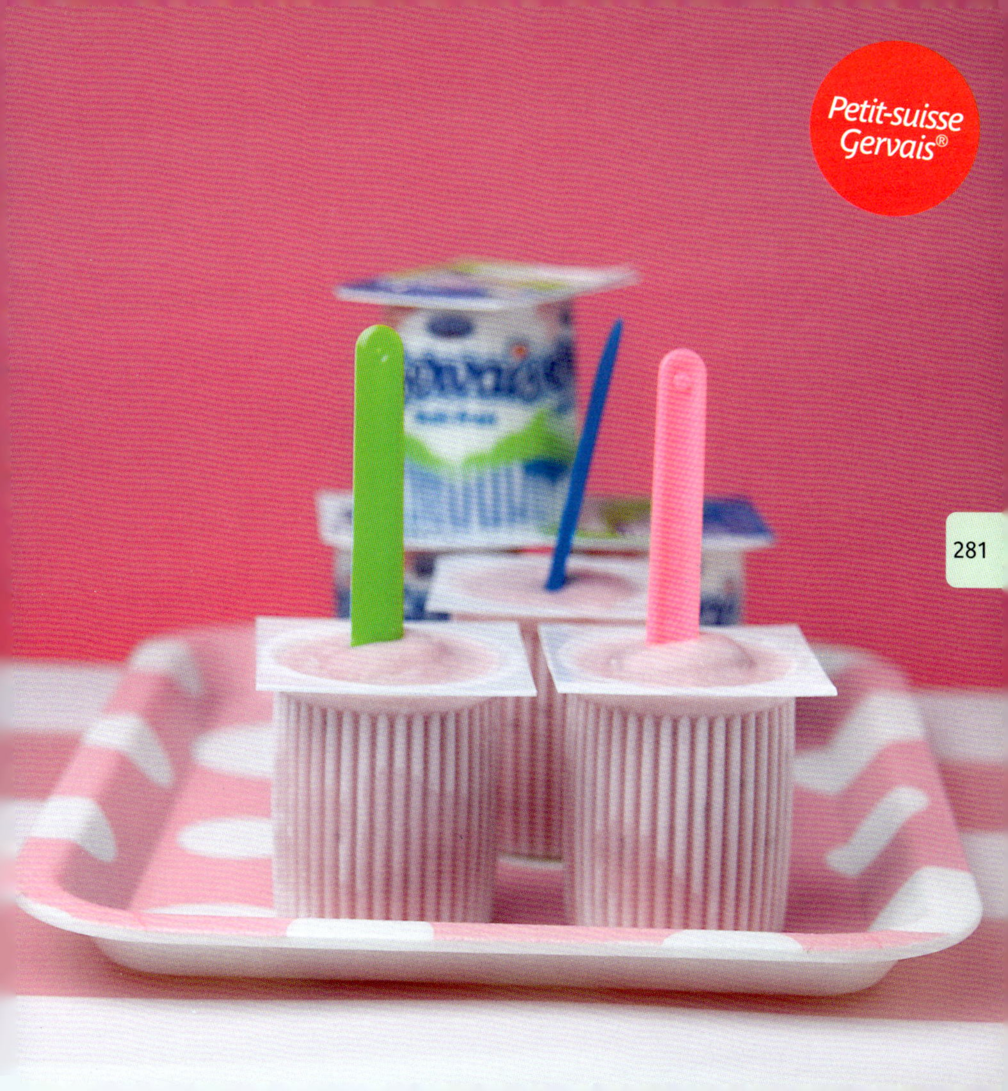

Petit-suisse Gervais®

CAKE AU BROCOLI

Préparation : 20 min • **Cuisson :** 1 h 10 • **Pour 4 personnes**

1 petite tête de brocoli • 3 tranches de pain de mie • 10 cl de lait
4 c. à s. d'huile d'olive • 1 petit-suisse Gervais® nature
3 œufs • sel et poivre

- Lavez le brocoli et séparez les bouquets. Faites-les cuire dans de l'eau bouillante salée pendant 10 min. Égouttez-les.
- Préchauffez le four à 210 °C.
- Détaillez le pain de mie en morceaux. Mettez-les dans le bol du mixeur avec le brocoli cuit, le lait, un peu d'huile, du sel et du poivre, puis mixez grossièrement.
- Versez la préparation dans un saladier, puis ajoutez le petit-suisse Gervais®, les œufs et le reste d'huile d'olive. Mélangez.
- Versez le mélange dans un moule à cake et placez-le dans un plat à four. Ajoutez de l'eau jusqu'aux 2/3 de la hauteur du moule à cake.
- Faites cuire pendant 1 h.
- Servez chaud.

Cake au brocoli et aux herbes

Ajoutez 6 brins de persil et 10 brins de ciboulette ciselés à la préparation en même temps que le petit-suisse.

Cake au brocoli et aux lardons

Ajoutez 150 g de lardons fumés revenus à la poêle à la préparation. Vous pouvez aussi utiliser des lamelles de jambon sec ou du bacon grillé.

Cake au chou romanesco et à la muscade

Remplacez le brocoli par du chou romanesco, et ajoutez 1 pincée de noix muscade râpée à la préparation.

Cake à la carotte et à la coriandre

Remplacez le brocoli par 400 g de carottes pelées, coupées en rondelles et cuites à la vapeur. Ajoutez les feuilles de 10 brins de coriandre à la préparation.

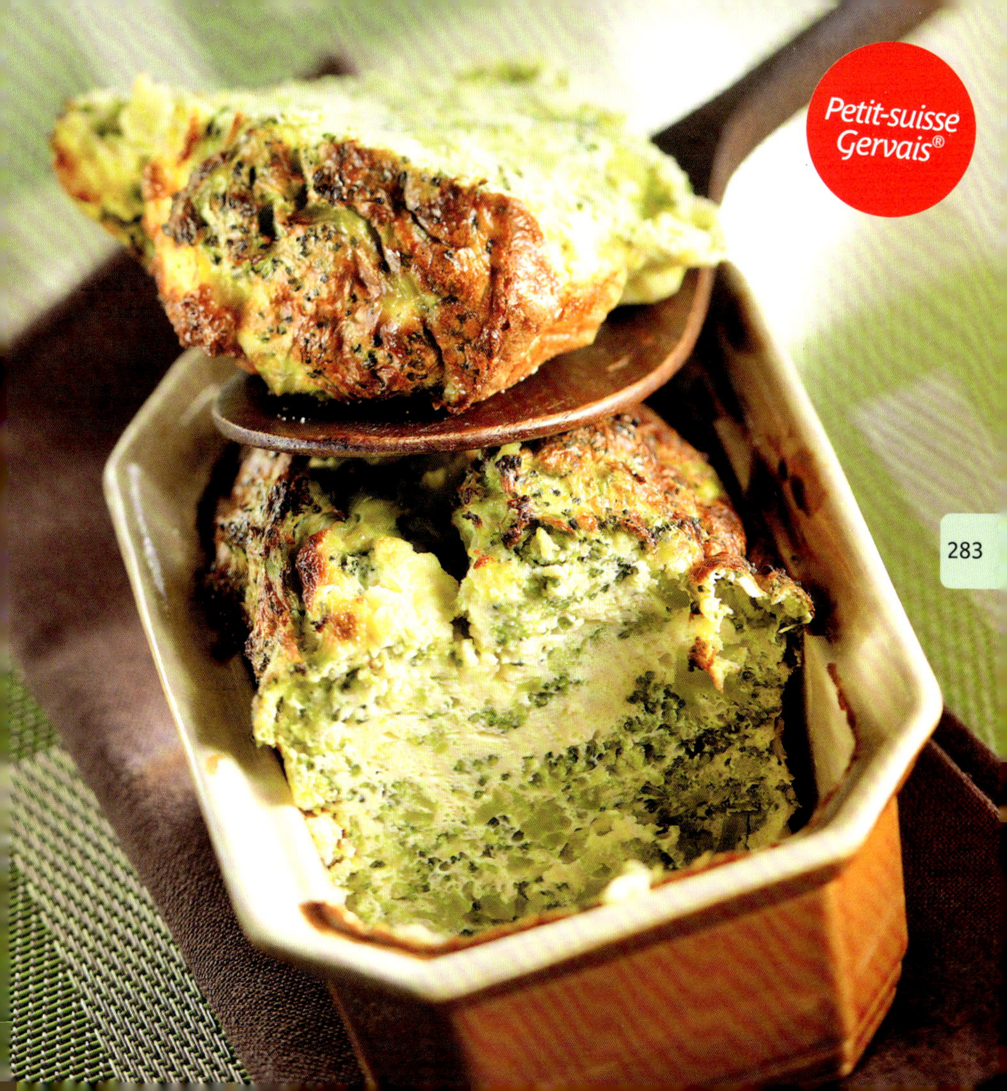

Petit-suisse Gervais®

Gâteau à l'ananas et au chocolat
Remplacez les bananes par 6 tranches d'ananas frais ou au sirop.

Gâteau au thé vert matcha et au chocolat
Remplacez les bananes par 2 c. à c. de thé vert matcha dilué dans 10 cl de lait bouillant.

Gâteau à la cerise et à la pistache
Remplacez les bananes par 300 g de cerises dénoyautées, et le chocolat par 75 g de pistaches non salées décortiquées.

Smoothie à la banane et aux dattes
Mixez 1 banane pelée avec 4 dattes dénoyautées, 15 cl de jus de pomme et 4 glaçons. Servez avec le gâteau.

Petit-suisse Gervais®

GÂTEAU À LA BANANE ET AU CHOCOLAT

Préparation : 15 min • **Cuisson** : 45 min • **Pour 6 à 8 personnes**

2 petits-suisses Gervais® nature • 3 œufs • 125 g de sucre
170 g de farine • 85 g de fécule de pomme de terre
1 sachet de levure chimique • 2 c. à s. d'huile de tournesol • 2 bananes
100 g de chocolat noir à pâtisserie • beurre, pour le moule

- Préchauffez le four à 180 °C.
- Mettez les petits-suisses Gervais® dans un saladier avec les œufs et le sucre, puis battez énergiquement au fouet.
- Incorporez la farine, la fécule de pomme de terre, la levure et l'huile, et remuez bien.
- Pelez les bananes et coupez-les en rondelles. Coupez le chocolat en petits morceaux. Incorporez-les à la pâte.
- Versez la préparation dans un moule à manqué préalablement beurré.
- Faites cuire au four pendant 45 min environ.
- Laissez refroidir avant de déguster.

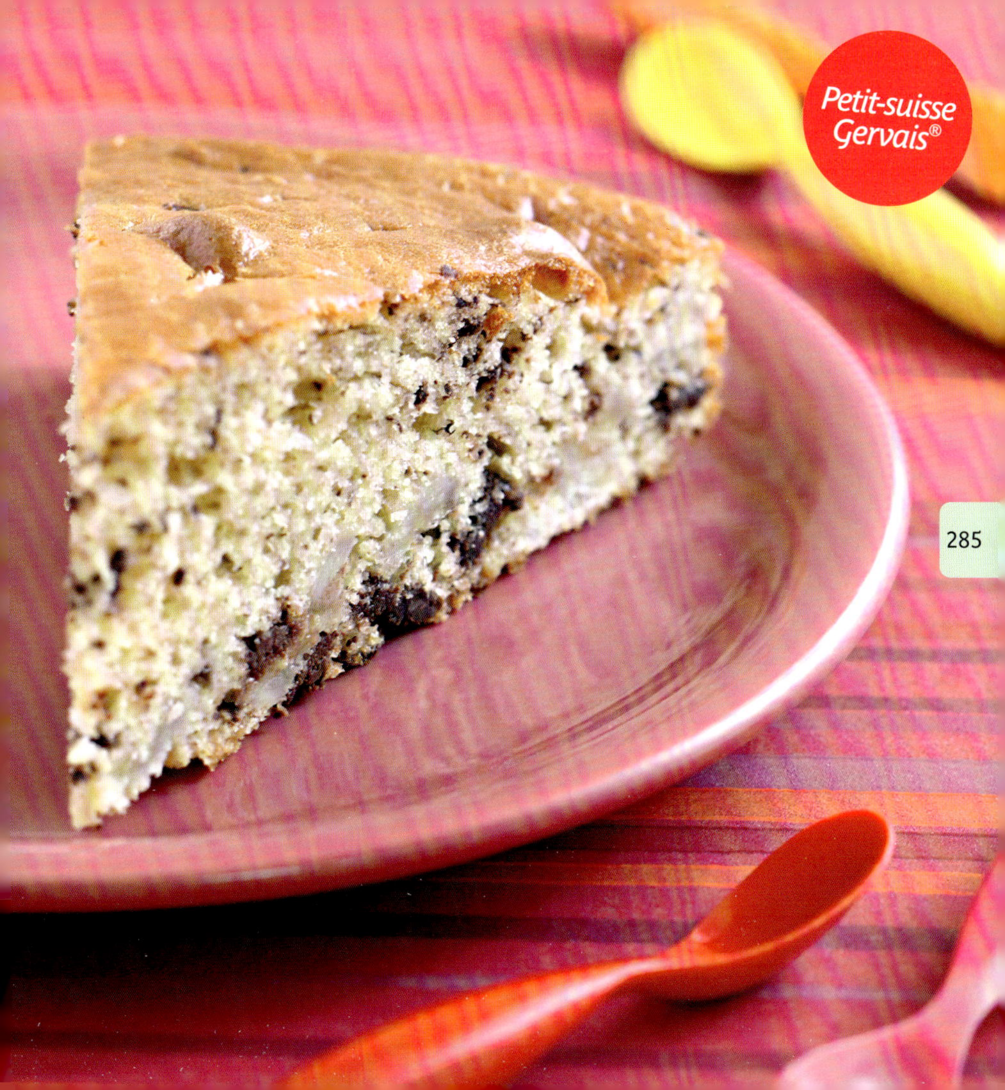
Petit-suisse
Gervais®

MUFFINS AU PETIT-SUISSE ET À LA POIRE

Préparation : 15 min • **Cuisson** : 30 min • **Pour 12 muffins**

2 poires • 1 œuf • 60 g de sucre en poudre • 7 g de sucre vanillé
4 petits-suisses Gervais® nature • 2 c. à s. d'huile • le zeste de 1 citron
le zeste de 1/2 orange • le jus de 1 orange • 200 g de farine
2 c. à c. de levure chimique

- Préchauffez le four à 200 °C.
- Pelez les poires, ôtez la partie dure au centre, puis mixez la chair.
- Mettez-la dans un saladier avec l'œuf, les sucres, les petits-suisses Gervais®, l'huile, les zestes d'agrumes et le jus d'orange. Battez au fouet.
- Mélangez la farine et la levure, puis incorporez au mélange.
- Déposez de petites caissettes en papier dans 12 alvéoles d'un moule à muffin. Répartissez la pâte dans les caissettes.
- Faites cuire au four pendant 30 min.
- Laissez refroidir avant de servir.

Muffins à la verveine
Remplacez le jus d'orange par 10 cl de lait, dans lequel vous aurez fait infuser 2 sachets de verveine pendant 15 min.

Muffins à la châtaigne
Remplacez la farine par de la farine de châtaigne. Ajoutez 50 g de marrons confits grossièrement broyés à la préparation.

Muffins à la confiture de lait
Nappez les muffins de 1 ou 2 c. à c. de confiture de lait dès la sortie du four, et laissez refroidir.

Confiture de roses
Mettez 350 g de pétales de rose comestibles dans un faitout avec le jus de 2 citrons, 50 cl d'eau, et faites cuire à feu doux jusqu'à évaporation du liquide. Ajoutez 550 g de sucre cristallisé, et faites chauffer en remuant sur feu doux jusqu'à ce que le sucre soit dissous. Laissez refroidir. Servez avec les muffins.

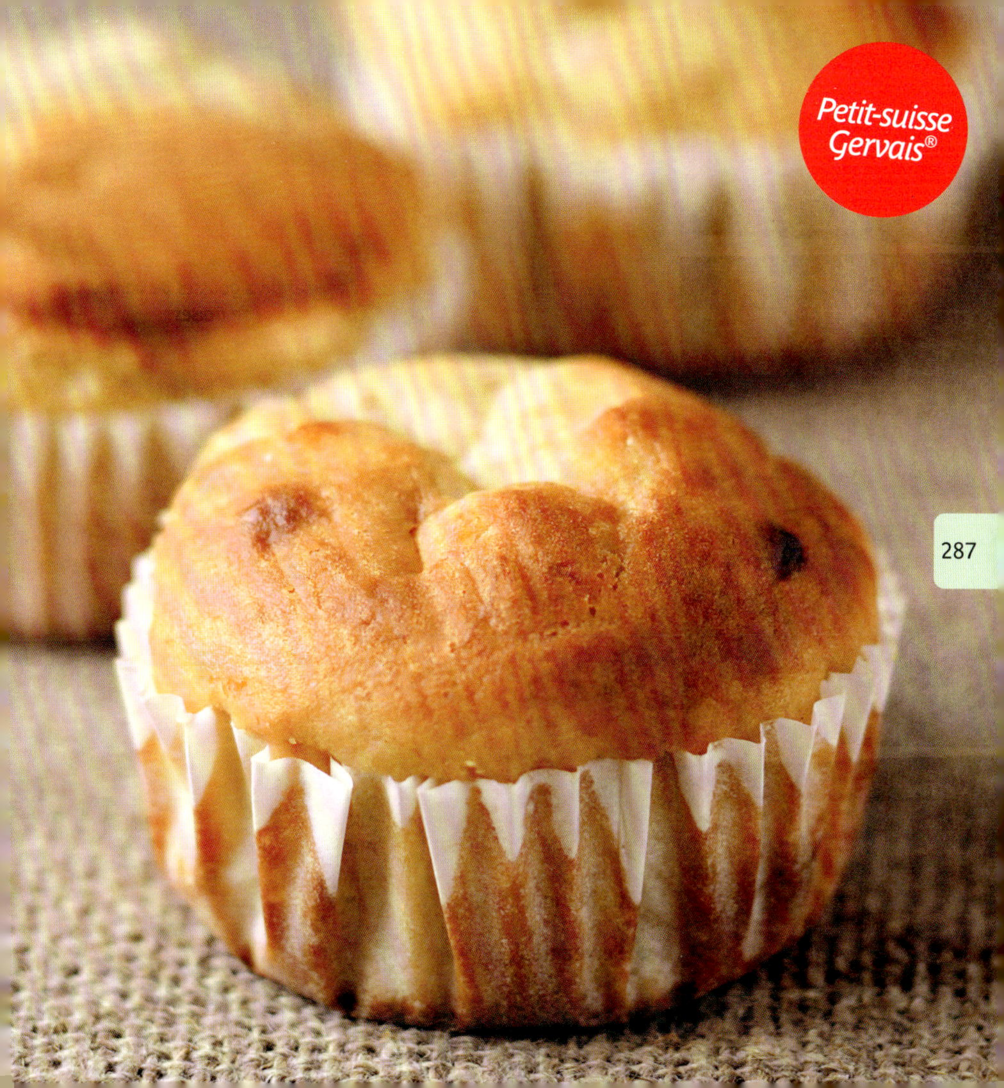
Petit-suisse
Gervais®

VERRINES À LA FRAISE ET À LA RHUBARBE

Préparation : 15 min • **Cuisson :** 8 à 10 min • **Congélation :** 15 min
Pour 4 personnes

8 tiges de rhubarbe rose • 8 cl de liqueur de fraise
4 petits-suisses Gervais® • les graines de 2 gousses de vanille
90 g de meringues • confiture de fraises

- Rincez la rhubarbe, puis taillez-la en tronçons de 4 cm.
- Mettez-les dans une casserole avec la liqueur de fraise, et faites chauffer à couvert, à feu moyen, de 8 à 10 min, jusqu'à ce que la rhubarbe soit tendre.
- Retirez la casserole du feu et étalez le mélange sur un plateau pour le laisser refroidir. Mettez-le ensuite dans un récipient en plastique, et laissez-le au congélateur pendant 15 min.
- Pendant ce temps, mettez les petits-suisses Gervais® et les graines de vanille dans un saladier, et battez jusqu'à ce que des pointes se forment.
- Cassez les meringues en morceaux.
- Placez la moitié des morceaux de meringue au fond de 4 verrines, nappez d'une couche de rhubarbe, puis de confiture de fraises, puis de petits-suisses à la vanille, puis recommencez avec 1 couche de meringue, etc., en terminant par les petits-suisses à la vanille.
- Servez très frais.

Verrines aux biscuits roses

Remplacez les meringues par des biscuits roses de Reims émiettés. Remplacez la liqueur de fraise par de l'eau de rose.

Verrines à l'abricot et à la violette

Remplacez la rhubarbe cuite par 12 abricots frais dénoyautés et taillés en dés, et la confiture de fraises par de la confiture de violettes.

Verrines à l'abricot et à la lavande

Reprenez la recette ci-dessus en remplaçant la confiture de violettes par de la gelée d'abricot. Remplacez la vanille par 1 c. à s. de fleurs de lavande séchées.

Verrines au lemon curd et aux sablés

Remplacez la rhubarbe et la confiture par du lemon curd, et les meringues par des sablés au beurre grossièrement émiettés.

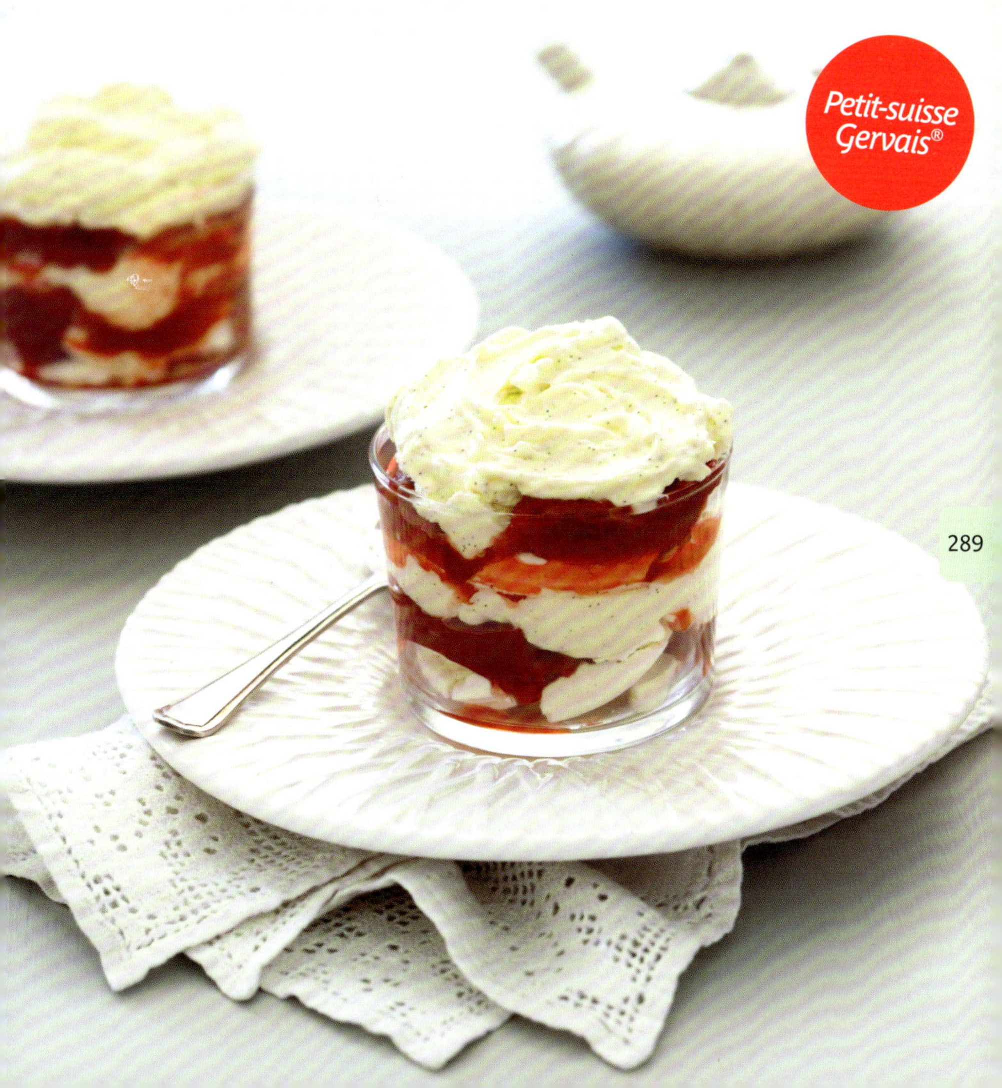
Petit-suisse Gervais®

CHEESECAKE AU CITRON ET AUX CERISES

Préparation : 20 min • **Cuisson :** aucune • **Réfrigération :** 5 h
Pour 8 personnes

pour la base : 175 g de biscuits secs • 55 g de beurre
pour la garniture : 2 sachets de 11 g de gélatine en poudre
10 cl de jus d'orange • le jus de 1 citron • 350 g de Philadelphia®
1 yaourt brassé nature • 55 g de sucre en poudre • 55 g de raisins secs
115 g de cerises noires bien mûres • 2 c. à c. de sucre glace

- Pour la base, écrasez grossièrement les biscuits, puis mélangez-les avec le beurre pour former une pâte. Étalez-la dans un moule à fond amovible, pressez bien, puis réservez au réfrigérateur pendant 1 h.
- Pendant ce temps, dissolvez la gélatine dans le jus d'orange.
- Mettez-la dans un blender avec le jus de citron, le Philadelphia®, le yaourt et le sucre. Mixez pendant quelques secondes, puis versez le mélange dans un saladier. Incorporez les raisins secs.
- Versez cette préparation sur la base en biscuits, puis réservez au réfrigérateur pendant 2 h.
- Saupoudrez les cerises de sucre glace, puis placez-les sur le cheesecake. Replacez au réfrigérateur pour 2 h environ, jusqu'à ce que la crème ait bien pris.

Cheesecake aux fraises et à la rose

Remplacez le jus de citron par 1 c. à c. d'eau de rose, et les cerises par des fraises équeutées.

Cheesecake aux myrtilles et aux framboises

Remplacez les raisins secs par des myrtilles, et les cerises par des framboises.

Cheesecake au gingembre et aux fruits de la Passion

Remplacez les raisins secs par 30 g de gingembre confit émietté, et les cerises par un coulis de fruits de la Passion : faites un caramel à sec avec 50 g de sucre. Hors du feu, ajoutez le jus et les graines de 1 fruit de la Passion, le jus de 1 citron vert, et battez au fouet. Ajoutez 1 c. à s. de lait entier et laissez épaissir sur feu doux de 2 à 3 min. Laissez refroidir, puis nappez le cheesecake de ce coulis. Remettez au frais pour 2 h.

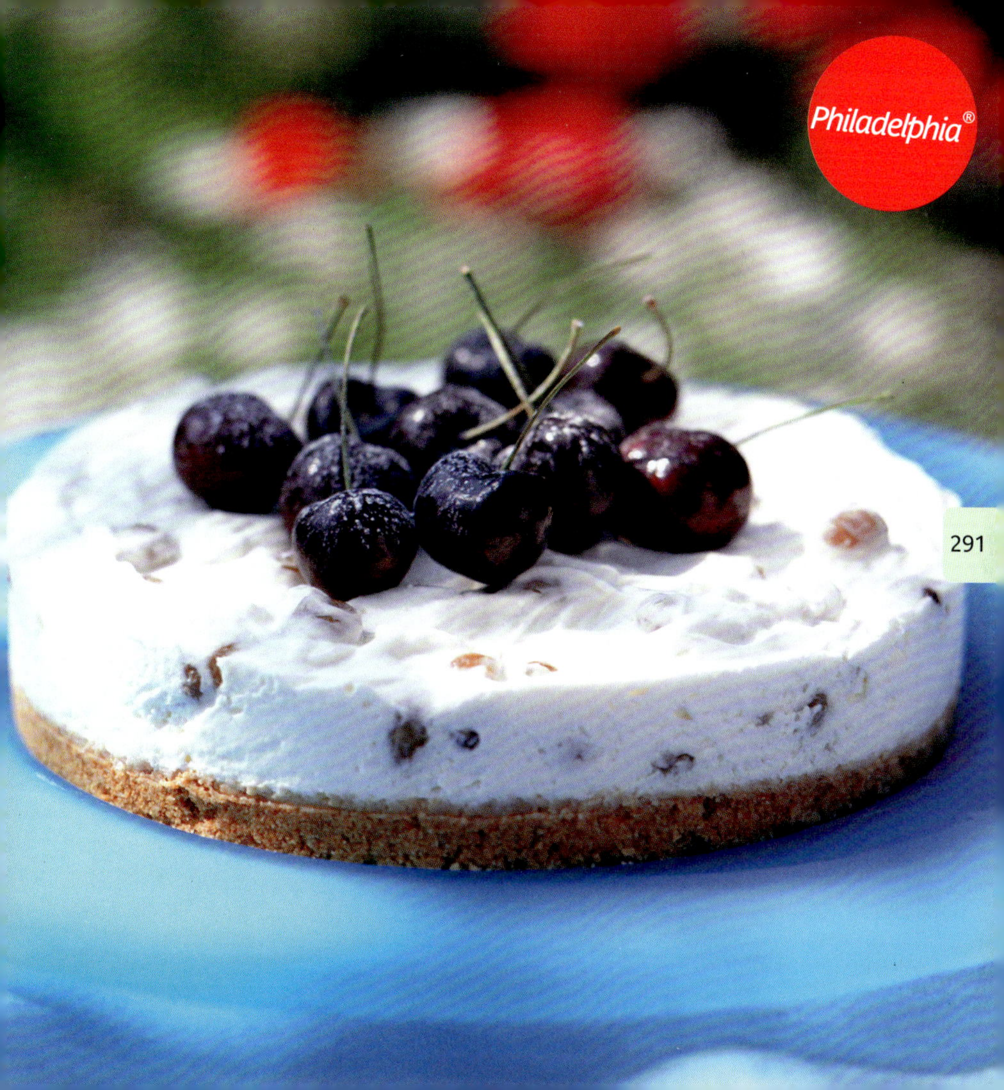
Philadelphia®

CRÉMEUX DE CHOU-FLEUR AU PHILADELPHIA®

Préparation : 15 min • **Cuisson :** 20 min • **Pour 3 ou 4 personnes**

1 gros chou-fleur • 2 blancs de poireau • 2 c. à s. d'huile d'olive
1 cube de bouillon de bœuf • 150 g de Philadelphia®
10 cl de lait + un peu si besoin • 1 pincée de noix muscade râpée • sel

- Séparez les bouquets de chou-fleur, puis faites-les cuire à la vapeur pendant 20 min.
- Pendant ce temps, coupez les blancs de poireau en rondelles et mettez-les dans une cocotte avec l'huile d'olive.
- Faites-les cuire pendant 10 min environ, puis ajoutez le cube de bouillon et un peu d'eau pour le dissoudre.
- Éteignez le feu, puis ajoutez le chou-fleur, le Philadelphia® et le lait.
- Mixez le tout à l'aide d'un mixeur girafe. Ajoutez un peu de lait si le crémeux est trop épais.
- Goûtez, salez et ajoutez la noix muscade.
- Répartissez dans des bols et servez.

Crémeux au bacon grillé

Taillez 4 à 6 tranches de bacon en fines lamelles, puis faites-les revenir à la poêle pendant quelques minutes, sans matière grasse, jusqu'à ce qu'elles soient bien dorées. Ajoutez sur le crémeux juste avant de servir.

Crémeux de topinambour

Remplacez le chou-fleur par 600 g de topinambours pelés et cuits à l'eau pendant 30 min. Parsemez de copeaux de fourme d'Ambert juste avant de servir.

Crémeux de chou-fleur aux crevettes sautées

Faites revenir 12 crevettes roses décortiquées à la poêle avec 1 filet d'huile d'olive. Répartissez-les dans les bols juste avant de servir.

Crémeux de chou-fleur et brocoli

Remplacez la moitié du chou-fleur par 1/2 tête de brocoli. Remplacez la noix muscade par 1 c. à c. d'herbes de Provence.

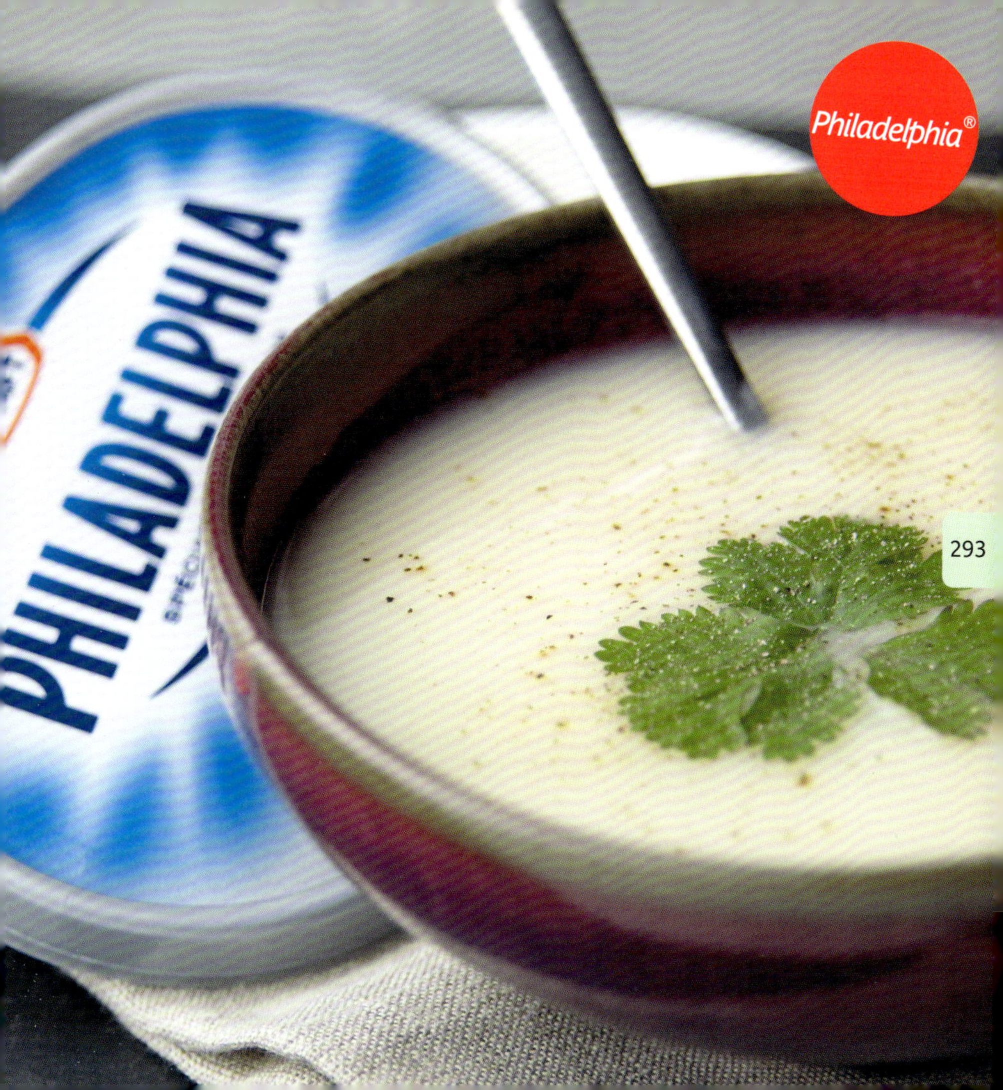
PHILADELPHIA

Gâteau de crêpes au thon et au maïs

Remplacez le saumon fumé par du thon au naturel émietté et les câpres et l'aneth par du maïs doux. Intercalez des feuilles de salade verte entre les crêpes.

Gâteau de crêpes au saumon et à l'avocat

Remplacez les câpres et l'aneth par la chair écrasée de 2 avocats bien mûrs. Ajoutez le jus de 1/2 citron.

Gâteau de crêpes au poulet et au concombre

Remplacez le saumon fumé par du jambon de poulet. Remplacez les échalotes, l'aneth et les câpres par 2 gousses d'ail, 10 brins de menthe et 1 concombre hachés.

Gâteau de crêpes au jambon et aux figues

Remplacez le saumon fumé par du jambon sec. Remplacez les échalotes, l'aneth et les câpres par la chair de 10 figues fraîches mixée.

Philadelphia®

GÂTEAU DE CRÊPES AU SAUMON FUMÉ

Préparation : 15 min • **Cuisson :** aucune • **Réfrigération :** 12 h
Pour 8 personnes

250 g de Philadelphia® • 6 échalotes + quelques-unes pour accompagner
10 brins d'aneth + quelques-uns pour accompagner
2 c. à s. de câpres • 7 ou 8 crêpes • 300 g de saumon fumé
quartiers de citron pour accompagner

- Sortez le Philadelphia® du réfrigérateur 30 min avant de commencer la recette.
- Épluchez les échalotes, puis émincez-les finement. Rincez l'aneth, essuyez-le avec du papier absorbant, puis hachez-le.
- Battez le Philadelphia® dans un saladier avec une spatule en bois jusqu'à ce qu'il soit bien lisse. Ajoutez les échalotes, les câpres et l'aneth, puis mélangez bien.
- Disposez 1 crêpe sur un grand morceau de film alimentaire, tartinez-la de préparation au fromage et recouvrez-la de 2 tranches de saumon fumé. Répétez l'opération jusqu'à épuisement des ingrédients, en terminant par une crêpe.
- Enveloppez le gâteau dans le film alimentaire et réservez au réfrigérateur pendant plusieurs heures, voire toute une nuit, jusqu'à ce que le gâteau soit bien ferme.
- Déballez le gâteau de crêpes et transférez-le sur un plat de service. Servez avec quelques câpres, des quartiers de citron et de l'aneth.

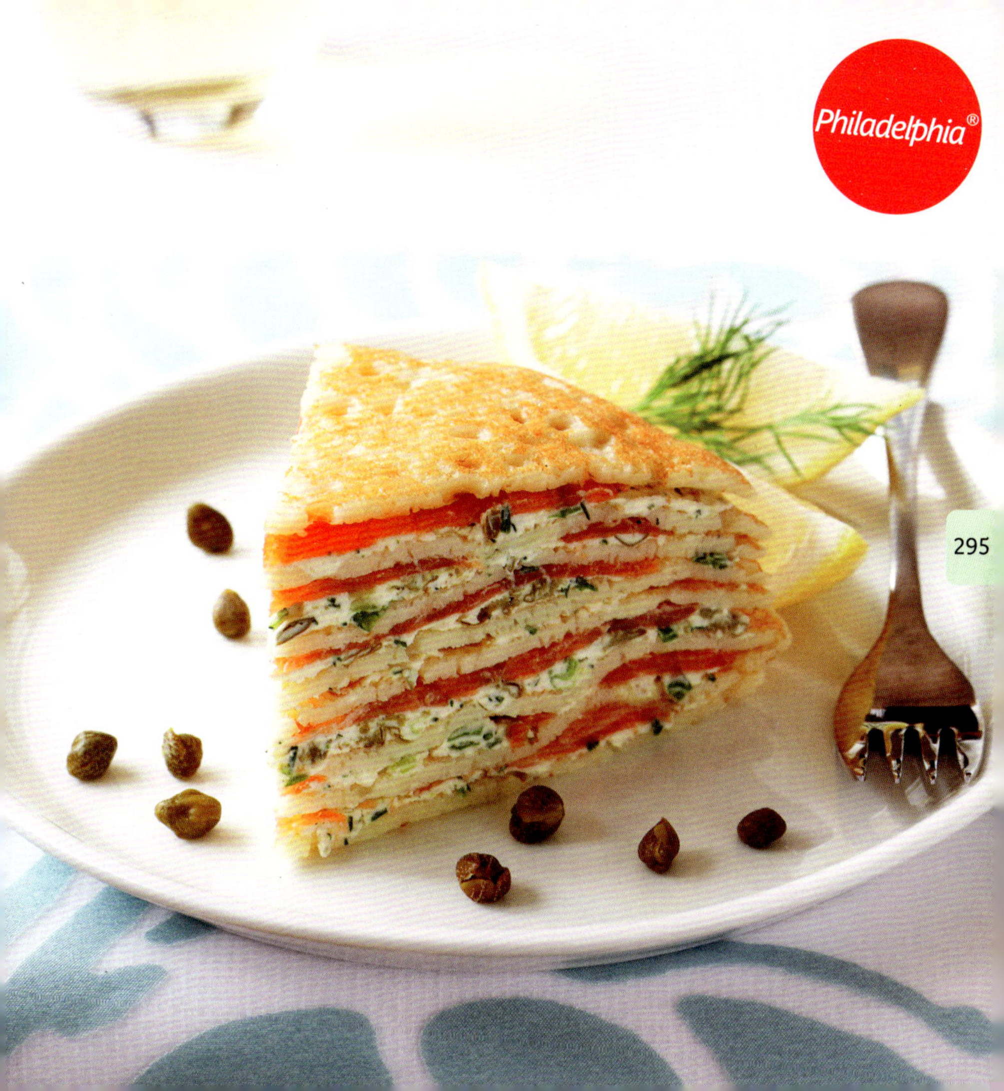
Philadelphia®

Philadelphia®

QUICHE AUX CHAMPIGNONS ET AUX TOMATES

Préparation : 10 min • **Cuisson :** 45 min • **Pour 6 personnes**

4 tomates moyennes • 300 g de champignons de Paris
10 brins de persil • 4 œufs • 100 g de Philadelphia®
1 rouleau de pâte brisée • sel et poivre

- Lavez les tomates et les champignons de Paris, puis coupez-les en morceaux.
- Faites-les réduire à la poêle sans matière grasse pendant 10 min.
- Rincez le persil, épongez-le sur du papier absorbant, puis ciselez-le. Ajoutez-le dans la poêle en fin de cuisson. Retirez la poêle du feu.
- Préchauffez le four à 180 °C.
- Fouettez les œufs avec le Philadelphia®. Salez et poivrez. Ajoutez les légumes.
- Déroulez la pâte et tapissez-en un moule à tarte recouvert de papier sulfurisé. Versez la garniture par-dessus.
- Faites cuire au four pendant 35 min environ.
- Servez chaud ou froid.

Quiche à la moutarde
Ajoutez 2 c. à s. de moutarde à la préparation en même temps que le Philadelphia®.

Quiche aux 3 poivrons
Remplacez les tomates et les champignons par 3 poivrons : 1 rouge, 1 jaune et 1 orange, taillés en dés et revenus à la poêle avec 1 filet d'huile d'olive.

Quiche aux pommes de terre et aux champignons
Remplacez les tomates par 3 pommes de terre cuites à l'eau et taillées en dés. Faites revenir les champignons à la poêle avec 2 échalotes émincées et un peu d'huile de tournesol.

Quiche aux tomates cerises et au roquefort
Remplacez les tomates par 400 g de tomates cerises coupées en deux. Supprimez les champignons et ajoutez 200 g de roquefort à la préparation en même temps que le Philadelphia®.

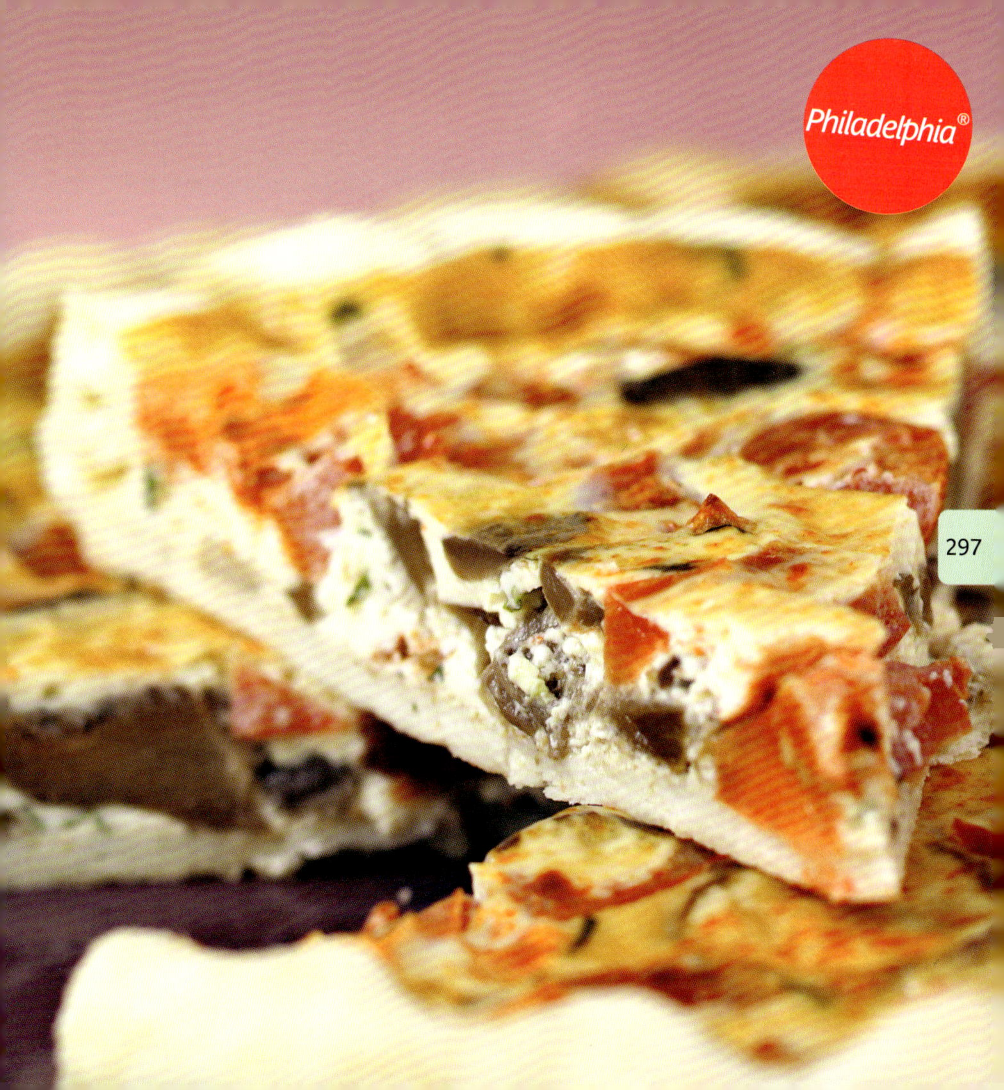

TARTINADE AU THON ET À L'AVOCAT

Préparation : 15 min • **Cuisson** : aucune • **Pour 1 bol**

1 avocat bien mûr • 1 oignon • 15 brins de persil • 1 c. à c. de moutarde
150 g de Philadelphia® • 170 g de thon au naturel
1 c. à s. de jus de citron • tranches de pain, pour accompagner
sel et poivre

- Coupez l'avocat en deux, dénoyautez-le, puis prélevez la chair. Épluchez l'oignon, puis hachez-le. Rincez le persil, épongez-le sur du papier absorbant, puis ciselez-le.
- Mettez la chair d'avocat dans un bol, puis écrasez-la à la fourchette avec la moutarde et le Philadelphia®.
- Ajoutez le thon égoutté et émiettez-le. Incorporez l'oignon, le jus de citron et le persil, puis mélangez bien. Salez et poivrez.
- Couvrez de film alimentaire et réservez au frais jusqu'au moment de servir.
- Faites griller les tranches de pain et tartinez-les de la préparation.

Tartinade à l'artichaut
Remplacez l'avocat et le thon par le contenu de 1 bocal d'artichauts (sans l'huile). Mixez le tout.

Tartinade au surimi
Remplacez le thon par 10 bâtonnets de surimi hachés, et l'avocat par 1 c. à s. de ketchup, 1 trait de Tabasco® et 3 brins de ciboulette.

Tartinade de haricots rouges
Remplacez le thon et l'avocat par 250 g de haricots rouges mixés. Ajoutez 1 c. à s. de concentré de tomate et 1 trait de sauce soja. Supprimez le persil.

Roulés de saumon à la tartinade
Nappez des tranches de saumon fumé de tartinade, puis roulez-les et maintenez-les avec des piques à cocktail.

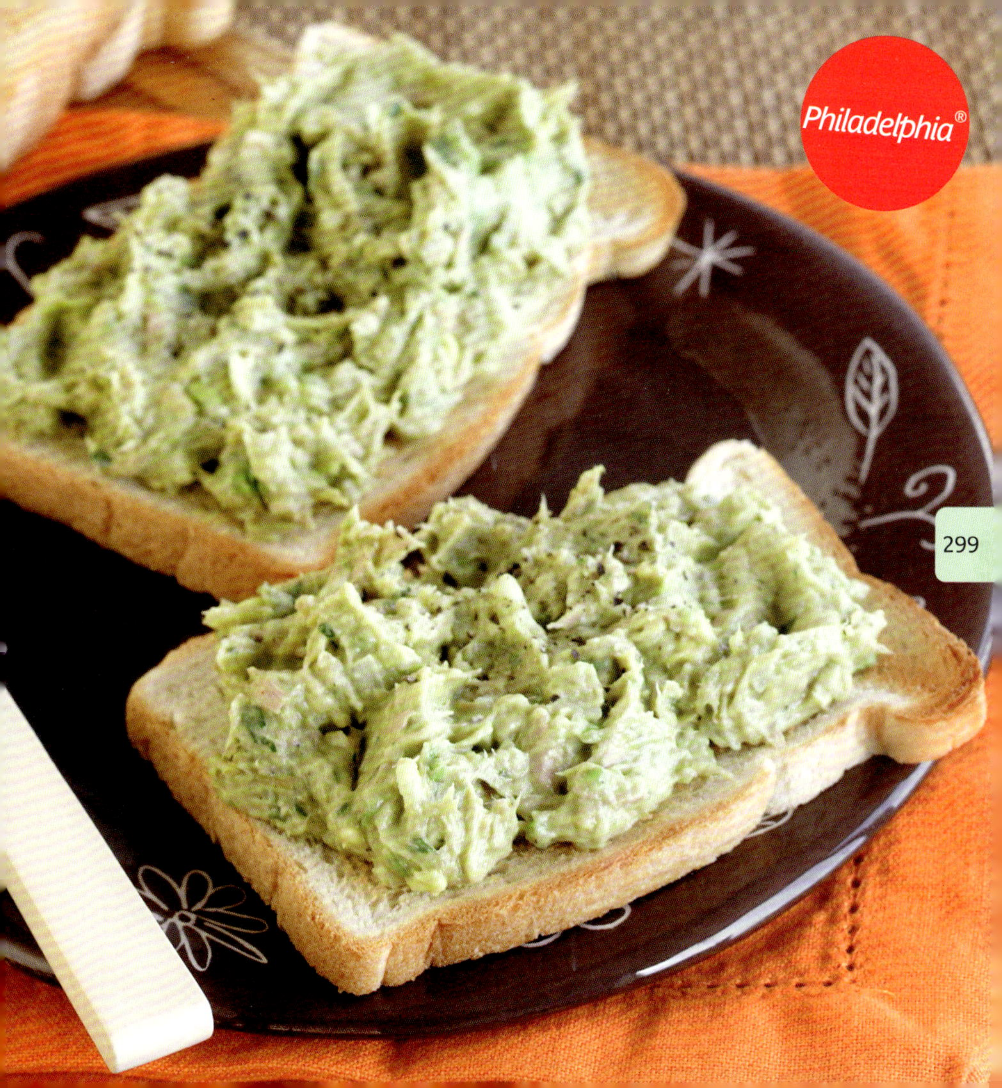
Philadelphia®

BEIGNETS AU RICARD®

Préparation : 25 min • **Cuisson** : 20 min • **Repos** : 30 min
Pour 12 beignets

250 g de farine • 1 sachet de levure rapide • 2 jaunes d'œufs
30 g de sucre en poudre + un peu pour saupoudrer • 2 c. à s. de lait
5 cl de Ricard® • huile de friture

- Mettez la farine, la levure, les jaunes d'œufs, le sucre, le lait, le Ricard® et 8 cl d'eau dans un saladier, puis pétrissez la pâte à la main.
- Formez une boule, recouvrez le saladier d'un torchon, puis laissez lever dans un endroit tiède pendant 30 min.
- Séparez la pâte en 10 boules et donnez-leur une forme de donut, en faisant un trou au centre.
- Faites chauffer un bain de friture à 180 °C et déposez-y les beignets 3 par 3. Retournez-les pendant la cuisson.
- Lorsqu'ils sont bien dorés, déposez les beignets sur une feuille de papier absorbant, et saupoudrez de sucre.

Beignets aux pommes et au Ricard®
Incorporez 2 pommes pelées, épépinées et taillées en dés à la pâte une fois qu'elle a levé.

Glaçage au sucre
Mélangez 200 g de sucre glace et 10 cl d'eau dans un bol. Nappez les beignets encore chauds de ce glaçage et laissez refroidir sur une grille.

Glaçage au chocolat et à la mélasse
Faites fondre 75 g de chocolat noir avec 50 g de beurre, 100 g de mélasse et 1 c. à s. de crème fraîche. Hors du feu, ajoutez 175 g de sucre glace. Décorez les beignets refroidis de ce glaçage.

Beignets fourrés
Coupez les beignets cuits et refroidis en deux, puis garnissez-les de lemon curd, de caramel au beurre salé ou de confiture d'abricots.

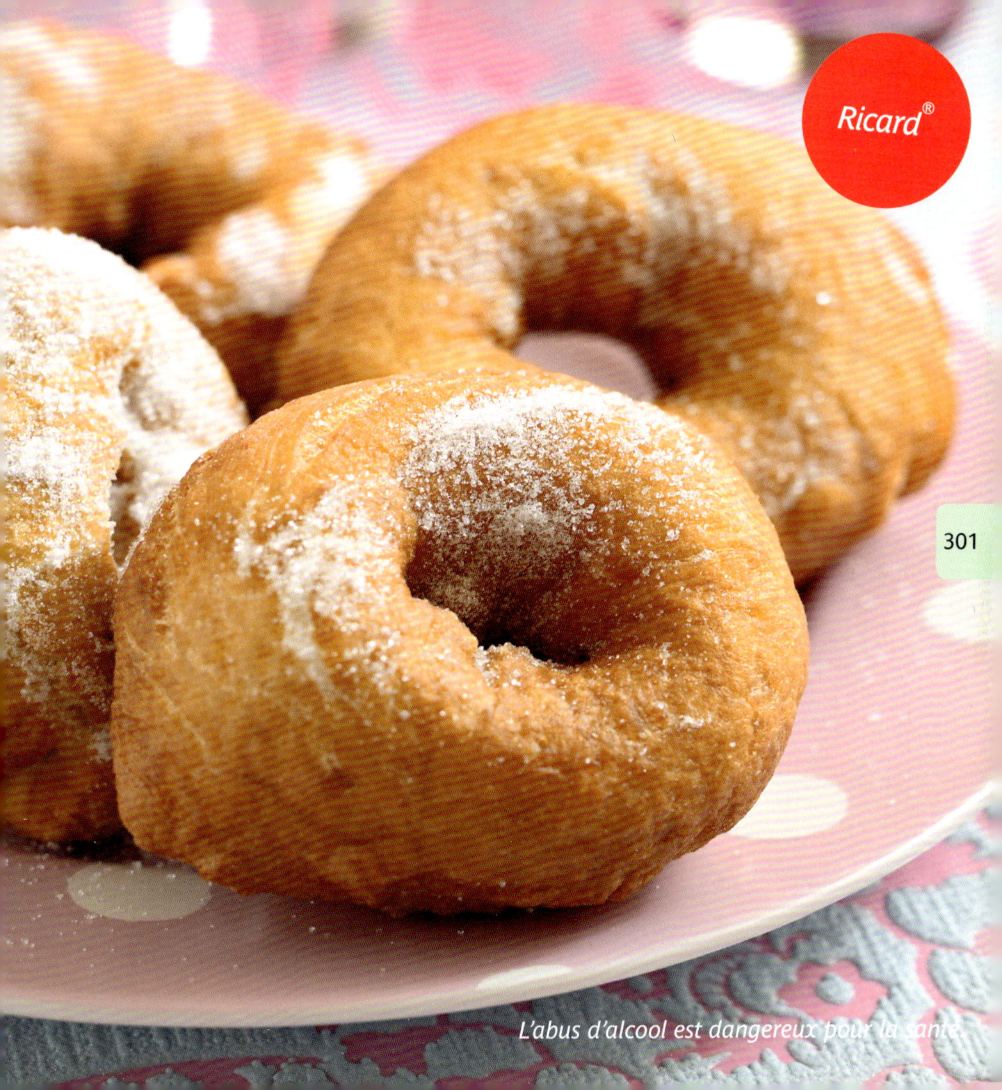
Ricard®

GAMBAS SAUTÉES AU RICARD®

Préparation : 15 min • **Cuisson :** 3 min • **Pour 6 personnes**

1 kg de gambas épluchées mais avec la queue • 2 gousses d'ail
1 c. à s. d'huile d'olive • 1 bon trait de Ricard® • feuilles de persil
tranches de citron

- Décortiquez les gambas en laissant le bout de la queue. Pratiquez une incision au couteau sur le dos de chaque gamba, puis aplatissez-les avec le plat du couteau.
- Épluchez l'ail et hachez-le.
- Faites chauffer l'huile dans une grande poêle à feu vif. Ajoutez l'ail et les gambas et faites-les sauter pendant 3 min en remuant.
- Ajoutez le Ricard® dans la poêle et flambez.
- Égouttez les gambas sur du papier absorbant, puis servez-les, accompagnées de feuilles de persil et de tranches de citron.

Gambas sautées au Ricard® et à la crème

Retirez les gambas cuites et flambées de la poêle, puis ajoutez 20 cl de crème fraîche liquide dans celle-ci. Baissez le feu et laissez réduire. Nappez les gambas de cette sauce avant de servir.

Noix de saint-jacques au Ricard®

Remplacez les gambas par des noix de saint-jacques, que vous ferez cuire pendant 1 min au maximum sur chaque face.

Gambas au Ricard® et à la tomate

Faites chauffer 1 boîte de concentré de tomate avec 10 cl d'eau. Ajoutez les gambas, 1 c. à s. d'herbes de Provence, 1 c. à s. de graines de fenouil, 1 gousse d'ail hachée, 20 cl de Ricard®, du sel et du poivre. Laissez mijoter pendant 20 min à feu doux. Ajoutez 10 cl de Ricard® en fin de cuisson, puis flambez. Servez avec du riz.

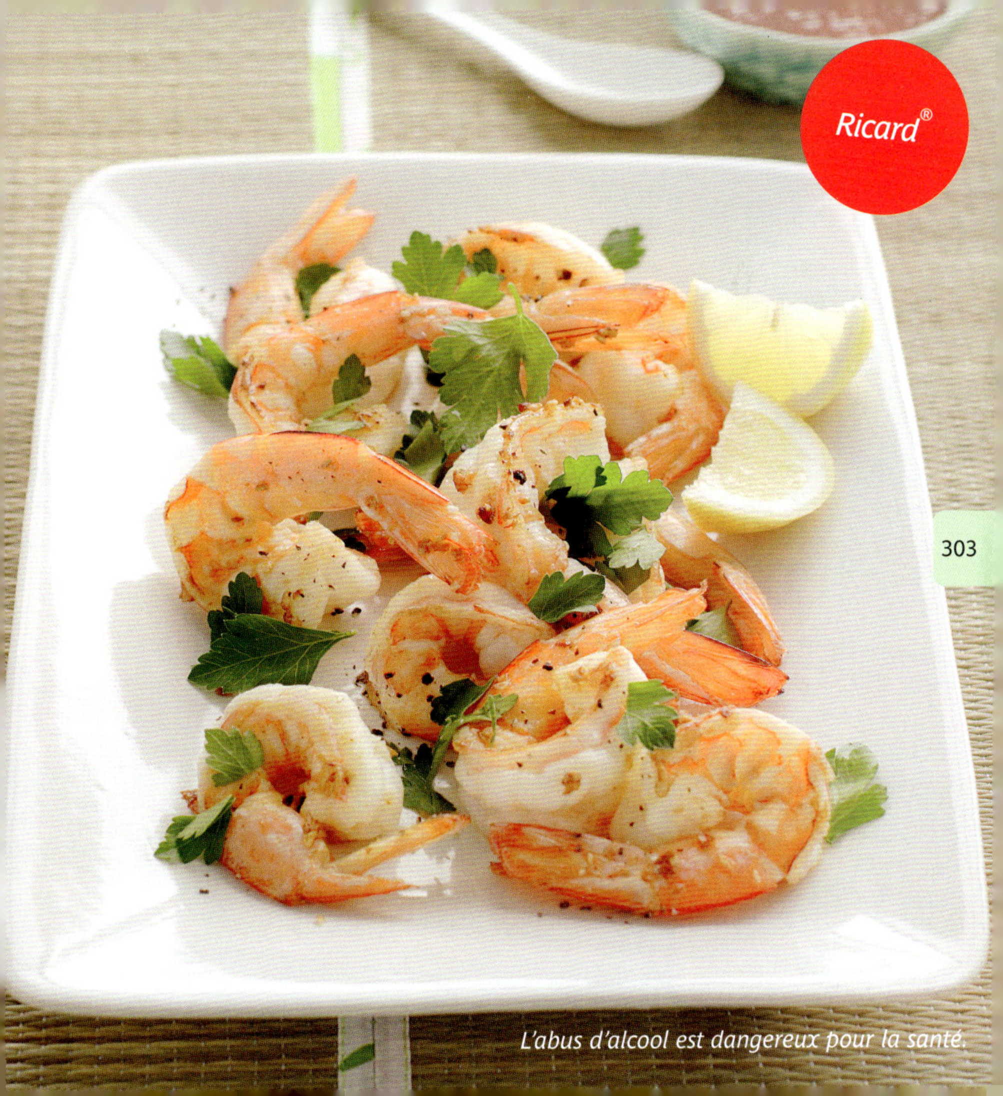
Ricard®

NAGE DE MELON AU RICARD®

Préparation : 15 min • **Cuisson :** 5 min • **Réfrigération** : 2 h
Pour 4 personnes

2 melons • 30 g de sucre en poudre • 10 cl de Ricard®
quelques feuilles de menthe

- Coupez les melons en deux et prélevez des billes de chair à l'aide d'une cuillère parisienne.
- Mettez-les dans un saladier.
- Mettez le sucre dans une casserole et ajoutez 20 cl d'eau. Portez à ébullition pour dissoudre le sucre et obtenir un sirop.
- Hors du feu, ajoutez le Ricard® et 20 cl d'eau.
- Versez ce sirop au Ricard® dans le saladier.
- Réservez au réfrigérateur pendant 2 h.
- Lavez les feuilles de menthe et essuyez-les avec du papier absorbant.
- Répartissez la nage de melon dans des verres et ornez-les de feuilles de menthe.
- Servez sans attendre.

Nage de pastèque au Ricard®

Remplacez les melons par 1 gros morceau de pastèque, dont vous prélèverez la chair en billes. Supprimez les graines.

Granité de melon au Ricard®

Mixez la chair des melons, puis ajoutez le Ricard® et le sirop de sucre. Mettez le mélange dans un plat supportant le froid et mettez au congélateur. Grattez le mélange toutes les heures à la fourchette, jusqu'à l'obtention d'un granité.

Soupe salée au melon et au Ricard®

Remplacez le sucre par du sel, du poivre et des baies roses. Servez avec du jambon sec taillé en lamelles.

Cocktail au melon et au Ricard®

Mixez les billes de melon avec 15 cl de Ricard®, 1 sirop de sucre infusé à l'estragon et 10 glaçons. Versez dans des verres à Ricard® et servez sans attendre.

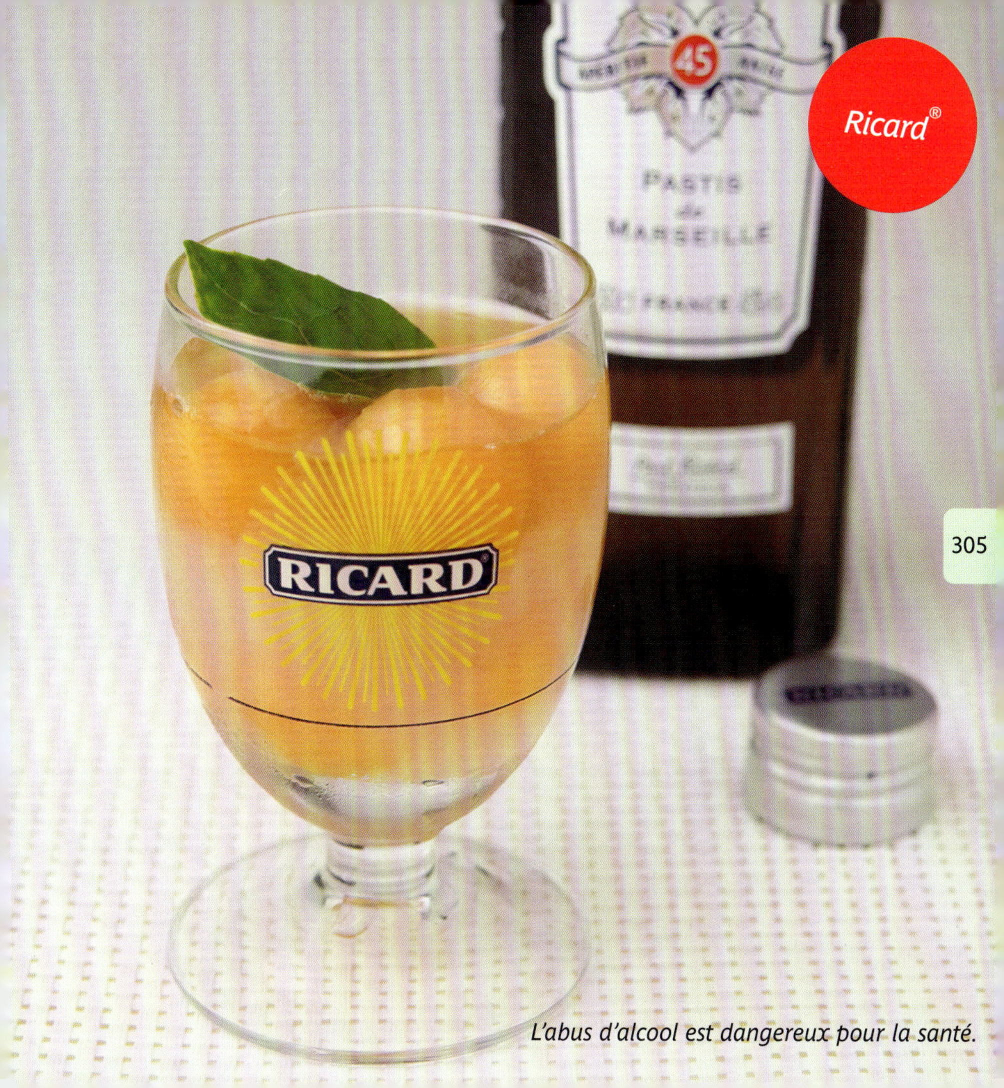

L'abus d'alcool est dangereux pour la santé.

PAPILLOTES DE ROUGET AU FENOUIL ET AU RICARD®

Préparation : 15 min • **Cuisson :** 25 min • **Pour 4 personnes**

2 bulbes de fenouil • 2 tomates • 2 c. à s. d'huile d'olive
1 c. à s. de Ricard® • 12 filets de rouget • sel et poivre

- Lavez les bulbes de fenouil et les tomates. Émincez finement le fenouil, et coupez les tomates en rondelles.
- Faites-les fondre dans une sauteuse sur feu moyen, pendant 15 min environ, avec l'huile d'olive.
- Ajoutez le Ricard®, salez, et laissez le jus réduire.
- Préchauffez le four à 180 °C.
- Découpez 4 feuilles de papier sulfurisé. Répartissez les légumes et les filets de rouget sur chacune. Salez et poivrez. Refermez les papillotes.
- Faites cuire au four pendant 10 min environ.
- Servez sans attendre.

Rougets et fenouil grillés au Ricard®
Faites griller le fenouil émincé au barbecue pendant quelques minutes. Saisissez rapidement les filets de rouget, puis faites flamber au Ricard®.

Papillotes de poireau et fenouil
Remplacez les tomates par 2 blancs de poireau émincés.

Papillotes de saumon
Remplacez les filets de rouget par 4 pavés de saumon. Faites cuire au four pendant 25 min.

Papillotes de cabillaud
Supprimez les tomates. Faites revenir le fenouil avec 200 g de lardons. Ajoutez 1 carotte, 1 gousse d'ail et 2 échalotes hachées. Remplacez les filets de rouget par 4 pavés de cabillaud. Faites cuire au four pendant 30 min.

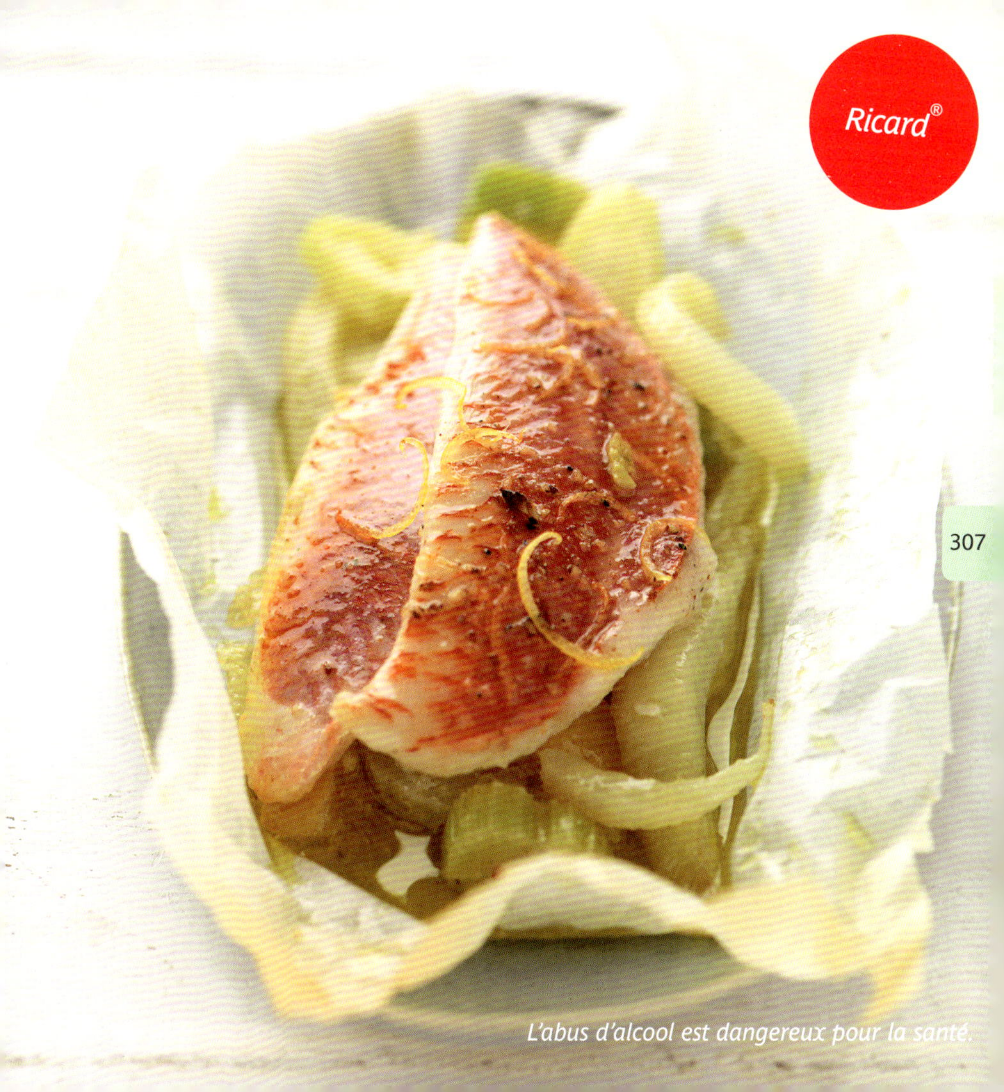

Rillettes Bordeau Chesnel®

BOUCHÉES AUX RILLETTES

Préparation : 20 min • **Cuisson :** 30 min • **Pour 6 personnes**

3 gousses d'ail • 1 oignon • 1 pot de rillettes du Mans Bordeau Chesnel®
1 c. à s. de clous de girofle moulus • 100 g de chapelure
1 rouleau de pâte feuilletée • 1 œuf • graines de sésame
sauce piment pour accompagner • sel et poivre

- Préchauffez le four à 220 °C.
- Épluchez l'ail et l'oignon. Écrasez l'ail et hachez l'oignon.
- Dans un grand saladier, mélangez les rillettes Bordeau Chesnel®, l'ail, l'oignon, les clous de girofle et la chapelure. Salez et poivrez.
- Déroulez la pâte feuilletée, puis coupez-la en deux. Divisez la farce en deux, puis étalez chaque part sur une moitié de pâte, en formant un boudin.
- Séparez le blanc du jaune d'œuf. Badigeonnez les parties de pâte sans farce avec du blanc d'œuf, puis repliez-les sur la viande pour l'enfermer. Pincez les bords de pâte pour bien refermer, brossez avec le jaune d'œuf battu, et parsemez de graines de sésame. Salez et poivrez.
- Coupez les boudins de pâte farcis en tronçons de 3 cm. Placez-les, sur une plaque à pâtisserie recouverte de papier sulfurisé.
- Faites cuire au four pendant 30 min environ, jusqu'à ce que les roulés soient bien dorés.
- Servez avec de la sauce piment.

Bouchées aux rillettes à la pomme
Ajoutez 1 pomme rouge râpée à la farce.

Bouchées aux rillettes et à la sauge
Ajoutez 10 brins de sauge ciselés à la farce. À défaut, utilisez du romarin frais ou de l'origan déshydraté.

Bouchées aux rillettes aux épices
Ajoutez 1 c. à c. de paprika doux, 1 c. à c. de piment d'Espelette et 1 pincée de piment de Cayenne à la farce.

Sauce piment maison
Mixez 2 petits piments rouges avec 1 morceau de 5 cm de blanc de poireau, 1 gousse d'ail et 1 morceau de 2 cm de gingembre frais. Salez, poivrez, ajoutez 1 cube de bouillon de bœuf dilué dans de l'eau et 4 c. à s. d'huile. Servez en accompagnement des bouchées.

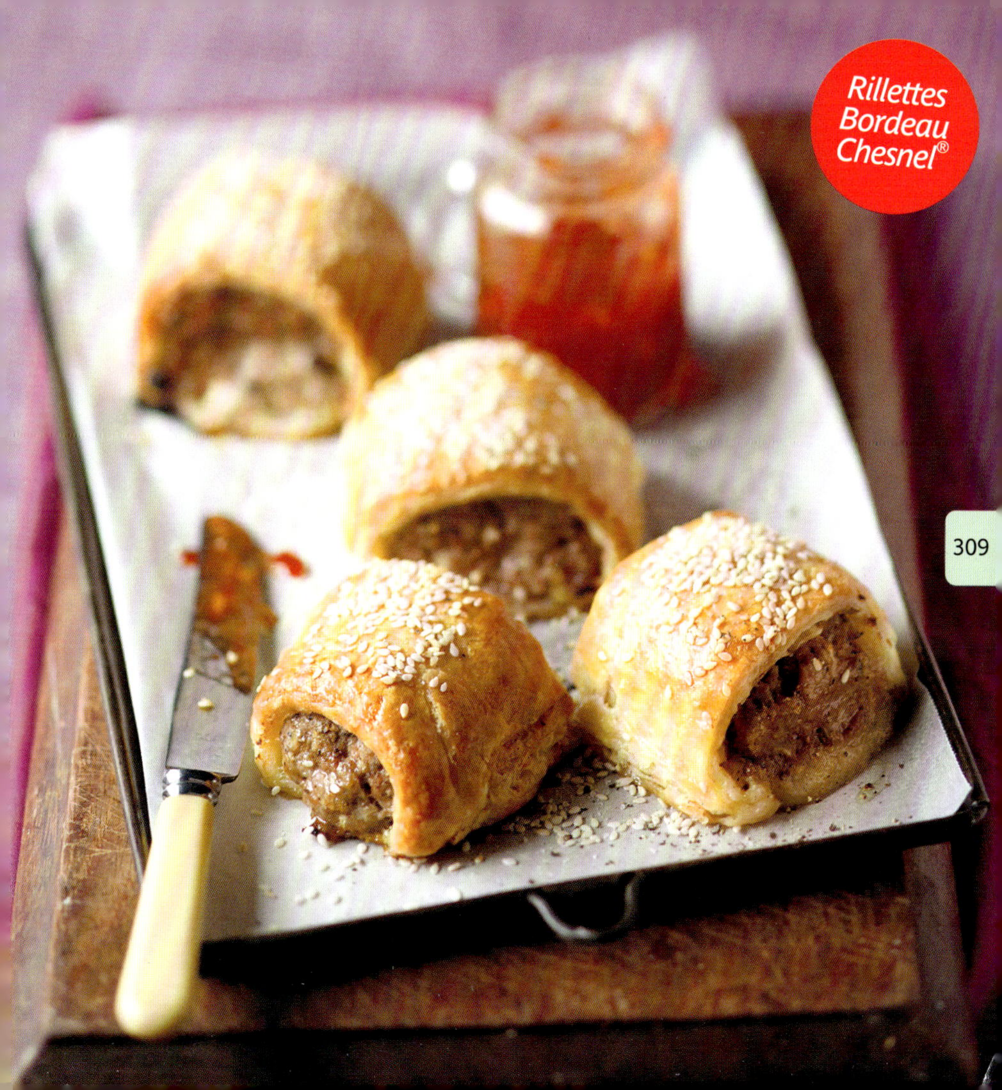
Rillettes
Bordeau
Chesnel®

CAKE AUX RILLETTES

Préparation : 15min • **Cuisson :** 50 min • **Pour 6 personnes**

200 g de farine • 1 sachet de levure chimique • 100 g de gruyère râpé
10 cl de lait • 3 œufs • 200 g de rillettes du Mans Bordeau Chesnel®
sel et poivre

- Préchauffez le four à 180 °C.
- Mélangez la farine, la levure, le gruyère râpé, le lait, les œufs, du sel et du poivre dans un saladier.
- Faites chauffer les rillettes Bordeau Chesnel® à la poêle, à feu doux, pour les faire fondre. Retirez la graisse rendue, puis ajoutez les rillettes à la pâte.
- Versez la préparation dans un moule à cake.
- Faites cuire au four pendant 45 min environ.

Cake aux rillettes et aux raisins secs

Ajoutez 75 g de raisins secs à la préparation. Assaisonnez avec des baies roses.

Cake aux rillettes et aux pruneaux

Ajoutez 75 g de pruneaux dénoyautés et coupés en dés à la pâte.

Muffins aux rillettes et aux pistaches

Ajoutez 75 g de pistaches non salées concassées à la pâte. Répartissez-la dans les alvéoles d'un moule à muffin et faites cuire au four de 25 à 30 min.

Cake aux rillettes, au persil et aux pignons

Ajoutez 75 g de pignons de pin grillés à sec et 1/2 bouquet de persil plat ciselé à la préparation.

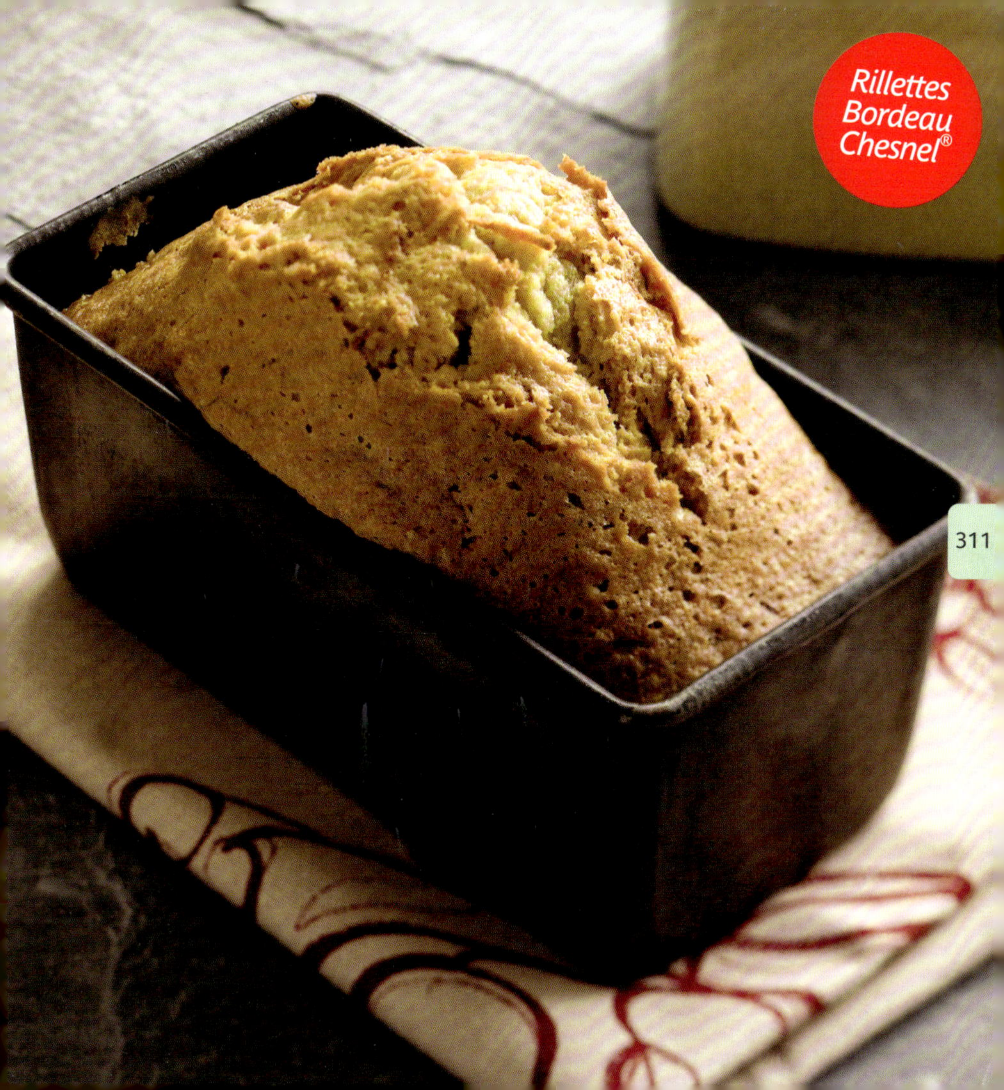
Rillettes
Bordeau
Chesnel®

WRAPS AUX RILLETTES

Préparation : 10 min • **Cuisson** : aucune • **Pour 4 personnes**

1 concombre • 2 tomates • 8 lanières de poivron grillé à l'huile
1 petite boîte de grains de maïs • 4 feuilles de laitue • 4 tortillas de blé
1 pot de rillettes de poulet rôti Bordeau Chesnel®

- Pelez le concombre, épépinez-le et taillez-le en tout petits dés.
- Plongez les tomates dans de l'eau bouillante pendant 30 sec, puis passez-les sous l'eau froide pour arrêter la cuisson. Pelez-les, puis épépinez-les et concassez-les.
- Taillez les lanières de poivron grillé en petits dés.
- Égouttez les grains de maïs et rincez-les.
- Déposez une feuille de salade sur chaque tortilla.
- Nappez chaque feuille de salade de rillettes Bordeau Chesnel®, puis répartissez les dés de tomate, de concombre et de poivron grillé, ainsi que les grains de maïs, par-dessus.
- Enroulez les tortillas de blé sur la farce, et maintenez les rouleaux à l'aide de piques à cocktail.
- Servez ou mettez-les dans une lunch box pour le repas de midi.

Wraps à l'italienne
Remplacez le concombre par 4 tranches d'aubergine grillée taillées en dés. Remplacez le maïs par 4 tomates séchées émincées, et la laitue par de la roquette.

Wraps aux tagliatelles de légumes et aux rillettes
Remplacez les légumes par 2 petites courgettes et 2 carottes détaillées en tagliatelles à l'aide d'une mandoline.

Galettes aux rillettes et aux tomates fraîches
Remplacez les tortillas par des galettes de sarrasin. Recouvrez-les de rillettes, de rondelles de tomate et de gruyère râpé. Repliez les bords des galettes sur la farce, et faites cuire au four préchauffé à 180 °C pendant 15 min.

Galettes aux rillettes et au miel
Reprenez la recette ci-dessus en ajoutant 1 c. à s. de miel sur les tomates avant de plier. Remplacez le fromage râpé par de la bûche de chèvre.

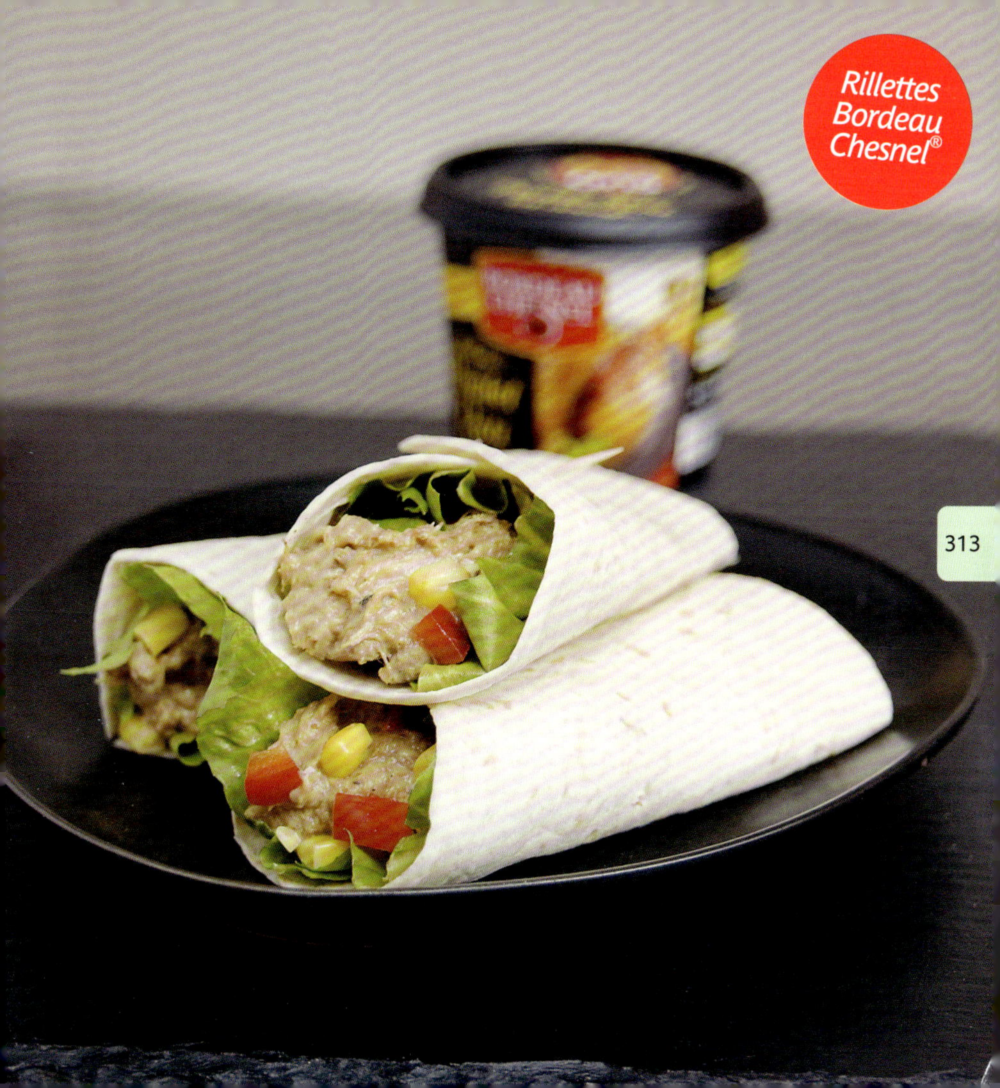
Rillettes
Bordeau
Chesnel®

CROQUETTES DE RIZ AUX TOMATES CONFITES

Préparation: 20 min • **Cuisson**: 40 min • **Repos**: 30 min • **Pour 6 personnes**

pour les croquettes : *1 petit oignon • 1 gousse d'ail • 1 bouquet de basilic 2 c. à s. d'huile d'olive • 230 g de riz long grain Uncle Ben's® • 6 cl de vin blanc sec • 30 cl de bouillon de poulet • 80 g de parmesan râpé • 50 g de tomates confites • 40 g de farine • feuilles de roquette, pour accompagner*
pour la mayonnaise : *80 g de mayonnaise • le jus de 1/2 citron quelques feuilles de basilic hachées • sel et poivre*

- Épluchez l'oignon et l'ail. Émincez l'oignon et écrasez l'ail. Rincez le basilic, essuyez-le sur du papier absorbant, puis ciselez-le.
- Faites chauffer 1 c. à s. d'huile d'olive dans une casserole à feu vif, et faites-y revenir l'ail et l'oignon pendant 4 min environ, jusqu'à ce qu'ils soient bien tendres. Ajoutez le riz Uncle Ben's® et faites cuire en remuant pendant 1 min environ pour bien imprégner les grains. Incorporez le vin et faites cuire en remuant, jusqu'à ce que le liquide soit absorbé.
- Incorporez le bouillon et 15 cl d'eau. Portez à ébullition, puis réduisez le feu et laissez mijoter de 20 à 25 min, en remuant de temps en temps, jusqu'à ce que le riz soit bien tendre et que le liquide soit absorbé. Incorporez le parmesan, les tomates et le basilic, salez et poivrez. Laissez refroidir pendant 30 min.
- Mélangez tous les ingrédients pour la mayonnaise.
- Quand le riz a un peu refroidi, formez 8 galettes. Enrobez-les de farine, puis secouez-les pour en ôter l'excès. Faites chauffer le reste d'huile dans une grande poêle à feu vif, et faites cuire les galettes en deux fois, en les faisant dorer de 3 à 4 min sur chaque face. Servez avec la mayonnaise et la roquette.

Croquettes de riz au jambon et au paprika

Remplacez les tomates confites par 2 tranches de jambon blanc taillées en petits morceaux. Remplacez le basilic par 1 c. à c. de paprika que vous ajouterez en même temps que le riz.

Croquettes de riz à la mozzarella et au safran

Remplacez les tomates confites par 100 g de mozzarella taillée en dés. Remplacez le basilic par 1 pincée de safran, que vous ajouterez en même temps que le riz.

Croquettes de riz aux crevettes

Remplacez les tomates confites par 100 g de crevettes roses décortiquées, taillées en morceaux. Remplacez le basilic par de la coriandre.

Sauce tomate pimentée

Faites revenir 1 oignon haché à l'huile d'olive, puis ajoutez 4 tomates concassées, et laissez mijoter pendant 20 min. Ajoutez 1/2 c. à c. de purée de piment et 1 pincée de sel. Laissez refroidir et servez avec les croquettes.

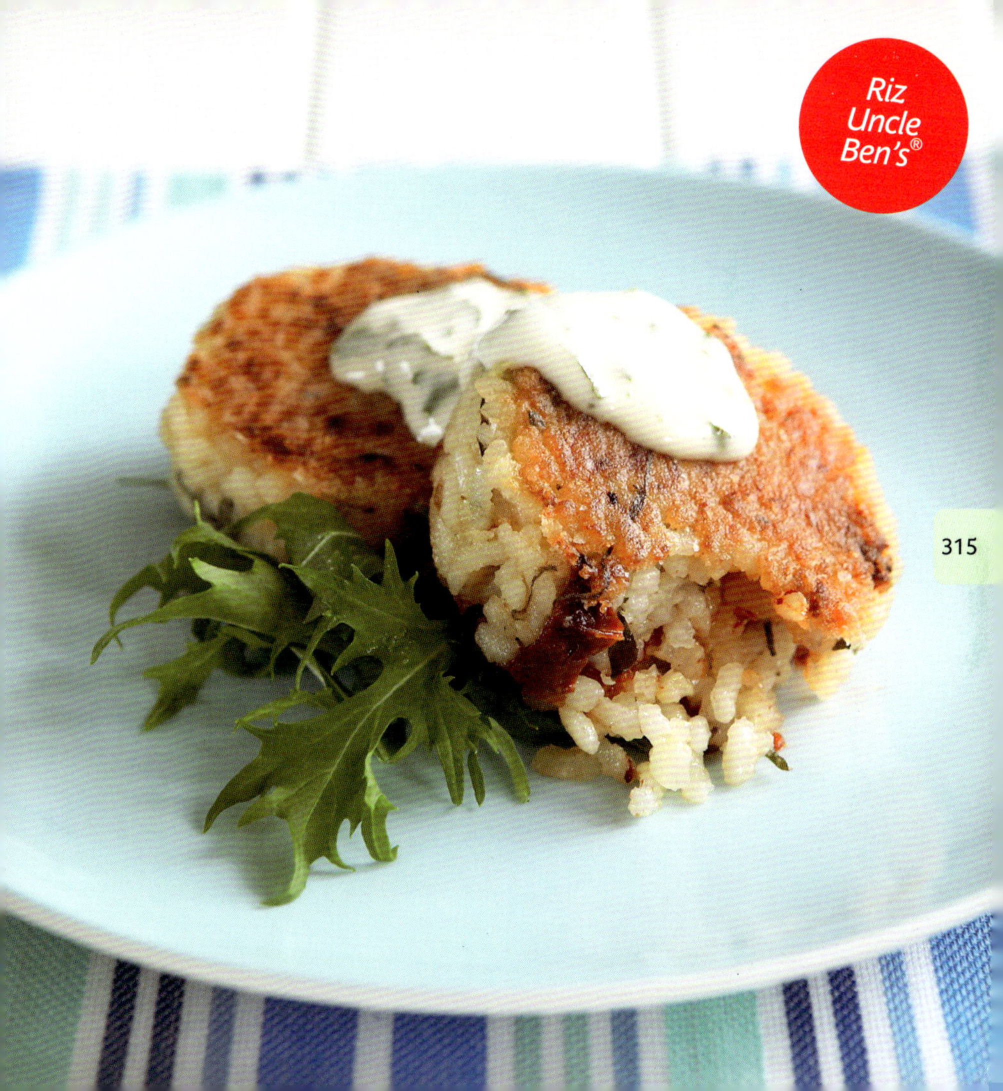
Riz
Uncle
Ben's®

RISOTTO AUX PETITS POIS

Préparation : 5 min • **Cuisson :** 25 min • **Pour 2 personnes**

1 oignon • huile d'olive • 200 g de riz Uncle Ben's pour risotto
5 cl de vin blanc • 70 cl de bouillon de volaille • 1/2 bouquet de coriandre
1/2 bouquet de menthe • 125 g de petits pois frais ou surgelés
20 g de parmesan • 2 c. à s. de crème liquide • sel et poivre

- Épluchez l'oignon, puis émincez-le finement. Faites-le revenir dans une sauteuse avec 1 filet d'huile d'olive pendant 10 min.
- Ajoutez le riz Uncle Ben's® et remuez jusqu'à ce qu'il devienne légèrement translucide.
- Versez le vin blanc, et laissez cuire jusqu'à ce qu'il soit complètement absorbé.
- Versez le bouillon petit à petit, en laissant le riz l'absorber complètement avant d'en ajouter de nouveau, et en remuant souvent. Faites cuire pendant 15 min.
- Pendant ce temps, rincez la coriandre et la menthe, puis hachez-les. Ajoutez-les dans la sauteuse avec les petits pois, salez, poivrez et poursuivez la cuisson pendant 5 min.
- Hors du feu, incorporez le parmesan et la crème liquide.
- Laissez reposer pendant 2 min avant de servir.

Risotto aux tomates cerises et au persil

Remplacez les herbes par 1 bouquet de persil, et les petits pois par 250 g de tomates cerises entières.

Risotto au potiron

Faites revenir 400 g de potiron taillé en dés avec l'oignon, puis ajoutez un peu de bouillon et laissez cuire jusqu'à ce qu'il soit tendre avant de poursuivre la recette. Supprimez les herbes.

Risotto au potiron et au lait de soja

Reprenez la recette ci-dessus en remplaçant 15 cl de bouillon et le vin par 20 cl de lait de soja.

Risotto cantonais

Supprimez les herbes. Faites cuire 2 œufs en omelette, puis taillez-la en petits morceaux. Faites revenir 200 g de lardons fumés à la poêle sans matière grasse. Ajoutez le tout dans la sauteuse en même temps que le parmesan.

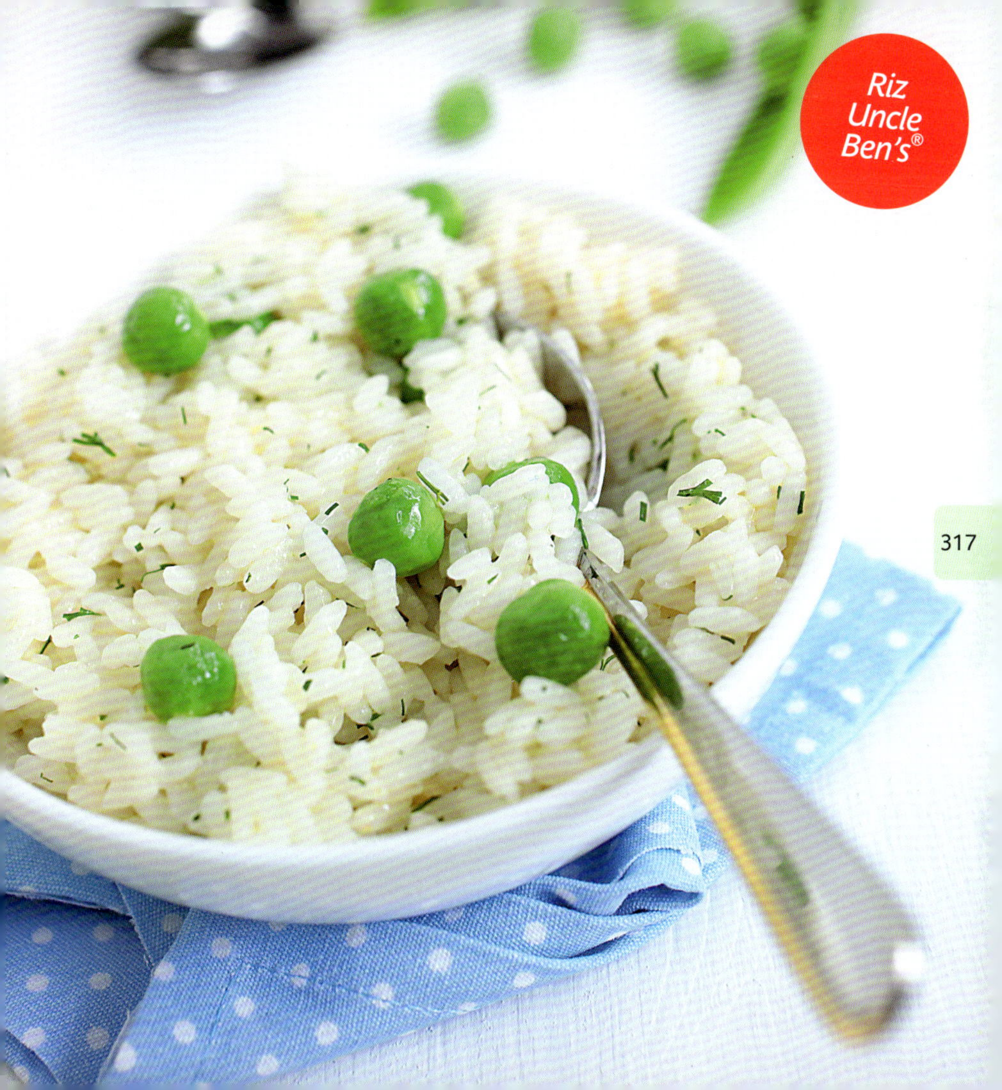
Riz Uncle Ben's®

RIZ AUX LÉGUMES ET AUX ÉPICES

Préparation : 15 min • **Cuisson :** 35 min • **Pour 8 personnes**

3 oignons jaunes • 2 gousses d'ail • 1 chou-fleur • 2 grosses pommes de terre 2 carottes • 250 g de haricots verts • 2 c. à s. de ghee ou de beurre 1 c. à s. de cumin • 1 c. à c. de curcuma • 3 gousses de cardamome écrasées 1 bâton de cannelle • 700 g de riz long grain Uncle Ben's® 1,5 l de bouillon de légumes • feuilles de coriandre, pour décorer

- Épluchez les oignons et l'ail. Émincez l'oignon et écrasez l'ail. Séparez les bouquets de chou-fleur. Pelez les pommes de terre et les carottes, puis coupez-les en rondelles. Lavez les haricots verts, puis coupez-les en tronçons de 5 cm.
- Faites chauffer la moitié du ghee ou du beurre dans une sauteuse. Ajoutez-y l'ail et la moitié des oignons, et laissez cuire en remuant pendant 3 min. Ajoutez le cumin, le curcuma, les gousses de cardamome écrasées et la cannelle, puis faites cuire pendant 30 sec.
- Ajoutez le chou-fleur, les pommes de terre et les carottes. Faites cuire en remuant pendant 5 min, jusqu'à ce que les légumes soient bien enrobés d'épices. Ajoutez le riz Uncle Ben's®, mélangez, puis incorporez le bouillon. Portez à ébullition, puis baissez le feu et laissez mijoter à couvert pendant 10 min. Ajoutez les haricots verts, et poursuivez la cuisson pendant encore 5 min jusqu'à ce que le riz soit cuit, et les légumes bien tendres.
- Faites fondre le ghee restant dans une petite poêle à feu moyen. Ajoutez le reste des oignons et laissez cuire en remuant de temps en temps pendant 10 min, jusqu'à ce qu'ils soient bien dorés.
- Servez le riz avec les oignons et parsemez de feuilles de coriandre.

Riz aux légumes et au poulet

Taillez 4 blancs de poulet en dés et faites-les dorer à la poêle avec le reste des oignons. Ajoutez-les sur le riz avant de servir.

Riz à l'ananas et aux noix de cajou

Remplacez les pommes de terre et le chou-fleur par la chair de 2 ananas taillée en dés. Parsemez le riz de noix de cajou juste avant de servir.

Riz aux légumes et à l'agneau

Faites revenir 600 g d'épaule d'agneau taillée en dés dans la sauteuse avec les oignons, l'ail et les épices, puis ajoutez 1 yaourt brassé et laissez mijoter pendant 15 min avant d'ajouter les autres ingrédients.

Lassi à l'indienne

Battez au fouet 8 yaourts brassés avec 20 cl de lait, 1 pincée de sel, 1 pincée de cardamome et 3 gouttes d'eau de rose. Servez très frais, avec le riz.

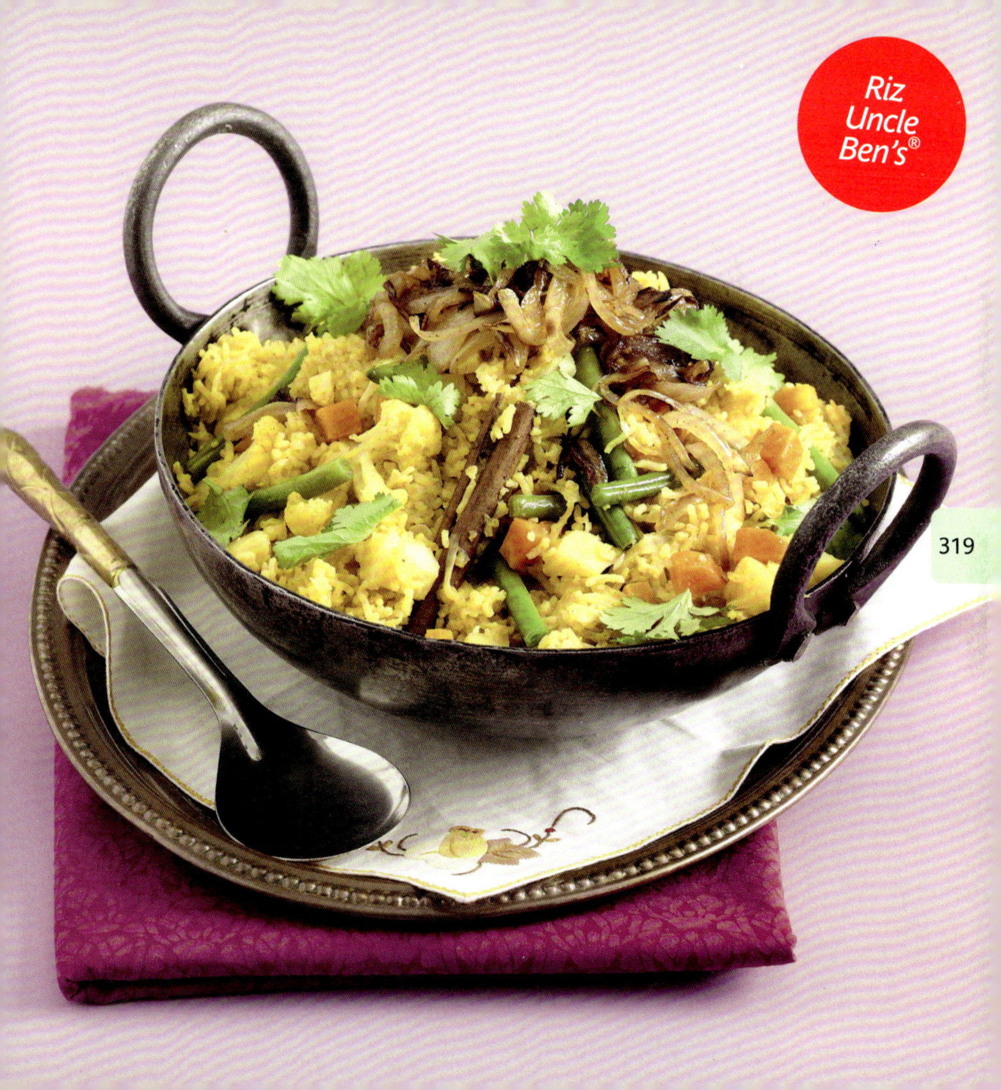
Riz
Uncle
Ben's®

Salade de riz au melon et au jambon
Remplacez l'ananas par 1 melon, dont vous détaillerez la chair en dés. Remplacez le surimi par 8 tranches de jambon sec coupées en allumettes.

Salade de riz à la truite et à l'orange
Remplacez le surimi par 4 tranches de truite fumée taillées en dés, et l'ananas par 2 oranges pelées et séparées en quartiers. Supprimez les olives.

Salade de riz aux gambas et aux poivrons
Remplacez le surimi par 16 gambas cuites décortiquées et coupées en deux. Remplacez l'ananas, le maïs et les olives par 1 poivron rouge et 1 poivron vert pelés et taillés en dés.

Salade de riz aux œufs durs et à l'avocat
Remplacez le surimi par 4 à 6 œufs durs coupés en quatre, et l'ananas par 2 avocats bien mûrs, dont vous détaillerez la chair en dés.

Riz Uncle Ben's®

SALADE DE RIZ À L'ANANAS ET AU SURIMI

Préparation : 15 min • **Cuisson** : 10 min • **Repos** : 1 h • **Pour 4 personnes**

150 g de riz Uncle Ben's® cuisson rapide • 2 c. à s. de raisins secs
8 bâtonnets de surimi au crabe • 1 ananas victoria
100 g de grains de maïs • 50 g de noix de cajou • 50 g d'olives vertes
le jus de 1/2 citron • 5 c. à s. de mayonnaise • 4 ou 5 brins de ciboulette • sel

- Faites cuire le riz Uncle Ben's® dans 2 fois son volume d'eau salée. Égouttez-le et mettez-le dans un saladier. Laissez-le refroidir complètement.
- Faites tremper les raisins secs dans de l'eau tiède pendant 15 min, puis égouttez-les.
- Coupez le surimi en cubes.
- Retirez l'écorce de l'ananas et ôtez les yeux avec la pointe d'un couteau. Taillez la chair en dés.
- Rincez les grains de maïs et égouttez-les.
- Une fois que le riz a refroidi, ajoutez-y le surimi, les dés d'ananas, les raisins secs, les grains de maïs, les noix de cajou, les olives vertes, le jus de citron et la mayonnaise.
- Rincez la ciboulette et hachez-la. Ajoutez-la à la salade.
- Servez froid.

Riz Uncle Ben's®

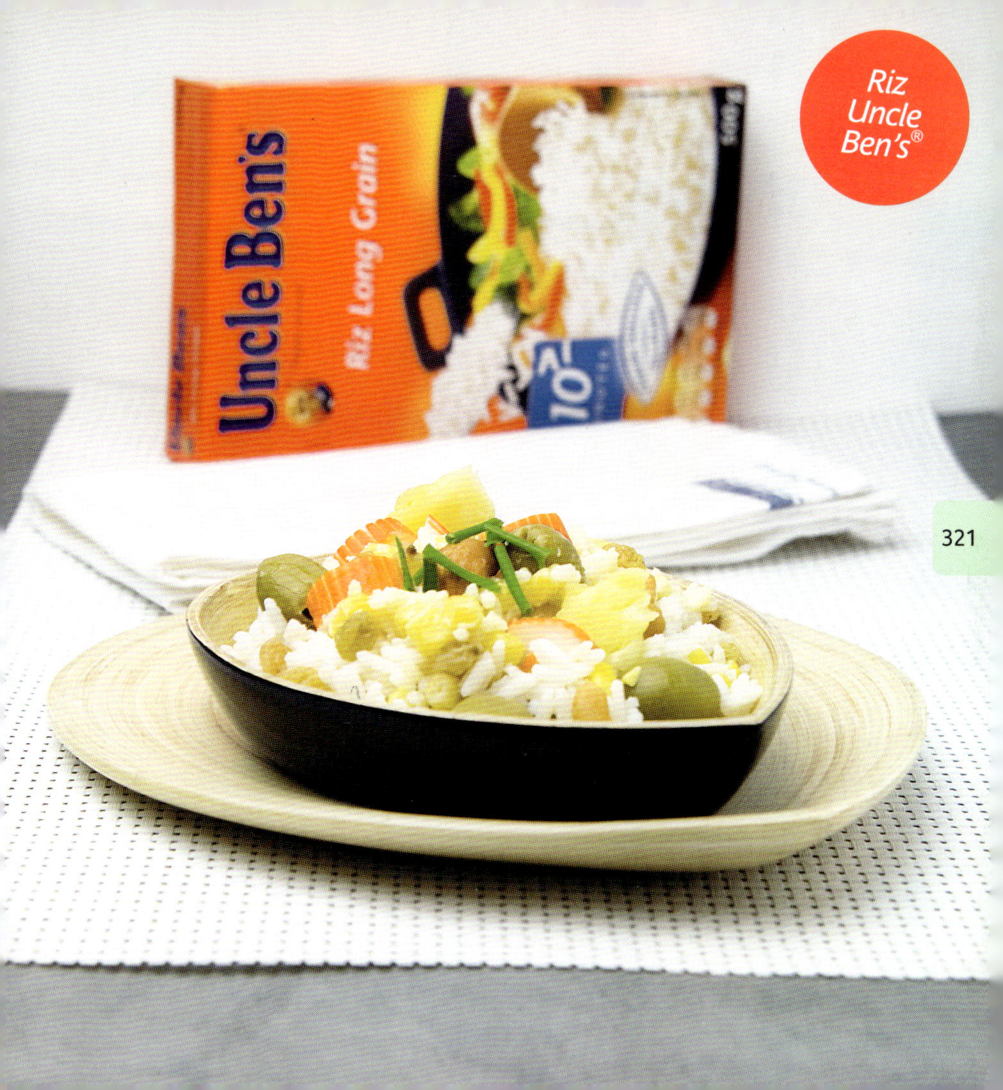

SOUPE MAROCAINE HARIRA

Préparation : 15 min • **Cuisson :** 30 min • **Pour 4 à 6 personnes**

150 g d'épaule d'agneau • 1 oignon • 2 c. à s. d'huile d'olive
50 g de lentilles • 100 g de pois chiches en boîte
50 g de riz long grain Uncle Ben's® • 400 g de tomates concassées
1/2 c. à s. de cumin en poudre • 1/2 bouquet de coriandre • sel et poivre

- Coupez l'agneau en petits cubes. Épluchez l'oignon et émincez-le finement.
- Faites dorer l'oignon et la viande dans une cocotte avec l'huile. Salez et poivrez.
- Ajoutez tous les ingrédients à l'exception de la coriandre. Versez 40 cl d'eau et portez à ébullition. Baissez le feu et laissez mijoter pendant 30 min à couvert.
- Rincez la coriandre, épongez-la avec du papier absorbant, puis ciselez-la.
- Rectifiez l'assaisonnement de la soupe, puis ajoutez la coriandre.
- Servez chaud.

Soupe Harira aux épices
Ajoutez 1 c. à s. de ras-el-hanout, 1 c. à c. de gingembre en poudre et 1 c. à c. de paprika. Ajoutez, éventuellement, 1 pincée de piment de Cayenne.

Soupe Harira au céleri
Remplacez les lentilles par 2 branches de céleri hachées, que vous ferez revenir avec les légumes secs.

Soupe Harira aux fèves et au citron
Remplacez les pois chiches par 100 g de fèves en boîte. Ajoutez le jus de 1/2 citron à la préparation.

Soupe Harira à l'œuf
Cassez 2 œufs et incorporez-les dans la soupe 2 min avant la fin de la cuisson.

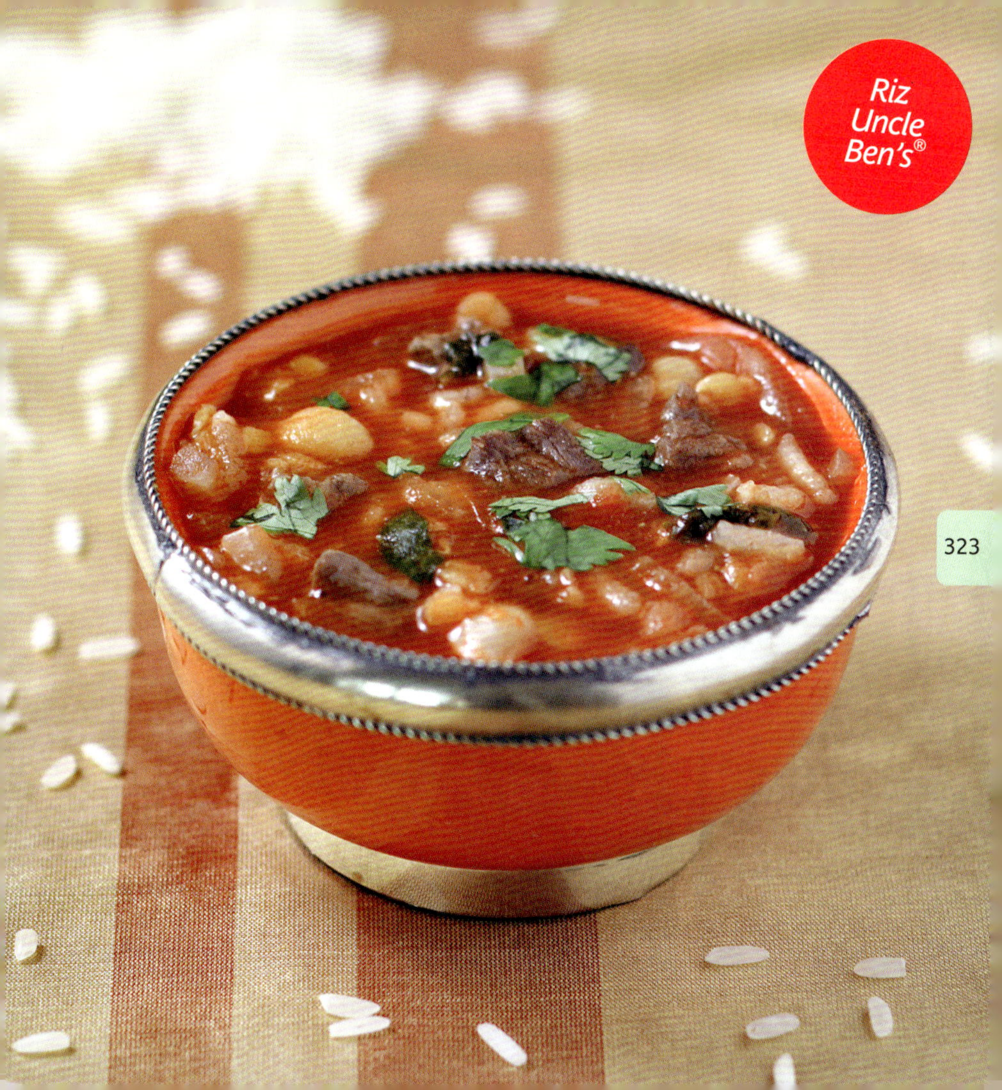
Riz
Uncle
Ben's®

CROQUE-MONSIEUR AUX SARDINES

Préparation : 10 min • **Cuisson** : 9 min • **Pour 4 personnes**

4 petites tranches de pain de campagne • huile d'olive
2 boîtes de sardines à l'huile Connétable® • 2 crottins de Chavignol
4 c. à c. de câpres

- Préchauffez le gril du four.
- Faites griller les tranches de pain de campagne au grille-pain. Coupez-les en deux.
- Déposez-en 4 sur une plaque à pâtisserie recouverte de papier sulfurisé, puis arrosez-les d'un petit filet d'huile d'olive.
- Émiettez le contenu des boîtes de sardines Connétable® et répartissez-le sur les tranches de pain.
- Coupez les crottins en deux dans l'épaisseur, et déposez-en un sur chaque croque.
- Ajoutez 1 c. à c. de câpres par-dessus.
- Passez sous le gril du four de 5 à 7 min. Le fromage doit commencer à fondre et à dorer.
- Recouvrez les croques avec les demi-tranches de pain restantes, et repassez sous le gril pendant 2 min.
- Servez sans attendre.

Croque-monsieur sardine-tapenade

Nappez les tranches de pain de tapenade noire avant d'ajouter les sardines.

Croque-monsieur sardine-poivron grillé

Mixez le contenu de 1 boîte de poivrons grillés (sans l'huile), puis nappez-en les tranches de pain avant d'ajouter les sardines.

Croque-monsieur sardine-tzatziki

Remplacez les crottins de Chavignol par du tzatziki.

Club-sandwiches aux sardines

Coupez 6 tranches de pain de mie grillées en deux, en diagonale. Nappez-en 4 de mayonnaise, ajoutez par-dessus 2 rondelles de tomates et 2 sardines, couvrez de 4 autres tranches de pain, surmontez de salade verte, de 2 rondelles d'œuf dur et de 2 sardines. Couvrez avec le pain restant. Maintenez avec des piques à cocktail.

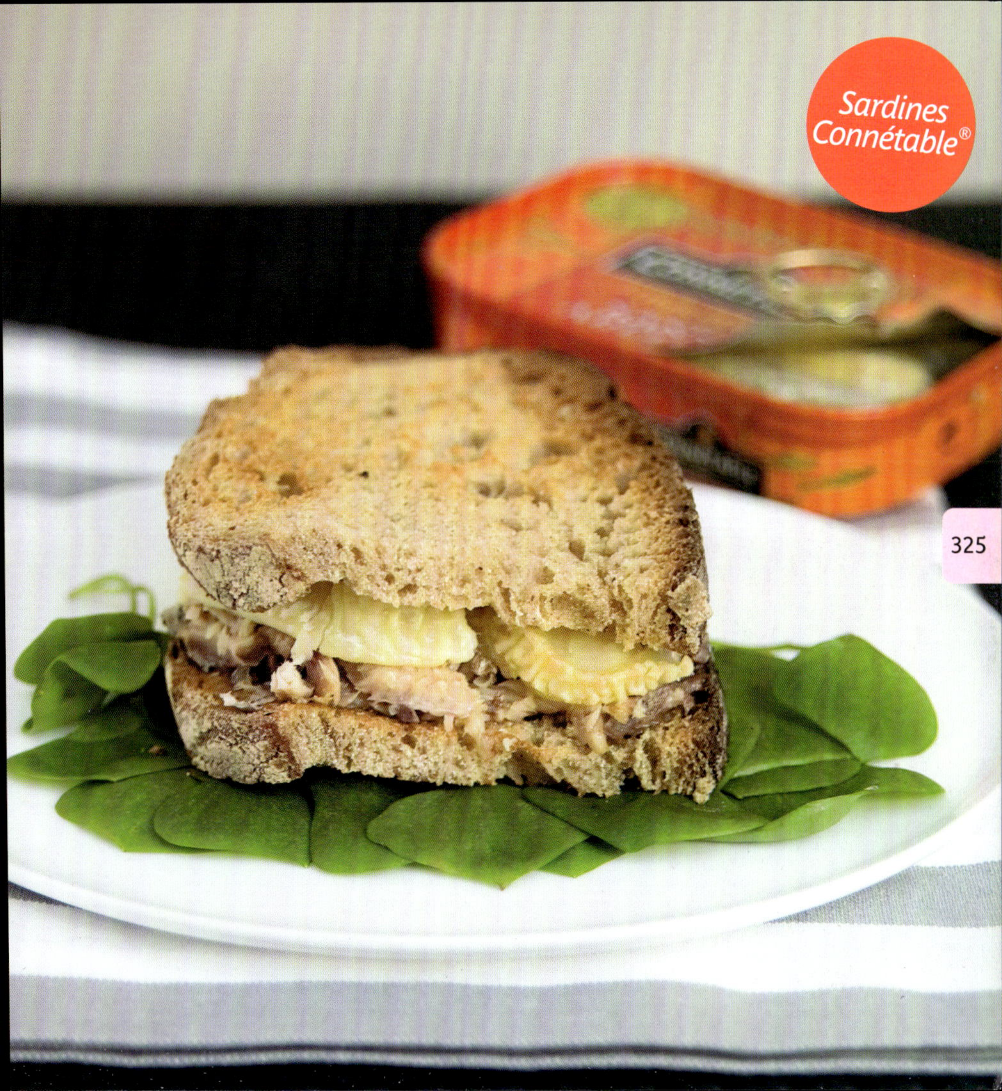
Sardines
Connétable®

ROULEAUX DE PRINTEMPS À LA SARDINE

Préparation : 20 min • **Cuisson :** aucune • **Réfrigération :** 1 h
Pour 4 personnes

1/2 concombre • 1 carotte • 8 feuilles de laitue
8 feuilles de menthe • 1 poignée de germes de soja
8 galettes de riz • 8 sardines à l'huile Connétable®

- Pelez le demi-concombre et la carotte, et taillez-les en fins bâtonnets. Lavez la laitue, la menthe et les germes de soja, puis essuyez-les avec du papier absorbant.
- Trempez 1 feuille de riz dans de l'eau chaude pendant quelques secondes pour la ramollir, puis étalez-la sur un torchon.
- Posez 1 feuille de laitue, quelques bâtonnets de carottes et de concombre, quelques germes de soja et 1 sardine Connétable® par-dessus, et terminez par 1 feuille de menthe.
- Repliez les bords de la feuille de riz vers le centre, puis roulez pour former le rouleau de printemps. Enveloppez-le dans du film alimentaire.
- Renouvelez l'opération pour les 7 autres rouleaux, puis réservez au réfrigérateur pendant 1 h.
- Servez bien frais.

Rouleaux à la sardine et à la cive
Ajoutez 4 cives finement émincées à la garniture.

Rouleaux à la sardine et aux vermicelles de riz
Faites tremper 50 g de vermicelles de riz dans de l'eau très chaude. Égouttez-les, puis taillez-les en tronçons. Répartissez-les dans les rouleaux de printemps.

Rouleaux à la sardine et aux champignons noirs
Faites tremper 10 g de champignons noirs déshydratés dans de l'eau chaude, et laissez-les gonfler. Égouttez-les, émincez-les, puis répartissez-les dans les rouleaux de printemps.

Sauce pour rouleaux de printemps
Mélangez 1/2 carotte râpée, 6 feuilles de menthe ciselées, le jus de 1/2 citron, 4 c. à s. de sauce soja, 1 c. à s. de vinaigre de riz et 3 c. à s. d'eau. Trempez les rouleaux dans cette sauce.

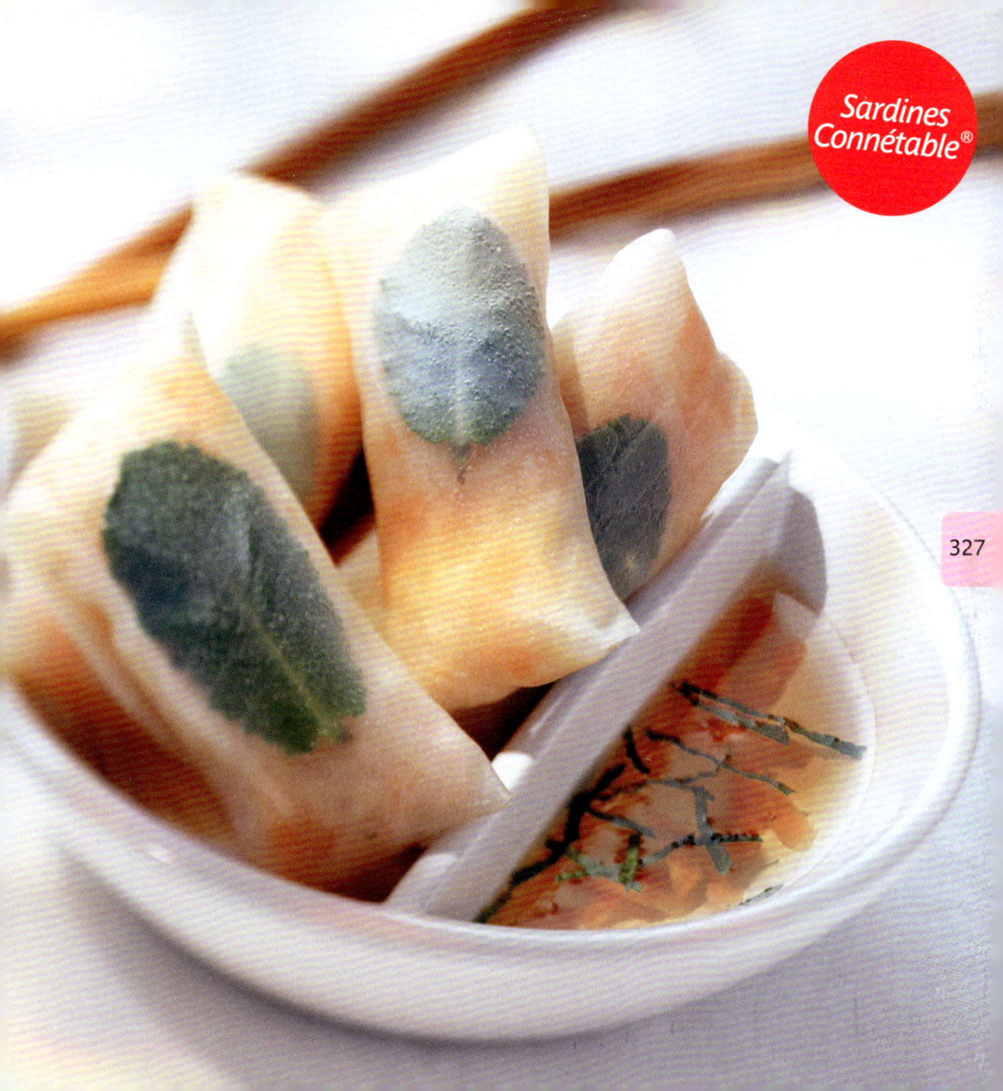
Sardines
Connétable®

SALADE AUX SARDINES ET AUX POMMES

Préparation : 15 min • **Cuisson** : aucune • **Pour 4 personnes**

pour la salade : 1 concombre • 1/4 de chou rouge • 2 pommes rouges
1 branche de céleri • 1 carotte • 1 boîte de sardines à l'huile Connétable®
40 g de cacahuètes
pour la vinaigrette : 1 ciboule • 1 c. à s. de sauce soja
3 c. à s. d'huile d'arachide • 1 c. à s. de vinaigre de vin • sel et poivre

- Lavez soigneusement le concombre, le chou rouge, les pommes et le céleri. Pelez la carotte.
- Coupez le concombre en fines rondelles, puis coupez celles-ci en deux. Évidez les pommes à l'aide d'un vide-pomme, puis taillez-les également en fines rondelles, et coupez celles-ci en deux.
- Émincez finement le chou. Taillez le céleri en très fins bâtonnets, et râpez la carotte.
- Pour la vinaigrette, rincez la ciboule, puis hachez-la finement. Mettez-la dans un bol avec tous les autres ingrédients et mélangez bien.
- Mettez les légumes et les pommes dans un saladier. Arrosez-les de vinaigrette et mélangez.
- Mettez la salade dans des assiettes. Répartissez les sardines Connétable® par-dessus. Broyez grossièrement les cacahuètes, puis ajoutez-les à la salade.
- Servez sans attendre.

Salade de mesclun aux sardines

Remplacez le chou rouge et le céleri par 3 grosses poignées de mesclun. Remplacez les pommes par 200 g de tomates cerises, et les cacahuètes par des olives noires.

Salade de pommes de terre aux sardines

Mélangez 400 g de pommes de terre cuites à l'eau refroidies et taillées en dés avec 1 oignon rouge émincé, 3 c. à s. de mayonnaise et le contenu de 1 boîte de sardines Connétable®.

Salade de pâtes aux sardines

Mélangez 400 g de fusillis cuits et refroidis avec 2 œufs durs taillés en quartiers, 8 poivrons rouges grillés taillés en lamelles, quelques olives vertes et le contenu de 1 boîte de sardines Connétable®. Arrosez de vinaigrette à l'huile d'olive.

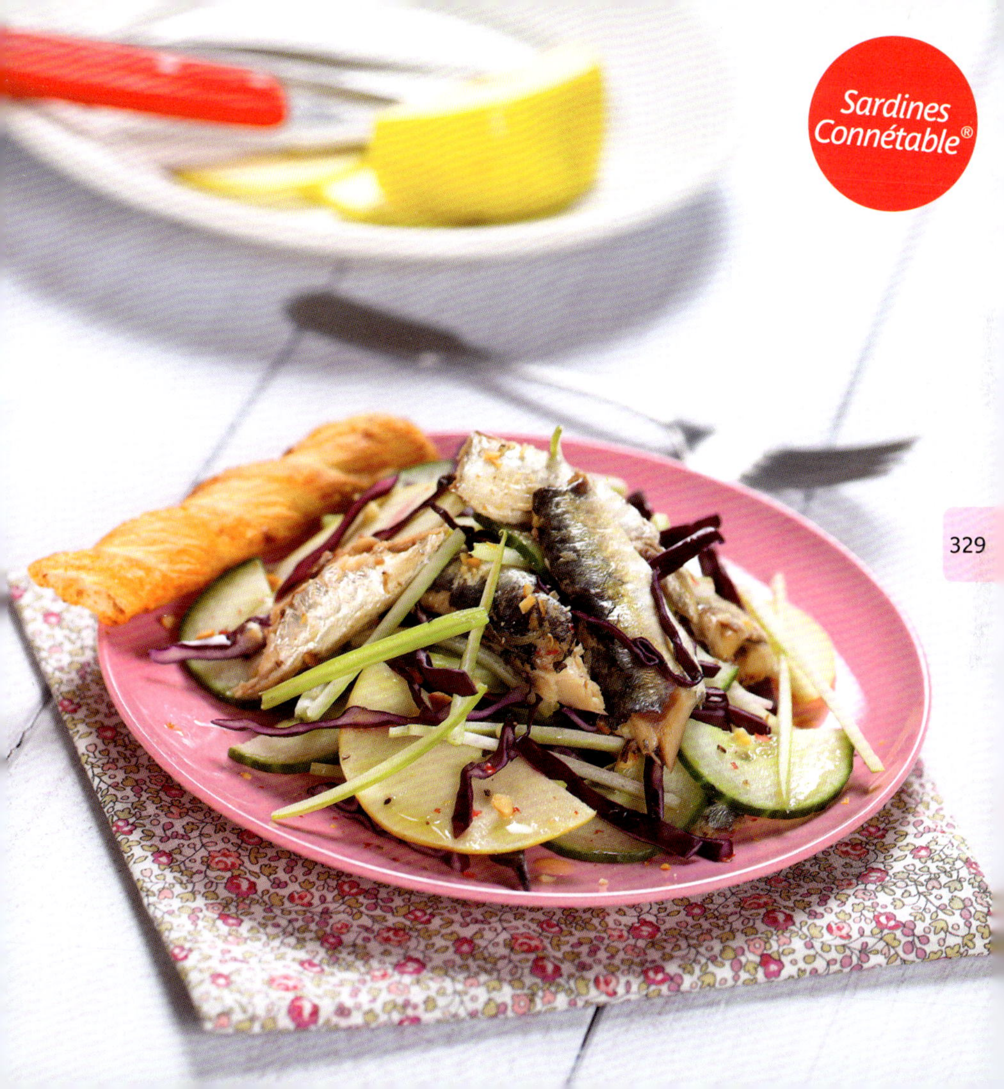

Sardines Connétable®

SAMOUSSAS AUX SARDINES

Préparation : 20 min • **Cuisson** : 20 min • **Pour 4 personnes**

1 poivron rouge • 2 gousses d'ail • 1 bouquet de basilic • 10 olives noires
2 boîtes de sardines Connétable® à l'huile d'olive et au piment d'Espelette
2 c. à s. de câpres • 4 feuilles de brick • huile d'olive • huile de friture
sel et poivre

- Préchauffez le gril du four.
- Coupez le poivron en deux, épépinez-le, puis placez-le sur une grille, côté coupé vers le bas, puis faites griller jusqu'à ce que la peau craquelle et noircisse. Glissez le poivron dans un sac à congélation, nouez et laissez reposer pendant quelques minutes, puis pelez le poivron.
- Épluchez l'ail et hachez-le. Rincez le basilic, épongez-le sur du papier absorbant, puis ciselez-le. Taillez le poivron et les olives en petits morceaux.
- Émiettez les sardines Connétable® dans un saladier. Ajoutez 1 c. à s. d'huile de la boîte, les câpres, l'ail, le basilic ainsi que poivron et olives émincés. Salez, poivrez et mélangez.
- Coupez les feuilles de brick en quatre. Pliez en deux pour obtenir un triangle. Huilez la surface au pinceau, puis déposez un peu de farce à la sardine au centre. Refermez en rabattant chacune des 3 pointes vers le centre.
- Faites dorer dans l'huile de friture de 2 à 3 min sur chaque face. Servez chaud.

Samoussas aux sardines et aux tomates

Remplacez le poivron et le basilic par 3 petites tomates épépinées et taillées en petits dés.
Ajoutez 1 filet de jus de citron à la farce.

Samoussas aux sardines et au fromage frais

Mélangez les sardines avec 150 g de fromage frais, 1/2 bouquet de persil ciselé et 50 g de fromage râpé.
Garnissez les feuilles de brick de ce mélange.

Samoussas aux sardines et à la feta

Mélangez les sardines avec 200 g de feta émiettée et 1 c. à c. de curry.
Garnissez les feuilles de brick de ce mélange.

Croissants aux sardines

Remplacez les feuilles de brick par 1 rouleau de pâte feuilletée, que vous couperez en 16 triangles. Garnissez chacun de 1 c. à c. de farce, puis roulez pour former des croissants.
Faites cuire au four préchauffé à 200 °C pendant 15 min.

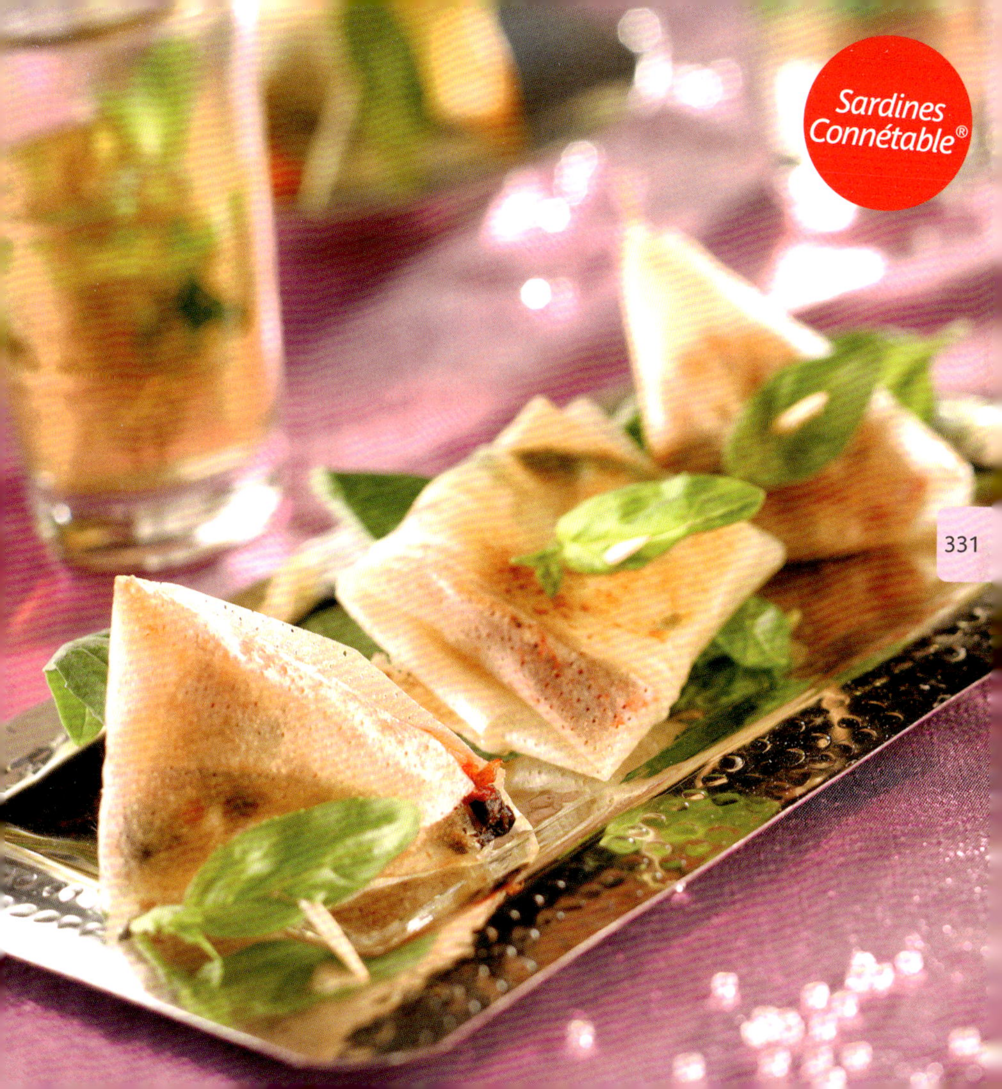
Sardines Connétable®

NOIX DE SAINT-JACQUES À LA SAVORA®

Préparation : 10 min • **Cuisson** : 7 min • **Pour 2 personnes**

10 noix de saint-jacques • 1 gousse d'ail • 2 échalotes
3 c. à s. d'huile d'olive • 1 c. à s. de vinaigre blanc
1 c. à s. de Savora® • 55 g de sucre en poudre • 20 g de beurre
feuilles de cresson • sel et poivre

- Rincez les noix de saint-jacques, puis égouttez-les sur du papier absorbant.
- Épluchez l'ail et les échalotes. Écrasez l'ail et émincez les échalotes.
- Mettez 1 c. à s. d'huile, le vinaigre, la Savora® et le sucre dans une jatte, et battez au fouet. Salez et poivrez.
- Faites chauffer le reste d'huile avec le beurre dans une poêle. Faites-y revenir l'ail et les échalotes pendant 5 min.
- Ajoutez les noix de saint-jacques et faites-les cuire pendant 1 min sur chaque face.
- Rincez le cresson et répartissez-le dans 2 assiettes. Déposez les noix de saint-jacques par-dessus, puis arrosez de sauce et poivrez.
- Servez sans attendre.

Saint-jacques au lard et à la Savora®
Entourez chaque noix de saint-jacques d'une fine tranche de lard, que vous maintiendrez avec une pique à cocktail, avant de faire cuire.

Saint-jacques flambées à la Savora®
Une fois les saint-jacques cuites, ajoutez 5 cl de cognac dans la poêle et faites flamber.

Saint-jacques en sauce crémeuse à la Savora®
Une fois les saint-jacques cuites, mettez 1 c. à s. de Savora®, 15 cl de crème liquide et 1 pincée de cumin dans la poêle. Faites chauffer pendant 2 min, puis servez avec les saint-jacques.

Brochettes de crevettes à la Savora®
Enfilez, 3 par 3, 12 crevettes roses décortiquées sur des brochettes, puis faites-les dorer rapidement à la poêle avec un peu d'huile ou sur une poêle-gril. Servez avec la sauce à la Savora®.

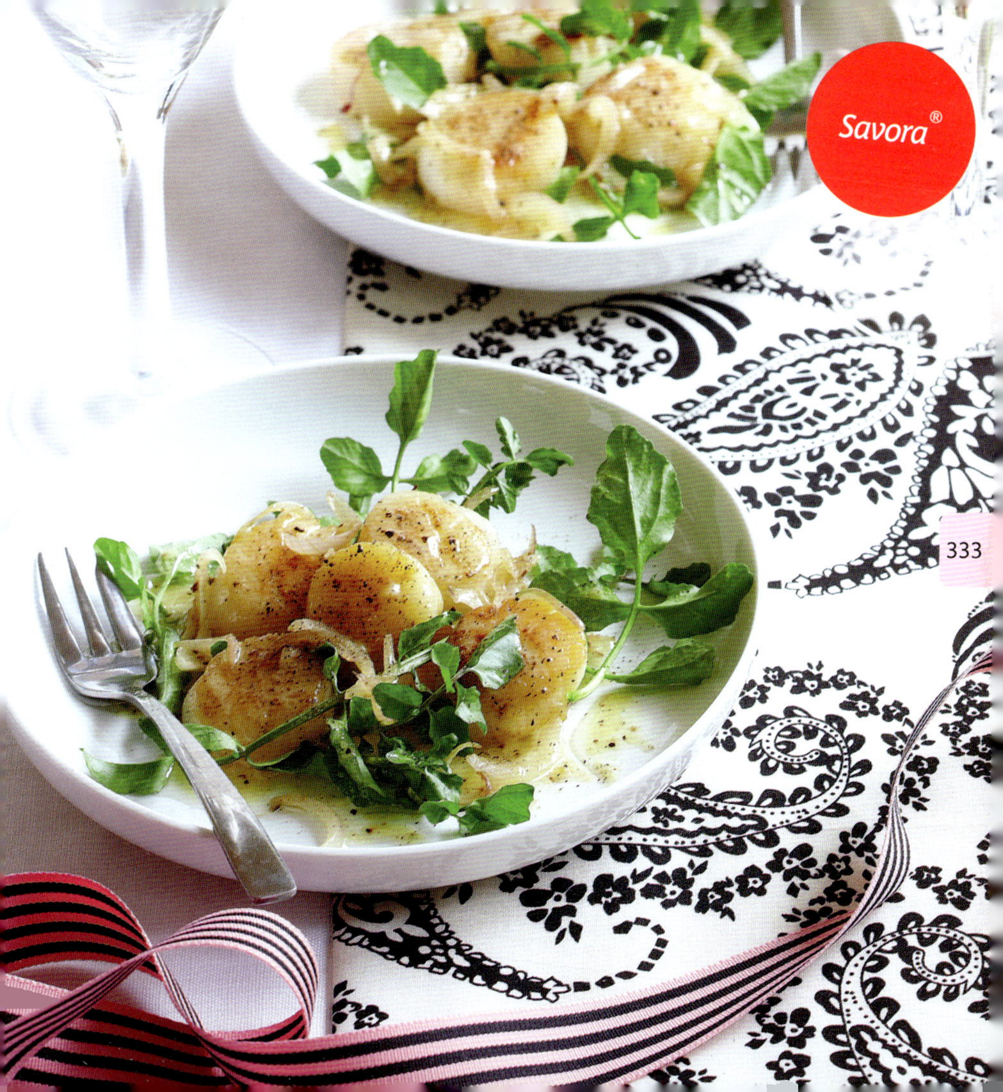
Savora®

PAPILLOTES DE CABILLAUD À LA SAVORA®

Préparation : 15 min • **Cuisson** : 35 min • **Pour 4 personnes**

1 gros oignon • 4 blancs de poireau • 30 g de beurre
200 g de crème fraîche épaisse • 2 ou 3 c. à s. de Savora®
4 morceaux de dos de cabillaud • sel et poivre

- Épluchez l'oignon et émincez-le.
- Lavez les blancs de poireau et coupez-les en rondelles.
- Faites fondre le beurre dans une poêle, puis faites-y revenir l'oignon pendant 5 min, puis ajoutez les poireaux et faites cuire pendant 10 min. Salez et poivrez.
- Préchauffez le four à 210 °C.
- Dans un bol, mélangez la crème fraîche et la Savora®.
- Découpez 4 morceaux de papier sulfurisé et répartissez les blancs de poireau par-dessus.
- Déposez un morceau de dos de cabillaud dans chaque papillote, et nappez de crème à la Savora®. Salez et poivrez.
- Fermez les papillotes. Mettez-les dans un plat supportant la chaleur, puis faites cuire au four pendant 20 min.
- Servez chaud.

Papillotes de cabillaud aux petits légumes

Remplacez les blancs de poireau par 2 carottes, 1 courgette et 1 branche de céleri taillées en tout petits dés.

Papillotes de cabillaud au fenouil

Remplacez les blancs de poireau par 1 gros bulbe de fenouil (ou 2 petits) finement émincé. Poivrez généreusement avant de servir.

Papillotes de cabillaud à la fondue d'échalotes

Remplacez les poireaux et l'oignon par 10 échalotes épluchées, finement émincées et revenues à la poêle à feu très doux avec un peu d'huile d'olive. Répartissez-les dans les papillotes une fois qu'elles sont fondantes.

Papillotes de poulet à la Savora®

Remplacez le cabillaud par 500 g de filets de poulet taillés en lamelles. Faites cuire pendant 15 min.

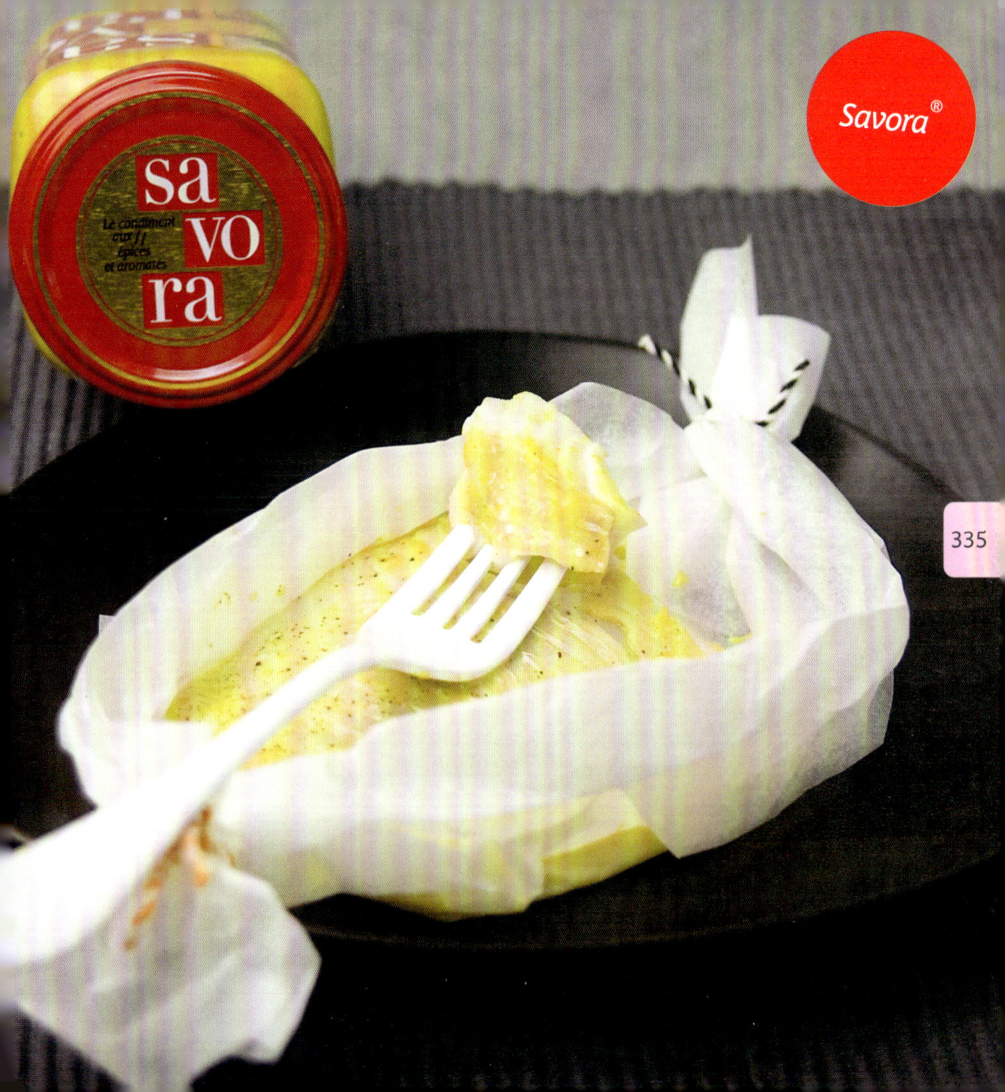

Savora®

PILONS DE POULET À L'INDIENNE

Préparation : 20 min • **Cuisson :** 25 min • **Marinade :** 2 h
Pour 4 personnes

3 gousses d'ail • 2 feuilles de laurier • 1 c. à s. de gingembre râpé • 4 c. à s. de Savora® • 1 c. à s. de vinaigre de vin • 3 c. à s. d'huile • 8 pilons de poulet • 1 oignon • 15 cl de bouillon de volaille • sel et poivre

- Épluchez l'ail et hachez-le. Émiettez le laurier.
- Préparez une marinade en mélangeant dans un plat l'ail, le gingembre, le laurier, 3 c. à s. de Savora®, le vinaigre et l'huile.
- Ajoutez les pilons dans le plat, imprégnez-les bien de la marinade, puis réservez au réfrigérateur pendant 2 h, en retournant les pilons 2 ou 3 fois.
- Préchauffez le four à 200 °C.
- Épluchez l'oignon et émincez-le.
- Égouttez les pilons, puis mettez-les dans un plat à four avec l'oignon.
- Faites cuire au four pendant 25 min en retournant les pilons à mi-cuisson.
- Mélangez la marinade avec le bouillon de volaille dans une petite casserole, et portez à ébullition. Hors du feu, incorporez le reste de Savora®, du sel et du poivre.
- Nappez les pilons de poulet de cette sauce avant de servir.

Pilons marinés à la citronnelle
Ajoutez à la marinade le jus de 1/2 citron ainsi que 1 bâton de citronnelle finement émincé.

Pilons marinés au curry
Remplacez le gingembre, le laurier et le vinaigre par 2 c. à s. de sauce soja et 2 c. à c. de curry en poudre.

Remplacez le gingembre, le laurier et le vinaigre par 1 c. à s. de concentré de tomate, 1 c. à s. de ketchup et 1 trait de sauce piquante mexicaine.

Pilons marinés au sésame
Passez les pilons de poulet marinés et égouttés dans une assiette remplie de graines de sésame avant de faire cuire au four.

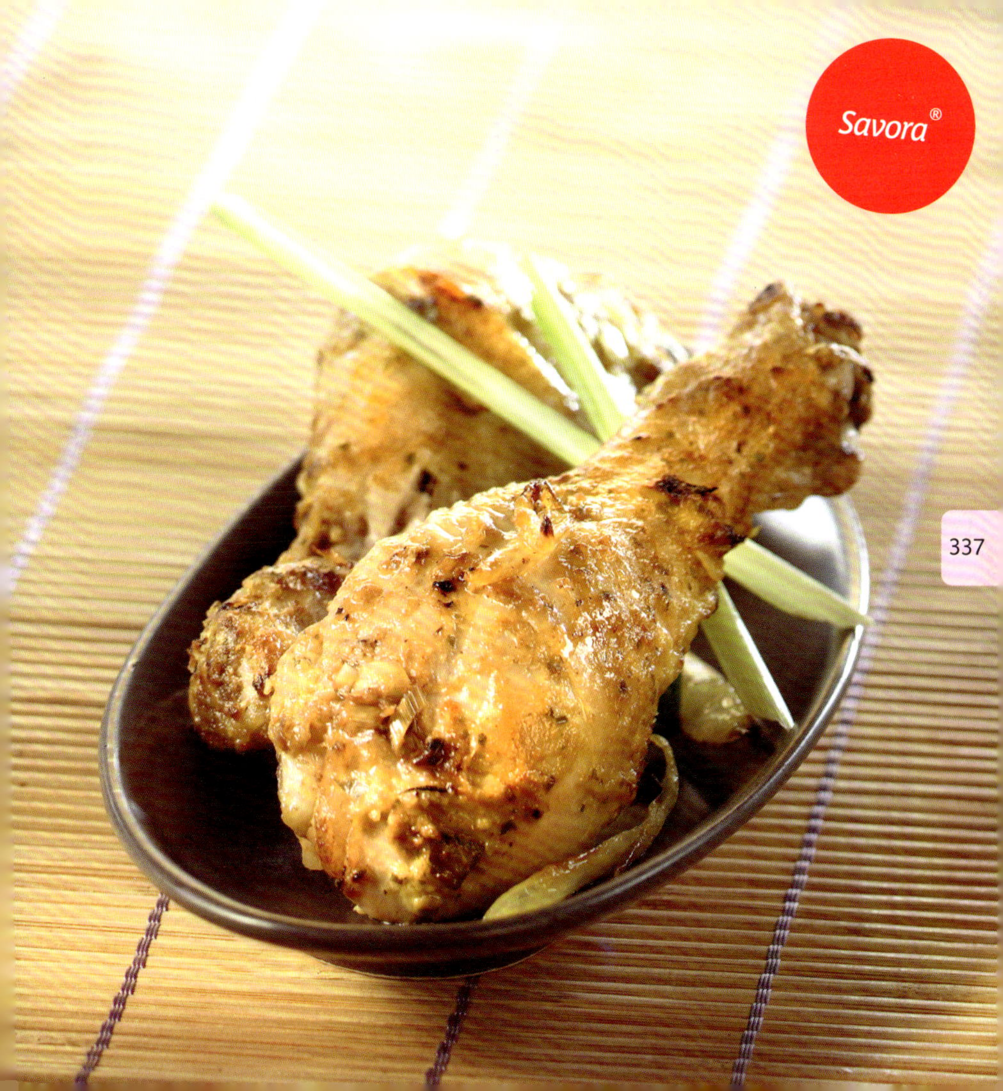
Savora®

Scones au whisky et aux tomates confites

Battez le lait avec 5 cl de whisky avant de l'incorporer à la pâte. Ajoutez 10 tomates confites égouttées et hachées au mélange.

Scones aux carottes

Remplacez le cheddar et les flocons d'avoine par 2 carottes pelées et râpées. Ajoutez 1 c. à s. de graines de cumin à la pâte.

Scones au jambon sec

Ajoutez 4 tranches de jambon sec taillées en lamelles à la préparation.

Sandwiches de scones au saumon

Coupez les scones cuits en deux, puis garnissez-les de 1/2 tranche de saumon fumé et de crème fraîche épaisse agrémentée de 1 c. à c. de graines de moutarde.

SCONES À LA SAVORA®

Préparation : 15 min • **Cuisson :** 15 min • **Réfrigération :** 1 h
Pour 15 scones

60 g de cheddar • 250 g de farine + un peu pour le plan de travail
40 g de flocons d'avoine • 60 g de beurre ramolli • 1 œuf
15 cl de lait • 1 c. à s. de Savora® • sel et poivre

- Râpez finement le cheddar.
- Dans un saladier, réunissez la farine, les flocons d'avoine et le beurre. Travaillez le mélange du bout des doigts, jusqu'à l'obtention d'un mélange sableux.
- Incorporez le reste des ingrédients, salez et poivrez. Formez une boule de pâte, enveloppez-la dans du film alimentaire et laissez-la reposer au réfrigérateur pendant 1 h.
- Préchauffez le four à 180 °C.
- Sur le plan de travail fariné, étalez la pâte sur 1 cm d'épaisseur environ. Découpez de petits tas arrondis à l'aide d'un emporte-pièce.
- Posez-les sur une plaque recouverte de papier sulfurisé.
- Faites cuire au four pendant 15 min environ, jusqu'à ce que les scones soient dorés.
- Laissez refroidir avant de déguster.

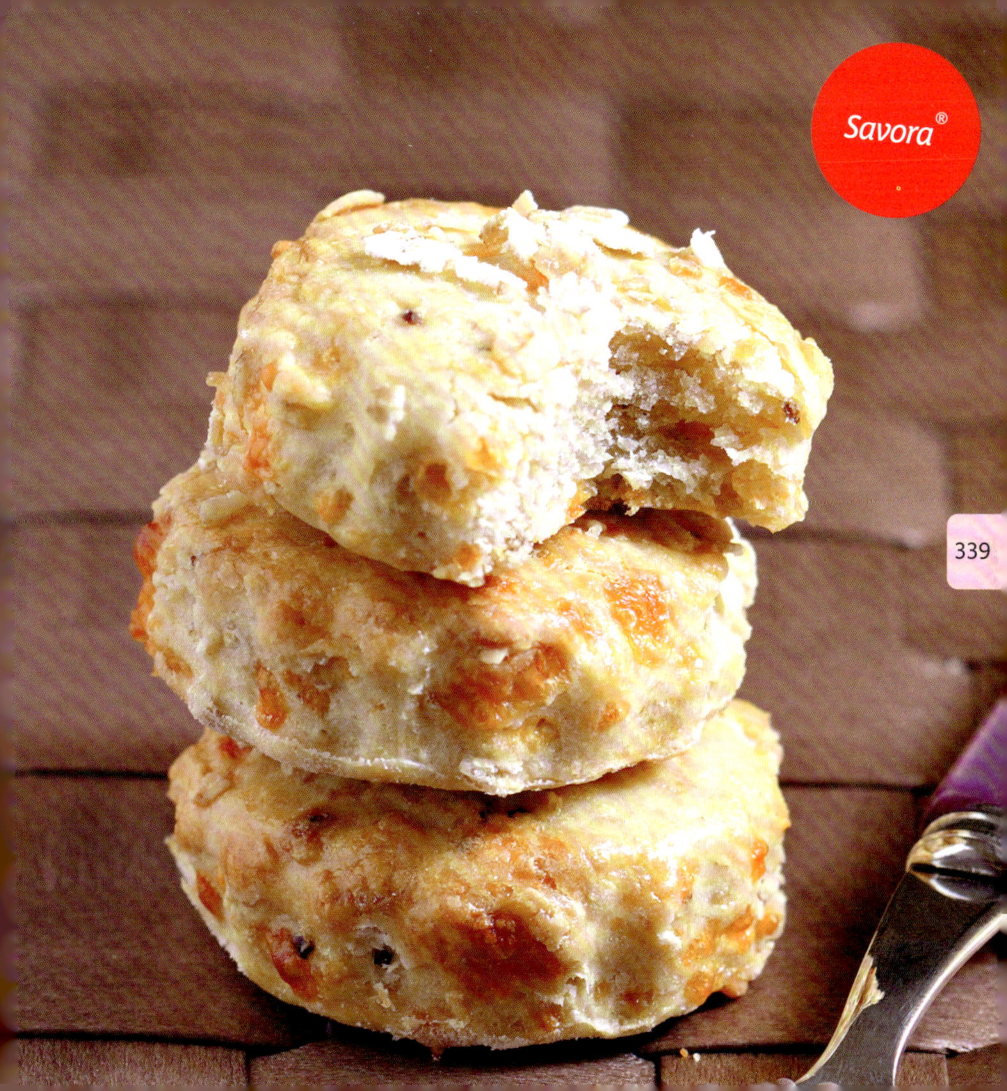
Savora®

TARTE FINE AUX POMMES DE TERRE ET À LA SAVORA®

Préparation : 20 min • **Cuisson** : 55 min • **Pour 1 tarte**

1 oignon • 750 g de pommes de terre • 5 brins de romarin
3 c. à s. de Savora® • 125 g de gruyère râpé

- Préchauffez le four à 200 °C.
- Épluchez l'oignon et émincez-le. Pelez les pommes de terre, puis taillez-les en tranches très fines à l'aide d'une mandoline. Émiettez le romarin. Faites revenir l'oignon dans une poêle, jusqu'à ce qu'il soit bien doré. Retirez-le de la poêle et réservez-le.
- Badigeonnez le fond d'un plat rond d'une fine couche de Savora®. Recouvrez d'une couche de pommes de terre en formant une rosace, et badigeonnez de Savora®. Répétez l'opération jusqu'à ce que la moitié des pommes de terre soient disposées dans le plat, en appuyant fermement après chaque ajout.
- Mélangez le romarin, le gruyère râpé, l'oignon et 1 c. à s. de Savora®. Étalez cette préparation sur la première couche puis continuez à disposer les pommes de terre et la Savora® alternativement, comme précédemment, jusqu'à l'épuisement des ingrédients.
- Faites cuire au four de 45 à 50 min, jusqu'à ce que le dessus de la tarte soit bien doré, et les pommes de terre, tendres.
- Retirez la tarte du four et laissez reposer pendant 5 min avant de retourner délicatement sur un plat.

Tarte fine au bacon
Taillez 150 g de bacon en allumettes et intercalez-les entre chaque couche de pommes de terre.

Tarte fine de pommes de terre et patates douces
Remplacez la moitié des pommes de terre par 400 g environ de patates douces, que vous préparerez de la même manière que les pommes de terre.

Tarte fine aux échalotes
Remplacez l'oignon par 10 petites échalotes épluchées et finement émincées.

Rösti à la Savora®
Râpez les pommes de terre. Mélangez tous les ingrédients dans un saladier, puis déposez 1 grosse poignée de la préparation dans une poêle, avec de l'huile de tournesol, et faites cuire pendant 7 min environ sur chaque face, jusqu'à ce que la galette soit bien dorée. Maintenez au chaud le temps de préparer les autres rösti.

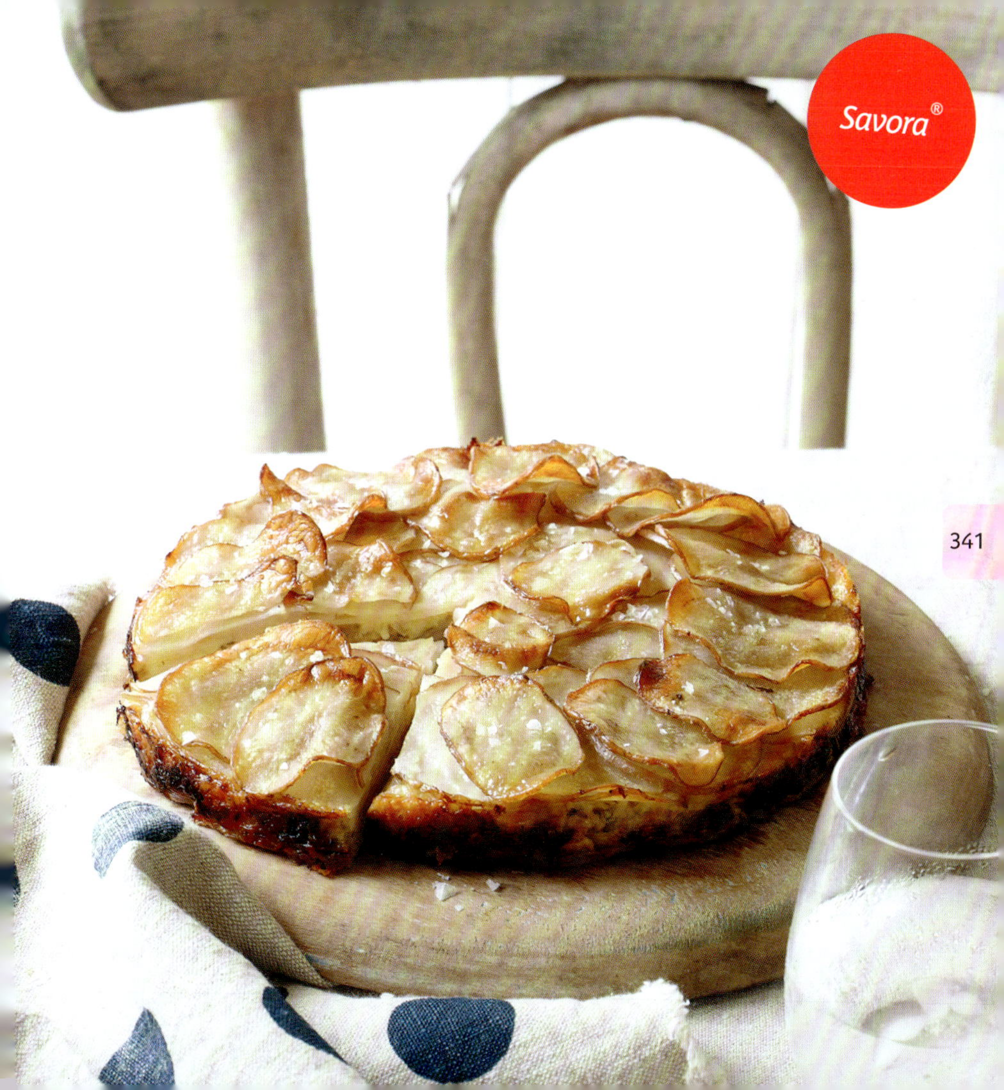
Savora®

BONSHOMMES AUX SMARTIES®

Préparation : 30 min • **Cuisson :** 10 min • **Repos :** 1 h 30
Pour 8 bonshommes

pour les bonshommes : 20 Smarties® + quelques-uns pour décorer
260 g de farine + un peu pour le plan de travail • 80 g de sucre
2 sachets de levure chimique • 12 cl de lait + 1 c. à s. • 2 c. à c. d'extrait de vanille liquide • 30 g de beurre fondu • 1 œuf • billes de sucre
pour le glaçage : 350 g de sucre glace

- Broyez les Smarties®, puis mélangez-les avec la farine, le sucre et la levure dans un saladier. Creusez un puits au centre. Versez le lait dans un autre saladier, puis ajoutez la vanille, le beurre et l'œuf, et battez au fouet. Versez le tout dans le puits. Travaillez à la spatule, jusqu'à l'obtention d'une pâte épaisse.
- Déposez-la sur le plan de travail fariné et pétrissez pendant 5 min. Mettez la pâte dans une jatte, couvrez et laissez reposer pendant 1 h. Elle doit doubler de volume.
- Pétrissez de nouveau, puis étalez la pâte sur 1 cm d'épaisseur. Découpez les bonshommes à l'aide d'un emporte-pièce. Déposez-les sur une plaque recouverte de papier sulfurisé, en les espaçant de 2 cm. Couvrez de papier sulfurisé. Laissez reposer pendant 30 min.
- Préchauffez le four à 180 °C. Badigeonnez les bonshommes avec un peu de lait, et faites-les cuire pendant 10 min, jusqu'à ce qu'ils soient dorés. Laissez refroidir.
- Pour le glaçage, faites fondre le sucre au bain-marie avec 2 c. à s. d'eau. Recouvrez-en les bonshommes. Décorez sans attendre de Smarties® et de billes de sucre. Laissez prendre, puis servez.

Bonshommes à la fleur d'oranger
Remplacez l'extrait de vanille liquide par 1 c. à s. d'eau de fleur d'oranger. Vous pouvez également utiliser de la liqueur d'orange.

Bonshommes à la cannelle
Remplacez l'extrait de vanille liquide par 1 c. à c. de cannelle en poudre.

Bonshommes au chocolat
Ajoutez 2 c. à c. de cacao amer à la préparation. Nappez les bonshommes d'un glaçage réalisé en faisant fondre 100 g de chocolat noir avec 15 cl de crème fraîche.

Bonshommes roses
Préparez le glaçage en faisant fondre au bain-marie le sucre glace avec 30 cl de lait, 1 c. à c. d'extrait de vanille liquide et 2 gouttes de colorant alimentaire rouge.

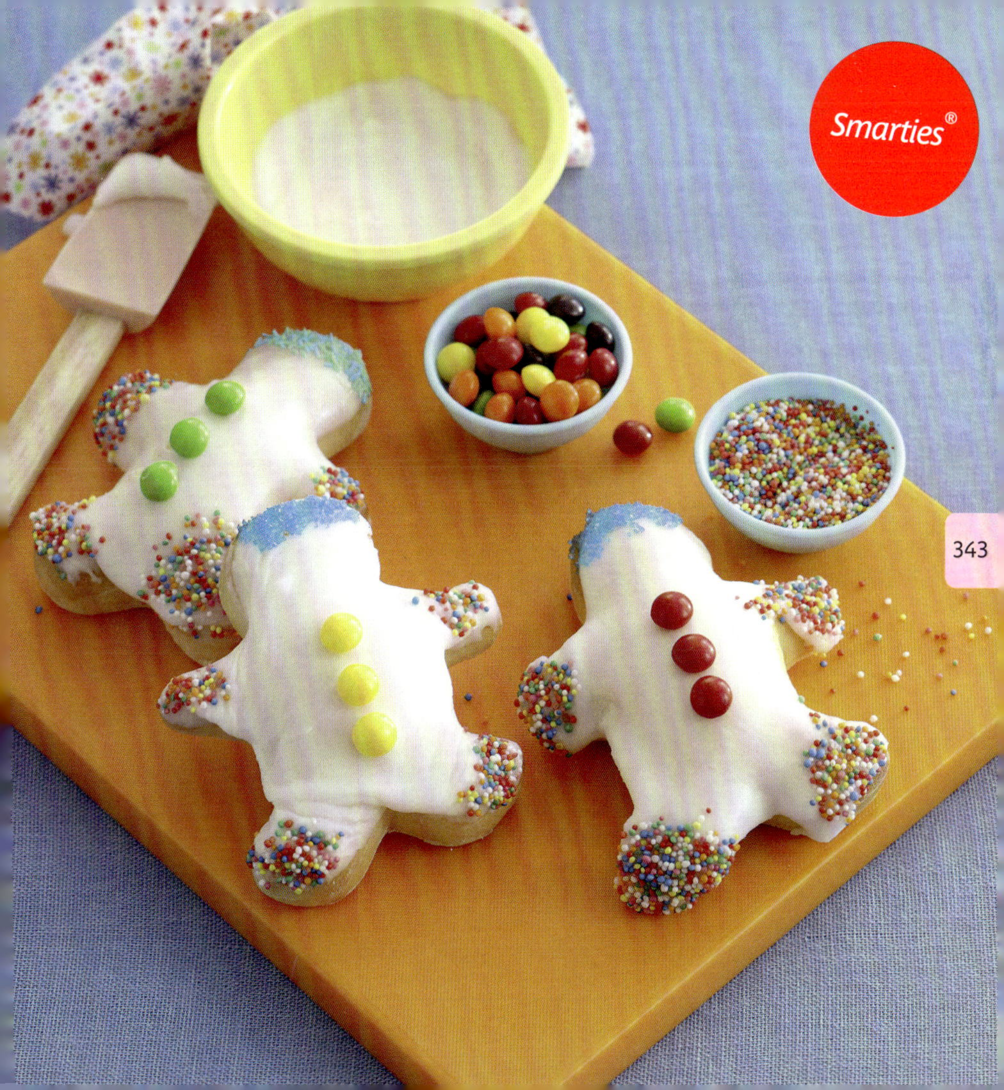
Smarties®

MUFFINS AUX SMARTIES®

Préparation : 15 min • **Cuisson** : 20 min • **Pour 12 muffins**

100 g de beurre • 280 g de farine • ½ sachet de levure chimique
120 g de sucre roux • 2 œufs • 10 cl de lait • 200 g de Smarties® • sel

- Préchauffez le four à 180 °C.
- Faites fondre le beurre dans une petite casserole.
- Mettez la farine, la levure, le sucre et 1 pincée de sel dans un saladier.
- Battez les œufs au fouet dans une jatte. Ajoutez le beurre fondu et le lait, puis mélangez.
- Réunissez les 2 préparations et mélangez délicatement à l'aide d'une spatule en bois. Incorporez les Smarties® sans trop travailler la pâte.
- Répartissez le mélange dans les alvéoles d'un moule à muffin, en les remplissant aux 2/3.
- Faites cuire au four pendant 20 min.
- Laissez refroidir sur une grille.

Muffins à la mélasse et aux Smarties®

Remplacez le sucre par de la mélasse, et ajoutez 1 c. à c. de gingembre en poudre à la préparation.

Muffins à la figue et aux Smarties®

Ajoutez 200 g de figues fraîches coupées en petits morceaux à la préparation. Remplacez le lait et 30 g de beurre par 1 yaourt brassé nature.

Muffins aux flocons d'avoine et aux Smarties®

Remplacez 100 g de farine par 100 g de flocons d'avoine. Ajoutez 1 pincée de cannelle à la préparation.

Crème au pamplemousse

Battez 6 jaunes d'œufs avec 200 g de sucre en poudre dans une casserole. Ajoutez le jus de 2 pamplemousses. Faites épaissir sur feu doux, sans laisser bouillir. Hors du feu, ajoutez 180 g de beurre coupé en dés et fouettez. Laissez refroidir. Servez avec les muffins.

Smarties®

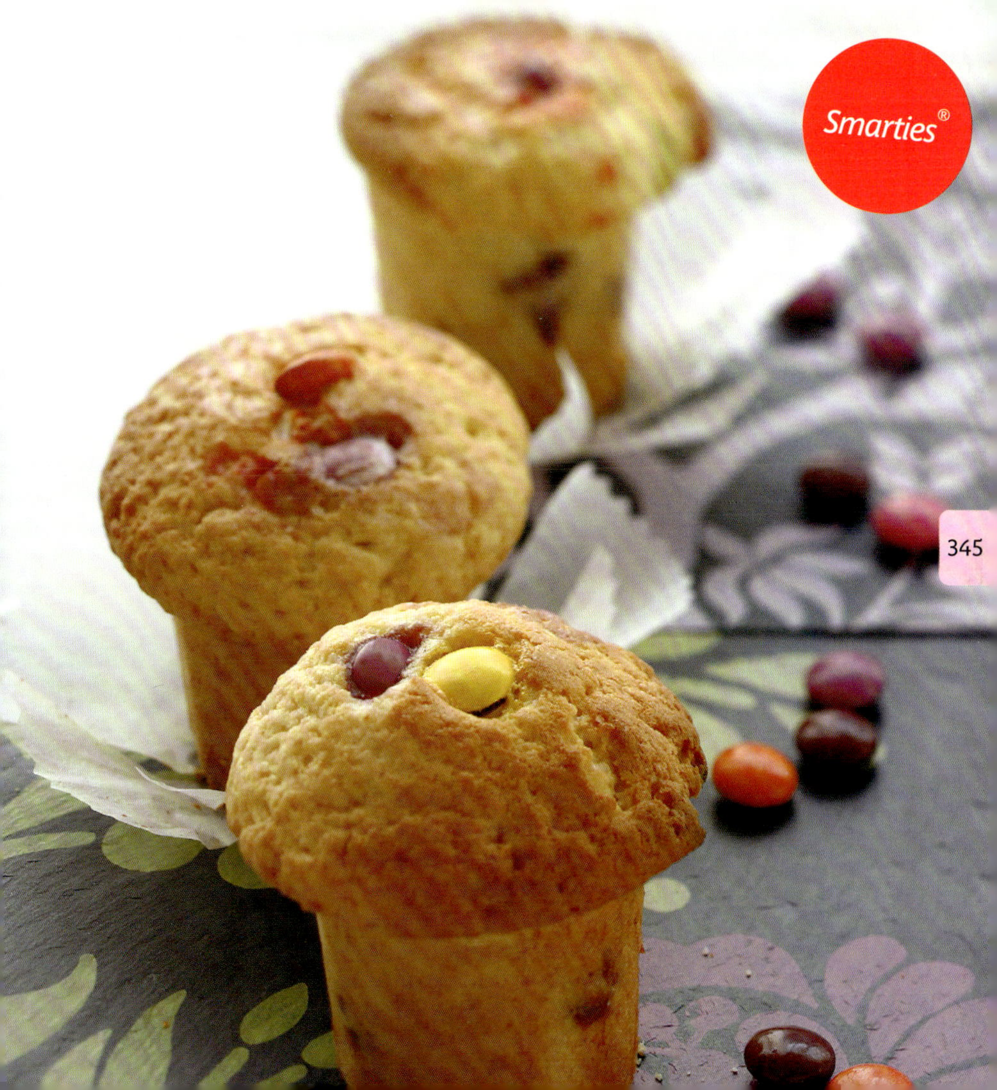

Galettes de spaghetti façon pizza
Remplacez le pesto par du coulis de tomates, et les crottins de Chavignol par de la mozzarella taillée en rondelles.

Galettes de spaghetti à l'aubergine
Remplacez le pesto par du caviar d'aubergine, et les crottins de Chavignol par de la feta.

Galettes de spaghetti aux figues
Remplacez le pesto par de la confiture de figues ou par des figues fraîches taillées en quartiers, et utilisez du comté à la place des crottins de Chavignol.

Galettes de spaghetti à la tapenade
Remplacez le pesto par de la tapenade verte, et les crottins de Chavignol par de l'emmental.

Spaghetti Panzani®

PETITES GALETTES DE SPAGHETTI AU PESTO DE PERSIL

Préparation: 15 min • **Cuisson**: 20 min • **Pour 12 galettes**

pour le pesto : *1 bouquet de persil plat • 1 gousse d'ail*
100 g de copeaux de parmesan • 50 g de pignons de pin
20 cl d'huile d'olive • gros sel
pour les galettes : *120 g de spaghetti Panzani® • 2 c. à s. d'huile d'olive*
+ un peu si besoin • 4 crottins de Chavignol • sel

- Pour le pesto, lavez le persil, puis essuyez-le avec du papier absorbant. Coupez les tiges pour ne garder que les feuilles. Épluchez la gousse d'ail et hachez-la grossièrement.

- Mettez le persil et l'ail dans le bol du mixeur, et ajoutez le parmesan, les pignons et un peu de gros sel. Mixez en incorporant petit à petit l'huile d'olive en filet .

- Pour les galettes, faites cuire les spaghettis dans une grande quantité d'eau bouillante salée. Égouttez-les. Préchauffez le four à 150 °C. Faites chauffer l'huile dans une grande poêle.

- Façonnez de petites galettes de spaghetti Panzani® et faites-les revenir à la poêle, par petite quantité. Ajoutez un peu d'huile si besoin. Quand elles sont dorées, égouttez-les sur du papier absorbant, puis déposez-en la moitié sur une plaque à pâtisserie recouverte de papier sulfurisé.

- Nappez ces galettes de pesto de persil. Coupez les crottins en trois dans le sens de l'épaisseur et déposez un morceau sur chaque galette. Recouvrez avec les galettes restantes.

- Faites cuire au four pendant 5 min environ. Le fromage doit être fondu. Servez sans attendre.

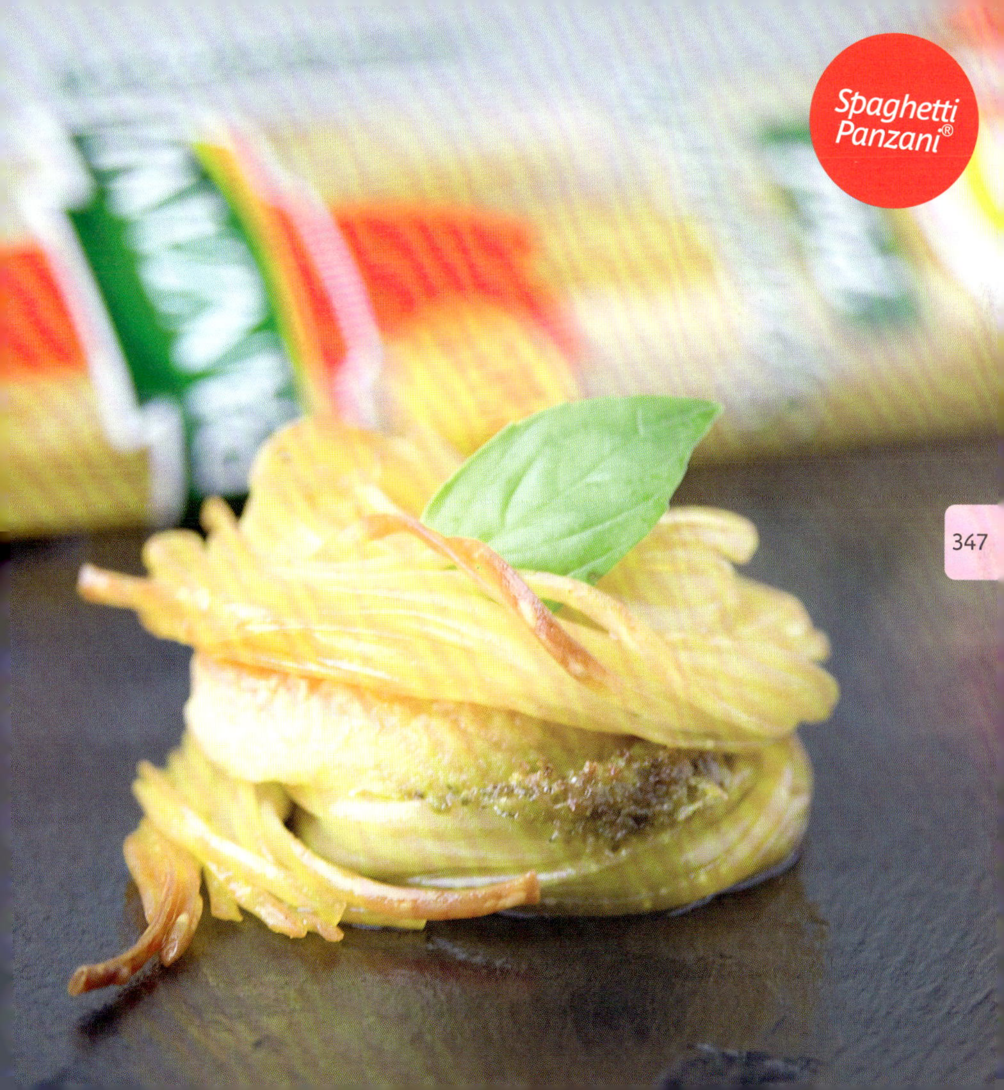
Spaghetti
Panzani®

SPAGHETTI AUX AUBERGINES

Préparation : 10 min • **Cuisson** : 25 min • **Repos** : 15 min
Pour 2 personnes

1 aubergine • 5 c. à s. d'huile d'olive • 2 gousses d'ail
440 g de tomates pelées en conserve • 12 feuilles de basilic
12 olives dénoyautées • 2 c. à s. de petites câpres
250 g de spaghetti Panzani® • parmesan râpé • sel

- Coupez les extrémités de l'aubergine et coupez-la en deux dans le sens de la longueur, puis coupez chaque moitié en tranches de 5 mm. Disposez-les sur du papier absorbant, puis salez-les généreusement. Laissez dégorger pendant 15 min.
- Essuyez les morceaux d'aubergines avec du papier absorbant. Faites chauffer 3 c. à s. d'huile d'olive dans une grande poêle et faites-y revenir les tranches d'aubergine jusqu'à ce qu'elles soient bien dorées et tendres. Retirez de la poêle et réservez.
- Épluchez les gousses d'ail. Faites chauffer le reste d'huile dans une casserole, ajoutez-y l'ail, et faites cuire pendant 1 min. Ajoutez les morceaux d'aubergine et les tomates, et faites cuire à couvert pendant 10 min à feu doux.
- Rincez le basilic, épongez-le avec du papier absorbant, puis ciselez-le. Ajoutez les olives, les câpres et le basilic dans la casserole, et laissez mijoter pendant encore 10 min sans couvercle.
- Pendant ce temps, faites cuire les spaghetti Panzani® al dente dans une grande quantité d'eau bouillante salée. Égouttez-les, puis mélangez-les à la sauce.
- Servez sans attendre, avec du parmesan râpé.

Spaghetti aux légumes grillés
Remplacez l'aubergine par 2 tranches d'aubergine grillée surgelées, que vous ferez décongeler et cuire très rapidement à la poêle. Ajoutez 150 g de poivrons grillés taillés en lamelles en fin de cuisson.

Spaghetti aux aubergines et aux anchois
Remplacez le basilic par 4 petits filets d'anchois taillés en morceaux. Vous pouvez également utiliser des sardines.

Spaghetti aux aubergines et à la feta
Ajoutez 150 g de feta coupée en dés dans la casserole 5 min avant la fin de la cuisson. Vous pouvez également utiliser de la mozzarella.

Spaghetti aux aubergines, aux carottes et aux épinards
Faites cuire 1 petite carotte taillée en dés en même temps que les morceaux d'aubergine. Remplacez les câpres et le basilic par 1 petite poignée de jeunes pousses d'épinards.

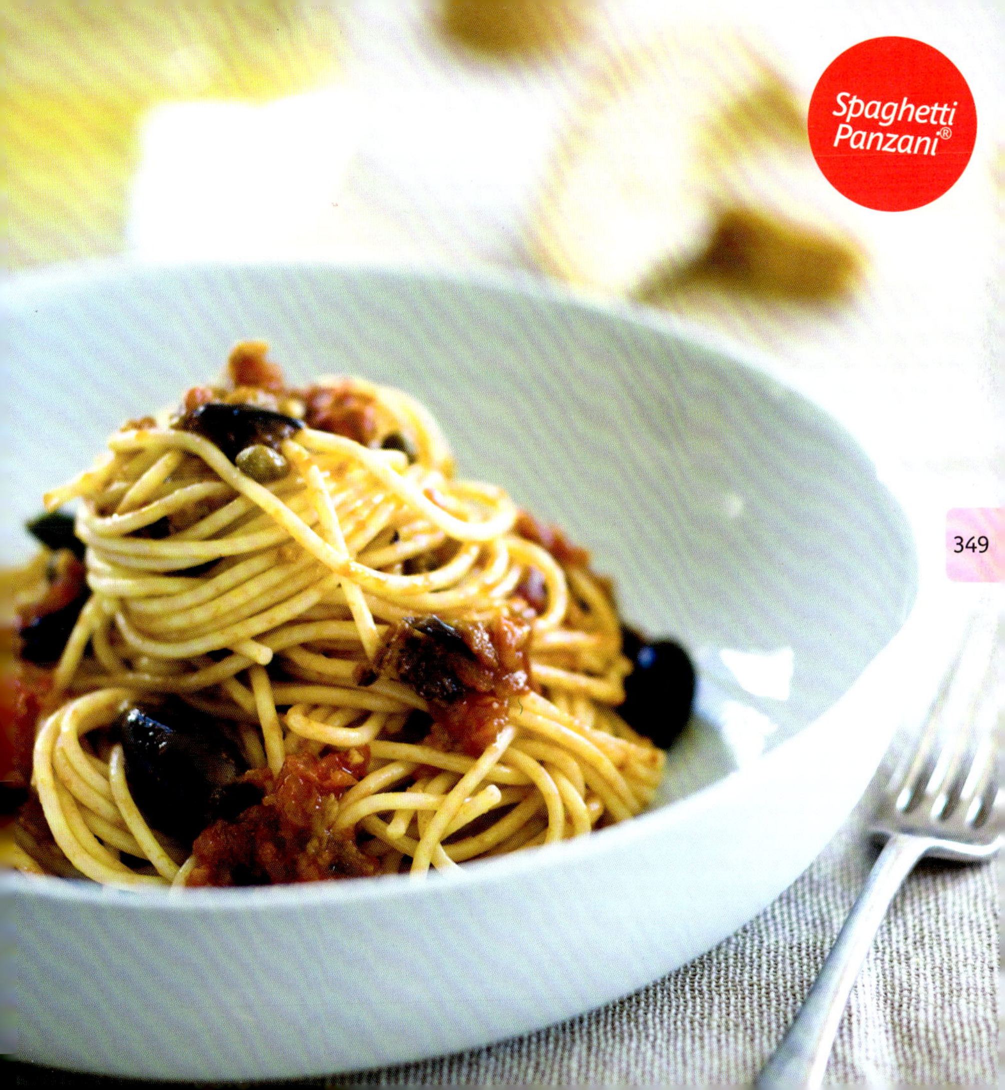
Spaghetti Panzani®

SPAGHETTI EN SAUCE TOMATE PIMENTÉE

Préparation : 15 min • **Cuisson :** 1 h 15 • **Pour 4 personnes**

2 gousses d'ail • 1 oignon • 2 piments oiseaux • 1/2 bouquet de basilic
1 c. à s. d'huile d'olive • 1 boîte de tomates concassées
2 c. à c. de concentré de tomate • 1 c. à s. de vinaigre balsamique
400 g de spaghetti Panzani® • copeaux de parmesan • sel et poivre

- Épluchez l'ail et l'oignon. Hachez l'ail et émincez l'oignon. Rincez les piments, épépinez-les et hachez-les. Rincez le basilic, épongez-le sur du papier absorbant, puis ciselez-le.
- Faites revenir l'ail et l'oignon dans une sauteuse avec l'huile d'olive. Une fois qu'ils sont translucides, ajoutez le piment et faites revenir pendant 5 min.
- Ajoutez les tomates concassées, le concentré de tomate, le basilic, le vinaigre, du sel et du poivre.
- Laissez mijoter à feu doux pendant 1 h.
- Faites cuire les spaghetti Panzani® al dente dans une grande quantité d'eau bouillante salée. Égouttez-les.
- Répartissez les spaghetti dans 4 assiettes, nappez de sauce et parsemez de copeaux de parmesan juste avant de servir.

Spaghetti en sauce pimentée aux olives
Ajoutez 60 g d'olives noires dénoyautées et taillées en rondelles à la sauce en même temps que les tomates concassées.

Spaghetti en sauce pimentée aux palourdes
Quelques minutes avant de servir, faites cuire 1 livre de palourdes nettoyées dans une cocotte, à sec, jusqu'à ce qu'elles s'ouvrent. Ajoutez-les à la sauce, décoquillées ou non, et servez.

Spaghetti en sauce pimentée au thon
Ajoutez 1 boîte de thon au naturel émietté dans la sauteuse en même temps que le piment. Ajoutez éventuellement 1 c. à s. de câpres avec les tomates.

Spaghetti en sauce pimentée à la pancetta
Ajoutez 125 g de pancetta taillée en dés à la préparation en même temps que l'oignon. À défaut, utilisez du bacon.

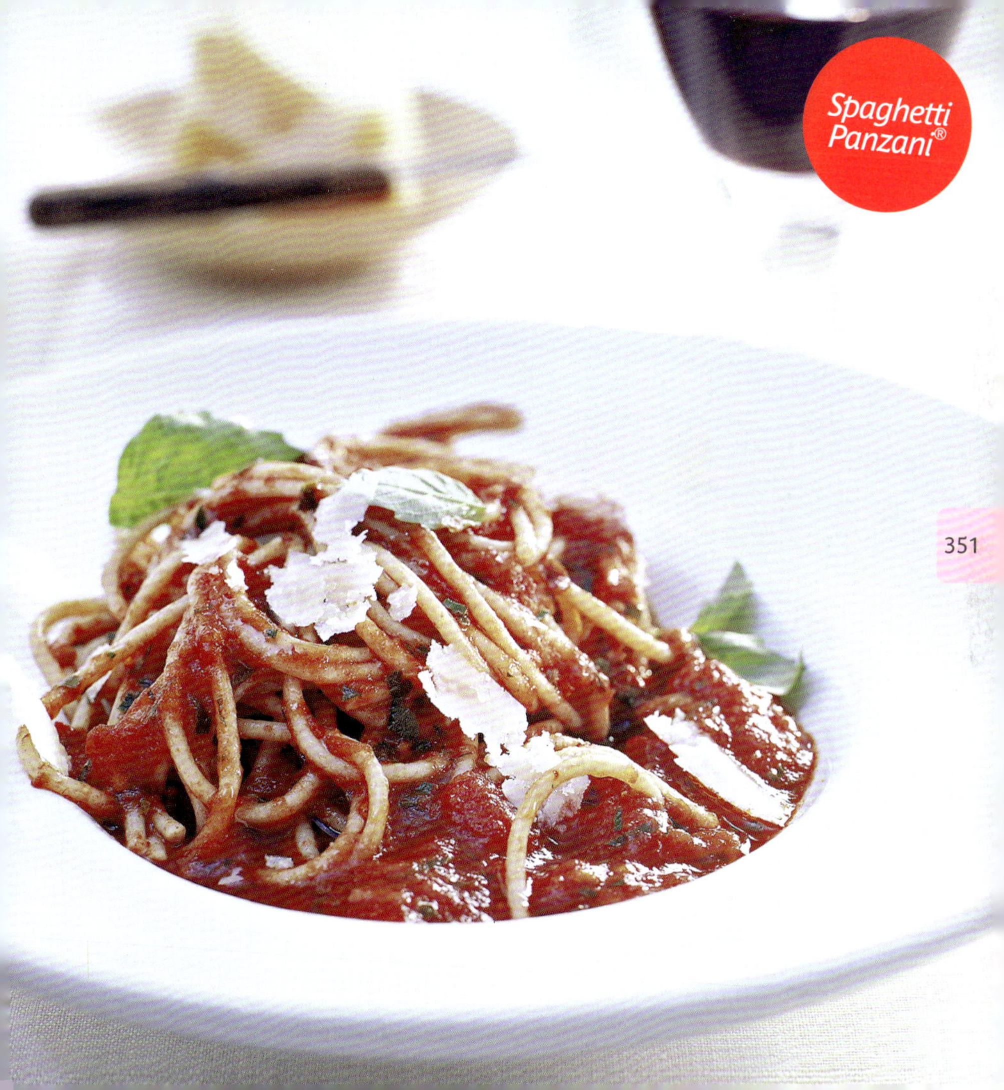
Spaghetti
Panzani®

Spaghetti au cabillaud et aux poireaux
Supprimez le basilic. Faites revenir 4 blancs de poireau taillés en rondelles dans une sauteuse pendant 15 min puis ajoutez-les dans les assiettes avec les spaghetti et le poisson.

Spaghetti au poulet et aux herbes
Remplacez le cabillaud par 4 filets de poulet taillés en lamelles.

Spaghetti aux calamars
Remplacez le cabillaud par 500 g d'anneaux de calamar, que vous ferez cuire pendant 5 min. Ajoutez 3 c. à s. de crème fraîche épaisse en toute fin de cuisson.

SPAGHETTI AU CABILLAUD ET AUX HERBES

Préparation : 10 min • **Cuisson** : 15 min • **Réfrigération** : 2 h
Pour 4 personnes

1 bouquet de basilic • 1/2 bouquet de persil • 2 piments oiseaux
4 filets de cabillaud • le jus et le zeste de 1 citron • 4 c. à s. d'huile d'olive
400 g de spaghetti Panzani® • 2 c. à s. de câpres • sel et poivre

- Rincez le basilic et le persil, épongez-les sur du papier absorbant. Ciselez le persil et un quart du basilic. Rincez les piments, puis hachez-les.

- Mettez le poisson dans un plat. Mélangez le zeste et le jus de citron avec 1 c. à s. d'huile d'olive, le basilic, le persil et le piment. Versez sur le poisson. Réservez au frais pendant 2 h.

- Au bout de ce temps, faites cuire les spaghetti Panzani® al dente dans une grande quantité d'eau bouillante salée. Égouttez-les.

- Faites pocher les feuilles de basilic restantes pendant 15 sec. Faites chauffer 1 autre c. à s. d'huile dans une casserole sur feu moyen. Ajoutez-y les feuilles de basilic égouttées et faites-les frire pendant 5 sec. Égouttez-les sur du papier absorbant.

- Faites chauffer 1 autre c. à s. d'huile d'olive dans une poêle sur feu moyen. Ôtez le poisson de la marinade et réservez-la. Faites cuire le poisson pendant 2 min sur chaque face, jusqu'à ce qu'il soit doré. Retirez-le de la poêle et réservez-le au chaud.

- Versez la marinade dans la poêle et faites cuire à feu vif pendant 1 min. Ajoutez-la aux spaghetti chauds avec le reste d'huile d'olive. Salez et poivrez, puis mélangez. Servez les spaghetti dans les assiettes, et couvrez d'un filet de poisson, puis parsemez de basilic frit et de câpres. Servez.

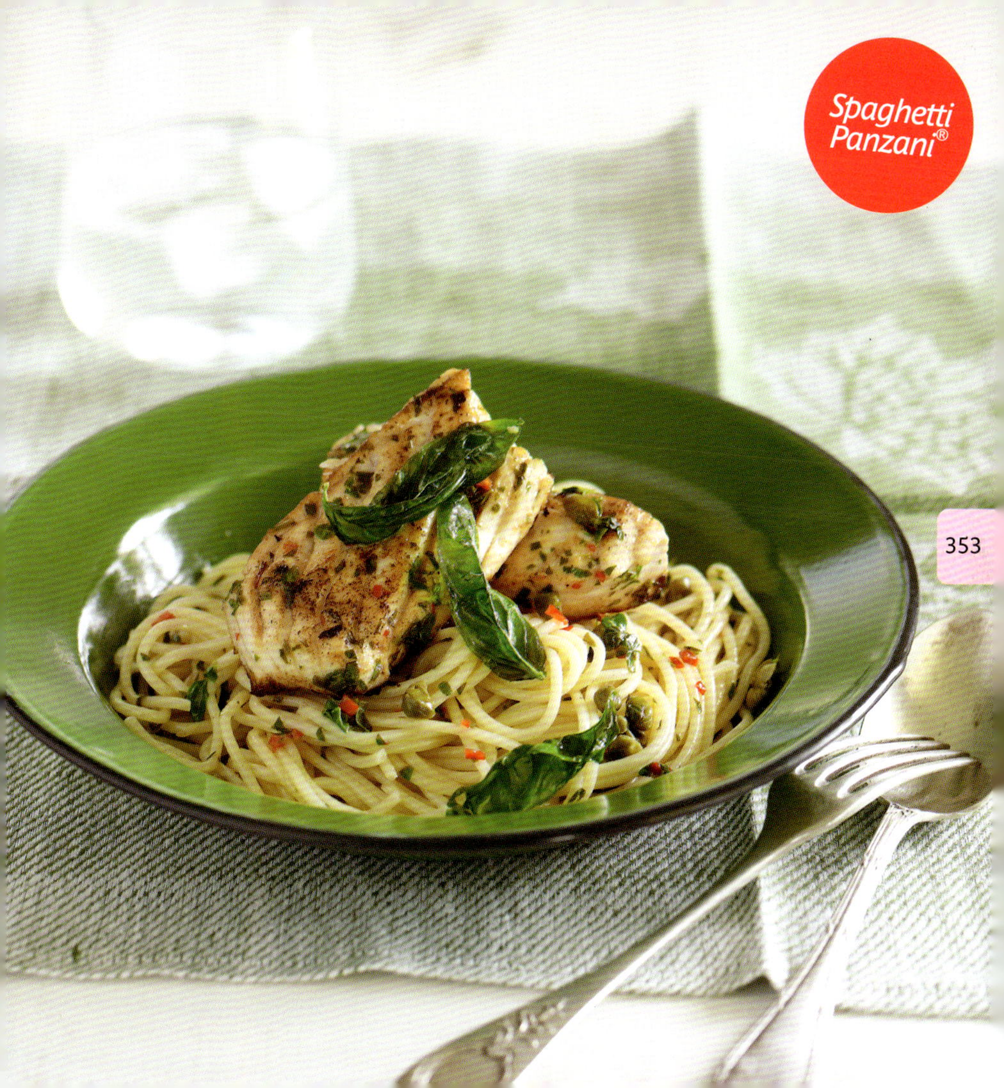
Spaghetti
Panzani®

SPAGHETTI AUX FÈVES ET AUX TOMATES SÉCHÉES

Préparation : 20 min • **Cuisson :** 10 min • **Pour 4 personnes**

200 g de fèves fraîches • 2 échalotes • 1 c. à s. d'huile d'olive + un peu pour arroser les pâtes • 400 g de spaghetti Panzani® 1 bocal de tomates séchées à l'huile • 4 brins de persil • sel et poivre

- Écossez les fèves, puis faites-les blanchir dans de l'eau bouillante salée pendant 3 min.
- Pendant ce temps, épluchez les échalotes et émincez-les.
- Faites chauffer l'huile dans une poêle et faites-y revenir les échalotes pendant 5 min, puis ajoutez les fèves égouttées dans la poêle et faites revenir de 2 à 3 min.
- En parallèle, faites cuire les spaghetti Panzani® al dente dans une grande quantité d'eau bouillante salée.
- Égouttez les tomates séchées, puis ajoutez-les dans la poêle pour 2 min.
- Rincez le persil, épongez-le sur du papier absorbant, puis séparez les feuilles.
- Égouttez les pâtes, puis répartissez-les dans des assiettes. Arrosez-les d'huile d'olive, puis ajoutez les fèves et les tomates. Poivrez généreusement. Parsemez de persil et servez.

Spaghetti aux fèves et aux asperges

Faites blanchir 8 asperges vertes coupées en morceaux de 2 cm pendant 3 min, puis égouttez-les et ajoutez-les dans la poêle en même temps que les fèves.

Spaghetti aux fèves et à la ricotta

Ajoutez 150 g de ricotta dans la poêle en même temps que les tomates séchées.

Spaghetti aux poivrons et aux crevettes

Remplacez les tomates séchées par 1 poivron jaune taillé en lamelles, revenues à la poêle avec les fèves. Ajoutez 200 g de crevettes roses décortiquées pour les 2 dernières min de cuisson.

Tomates séchées maison

Répartissez 250 g de tomates cerises lavées et coupées en deux sur une plaque recouverte de papier sulfurisé, côté coupé vers le haut. Parsemez de 2 c. à c. de sucre et salez. Faites cuire au four préchauffé à 90 °C pendant 4 h.

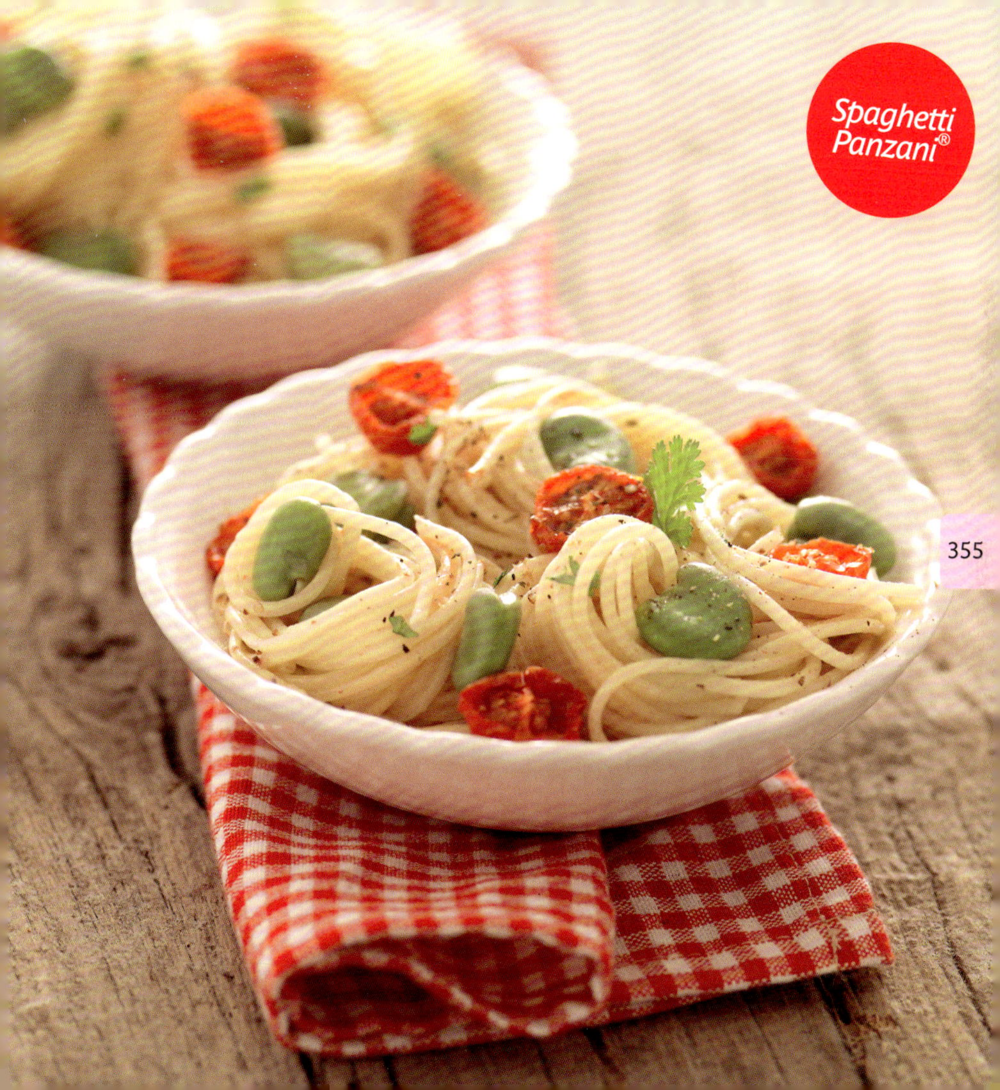
Spaghetti
Panzani®

Speculoos Lotus®

BOUCHÉES AU MASCARPONE ET AUX SPECULOOS

Préparation : 15 min • **Cuisson** : 45 min • **Repos** : 30 min
Réfrigération : 24 h • **Pour 4 personnes**

100 g de Speculoos Lotus® • 40 g de beurre ramolli
270 g de mascarpone • 270 g de fromage blanc
100 g de sucre en poudre • 2 œufs • 3 cm de gingembre frais râpé
le jus de 1 citron

- Préchauffez le four à 180 °C.
- Placez les Speculoos Lotus® dans un sac à congélation, fermez-le, puis écrasez-le à l'aide d'un rouleau à pâtisserie de façon à écraser grossièrement les biscuits.
- Mettez-les dans un saladier et ajoutez le beurre. Mélangez puis tapissez le fond d'un moule carré de cette préparation, et tassez bien.
- Dans un autre saladier, mélangez le mascarpone, le fromage blanc, le sucre, les œufs, le gingembre et le jus de citron. Versez ce mélange dans le moule.
- Faites cuire au four pendant 45 min.
- Laissez reposer dans le four, porte ouverte, pendant 30 min, puis laissez refroidir complètement à température ambiante. Couvrez de film alimentaire et réservez au frais pendant 24 h.
- Découpez en petites bouchées avant de servir.

Petites bouchées aux Speculoos et au café

Ajoutez 2 c. à c. de café soluble dilué, dans 1 c. à s. d'eau à la préparation au mascarpone. Vous pouvez aussi utiliser 5 cl de liqueur de café.

Petites bouchées aux Speculoos et aux poires

Coupez 4 demi-poires au sirop bien égouttées en cubes. Répartissez-les sur la base aux Speculoos avant d'ajouter la préparation au mascarpone.

Petites bouchées aux Speculoos et au lemon curd

Nappez la base aux Speculoos d'une couche généreuse de lemon curd avant d'ajouter la préparation au mascarpone.

Coulis aux Speculoos

Mélangez 100 g de Speculoos mixés avec 5 cl de sirop de sucre de canne. Laissez prendre au frais, puis faites fondre dans une petite casserole. Ajoutez 25 cl de crème liquide, en battant au fouet. Laissez refroidir, puis servez les bouchées arrosées de coulis.

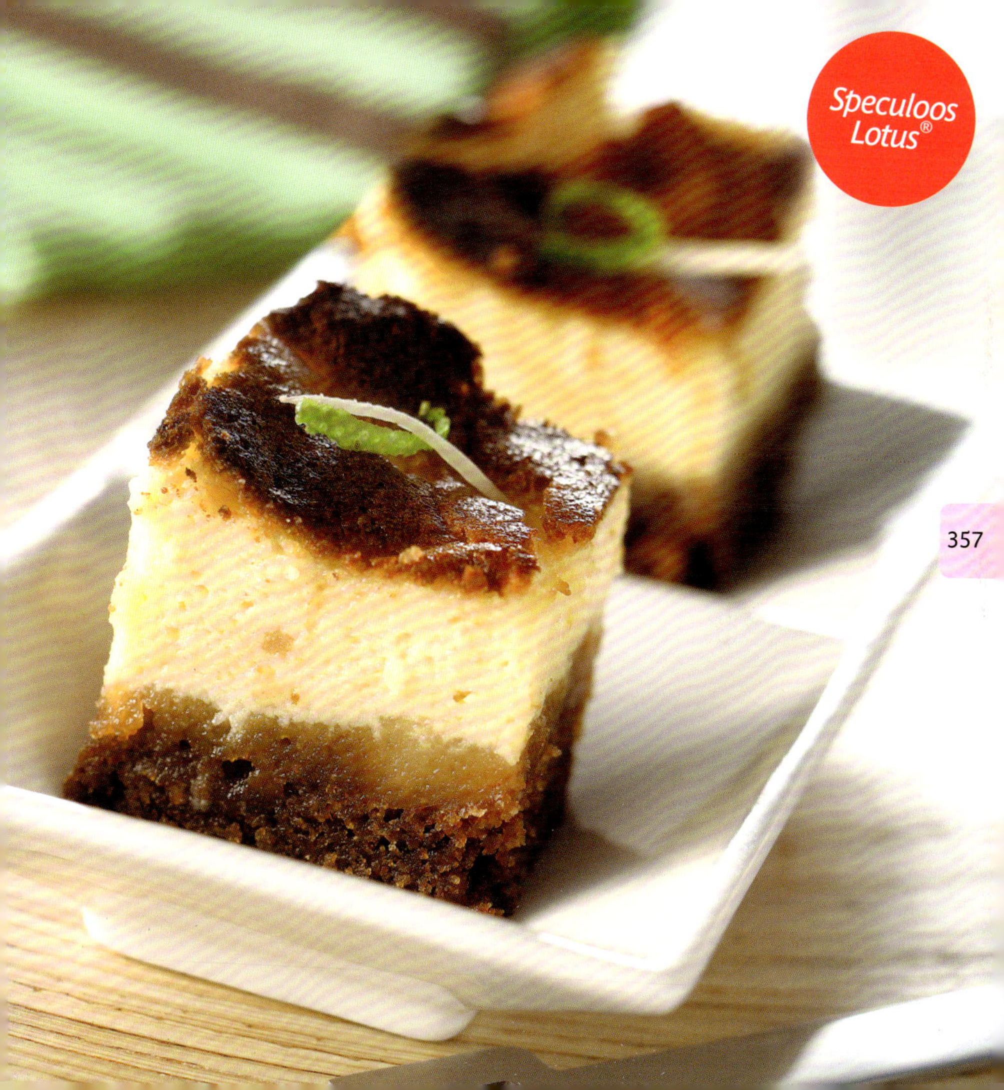
Speculoos
Lotus®

CHEESECAKE À LA RHUBARBE ET AUX SPECULOOS

Préparation : 20 min • **Cuisson** : 1 h 05 • **Pour 6 à 8 personnes**

__pour la base :__ 20 g de graines de sésame
250 g de Speculoos Lotus® • 80 g de beurre
__pour la garniture :__ 450 g de rhubarbe • 160 g de sucre
500 g de mascarpone • 3 œufs • 2 c. à s. de fécule de pomme de terre
amandes effilées, pour décorer

- Pour la garniture, pelez la rhubarbe et coupez-la en tronçons de 2 cm. Faites-les cuire avec 50 g de sucre et 5 cl d'eau pendant 20 min environ, jusqu'à ce qu'ils soient tendres. Passez la préparation au tamis pour en extraire le jus.
- Préchauffez le four à 180 °C.
- Pour la base, faites dorer les graines de sésame dans une poêle antiadhésive sans matière grasse. Mixez les Speculoos Lotus® avec le beurre jusqu'à l'obtention d'un mélange homogène. Ajoutez les graines de sésame.
- Répartissez cette préparation au fond d'un moule à base amovible, et pressez bien.
- Mixez le reste de sucre avec le mascarpone et les œufs jusqu'à l'obtention d'un mélange lisse. Versez dans un saladier, et incorporez la fécule de pomme de terre et la rhubarbe. Versez dans le moule et lissez à la spatule.
- Faites cuire au four de 35 à 45 min. La surface doit être bien dorée. Laissez refroidir avant de servir. Parsemez d'amandes effilées.

Cheesecake à la rhubarbe et aux fraises séchées

Remplacez 50 g de rhubarbe par 50 g de fraises séchées, que vous mixerez avec le mascarpone.

Cheesecake à la ricotta et aux framboises

Remplacez le mascarpone par de la ricotta. Une fois le gâteau cuit et refroidi, ornez toute la surface de framboises fraîches.

Coulis de fruits rouges

Mettez 400 g de fruits rouges surgelés décongelés dans une casserole avec 5 cl d'eau et 50 g de sucre. Faites cuire pendant 15 min à feu doux. Mixez, puis laissez refroidir puis servez avec le cheesecake.

Coulis de fraises à l'huile d'olive

Mixez 400 g de fraises fraîches lavées et équeutées avec 2 c. à s. de sucre glace et 4 c. à s. d'huile d'olive. Laissez refroidir, puis servez avec le cheesecake.

Speculoos Lotus®

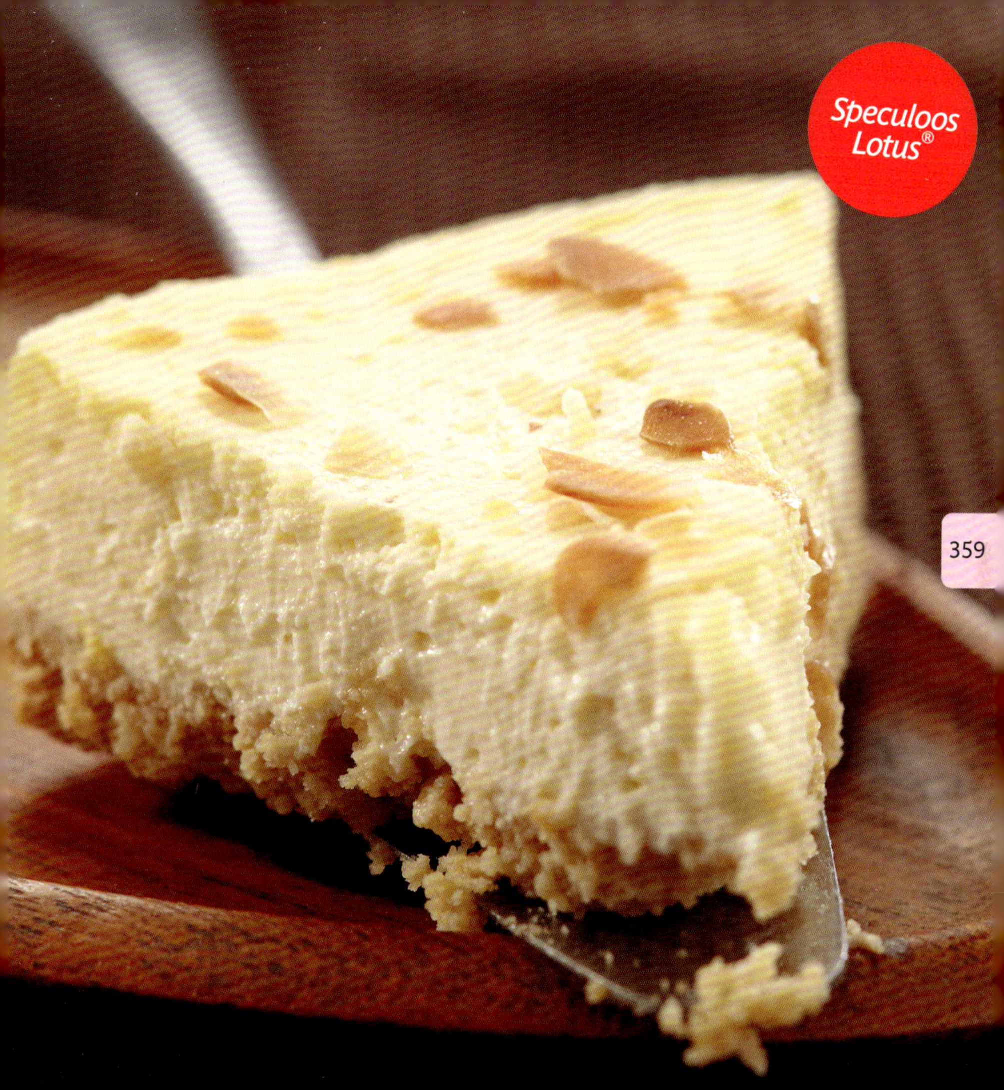

GLACE AUX SPECULOOS

Préparation : 25 min • **Cuisson :** 10 min • **Turbine :** 40 min • **Pour 1 litre**

4 jaunes d'œufs • 120 g de sucre en poudre • 2 sachets de sucre vanillé
40 cl de lait • 200 g de Speculoos Lotus®
25 cl de crème liquide entière très froide

- Mettez les jaunes d'œufs, le sucre et le sucre vanillé dans une jatte supportant la chaleur, et battez au fouet jusqu'à ce que le mélange soit mousseux. Ajoutez le lait et mélangez.
- Faites chauffer au bain-marie, à feu doux, en remuant sans cesse à la cuillère en bois, jusqu'à ce que le mélange épaississe.
- Émiettez les Speculoos Lotus®. Ajoutez-les à la préparation précédente et mélangez. Laissez refroidir en remuant de temps à autre.
- Quand la préparation a refroidi, montez la crème liquide en chantilly. Incorporez-la délicatement à la crème.
- Faites turbiner en sorbetière et réservez au congélateur.

Glace aux Speculoos express

Remplacez la préparation liquide par 50 cl de crème anglaise prête à l'emploi.

Glace aux Speculoos et au caramel

Portez à ébullition 12 cl d'eau, 500 g de sucre, 1 c. à s. de vinaigre blanc, et laissez cuire à feu doux jusqu'à ce que le caramel soit roux. Incorporez délicatement (en prenant garde aux projections) 50 cl d'eau bouillante. Faites chauffer pendant 1 min, et laissez refroidir. Ajoutez dans l'appareil à glace, en formant des marbrures.

Milk-shake banane-Speculoos

Mixez 4 boules de glace aux Speculoos avec 2 bananes pelées et coupées en rondelles, 6 glaçons et 15 cl de lait. Répartissez dans des verres et servez sans attendre, avec des pailles.

Milk-shake chocolat-Speculoos

Reprenez la recette ci-dessus en remplaçant les bananes par 2 boules de glace au chocolat.

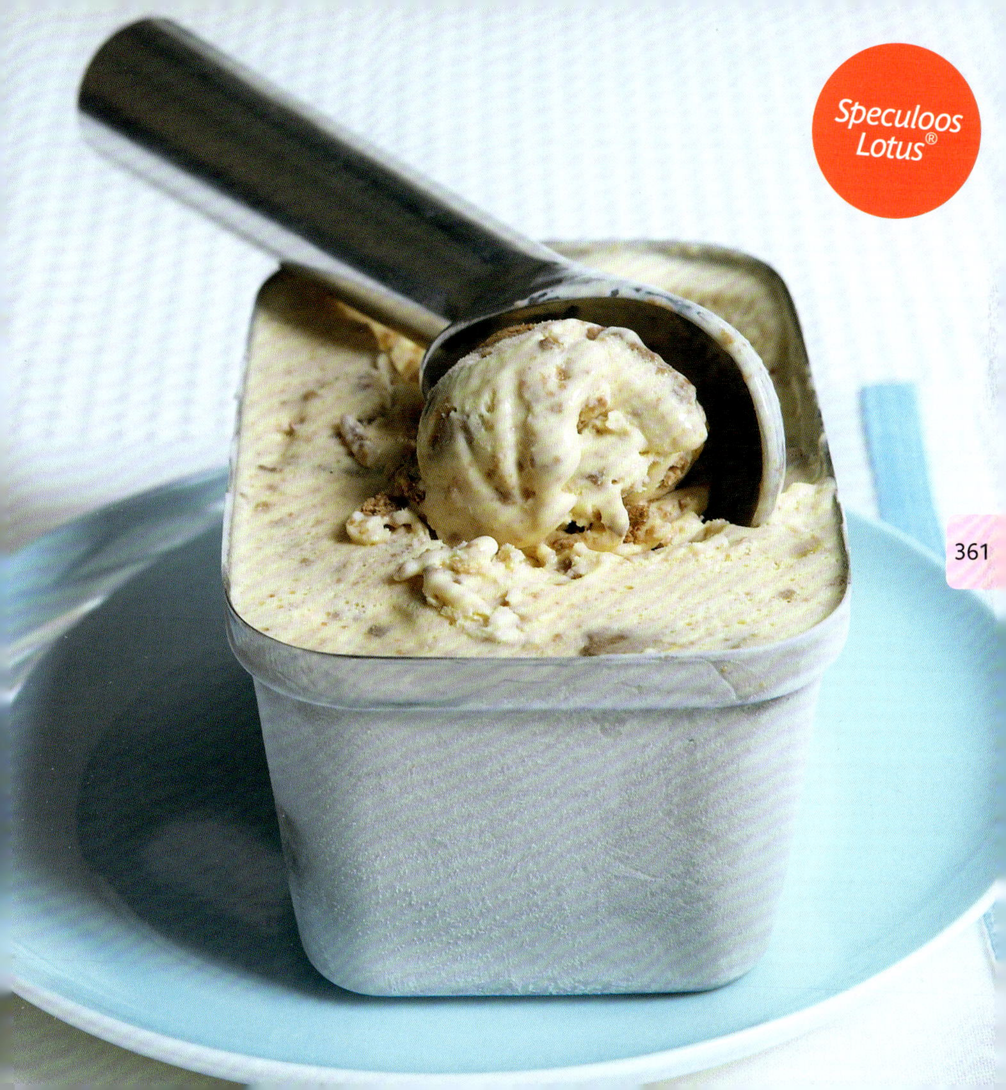

Speculoos Lotus®

MOUSSE AU CHOCOLAT NOIR ET AUX SPECULOOS

Préparation : 15 min • **Cuisson** : 5 min • **Réfrigération** : 2 h
Pour 6 personnes

100 g de Speculoos Lotus® • 200 g de chocolat • 40 g de beurre doux
4 œufs • 40 g de sucre glace

- Mixez les Speculoos Lotus® puis passez la poudre au tamis pour en affiner le grain.
- Coupez le chocolat en morceaux, puis faites-les fondre dans une casserole avec le beurre taillé en parcelles.
- Séparez les blancs des jaunes d'œufs. Incorporez les jaunes d'œufs et la poudre de biscuits dans la casserole, et remuez bien.
- Montez les blancs d'œufs en neige ferme, puis incorporez délicatement le sucre glace pour former une meringue.
- Incorporez-la délicatement à la spatule à la préparation précédente.
- Versez dans des ramequins. Laissez prendre au réfrigérateur pendant 2 h.

Mousse aux Speculoos et à l'orange

Mixez les Speculoos avec le zeste de 1/2 orange non traitée. Vous pouvez également utiliser du zeste de pamplemousse ou de clémentine.

Mousse aux Speculoos et au mascarpone

Remplacez le chocolat et le beurre par 300 g de mascarpone, que vous mélangerez sans le faire chauffer avec les jaunes d'œufs et la poudre de Speculoos, avant d'incorporer la meringue.

Mousse aux Speculoos et au café

Reprenez la recette ci-dessus en mélangeant la poudre de Speculoos avec 1 tasse de café noir avant de l'incorporer aux autres ingrédients.

Chantilly à la banane

Mixez 1 banane pelée et débarrassée des résidus blancs avec le jus de 1/2 citron. Montez 10 cl de crème liquide très froide en chantilly, puis incorporez-y la banane. Décorez les mousses de cette chantilly.

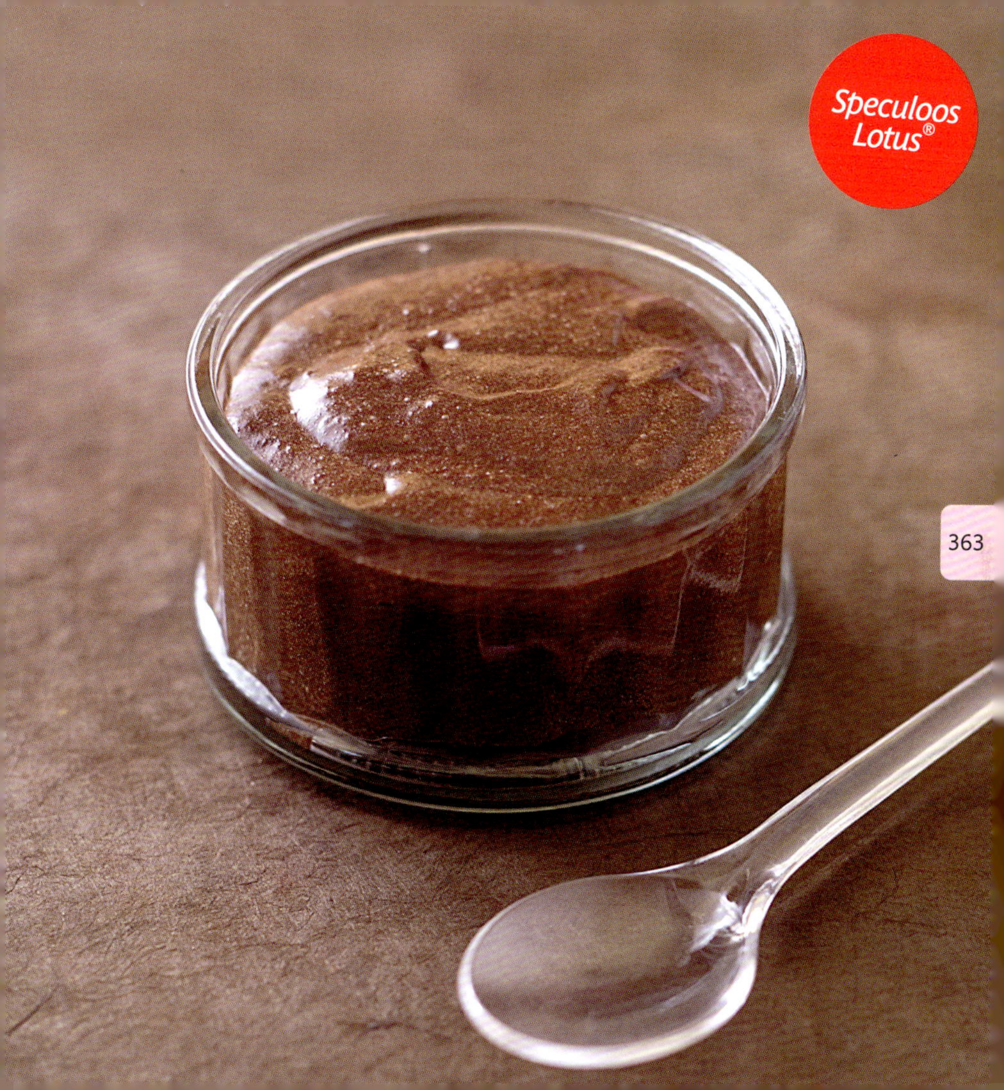

Speculoos Lotus®

VERRINES CHOCO-BANANE AUX SPECULOOS

Préparation : 15 min • **Cuisson :** 3 min • **Réfrigération :** 2 h
Pour 4 verrines

75 g de chocolat noir à pâtisserie • 2 œufs • 2 bananes
8 Speculoos Lotus® • 2 c. à s. de miel

- Séparez les carreaux de chocolat, mettez-les dans une jatte supportant la chaleur, et faites-les fondre au bain-marie.
- Séparez les blancs des jaunes d'œufs. Hors du feu, ajoutez les jaunes au chocolat fondu et mélangez.
- Dans une autre jatte, montez les blancs en neige ferme. Incorporez-les délicatement au mélange au chocolat à l'aide d'une cuillère en bois.
- Répartissez la préparation dans 4 verrines. Réservez au réfrigérateur pendant 2 h.
- Quelques minutes avant de servir, pelez les bananes et coupez-les en rondelles très fines. Mixez finement 3 Speculoos Lotus®.
- Mettez le tout dans une poêle, ajoutez le miel et faites caraméliser de 2 à 3 min, à feu moyen, en retournant les rondelles en cours de cuisson.
- Sortez les verrines du réfrigérateur. Répartissez les rondelles de banane dans les verrines. Écrasez grossièrement les Speculoos Lotus® restants et parsemez-en les bananes.
- Servez aussitôt.

Verrines choco-banane flambées aux Speculoos

Ajoutez 5 cl de rhum ambré dans la poêle une fois les bananes caramélisées, puis faites flamber rapidement.

Verrines vanille-poires aux Speculoos

Remplacez la crème au chocolat par de la crème dessert à la vanille, et les bananes par 2 poires pelées, coupées en morceaux et caramélisées au miel additionné de 1 capsule de cardamome pilée.

Aumônières choco-banane aux Speculoos

Garnissez le centre de 4 crêpes de crème au chocolat, de rondelles de banane et de brisures de Speculoos puis repliez les bords vers le centre et nouez avec du fil de cuisine.

Sablés choco-banane aux Speculoos

Mixez 200 g de Speculoos avec 100 g de beurre et 3 c. à s. d'eau tiède. Garnissez des moules à tartelette de cette pâte et faites durcir au réfrigérateur. Garnissez de crème au chocolat et de bananes caramélisées.

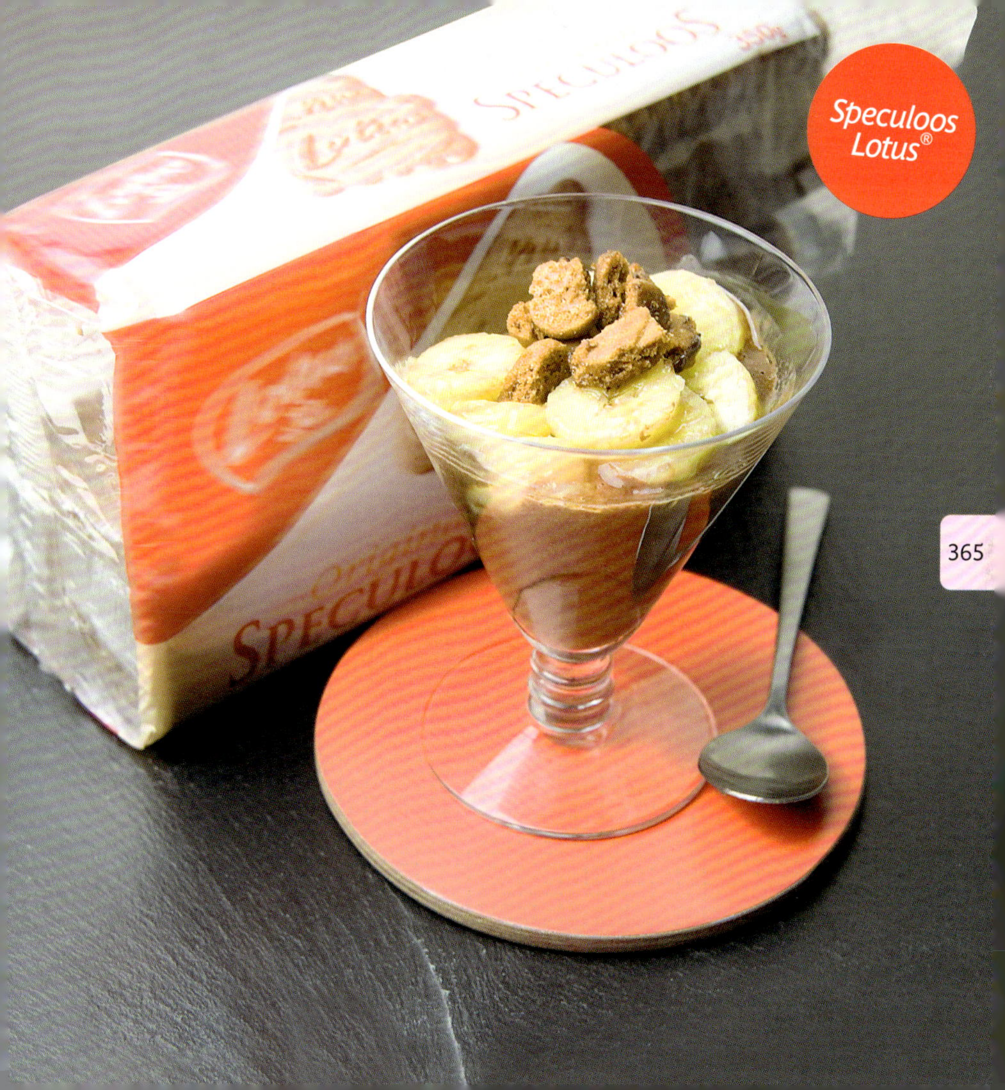

Speculoos Lotus®

Thé Lipton®

AIGUILLETTES DE POULET AU THÉ ET À LA MANDARINE

Préparation : 15 min • **Cuisson :** 35 min • **Infusion** : 10 min • **Pour 4 personnes**

2 sachets de thé Lipton® Yellow Label Tea • 4 carottes • 3 échalotes
1 c. à s. d'huile d'olive • 15 cl de bouillon de volaille
le jus de 4 mandarines • 1 c. à s. de miel • 1 c. à s. de concentré de tomate
4 blancs de poulet • sel et poivre

- Portez 10 cl d'eau à ébullition. Hors du feu, plongez-y les sachets de thé Lipton® et laissez infuser pendant 10 min. Retirez les sachets.
- Pelez les carottes, puis faites-les cuire pendant 10 min dans de l'eau bouillante salée.
- Épluchez les échalotes, puis émincez-les finement. Faites-les cuire dans une sauteuse avec l'huile d'olive à feu moyen.
- Ajoutez le thé et le bouillon de volaille, et laissez bouillir pendant 3 min.
- Prélevez le jus des mandarines. Ajoutez-le dans la sauteuse avec le miel et le concentré de tomate. Salez et poivrez. Laissez réduire pendant 5 min et réservez.
- Taillez les blancs de poulet en aiguillettes. Faites-les revenir dans une autre poêle, de 3 à 4 min.
- Égouttez les carottes, passez-les sous l'eau froide et coupez-les en bâtonnets.
- Faites réchauffer les bâtonnets de carotte et les morceaux de poulet pendant quelques minutes dans la sauce, et servez bien chaud.

Poulet au thé et au citron
Remplacez le jus de mandarine par le jus de 4 citrons. Vous pouvez également utiliser du jus de citron vert.

Canard au thé et à l'orange
Remplacez le poulet par 600 g d'aiguillettes de canard, et les mandarines par 2 oranges.

Poulet au thé et à la cannelle
Ajoutez 2 c. à c. de cannelle et 1 c. à c. de cumin à la sauce. Vous pouvez également utiliser un bâton de cannelle, que vous retirerez en fin de cuisson.

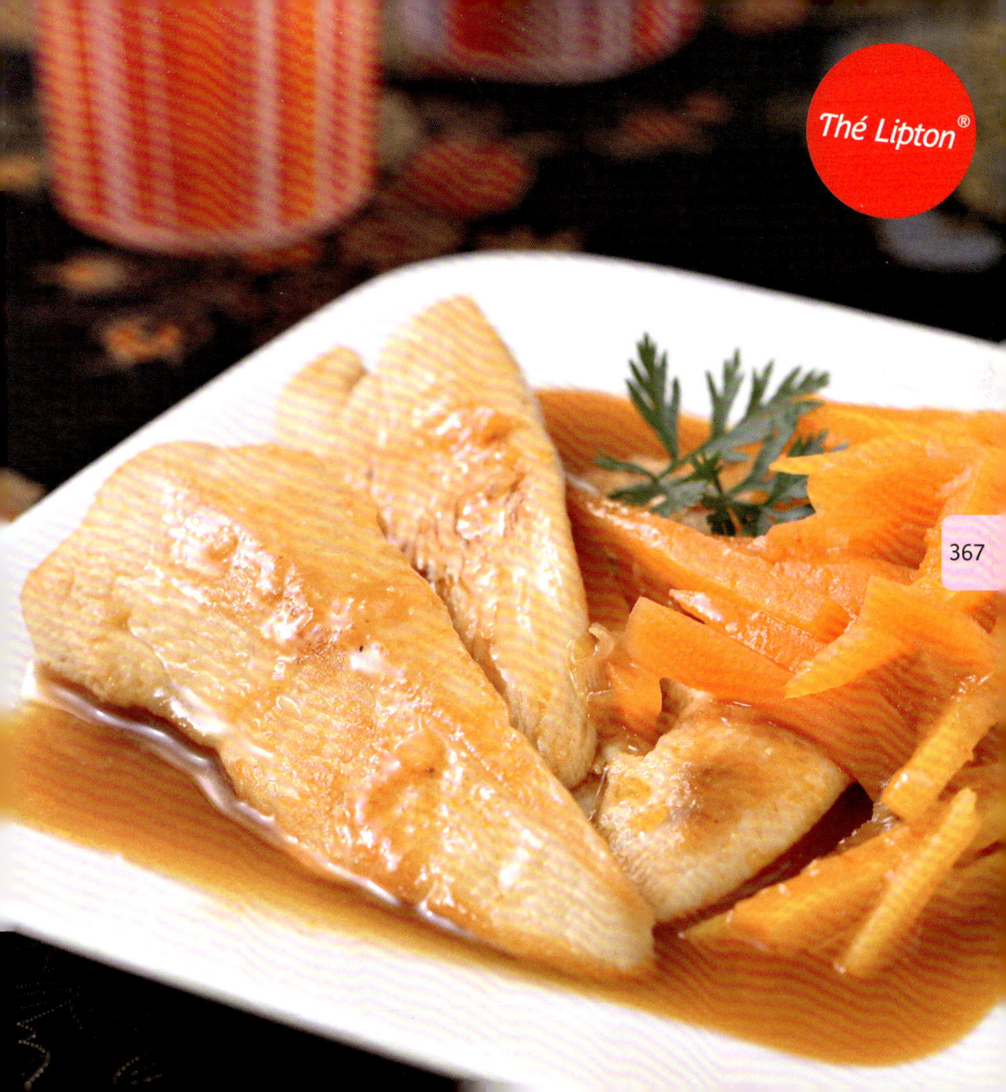
Thé Lipton®

GALETTE AU SUCRE ET AU THÉ

Préparation : 25 min • **Cuisson** : 30 min • **Infusion** : 15 min
Repos : 2 h • **Pour 8 personnes**

10 cl de lait • 2 c. à s. de thé Lipton® Russian Earl Grey
1 sachet de levure de boulanger • 250 g de farine • 1 œuf
130 g de beurre + un peu pour le moule
100 g de sucre en poudre • sel

- Portez le lait à ébullition, puis retirez du feu, et faites-y infuser le thé Lipton® Russian Earl Grey pendant 15 min. Filtrez le mélange.
- Dissolvez la levure dans le lait. Versez la farine et 1 pincée de sel dans un saladier. Faites un puits et incorporez l'œuf préalablement battu. Ajoutez le lait. Faites fondre 100 g de beurre et ajoutez-le à la pâte.
- Pétrissez la pâte à la main de 10 à 15 min, jusqu'à ce qu'elle soit souple et homogène. Laissez reposer pendant 2 h.
- Préchauffez le four à 210 °C.
- Beurrez un moule à tarte, puis étalez-y la pâte.
- Pour la garniture, saupoudrez la pâte de sucre, puis coupez le reste de beurre en parcelles et répartissez-le par-dessus.
- Faites cuire au four pendant 15 min environ.
- Servez tiède.

Galette au sucre et au citron

Utilisez du thé Lipton® au citron, et ajoutez le zeste de 1/2 citron à la préparation.

Galette au sucre et au caramel

Utilisez du thé Lipton® au caramel. Ajoutez 5 bonbons au caramel broyés à la pâte.

Infusion glacée à la rose et au litchi

Faites infuser 2 sachets d'infusion Lipton® à la rose et au litchi dans 90 cl d'eau. Ajoutez 50 g de sucre en poudre et le jus de 1 boîte de litchis. Réservez au frais. Servez glacé, avec la galette.

Thé à la pomme et au caramel

Portez à frémissements 8 cl de thé Lipton® Yellow, 8 cl de jus de pomme, 1/2 bâton de cannelle et 1 c. à c. de miel. Retirez le bâton de cannelle, et servez dans un verre épais, avec la galette.

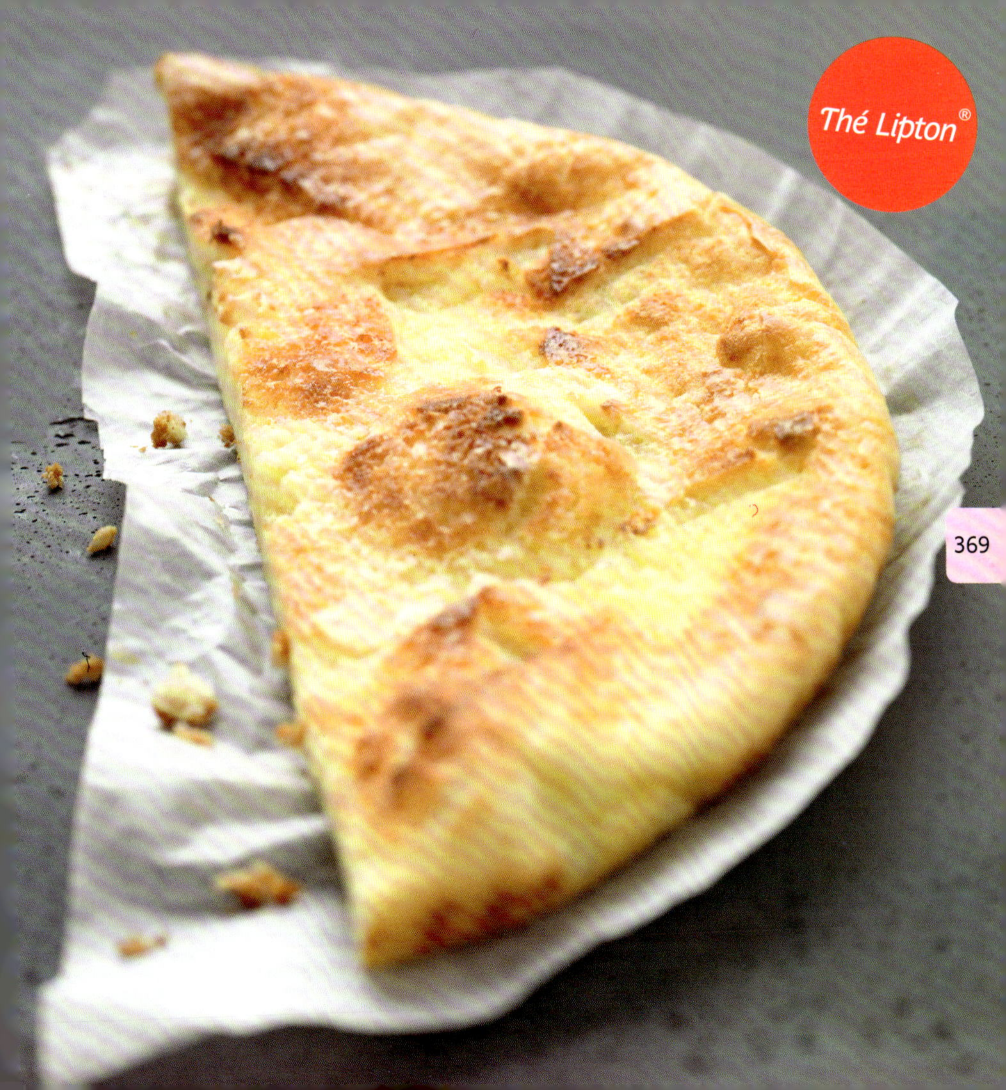
Thé Lipton®

GRANITÉ DE PASTÈQUE AU THÉ

Préparation : 15 min • **Cuisson** : 5 min • **Congélation** : 4 h
Pour 6 personnes

2 sachets de thé vert Lipton® à la menthe • 1,5 kg de pastèque
75 g de sucre • 12 feuilles de menthe

- Portez à ébullition 10 cl d'eau, puis retirez du feu et faites-y infuser les sachets de thé Lipton® à la menthe pendant 15 min.
- Pendant ce temps, retirez la peau de la pastèque. Épépinez-la et coupez-la en cubes de 1 cm de côté. Mixez 1 kg de pastèque (réservez le reste au réfrigérateur), jusqu'à ce que le mélange soit le plus lisse possible.
- Retirez les sachets de thé de l'eau. Remettez celle-ci sur le feu avec le sucre, et faites chauffer à feu moyen en remuant jusqu'à ce que le sucre soit fondu. Laissez refroidir.
- Mélangez la purée de pastèque et le sirop dans un saladier. Versez le mélange dans un récipient supportant le froid et mettez au congélateur pour 4 h. Grattez toutes les heures avec les dents d'une fourchette.
- Répartissez les morceaux de pastèque réservés dans des verrines, recouvrez de granité et de quelques feuilles de menthe, préalablement rincées et épongées sur du papier absorbant.

Granité de melon au poivre

Remplacez la pastèque par 1,5 kg de melon. Poivrez la préparation au moulin juste avant de congeler.

Granité de pamplemousse à la rose et au litchi

Remplacez la pastèque par la pulpe de 1,5 kg de pamplemousses roses, et le thé par de l'infusion Lipton® à la rose et au litchi.

Granité de brugnon à l'Earl Grey

Remplacez la pastèque par la chair de 1,5 kg de brugnons et le thé par 2 c. à s. de thé Lipton® Finest Earl Grey.

Granité de thé à la pastèque

Préparez une théière de thé avec 2 sachets de thé Lipton® de votre choix et sucrez généreusement. Mettez au congélateur et grattez toutes les heures. Servez avec des billes de pastèque.

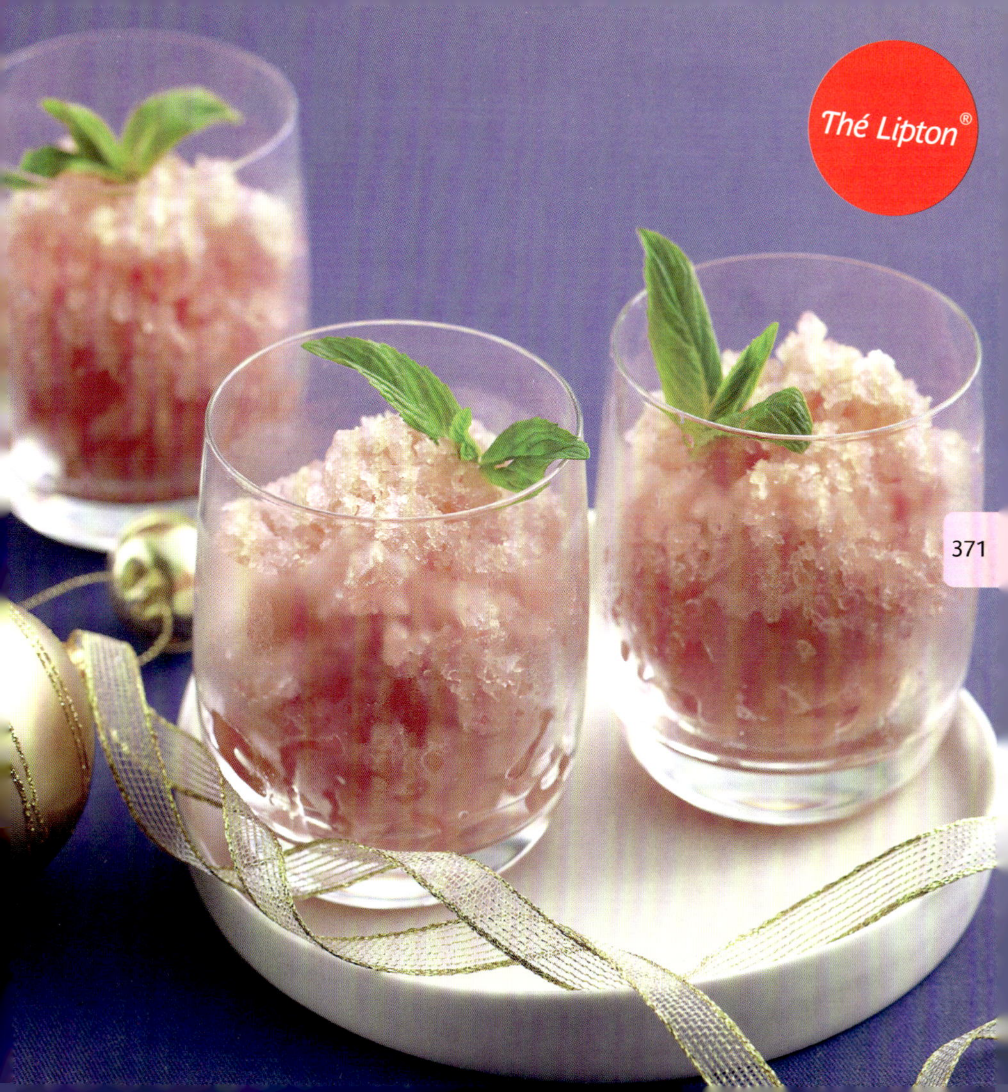
Thé Lipton®

MADELEINES AU THÉ ET AU MIEL

Préparation : 10 min • **Cuisson** : 15 min • **Réfrigération** : 1 h
Pour 24 madeleines

*20 cl de lait • 3 sachets de thé Lipton® Yellow Label Tea • 4 œufs
150 g de sucre roux • 160 g de beurre + un peu pour les moules
4 c. à s. de miel d'acacia • 200 g de farine
1/2 sachet de levure chimique • le jus de 1 citron*

- Versez le lait dans une casserole et portez à ébullition. Hors du feu, plongez-y les sachets de thé et laissez infuser pendant 10 min. Retirez les sachets.
- Mettez les œufs et le sucre dans un saladier, puis battez jusqu'à l'obtention d'un mélange mousseux.
- Coupez le beurre en morceaux, faites-le fondre avec le miel puis versez-le dans le saladier. Remuez délicatement, puis incorporez la farine, la levure, le jus de citron et le lait infusé. Mélangez.
- Recouvrez de film alimentaire et réservez au réfrigérateur pendant 1 h.
- Préchauffez le four à 180 °C.
- Beurrez les alvéoles d'un moule à madeleine et versez-y la pâte (il y a suffisamment de pâte pour 2 fournées).
- Faites cuire de 8 à 10 min, jusqu'à ce que les madeleines prennent une couleur légèrement dorée.
- Démoulez-les dès la sortie du four, et laissez refroidir.

Madeleines au thé et au chocolat

Remplacez le miel par 70 g de chocolat noir fondu. Vous pouvez également utiliser du chocolat au lait.

Madeleines au thé et à l'orange

Remplacez le jus de citron par le jus de 1/2 orange et ajoutez le zeste de l'orange à la préparation. Vous pouvez également utiliser 1/2 pamplemousse.

Madeleines au thé et au lemon curd

Coupez un chapeau aux madeleines et garnissez-les de 1 c. à c. de lemon curd. Reconstituez-les.

Madeleines au thé et à la confiture de lait

Coupez un chapeau aux madeleines et garnissez-les de 1 c. à c. de confiture de lait. Reconstituez-les.

Thé Lipton®

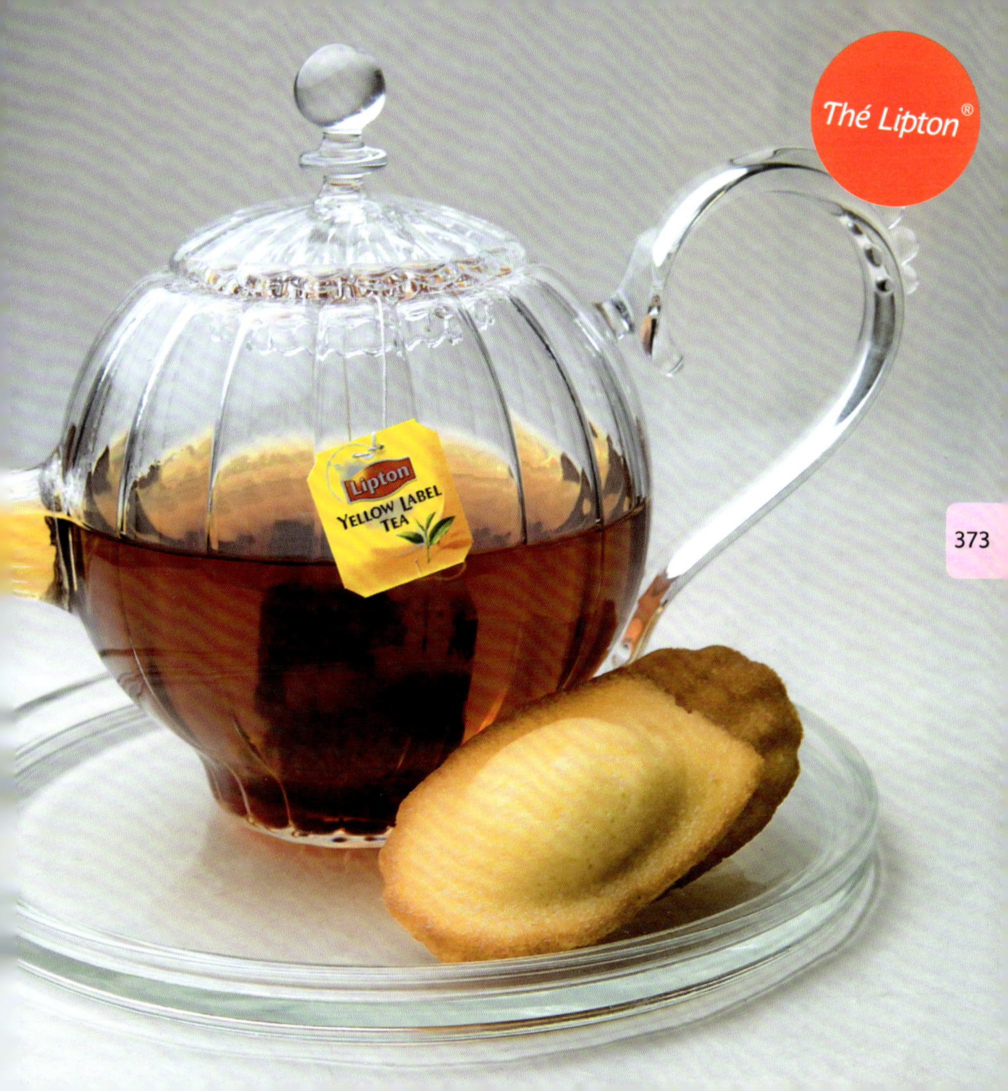

Thon Petit Navire® *(Une marque du groupe MW Brands)*

CAKE AU THON ET AUX OLIVES

Préparation : 10 min • **Cuisson** : 50 min • **Pour 1 cake**

180 g de farine + un peu pour le moule • 1 sachet de levure chimique
3 œufs • 10 cl d'huile d'olive • 10 cl de crème liquide
180 g de thon au naturel Petit Navire® • 75 g d'olives vertes dénoyautées
75 g d'olives noires dénoyautées • 100 g de gruyère râpé
beurre pour le moule • sel et poivre

- Préchauffez le four à 180 °C.
- Mélangez la farine et la levure dans un saladier.
- Dans un autre saladier, battez les œufs au fouet avec l'huile et la crème liquide. Salez et poivrez, puis versez le mélange dans le premier saladier, et mélangez jusqu'à l'obtention d'une préparation homogène.
- Égouttez le thon Petit Navire® puis émiettez-le. Ajoutez-le à la pâte avec les olives et le fromage râpé. Mélangez bien.
- Beurrez et farinez un moule à cake, puis versez-y la préparation.
- Faites cuire au four pendant 50 min. Vérifiez la cuisson en piquant le cake avec la lame d'un couteau : elle doit ressortir sèche.
- Laissez refroidir avant de démouler.

Cake au thon et à la tomate

Ajoutez 3 tomates épépinées et coupées en dés à la préparation. Vous pouvez également utiliser 1 boîte de thon Petit Navire® à la tomate.

Cake au thon et aux légumes

Remplacez les olives par 2 petites courgettes lavées et 1 poivron rouge lavé et épépiné. Coupez les légumes en dés avant de les incorporer à la préparation.

Cake au thon et à la ciboulette

Remplacez les olives par 6 brins de ciboulette ciselés.

Muffins au thon et aux olives

Mélangez 150 g de farine avec 1 sachet de levure chimique, 2 œufs, 10 cl de lait et 10 cl d'huile d'olive. Incorporez 120 g de thon au naturel Petit Navire® émietté, 100 g de gruyère râpé et 80 g d'olives vertes dénoyautées. Salez et poivrez. Répartissez dans les alvéoles d'un moule à muffin, et faites cuire au four préchauffé à 180 °C de 20 à 25 min.

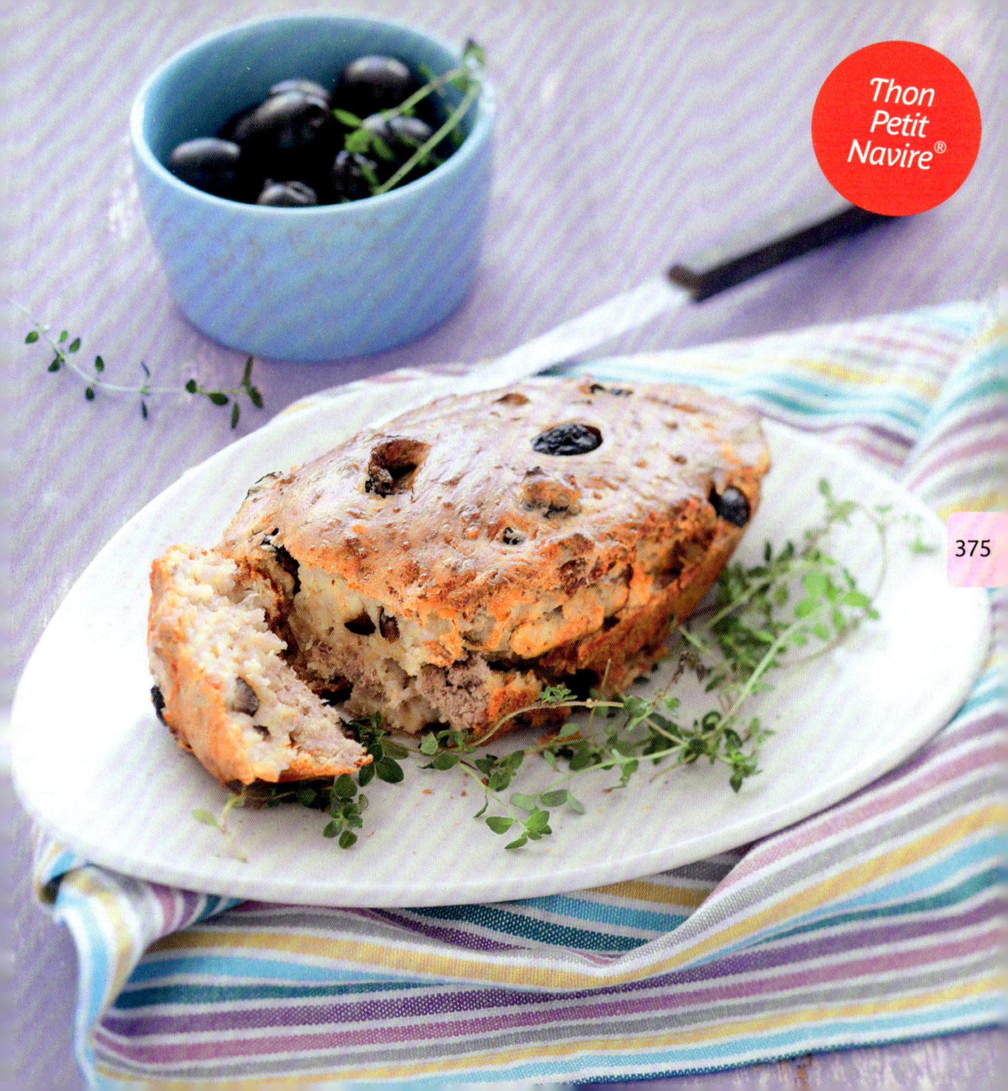
Thon Petit Navire®

Thon Petit Navire® *(Une marque du groupe MW Brands)*

LASAGNES AU THON ET AU FENOUIL

Préparation : 15 min • **Cuisson** : 50 min • **Pour 3 ou 4 personnes**

1/2 bulbe de fenouil • 3 petits blancs de poireau • 200 g de thon au naturel Petit Navire® • 3 feuilles de laurier • 50 cl de lait écrémé 25 g de beurre • 25 g de farine • huile pour graisser le moule 6 à 9 feuilles de lasagnes • 25 g de gruyère râpé • sel et poivre

- Préchauffez le four à 180 °C.
- Lavez le fenouil et les poireaux. Émincez le fenouil et taillez les poireaux en rondelles. Émiettez le thon Petit Navire®.
- Placez les feuilles de laurier, les poireaux et le fenouil dans une casserole, ajoutez le lait, et faites chauffer à feu doux pendant 10 min. Retirez les poireaux et le fenouil, et réservez-les. Jetez les feuilles de laurier. Versez le lait dans une carafe.
- Mettez le beurre et la farine dans une casserole, et faites chauffer à feu doux en mélangeant bien. Ajoutez le lait chaud petit à petit en remuant sans cesse. Portez à ébullition et laissez épaissir. Salez et poivrez. Réservez 3 c. à s. de cette sauce et mélangez le reste avec les légumes.
- Huilez un plat allant au four. Déposez 2 feuilles de lasagnes au fond du plat, puis recouvrez de la moitié du mélange aux légumes et de la moitié du thon. Renouvelez l'opération une fois et terminez par une nouvelle couche de lasagnes. Nappez-la de la sauce réservée, et parsemez de gruyère râpé.
- Faites cuire au four de 35 à 40 min, ou jusqu'à ce que le dessus soit fondu et doré, et que les pâtes soient cuites.

Lasagnes au thon et aux épinards

Faites blanchir, à l'eau bouillante, 1 kg d'épinards frais lavés, égouttés, débarrassés des tiges et retirez-les du feu dès l'ébullition. Transvasez dans de l'eau glacée, égouttez, puis faites revenir avec 1 noix de beurre, de 1 à 2 min. Remplacez le fenouil et les poireaux par les épinards.

Lasagnes au thon et à la ratatouille

Préparez une ratatouille en faisant revenir 1 oignon, 1 poivron rouge, 2 petites courgettes, 1 petite aubergine et 4 tomates. Remplacez le fenouil et les poireaux par la ratatouille.

Lasagnes au thon et aux courgettes

Remplacez le fenouil et les poireaux par 5 petites courgettes taillées en rondelles et revenues à la poêle.

Lasagnes au thon, aux courgettes et à la ricotta

Reprenez la recette ci-dessus en remplaçant la béchamel par de la ricotta.

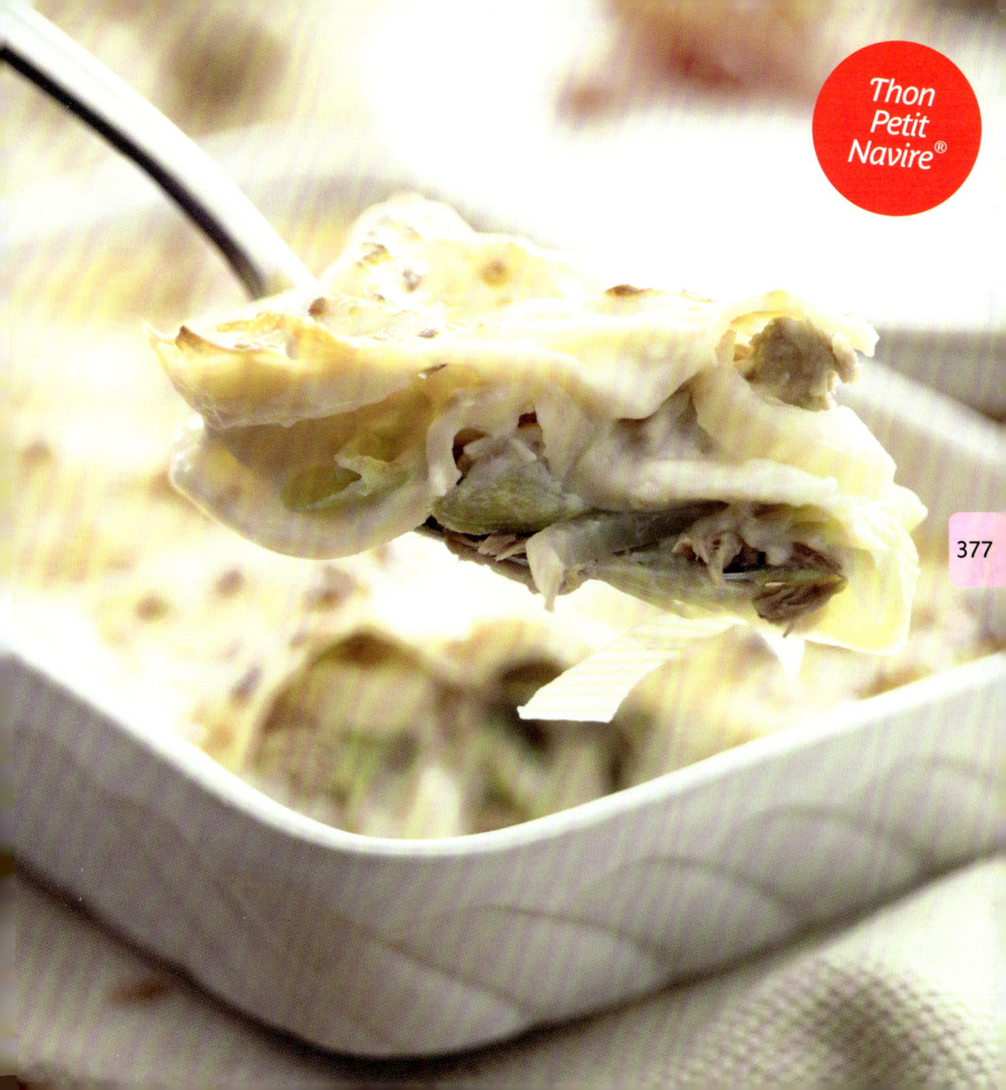
Thon
Petit
Navire®

Thon Petit Navire® *(Une marque du groupe MW Brands)*

PIZZETTE AU THON ET AUX CÂPRES

Préparation : 10 min • **Cuisson** : 10 min • **Pour 6 personnes**

1 rouleau de pâte à pizza de 250 g • 2 tomates
100 g de thon au naturel Petit Navire® • 2 c. à s. de câpres

- Préchauffez le four à 200 °C.
- Déroulez la pâte à pizza. Découpez-la en triangles.
- Lavez les tomates, puis coupez-les en petits dés. Répartissez-les sur les morceaux de pâte.
- Émiettez le thon Petit Navire® et répartissez-le sur les pizzette.
- Parsemez de câpres.
- Faites cuire au four pendant 10 min.
- Servez chaud ou froid.

Pizzette au thon et à la mozzarella
Déposez 1 petite lamelle de mozzarella sur chaque pizzette avant d'ajouter les autres ingrédients.

Pizzette au thon et à la moutarde
Badigeonnez légèrement les pizzettes de moutarde avant d'ajouter les autres ingrédients.

Pizzette au thon et au chèvre
Remplacez les câpres par 2 petits oignons émincés et revenus à la poêle avec de l'huile d'olive. Ajoutez 1 petite rondelle de bûche de chèvre sur chaque pizzette.

Pizzette au poivron
Nappez les pizzettes de poivronade (au rayon sauces) avant d'ajouter les autres ingrédients. Vous pouvez également remplacer les tomates par des dés de poivron cru ou grillé.

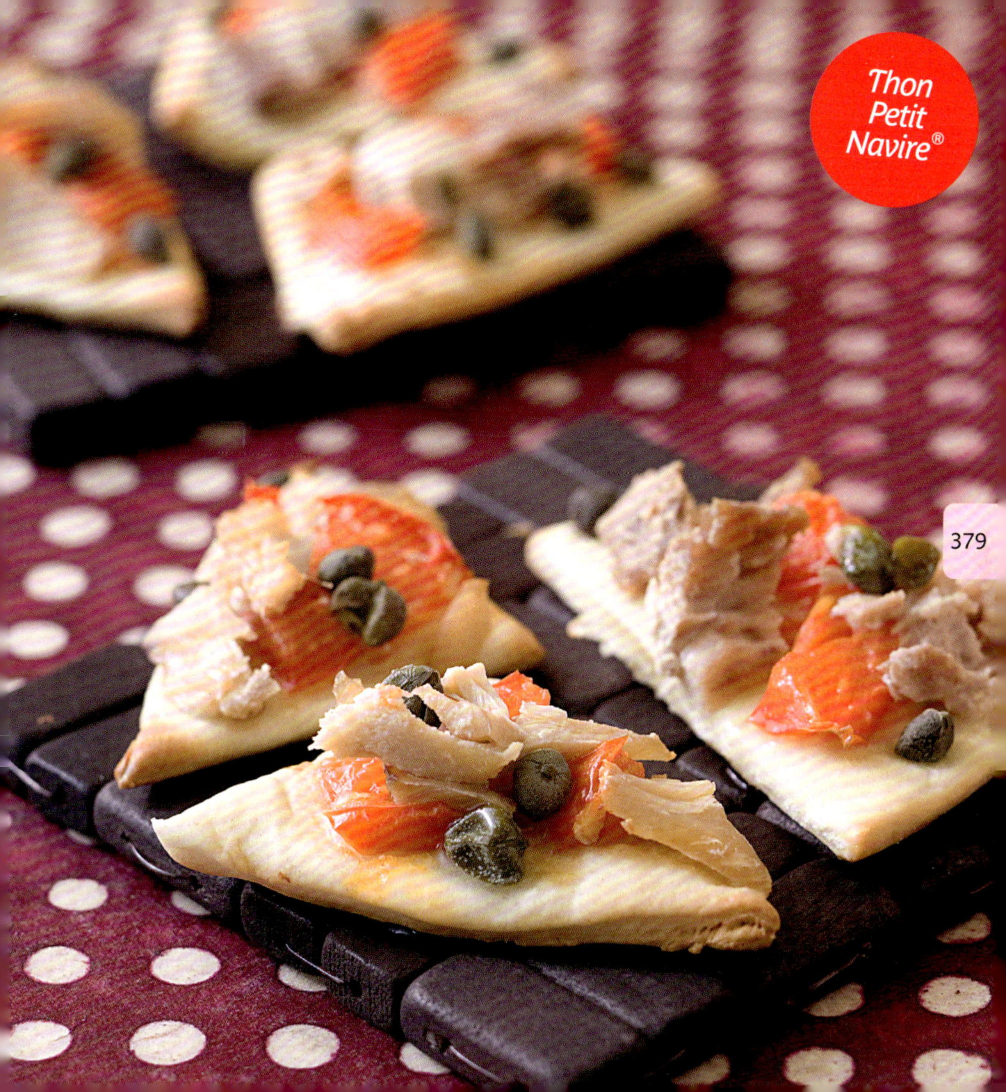

Thon Petit Navire®

Salade de quinoa aux épinards
Faites cuire 250 g de quinoa dans 50 cl d'eau pendant 10 min. Couvrez et laissez gonfler hors du feu. Laissez refroidir. Remplacez le riz par le quinoa.

Salade de riz croquante
Remplacez les petits pois par 50 g de cœurs de palmier et 1/2 concombre pelé, épépiné et taillé en dés. Remplacez les câpres par 1 petite poignée de germes de soja.

Salade de riz au pamplemousse
Remplacez les petits pois par 1 pamplemousse pelé et séparé en quartiers, dont vous retirerez la fine membrane blanche. Remplacez le zeste de citron par du zeste de pamplemousse.

Salade de riz aux champignons et au maïs
Remplacez les petits pois par le contenu de 1 petite boîte de champignons de Paris entiers égouttés. Remplacez les câpres par 1 petite boîte de maïs doux égoutté. Ajoutez quelques cornichons taillés en rondelles.

Thon Petit Navire® (Une marque du groupe MW Brands)

SALADE DE RIZ AUX ÉPINARDS

Préparation: 15 min • **Cuisson**: 30 min • **Pour 4 personnes**

250 g de riz long grain • 120 g de petits pois • 1 citron (non traité)
1 c. à s. de vinaigre • 3 c. à s. d'huile d'olive • 1 oignon blanc
20 g de câpres • 50 g de jeunes pousses d'épinards
350 g de thon au naturel Petit Navire® • sel et poivre

- Faites cuire le riz dans de l'eau bouillante salée pendant 20 min environ. Rincez-le, puis égouttez-le. Laissez-le refroidir.
- En parallèle, faites cuire les petits pois dans de l'eau bouillante salée pendant 10 min. Égouttez-les.
- Lavez le citron, puis prélevez le zeste et taillez-le en fines lamelles.
- Pressez le jus dans un bol, ajoutez le vinaigre, du sel, du poivre et l'huile en fouettant, pour bien émulsionner.
- Épluchez l'oignon et émincez-le. Ajoutez-le à la vinaigrette avec les câpres.
- Lavez et égouttez les épinards. Égouttez le thon Petit Navire® et séparez les lamelles.
- Placez le riz dans un saladier avec le thon et les petits pois. Ajoutez la vinaigrette et mélangez délicatement.
- Tapissez le fond de petits bols individuels de jeunes pousses d'épinards, puis ajoutez la salade de riz. Servez frais.

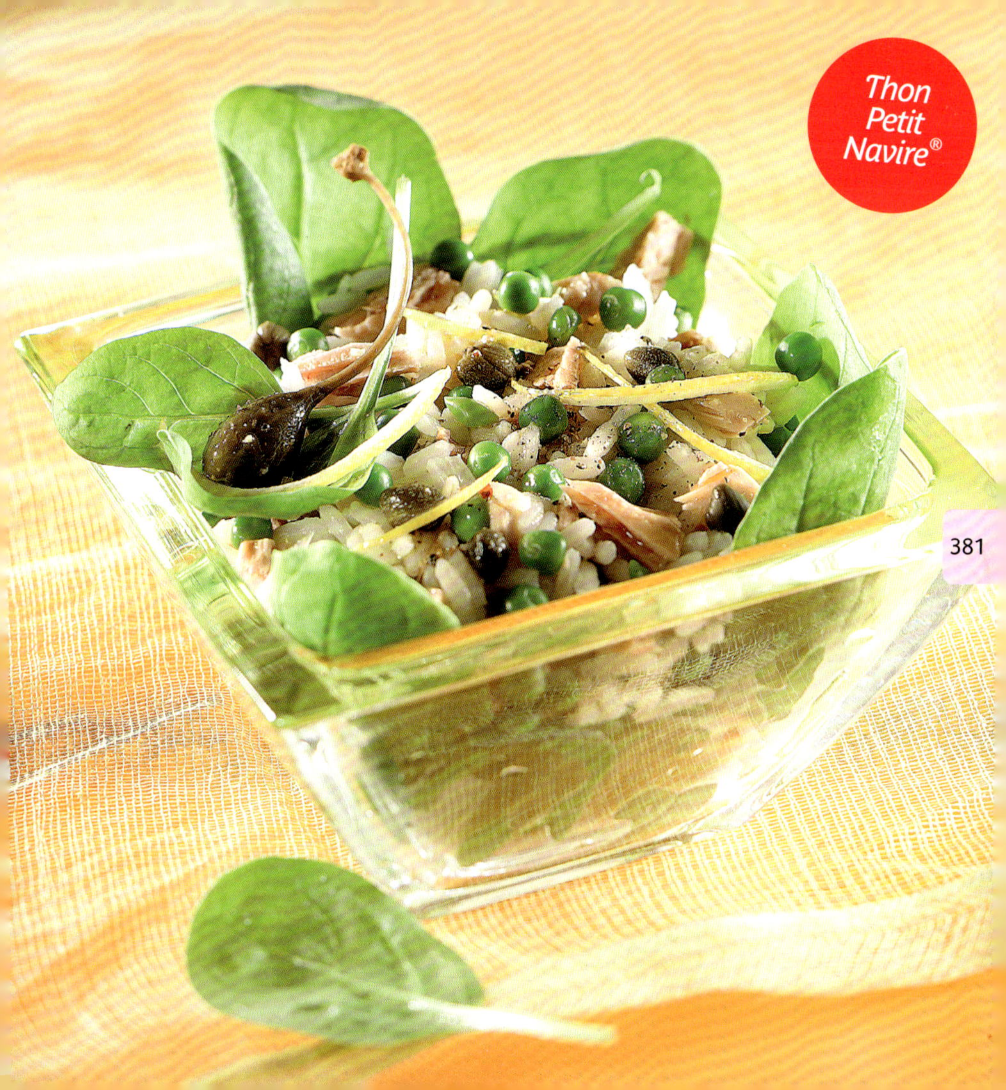
Thon
Petit
Navire®

Thon Petit Navire® (Une marque du groupe MW Brands)

TIMBALES ESTIVALES AU THON

Préparation : 10 min • **Cuisson** : 30 sec • **Pour 4 personnes**

1 concombre • 3 tomates • 1 boîte de thon Petit Navire® de 90 g
100 g de fromage frais • 6 brins de ciboulette

- Pelez le concombre, ouvrez-le en deux dans le sens de la longueur, et épépinez-le. Détaillez la chair en petits dés.
- Plongez les tomates dans une casserole d'eau bouillante pendant 30 sec, puis passez-les sous l'eau froide pour arrêter la cuisson. Pelez-les, épépinez-les et taillez-les en petits dés.
- Égouttez le thon Petit Navire® et émiettez-le. Mettez-le dans une jatte.
- Ajoutez le fromage frais, le concombre et les tomates.
- Lavez la ciboulette, puis essuyez-la avec du papier absorbant. Ciselez-la finement. Ajoutez-la à la préparation. Remuez bien.
- Répartissez ce mélange dans des ramequins.
- Réservez au frais jusqu'au moment de servir.

Verrines tricolores

Ne mélangez pas le concombre et les tomates avec la préparation au thon. Superposez dans des verrines 1 couche de dés de concombre, 1 couche de dés de tomate et 1 couche de mélange au thon. Renouvelez l'opération une fois.

Verrines à l'avocat et au thon

Écrasez la chair de 2 avocats avec 1 échalote hachée et le jus de 1 citron vert. Alternez dans des verrines les couches de mélange au thon et de préparation à l'avocat.

Endives garnies au thon

Supprimez le concombre et les tomates. Séparez les feuilles de 3 endives bien lavées et garnissez-les de mélange au thon.

Verrines à la betterave, au thon et à l'alfalfa

Garnissez 4 verrines de dés de betterave cuite, surmontez de mélange au thon et terminez par un peu d'alfalfa (graines germées que l'on trouve en épicerie bio).

Thon Petit Navire®

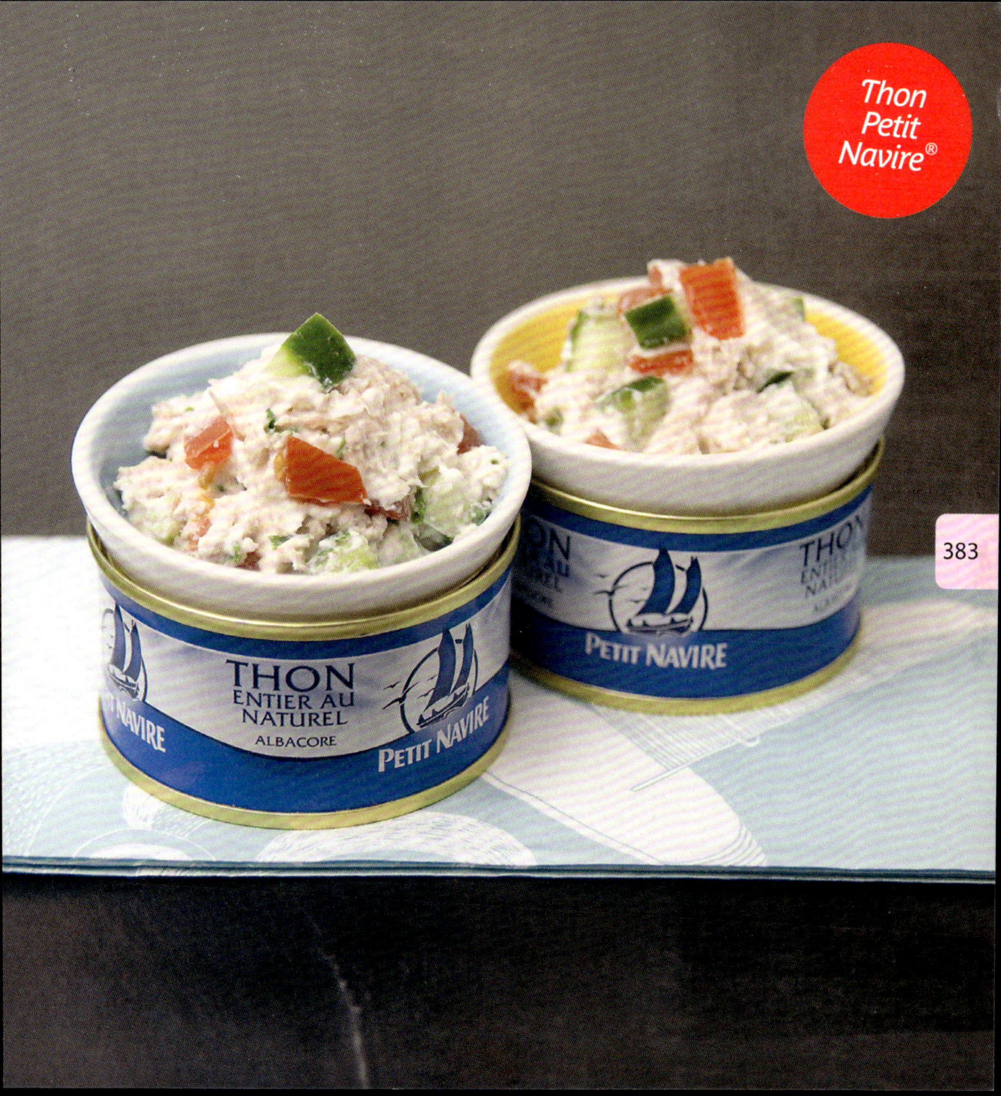

Thon Petit Navire® *(Une marque du groupe MW Brands)*

TORTILLAS ROULÉES AU THON

Préparation : 20 min • **Cuisson** : 10 min • **Réfrigération** : 1 h
Pour 4 personnes

2 œufs • 1 concombre • 2 brins de persil
1 grande boîte de thon au naturel Petit Navire®
4 c. à s. de mayonnaise • 4 tortillas

- Portez à ébullition une petite casserole d'eau. À l'ébullition, déposez-y délicatement les œufs et faites cuire pendant 8 min à partir de la reprise de l'ébullition. Retirez-les à l'aide d'une écumoire, puis passez-les sous l'eau froide pour stopper la cuisson.
- Lavez le concombre, coupez-le en quatre pour l'épépiner puis taillez-le en fins bâtonnets.
- Rincez le persil, épongez-le sur du papier absorbant puis ciselez-le.
- Écrasez les œufs durs. Égouttez le thon Petit Navire® puis émiettez-le. Mélangez-les avec la mayonnaise et le persil.
- Coupez les tortillas en trois. Tartinez-les de préparation au thon. Déposez un petit fagot de concombre près d'un bord, et roulez très serré.
- Enveloppez chaque roulé dans du film alimentaire, et réservez au frais pendant au moins 1 h avant de servir.

Tortillas aux carottes et au soja

Remplacez le concombre par 2 carottes pelées et taillées en fins bâtonnets. Garnissez les tortillas de fagots de carottes et de germes de soja.

Tortillas à la macédoine

Pour une version express, remplacez le concombre par le contenu de 1 boîte moyenne de macédoine de légumes, que vous mélangerez avec la préparation à base de thon et de mayonnaise.

Rouleaux de printemps au thon

Remplacez les tortillas par 4 feuilles de riz pour rouleaux de printemps. Ajoutez 1 c. à c. de sauce soja à la préparation au thon.

Wraps au thon et à l'avocat

Remplacez le concombre par la chair de 2 avocats taillée en dés. Mélangez-les à la préparation au thon. Ajoutez également le contenu de 1 petite boîte de maïs doux égoutté.

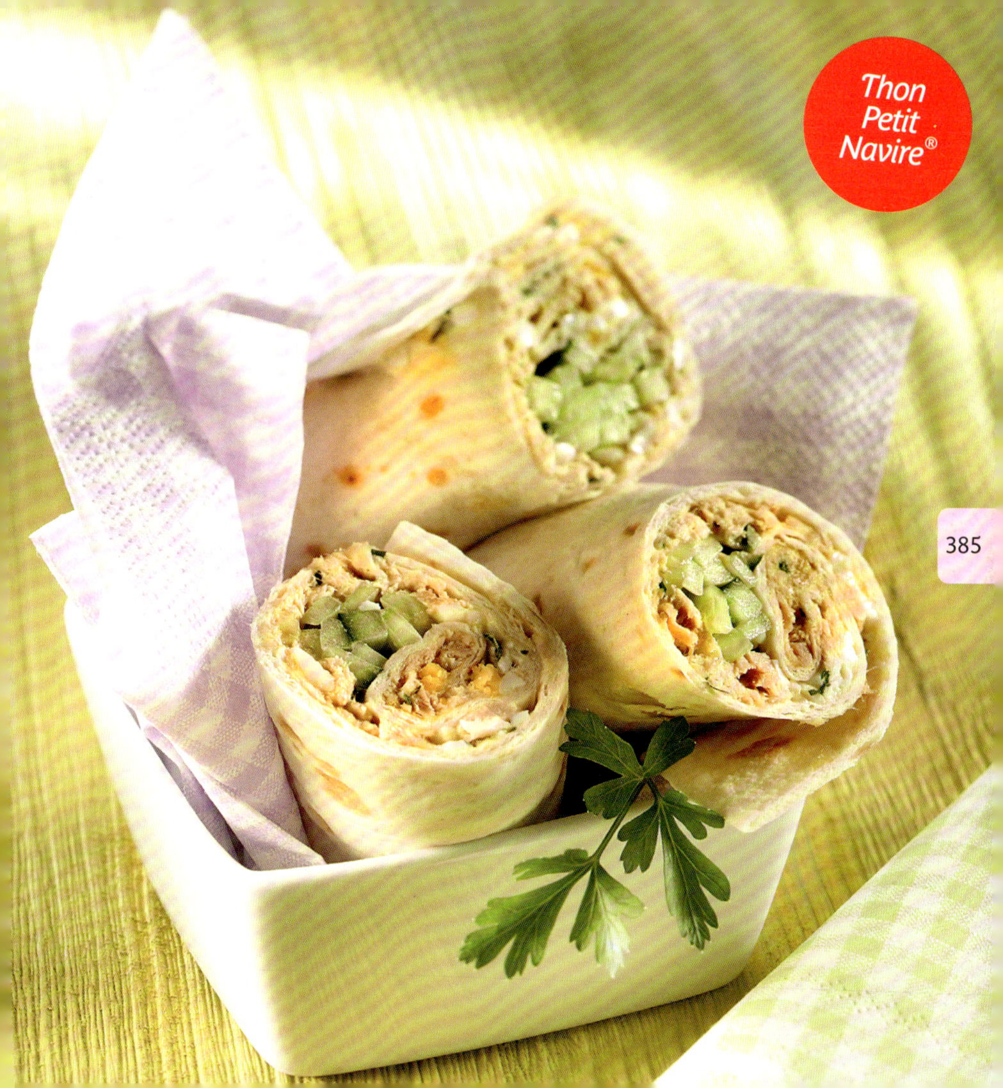
Thon
Petit
Navire®

COOKIES AU TOBLERONE®

Préparation : 15 min • **Cuisson :** 10 min • **Pour 20 cookies**

160 g de Toblerone® noir • 120 g de beurre ramolli • 100 g de sucre roux en poudre • 150 g de farine • 1/2 sachet de levure chimique 2 c. à s. de cacao amer en poudre • 1 œuf • sel

- Préchauffez le four à 180 °C.
- Concassez grossièrement le Toblerone® noir.
- Mettez le beurre et le sucre dans un saladier, et battez au fouet jusqu'à ce que le mélange blanchisse.
- Ajoutez la farine, la levure, le cacao, l'œuf et 1/2 c. à c. de sel.
- Incorporez les morceaux de Toblerone® puis mélangez de nouveau.
- Prélevez des boules de pâte et déposez-les sur une plaque à pâtisserie recouverte de papier sulfurisé, en les espaçant bien.
- Faites cuire au four pendant 10 min.
- Laissez refroidir légèrement avant de déguster.

Cookies au Toblerone® et à la nougatine

Supprimez le cacao amer.
Ajoutez 50 g de pépites de nougatine à la préparation.

Cookies aux flocons d'avoine

Ajoutez 40 g de flocons d'avoine à la préparation.
Vous pouvez également utiliser des flocons de petit épeautre (en épicerie bio).

Cookies au potimarron

Remplacez le beurre par 120 g de purée de potimarrons.
Ajoutez 20 g de sucre à la préparation.

Cookies à l'amande blanche et au muesli

Remplacez le beurre par 120 g de purée d'amandes.
Ajoutez 60 g de muesli à la préparation.

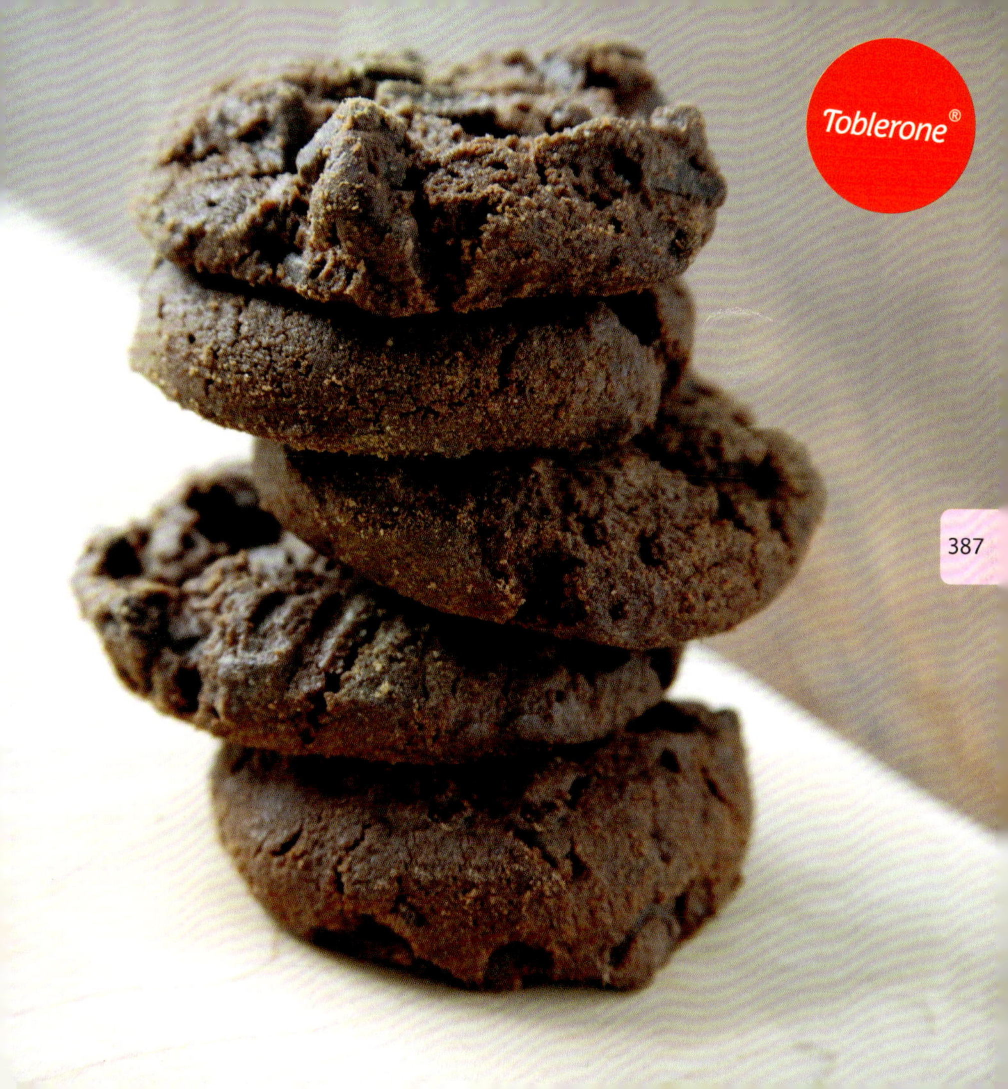
Toblerone®

CRUMBLE AUX POIRES ET AU TOBLERONE®

Préparation : 15 min • **Cuisson** : 35 min • **Pour 4 personnes**

3 poires bien mûres • 50 g de Toblerone® • 125 g de farine
100 g de sucre • 80 g de beurre

- Préchauffez le four à 190 °C.
- Pelez les poires, ôtez le cœur et coupez-les en petits cubes.
- Cassez le Toblerone® en petits morceaux et mélangez-les aux poires. Mettez le tout dans un plat allant au four.
- Dans un saladier, mélangez la farine et le sucre.
- Détaillez le beurre en parcelles et ajoutez-le dans le saladier.
- Travaillez le mélange du bout des doigts jusqu'à ce qu'il forme des miettes.
- Répartissez la pâte sur les poires et le Toblerone®, puis faites cuire au four pendant 35 min environ.
- Dégustez tiède.

Crumble aux poires, Toblerone® et caramel

Faites un caramel en faisant chauffer 150 g de sucre avec un peu d'eau. Hors du feu, incorporez 20 cl de crème liquide frémissante. Nappez les poires et le Toblerone® de caramel avant d'ajouter la pâte à crumble.

Crumble aux poires, Toblerone® et cacahuètes

Ajoutez 60 g de cacahuètes décortiquées non salées dans la pâte à crumble.

Crumble sans gluten

Remplacez la farine par 60 g de poudre d'amandes et 65 g de farine de riz ou de quinoa. Vous pouvez aussi utiliser de la Maïzena.

Crumble aux quetsches

Remplacez les poires par 450 g de quetsches lavées, dénoyautées et coupées en deux. Vous pouvez aussi utiliser des mirabelles.

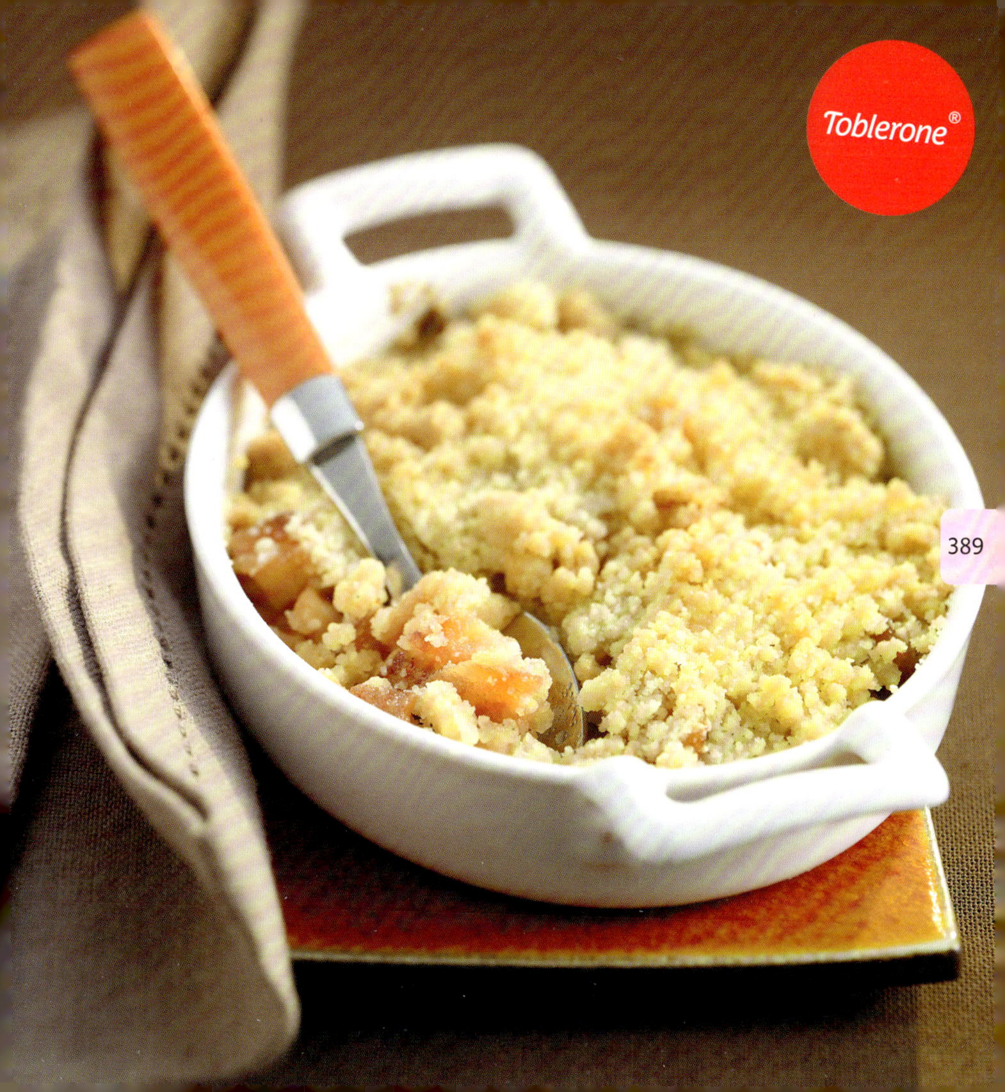
Toblerone®

FONDUE AU TOBLERONE®

Préparation : 10 min • **Cuisson** : 5 min • **Pour 6 personnes**

500 g de Toblerone® au chocolat au lait • 25 cl de crème liquide
500 g de cerises fraîches • 400 g de petits macarons

- Faites fondre le Toblerone® dans le caquelon à feu doux, en remuant régulièrement.
- Incorporez la crème liquide et remuez de nouveau.
- Lavez les cerises, équeutez-les et dénoyautez-les.
- Pour la dégustation, piquez 1 cerise ou 1 macaron sur une pique à fondue, puis trempez-les dans la fondue au Toblerone®.
- Dégustez bien chaud.

Fondue au Toblerone® et au lait concentré

Remplacez la crème liquide par du lait concentré non sucré dans une version pour adultes, sucré pour des enfants.

Fondue au Toblerone® et au kirsch

Ajoutez 5 cl de kirsch dans la fondue, et remuez bien. Vous pouvez également utiliser du Cointreau.

Fondue au Toblerone® et aux fruits secs

Remplacez les cerises et les macarons par des pruneaux, des abricots secs, des bananes séchées ou des noix.

Fondue gourmande au Toblerone®

En plus des cerises et des macarons, proposez dans des ramequins des morceaux de guimauve, des madeleines, des meringues, des morceaux de pain d'épice et de brioche. Proposez également des morceaux de pêche, de kiwi et de poire ainsi que des fraises.

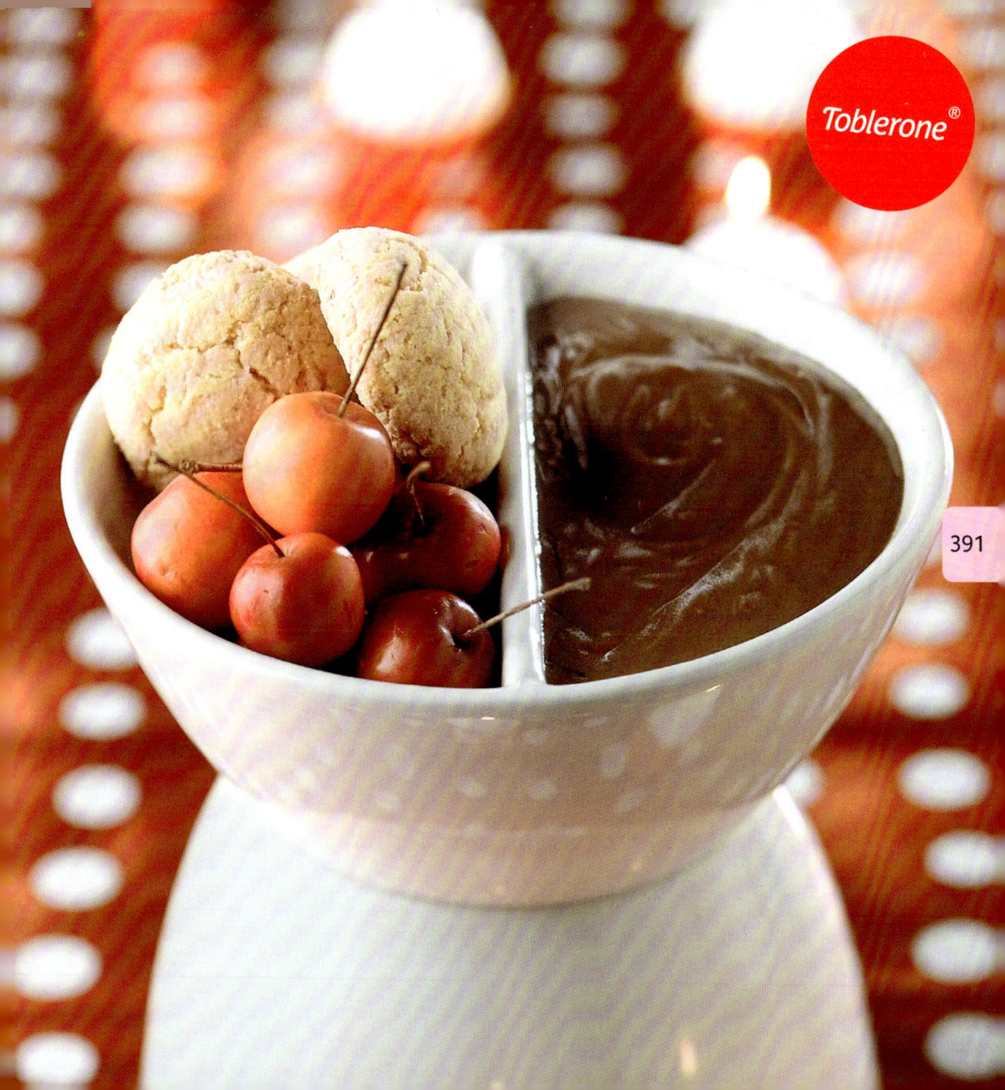
Toblerone®

Marbré au Toblerone® et au thé matcha
Remplacez l'extrait de vanille liquide par 2 c. à c. de thé vert matcha en poudre.

Marbré au Toblerone® et aux pistaches
Mixez 80 g de pistaches non salées, et remplacez l'extrait de vanille liquide par cette poudre.

Marbré au Toblerone®, au citron et au rhum
Remplacez l'extrait de vanille liquide par le jus de 2 citrons et 2 c. à c. de rhum.

Marbré italien
Utilisez un moule à manqué. Versez-y alternativement les 2 pâtes, cuillerée par cuillerée, en commençant au centre du moule.

MARBRÉ AU TOBLERONE®

Préparation : 20 min • **Cuisson :** 45 min • **Pour 4 personnes**

125 g de beurre + un peu pour le moule • 3 œufs • 50 g de Toblerone®
200 g de sucre en poudre • 6 c. à s. de lait • 200 g de farine
1 sachet de levure chimique • 1 c. à c. d'extrait de vanille liquide

- Préchauffez le four à 180 °C.
- Faites fondre le beurre dans une casserole. Séparez les blancs des jaunes d'œufs. Cassez le Toblerone® en morceaux et faites-les fondre dans une autre casserole.
- Versez le beurre fondu dans un saladier et mélangez-le avec le sucre à l'aide d'une cuillère en bois. Ajoutez les jaunes d'œufs, le lait, la farine et la levure. Remuez bien.
- Montez les blancs d'œufs en neige ferme, puis incorporez-les à la pâte.
- Séparez la pâte en deux parties, parfumez l'une avec l'extrait de vanille, l'autre avec le Toblerone® fondu.
- Beurrez un moule à cake et versez-y la préparation en alternant les couches de pâte à la vanille et de pâte au Toblerone®.
- Faites cuire au four pendant 40 min.
- Laissez refroidir complètement avant de démouler.

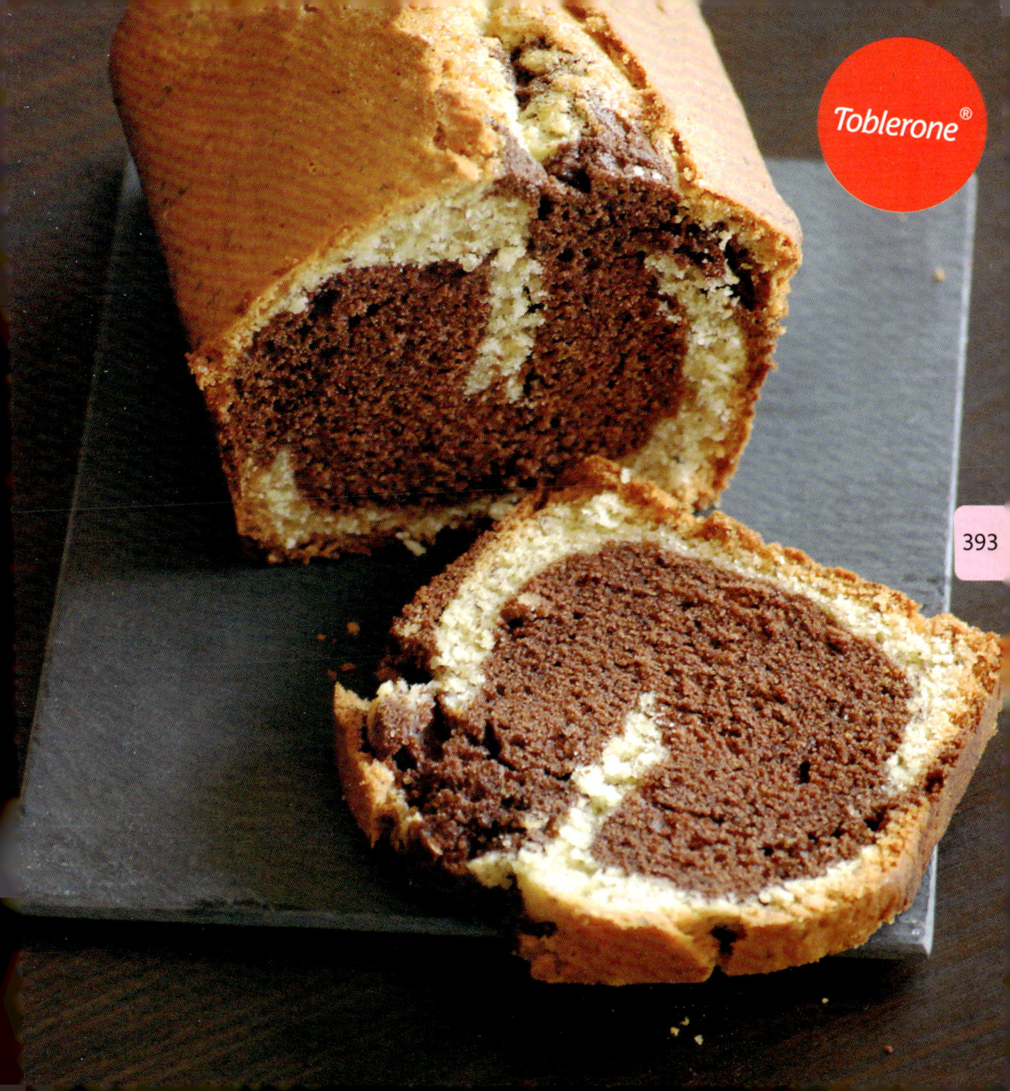
Toblerone®

PETITS POTS DE CRÈME AU TOBLERONE®

Préparation : 10 min • **Cuisson** : 35 min • **Pour 6 personnes**

3 œufs • 75 g de sucre roux en poudre
200 g de Toblerone® au chocolat au lait • 20 cl de lait
30 cl de crème liquide

- Préchauffez le four à 120 °C.
- Mettez les œufs et le sucre roux dans un saladier, et battez au fouet.
- Cassez le Toblerone® en morceaux, puis mettez-les dans une casserole avec le lait et la crème liquide. Faites fondre à feu doux, en remuant régulièrement.
- Versez délicatement le Toblerone® fondu dans le saladier et mélangez.
- Répartissez la crème dans des petits ramequins (ou verres supportant la chaleur), placez-les dans un grand plat à four, que vous remplirez d'eau jusqu'à mi-hauteur des ramequins.
- Faites cuire au four pendant 30 min.
- Laissez refroidir à température ambiante, puis réservez au réfrigérateur.
- Servez très frais.

Petits pots au Toblerone® et aux noisettes

Ajoutez 50 g de noisettes concassées à la préparation. Vous pouvez également utiliser des amandes concassées.

Petits pots au Toblerone® et à la fève tonka

Râpez 1 fève tonka et ajoutez-la au Toblerone® fondu, hors du feu. Mélangez bien. Vous pouvez ajouter les graines grattées de 1 gousse de vanille.

Petits pots au Toblerone® et au café

Ajoutez 2 c. à c. de café lyophilisé diluées dans 1 c. à s. d'eau au chocolat fondu, hors du feu. Vous pouvez également utiliser 1 c. à c. d'extrait de café liquide.

Petits pots au Toblerone® et au calvados

Reprenez la recette ci-dessus en ajoutant 1 c. à s. de calvados au chocolat fondu, hors du feu.

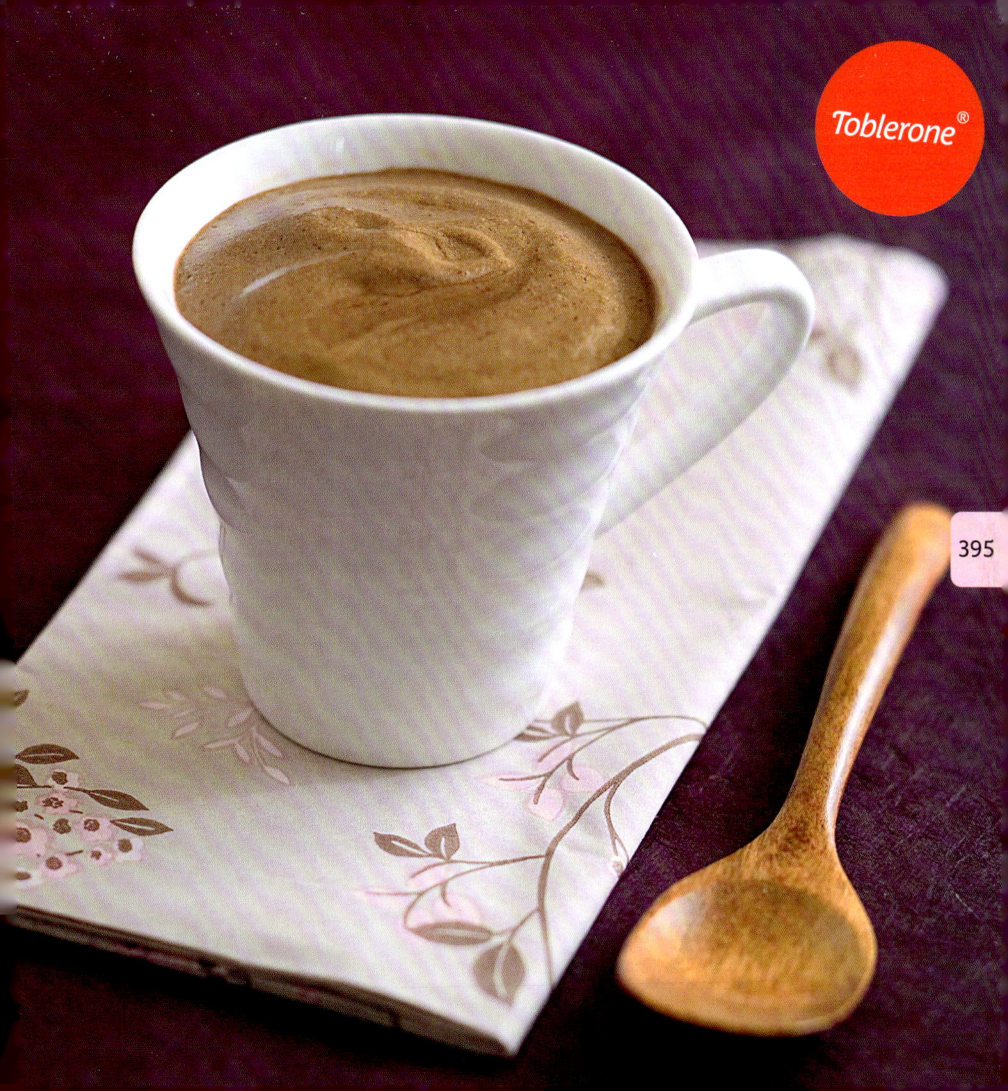

Toblerone®

ROULÉS DE CRÊPE AU TOBLERONE®

Préparation : 15 min • **Cuisson :** 10 min • **Repos :** 1 h • **Pour 6 personnes**

pour la crème de Toblerone® : *100 g de Toblerone® • 50 g de chocolat noir à pâtisserie • 5 cl de crème liquide entière • 10 cl de lait concentré sucré*
pour les roulés : *6 crêpes bretonnes*

- Pour la crème de Toblerone®, séparez les morceaux de Toblerone® et de chocolat noir, puis mettez-les dans une jatte supportant la chaleur.
- Faites-les fondre au bain-marie.
- Ajoutez la crème liquide et mélangez bien.
- Hors du feu, ajoutez le lait concentré sucré et mélangez.
- Laissez refroidir à température ambiante pendant 1 h.
- Nappez les crêpes de crème de Toblerone® puis roulez-les.
- Coupez-les en tronçons de 3 cm de largeur, et maintenez-les avec des piques à cocktail.
- Conservez le reste de crème de Toblerone® dans un bocal de verre fermé hermétiquement.

Chouquettes au Toblerone®
Faites une incision sur le côté d'une vingtaine de chouquettes, puis garnissez chacune de 1 c. à c. de crème au Toblerone®.

Roulés de pain de mie au Toblerone®
Aplatissez 10 à 12 tranches de pain de mie sans croûte au rouleau à pâtisserie, puis nappez-les de crème au Toblerone®. Roulez, coupez en quatre, et maintenez chaque roulé avec une pique à cocktail.

Madeleines à la crème de Toblerone®
Battez 2 œufs avec 80 g de sucre jusqu'à ce que le mélange blanchisse, ajoutez 80 g de farine, 1/2 c. à s. de levure et 80 g de beurre fondu. Ajoutez 5 c. à s. de crème au Toblerone®. Répartissez dans les alvéoles d'un moule à madeleine. Faites cuire au four préchauffé à 180 °C pendant 15 min.

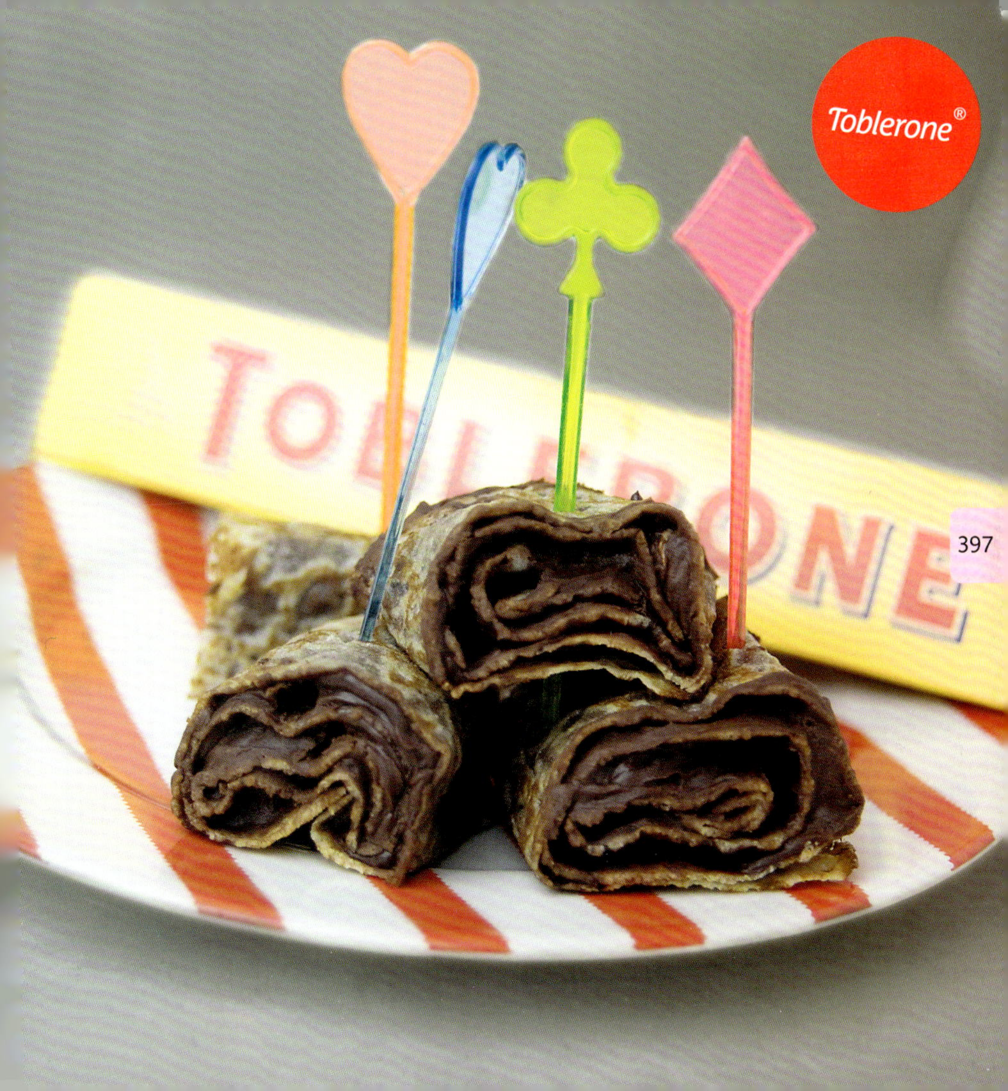

Toblerone®

BROCHETTES DE POULET THAÏ

Préparation : 15 min • **Cuisson** : 10 min • **Marinade** : 3 h
Pour 4 personnes

50 g de coriandre • 1 morceau de gingembre de 5 cm
1 tige de citronnelle • 2 petits piments rouges • 4 escalopes de poulet
1 yaourt nature Danone® • 2 c. à c. de sauce nuoc-mâm
1 c. à c. de cumin moulu • tranches de citron vert

- Rincez la coriandre, épongez-la sur du papier absorbant et émincez-la. Râpez le gingembre. Rincez la citronnelle et émincez-la. Rincez les piments et émincez-les. Taillez les escalopes de poulet en deux dans le sens de la longueur.
- Dans un saladier, mélangez le yaourt nature Danone®, la coriandre, le gingembre, la citronnelle, le piment, le nuoc-mâm et le cumin. Ajoutez le poulet et mélangez pour bien l'imprégner du mélange. Laissez mariner pendant 3 h au réfrigérateur.
- Enfilez chaque morceau de poulet sur une brochette.
- Faites chauffer un barbecue, une plancha ou une poêle gril, et faites cuire les brochettes de 4 à 5 min sur chaque face.
- Servez avec les tranches de citron vert.

Brochettes de poulet à l'indienne

Mélangez le jus de 1/2 citron, 3 yaourts nature Danone®, 1 c. à c. de garam masala, 1 c. à c. de curcuma, 1/2 c. à c. de cumin et faites-y mariner les morceaux de poulet pendant 3 h.

Brochettes de poulet au curry et aux agrumes

Mélangez le jus de 1 citron, le zeste de 1/2 orange, 1 yaourt brassé nature, 1 gousse d'ail écrasée, 2 c. à c. de curry et 1 c. à c. de paprika, et faites-y mariner les morceaux de poulet pendant 3 h.

Brochettes de poisson thaï

Remplacez le poulet par 4 pavés de saumon, de cabillaud, de loup, ou par 4 morceaux de dos de lotte.

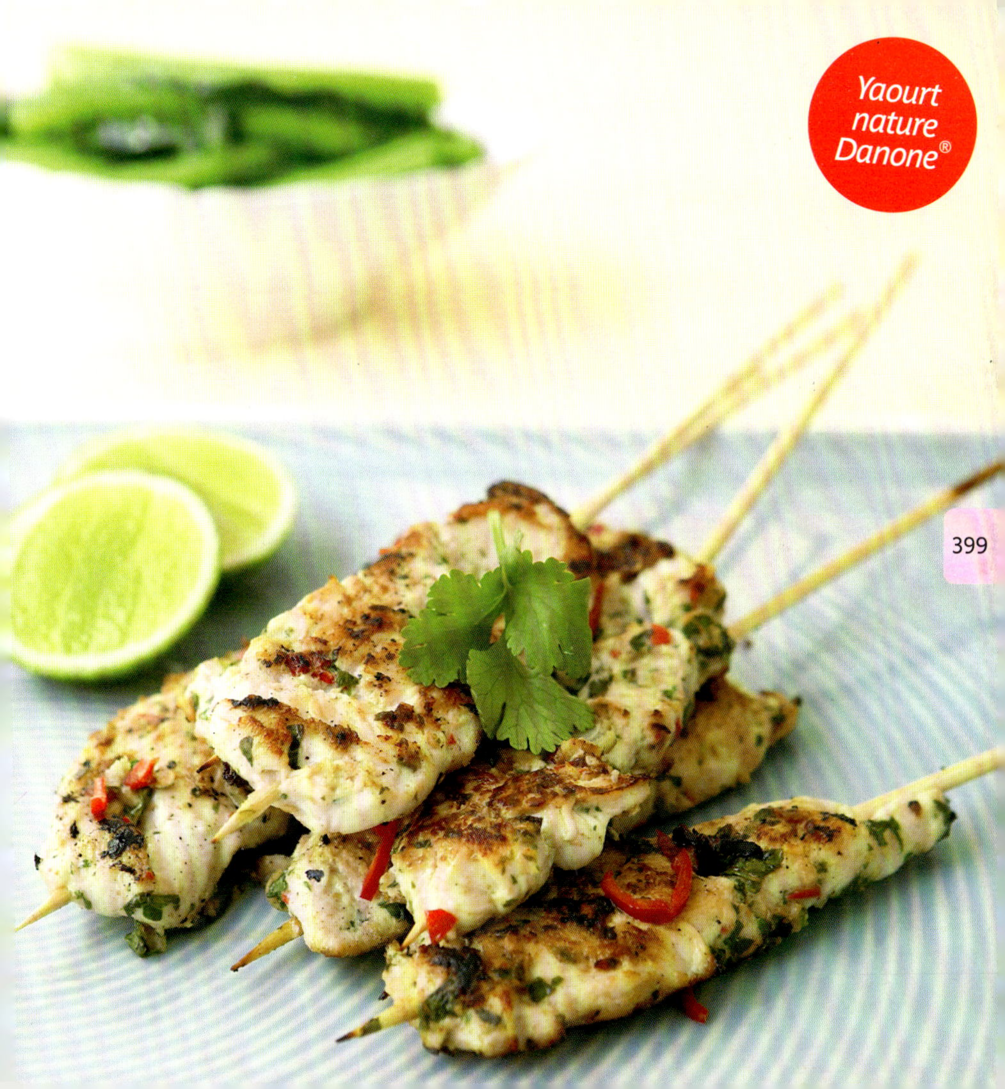
Yaourt nature Danone®

Yaourt nature Danone®

PANCAKES À LA VANILLE ET AUX FRUITS ROUGES

Préparation : 10 min • **Cuisson :** 16 min • **Pour 4 personnes**

160 g de farine • 1/4 de c. à c. de levure • 2 pots de yaourt nature Danone®
1 œuf • 1 c. à c. d'extrait de vanille liquide
500 g de fruits rouges frais mélangés • sirop d'érable

- Versez la farine et la levure dans un saladier. Faites un puits au centre et versez-y les yaourts nature Danone®, l'œuf et l'extrait de vanille liquide. Mélangez jusqu'à ce que la pâte soit homogène et sans grumeaux.
- Faites chauffer une grande poêle à feu moyen, et huilez-la légèrement. Versez 4 c. à s. de pâte dans la poêle en les espaçant légèrement, et faites cuire de 1 à 2 min, jusqu'à ce que des bulles apparaissent.
- Retournez et faites cuire pendant encore 1 ou 2 min, jusqu'à ce que les pancakes soient bien dorés.
- Placez-les sur une assiette et répétez l'opération jusqu'à épuisement des ingrédients.
- Servez les pancakes chauds, avec les fruits rouges préalablement lavés, et arrosez de sirop d'érable.

Pancakes à la banane
Ajoutez la chair de 1 banane écrasée à la préparation.
Vous pouvez également incorporer la banane simplement taillée en rondelles.

Pancakes à l'orange et à la pomme
Ajoutez 1 pomme pelée, épépinée et râpée, ainsi que le jus de 1 orange, à la préparation.

Pancakes aux myrtilles
Ajoutez 100 g de myrtilles fraîches ou décongelées à la pâte, et mixez le tout avant de faire cuire.

Gâteau de pancake à la confiture de lait
Superposez les pancakes 4 par 4, en intercalant 1 couche généreuse de confiture de lait entre chacun.
Vous pouvez également utiliser du caramel au beurre salé ou du sirop d'érable.

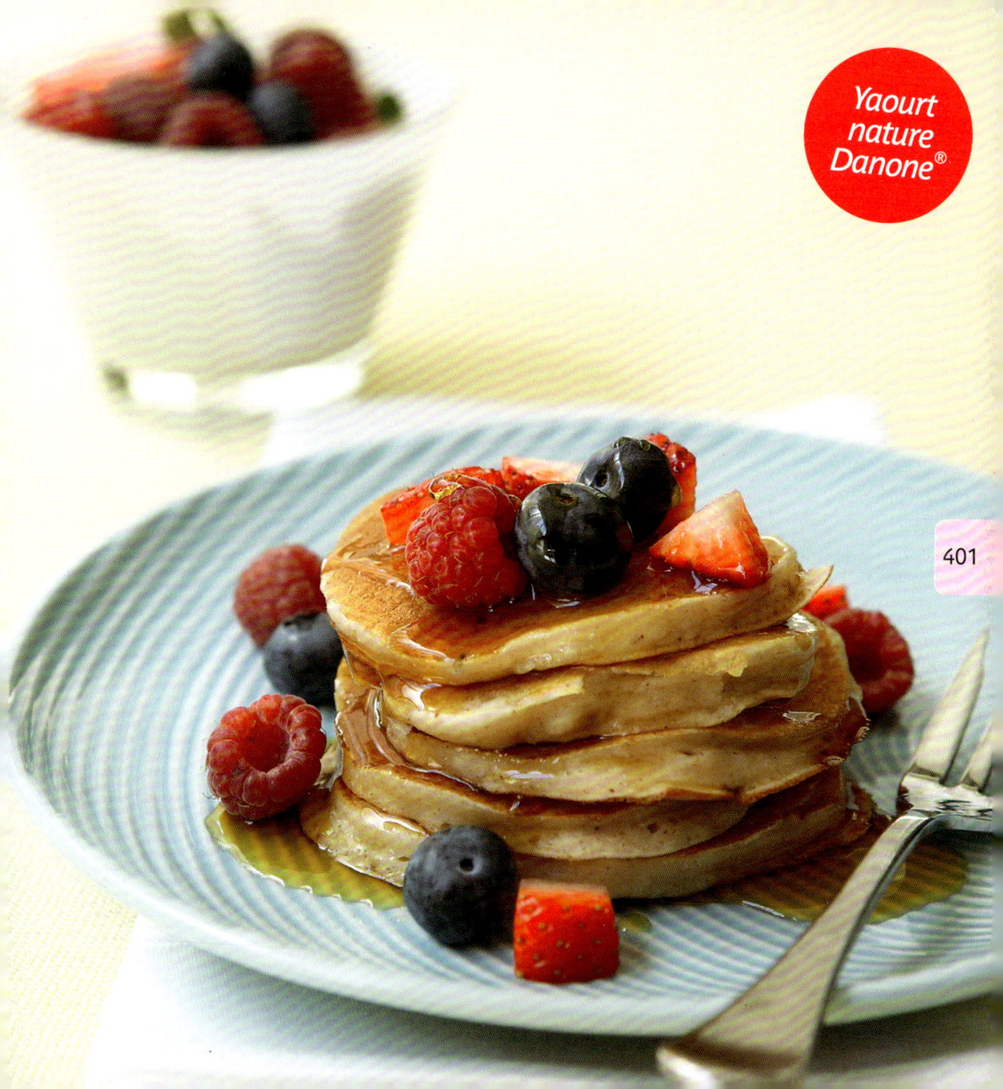
Yaourt
nature
Danone®

Yaourt nature Danone®

RAÏTA DE POIVRON

Préparation : 20 min • **Cuisson** : 30 min • **Réfrigération** : 4 h
Pour 1 bol de raïta

1 poivron rouge • 2 tomates • 1 échalote • 1 c. à s. d'huile d'olive • 1 ou 2 c. à c. de curcuma • 2 yaourts nature Danone® • sel

- Préchauffez le gril du four. Lavez le poivron et passez-le sous le gril du four. Dès qu'un côté commence à noircir, tournez-le d'un quart de tour. Continuez ainsi jusqu'à ce que le poivron soit noirci de toute part.
- Sortez-le du four et mettez-le sans attendre dans un sac à congélation, fermez-le, puis laissez refroidir pendant 15 min. Retirez-le du sac et pelez-le. Coupez-le en morceaux.
- Plongez les tomates dans de l'eau bouillante pendant 30 s, puis passez-les sous l'eau froide pour arrêter la cuisson. Pelez-les, épépinez-les et concassez-les grossièrement.
- Épluchez l'échalote et hachez-la. Faites chauffer l'huile d'olive dans une poêle, puis ajoutez-y l'échalote et le poivron.
- Laissez suer pendant 8 min environ, puis ajoutez les tomates, le curcuma et un peu de sel, puis poursuivez la cuisson pendant 5 min.
- Laissez refroidir légèrement, puis versez la préparation dans le bol du mixeur avec les yaourts nature Danone®.
- Mixez, puis versez le raïta dans un bol, et réservez-le au frais pendant 4 h.
- Servez comme dip à l'apéritif.

Raïta de concombre
Remplacez le poivron par 1 concombre épluché, fendu en deux et débarrassé des graines, puis râpé. Ajoutez 1 gousse d'ail hachée à la préparation.

Raïta de concombre à la menthe
Reprenez la recette ci-dessus en supprimant l'échalote et l'ail. Ajoutez 20 feuilles de menthe fraîche ciselées et 1 c. à s. de miel à la préparation.

Raïta d'avocat
Remplacez le poivron et les tomates par la chair de 2 avocats. Ajoutez 1 piment vert haché, 1 gousse d'ail, le jus de 1/2 citron vert et 1 trait de Tabasco®.

Salade au raïta de poivron
Mélangez les feuilles lavées de 1/2 laitue avec 2 tomates taillées en dés, 2 filets de poulet coupés en dés et revenus à la poêle, 20 g de pignons de pin grillés à sec. Servez avec le raïta en guise de vinaigrette.

Yaourt nature Danone®

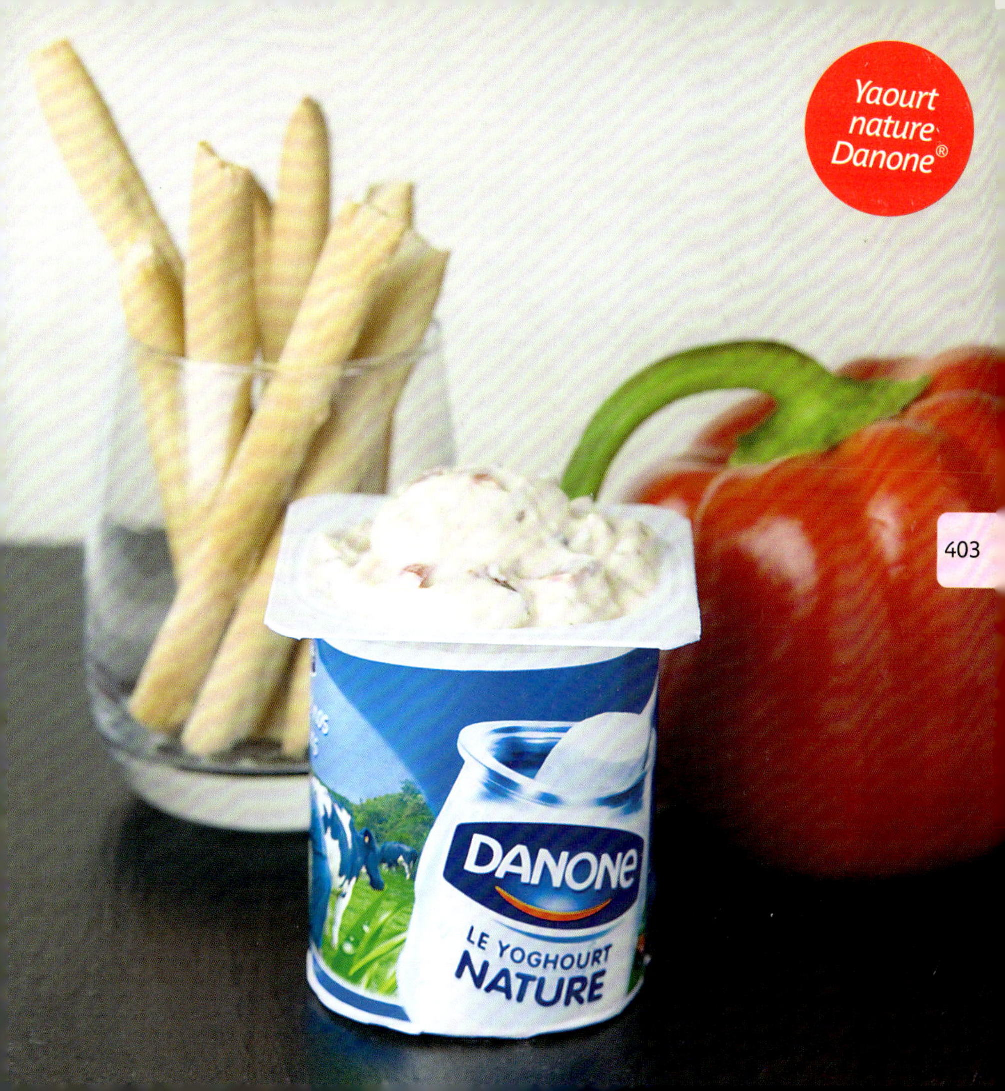

Salade composée estivale
Remplacez le céleri par 1 concombre, les pommes par des pêches, et la laitue iceberg par de la sucrine.

Salade composée aux choux
Remplacez le céleri par 1/2 tête de chou-fleur séparé en bouquets, et les pommes par 100 g de chou blanc et 100 g de chou rouge ciselé.

Sauce au yaourt asiatique
Pour la sauce, remplacez la ciboulette par 1/2 carotte râpée, la mayonnaise par 2 c. à s. de crème fraîche épaisse, et le jus de citron par de la sauce soja. Ajoutez 2 c. à s. de cacahuètes concassées.

Sauce au yaourt et à la moutarde
Remplacez la mayonnaise par 1 c. à s. de moutarde à l'ancienne. Ajoutez 1 échalote hachée à la préparation.

Yaourt nature Danone®

SALADE COMPOSÉE, SAUCE AU YAOURT

Préparation : 15 min • **Cuisson :** aucune • **Pour 6 personnes**

pour la salade : *3 branches de céleri • 1 pomme rouge*
1 pomme verte • 1 petite laitue iceberg • 100 g de cerneaux de noix
100 g d'emmental • 6 tranches de pain brioché
pour la sauce : *2 c. à s. de ciboulette finement hachée*
1 pot de yaourt nature Danone® • 2 c. à s. de mayonnaise
2 c. à s. de jus de citron • sel et poivre

- Pour la salade, rincez le céleri, puis taillez-le en morceaux de 1 cm de côté.
- Lavez les pommes, sans les peler, puis coupez-les en quatre, épépinez-les et supprimez la partie dure au centre, puis taillez-les en fines tranches.
- Lavez la salade, puis essorez-la. Coupez les feuilles en lanières.
- Concassez grossièrement les noix puis faites-les rapidement griller à sec dans une poêle. Taillez le fromage en dés.
- Mettez le céleri, les pommes, la laitue, les noix et le fromage dans un grand saladier, et mélangez bien.
- Pour la sauce, rincez la ciboulette, essuyez-la sur du papier absorbant, puis ciselez-la finement. Mettez-la dans un bol avec le yaourt nature Danone®, la mayonnaise et le jus de citron. Mélangez vivement de façon à obtenir une sauce homogène. Salez et poivrez. Versez la sauce sur la salade et remuez bien.
- Faites griller rapidement les tranches de pain brioché et servez avec la salade.

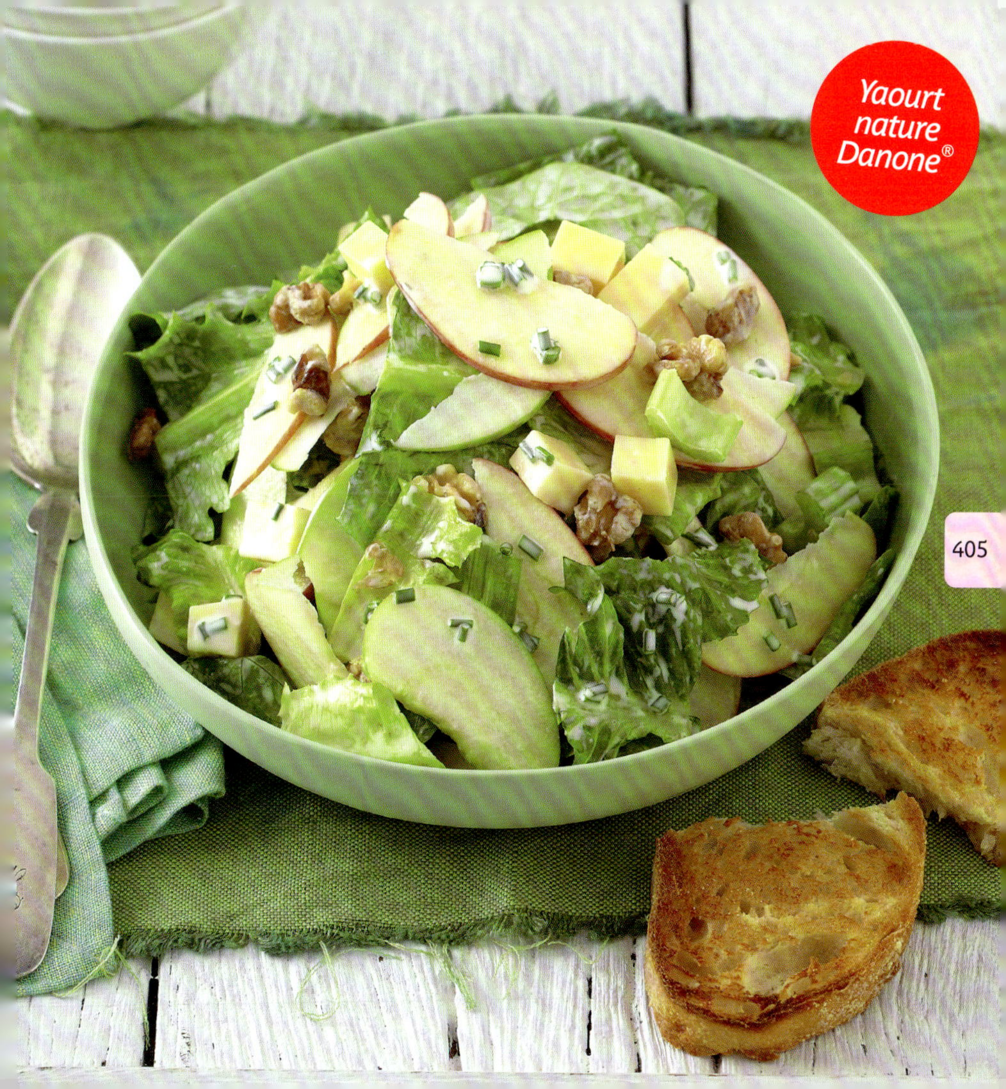
Yaourt
nature
Danone®

SMOOTHIE AU YAOURT ET AU FRUIT DE LA PASSION

Préparation : 5 min • **Cuisson :** aucune • **Pour 3 personnes**

1 yaourt nature Danone® • 40 cl de jus de fruit de la Passion + un peu
6 boules de glace vanille

- Mettez le yaourt Danone® et le jus de fruit de la Passion dans un blender et mixez.
- Répartissez les boules de glace dans 3 verres, puis ajoutez la préparation précédente en remplissant les verres jusqu'aux 3/4.
- Lorsque le cocktail commence à mousser, recouvrez d'un peu de jus de fruit de la Passion supplémentaire, et servez sans attendre.

Smoothie à la pêche et au yaourt
Remplacez le jus de fruit de la Passion par la chair de 3 ou 4 pêches.

Smoothie au rhum et au raisin
Remplacez le jus de fruit de la Passion par du jus de raisin, et la glace à la vanille par de la glace rhum-raisins.

Smoothie à la pomme et à la vodka
Remplacez le jus de fruit de la Passion par du jus de pomme, et la glace à la vanille par du sorbet à la pomme verte. Arrosez d'un peu de vodka très froide avant de servir.

Smoothie triple pomme
Reprenez la recette ci-dessus en remplaçant la vodka par de la liqueur de pomme glacée.

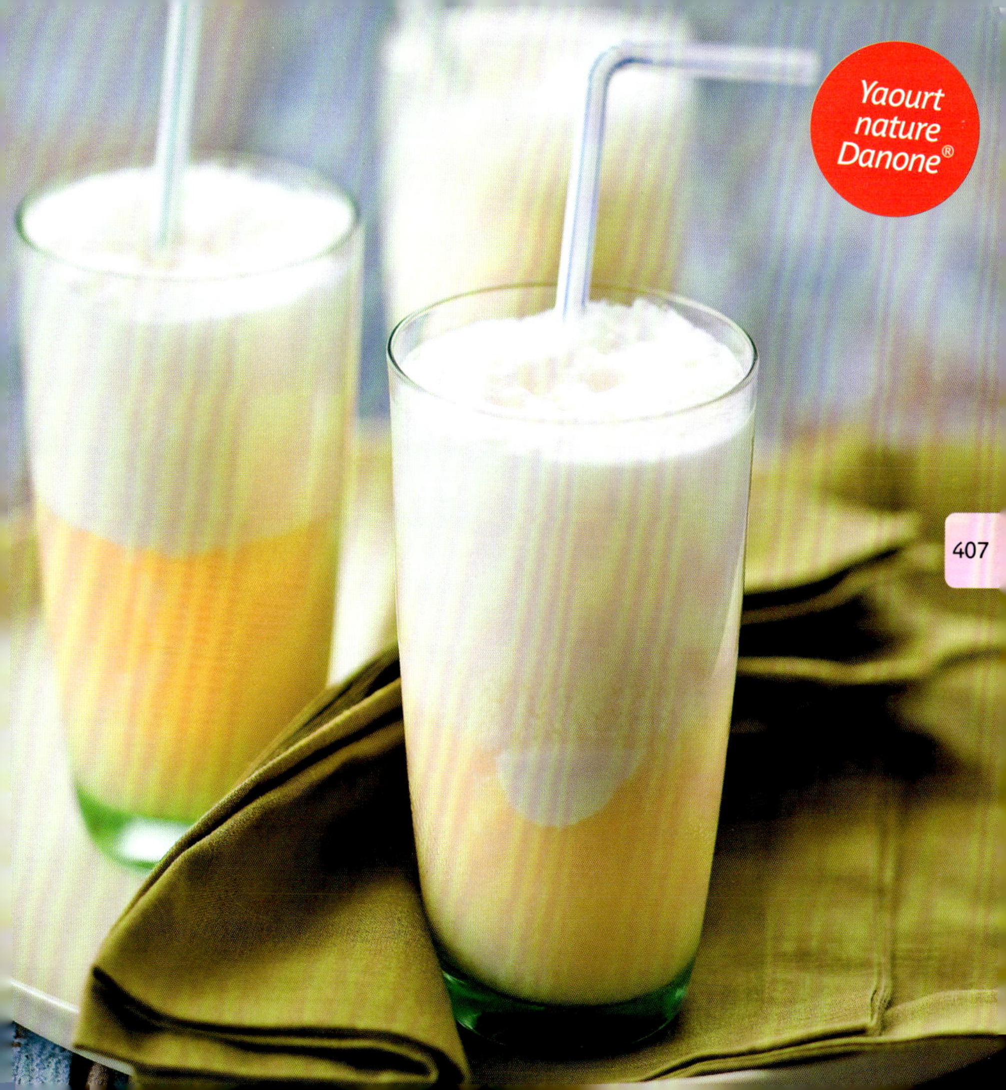
Yaourt
nature
Danone®

Yaourt nature Danone®

VERRINES EXOTIQUES AU YAOURT

Préparation : 10 min • **Cuisson :** aucune • **Pour 2 personnes**

1/2 papaye • 2 fruits de la Passion • 25 cl de crème fraîche épaisse
15 cl de crème anglaise • 2 yaourts nature Danone®
6 petites meringues écrasées

- Pelez la papaye, coupez-la en deux, épépinez-la, puis taillez-la en cubes. Réservez 2 c. à s. de chair.
- Prélevez la pulpe des fruits de la Passion et réservez-en 1 c. à s.
- Battez la crème au fouet électrique dans un grand saladier. Incorporez doucement la crème anglaise, le yaourt nature Danone® et la pulpe de fruit de la Passion.
- Ajoutez les meringues en mélangeant bien, jusqu'à ce que la préparation soit homogène.
- Versez la préparation dans des verrines et recouvrez avec les fruits réservés. Servez immédiatement.

Verrines exotiques au sirop d'érable

Ajoutez 2 c. à s. de sirop d'érable à la préparation une fois qu'elle est bien homogène. Ne remuez pas trop, de façon que le sirop d'érable forme des volutes dans le mélange.

Verrines des sous-bois

Remplacez la papaye par 200 g de mûres, et les fruits de la Passion par 200 g de fraises des bois.

Verrines exotiques au tapioca

Mélangez 65 g de tapioca, 12 cl de lait de coco, 25 cl d'eau et 60 g de sucre dans une casserole. Faites chauffer à feu moyen pendant 20 min. Répartissez au fond de 2 verrines avant d'ajouter le mélange au yaourt.

Verrines exotiques à la noix de coco

Ajoutez 4 c. à s. de noix de coco râpée à la préparation. Vous pouvez remplacer la crème fraîche par du lait de coco.

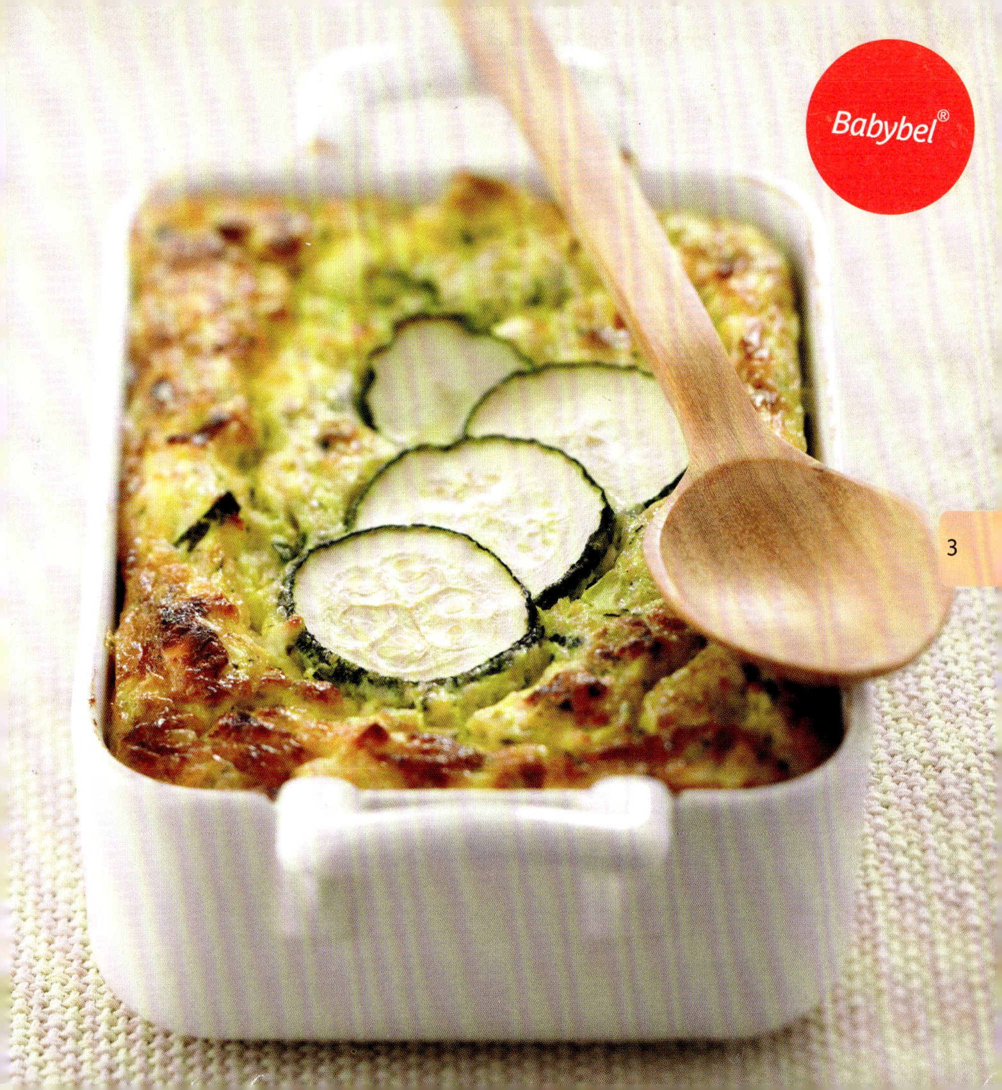
Babybel®

GRESSINS AU BABYBEL®

Préparation : 20 min • **Repos :** 1 h 40 • **Cuisson :** 15 min • **Pour 16 gressins**

2 Mini Babybel® • 250 g de farine • 1 sachet de levure de boulanger
2 c. à s. d'huile d'olive • 5 g de sel

- Retirez la coque des Mini Babybel® puis râpez-les grossièrement ou détaillez-les en tout petits morceaux.
- Dans un saladier, mettez la farine, la levure, le sel, le fromage et l'huile, puis pétrissez pendant 10 min, en incorporant 15 cl d'eau progressivement, jusqu'à l'obtention d'une pâte lisse qui ne colle pas aux mains.
- Formez une boule, mettez-la dans le saladier, couvrez d'un torchon et laissez lever pendant 1 h.
- Prélevez des parts de 20 g de pâte, enroulez-les en boudins très fins de 30 cm puis entortillez-les.
- Posez-les sur une plaque à pâtisserie et laissez lever pendant 40 min.
- Préchauffez le four à 230 °C, après avoir posé une coupelle d'eau sur la lèchefrite.
- Faites cuire au four pendant 7 min puis retournez les gressins et poursuivez la cuisson pendant 8 min, jusqu'à ce qu'ils soient dorés.

Gressins au Babybel® et au pavot

Ajoutez à la pâte 1 c. à s. de graines de pavot. Vous pouvez également utiliser des graines de sésame.

Gressins au Babybel® express

Remplacez la pâte à pain par 1 rouleau de pâte feuilletée. Parsemez de Babybel® râpé. Coupez la pâte en deux puis en lamelles de 3 cm. Entortillez-les puis faites-les cuire au four préchauffé à 220 °C de 8 à 10 min.

Croissants au Babybel®

Découpez 1 rouleau de pâte feuilletée en 16 triangles. Déposez 1/2 Mini Babybel® à la base de chacun puis enroulez chaque triangle de façon à former des croissants. Faites cuire au four préchauffé à 200 °C pendant 15 min.

Croissants au Babybel® et au jambon

Reprenez la recette ci-dessus en enroulant chaque 1/2 Mini Babybel® dans 1 lamelle de jambon blanc.

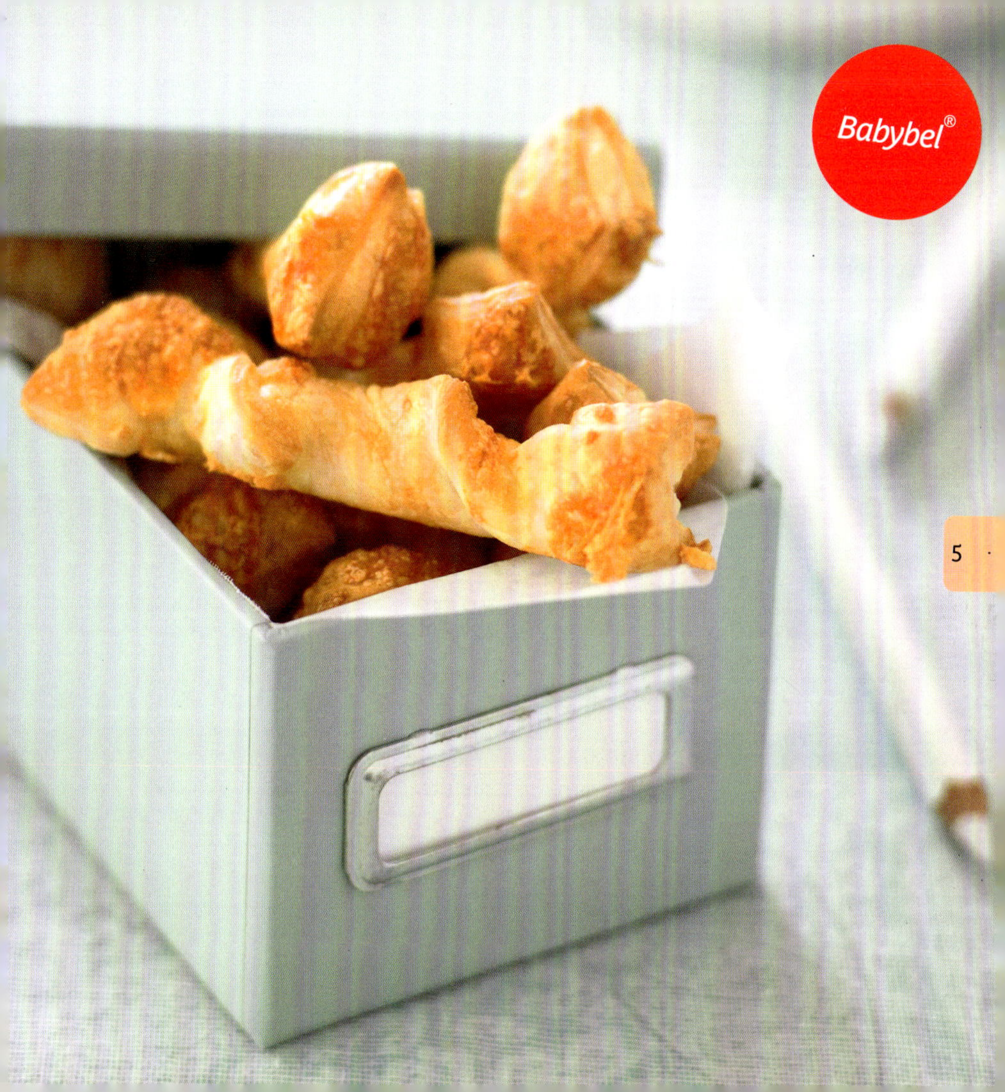

PAIN AUX LARDONS ET AU BABYBEL®

Préparation : 20 min • **Cuisson :** 45 min • **Pour 6 personnes**

250 g de lardons fumés • 480 g de farine + un peu pour le plan de travail
1 sachet de levure de boulanger • 1/4 de c. à c. de piment de Cayenne
40 g de beurre + un peu pour le moule • 125 g de maïs doux
4 Mini Babybel® • 12 cl de lait + un peu pour badigeonner le pain
1/2 c. à c. de sel

- Préchauffez le four à 200 °C.
- Hachez les lardons. Faites-les revenir à la poêle pendant 5 min, puis égouttez-les sur du papier absorbant.
- Versez la farine, la levure, le piment et le sel dans un grand saladier, puis ajoutez le beurre détaillé en parcelles et pétrissez.
- Incorporez la moitié des lardons et le maïs. Retirez les Mini Babybel® de leur coque puis coupez-les en petits morceaux. Ajoutez-en la moitié à la pâte. Faites un puits au centre. Incorporez le lait et 25 cl d'eau petit à petit, puis mélangez bien à la spatule de façon à obtenir une pâte lisse et légèrement collante.
- Placez la pâte sur le plan de travail fariné et pétrissez-la afin de bien mélanger les ingrédients.
- Divisez la pâte en 6 morceaux, et roulez chacun de manière à façonner de petites boules. Placez-les dans le moule préalablement beurré. Badigeonnez la surface d'un peu de lait. Parsemez du reste de lardons, de maïs et de fromage.
- Faites cuire au four de 35 à 40 min, jusqu'à ce que le pain soit doré. Laissez refroidir.

Pain fourré au Babybel®
Pour un goût plus fort en Babybel, glissez 1 Mini Babybel® au cœur de chaque boule de pâte juste avant de la placer dans le moule.

Pain au Babybel® à l'espagnole
Remplacez les lardons par 250 g de chorizo fort pelé et coupé en petits morceaux, et le maïs par des olives dénoyautées coupées en deux.

Pain sucré-salé au Babybel®
Remplacez les lardons par 6 tranches de jambon sec émincé, et le maïs par 100 g de figues fraîches coupées en quatre.

Pain aux légumes grillés et au Babybel®
Remplacez les lardons et le maïs par 100 g d'aubergines grillées, 100 g de courgettes grillées, 100 g de poivrons grillés et 50 g de tomates séchées.

Babybel®

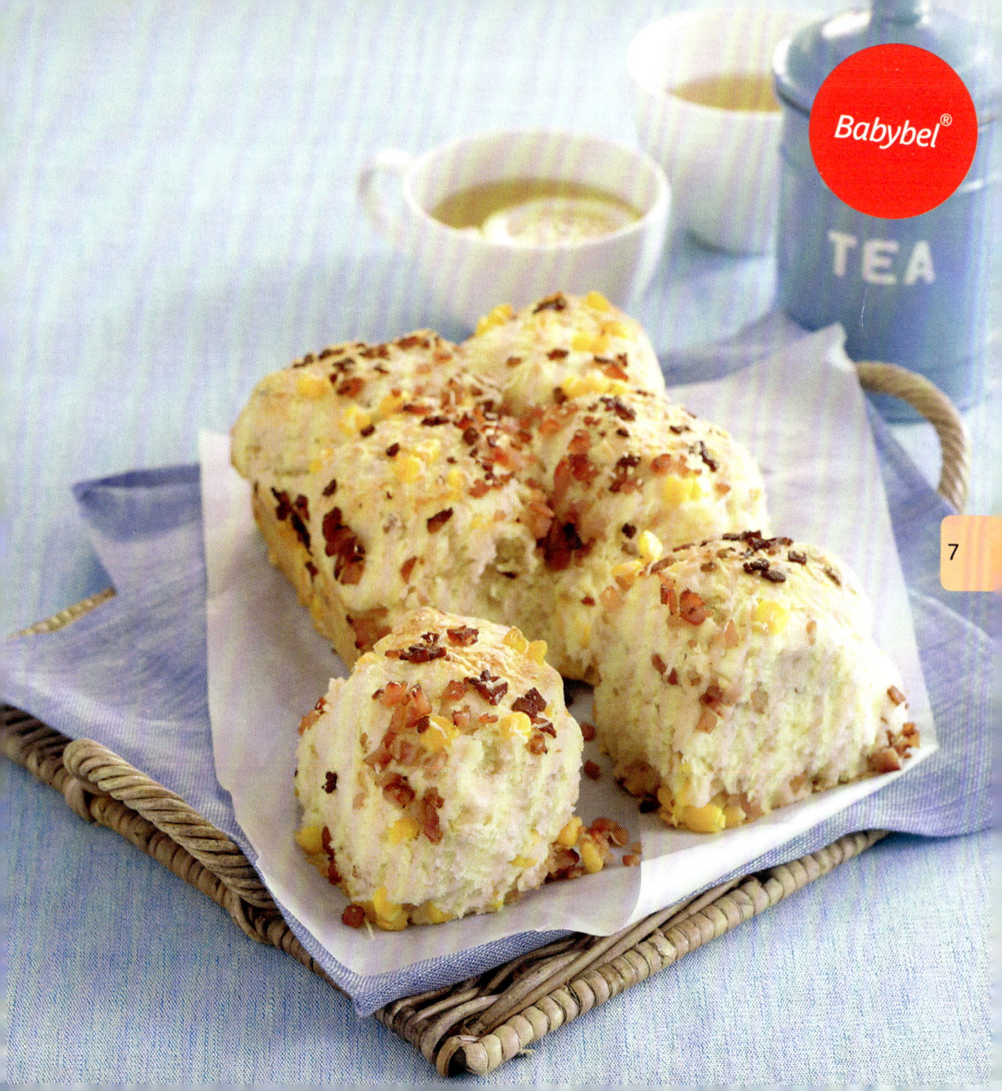

7

POMPONETTES AU BABYBEL® ET AUX TOMATES SÉCHÉES

Préparation : 20 min • **Cuisson :** 25 min • **Pour 4 personnes**

150 g de Babybel® • 8 tomates séchées à l'huile • 10 brins de ciboulette
2 œufs • 2 c. à s. de crème fraîche • 2 c. à s. d'huile d'olive
1 c. à c. rase de curry • 150 g de farine • 1/2 paquet de levure chimique
sel et poivre

- Préchauffez le four à 180 °C.
- Découpez les Babybel® et les tomates séchées en petits morceaux. Rincez la ciboulette, essuyez-la sur du papier absorbant puis ciselez-la finement.
- Mettez ces ingrédients dans un saladier, puis ajoutez les œufs, la crème fraîche, l'huile, le curry, du sel et du poivre. Mélangez.
- Ajoutez la farine et la levure. Mélangez rapidement le tout.
- Remplissez aux 3/4 les alvéoles d'un moule à muffins de cette préparation.
- Faites cuire au four pendant 25 min.

Pomponettes au Babybel®, aux tomates et aux câpres
Remplacez 4 tomates séchées par 2 c. à s. de câpres égouttées.

Pomponettes au Babybel® et aux herbes
Remplacez les tomates séchées par 1/2 bouquet de basilic et 1/2 bouquet de coriandre ciselés.

Pomponettes au pesto et au Babybel®
Mixez les feuilles de 1/2 bouquet de basilic avec 25 g de pignons de pin, 50 g de parmesan et 1/2 c. à c. de gros sel. Robot toujours en marche, incorporez 7 cl d'huile d'olive. Remplacez les tomates séchées par cette sauce.

Pomponettes à la tapenade verte et au Babybel®
Mixez 50 g d'olives vertes, 20 g de filets d'anchois et 30 g de câpres. Robot toujours en marche, incorporez 7 cl d'huile d'olive. Remplacez les tomates séchées par cette sauce.

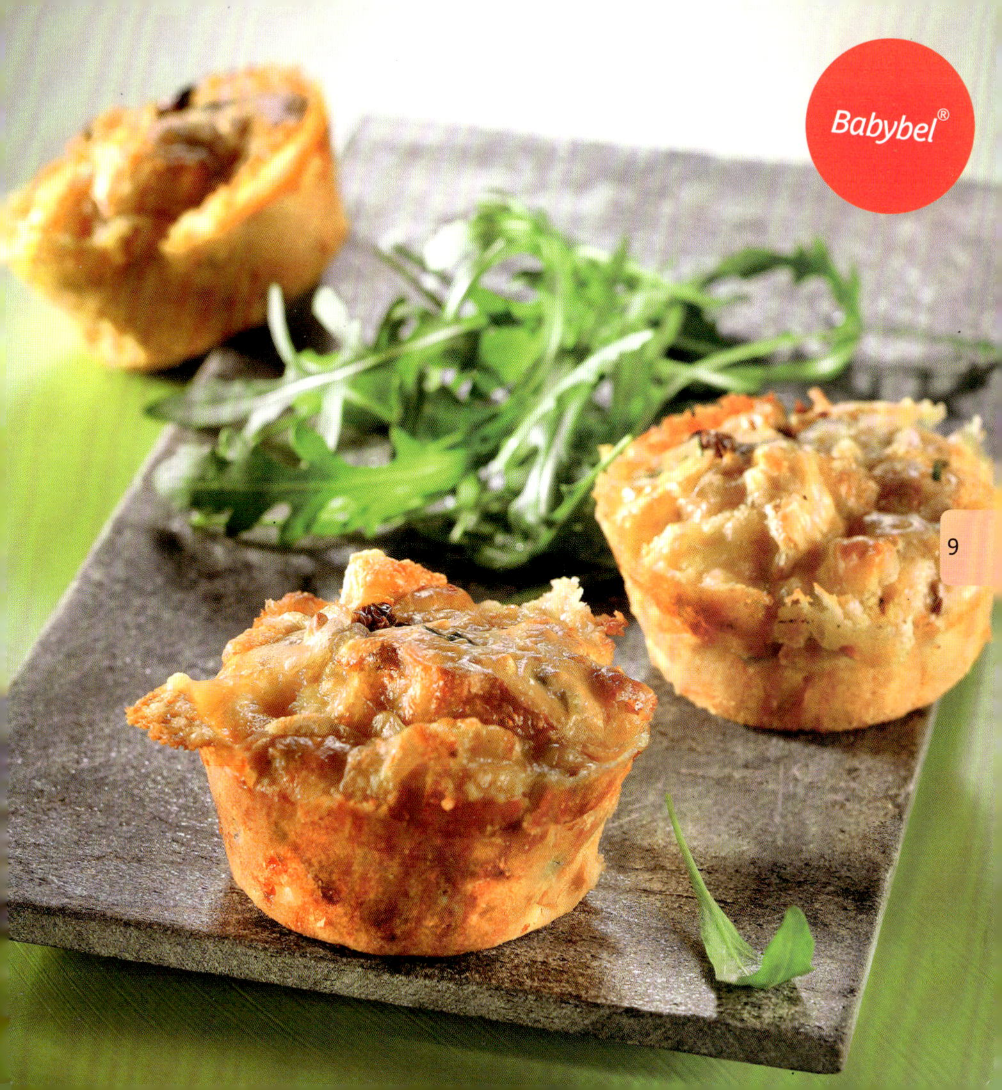
Babybel®

TORTILLA AUX LÉGUMES VERTS ET AU BABYBEL®

Préparation : 15 min • **Cuisson** : 38 min • **Pour 1 tortilla**

3 pommes de terre • 2 courgettes • 2 poivrons verts • 1 gros oignon
3 c. à s. d'huile d'olive • 6 œufs • 1 pincée de noix muscade râpée
1 pincée de piment d'Espelette • 1 c. à s. de lait
4 Mini Babybel® • sel et poivre

- Pelez les pommes de terre et les courgettes, puis coupez-les en cubes. Rincez les poivrons et coupez-les en dés.
- Épluchez l'oignon et émincez-le. Faites-le revenir dans une sauteuse avec 1 c. à s. d'huile d'olive, puis ajoutez les pommes de terre. Faites-les cuire à feu moyen pendant 20 min environ, en remuant régulièrement.
- Pendant ce temps, faites revenir les poivrons dans une poêle à feu moyen, avec 1 c. à s. d'huile d'olive, pendant 15 min. À mi-cuisson, ajoutez les courgettes. Remuez régulièrement.
- Cassez les œufs et mettez-les dans un saladier. Salez, poivrez, ajoutez la noix muscade et le piment d'Espelette. Battez au fouet. Ajoutez le lait, les pommes de terre et les légumes verts. Retirez la coque des Mini Babybel® et coupez-les en petits morceaux. Ajoutez-les dans le saladier.
- Faites chauffer le reste d'huile dans une poêle, puis versez-y le contenu du saladier.
- Faites cuire pendant 10 min environ sur feu doux à moyen. Retournez la tortilla et poursuivez la cuisson de 6 à 8 min. Laissez tiédir légèrement avant de déguster la tortilla, coupée en cubes.

Tortilla aux légumes rouges et au Babybel®
Remplacez les poivrons verts par des poivrons rouges, et les courgettes par 5 tomates débarrassées de leur pulpe.

Tortilla printanière au Babybel®
Remplacez les courgettes par 200 g de petits pois, et les poivrons par 2 carottes.

Tortilla au poulet et au Babybel®
Remplacez les courgettes par 250 g de filets de poulet détaillés en dés. Faites-les revenir à part à la poêle avec un peu d'huile d'olive.

Tortilla pimentée au Babybel®
Remplacez la noix muscade par 1/2 piment oiseau très finement haché. À défaut, utilisez 1 pincée de piment de Cayenne.

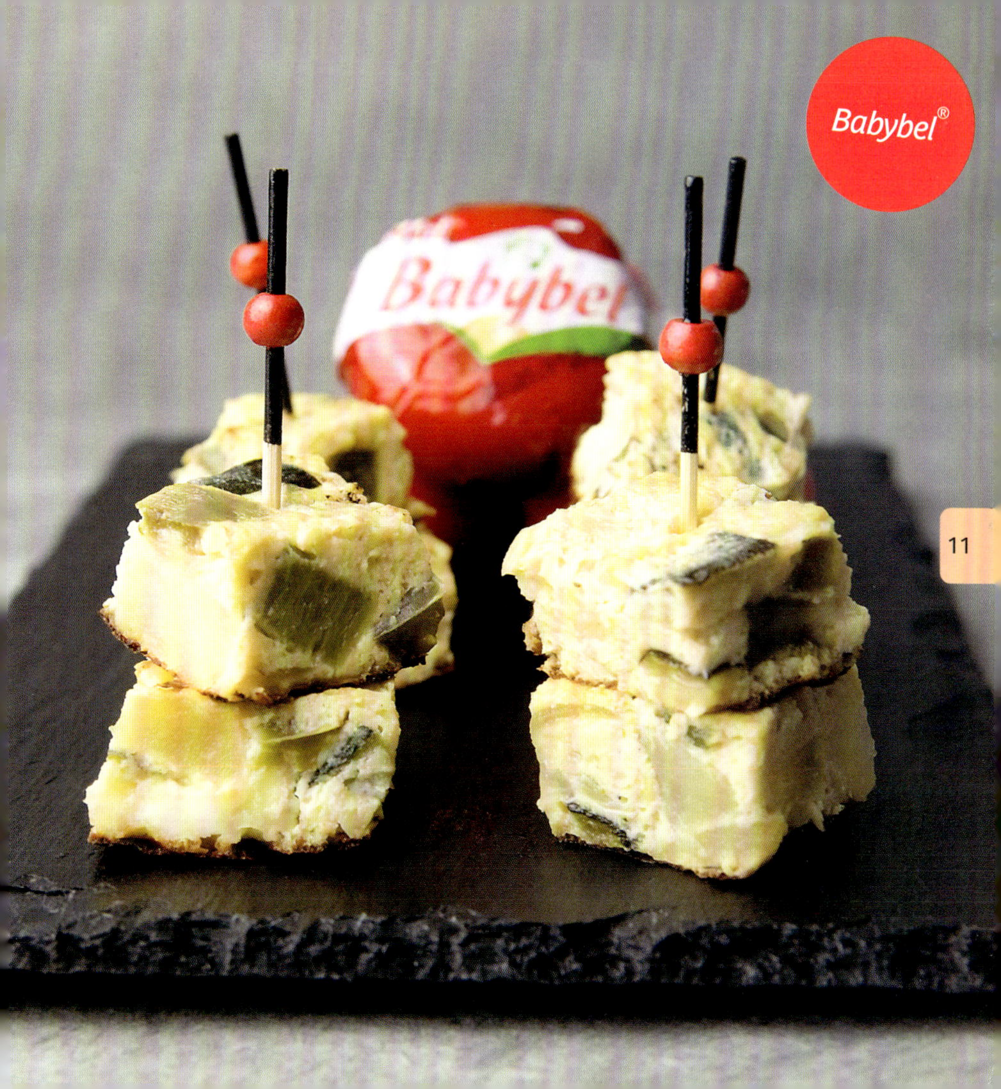

Babybel®

COCKTAIL B-52

Préparation : 2 min • **Cuisson :** aucune • **Pour 2 verres**

6 cl de liqueur de café • 6 cl de Baileys® • 6 cl de triple sec

- Répartissez la liqueur de café au fond de 2 verres à shot.
- Ajoutez très délicatement le Baileys® par-dessus, en le faisant couler le long du dos d'une cuillère à cocktail.
- Déposez de la même manière le triple sec sur le Baileys®.
- Faites flamber pendant 1 min.
- Plantez 1 paille dans chaque verre et buvez d'un trait.

Cocktail B-51
Remplacez le triple sec par du rhum blanc.

Cocktail B-55
Remplacez le triple sec par de l'absinthe.

Gelée de B-52
Faites bouillir 15 cl d'eau et ajoutez 3 g de gélatine en poudre. Hors du feu, répartissez le mélange dans 3 gobelets. Répartissez 5 cl de chaque ingrédient du B-52 dans chaque gobelet. Versez le mélange à la liqueur de café dans un moule à fond plat. Laissez refroidir pendant 1 min puis déposez le mélange au Baileys® par-dessus, laissez refroidir puis ajoutez le mélange de triple sec. Laissez durcir pendant 2 h. Découpez en morceaux et servez.

Cocktail Bazooka
Superposez délicatement dans un verre à shot 1 cl de curaçao, 3 cl de Baileys® et 2 cl de vodka. Buvez d'un trait.

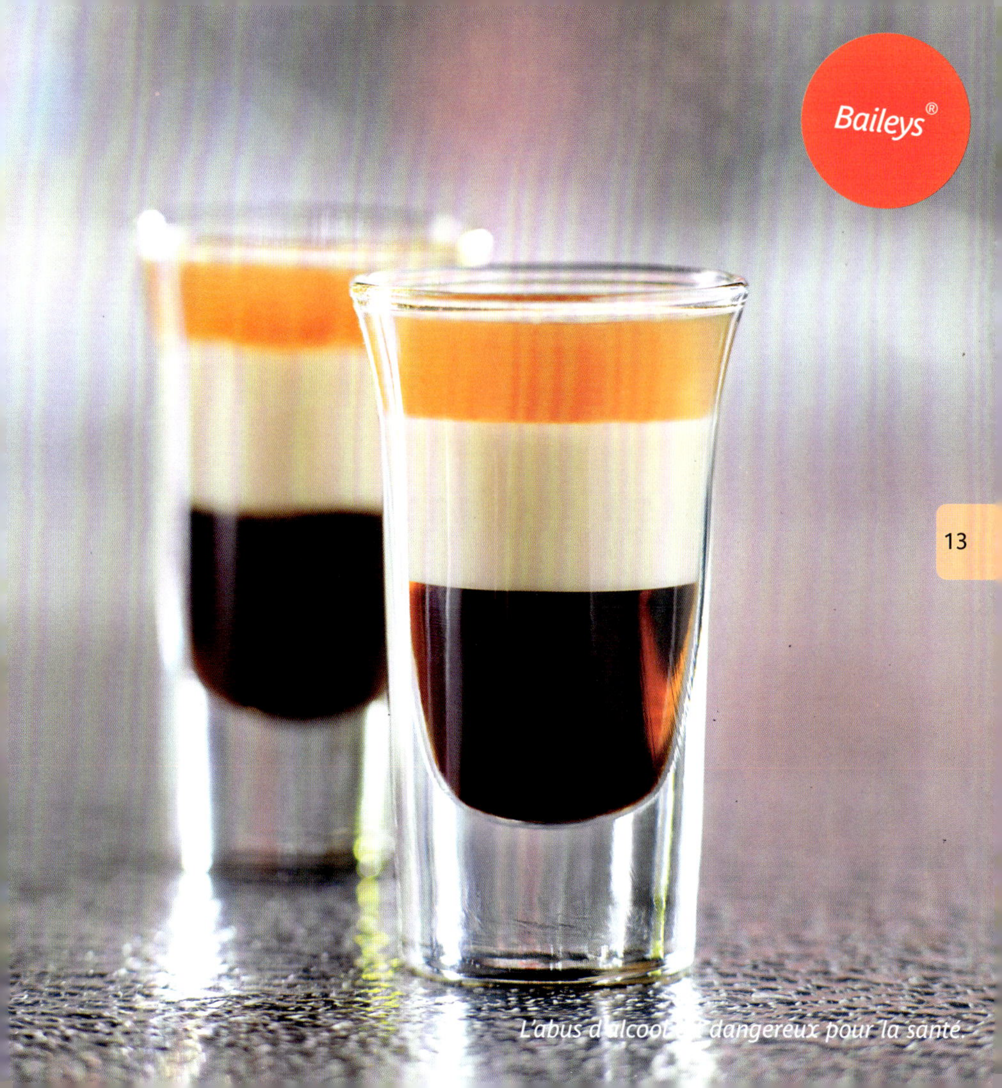
Baileys®
L'abus d'alcool est dangereux pour la santé.

Crème au chocolat noir et au Baileys®
Remplacez le chocolat blanc par du chocolat noir.

Crème au chocolat blanc sur lit de Baileys®
Versez 1 c. à c. de Baileys® au fond de 6 verrines puis déposez la mousse par-dessus. Laissez ensuite prendre au frais.

Crème au chocolat noir et coulis de Baileys®
Supprimez le Baileys® de la recette. Faites fondre 70 g de chocolat noir avec 10 cl de crème liquide et 10 cl de Baileys®. Laissez refroidir. Nappez les mousses de ce coulis juste avant de servir.

Crème au Baileys® au mascarpone
Fouettez 2 jaunes d'œufs avec 60 g de sucre, puis ajoutez 250 g de mascarpone. Mélangez 10 cl de Baileys® frémissant avec 2 feuilles de gélatine ramollies. Ajoutez au mélange précédent, puis incorporez 2 blancs d'œufs montés en neige. Répartissez dans des ramequins et laissez prendre au frais de 2 à 3 h.

CRÈME AU CHOCOLAT BLANC ET AU BAILEYS®

Préparation : 15 min • **Repos :** 2 à 3 h • **Cuisson :** 5 min • **Pour 6 personnes**

250 g de chocolat blanc • 40 g de beurre doux • 6 œufs
50 g de sucre en poudre • 5 cl de Baileys® • sel

- Cassez le chocolat en morceaux. Détaillez le beurre en parcelles.
- Faites-les fondre au bain-marie en remuant régulièrement.
- Séparez les blancs des jaunes d'œufs. Montez les blancs en neige ferme avec 1 pincée de sel.
- Hors du feu, ajoutez le sucre au chocolat fondu. Incorporez ensuite les jaunes d'œufs et mélangez à la spatule. Versez le Baileys®. Remuez de nouveau.
- Incorporez délicatement les blancs en neige à la base de chocolat à l'aide de la spatule.
- Répartissez le mélange dans des ramequins individuels. Laissez prendre au réfrigérateur de 2 à 3 h.

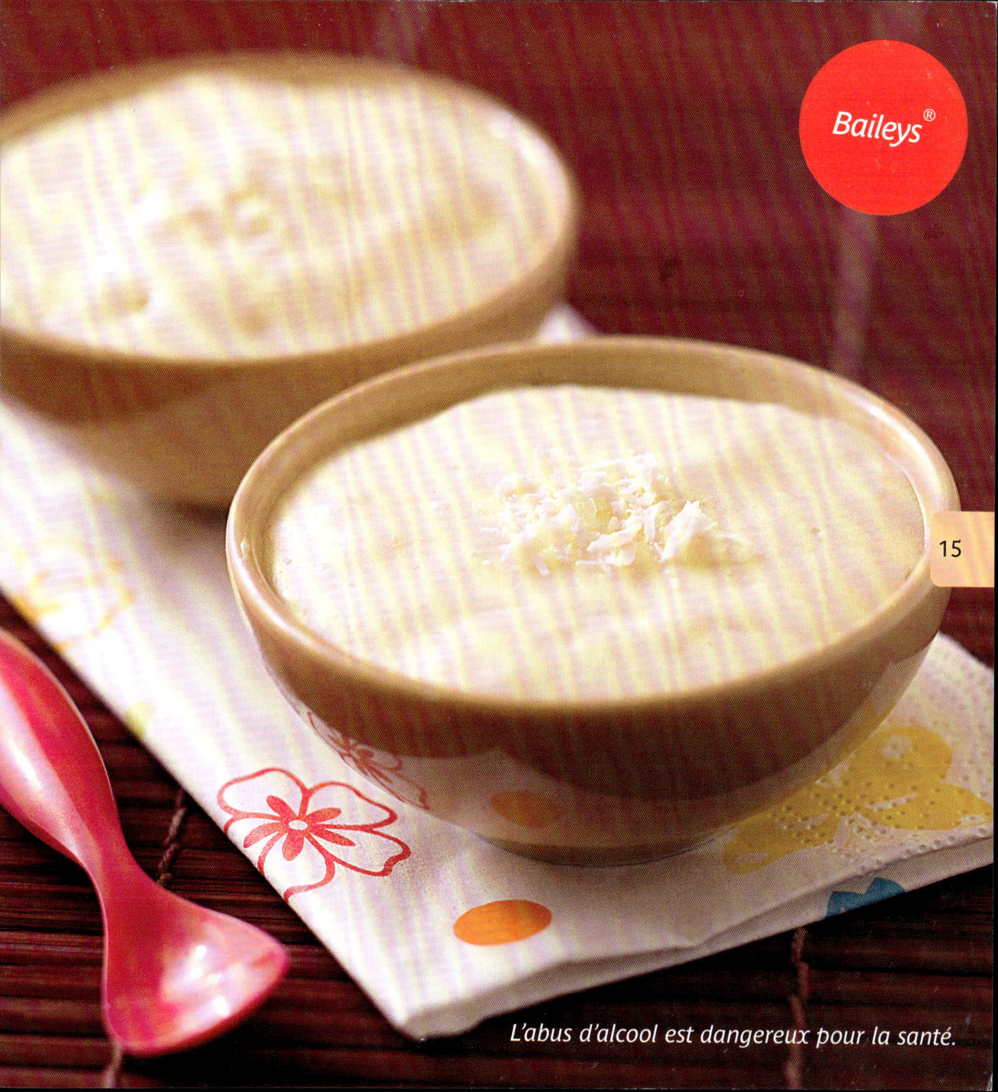

Baileys®

L'abus d'alcool est dangereux pour la santé.

FRUITS ROUGES AU SABAYON AU BAILEYS®

Préparation : 15 min • **Cuisson** : 10 min • **Pour 4 personnes**

pour les fruits : 100 g de framboises • 100 g de fraises • 100 g de mûres 100 g de groseilles

pour le sabayon : 4 jaunes d'œufs • 80 g de sucre en poudre 20 cl de Baileys®

- Rincez les fruits. Équeutez les fraises et coupez-les en deux ou en quatre si elles sont grosses.
- Répartissez-les dans 4 verrines ou ramequins, et réservez au frais.
- Mettez les ingrédients pour le sabayon dans une jatte.
- Faites chauffer au bain-marie dans une casserole remplie d'eau, à feu très doux. L'eau ne doit pas bouillir.
- Fouettez la préparation sans cesse, jusqu'à ce que le sabayon épaississe et soit légèrement mousseux.
- Retirez la jatte du feu dès que des bulles se forment sur les bords et continuez à fouetter pendant 1 min.
- Laissez tiédir légèrement, puis répartissez le sabayon sur les fruits rouges.
- Servez sans attendre.

Fruits rouges au sabayon au Baileys® gratinés
Parsemez les fruits recouverts de sabayon de sucre roux en poudre, puis passez les ramequins sous le gril du four pendant 5 min.

Fruits rouges à la sauce au Baileys®
Mélangez 100 g de sucre roux, 100 g de beurre, 20 cl de crème liquide entière et 7 cl de Baileys®. Portez à ébullition et laissez frémir en fouettant sans cesse. Remplacez le sabayon par cette sauce avec les fruits.

Fruits rouges au sabayon glacé au Baileys®
Ajoutez 60 cl de lait à la préparation pour le sabayon. Mélangez bien, puis faites turbiner en sorbetière. Servez avec les fruits.

Fruits jaunes au sabayon au Baileys®
Remplacez les fruits rouges par 1 pêche, 1 nectarine, 3 abricots pelés, dénoyautés et taillés en dés, et 1 orange pelée et séparée en quartiers.

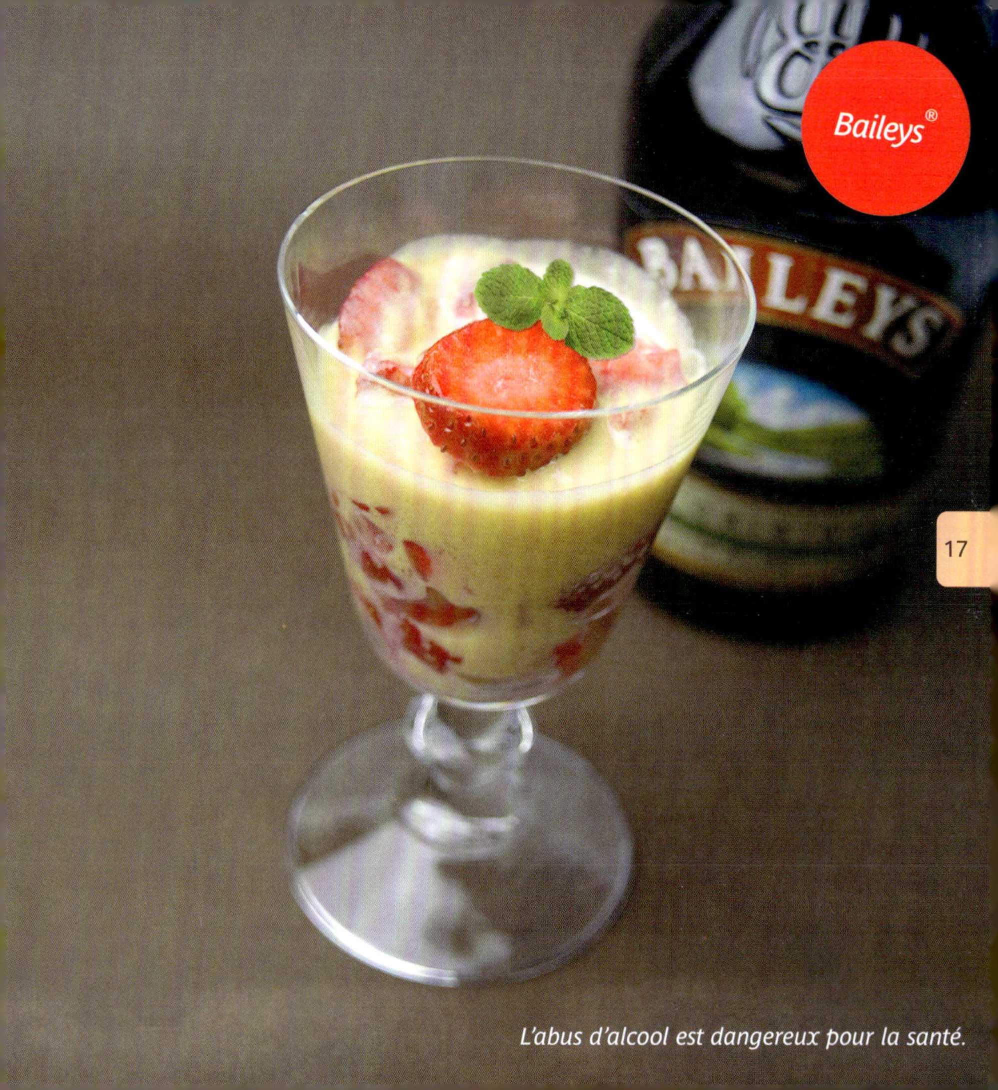

L'abus d'alcool est dangereux pour la santé.

LECHE MERENGADA AU BAILEYS®

Préparation : 15 min • **Cuisson :** 40 min • **Turbine :** 25 min • **Pour 6 personnes**

pour la crème : *75 cl de lait • 25 cl de crème fraîche • 160 g de sucre en poudre blanc + 2 c. à s. • 7 cl de Baileys® • 4 blancs d'œufs 1/4 de c. à s. de jus de citron*

pour les amandes caramélisées : *160 g d'amandes entières 110 g de sucre blanc • 1/4 de c. à s. de cannelle en poudre*

- Pour la crème, mettez le lait, la crème fraîche, 160 g de sucre et le Baileys® dans une casserole. Portez à ébullition, puis baissez le feu et laissez frémir pendant 5 min. Laissez refroidir complètement.
- Battez les blancs d'œufs en neige avec le jus de citron. Ajoutez les 2 c. à s. de sucre restantes et battez de nouveau. Incorporez-les à la préparation.
- Versez le mélange dans la cuve de la sorbetière, puis laissez turbiner.
- Pour les amandes caramélisées, mélangez tous les ingrédients dans une poêle et faites griller à feu vif de 5 à 10 min, ou jusqu'à l'obtention d'un caramel foncé.
- Étalez la préparation sur une plaque à pâtisserie recouverte de papier sulfurisé. Laissez refroidir, puis cassez grossièrement en petits morceaux et réservez.
- Versez la leche merengada dans des verres, et parsemez d'amandes caramélisées avant de servir.

Baileys® coffee à la leche merengada

Versez du café chaud dans une tasse, ajoutez 1 morceau de sucre, 1 c. à s. de Baileys® et 1 boule de leche merengada.

Milk-shake à la leche merengada

Mixez 1 l de lait avec 10 c. à s. de leche merengada au Baileys®. Ajoutez 3 gouttes d'extrait de vanille liquide et répartissez dans 4 verres. Parsemez d'amandes caramélisées.

Sandwich glacé à la leche merengada

Accolez 2 shortbreads en déposant 1 boule de leche merengada au Baileys® entre eux.

Leche merengada en coupe de chocolat

Faites fondre 200 g de chocolat noir. Formez des disques sur une plaque recouverte de papier sulfurisé, par rangées de 4. Quand le chocolat commence à se figer, découpez des bandes de papier et posez-les sur une bouteille. Laissez durcir. Déposez 1 boule de leche merengada au Baileys® sur chaque tuile.

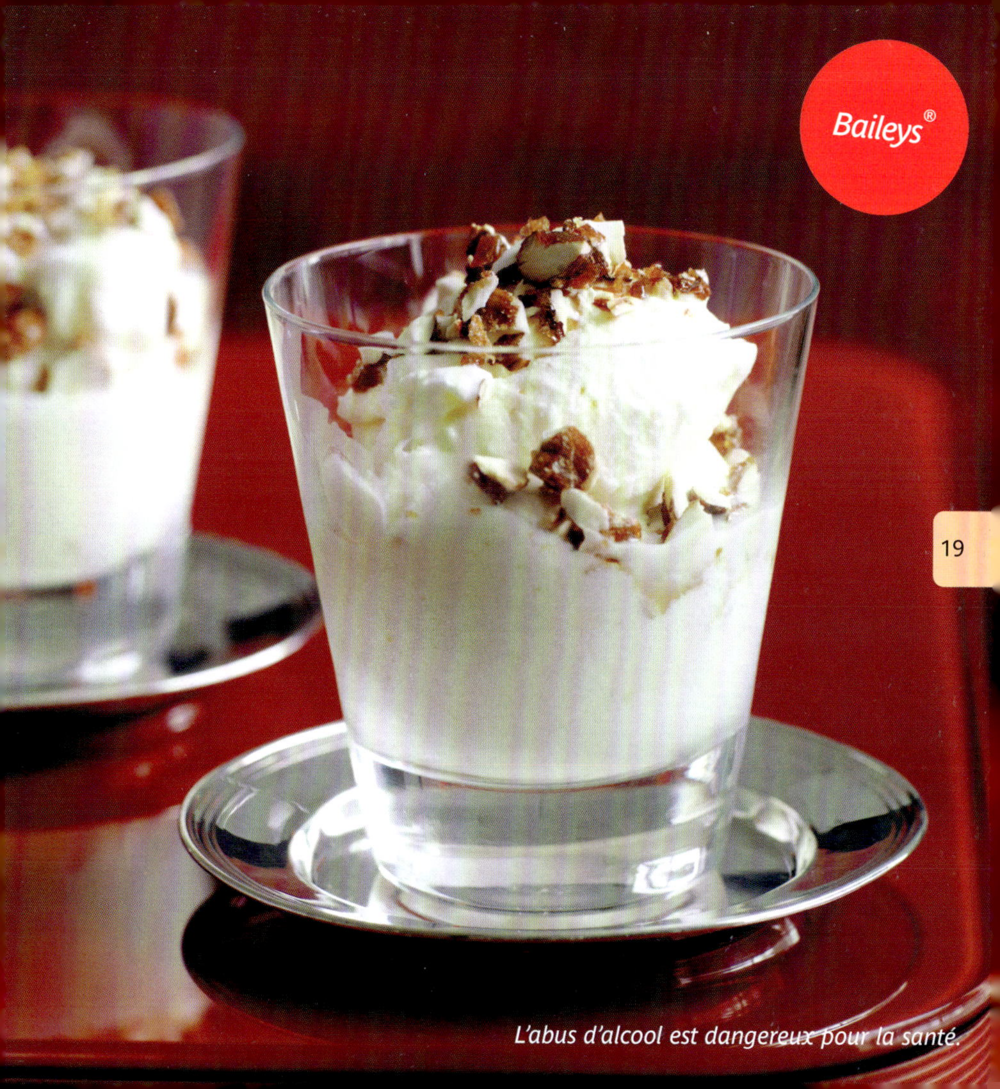

Banania®

GÂTEAU ROULÉ AU CHOCOLAT ET À LA VANILLE

Préparation : 25 min • **Cuisson :** 35 min • **Pour 8 personnes**

pour le gâteau : *60 g de beurre • 4 œufs • 75 g de sucre en poudre 75 g de farine • 75 g de chocolat en poudre Banania® • sucre glace*
pour la crème à la vanille : *50 cl de lait • 1 gousse de vanille 4 jaunes d'œufs • 50 g de sucre glace • 30 g de farine • sel*

- Pour la génoise, préchauffez le four à 180 °C. Coupez le beurre en parcelles, puis faites-le fondre. Laissez-le refroidir. Séparez les blancs des jaunes d'œufs. Battez les jaunes au fouet avec 2 c. à s. de sucre. Battez les blancs en neige avec le reste de sucre. Ajoutez la farine, le chocolat en poudre et le beurre aux jaunes d'œufs et mélangez. Incorporez délicatement les blancs en neige. Étalez la pâte sur une plaque à pâtisserie recouverte de papier sulfurisé. Faites cuire au four pendant 30 min.

- Préparez la crème à la vanille. Portez le lait à ébullition dans une casserole. Ajoutez la gousse de vanille fendue en deux et grattée ainsi que 1 pincée de sel. Retirez du feu et filtrez. Dans un saladier, mélangez les jaunes d'œufs avec le sucre glace jusqu'à ce que le mélange blanchisse. Incorporez-y petit à petit la farine, puis le lait bouillant. Reversez ce mélange dans une casserole. Faites chauffer à feu doux en remuant avec une cuillère en bois jusqu'à ce que la crème épaississe. Laissez bouillir pendant quelques instants en continuant de tourner. Versez la préparation dans un saladier et laissez refroidir, recouvert de film alimentaire.

- Sortez la génoise du four, retournez-la sur une grille et ôtez le papier. Roulez-la sur elle-même et laissez-la refroidir. Déroulez-la, nappez-la de crème, roulez-la de nouveau et disposez-la sur un plat, jointure vers le bas. Parsemez de sucre glace et servez.

Gâteau roulé léger

Pour le gâteau, remplacez le sucre par 3 c. à s. d'édulcorant liquide, la farine par de la fécule de pomme de terre et le beurre par de la margarine allégée.

Gâteau roulé au chocolat et au café

Ajoutez 1 à 2 c. à c. d'extrait de café liquide à la préparation.

Gâteau roulé tout chocolat

Battez au fouet 3 jaunes d'œufs avec 70 g de sucre jusqu'à ce que le mélange blanchisse. Ajoutez 40 g de farine et 3 c. à s. de chocolat en poudre Banania®. Délayez avec 50 cl de lait bouillant. Versez dans une casserole et faites chauffer en battant sans cesse jusqu'à épaississement. Laissez refroidir. Remplacez la crème à la vanille par cette préparation.

Glaçage au Banania®

Mélangez 60 g de sucre glace, 1 c. à s. de chocolat en poudre Banania®, 1/2 sachet de sucre vanillé et 25 g de beurre fondu refroidi. Nappez le gâteau roulé refroidi de ce glaçage.

Banania®

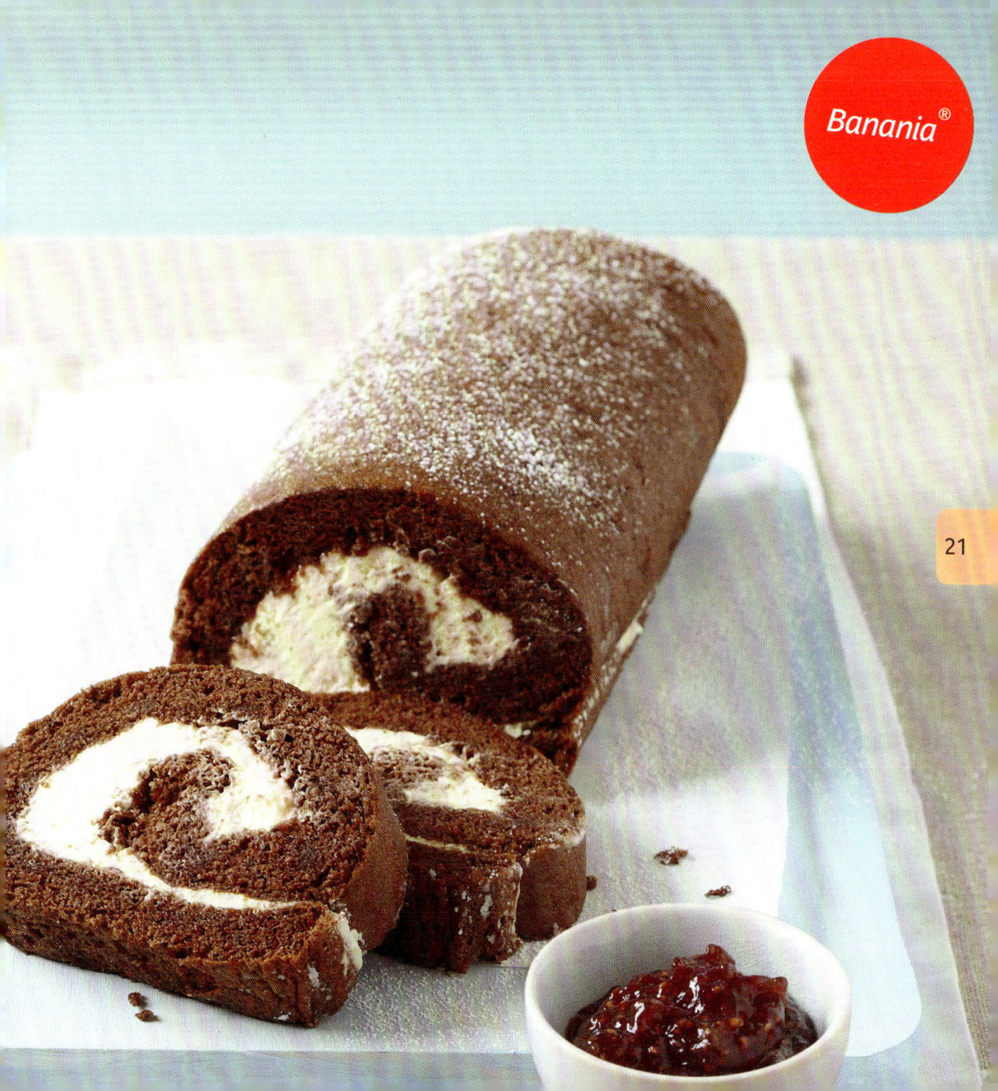

PARFAIT AU CHOCOLAT ET SALADE D'ORANGES

Préparation : 30 min • **Repos** : 12 h • **Cuisson** : 5 min • **Pour 6 personnes**

pour le parfait : 150 g de sucre en poudre • 4 jaunes d'œufs
1 yaourt brassé nature • 45 cl de crème fraîche épaisse
70 g de chocolat en poudre Banania® + un peu pour décorer
1 c. à s. de cognac • 40 g d'amandes effilées et toastées
pour la salade d'oranges : 3 oranges de taille moyenne • 1 c. à s. de miel
1 ou 2 c. à s. de cacao en poudre Banania®

- Pour le parfait, mettez le sucre et 15 cl d'eau dans une petite casserole. Faites chauffer à feu moyen, sans laisser bouillir, jusqu'à ce que le sucre soit dissous. Portez ensuite à ébullition et laissez frémir, sans couvrir, pendant 3 minutes. Retirez du feu.

- Battez les jaunes d'œufs avec le yaourt au fouet électrique jusqu'à ce qu'ils blanchissent. Incorporez petit à petit le sirop en remuant sans cesse jusqu'à ce que le mélange refroidisse. Fouettez la crème fraîche. Incorporez-la au mélange avec le chocolat en poudre Banania®, le cognac et les amandes.

- Versez la préparation dans un moule à terrine tapissé de papier sulfurisé et couvrez-le de film alimentaire. Réservez au réfrigérateur pour toute une nuit.

- Pour la salade, pelez les oranges et découpez chaque quartier en deux, déposez les morceaux dans un bol sans en perdre le jus. Versez le miel en filet sur les quartiers.

- Au moment de servir, retournez le parfait sur un grand plat et coupez-le en 6 tranches. Répartissez-les dans des assiettes. Accompagnez de salade d'oranges et saupoudrez le tout de chocolat en poudre Banania®.

Salade d'oranges au chocolat Banania®

Mélangez 75 g de chocolat en poudre Banania® avec 25 g de beurre fondu et refroidi, et 2 c. à s. de café fort refroidi. Passez les oranges dans ce mélange juste avant de servir.

Cocktail au chocolat Banania® et à l'orange

Mélangez 1 l de lait très chaud avec 3 c. à s. de chocolat en poudre Banania®. Versez le mélange dans un shaker avec 2 c. à s. de miel, le zeste râpé de 1 orange et 1 c. à c. de cannelle en poudre. Réservez au congélateur pendant 15 min, puis secouez énergiquement. Répartissez dans 6 verres à cocktail. Servez avec le parfait.

Cocktail au chocolat Banania® et au rhum

Reprenez la recette ci-dessus et ajoutez 10 cl de rhum dans le shaker. Servez avec le parfait.

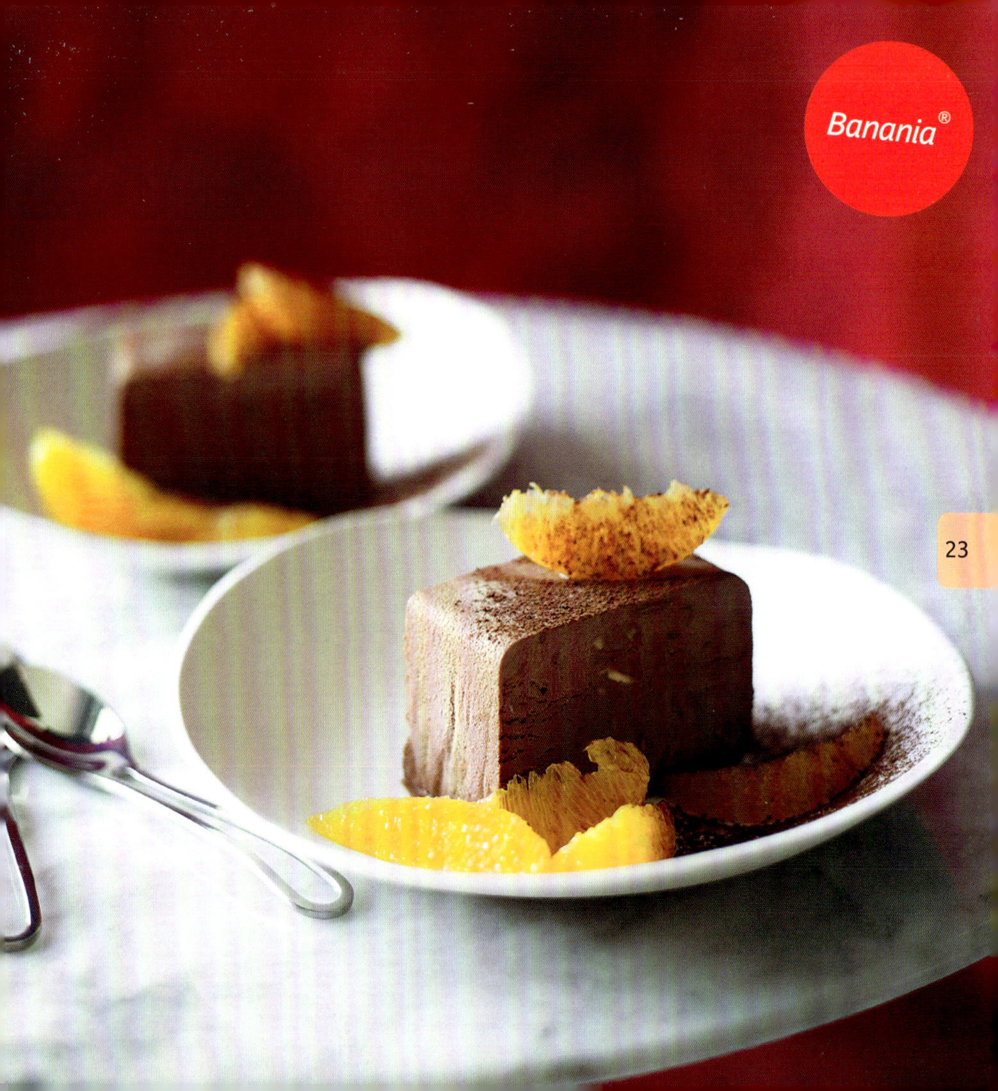
Banania®

Banania®

PROFITEROLES AU CHOCOLAT

Préparation : 25 min • **Cuisson** : 40 min • **Pour 16 profiteroles**

***pour les choux** : 75 g de beurre • 240 g de farine • 1 c. à s. de chocolat en poudre Banania® • 4 œufs • sucre glace • sel*
***pour la garniture** : crème glacée à la vanille*
***pour la sauce au chocolat** : 150 g de chocolat en poudre Banania® 15 cl de crème liquide*

- Préchauffez le four à 200 °C. Pour les choux, détaillez le beurre en parcelles. Mettez-le dans une casserole avec 25 cl d'eau, à feu moyen, et portez doucement à ébullition. Mélangez la farine, le chocolat en poudre Banania® et 1 pincée de sel dans une jatte, puis ajoutez-les dans la casserole. Remuez à l'aide d'une cuillère en bois pendant 1 min jusqu'à ce que la préparation se décolle des bords. Versez dans un saladier et laissez refroidir pendant 5 min. Incorporez les œufs un à un, en battant au fouet entre chaque ajout, jusqu'à l'obtention d'une pâte bien lisse et brillante. Versez le mélange dans une poche munie d'une douille. Formez de petits tas de pâte sur 2 plaques de cuisson recouvertes de papier sulfurisé, en les espaçant de 3 cm. Aplatissez légèrement chaque chou.

- Faites cuire pendant 10 min, puis baissez la température du four à 180 °C et poursuivez la cuisson de 20 à 25 min, jusqu'à ce que les choux soient fermes au toucher. Pratiquez une petite incision sur le côté de chaque chou, puis laissez-les refroidir dans le four éteint. Coupez les choux en deux. Garnissez chacun de 1 à 2 c. à s. de crème glacée à la vanille.

- Pour la sauce, mettez le chocolat en poudre Banania® dans une casserole avec la crème liquide et faites fondre en remuant à la spatule. Faites couler la sauce sur les choux. Saupoudrez-les de sucre glace et servez.

Profiteroles à la menthe

Remplacez la crème glacée à la vanille par de la glace à la menthe et aux pépites de chocolat.

Profiteroles à la glace au chocolat

Remplacez la crème glacée à la vanille par de la glace au chocolat.

Crème pâtissière au Banania®

Portez à ébullition 50 cl de lait entier dans une casserole. Dans un saladier, battez 6 jaunes d'œufs et 100 g de sucre jusqu'à ce que le mélange blanchisse. Incorporez 50 g de farine et 2 c. à s. de Banania®. Versez la moitié du lait dans le saladier, en fouettant. Reversez le tout dans la casserole et laissez épaissir, en fouettant. Versez dans un saladier. Laissez refroidir puis garnissez les choux de crème.

Mousse au Banania®

Battez 4 jaunes d'œufs au fouet électrique avec 200 g de chocolat en poudre Banania®. Incorporez 6 blancs d'œufs en neige au mélange. Réservez au frais pendant 3 h. Garnissez les choux de cette mousse.

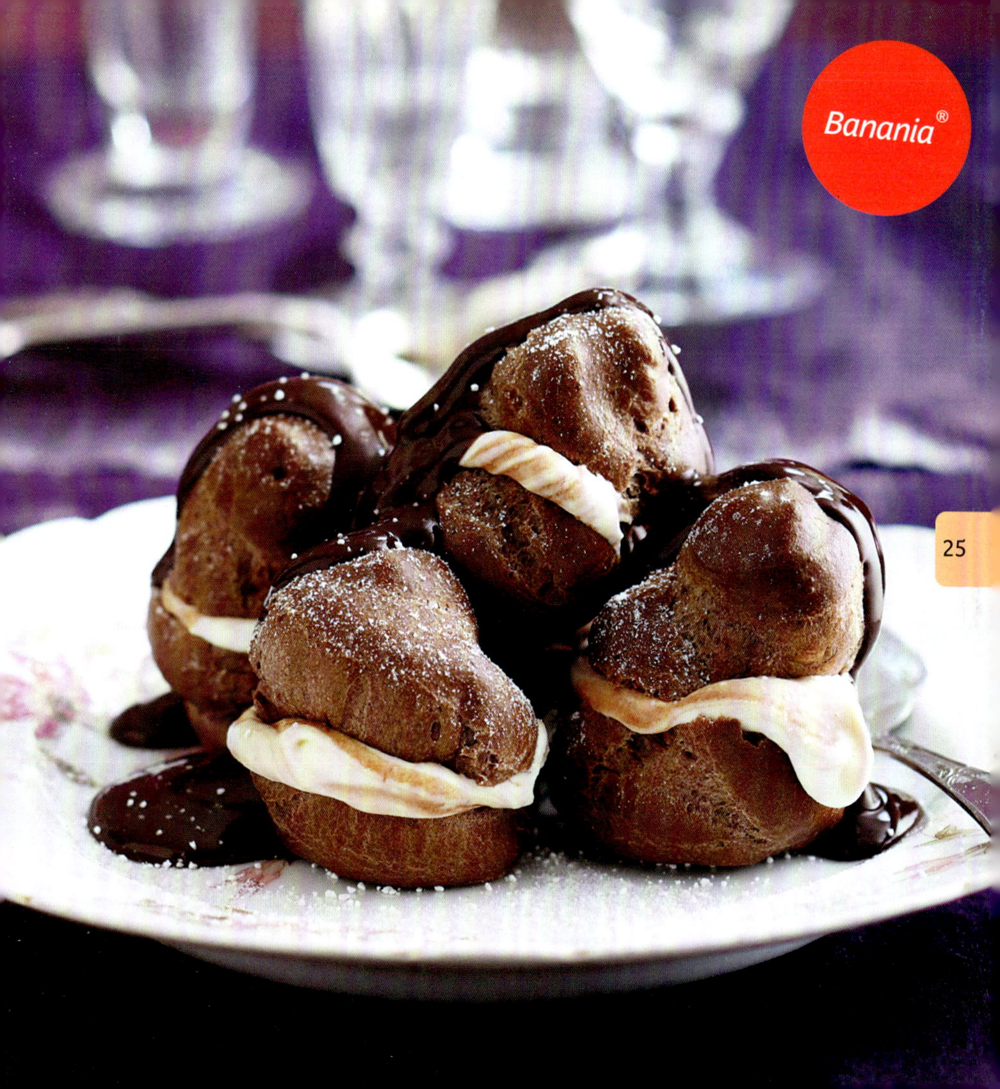
Banania®

TARTELETTES AU BANANIA® ET AU PIMENT D'ESPELETTE

Préparation : 10 min • **Cuisson :** 23 min • **Pour 6 personnes**

1 rouleau de pâte sablée • 180 g de chocolat en poudre Banania® + un peu pour la décoration • 20 cl de crème liquide 1 pincée de piment d'Espelette • 1 œuf

- Préchauffez le four à 180 °C.
- Déroulez la pâte sablée et découpez-y 6 disques à l'aide d'un emporte-pièce.
- Étalez les disques de tarte dans des moules à tartelette. Piquez le fond avec une fourchette. Parsemez de haricots secs ou de grains de riz.
- Faites cuire à blanc dans le four pendant 10 min.
- Sortez les fonds de tarte du four et retirez les haricots ou le riz. Laissez refroidir.
- Mettez le chocolat Banania® et la crème liquide dans une casserole. Ajoutez le piment d'Espelette et faites cuire pendant 3 min en remuant.
- Laissez refroidir, puis ajoutez l'œuf.
- Répartissez le mélange sur les fonds de tarte.
- Faites cuire au four à 180 °C de 10 à 12 min.
- Laissez refroidir, puis parsemez de chocolat en poudre Banania® avant de servir.

Pâte sablée au Banania®

Mettez 250 g de farine dans un saladier avec 1 pincée de sel, 50 g de sucre, 2 c. à s. de Banania® et mélangez. Incorporez 125 g de beurre coupé en parcelles. Travaillez du bout des doigts pour obtenir du sable. Faites un puits au centre et versez 1 c. à c. de crème fraîche et 1 œuf battu. Mélangez, formez une boule, enveloppez-la dans du film alimentaire et réservez au frais pendant 1 h avant utilisation.

Tartelettes au Banania® et à l'amande

Ajoutez 1 c. à c. d'extrait d'amande amère à la préparation. Parsemez la pâte sablée d'amandes effilées avant d'ajouter la crème.

Tartelettes au Banania® et aux noisettes

Ajoutez 125 g de noisettes concassées à la préparation.

Tartelettes au Banania® et à l'orange confite

Ajoutez 100 g d'écorces d'orange confites taillées en dés à la préparation.

Banania®

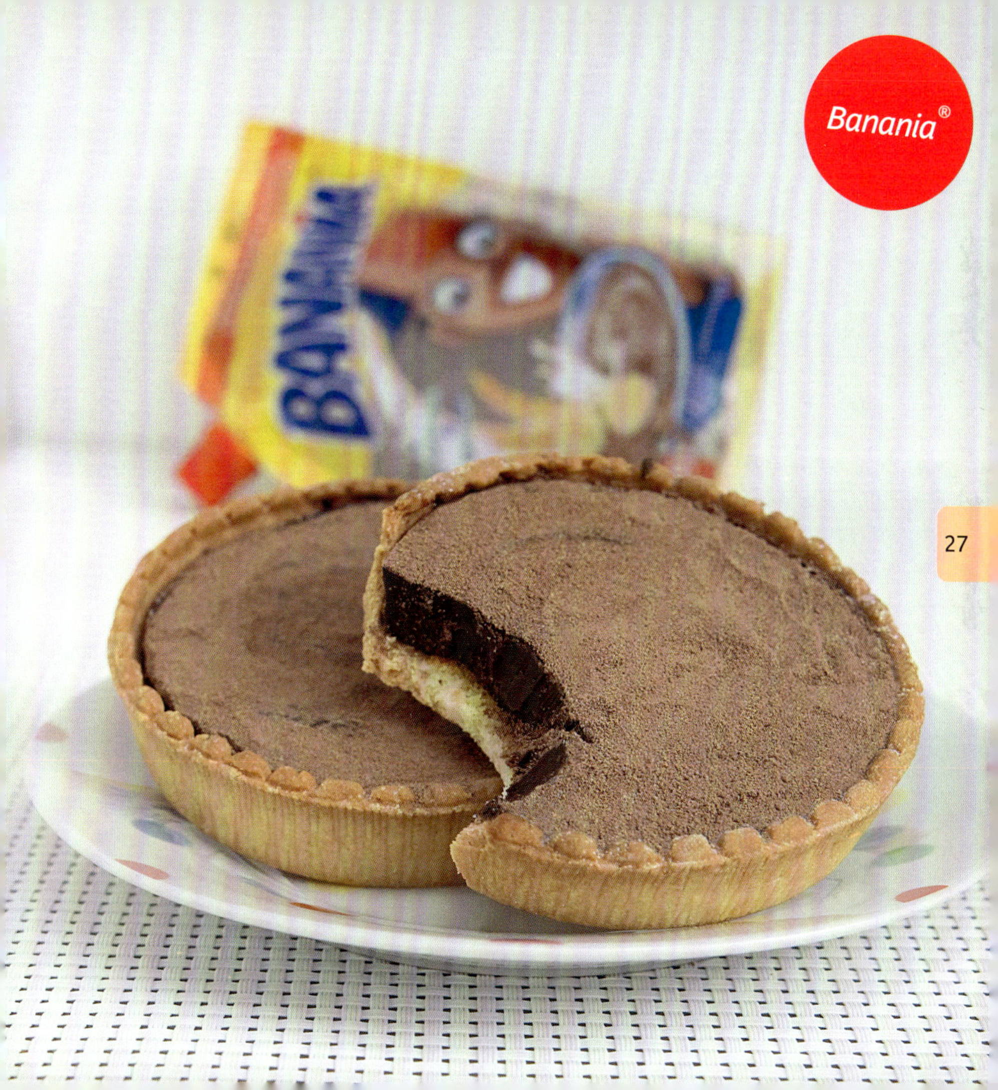

CABILLAUD CROUSTILLANT AUX HERBES

Préparation : 15 min • **Cuisson** : 15 min • **Pour 2 personnes**

12 biscottes Heudebert® • 15 brins de persil • 15 brins d'aneth 20 g de parmesan râpé • le zeste de 1 citron • 1 c. à s. d'huile d'olive + 1 filet • 2 filets de cabillaud • sel et poivre

- Préchauffez le four à 180 °C.
- Placez les biscottes Heudebert® dans un sac à congélation, fermez-le, puis écrasez-le à l'aide d'un rouleau à pâtisserie, de façon à obtenir une chapelure grossière.
- Rincez les herbes, essuyez-les sur du papier absorbant, puis ciselez-les finement.
- Dans un saladier, mélangez la chapelure, le parmesan, le zeste de citron, les herbes, du sel, du poivre et l'huile d'olive. Mélangez bien le tout.
- Déposez les filets de poisson sur une plaque de cuisson tapissée de papier sulfurisé. Arrosez-les de 1 filet d'huile d'olive, puis recouvrez-les de la chapelure aux herbes.
- Faites cuire de 15 à 20 min, jusqu'à ce que le poisson soit cuit à l'intérieur.
- Servez sans attendre, avec des haricots verts, par exemple.

Cabillaud pané aux herbes

Passez les filets de cabillaud dans de l'œuf battu, puis dans la chapelure aux herbes, pour les recouvrir de toute part. Faites-les cuire à la poêle, avec un peu d'huile de tournesol.

Cabillaud croustillant à l'indienne

Remplacez les herbes et le citron par 3/4 de c. à c. de cumin, 1/2 c. à c. de coriandre en poudre, 1/2 c. à c. de cardamome, 1/2 c. à c. de poivre, 1/4 de c. à c. de cannelle, 1 pincée de girofle et 1 pincée de noix muscade.

Cabillaud croustillant à la marocaine

Remplacez les herbes et le citron par 1,5 c. à s. de ras-el-hanout.

Poulet croustillant aux herbes

Remplacez l'aneth par de la coriandre et le citron par 1 gousse d'ail hachée revenue à la poêle avec un peu d'huile d'olive. Badigeonnez de moutarde 2 filets de poulet avant de les parsemer de chapelure aux herbes.

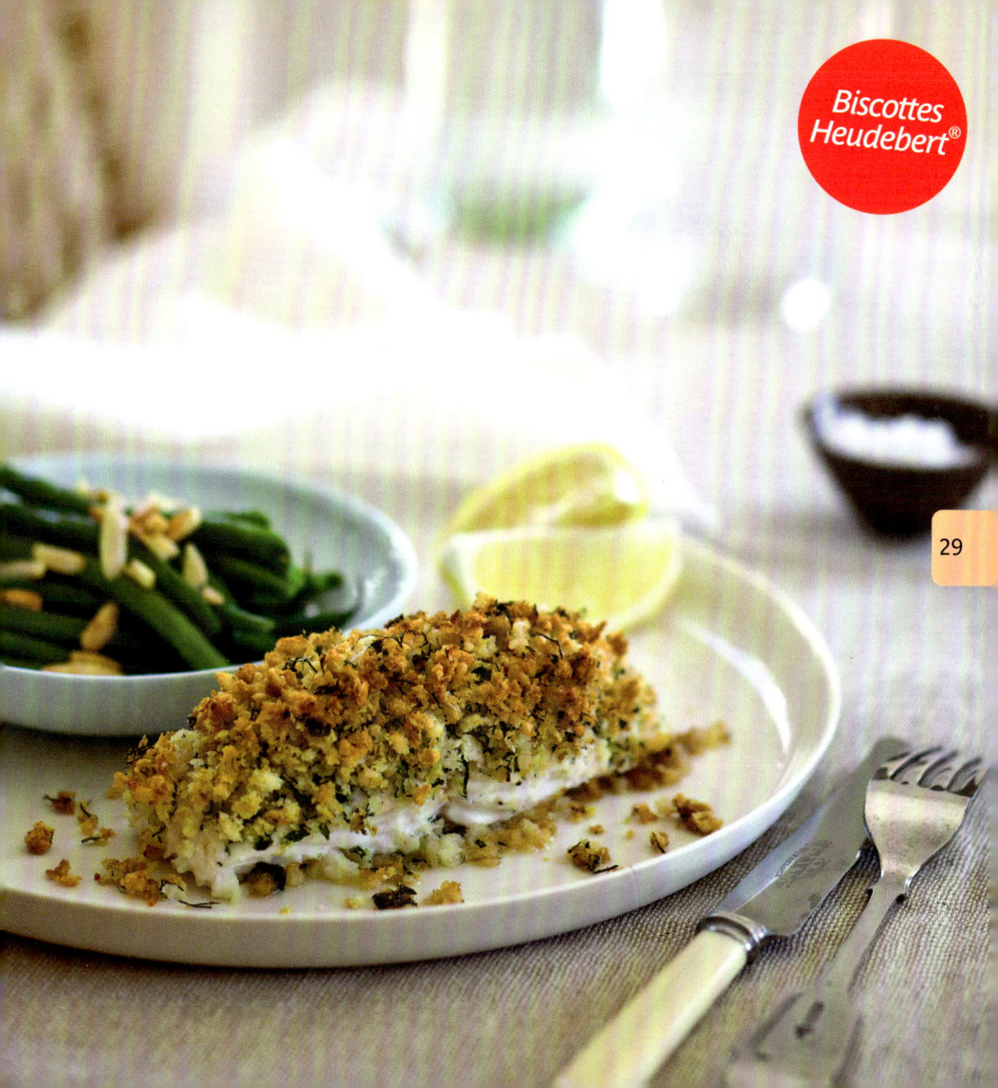
Biscottes
Heudebert®

CROQUANTS AUX BISCOTTES ET AUX NOISETTES

Préparation : 20 min • **Cuisson** : 30 min • **Réfrigération** : 30 min
Pour 20 biscuits

60 g de biscottes Heudebert® • 110 g de poudre de noisettes
150 g de beurre ramolli • 90 g de cassonade
1 c. à c. d'épices pour pain d'épice • 120 g de farine • sel

- Préchauffez le four à 190 °C.
- Placez les biscottes Heudebert® dans un sac à congélation, fermez-le, puis écrasez-le à l'aide d'un rouleau à pâtisserie, de façon à obtenir une chapelure grossière. Mélangez-la avec la poudre de noisettes, puis versez la préparation sur une plaque à pâtisserie recouverte de papier sulfurisé. Faites torréfier pendant 12 min environ, en remuant de temps en temps, jusqu'à ce que le mélange soit doré. Laissez refroidir.
- Dans une jatte, travaillez délicatement le beurre en pommade. Ajoutez la cassonade et les épices, et remuez bien. Incorporez le mélange chapelure-poudre de noisettes, la farine et 1 pincée de sel. Mélangez. Formez un ou deux boudin(s) de pâte de 4 à 5 cm de diamètre, puis enveloppez-le(s) dans du film alimentaire. Réservez au réfrigérateur pendant 30 min.
- Préchauffez le four à 180 °C. Taillez le(s) boudin(s) en rondelles de 1,5 cm d'épaisseur et répartissez-les sur une plaque à pâtisserie recouverte de papier sulfurisé.
- Faites cuire au four de 20 à 25 min, jusqu'à ce que les croquants soient bien dorés. Surveillez attentivement la cuisson, car ils ne doivent pas brunir. Laissez refroidir complètement.

Croquants aux biscottes et aux raisins secs

Supprimez 30 g de poudre de noisettes. Ajoutez 50 g de raisins secs à la préparation.

Croquants aux biscottes et aux amandes

Remplacez la poudre de noisettes par de la poudre d'amandes. Ajoutez 50 g d'amandes effilées à la préparation.

Croquants aux biscottes et à l'anis

Remplacez les épices pour pain d'épice par 2 c. à s. de graines d'anis vert.

Croquants aux biscottes et à la vanille

Remplacez les épices pour pain d'épice par les graines grattées de 2 gousses de vanille. À défaut, utilisez 2 c. à c. d'extrait de vanille liquide.

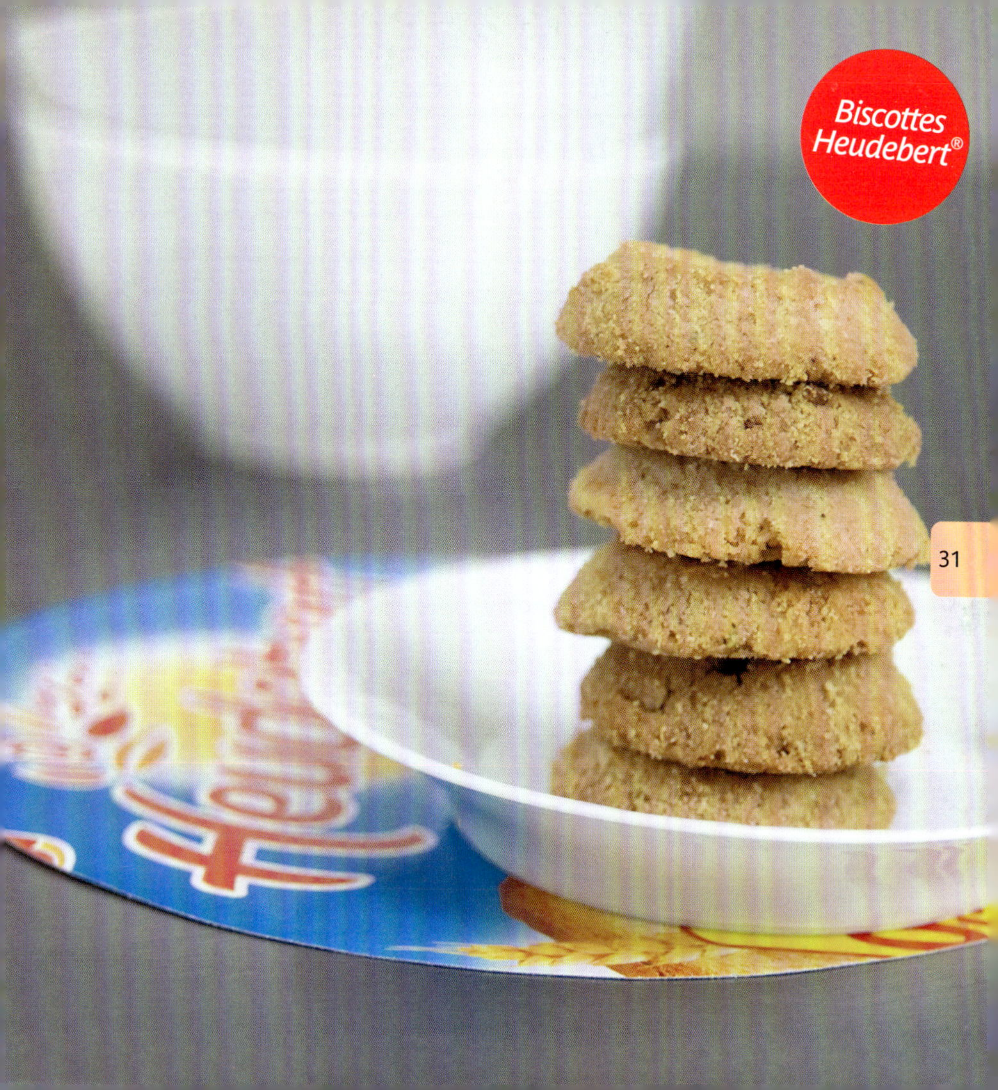
Biscottes Heudebert®

Galettes de saumon aux courgettes
Remplacez la moitié des pommes de terre par 300 g de courgettes lavées et râpées, que vous ferez revenir de 1 à 2 min à la poêle avec 1 filet d'huile d'olive.

Galettes de saumon aux carottes
Remplacez la moitié des pommes de terre par 300 g de carottes pelées et taillées en rondelles, que vous ferez cuire en même temps que les pommes de terre.

Galettes végétariennes
Remplacez le saumon par 150 g de tofu nature taillé en dés et 300 g de champignons de Paris frais, émincés et revenus à la poêle avec un peu d'huile d'olive.

Galettes au bœuf et aux pommes de terre
Remplacez le saumon par 400 g de bœuf haché revenu à la poêle sans matière grasse. Remplacez l'aneth par du persil ou de la coriandre.

Biscottes Heudebert®

GALETTES DE SAUMON AUX POMMES DE TERRE

Préparation: 20 min • **Réfrigération**: 20 min • **Cuisson**: 40 min
Pour 4 personnes

600 g de pommes de terre • 400 g de saumon • 2 gousses d'ail
1 oignon rouge • huile d'olive • 15 brins d'aneth • 2 œufs
le zeste de 1 citron • 8 biscottes Heudebert® • 40 g de farine • sel et poivre

- Épluchez les pommes de terre et taillez-les en rondelles. Faites-les bouillir dans une grande casserole d'eau bouillante salée, de 10 à 15 min, jusqu'à ce qu'elles soient bien tendres. Égouttez-les, puis écrasez-les. Laissez refroidir.

- Dans une autre casserole, faites pocher le saumon dans de l'eau frémissante salée, de 5 à 8 min. Égouttez-le puis détaillez la chair en morceaux.

- Épluchez l'ail et l'oignon, puis émincez-les. Faites-les revenir à la poêle, à feu vif, avec 1 c. à s. d'huile d'olive, de 3 à 4 min. Rincez l'aneth, essuyez-le avec du papier absorbant, puis émincez-le. Mettez-le dans le saladier contenant les pommes de terre avec l'ail et l'oignon, le saumon, 1 œuf et le zeste de citron. Salez, poivrez et mélangez. Formez 8 galettes avec cette préparation et réservez-les au réfrigérateur pendant 20 min.

- Écrasez finement les biscottes Heudebert® et mettez-les dans une assiette. Passez les galettes dans la farine, secouez-les pour retirer l'excès, puis trempez-les dans l'œuf battu restant et enrobez-les de chapelure, en appuyant fermement.

- Faites chauffer un peu d'huile dans la poêle à feu moyen. Faites cuire les galettes en deux fois, de 4 à 5 min de chaque côté, jusqu'à ce qu'elles soient bien dorées. Égouttez-les sur du papier absorbant, puis servez.

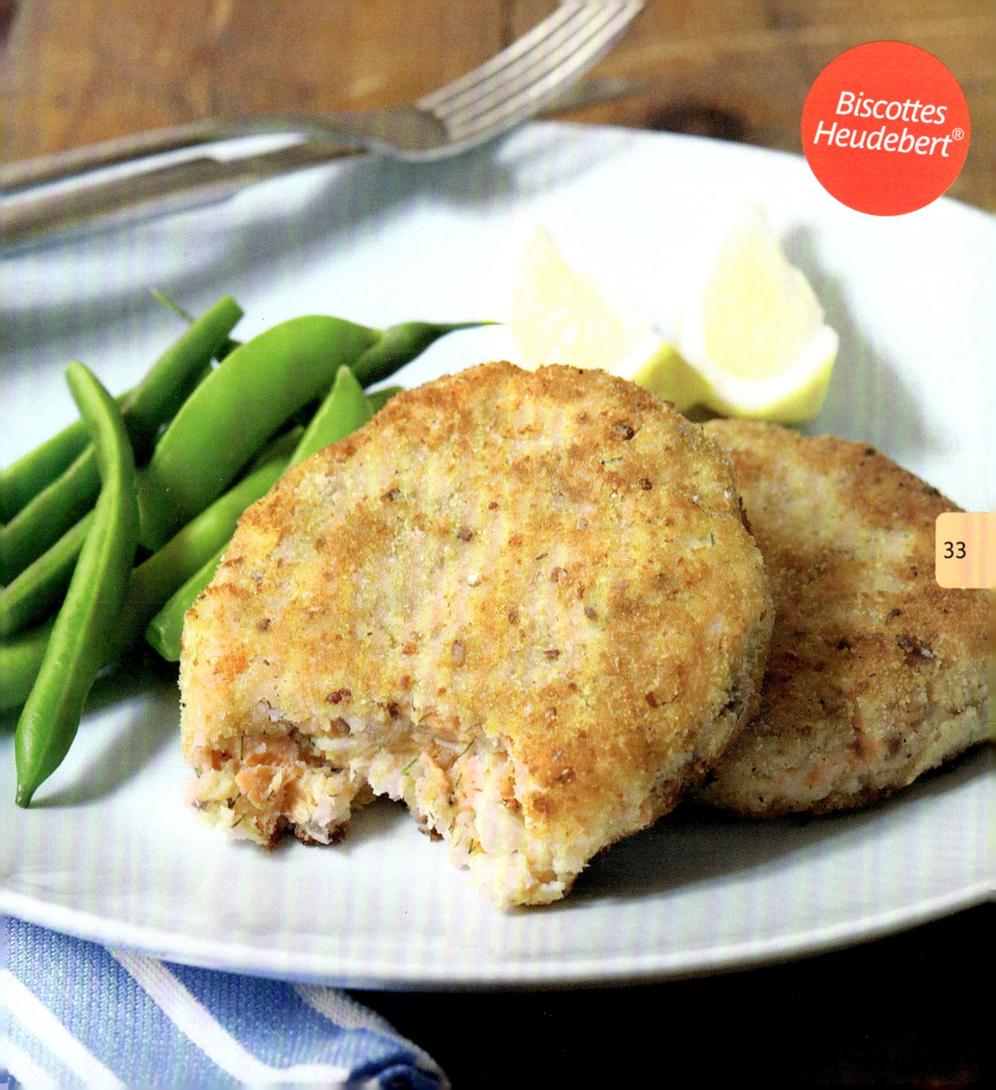
Biscottes
Heudebert®

Charlotte aux framboises
Remplacez les fraises par des framboises. Remplacez le sirop par 2 c. à s. de kirsch.

Charlotte aux pommes
Remplacez les fraises par des lamelles de pommes revenues à la poêle ave un peu de beurre et de sucre. Remplacez la crème pâtissière par de la crème fouettée à la vanille.

Charlotte à la crème aux fraises
Mixez 500 g de fraises en coulis et faites-en chauffer 1/4 dans une casserole avec 6 feuilles de gélatine ramollies et 60 g de sucre. Hors du feu, ajoutez le reste du coulis. Laissez refroidir. Mettez la casserole dans un saladier rempli de glaçons et faites épaissir à la cuillère en bois. Incorporez 40 cl de crème liquide montée en chantilly avec 1 sachet de sucre vanillé.

Charlotte au chocolat
Mélangez délicatement 250 g de chocolat noir fondu et 4 blancs d'œufs battus en neige avec 50 g de sucre en poudre. Remplacez la crème et les fraises par cette mousse.

Biscuits à la cuiller Brossard®

CHARLOTTE AUX FRAISES

Préparation : 45 min • **Réfrigération :** 12 h • **Cuisson :** 10 min
Pour 6 personnes

pour la crème pâtissière : *25 cl de lait • 1 gousse de vanille*
2 jaunes d'œufs • 40 g de sucre en poudre • 25 g de farine
pour le sirop : *100 g de sucre en poudre*
pour le gâteau : *500 g de fraises • 30 biscuits à la cuiller Brossard®*

- Pour la crème pâtissière, faites chauffer le lait avec les graines grattées de la gousse de vanille.
- Dans une jatte, battez les jaunes d'œufs au fouet électrique avec le sucre jusqu'à ce que le mélange blanchisse. Ajoutez la farine. Incorporez le lait chaud progressivement et laissez épaissir pendant 5 min en remuant sans cesse. Laissez refroidir complètement.
- Préparez un sirop en faisant chauffer le sucre et 25 cl d'eau dans une casserole.
- Lavez les fraises et équeutez-les, puis coupez-les en deux.
- Passez rapidement les biscuits à la cuiller dans le sirop de sucre puis tapissez-en les bords et le fond d'un moule à charlotte.
- Versez ensuite une couche de crème pâtissière dans le moule. Recouvrez-la de la moitié des fraises. Ajoutez une couche de crème pâtissière puis une couche de biscuits à la cuiller. Nappez du reste de crème et couvrez du reste des fraises.
- Couvrez la charlotte de film alimentaire, puis réservez-la au réfrigérateur pendant 12 h, avant de la servir.

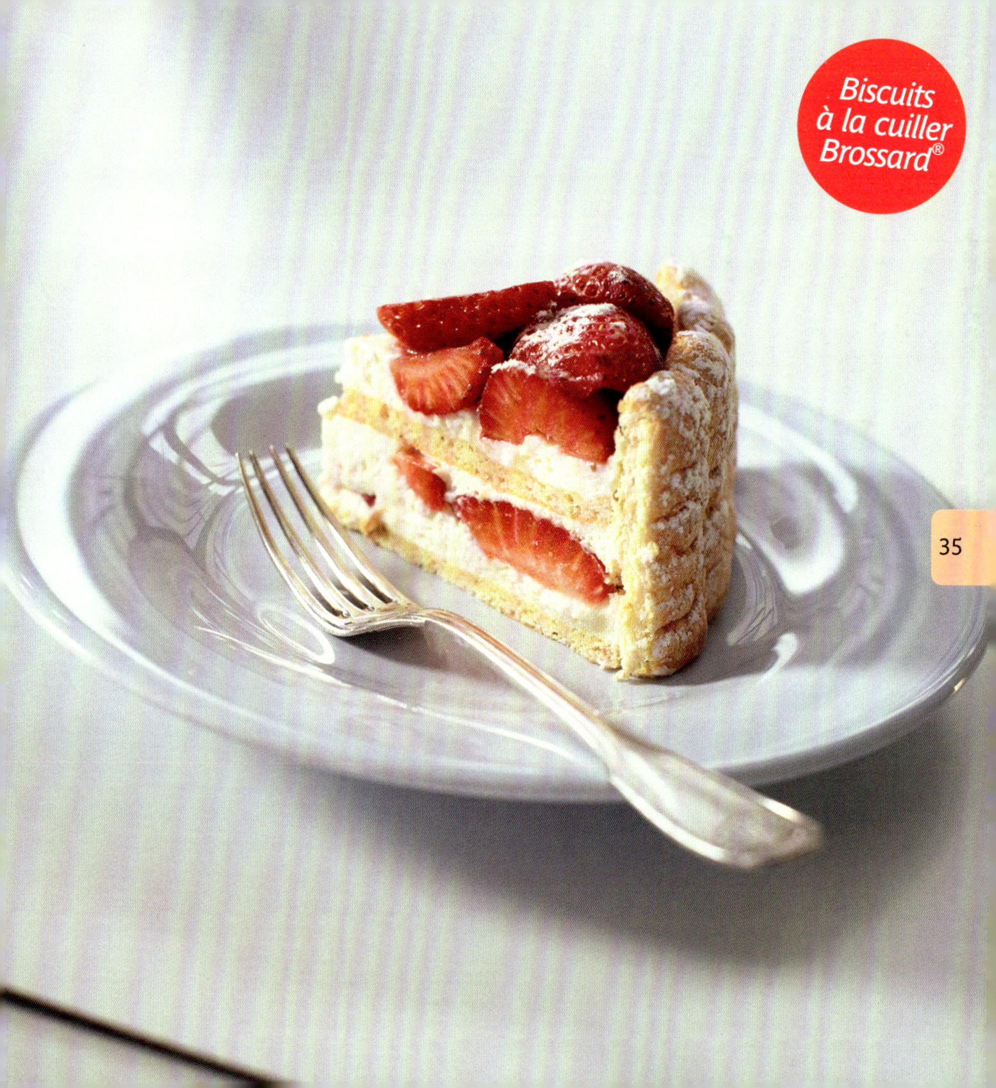
Biscuits
à la cuiller
Brossard®

Gâteau crémeux aux cerises
Ajoutez 125 g de cerises au sirop dénoyautées à la préparation à base de poudre d'amandes. Remplacez le lait au cognac par le sirop des cerises.

Gâteau crémeux à l'orange
Ajoutez le jus et le zeste de 1 orange à la préparation à base de poudre d'amandes. Remplacez le lait au cognac par du jus d'orange.

Gâteau crémeux à l'ananas et à la noix de coco
Remplacez la moitié de la poudre d'amandes par 100 g de noix de coco râpée. Ajoutez 125 g de dés d'ananas au sirop au mélange. Remplacez le lait au cognac par le sirop de l'ananas. Parsemez le gâteau de noix de coco râpée.

Tiramisu aux biscuits à la cuiller Brossard®
Remplacez la préparation à base de poudre d'amandes par 250 g de mascarpone auquel vous incorporerez 2 blancs d'œufs battus en neige. Remplacez le lait au cognac par du café fort.

GÂTEAU CRÉMEUX AUX BISCUITS À LA CUILLER

Préparation : 30 min • **Cuisson** : aucune • **Réfrigération** : 12 h
Pour 8 personnes

*125 g de beurre ramolli • 115 g de sucre + 1 c. à s. • 2 œufs
230 g de poudre d'amandes • 1/2 c. à c. d'extrait d'amande amère
25 cl de lait • 2 c. à s. de cognac • 250 g de biscuits à la cuiller Brossard®
350 g de crème fraîche • amandes effilées • copeaux de chocolat*

- Détaillez le beurre en parcelles, puis mettez-le dans un saladier avec le sucre. Battez au fouet électrique jusqu'à ce que le mélange soit clair et mousseux. Séparez les blancs des jaunes d'œufs. Incorporez les jaunes d'œufs à la préparation en fouettant bien après chaque ajout. Ajoutez la poudre d'amandes et l'extrait d'amande amère. Mélangez bien. Incorporez la moitié du lait petit à petit en battant sans cesse au fouet.

- Dans un bol, battez les blancs en neige au fouet électrique. Incorporez 1 c. à s. de sucre sans cesser de battre. Incorporez délicatement les blancs en neige à la préparation. Dans un petit saladier, mélangez le lait restant et le cognac.

- Coupez les biscuits à la cuiller Brossard® en deux dans le sens de l'épaisseur. Tapissez le fond d'un moule carré de demi-biscuits. Badigeonnez-les de lait au cognac puis nappez-les de crème. Renouvelez l'opération jusqu'à épuisement des ingrédients, en terminant par une couche de biscuits. Réservez au réfrigérateur pendant 12 h.

- Une heure avant de servir, sortez le plat du réfrigérateur. Battez la crème fraîche au fouet, puis recouvrez-en le gâteau. Parsemez-le d'amandes effilées et de copeaux de chocolat.

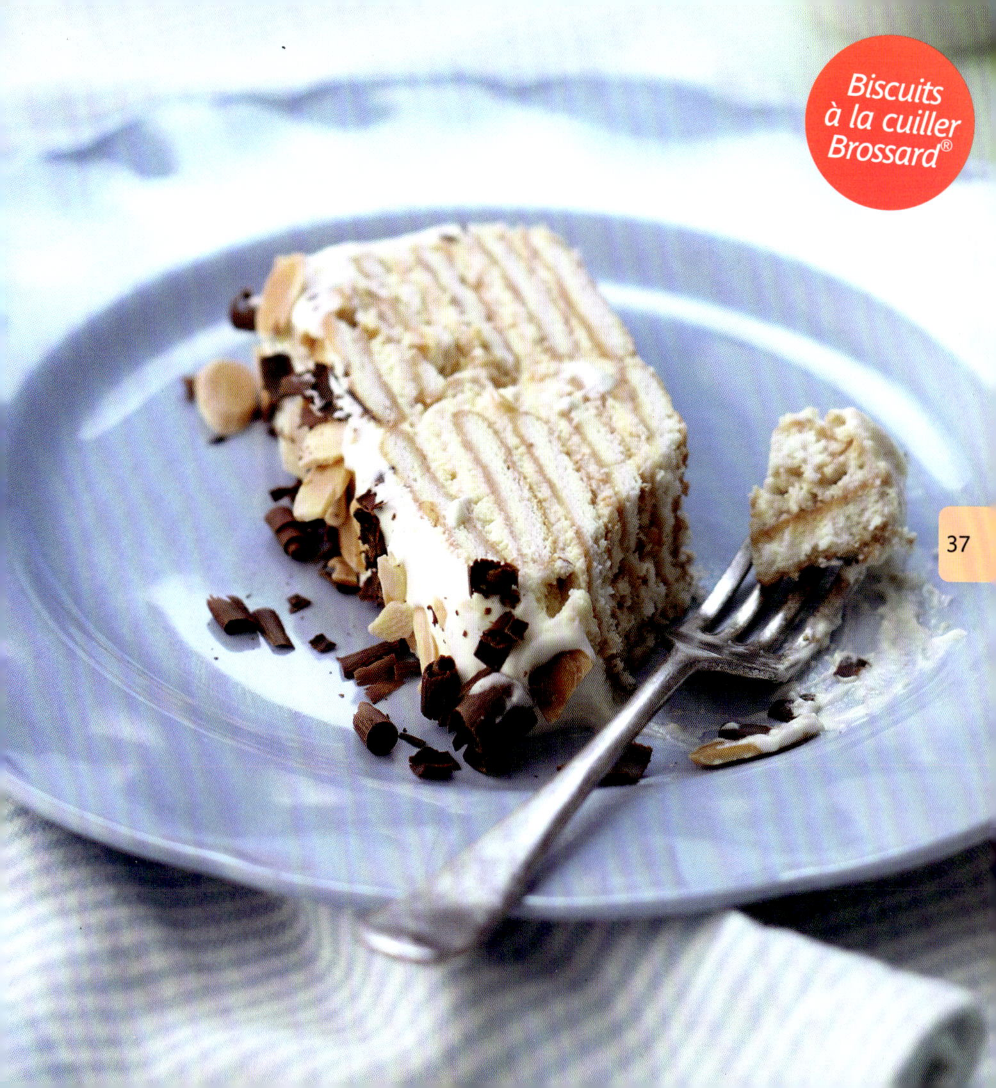
Biscuits
à la cuiller
Brossard®

Tiramisu express aux pêches
Utilisez des pêches au sirop et remplacez le sirop de sucre par le sirop des pêches.

Tiramisu aux poires et au caramel
Remplacez les pêches par 6 poires pelées et coupées en dés. Alternez les couches de fruits, de mélange au mascarpone et de biscuits avec du caramel au beurre salé.

Tiramisu aux fruits rouges
Remplacez les pêches par 200 g de framboises, 200 g de fraises équeutées et coupées en deux, 100 g de myrtilles et 100 g de mûres. Pour le sirop, portez à ébullition 15 cl d'eau avec 80 g de sucre. Laissez refroidir, puis ajoutez 1 c. à s. de liqueur de fraise.

Tiramisu au tofu
Délayez 1 c. à c. d'agar-agar dans 3 c. à s. de lait et faites bouillir pendant 30 s. Remplacez le mascarpone par du tofu soyeux et battez-le vigoureusement avec le lait bouillant, les jaunes d'œufs et le sucre, avant d'incorporer les blancs d'œufs.

Biscuits à la cuiller Brossard®

TIRAMISU AUX PÊCHES

Préparation : 20 min • **Cuisson** : 10 min • **Réfrigération** : 12 h
Pour 6 personnes

6 pêches • 45 g de sucre en poudre • 2 œufs • 250 g de mascarpone 200 g de biscuits à la cuiller Brossard® • noix de coco râpée, pour décorer

- Pelez les pêches, dénoyautez-les et coupez la chair en dés.
- Mettez la peau et les noyaux des pêches dans une casserole. Ajoutez 20 cl d'eau et 1 c. à s. de sucre en poudre, puis faites chauffer pendant 10 min, à feu doux, pour faire un sirop.
- Retirez du feu et laissez refroidir.
- Séparez les blancs des jaunes d'œufs.
- Versez les jaunes dans une jatte et battez-les avec le reste de sucre en poudre et le mascarpone, jusqu'à l'obtention d'une crème lisse.
- Dans une autre jatte, montez les blancs en neige ferme, puis incorporez-les très délicatement au mélange précédent.
- Retirez la peau et les noyaux de pêche du sirop. Passez les biscuits à la cuiller Brossard® dans le sirop, puis répartissez-en la moitié dans 6 verrines.
- Ajoutez ensuite une couche de dés de pêche, une couche de mélange au mascarpone, une couche de biscuits imbibés, une couche de dés de pêche et une couche de mélange au mascarpone.
- Réservez au réfrigérateur pendant au moins 12 h.
- Parsemez de noix de coco râpée juste avant de servir.

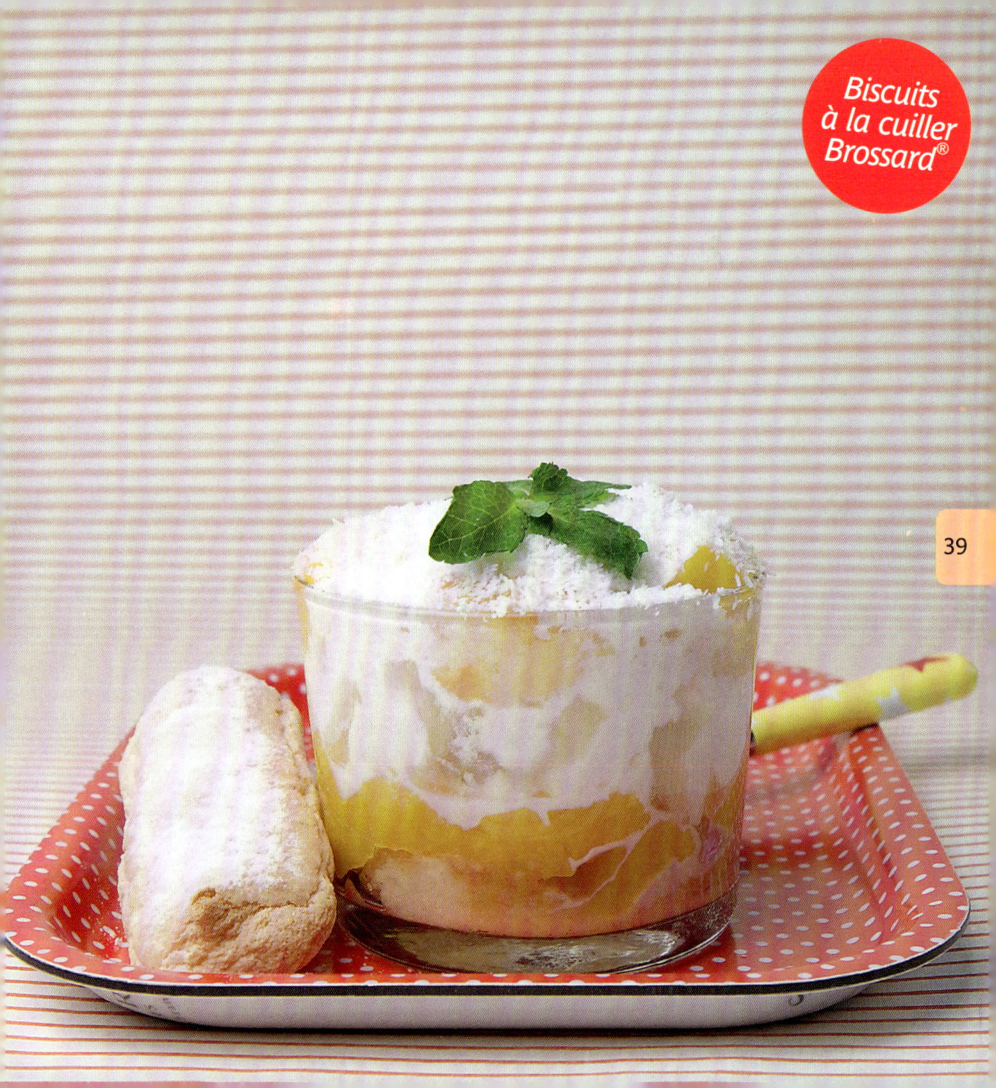
Biscuits
à la cuiller
Brossard®

TRIFLES AUX FRUITS ROUGES

Préparation: 25 min • **Cuisson**: 5 min • **Réfrigération**: 5 h
Pour 8 verrines

1 barquette de fraises • 1 barquette de framboises
1 barquette de myrtilles • 1 paquet de gelée en poudre à la framboise
50 cl de crème anglaise • 8 biscuits à la cuiller Brossard®
6 cl de cognac • 250 g de crème fraîche

- Lavez rapidement les fruits rouges. Équeutez les fraises et coupez-les en deux. Répartissez les fruits rouges dans 8 verrines. Réservez-en quelques-uns pour la décoration.
- Préparez la gelée en suivant les instructions sur le paquet, puis versez-la sur les fruits. Laissez prendre au réfrigérateur de 4 à 5 h.
- Nappez la gelée de crème anglaise.
- Émiettez grossièrement les biscuits à la cuiller Brossard®. Répartissez les morceaux dans les verrines, puis arrosez de cognac.
- Fouettez rapidement la crème fraîche. Déposez-en 1 c. à s. sur chaque verrine. Décorez avec les fruits réservés.
- Servez sans attendre.

Trifles à la mangue
Remplacez les fruits rouges par 4 ou 5 mangues bien mûres, pelées et taillées en dés. Remplacez la gelée à la framboise par de la gelée au citron.

Trifles au fromage blanc
Mélangez 400 g de fromage blanc avec 2 feuilles de gélatine ramollies, 2 blancs d'œufs montés en neige et 1 sachet de sucre vanillé. Remplacez la gelée par ce mélange. Supprimez la crème anglaise.

Trifles au chocolat blanc
Mélangez 200 g de chocolat blanc fondu avec 2 blancs d'œufs montés en neige et 500 g de mascarpone. Remplacez la gelée par ce mélange. Supprimez la crème anglaise.

Crème anglaise maison
Portez à ébullition 30 cl de lait avec les graines de 1 gousse de vanille. Dans une jatte, battez 3 jaunes d'œufs au fouet avec 50 g de sucre. Versez la moitié du lait sur les œufs en fouettant. Reversez le tout dans la casserole. En fouettant, faites épaissir sans laisser bouillir jusqu'à ce que la crème ne mousse plus. Laissez refroidir.

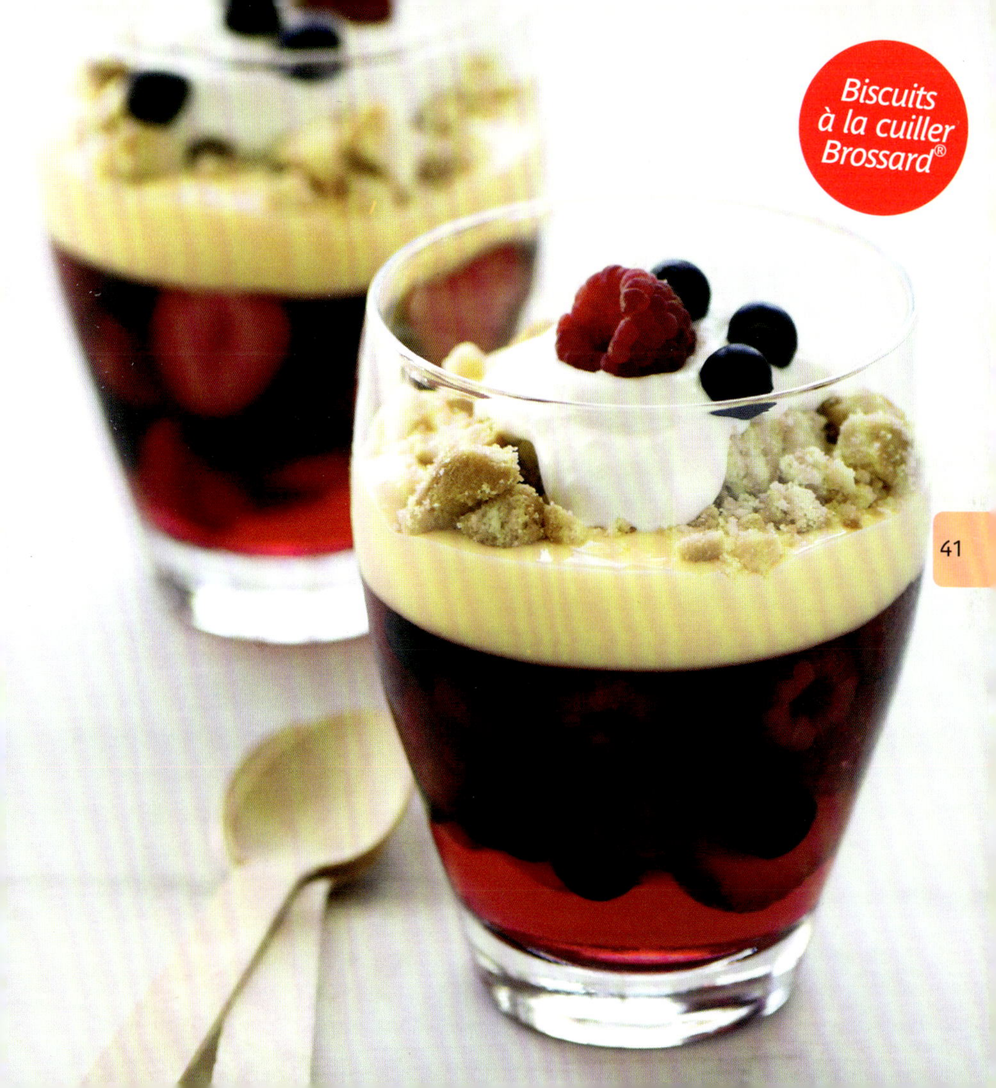
Biscuits
à la cuiller
Brossard®

Cocotte d'agneau aux aubergines et aux olives
Remplacez les haricots verts par 2 aubergines taillées en dés. Ajoutez 100 g d'olives vertes dénoyautées.

Cocotte d'agneau à la feta
Environ 15 min avant la fin de la cuisson, ajoutez 200 g de feta coupée en dés dans la cocotte.

Cocotte d'agneau aux pommes de terre
Remplacez les *risoni* et les haricots par 500 g de pommes de terre pelées et coupées en rondelles. Ajoutez 1 branche de thym et 2 feuilles de laurier à la préparation.

Cocotte d'agneau au fenouil
Remplacez les *risoni* et les haricots verts par 4 bulbes de fenouil coupés en 4. Ajoutez le jus du citron en plus du zeste.

Bouillon Kub® Or

COCOTTE D'AGNEAU À LA GRECQUE

Préparation : 15 min • **Cuisson** : 1 h 40 • **Pour 4 personnes**

*1 kg de sauté d'agneau • huile d'olive • 4 gousses d'ail • 2 oignons
1 boîte de tomates concassées • 1 c. à c. d'origan déshydraté
2 bouillons Kub® Or • 200 g de haricots verts • 100 g de risoni (petites pâtes en forme de grains de riz) • le zeste de 1 citron • sel et poivre*

- Préchauffez le four à 180 °C.
- Détaillez l'agneau en cubes. Faites chauffer un peu d'huile d'olive dans une poêle et faites-y dorer la viande de toute part.
- Pendant ce temps, épluchez l'ail et les oignons. Écrasez l'ail et émincez les oignons.
- Retirez l'agneau de la poêle et réservez-le. Faites chauffer encore un peu d'huile d'olive dans la poêle et faites-y revenir l'ail et l'oignon.
- Versez un peu d'huile d'olive dans une cocotte, puis mettez-y la viande, le mélange ail et oignon, puis les tomates et l'origan. Couvrez la cocotte et placez-la dans le four. Faites cuire pendant 1 h.
- Portez à ébullition 50 cl d'eau et délayez-y les bouillons Kub® Or. Coupez les haricots verts en tronçons de 3 cm.
- Ajoutez le bouillon dans la cocotte avec les *risoni* et les haricots verts.
- Couvrez et replacez au four pour 40 min, jusqu'à ce que la viande soit bien tendre. Incorporez le zeste de citron, salez et poivrez.

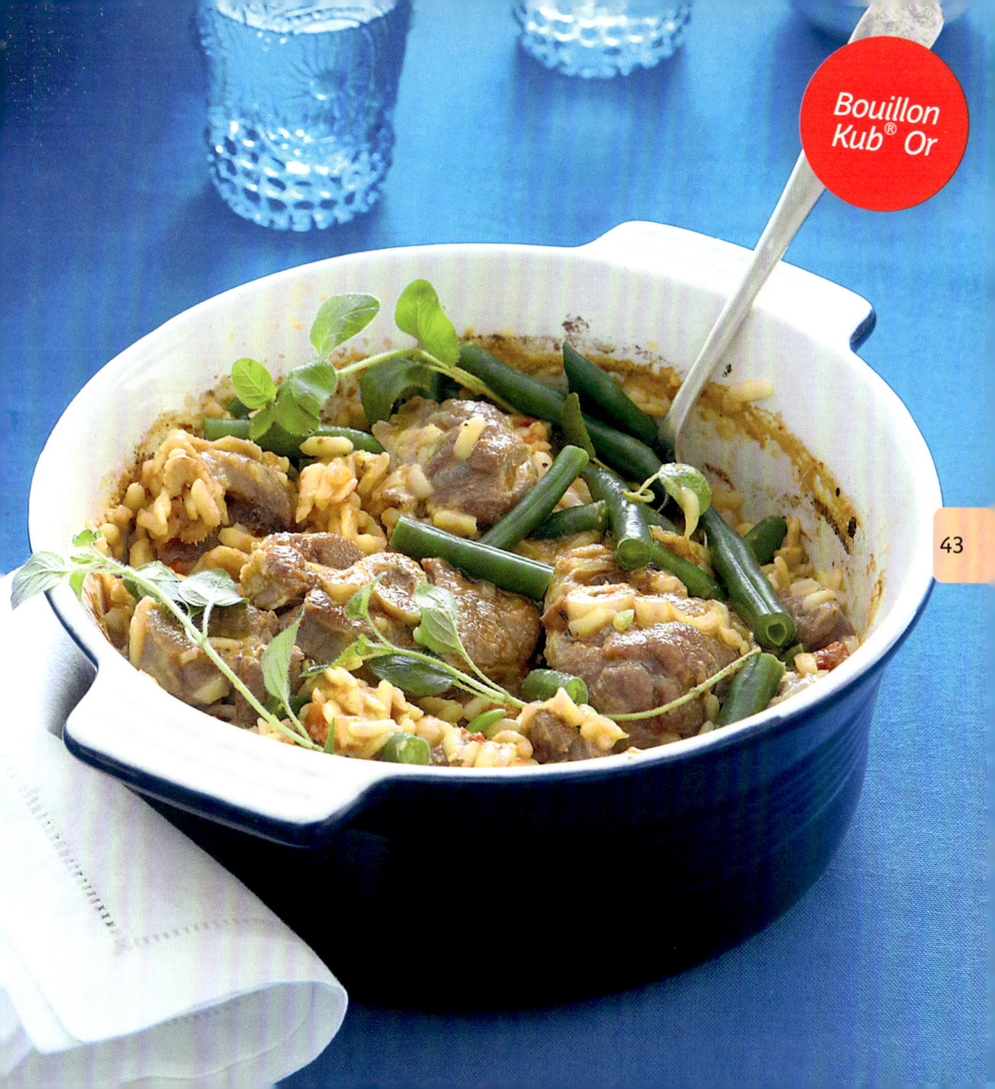
Bouillon
Kub® Or

MOULES EN BOUILLON PARFUMÉ

Préparation : 15 min • **Cuisson** : 20 min • **Pour 2 personnes**

500 g de moules • 100 g de haricots verts • 1 bouquet de coriandre
1 petite tomate • 2 c. à c. d'huile végétale • 2 c. à c. de pâte de curry vert
12 cl de vin blanc • 25 cl de lait de coco • 1 bouillon Kub® Or
2 c. à c. de sucre roux en poudre • 1 c. à s. de jus de citron vert
pain croustillant et tranches de citron vert, pour accompagner

- Nettoyez les moules et ébarbez-les. Équeutez les haricots verts et coupez-les en deux. Rincez la coriandre, essuyez-la sur du papier absorbant, puis détachez les feuilles. Lavez la tomate et taillez-la en dés.

- Faites chauffer un wok ou une grande poêle sur feu moyen. Ajoutez l'huile, puis la pâte de curry et faites cuire de 1 à 2 min avant d'ajouter le vin et le lait de coco. Portez à ébullition, puis baissez le feu et laissez mijoter à découvert pendant 5 min.

- Pendant ce temps, délayez le bouillon Kub® Or dans 15 cl d'eau bouillante. Ajoutez le bouillon dans le wok avec le sucre et faites chauffer pendant 2 min.

- Ajoutez alors les moules, couvrez et faites cuire de 5 à 8 min, jusqu'à ce que les moules s'ouvrent. Ajoutez les haricots verts pour les 2 dernières minutes de cuisson.

- Retirez et jetez toutes les moules non ouvertes. Ajoutez le jus de citron et la coriandre.

- Répartissez les moules et le bouillon dans des bols et parsemez de dés de tomate. Servez avec du pain croustillant et des tranches de citron vert.

Coques en bouillon parfumé

Remplacez les moules par des coques. Vous pouvez également utiliser des palourdes.

Moules en bouillon à la citronnelle et au gingembre

Ajoutez 5 tiges de citronnelle ciselées et 1 morceau de gingembre de 1 cm râpé dans le bouillon en même temps que la pâte de curry.

Moules en bouillon au safran

Remplacez la pâte de curry vert par 2 c. à c. de safran en poudre. À défaut, utilisez du curcuma.

Moules en bouillon aux nouilles

Supprimez la moitié des moules. Faites cuire 200 g de nouilles asiatiques aux œufs en suivant les indications sur le paquet. Répartissez-les dans les bols et couvrez-les de moules en bouillon parfumé.

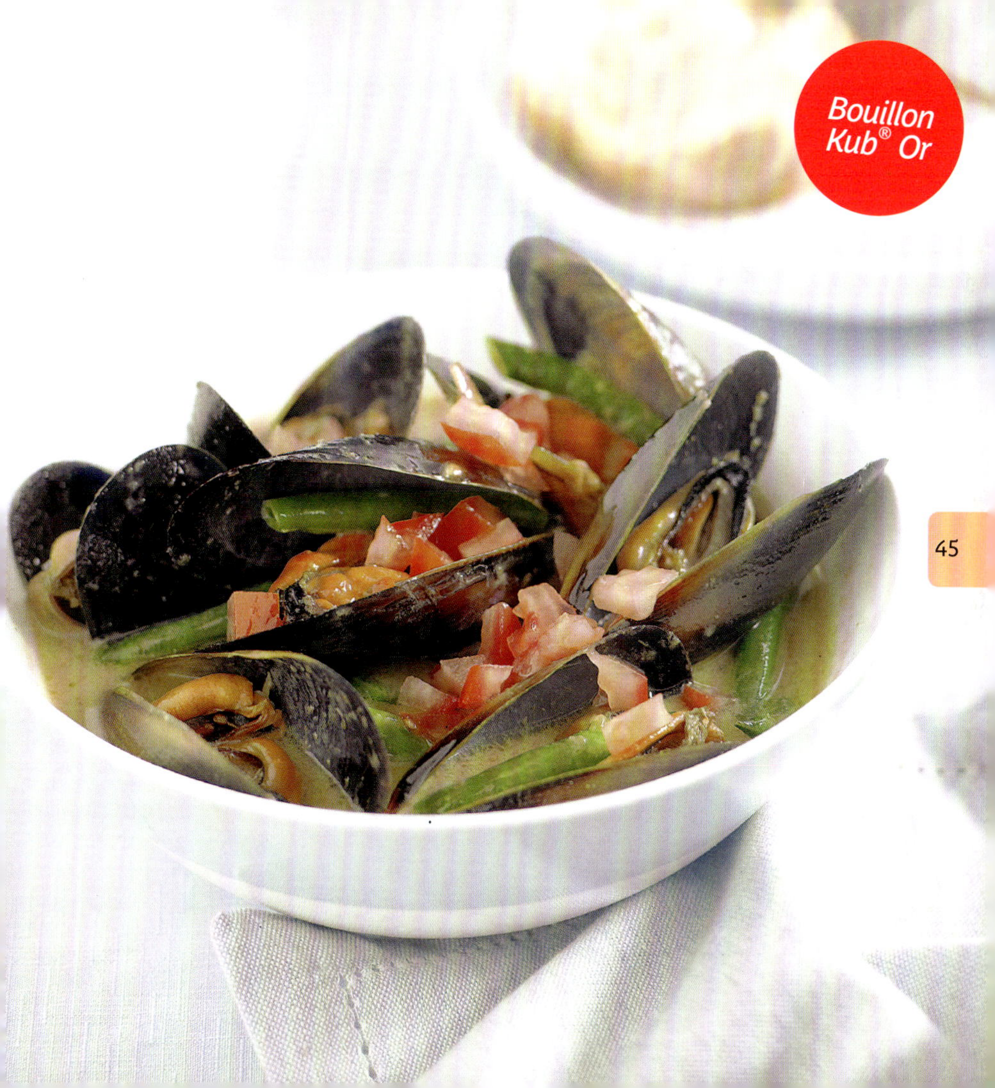

Bouillon Kub® Or

RISOTTO AUX CHAMPIGNONS ET AU CHORIZO

Préparation : 20 min • **Cuisson** : 25 min • **Pour 4 personnes**

1 bouillon Kub® Or • 1 gros oignon • 350 g de champignons de Paris
1 c. à s. d'huile d'olive • 250 g de riz rond
150 g de chorizo • 80 g de copeaux de parmesan

- Dans une petite casserole, portez à ébullition 1 l d'eau avec le bouillon Kub® Or.
- Épluchez l'oignon et émincez-le. Lavez les champignons, coupez-les en quartiers, puis en fines lamelles.
- Faites revenir l'oignon à feu doux dans une sauteuse avec l'huile d'olive. Lorsqu'il est translucide, versez le riz dans la sauteuse et remuez jusqu'à ce qu'il devienne transparent.
- Ajoutez les champignons ainsi qu'une louche de bouillon chaud, et faites chauffer à feu doux, en remuant régulièrement, jusqu'à l'absorption complète du bouillon. Versez le reste de bouillon petit à petit, en laissant le riz l'absorber avant d'en ajouter de nouveau et en remuant souvent. La cuisson doit durer 20 min environ.
- Pelez le chorizo et coupez-le en fines rondelles. Faites-le revenir à la poêle sans matière grasse. Jetez l'huile rendue.
- Lorsque le riz est cuit, mettez le chorizo et le parmesan dans la sauteuse. Remuez et laissez reposer pendant 2 min (il n'est pas nécessaire de saler, car le chorizo et le parmesan relèvent suffisamment le plat). Servez sans attendre.

Risotto de fête

Remplacez les champignons de Paris par des morilles déshydratées mises à tremper dans de l'eau tiède pendant 1 h. Faites-les revenir à la poêle avec un peu de beurre, avant de les ajouter au risotto en toute fin de cuisson. Remplacez le chorizo par des lamelles de magret séché.

Risotto au poulet et aux cèpes

Remplacez les champignons de Paris par des cèpes coupés en morceaux et le chorizo par 200 g de dés de blancs de poulet revenus à la poêle.

Risotto au poulet et aux courgettes

Reprenez la recette ci-dessus en remplaçant les cèpes par 3 courgettes taillées en cubes et revenues à la poêle à l'huile d'olive. Ajoutez-les en fin de cuisson.

Risotto aux crevettes et au curry

Remplacez le chorizo par des crevettes décortiquées. Ajoutez 1 c. à c. de curry en poudre en même temps que le parmesan.

Bouillon Kub® Or

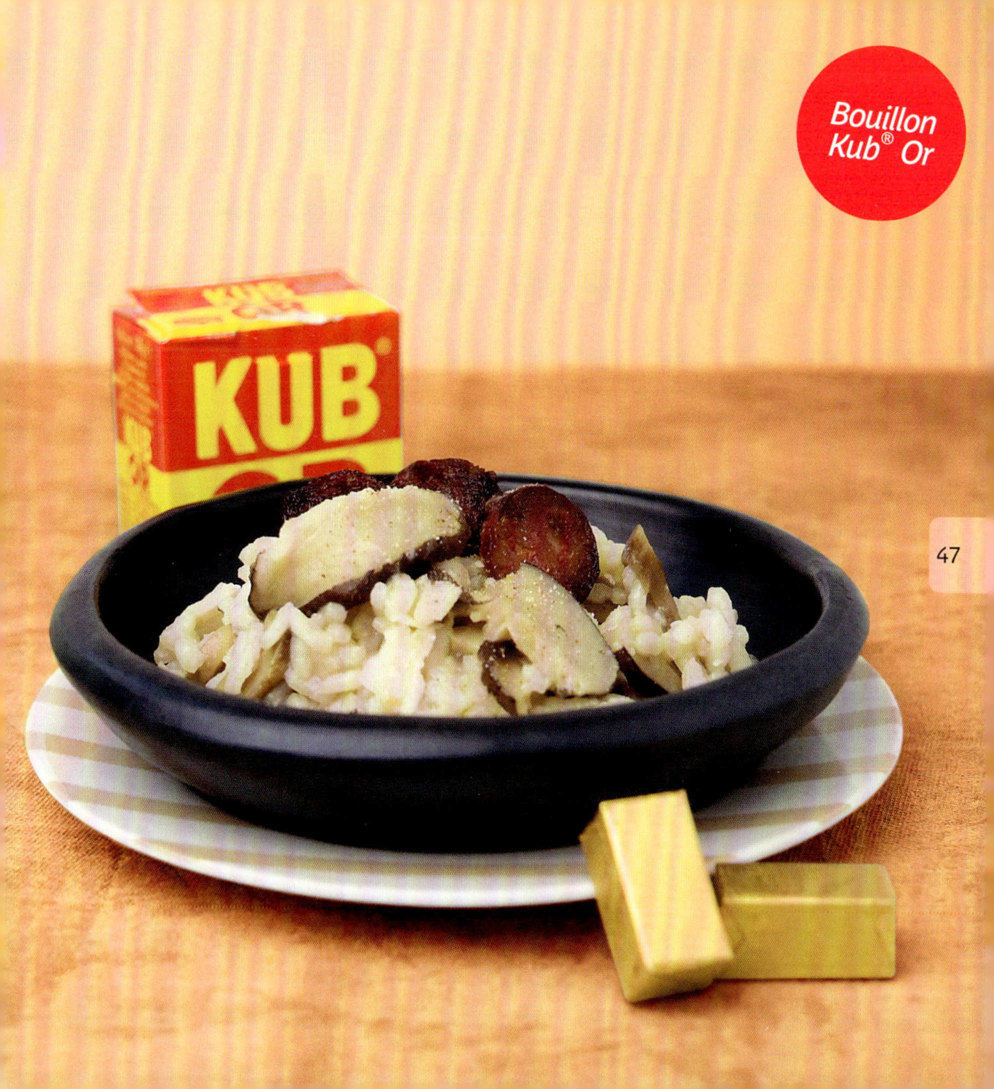

Bouillon Kub® Or

SOUPE MEXICAINE À L'AVOCAT

Préparation: 25 min • **Cuisson**: 35 min • **Pour 4 personnes**

8 grosses tomates • 2 branches de céleri • 3 poireaux • 2 carottes
2 gousses d'ail • 4 escalopes de poulet • 1/2 c. à c. de cumin en poudre
1/2 c. à c. de coriandre en poudre • 1 c. à s. d'huile d'avocat
2 c. à s. d'huile de tournesol • 2 bouillons Kub® Or • 125 g de grains
de maïs doux • coriandre fraîche • 1 avocat bien mûr • le jus
de 1 citron vert • chips mexicaines, pour accompagner • sel et poivre

- Préchauffez le gril du four. Lavez les tomates, le céleri et les poireaux. Pelez les carottes et épluchez l'ail. Coupez les tomates en deux, taillez le céleri, les poireaux en rondelles, râpez les carottes et hachez l'ail.
- Disposez les tomates, côté coupé vers le haut, et les escalopes dans un plat à four. Assaisonnez de cumin, de coriandre, de sel et de poivre, et arrosez d'huile d'avocat. Laissez cuire sous le gril de 15 à 20 min jusqu'à ce que le poulet soit cuit.
- Faites revenir rapidement tous les autres légumes préparés avec l'huile de tournesol dans une grande sauteuse. Portez à ébullition 1 l d'eau dans une grande casserole et ajoutez-y les bouillons Kub® Or.
- Écrasez les tomates grillées, ajoutez-les au bouillon avec le maïs et tous les légumes, puis laissez mijoter pendant 15 min.
- Coupez le poulet en lamelles. Lavez la coriandre, égouttez-la sur du papier absorbant, puis ciselez-la. Ajoutez-les au bouillon.
- Coupez l'avocat en deux, dénoyautez-le et détaillez la chair en dés. Versez la soupe dans des bols. Répartissez l'avocat et le jus de citron vert dans chacun. Servez avec des chips mexicaines.

Soupe mexicaine aux haricots rouges

Remplacez les poireaux et l'avocat par 1 grosse boîte de haricots rouges rincés et égouttés. Ajoutez-les dans la casserole en même temps que le maïs et les légumes sautés.

Soupe mexicaine pimentée

Taillez 1 piment vert en fines rondelles et faites-les revenir dans la sauteuse avec les autres légumes.

Soupe mexicaine aux croûtons

Détaillez 4 tranches de pain au maïs en cubes et frottez-les rapidement avec 1/2 gousse d'ail. Faites-les dorer sous le gril du four en les retournant à mi-cuisson. Ajoutez-les dans la soupe et supprimez les chips.

Soupe mexicaine aux pommes de terre et aux poivrons

Remplacez les poireaux et les carottes par 400 g de pommes de terre cuites à l'eau et 1 poivron rouge taillé en lamelles.

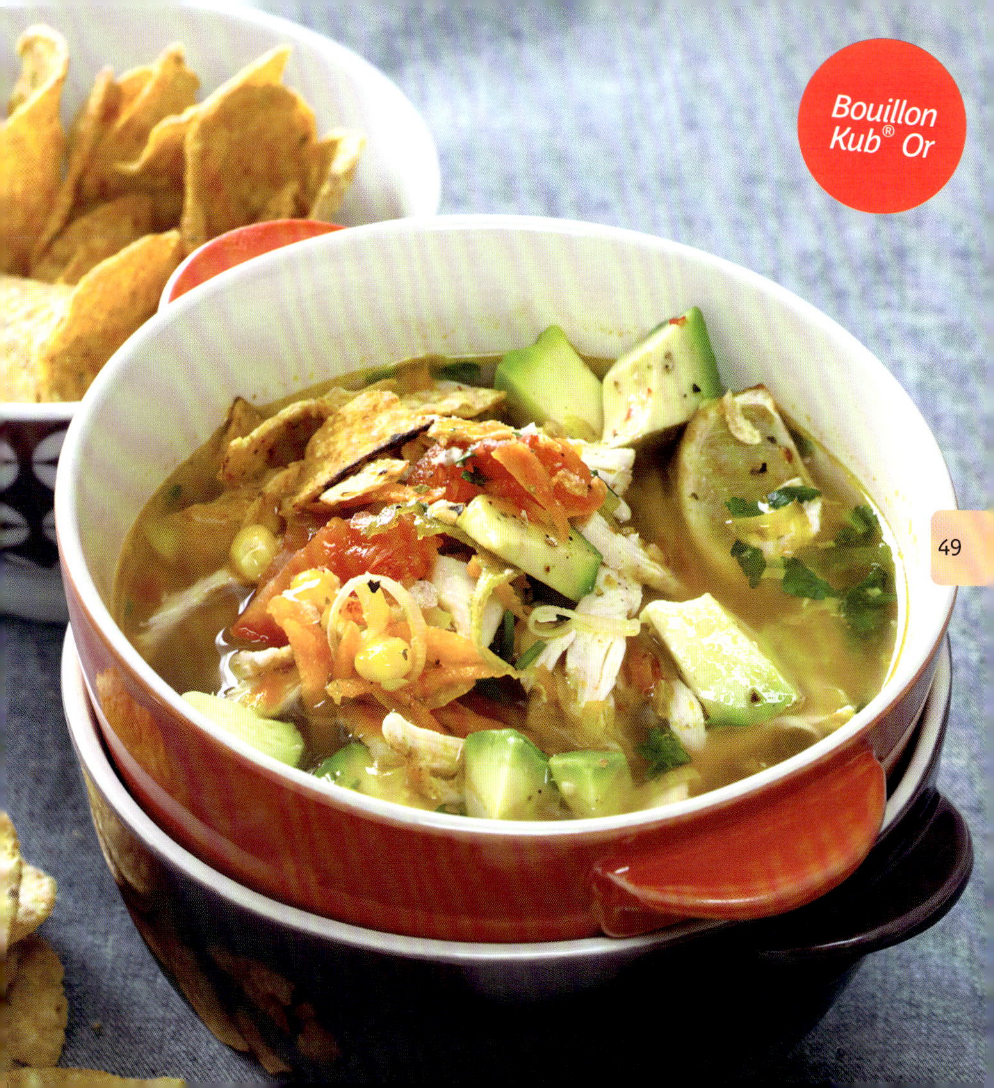
Bouillon
Kub® Or

WOK DE POULET AUX LÉGUMES VERTS

Préparation : 10 min • **Cuisson** : 10 min • **Pour 4 personnes**

500 g d'escalopes de poulet • 125 g de miniépis de maïs
8 cives • 2 gousses d'ail • 1 bouillon Kub® Or
2 c. à c. de fécule de pomme de terre • 2 c. à s. d'huile végétale
250 g de haricots mange-tout • 50 g de cerneaux de noix
1 c. à s. de pâte de piment vert • riz vapeur pour accompagner

- Détaillez les escalopes de poulet en lamelles. Coupez les miniépis de maïs en deux dans la longueur. Épluchez les cives et taillez-les en tronçons de 10 cm. Épluchez les gousses d'ail et hachez-les.
- Dans une jatte, dissolvez le bouillon Kub® Or dans 3 c. à s. d'eau bouilante. Ajoutez la fécule de pomme de terre et 2 c. à s. d'eau. Faites tremper les lamelles de poulet dans ce mélange et remuez de façon que le poulet soit entièrement recouvert.
- Faites chauffer l'huile dans un wok à feu vif. Faites-y revenir le poulet pendant 3 min, jusqu'à ce qu'il soit bien doré. Retirez-le du wok et réservez-le dans un bol.
- Versez les haricots mange-tout, les miniépis de maïs, les cives et les noix dans le wok, et faites sauter pendant 2 min environ, jusqu'à ce que les légumes soient tendres mais encore croquants.
- Replacez le poulet dans le wok avec l'ail et le piment, et faites sauter pendant 1 min environ. Ajoutez le reste du mélange au bouillon Kub® Or dans le wok et faites cuire pendant 1 min, jusqu'à ce que les légumes soient enrobés.
- Servez avec du riz vapeur.

Wok de bœuf aux légumes verts

Remplacez le poulet par du bœuf. Saisissez-le très rapidement au wok, pour qu'il reste saignant au centre.

Wok de crevettes aux légumes verts

Remplacez le poulet par 500 g de crevettes cuites décortiquées. Vous pouvez également utiliser des gambas. Faites-les cuire pendant 2 min seulement au wok. Ajoutez 1 c. à c. de sauce d'huître à la préparation.

Wok de saint-jacques aux légumes verts

Remplacez le poulet par 500 g de noix de saint-jacques. Faites-les revenir très rapidement au wok (1 min au maximum). Ajoutez 1 c. à c. de sauce d'huître à la préparation.

Wok de poulet aux noix de cajou

Remplacez les noix par des noix de cajou. Vous pouvez aussi utiliser des cacahuètes.

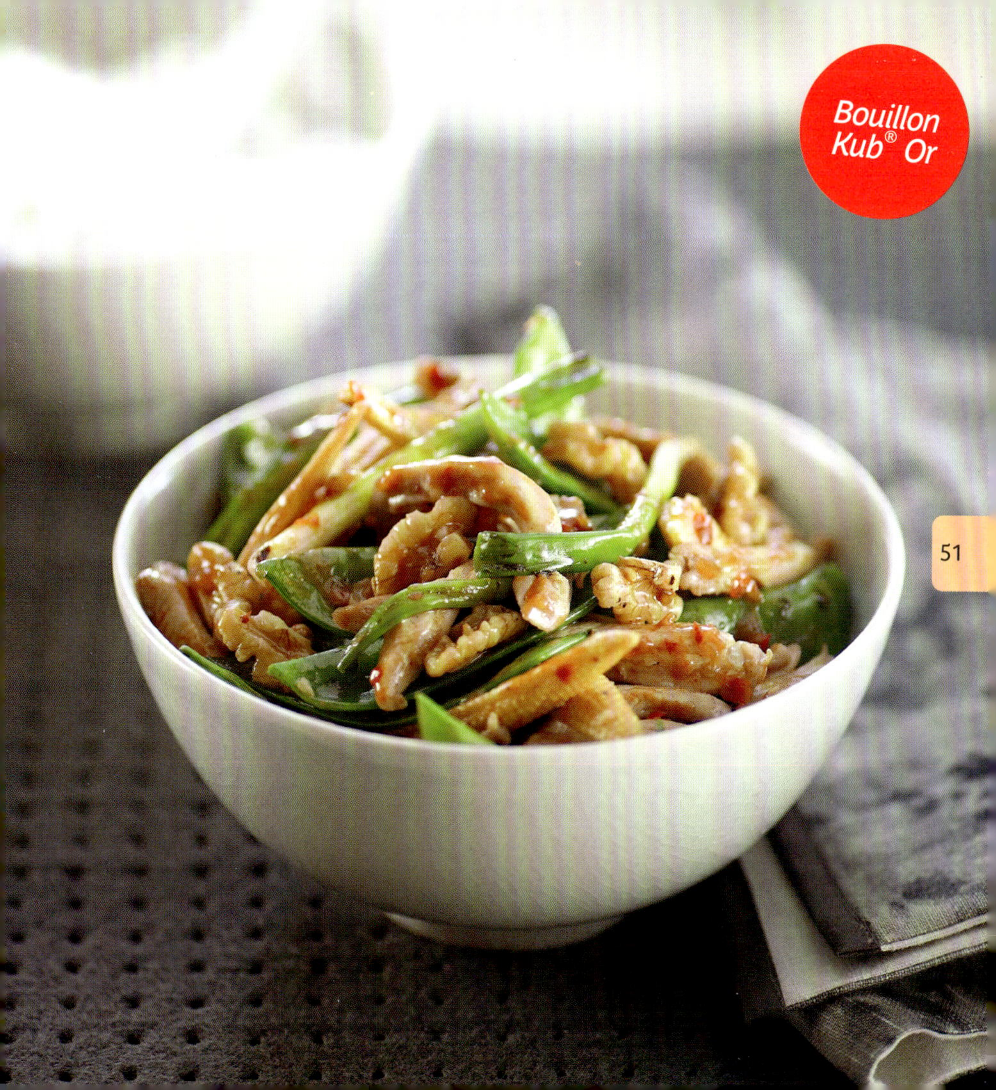

Bouillon Kub® Or

MILK-SHAKE AU BOUNTY®

Préparation : 5 min • **Cuisson** : aucune • **Pour 4 personnes**

10 glaçons • 4 barres Bounty® • 4 boules de glace à la vanille
2 c. à s. de crème fraîche épaisse • 10 cl de lait

- Pilez rapidement les glaçons au blender.
- Ajoutez les barres Bounty® coupées en morceaux, ainsi que la glace, la crème fraîche et le lait.
- Mixez pendant 1 min environ, jusqu'à ce que le mélange soit lisse et crémeux.
- Répartissez le milk-shake dans 4 verres.
- Servez sans attendre.

Milk-shake au Bounty® viennois

Nappez le milk-shake de sirop de chocolat, puis recouvrez de crème Chantilly.

Milk-shake au Bounty® et au rhum

Ajoutez 1 bouchon de rhum ambré à la préparation.

Duo de milk-shake Bounty®-chocolat

Divisez les quantités des ingrédients par deux. Préparez un autre milk-shake en mixant 2 boules de glace au chocolat avec 15 cl de lait. Répartissez le milk-shake au Bounty® dans les verres et déposez très délicatement le milk-shake au chocolat par-dessus, en le faisant couler le long d'une cuillère.

Milk-shake et brochette de fruits exotiques

Servez les milk-shakes accompagnés de brochettes, sur lesquelles vous alternerez des morceaux de kiwi, de banane, de mangue, d'ananas et de carambole.

Bounty®

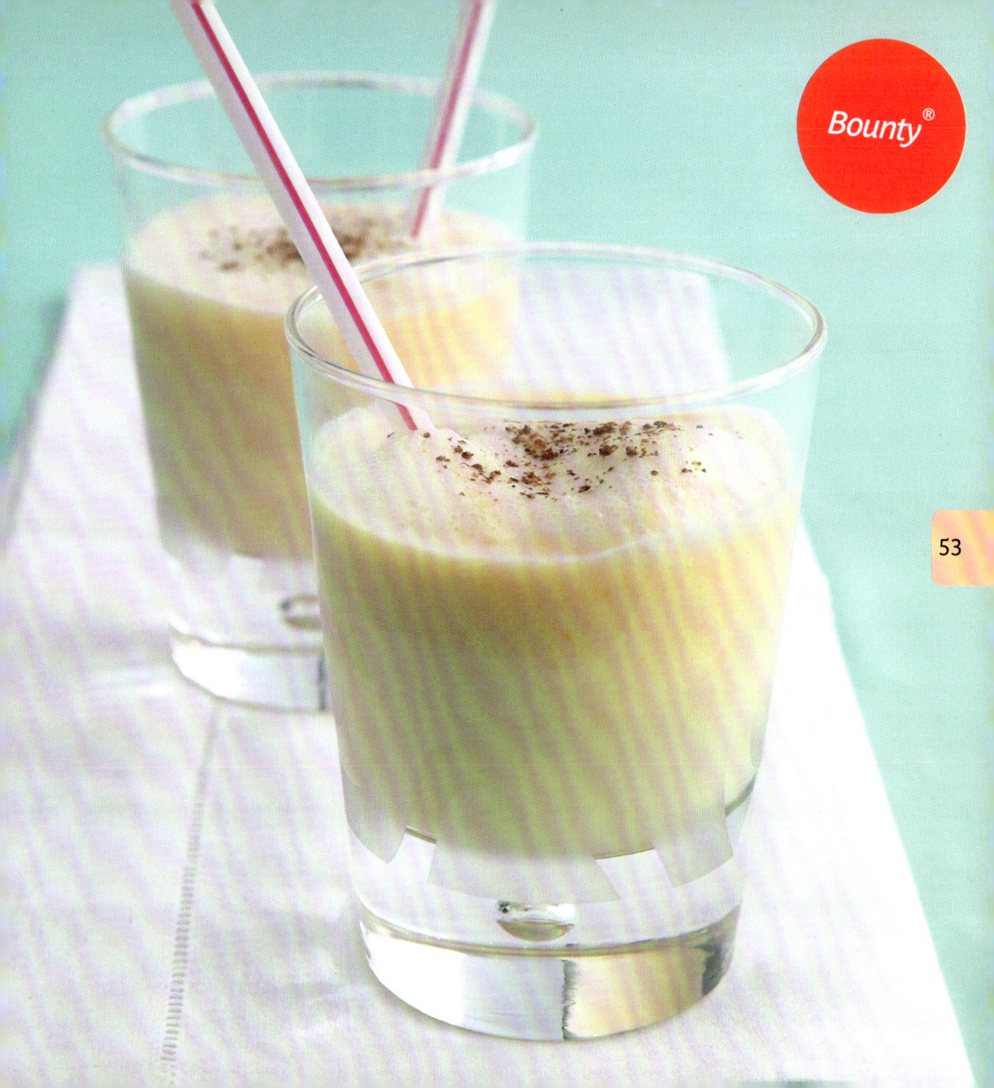

MOUSSE RÉGRESSIVE AU BOUNTY®

Préparation : 10 min • **Cuisson :** 5 min • **Réfrigération :** 3 h • **Pour 4 personnes**

3 barres Bounty® • 5 c. à s. de lait • 2 œufs + 1 blanc
3 c. à s. de crème fraîche épaisse

- Coupez les barres Bounty® en morceaux et mettez-les dans une casserole avec le lait. Faites fondre à feu doux en mélangeant régulièrement, puis retirez la casserole du feu.
- Séparez les blancs des jaunes d'œufs. Montez les 3 blancs d'œufs en neige ferme.
- Ajoutez les 2 jaunes ainsi que la crème fraîche dans la casserole contenant les Bounty® fondus. Mélangez bien. Incorporez délicatement les blancs en neige.
- Répartissez la préparation dans des ramequins. Réservez au réfrigérateur pendant 3 h avant de servir.

Mousse glacée au Bounty®

Versez la préparation dans une sorbetière et faites-la turbiner de façon à obtenir une crème glacée. Conservez-la au congélateur.

Ananas à la mousse au Bounty®

Faites caraméliser 8 tranches d'ananas nappées d'un sirop de sucre au four. Servez-les chaudes, accompagnées de 2 c. à s. de mousse au Bounty®.

Tartelettes de shortbreads au Bounty®

Mixez 1 paquet de shortbreads avec 100 g de beurre en parcelles et 3 c. à s. d'eau. Répartissez le mélange dans des moules à tartelette beurrés. Réservez au frais pendant 15 min. Garnissez les fonds de tarte de mousse au Bounty®. Réservez au frais jusqu'au moment de servir.

Mousse au Bounty® sur chips de mangue

Faites frire 2 mangues taillées en fines tranches en plusieurs fois. Égouttez-les, puis laissez-les refroidir. Garnissez chaque chips de 2 c. à s. de mousse au Bounty®.

Bounty®

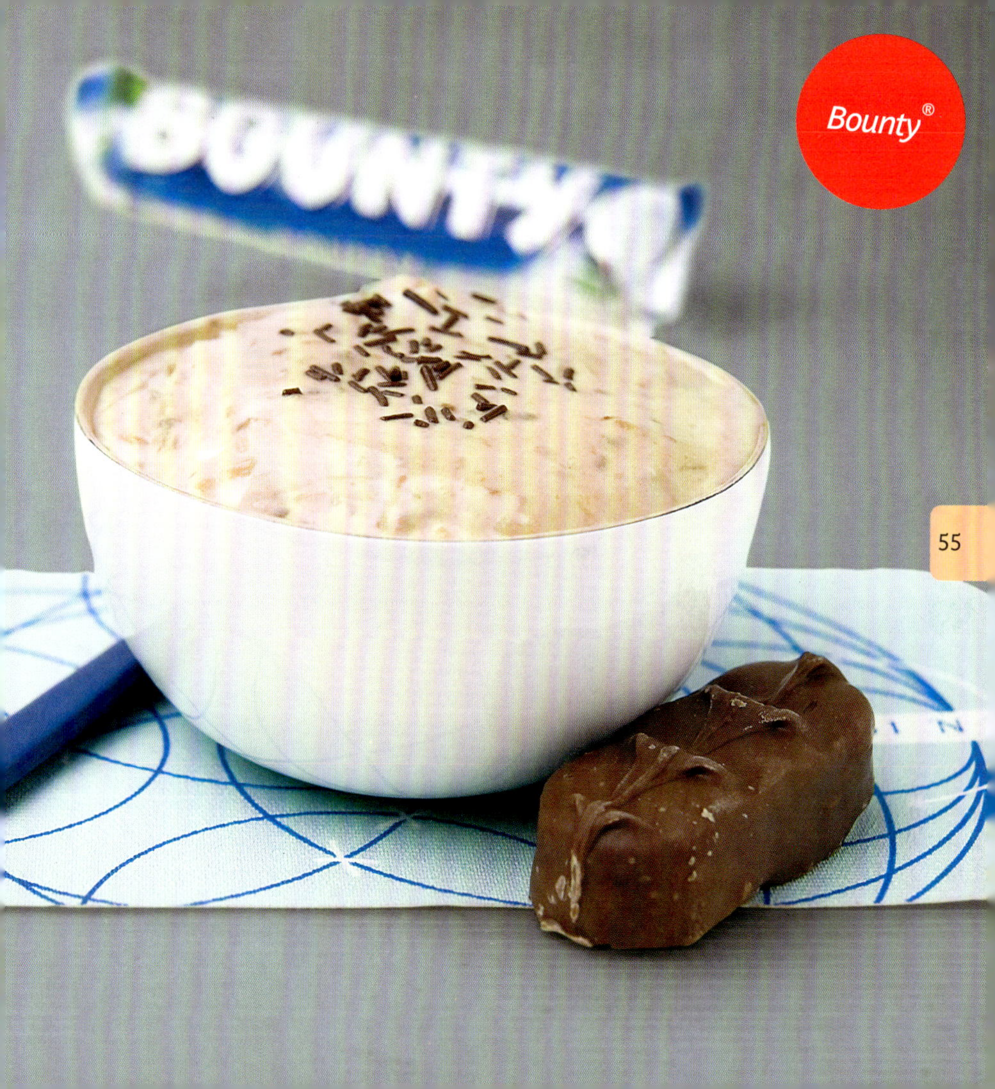

COCKTAIL VIENNOIS AU CAFÉ

Préparation : 5 min • **Cuisson** : aucune • **Pour 1 personne**

café moulu Jacques Vabre® Nectar • 10 cl de crème fraîche épaisse
glaçons • 6 cl de crème liquide • 1 cl de sirop de chocolat
1/2 c. à c. de cannelle • brisures de chocolat

- Préparez du café dans une cafetière avec le café moulu Jacques Vabre® Nectar et de l'eau. Laissez refroidir complètement.
- Battez la crème fraîche épaisse au fouet jusqu'à ce qu'elle épaississe légèrement.
- Remplissez la moitié d'un shaker de glaçons.
- Versez-y 12 cl du café refroidi, la crème liquide et le sirop de chocolat. Ajoutez la cannelle.
- Agitez énergiquement puis filtrez et versez dans un verre sans pied.
- Nappez le cocktail de crème fouettée, puis parsemez de brisures de chocolat.
- Servez sans attendre.

Irish Coffee

Faites chauffer 3 cl de whisky avec 2 morceaux de sucre sans laisser bouillir. Ajoutez 4 cl de café Jacques Vabre® Nectar chaud et remuez. Versez dans un verre et nappez de crème fouettée.

Café espagnol

Faites chauffer 1 cl de triple sec, 1 cl de rhum blanc et 1 cl de liqueur de café, puis flambez. Versez dans une tasse, recouvrez de café Jacques Vabre® Nectar chaud sucré, et nappez de crème fouettée.

Café glacé

Versez 2 cl de cognac, 2 cl de crème de vanille, 6 cl de café Jacques Vabre® Nectar froid, 3 cl de crème fraîche et 2 c. à s. de sucre en poudre dans un shaker. Frappez, puis versez dans un verre rempli de glaçons.

Café brésilien

Préparez un café Jacques Vabre® Nectar et versez-le dans une tasse. Ajoutez 2 cl de cognac, 2 cl de triple sec, 2 cl de liqueur de café, et nappez de crème fouettée.

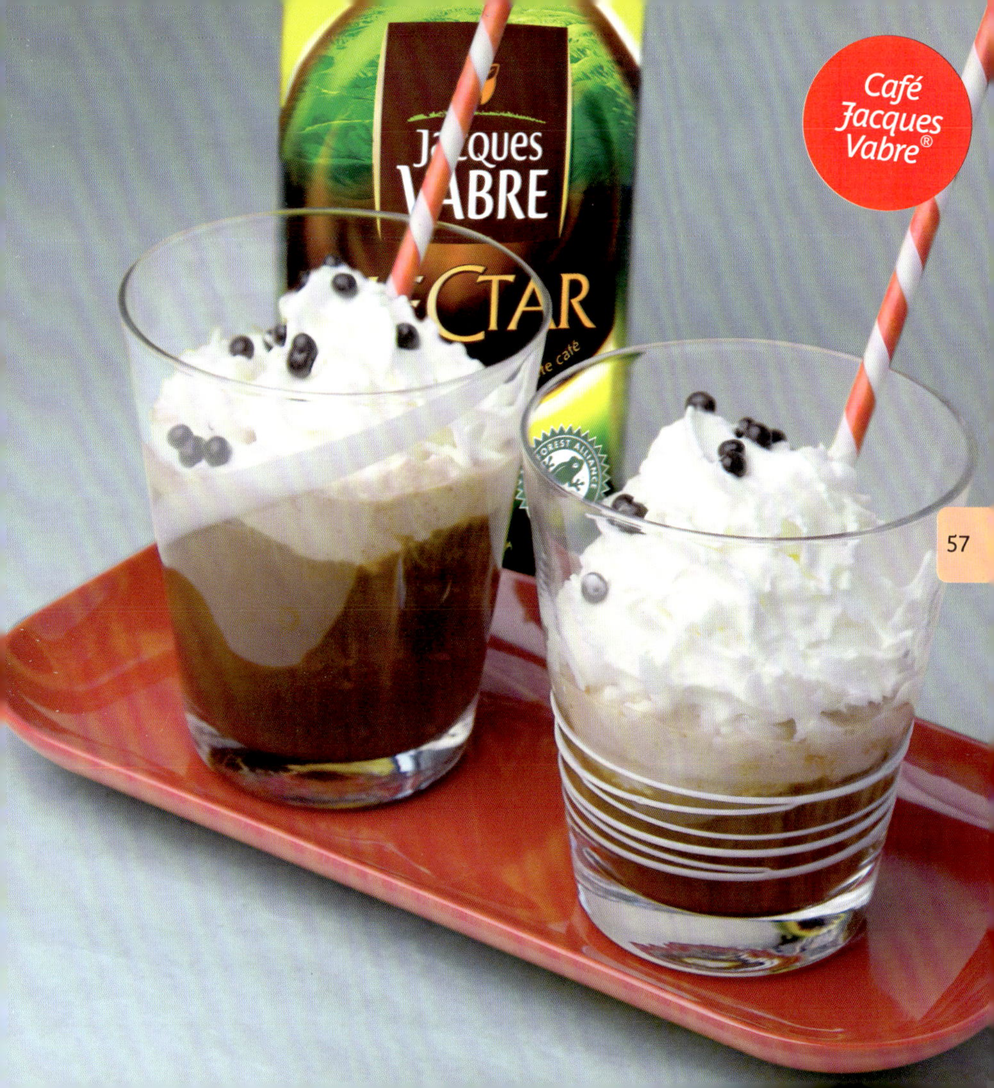

Café Jacques Vabre®

Crème renversée au café et à l'orange
Remplacez l'extrait de vanille liquide par le zeste râpé de 1 orange non traitée.

Crème renversée au café et aux épices
Remplacez l'extrait de vanille liquide par 1/2 c. à c. de cannelle, 1 pincée de cardamome et 1 pincée de gingembre en poudre.

Crème renversée au café et aux sablés
Émiettez grossièrement de 8 à 10 sablés bretons et parsemez-en le fond des ramequins avant d'y ajouter la préparation. Vous pouvez aussi utiliser des shortbreads.

Café Jacques Vabre®

CRÈME RENVERSÉE AU CAFÉ

Préparation : 20 min • **Cuisson :** 40 min • **Réfrigération :** 12 h
Pour 6 personnes

270 g de sucre en poudre • café moulu Jacques Vabre® Nectar
30 cl de lait • 25 cl de crème fraîche épaisse • 4 œufs
1 petite c. à s. d'extrait de vanille liquide

- Préchauffez le four à 160 °C.
- Préparez un sirop en faisant chauffer 12 cl d'eau et 225 g de sucre en poudre dans une casserole à feu vif, sans faire bouillir, jusqu'à ce que le sucre soit dissous. Portez ensuite à ébullition, puis laissez frémir sans mélanger jusqu'à ce que le sirop soit bien doré. Versez le sirop dans 6 ramequins supportant la chaleur en les faisant tourner pour bien en recouvrir les parois et le fond.
- Préparez un café fort avec le café moulu Jacques Vabre® Nectar. Versez le lait, la crème fraîche et 10 cl de café dans une casserole, et faites chauffer à feu moyen.
- Battez les œufs, la vanille et le reste de sucre dans un saladier puis incorporez petit à petit la préparation liquide, tout en remuant au fouet. Versez le mélange dans les ramequins.
- Posez les ramequins dans un grand plat à four et remplissez-le d'eau bouillante de façon que les ramequins soient immergés jusqu'à mi-hauteur. Faites cuire de 25 à 30 min, jusqu'à ce que les crèmes aient bien pris. Laissez refroidir complètement.
- Réservez au réfrigérateur pendant 12 h. Renversez les crèmes dans des assiettes juste avant de servir.

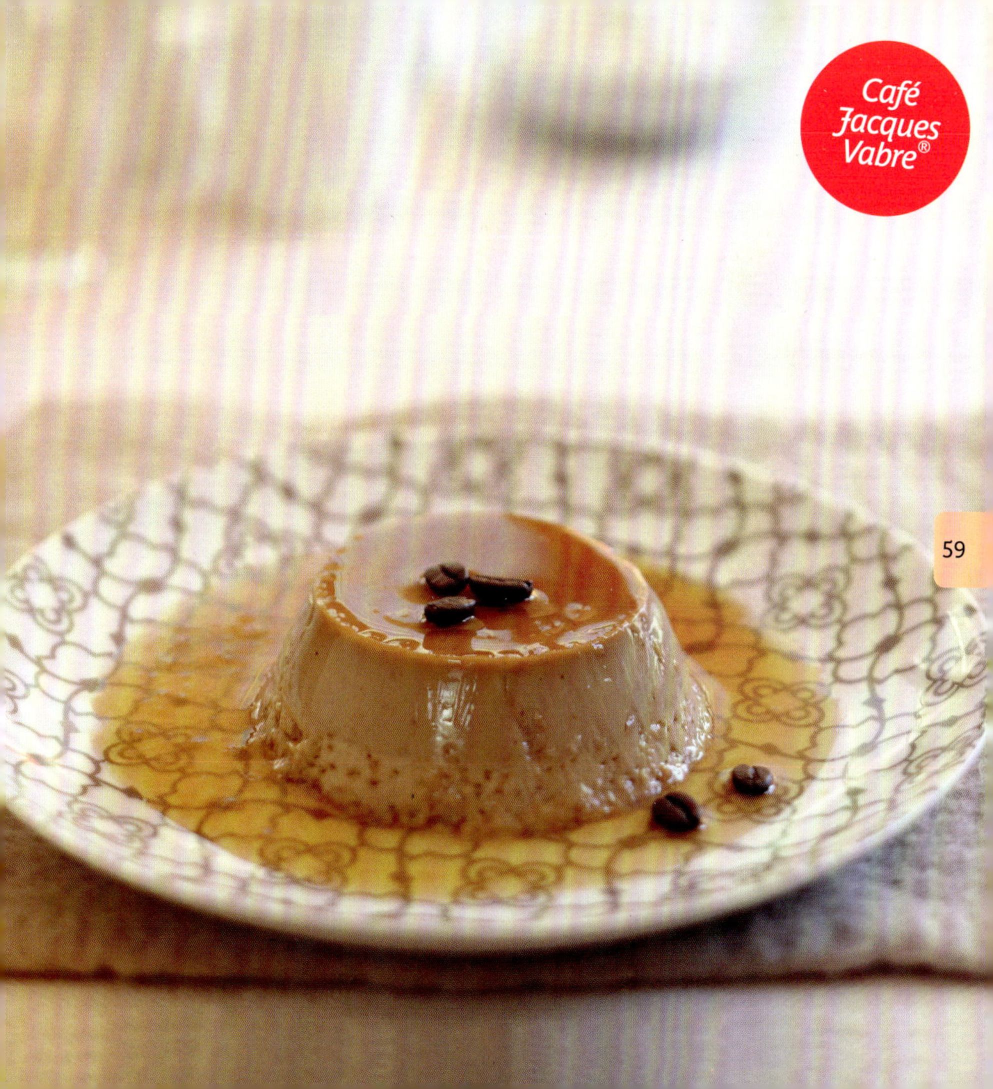
Café
Jacques
Vabre®

Café Jacques Vabre®

NAGE DE POISSONS ET CHANTILLY AU CAFÉ

Préparation : 15 min • **Cuisson** : 30 min • **Pour 6 personnes**

pour la nage de poissons *: 4 échalotes • 1 carotte • 1 blanc de poireau*
2 c. à s. d'huile d'olive • 1 pincée de noix muscade râpée
1 clou de girofle • 400 g de filets de saumon • 400 g de dos de cabillaud
400 g de filets de merlan • 18 crevettes • sel et poivre
pour la chantilly *: 15 cl de crème liquide très froide*
1 c. à c. de café soluble Jacques Vabre® • sel et poivre

- Épluchez les échalotes et pelez la carotte, puis hachez-les, ainsi que le poireau.
- Faites chauffer l'huile dans une cocotte, puis faites-y revenir le tout pendant 5 min. Ajoutez 1,5 l d'eau, les épices, du sel et du poivre. Portez à ébullition, puis laissez frémir pendant 20 min.
- Pendant ce temps, battez la crème liquide en chantilly avec le café soluble Jacques Vabre®. Salez et poivrez.
- Détaillez les poissons en cubes et décortiquez les crevettes.
- Filtrez la nage, puis remettez-la dans la cocotte. Portez à frémissements, puis plongez-y les filets de poissons et laissez frémir de 2 à 3 min, puis ajoutez les crevettes et poursuivez la cuisson pendant 2 min.
- Retirez les morceaux de poissons et les crevettes du bouillon à l'aide d'une écumoire, puis répartissez-les dans 6 assiettes creuses. Arrosez de bouillon.
- Déposez 1 c. à s. de chantilly au café sur chaque assiette et servez sans attendre.

Nage de poissons au citron vert
Ajoutez le jus de 2 citrons verts dans la nage après avoir retiré les morceaux de poissons et les crevettes. Remuez avant de verser dans les assiettes.

Nage de poissons pimentée
Ajoutez 1 pincée de piment de Cayenne en même temps que les épices. Vous pouvez également ajouter 1 petit piment rouge taillé en rondelles.

Nage de poissons au safran
Remplacez les épices et le piment par 1 c. à c. de filaments de safran.

Nage de fruits de mer
Remplacez les poissons par les mêmes quantités de queues de langoustines décortiquées, de noix de saint-jacques et de moules cuites décoquillées. Faites cuire les langoustines avec les crevettes, pendant 2 min, et le reste pendant 1 min.

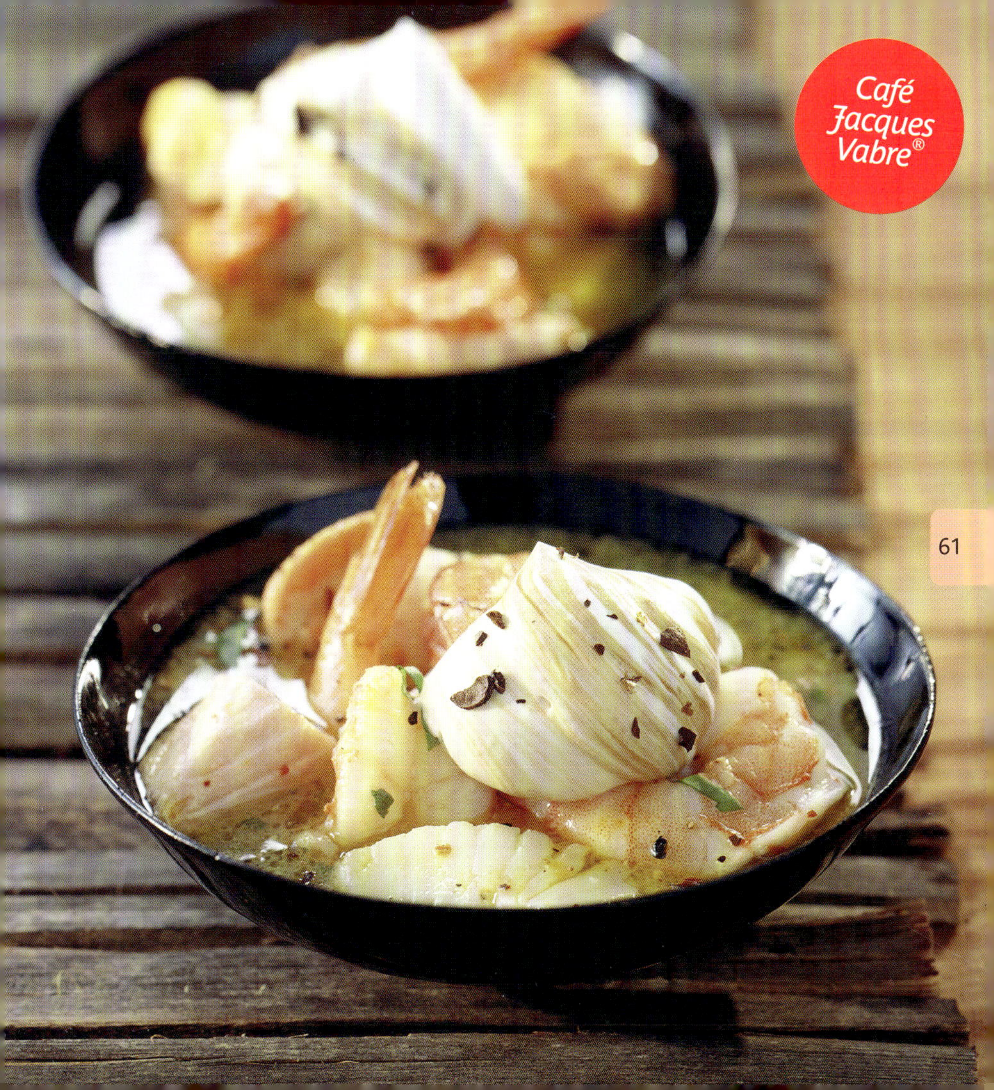
Café
Jacques
Vabre®

Café Jacques Vabre®

PAVLOVAS AU CAFÉ

Préparation : 15 min • **Cuisson :** 40 min • **Pour 6 pavlovas**

2 blancs d'œufs • 115 g de sucre glace • 100 g de chocolat
45 cl de crème fraîche épaisse • 1 c. à c. de café soluble Jacques Vabre®

- Préchauffez le four à 130 °C.
- Tapissez 2 plaques à pâtisserie de papier sulfurisé, puis dessinez les contours de 9 cercles de 7 cm de diamètre sur chaque feuille.
- Battez les blancs en neige dans un saladier à l'aide d'un fouet électrique. Incorporez petit à petit le sucre tout en continuant de battre à grande vitesse, jusqu'à ce que le sucre soit dissous, et la meringue, épaisse et brillante.
- Déposez 1 c. à s. de meringue au centre de chaque cercle, puis étalez la préparation de façon qu'elle remplisse le cercle.
- Faites cuire au four pendant 40 min, ou jusqu'à ce que les meringues soient fermes et sèches au toucher.
- Pendant ce temps, râpez le chocolat. Faites-le chauffer au bain-marie avec 15 cl de crème fraîche dans une petite casserole jusqu'à ce que le mélange soit lisse. Retirez du feu et réservez.
- Dissolvez le café soluble Jacques Vabre® dans 1 c. à s. d'eau. Battez le reste de crème avec le café dissous au fouet électrique jusqu'à ce que le mélange forme des pointes.
- Empilez les cercles de meringue trois par trois en déposant entre chaque une couche épaisse de crème au café.
- Servez-les nappés de sauce au chocolat.

Pavlovas au café et au chocolat

Pour les meringues, remplacez 15 g de sucre glace par 15 g de cacao amer en poudre.

Pavlovas au café et aux noisettes

Ajoutez 75 g de noisettes concassées à la crème au café.

Pavlovas à la mousse au café

Mélangez 2 jaunes d'œufs avec 40 g de sucre dans une casserole. Versez 7 cl de lait bouillant et mélangez jusqu'à ce que la crème nappe la cuillère. Ajoutez 1/2 c. à s. de café soluble Jacques Vabre® et réservez. Battez 2 blancs d'œufs en neige et incorporez-y 1 c. à s. de café soluble Jacques Vabre®. Mélangez les deux préparations. Remplacez la crème au café par ce mélange.

Coulis au café

Faites fondre 160 g de sucre roux avec 18 cl d'eau, puis laissez frémir de 7 à 8 min. Hors du feu, ajoutez 1 c. à s. de café soluble Jacques Vabre®. Mélangez et laissez refroidir. Servez les pavlovas nappés de ce coulis.

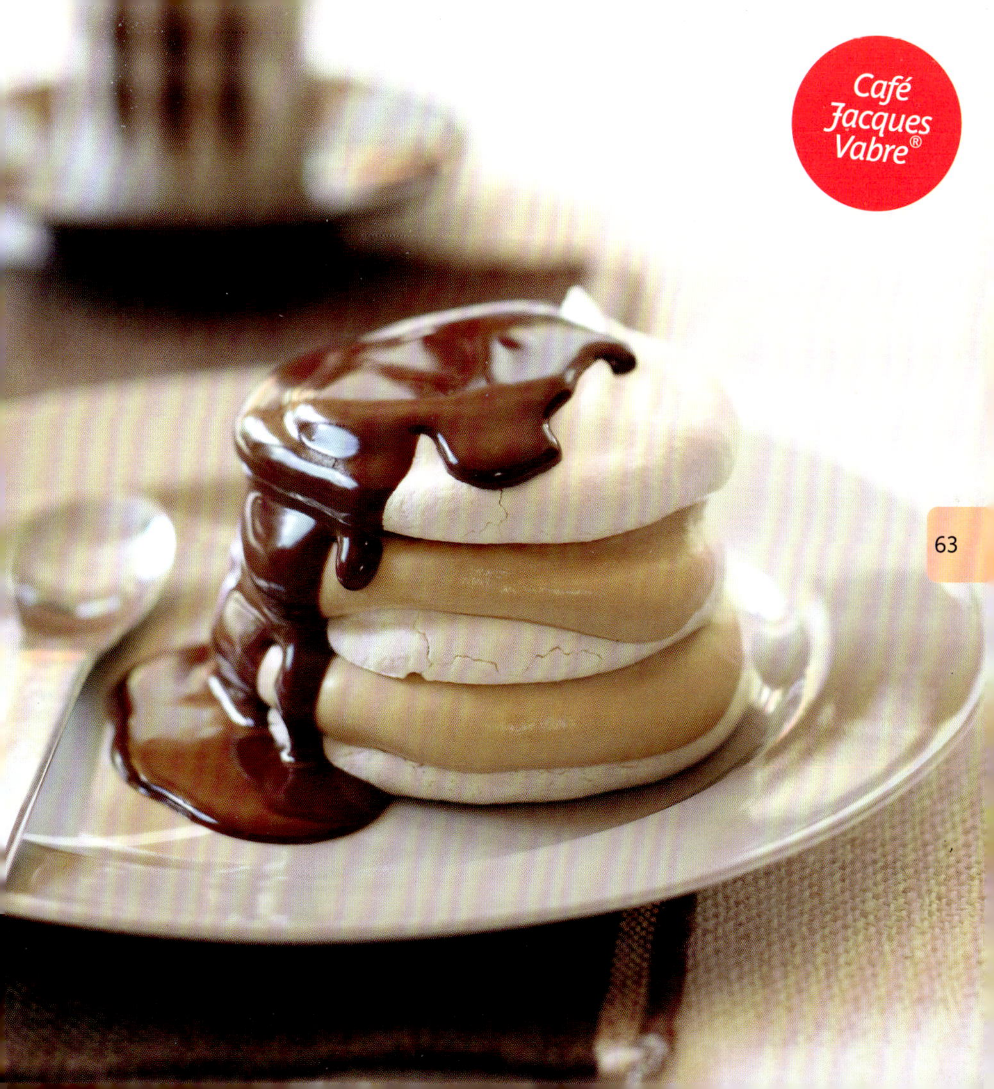
Café
Jacques
Vabre®

CIGARES AU CARAMBAR®

Préparation : 10 min • **Cuisson** : 10 min • **Pour 16 cigares**

1 rouleau de pâte feuilletée • 16 Carambar® au caramel
1 jaune d'œuf • 2 c. à s. de graines de sésame

- Préchauffez le four à 180 °C.
- Déroulez la pâte feuilletée et découpez-la en morceaux légèrement plus grands que les Carambar®.
- Déballez les Carambar® et déposez-en un sur chaque morceau de pâte feuilletée. Enroulez la pâte sur le caramel en soudant bien les bords.
- Badigeonnez chaque cigare de jaune d'œuf légèrement battu.
- Parsemez-les de graines de sésame, puis déposez-les sur une plaque à pâtisserie recouverte de papier sulfurisé.
- Faites cuire au four pendant 10 min.
- Laissez tiédir avant de déguster.

Cigares au Carambar® et aux pommes

Nappez les morceaux de pâte feuilletée d'une fine couche de compote de pommes avant d'ajouter les Carambar®.

Cigares au Carambar® et au chocolat

Faites fondre 80 g de chocolat noir à pâtisserie avec 15 cl de crème liquide. Nappez les morceaux de pâte de ce mélange avant d'ajouter les Carambar®.

Cigares au Carambar® aux grains de sucre

Remplacez les grains de sésame par des grains de sucre blanc. Vous pouvez également utiliser des grains de sucre colorés, que l'on trouve dans certaines épiceries fines.

Cigares au Carambar® aux amandes

Remplacez les graines de sésame par des amandes effilées. Vous pouvez éventuellement saupoudrer les morceaux de pâte de poudre d'amandes avant d'ajouter les Carambar®.

Carambar®

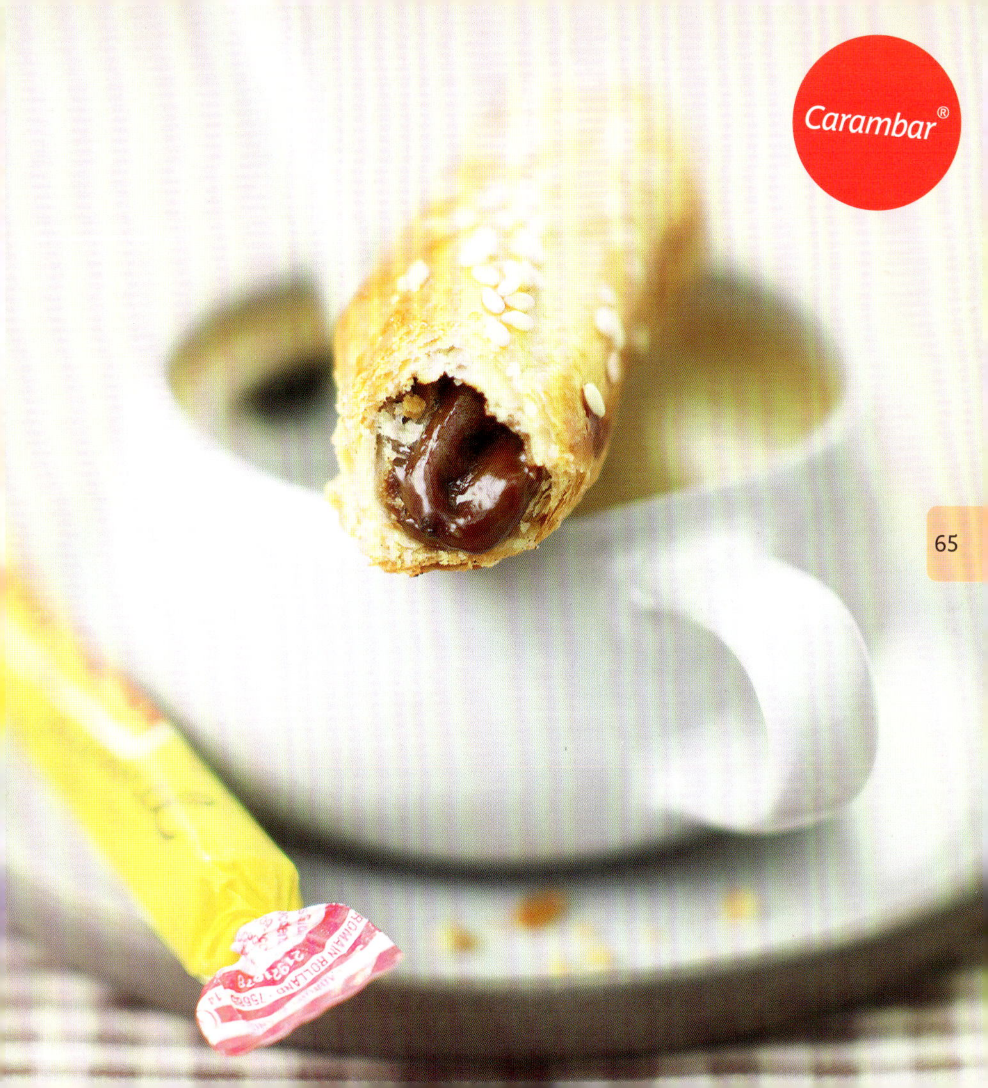

CRÈME BRÛLÉE AU CARAMBAR®

Préparation : 10 min • **Cuisson** : 1 h 10 • **Réfrigération** : 2 h
Pour 6 personnes

40 cl de crème liquide • 12 Carambar® au caramel • 4 jaunes d'œufs
60 g de sucre en poudre • 15 g de cassonade

- Préchauffez le four à 100 °C.
- Versez la crème liquide dans une casserole, portez à ébullition puis faites-y fondre les Carambar® en remuant régulièrement.
- Pendant ce temps, battez les jaunes d'œufs avec le sucre jusqu'à ce que le mélange blanchisse, puis ajoutez la crème au Carambar® bouillante. Remuez doucement, puis passez au chinois pour éliminer la mousse.
- Répartissez la préparation dans 6 ramequins supportant la chaleur. Déposez-les dans un grand plat à four. Remplissez-le d'eau chaude jusqu'à mi-hauteur des ramequins.
- Faites cuire au four pendant 1 h. La crème doit encore être légèrement tremblante.
- Laissez refroidir complètement, puis réservez les crèmes au réfrigérateur pendant 2 h.
- Au moment de servir, saupoudrez-les de cassonade et faites-les caraméliser au chalumeau de cuisine ou sous le gril du four.

Crème brûlée au Carambar® et au gingembre
Ajoutez 1/2 cm de gingembre frais râpé dans la crème liquide avant de porter à ébullition.

Crème brûlée au Carambar® et au rhum
Ajoutez 1 bouchon de rhum ambré à la crème liquide avant de porter à ébullition.

Espuma au Carambar®
Faites chauffer 15 cl de crème liquide et faites-y fondre 4 Carambar® à feu doux. Filtrez puis versez dans un siphon. Réservez au frais pendant 1 h. Placez une cartouche de gaz dans le siphon. Secouez vivement, puis déposez un peu d'espuma sur chaque crème brûlée juste avant de servir.

Espuma à la vanille
Reprenez la technique ci-dessus en remplaçant le mélange à base de Carambar® par 25 cl de crème anglaise à la vanille bien froide. Servez avec la crème brûlée au Carambar®.

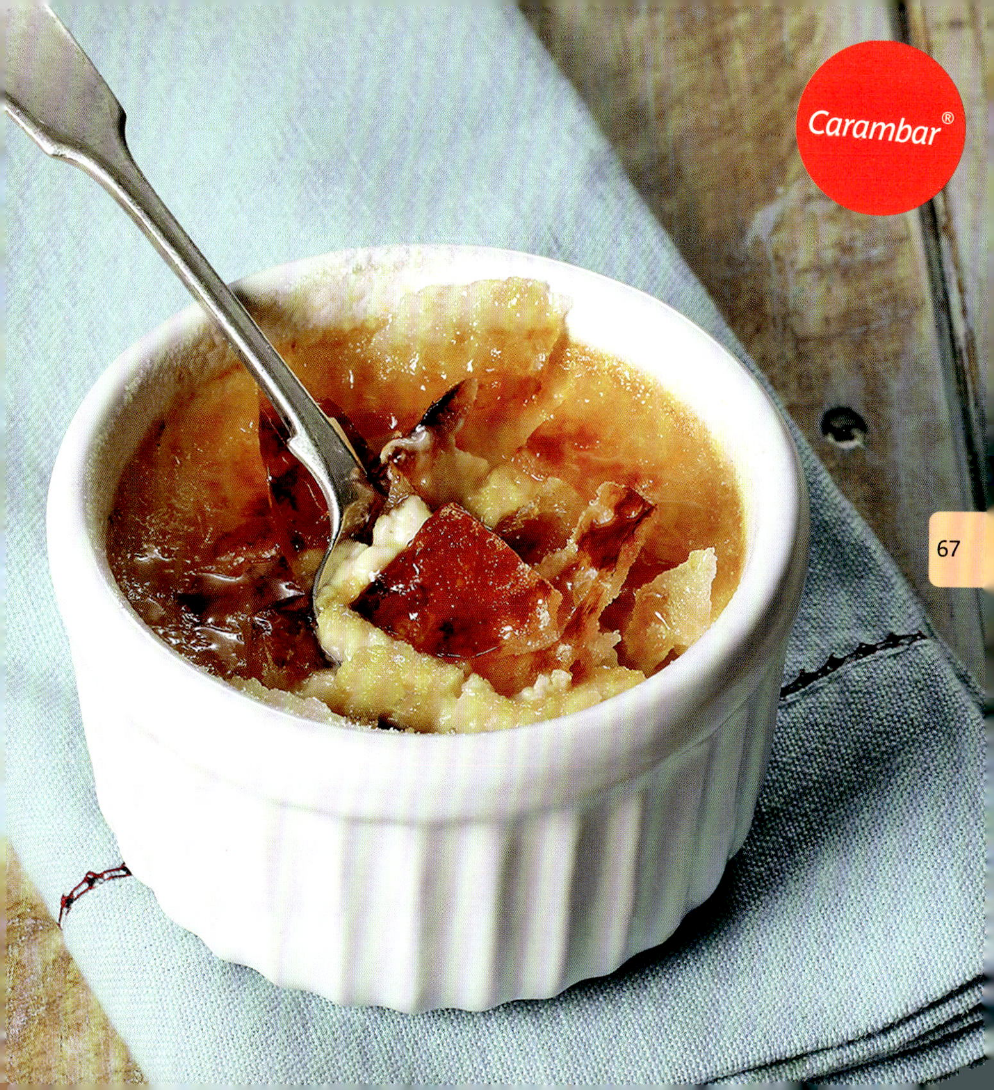

Carambar®

GÂTEAU AUX POIRES AU CARAMBAR®

Préparation : 20 min • **Cuisson** : 40 min • **Pour 6 personnes**

30 cl de crème liquide • 6 Carambar® au caramel • 1 pot de yaourt brassé nature • 125 g de sucre • 12,5 cl de crème liquide • 250 g de farine 1 sachet de levure chimique • 3 œufs • 2 poires

- Préchauffez le four à 180 °C.
- Versez la crème liquide dans une casserole, portez à ébullition, puis faites-y fondre les Carambar® en remuant régulièrement. Retirez du feu et laissez refroidir et durcir le temps de préparer le gâteau.
- Mettez le contenu du pot de yaourt dans un saladier. Ajoutez le sucre, la crème liquide, la farine et la levure. Mélangez bien.
- Incorporez les œufs un à un, en remuant entre chaque ajout.
- Coupez le caramel de Carambar® en carrés à l'aide d'une paire de ciseaux, puis incorporez-en les 2/3 à la pâte.
- Pelez les poires, coupez-les en quatre, retirez le cœur et les pépins, puis coupez-les en 12 morceaux.
- Versez la pâte dans un moule à manqué tapissé de papier sulfurisé, puis disposez les quartiers de poire par-dessus. Parsemez du reste de dés de caramel au Carambar®.
- Faites cuire au four pendant 40 min.
- Laissez refroidir avant de servir.

Gâteau poires-Carambar® aux amandes

Remplacez 90 g de farine par de la poudre d'amandes. Remplacez le yaourt brassé nature par 20 cl de lait d'amandes.

Gâteau aux abricots et au Carambar®

Remplacez les poires par 5 abricots dénoyautés et coupés en quatre. Vous pouvez aussi utiliser 2 pêches pelées et dénoyautées.

Gâteau au coing et au Carambar®

Remplacez les poires par 1 coing pelé, détaillé en morceaux et cuit à la casserole avec un peu d'eau pendant 15 min.

Glace à la cannelle

Faites bouillir 50 cl de lait avec 1 c. à s. de cannelle en poudre pendant 2 min. Battez 6 jaunes d'œufs et 150 g de sucre en poudre au fouet dans une jatte. Incorporez le lait petit à petit puis remettez le tout dans la casserole et faites épaissir en remuant, sur feu doux. Passez au chinois et laissez refroidir. Faites turbiner en sorbetière. Servez avec le gâteau.

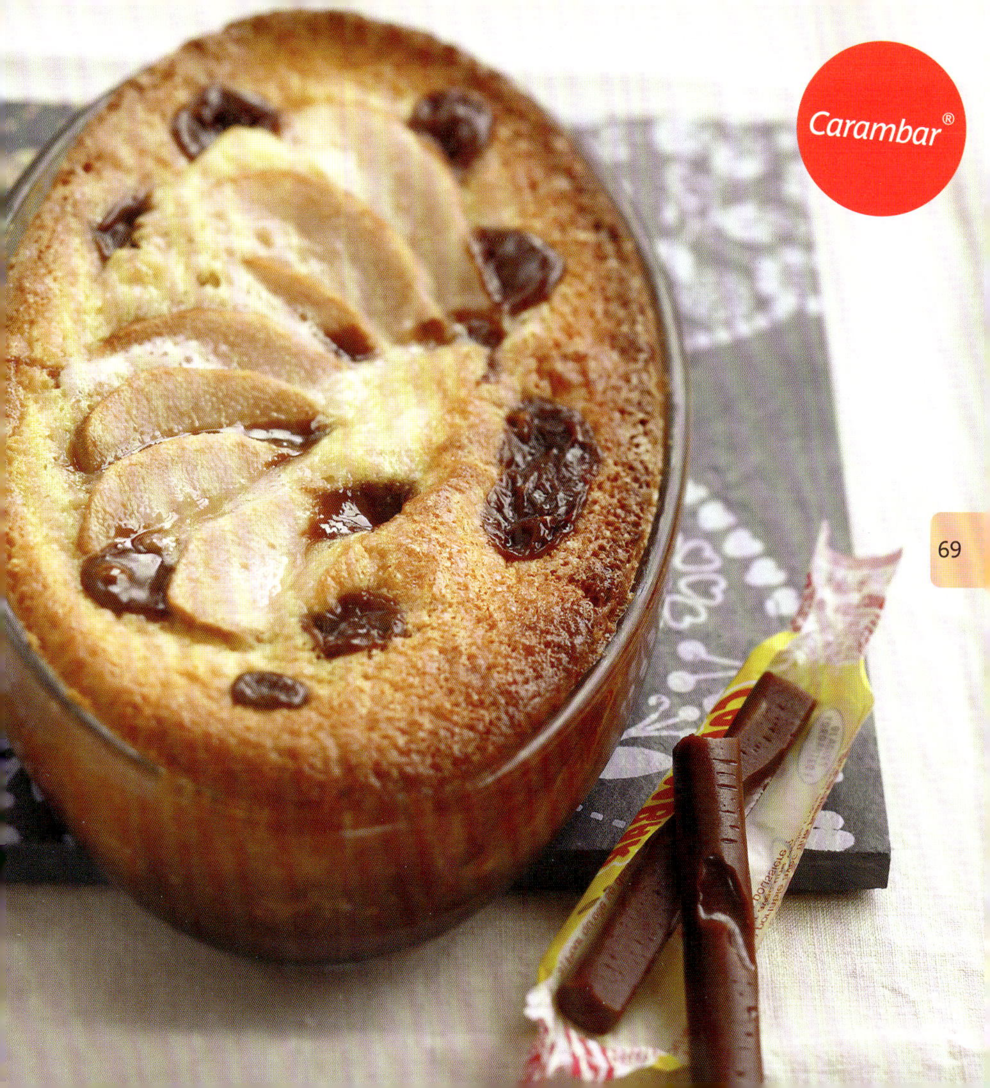
Carambar®

POIRES À LA VANILLE, SAUCE AU CARAMBAR®

Préparation : 15 min • **Cuisson** : 15 min • **Pour 4 personnes**

pour les poires au sirop : 4 poires • le jus de 1 citron
250 g de sucre en poudre • 2 gousses de vanille
pour la sauce au Carambar® : 12 Carambar® • 10 cl de crème liquide

- Pelez les poires, coupez-les en quatre, puis retirez le cœur et les pépins. Coupez la chair en cubes. Arrosez-les d'un peu de jus de citron.
- Mettez le sucre, 50 cl d'eau, le reste de jus de citron, les graines grattées des gousses de vanille ainsi que les gousses dans une casserole. Ajoutez les morceaux de poire.
- Portez à ébullition, puis laissez frémir de 10 à 15 min, jusqu'à ce que les morceaux de poire soient tendres.
- Laissez refroidir.
- Pendant ce temps, préparez la sauce au Carambar® : coupez les Carambar® en morceaux et mettez-les dans une casserole avec la crème liquide. Faites chauffer à feu doux en remuant, jusqu'à ce que les Carambar® soient fondus. Laissez tiédir.
- Répartissez les morceaux de poire dans des verrines. Arrosez d'un peu de sirop, puis nappez de sauce au Carambar®.

Poires aux épices douces
Ajoutez 1 clou de girofle, 2 capsules de cardamome, 1 bâton de cannelle et 1 étoile de badiane au sirop.

Sauce au Carambar® au beurre salé
Incorporez 35 g de beurre demi-sel à la sauce au Carambar® chaude. Faites fondre en remuant.

Samoussas aux poires et au Carambar®
Coupez 8 feuilles de brick en deux, puis encore en deux, pour former de longues bandes. Badigeonnez-les de beurre fondu. Déposez 1 c. à s. de morceaux de poire au sirop dans un angle, puis pliez de façon à former des samoussas. Faites dorer à la poêle avec un peu d'huile de tournesol. Servez-les nappés de sauce au Carambar®.

Tarte aux poires et au Carambar®
Doublez les quantités de Carambar® et de crème liquide pour la sauce. Incorporez-y 4 œufs. Répartissez les cubes de poire sur une pâte sablée, couvrez du mélange au Carambar®. Faites cuire au four à 180 °C de 35 à 40 min.

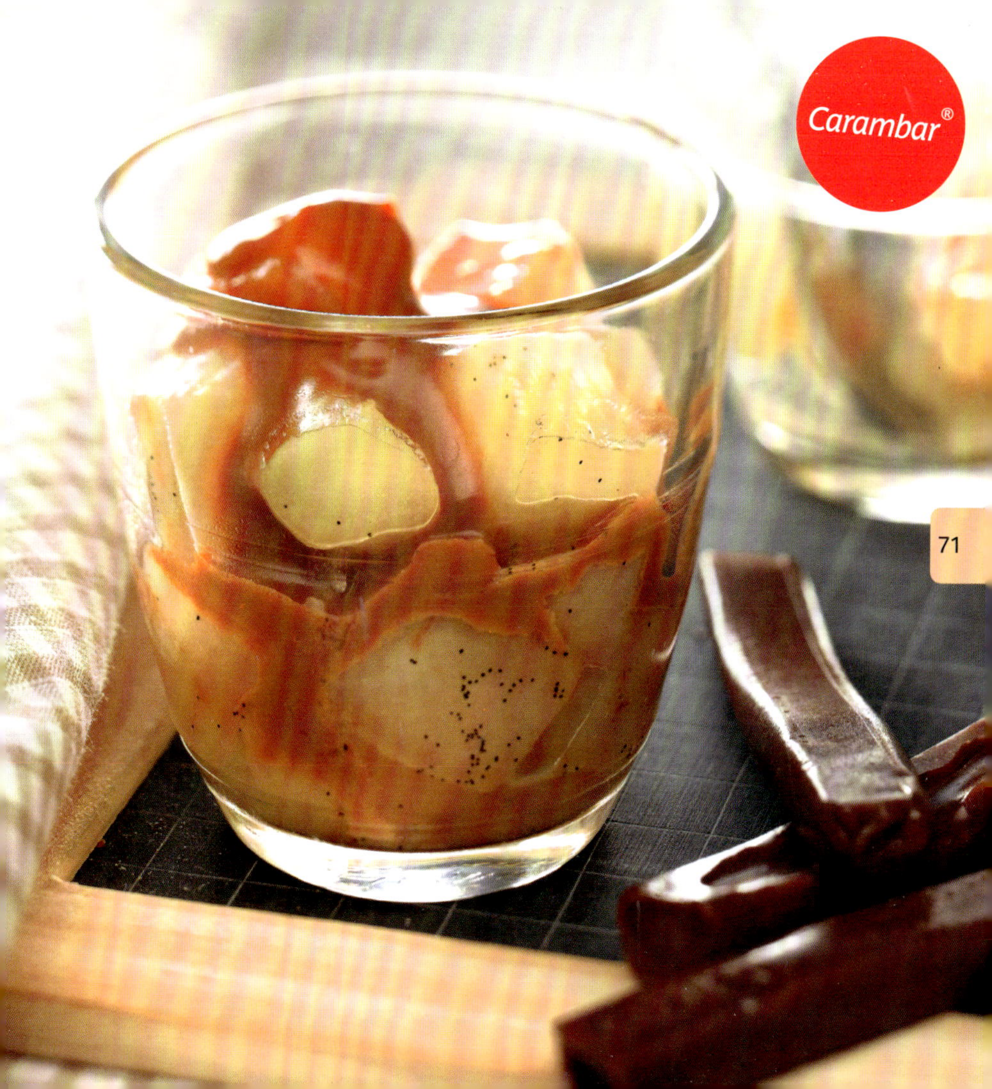
Carambar®

RIZ AU LAIT AU CARAMBAR®

Préparation : 5 min • **Cuisson :** 22 min • **Pour 2 ou 3 personnes**

100 g de riz rond • 50 cl de lait frais entier • 40 g de sucre • 6 Carambar®

- Faites cuire le riz pendant 2 min dans un grand volume d'eau bouillante, puis égouttez-le.
- Mettez-le dans une casserole avec le lait et faites cuire pendant 15 min en remuant régulièrement.
- Ajoutez le sucre et poursuivez la cuisson pendant 5 min.
- Laissez refroidir le riz ; il finira d'absorber le lait restant.
- Coupez les Carambar® en quatre. Incorporez-les au riz au lait tiède.
- Servez sans attendre.

Riz au lait de coco et aux mangues

Remplacez la moitié du lait par du lait de coco. Détaillez une mangue pelée et débarrassée de sa partie dure au centre en dés. Faites-les revenir à la poêle avec une noix de beurre. Ajoutez-les au riz au lait au Carambar® juste avant de servir.

Riz au lait à la fleur d'oranger et aux pistaches

Ajoutez 2 c. à c. d'eau de fleur d'oranger et 30 g de pistaches au riz au lait juste avant de servir.

Quinoa au lait de soja et au Carambar®

Remplacez le riz par 100 g de quinoa, et le lait par du lait de soja. Ajoutez éventuellement 1 sachet de sucre vanillé.

Riz au lait d'avoine et au chocolat

Remplacez le lait par du lait d'avoine (en épicerie bio) et ajoutez 3 c. à s. de cacao en poudre non sucré à la préparation.

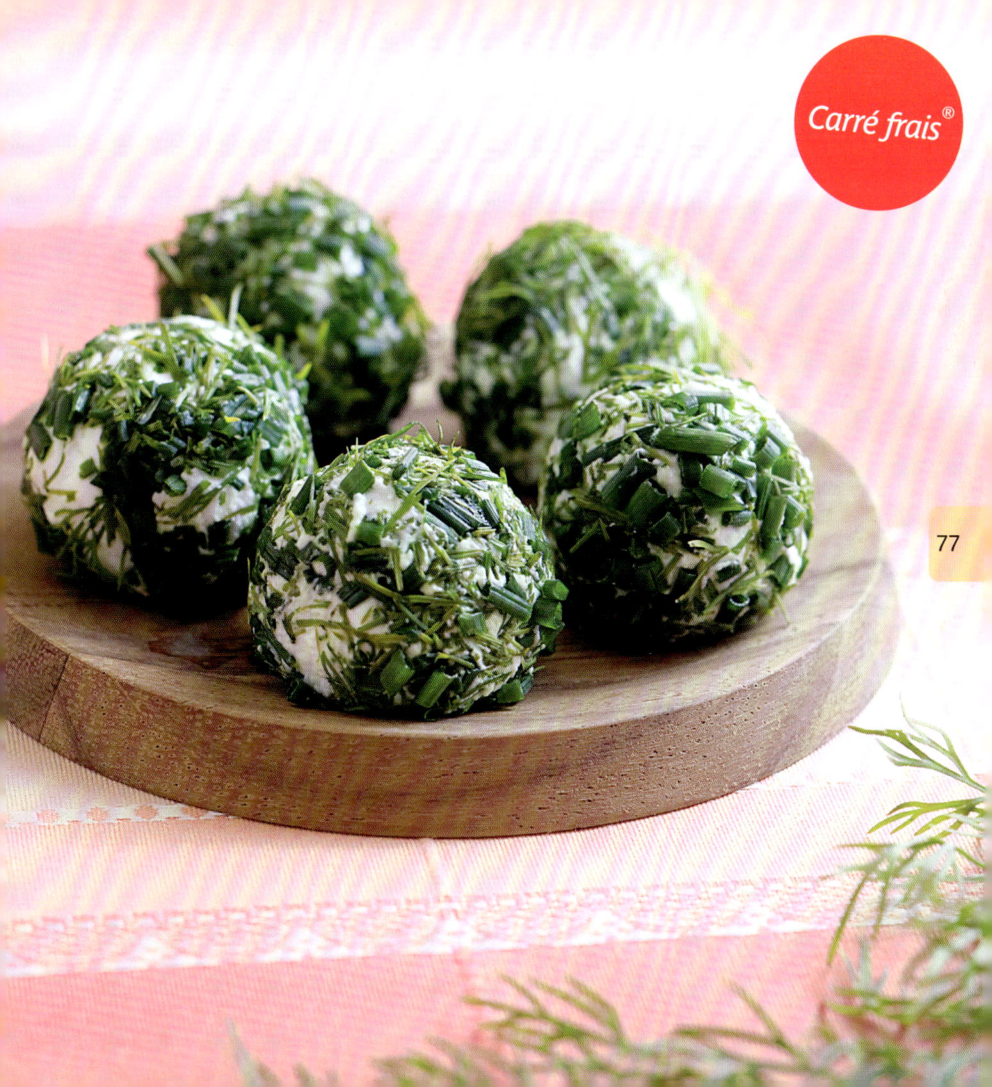

Carré frais®

CANAPÉS DE CONCOMBRE À LA COPPA ET AU TZATZIKI

Préparation : 15 min • **Cuisson :** aucune • **Pour 40 canapés**

pour le tzatziki : 1/2 concombre • 1 c. à s. de jus de citron • 1 gousse d'ail • 1 bouquet de menthe • 4 Carré frais® • 1 yaourt brassé nature • 1 c. à s. d'huile d'olive • sel et poivre

pour les canapés : 1 concombre • 10 tranches de coppa

- Pour le tzatziki, pelez le ½ concombre et coupez-le en tout petits dés. Arrosez-les de jus de citron. Salez et poivrez.
- Épluchez l'ail et hachez-le finement.
- Nettoyez soigneusement la menthe, égouttez-la sur du papier absorbant et hachez-la. Réservez-en un peu pour la décoration.
- Dans un saladier, mettez les Carré frais® et le yaourt brassé, puis fouettez.
- Ajoutez le concombre, l'ail, la menthe et l'huile d'olive. Salez et poivrez. Fouettez de nouveau pour bien mélanger.
- Pour les canapés, lavez soigneusement le concombre, sans le peler. Coupez-le en rondelles d'environ 5 mm d'épaisseur. Déposez-les sur un plat de service.
- Coupez les tranches de coppa en quatre.
- Placez 1 morceau de coppa sur chaque rondelle de concombre. Déposez l'équivalent de 1 c. à c. de tzatziki sur chaque canapé. Parsemez du reste de menthe hachée.
- Servez frais.

Sandwiches croquants au tzatziki
Coupez 40 tranches de pain croustillant suédois en deux. Déposez un canapé au concombre sur la moitié d'entre elles, surmontez d'une lamelle de coppa, d'une rondelle de concombre et d'une demi-tranche de pain croustillant.

Canapés de blinis au saumon et au tzatziki
Remplacez les rondelles de concombre par des miniblinis et la coppa par des lamelles de saumon fumé.

Verrines au concombre, aux crevettes et au tzatziki
Taillez 1 concombre pelé et épépiné en tout petits dés. Répartissez-les dans 6 petites verrines. Ajoutez de 8 à 10 crevettes cocktail, puis recouvrez de tzatziki.

Tzatziki de radis
Pour le tzatziki, remplacez le 1/2 concombre par 16 radis râpés. Remplacez la menthe par de la ciboulette. Servez sur des morceaux de pita.

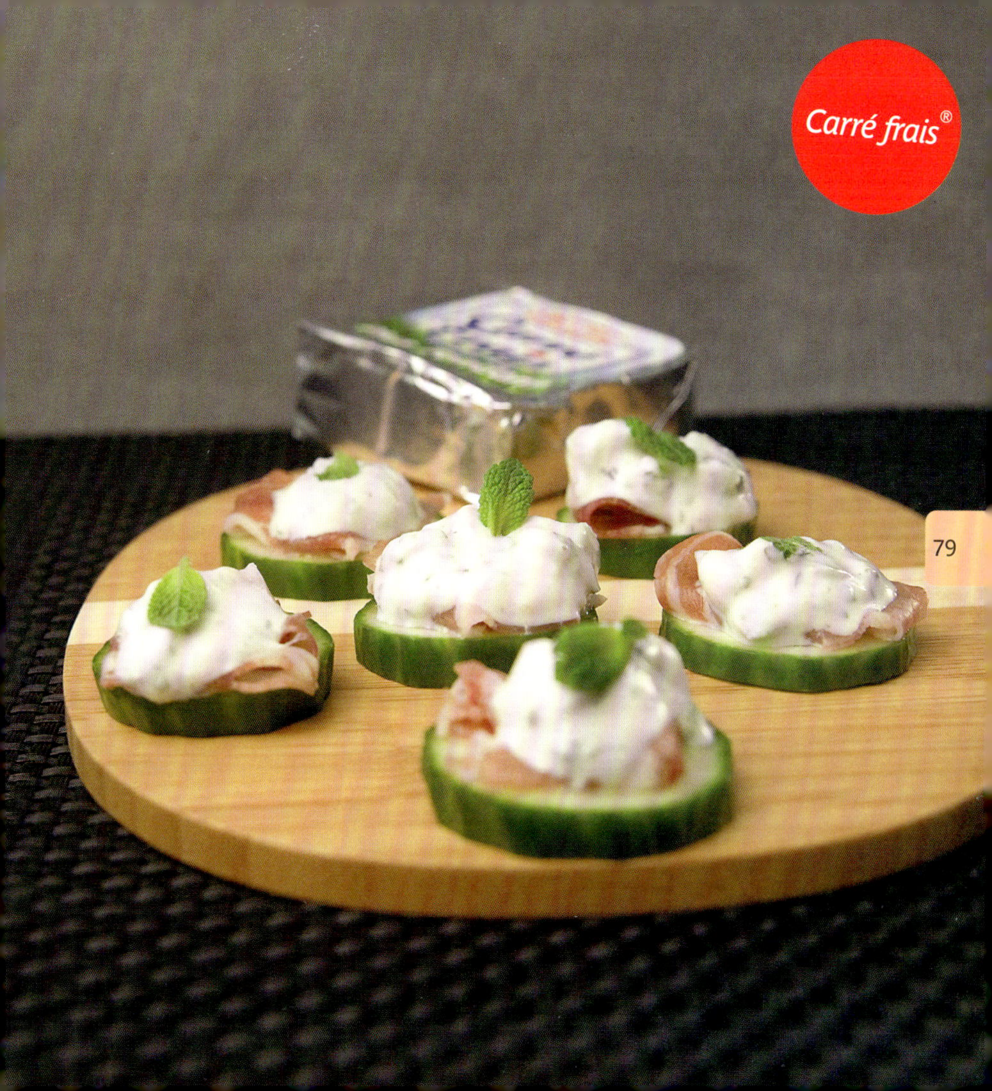

Carré frais®

Rillettes de canard au citron confit
Remplacez l'orange par 1 citron confit.

Rillettes de canard au piment d'Espelette
Remplacez l'orange et l'oignon par 2 gousses d'ail hachées, la coriandre par 1 brin de thym et 1 brin de laurier et le gingembre, par 1 c. à c. de piment d'Espelette.

Rillettes de canard aux abricots
Remplacez l'orange et les épices par 100 g d'abricots secs mis à tremper dans de l'eau chaude avec 2 brins de thym.

Rillettes de canard au poivre vert
Remplacez la coriandre et le gingembre par 1 brin de thym et 1 brin de laurier, et l'orange par 1 petite c. à c. de grains de poivre vert.

Carré frais®

RILLETTES DE CANARD À L'ORANGE

Préparation: 20 min • **Cuisson**: 35 min • **Pour 6 personnes**

2 cuisses de canard confites • 1 orange • 1 oignon
1/2 c. à c. de coriandre en poudre • 1/2 c. à c. de gingembre en poudre
1 c. à s. de cognac • 75 g de Carré frais®

- Préchauffez le four à 180 °C.
- Placez les cuisses de canard confites dans un plat allant au four et faites-les cuire pendant 20 min pour les dégraisser.
- Réservez 2 c. à s. de graisse et émiettez la chair.
- Prélevez la moitié du zeste de l'orange et la totalité de son jus.
- Épluchez l'oignon et émincez-le finement. Faites-le revenir à la poêle pendant quelques minutes avec 1 c. à s. de la graisse de canard réservée.
- Ajoutez la chair émiettée du canard, le jus et le zeste de l'orange, les épices et le cognac. Laissez cuire de 5 à 10 min pour bien mélanger les saveurs.
- Versez le mélange dans le bol du mixeur. Ajoutez le reste de graisse de canard réservée ainsi que le Carré frais® et mixez rapidement jusqu'à l'obtention d'une texture onctueuse.
- Conservez au frais jusqu'au moment de servir.

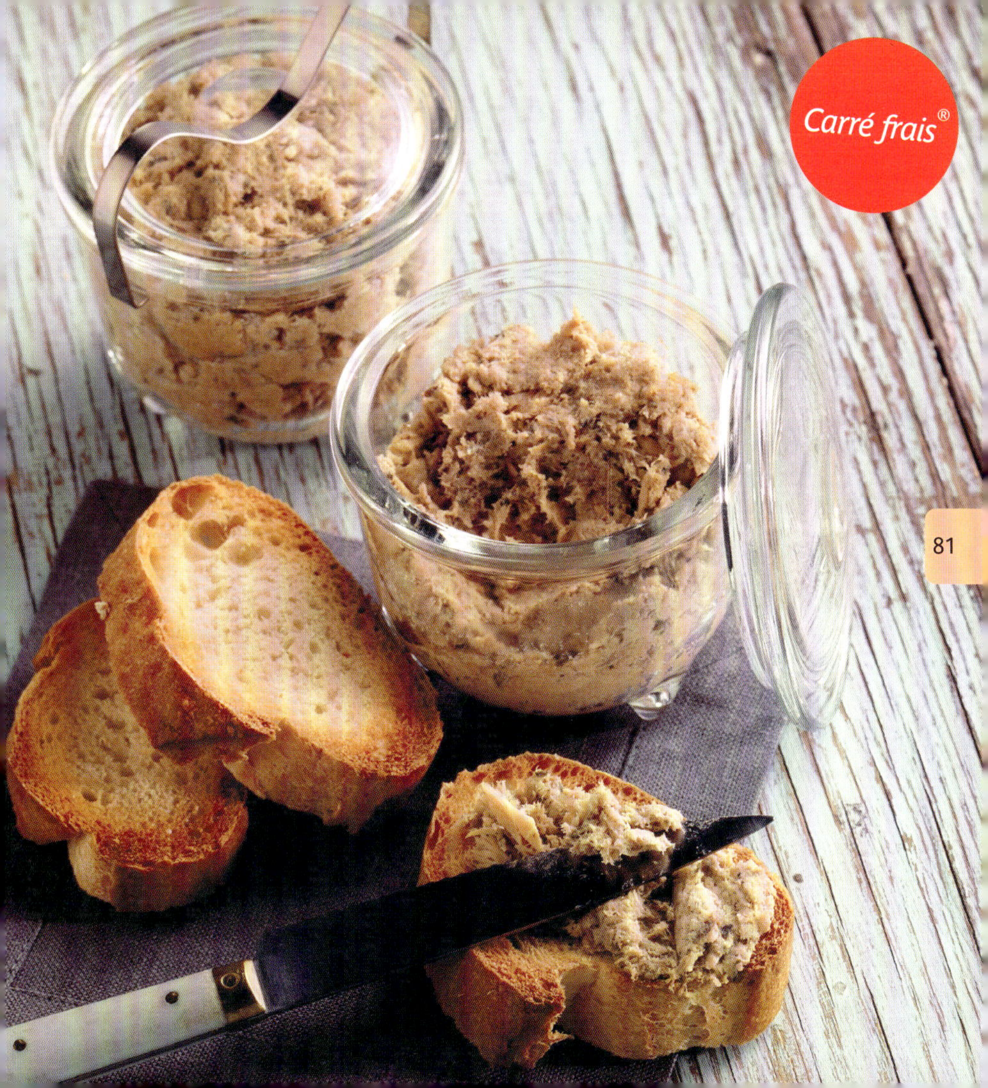
Carré frais®

Rouleaux de poivron rouge au cumin et à la coriandre
Ajoutez 1/2 c. à c. de cumin en poudre au Carré frais®. Remplacez les feuilles de basilic à l'intérieur des rouleaux par de la coriandre, et les feuilles extérieures par de la roquette.

Feuilles de vigne farcies au poivron
Faites blanchir 8 feuilles de vigne fraîches pendant 2 min dans de l'eau bouillante, puis passez-les sous l'eau froide et essuyez-les avec du papier absorbant. Laissez reposer pendant 1 journée. Remplacez les feuilles de basilic extérieures par les feuilles de vigne.

Rouleaux de poivron grillé aux abricots
Remplacez les poivrons frais par des poivrons grillés à l'huile bien égouttés. Ajoutez 6 abricots secs coupés en tout petits dés au Carré frais®.

Rouleaux d'aubergine grillée
Remplacez les poivrons par des aubergines grillées coupées en deux.

Carré frais®

ROULEAUX DE POIVRON ROUGE

Préparation : 20 min • **Cuisson :** 12 min • **Pour 4 personnes**

2 poivrons rouges • huile d'olive • 1 poignée de feuilles de basilic frais
150 g de Carré frais® • 4 tranches de jambon sec
roquette, pour accompagner

- Préchauffez le four à 200 °C.
- Coupez les poivrons en deux, retirez les pépins et la membrane blanche, puis arrosez la chair d'huile d'olive.
- Déposez les poivrons sur une plaque recouverte de papier sulfurisé et faites cuire pendant 12 min, jusqu'à ce qu'ils soient tendres.
- Pelez les poivrons, puis coupez chaque moitié en deux.
- Lavez les feuilles de basilic, puis essuyez-les avec du papier absorbant. Écrasez le Carré frais® à la fourchette. Coupez les tranches de jambon en deux.
- Disposez les feuilles de basilic trois par trois, côte à côte, sur une planche à découper. Déposez un quartier de poivron sur chaque trio de feuilles. Placez par-dessus les feuilles de basilic restantes, puis le fromage frais et, enfin, le jambon. Roulez.
- Servez sur un lit de roquette.

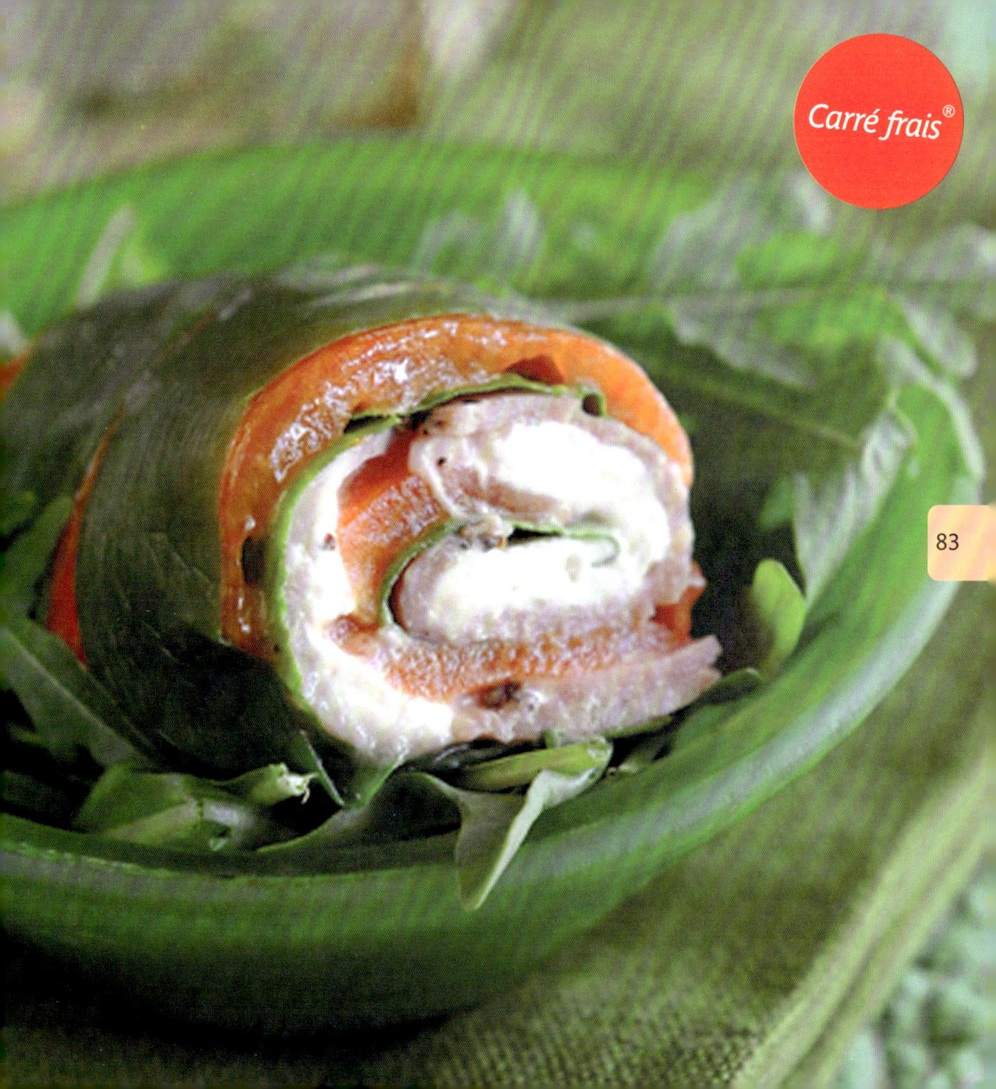
Carré frais®

ROULÉS DE SAUMON ET SAUCE À L'AVOCAT

Préparation : 25 min • **Cuisson** : aucune • **Pour 4 personnes**

pour les roulés : *1/2 concombre • 100 g de Carré frais®*
1 c. à c. de sucre • 4 galettes de riz • 4 tranches de saumon fumé
1/2 bouquet de ciboulette • 2 c. à c. d'œufs de saumon • sel et poivre
pour la sauce : *1 avocat • le jus de 2 petits citrons*
1 c. à c. de Tabasco® • sel

- Pour les roulés, pelez le concombre, épépinez-le et coupez-le en tout petits dés. Mélangez-les avec le Carré frais® dans un bol, salez et poivrez.
- Faites fondre le sucre dans un verre d'eau tiède. Déposez 1 galette de riz sur un torchon humide et badigeonnez-la d'eau sucrée, à l'aide d'un pinceau.
- Recouvrez de 1 tranche de saumon, puis nappez du mélange au concombre. Roulez la galette bien serrée en rentrant les bords, et enveloppez-la dans du film alimentaire bien tendu.
- Renouvelez l'opération avec les autres galettes. Réservez au frais.
- Pour la sauce, coupez l'avocat en deux, dénoyautez-le et mettez la chair dans le bol du mixeur avec le jus de citron, 2 pincées de sel et le Tabasco®. Réservez au frais.
- Avant de servir, retirez le film et coupez les roulés en tronçons, de biais. Attachez chaque morceau avec un brin de ciboulette. Décorez d'œufs de saumon et servez avec la sauce.

Roulés de jambon aux tomates

Remplacez le saumon fumé par du jambon sec, et le concombre par 1/2 barquette de tomates cerises épépinées et taillées en dés.

Roulés de viande des Grisons aux figues

Remplacez le saumon fumé par des tranches de viande des Grisons et le concombre par 8 à 10 figues séchées, mises à tremper dans de l'eau et coupées en petits dés.

Sauce au Carré frais® au raifort

Mélangez 75 g de Carré frais® avec 15 cl de crème fraîche épaisse, 1 c. à s. de raifort, 1 c. à s. de vinaigre de framboise, du sel et du poivre blanc. Servez avec les roulés.

Sauce au Carré frais® et à la moutarde

Mélangez 75 g de Carré frais® avec 25 cl de crème liquide, 1 ou 2 c. à s. de moutarde à l'ancienne et 5 brins de ciboulette hachés. Servez avec les roulés.

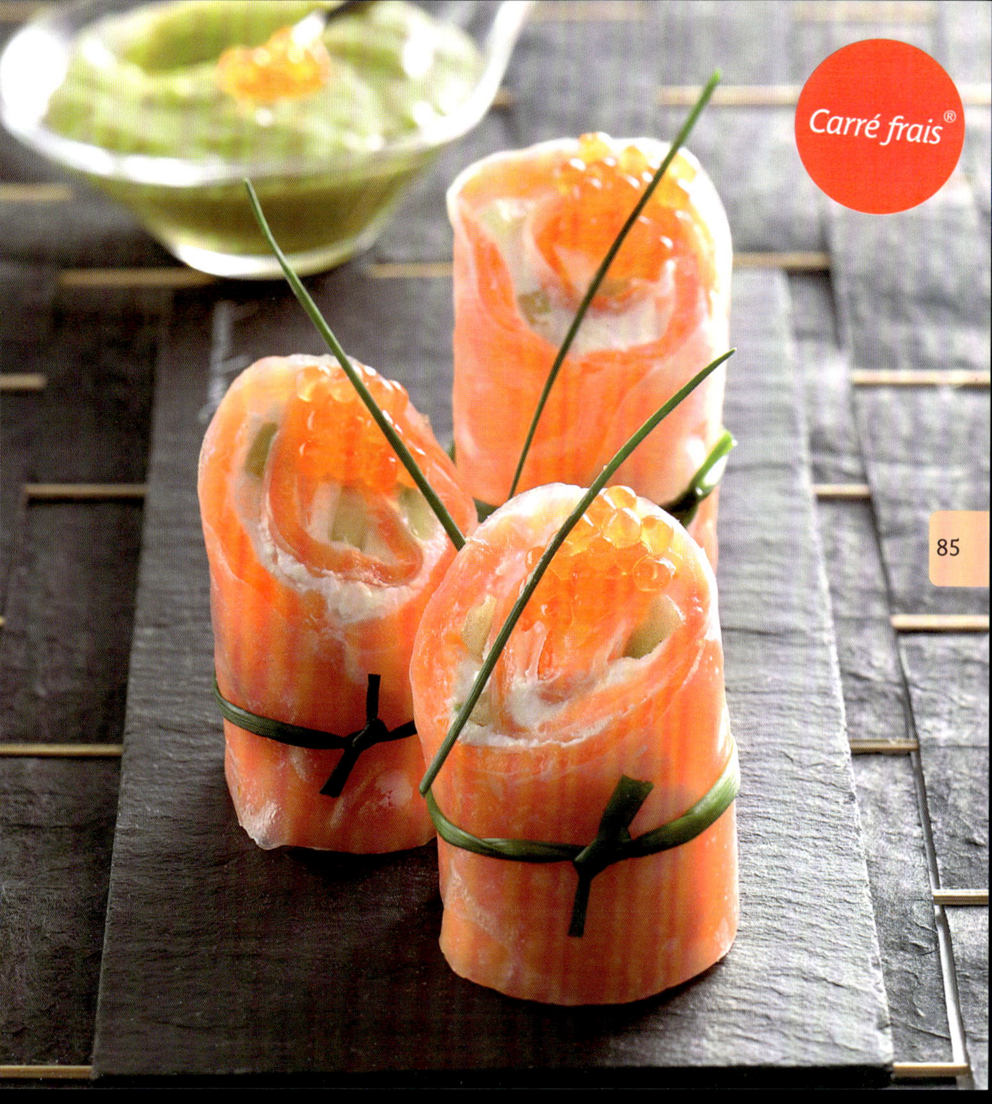
Carré frais®

CAKE AUX CHAMALLOWS® ET AU CHOCOLAT BLANC

Préparation: 10 min • **Cuisson**: 40 min • **Pour 6 personnes**

125 g de beurre • 3 œufs • 80 g de sucre • 180 g de farine
1/2 sachet de levure chimique • 10 cl de lait
75 g de chocolat blanc à pâtisserie • 100 g de Chamallows®

- Préchauffez le four à 180 °C. Détaillez le beurre en parcelles et faites-le fondre dans une petite casserole.
- Mettez les œufs et le sucre dans un saladier, et battez au fouet jusqu'à ce que le mélange blanchisse et devienne mousseux.
- Incorporez progressivement la farine et la levure, puis le beurre fondu et le lait. Mélangez jusqu'à l'obtention d'une pâte homogène.
- Cassez le chocolat en morceaux, puis broyez-les grossièrement à l'aide d'un rouleau à pâtisserie. Coupez les Chamallows® en quatre. Incorporez le tout à la préparation.
- Beurrez et farinez un moule à cake, puis versez-y le mélange.
- Faites cuire au four pendant 40 min. Pour vérifier la cuisson, piquez la pointe d'un couteau au centre du gâteau. Elle doit ressortir sèche.
- Laissez refroidir avant de déguster.

Cake aux Chamallows® et aux fruits rouges

Remplacez le chocolat blanc par 150 g de fruits rouges mélangés. Ajoutez, éventuellement, 20 cl de lait de coco à la préparation.

Cake au citron et au pavot

Ajoutez le jus de 2 citrons et le zeste de 1 citron à la préparation. Ajoutez également 1 c. à s. de graines de pavot.

Cake aux Chamallows® et aux carottes

Remplacez le chocolat blanc et le beurre par 150 g de carottes râpées. Ajoutez 1 pincée de gingembre en poudre au mélange.

Cake aux Chamallows® et au potimarron

Remplacez le chocolat blanc et la moitié du beurre par 200 g de purée de potimarrons. Ajoutez 50 g de pépites de chocolat noir.

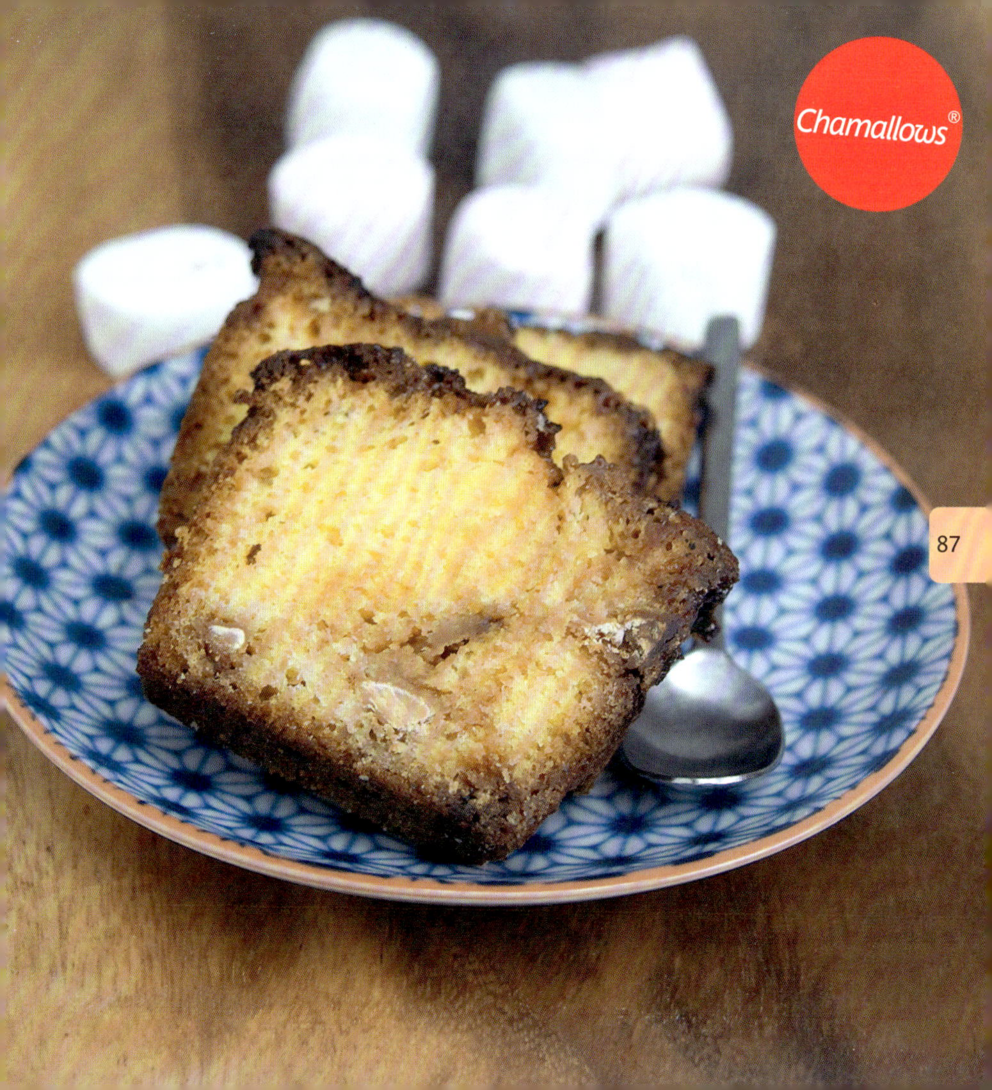
Chamallows®

CRÈME LITCHIS-FRAMBOISES AUX CHAMALLOWS®

Préparation: 20 min • **Cuisson**: 15 min • **Réfrigération**: 2 h
Pour 6 personnes

pour la crème : *150 g de litchis frais • 350 g de framboises 2 c. à s. de jus de betterave • 4 œufs • 150 g de fromage blanc 10 cl de crème liquide • 1 c. à s. de farine • 120 g de sucre glace • sel*
pour les brochettes : *18 Chamallows®*

- Retirez la peau et le noyau des litchis. Rincez rapidement les framboises. Mettez-les dans le bol du mixeur et mixez jusqu'à l'obtention d'un coulis. Ajoutez le jus de betterave, pour accentuer la couleur du coulis (le goût de la betterave ne sera pas détectable).

- Cassez les œufs et séparez les blancs des jaunes. Réservez les blancs. Versez les jaunes dans une casserole, ajoutez le fromage blanc, la crème liquide et la farine, et faites chauffer à feu doux en remuant au fouet. Retirez la casserole du feu dès que la crème commence à épaissir. Laissez refroidir complètement.

- Battez les blancs d'œufs en neige ferme au fouet électrique avec 1 pincée de sel. Incorporez le sucre glace sans cesser de battre. Ajoutez délicatement le coulis de framboises, puis la crème refroidie en battant au fouet manuel.

- Répartissez le mélange dans des bols individuels et réservez au réfrigérateur pendant 2 h.

- Préchauffez le gril du four. Prenez 6 piques en bois et enfilez 3 Chamallows® sur chacune d'elles. Faites dorer au four pendant 5 min.

- Déposez 1 brochette sur chaque bol et servez.

Crème aphrodisiaque aux framboises

Utilisez 500 g de framboises. Remplacez les litchis par 10 cl de liqueur de litchi et ajoutez 1 morceau de 1 cm de gingembre frais râpé à la préparation. Vous pouvez aussi utiliser du gingembre confit.

Crème express aux fraises

Mixez 500 g de fraises avec 30 cl de crème fleurette. Ajoutez 2 ou 3 c. à s. de sucre glace. Servez très froid, avec les brochettes.

Brochettes de Chamallows® au chocolat

Faites fondre 200 g de chocolat noir avec 3 c. à s. de crème fraîche. Passez les brochettes de Chamallows® dans le chocolat fondu, puis dans du vermicelle de sucre. Servez avec la crème.

Brochettes de fruits exotiques aux Chamallows®

Choisissez des piques plus grandes et alternez sur chacune d'elles des Chamallows® et des morceaux d'ananas, de mangue et de banane.

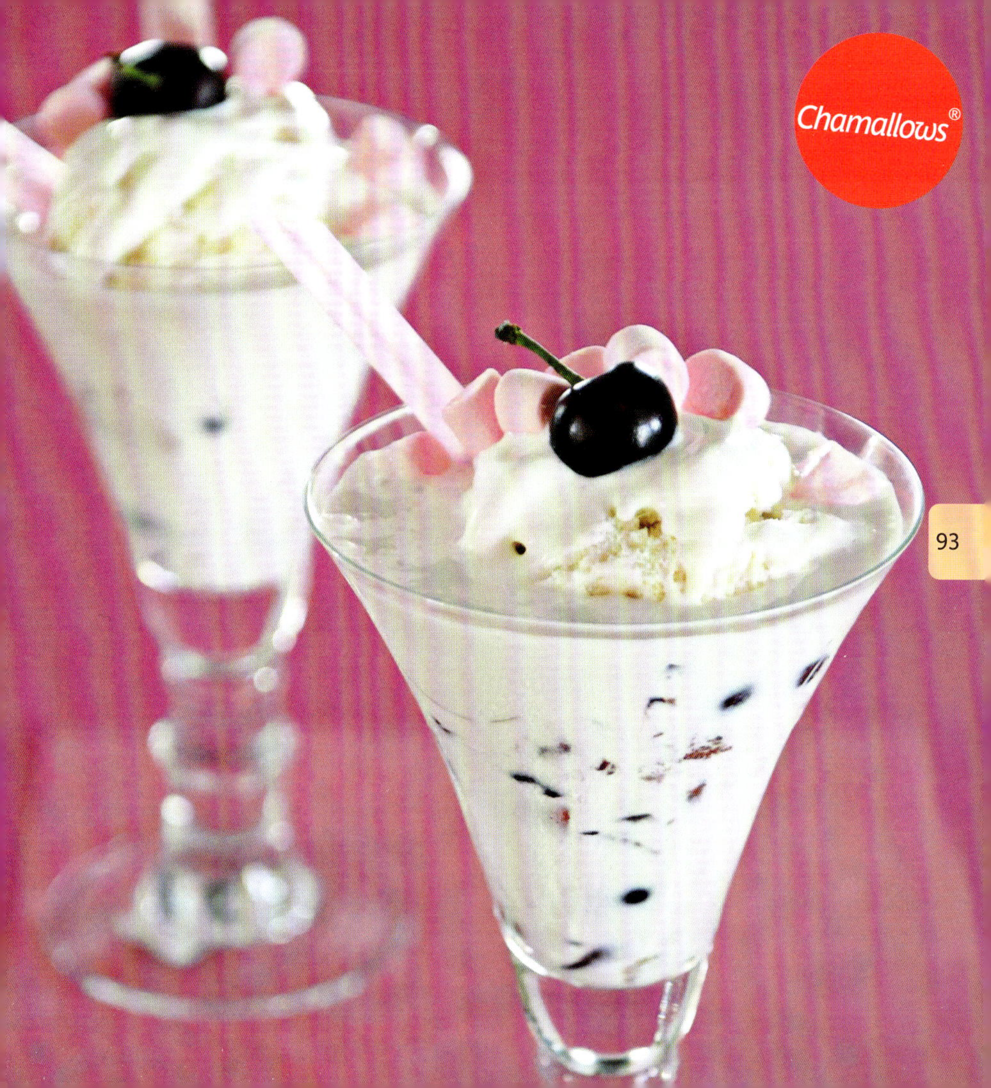
Chamallows®

CHICKEN WINGS CARAMÉLISÉES AU CITRON

Préparation : 10 min • **Cuisson** : 1 h 10 • **Marinade** : 6 h
Pour 4 personnes

12 ailes de poulet • 3 gousses d'ail • 5 oignons • 3 citrons
45 cl de Coca-Cola® • 3 c. à c. de sauce soja • 4 c. à s. d'huile d'olive
riz, pour accompagner • sel et poivre du moulin

- Taillez les ailes de poulet en deux au niveau des articulations. Épluchez l'ail et l'oignon. Hachez l'ail et émincez les oignons. Prélevez le zeste et le jus des citrons. Râpez finement les zestes.
- Mélangez le Coca-Cola®, la sauce soja, l'ail haché, les zestes et le jus des citrons, et du poivre, puis faites-y mariner les ailes de poulet pendant au moins 6 h.
- Faites chauffer l'huile dans une poêle et faites-y revenir les oignons à feu moyen jusqu'à ce qu'ils soient bien fondus. Salez et poivrez. S'ils colorent trop vite, versez un peu d'eau et laissez évaporer.
- Préchauffez le four à 220 °C.
- Mettez les ailes égouttées (gardez la marinade) dans un plat et faites cuire au four pendant 20 min. Retournez-les à mi-cuisson.
- Versez la marinade dans la poêle contenant les oignons et laissez cuire pendant 1 min.
- Versez le tout sur le poulet, mélangez et enfournez à mi-hauteur sous le gril. Laissez caraméliser pendant environ 40 min en remuant souvent pour que les ailes soient uniformément grillées.
- Servez avec du riz.

Chicken wings caramélisées aux épices

Remplacez l'ail et les citrons par 1/2 c. à c. de curry, 1/2 c. à c. de curcuma, 1/2 c. à c. de piment de Cayenne, 2 c. à s. de miel et 10 cl de coulis de tomates.

Crevettes caramélisées au citron

Remplacez les ailes de poulet par 24 grosses crevettes décortiquées. Vous pouvez également utiliser des gambas.

Riz pilaf aux échalotes

Faites revenir 4 échalotes épluchées et hachées dans une casserole avec un peu d'huile d'olive. Ajoutez l'équivalent de 1 verre de riz et de 2 verres d'eau. Salez. Faites cuire jusqu'à l'absorption complète du liquide. Servez avec les chicken wings.

Riz aux petits pois

Reprenez la recette ci-dessus en incorporant 500 g de petits pois surgelés cuits à l'eau 2 min avant la fin de la cuisson. Ajoutez 1 c. à c. de safran. Servez avec les chicken wings.

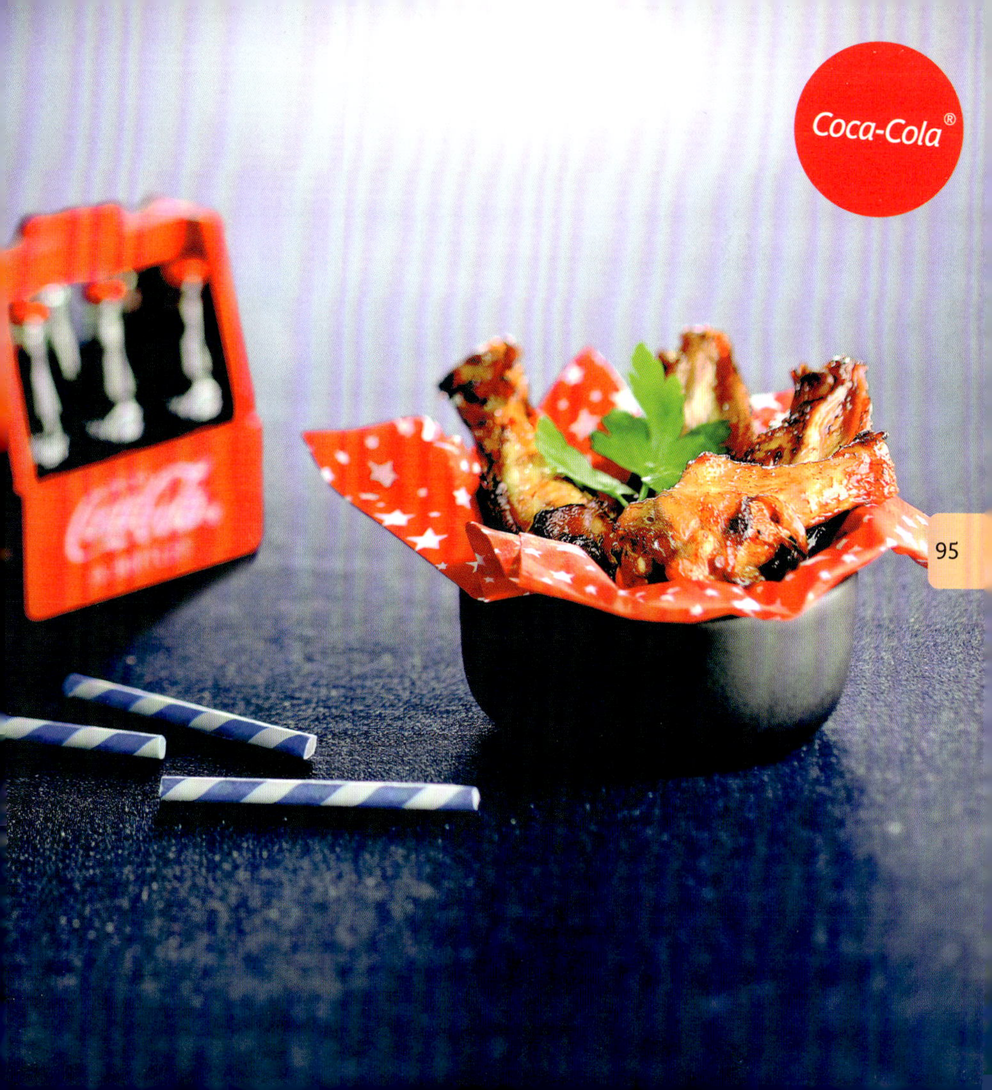

Coca-Cola®

PANNA COTTA AU LAIT DE COCO, GRANITÉ AU COCA-COLA®

Préparation : 20 min • **Cuisson** : 10 min • **Réfrigération** : 4 h
Pour 4 personnes

*3 feuilles de gélatine • 20 cl de crème liquide entière • 20 cl de lait de coco
90 g de sucre en poudre • 20 cl de Coca-Cola light® • 2 kiwis
4 c. à s. de jus de citron vert*

- Faites ramollir la gélatine dans de l'eau froide.
- Faites chauffer la crème avec le lait de coco et 80 g de sucre. Hors du feu, incorporez la gélatine essorée, mélangez bien et répartissez le tout dans 4 verres. Laissez refroidir et faites prendre pendant au moins 4 h au réfrigérateur.
- Portez 5 cl d'eau à ébullition avec le sucre restant, laissez frémir de 2 à 3 min, puis laissez refroidir. Incorporez 15 cl de Coca-Cola® light et mettez au congélateur.
- Avec les dents d'une fourchette, grattez ensuite toutes les heures pendant 4 h, afin de former des petits cristaux de granité.
- Pelez les kiwis, taillez-les en petits dés et faites-les mariner dans le reste de Coca-Cola® light mélangé au jus de citron vert. Réservez au frais.
- Pour servir, répartissez le kiwi sur la panna cotta, ajoutez 1 c. à c. de marinade et disposez le granité au Coca-Cola® par-dessus.

Panna cotta coco-mangue
Remplacez les kiwis par la chair de 1 mangue taillée en dés.

Panna cotta à la vanille
Supprimez le lait de coco et utilisez 40 cl de crème liquide entière. Faites-la chauffer avec les graines grattées de 2 gousses de vanille. Poursuivez ensuite la recette.

Panna cotta à la cannelle, pommes et granité
Reprenez la recette ci-dessus en remplaçant la vanille par 1 c. à c. de cannelle en poudre. Faites revenir 2 pommes pelées et coupées en dés à la poêle avec 1 noix de beurre. Utilisez-les à la place des kiwis.

Panna cotta à la gelée de Coca-Cola®
Mélangez 20 cl de Coca-Cola® sorti à l'avance pour le débarrasser de ses bulles, avec 4 feuilles de gélatine mises à tremper dans de l'eau froide. Versez sur la panna cotta et laissez prendre pendant 4 h.

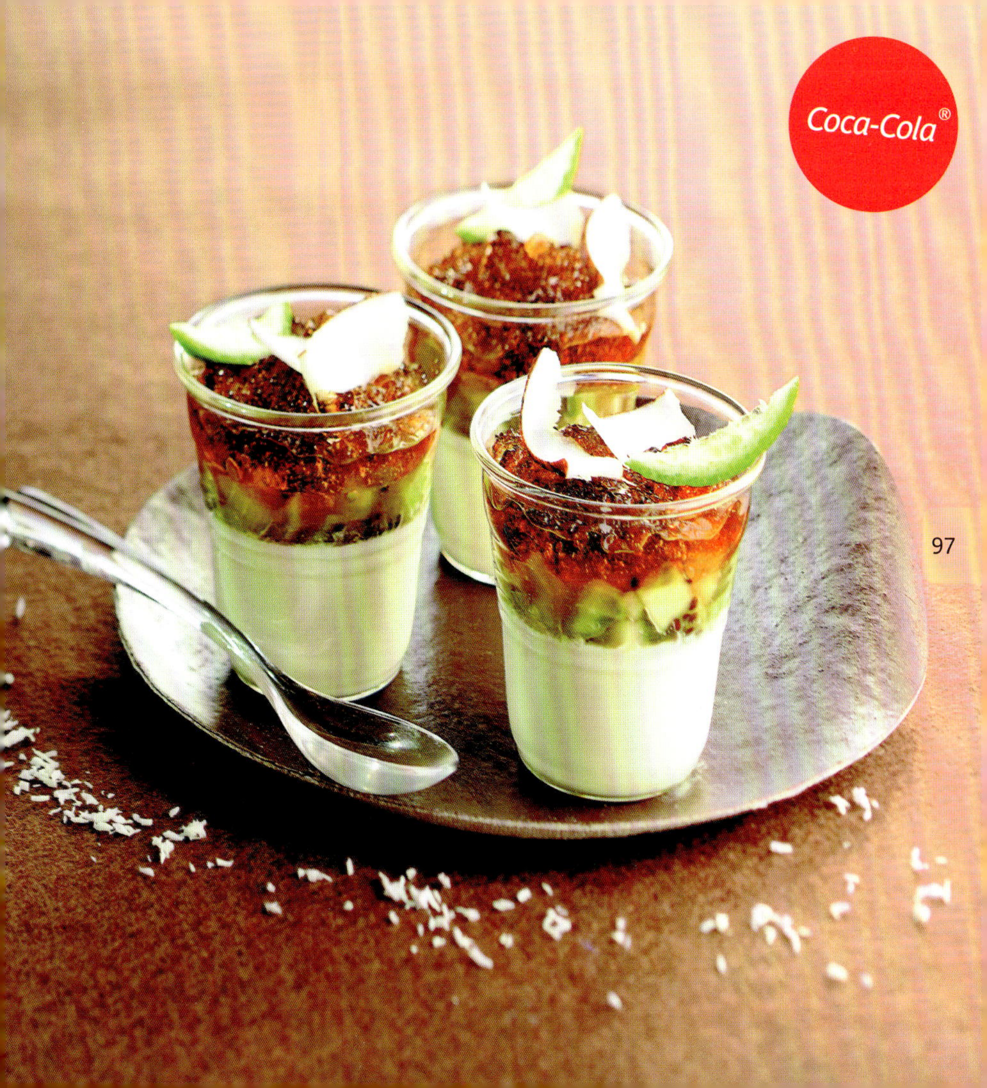
Coca-Cola®

PIZZA AUX POIVRONS ET AU CHORIZO

Préparation : 20 min • **Cuisson :** 1 h 15 • **Pour 4 personnes**

400 g de poivrons rouges • 1 gousse d'ail • 90 g de chorizo
150 g de mozzarella • 1 c. à s. d'huile d'olive • 1/2 c. à c. de thym
20 cl de Coca-Cola® • 1 rouleau de pâte à pizza
1 poignée de feuilles de roquette • sel et poivre

- Préchauffez le gril du four.
- Faites griller les poivrons sous le gril à mi-hauteur, de 30 à 45 min, en les retournant régulièrement pour que la cuisson soit uniforme. Enfermez-les ensuite pendant 5 min dans un sac en plastique, puis ôtez leur peau, retirez les graines et coupez-les en petits dés.
- Pendant ce temps, épluchez l'ail et hachez-le. Pelez le chorizo et taillez-le en fines tranches. Coupez la mozzarella en fines rondelles.
- Faites revenir les poivrons dans l'huile. Salez et poivrez. Ajoutez l'ail, la moitié du thym et le Coca-Cola®. Laissez mijoter jusqu'à ce que les poivrons aient presque absorbé tout le Coca-Cola®. Mixez à chaud de façon à obtenir un coulis très épais. Laissez tiédir.
- Préchauffez le four à 240 °C.
- Déroulez la pâte à pizza sur une plaque à pâtisserie tapissée de papier sulfurisé. Étalez le coulis de poivrons jusqu'à 1 cm du bord, puis répartissez le chorizo et recouvrez de rondelles de mozzarella. Parsemez de thym.
- Faites cuire au four de 15 à 20 min.
- Parsemez de feuilles de roquette et servez.

Pizza au jambon et au cantal

Remplacez le chorizo par 100 g de morceaux de jambon, et la mozzarella par des copeaux de cantal.

Pizza aux aubergines et au chèvre

Remplacez le chorizo par 150 g d'aubergines grillées taillées en dés, et la mozzarella par du fromage de chèvre.

Pizza aux poivron et aux champignons

Remplacez le chorizo par 400 g de champignons de Paris frais taillés en lamelles et revenus à la poêle pendant 10 min avec un peu d'huile et du persil haché.

Coulis de tomates au Coca-Cola®

Remplacez les poivrons par la même quantité de tomates pelées et débarrassées de leur pulpe. Faites revenir 2 échalotes épluchées et hachées en même temps que l'ail. Mixez. Remplacez le coulis de poivrons par cette préparation.

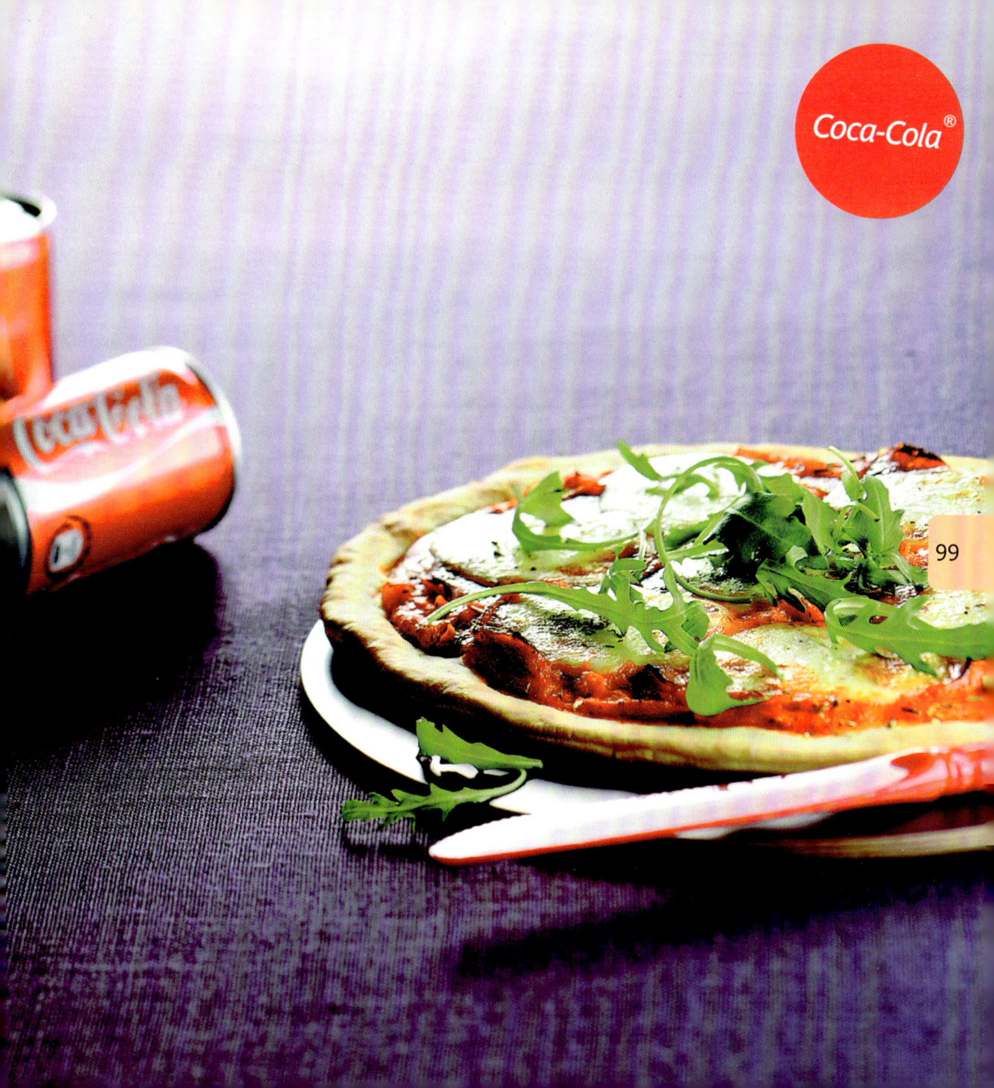
Coca-Cola®
Coca-Cola

TIRAMISU AUX FRAISES ET AU COCA-COLA®

Préparation : 25 min • **Cuisson :** aucune • **Réfrigération :** 15 h
Pour 4 personnes

350 g de fraises • 15 cl de Coca-Cola® zero • 2 c. à s. de jus de citron
50 g de sucre en poudre • 3 œufs • 180 g de mascarpone
10 biscuits roses de Reims + 1 pour la décoration • sel

- Lavez les fraises, équeutez-les et coupez-les en petits dés.
- Mélangez le Coca-Cola® zéro, le jus de citron, 10 g de sucre, les fraises coupées en petits dés, et laissez mariner au réfrigérateur pendant 3 h.
- Égouttez-les ensuite en veillant à réserver le jus de marinade.
- Séparez les blancs des jaunes d'œufs. Battez les jaunes au fouet avec le reste de sucre jusqu'à ce que le mélange blanchisse. Ajoutez le mascarpone, puis parfumez avec 4 c. à s. de marinade.
- Montez les blancs en neige ferme avec 1 pincée de sel, puis incorporez-les délicatement à la préparation.
- Répartissez la moitié des fraises au fond de 4 verres. Ajoutez une couche de biscuits cassés en morceaux, puis les fraises restantes. Versez 2 c. à s. de marinade dans chaque verre, tassez bien et nappez de crème au mascarpone.
- Couvrez et réservez au réfrigérateur pendant au moins 12 h. Émiettez le biscuit rose restant et parsemez-en le dessus des tiramisus. Servez bien frais.

Tiramisu aux fruits rouges
Remplacez les fraises par 100 g de framboises, 100 g de mûres, 100 g de myrtilles et 50 g de cassis.

Fraises marinées au basilic
Remplacez le jus de citron par les feuilles de 1/2 bouquet de basilic frais. Sucrez avec de la cassonade.

Crème au mascarpone et aux fraises
Pour accentuer le goût de fraise, mixez 150 g de fraises avec 25 g de sucre en poudre. Incorporez le coulis délicatement à la crème au mascarpone.

Melon mariné à la menthe
Remplacez les fraises par 350 g de billes de melons et le jus de citron par les feuilles de 1/2 bouquet de menthe fraîche.

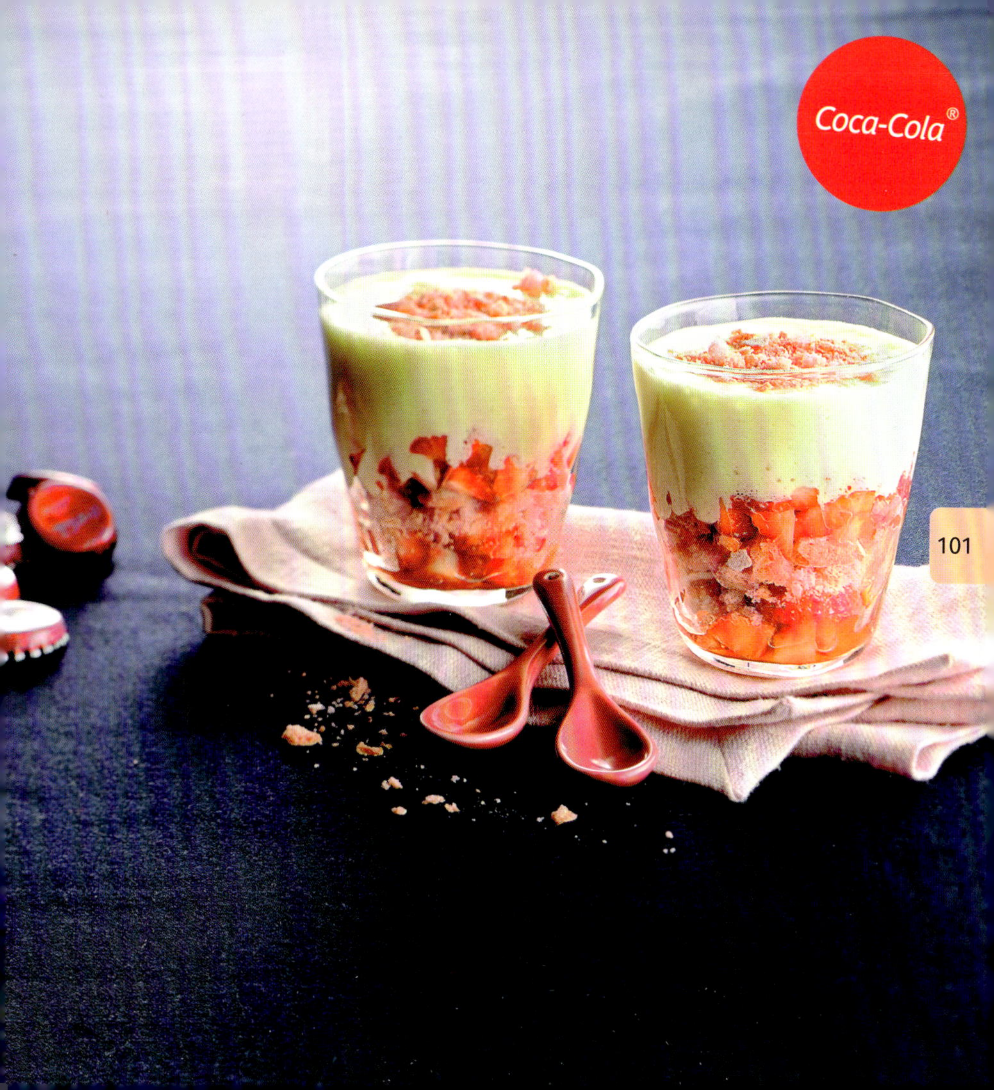
Coca-Cola®

COQUILLETTES À LA TRUFFE EN GRATIN

Préparation : 10 min • **Cuisson :** 15 min • **Pour 4 personnes**

400 g de coquillettes Lustucru® • 100 g de lardons
1 petit morceau de truffe • 1 c. à c. d'huile de truffe
2 c. à s. de crème fraîche épaisse • 70 g d'emmental râpé • sel

- Préchauffez le gril du four.
- Faites cuire les coquillettes Lustucru® al dente dans une grande casserole d'eau bouillante salée.
- Pendant ce temps, faites revenir les lardons à la poêle sans matière grasse.
- Râpez le morceau de truffe.
- Égouttez les coquillettes et remettez-les dans la casserole. Arrosez de l'huile de truffe et ajoutez la crème fraîche, les lardons et la truffe râpée.
- Mettez le tout dans un plat à gratin et parsemez d'emmental râpé.
- Faites dorer sous le gril du four de 6 à 8 min.
- Servez sans attendre.

Coquillettes à la pancetta et à la truffe
Remplacez les lardons par 5 tranches de pancetta taillées en lamelles.

Coquillettes au crabe
Remplacez la truffe et l'huile de truffe par 200 g de chair de crabe.

Coquillettes aux fèves et au jambon
Faites revenir 3 tranches de jambon émincées avec de l'huile pendant 2 min, puis ajoutez 150 g de fèves, et faites cuire jusqu'à ce qu'elles soient tendres. Remplacez la truffe et l'huile de truffe par ce mélange.

Coquillettes à la coriandre
Préparez un coulis de tomates en faisant chauffer à feu doux 6 tomates pelées et épépinées, 1 oignon émincé, du sel et du poivre. Mixez en coulis, puis ajoutez 1 poignée de feuilles de coriandre ciselées. Remplacez la truffe, l'huile de truffe et la crème fraîche par ce coulis.

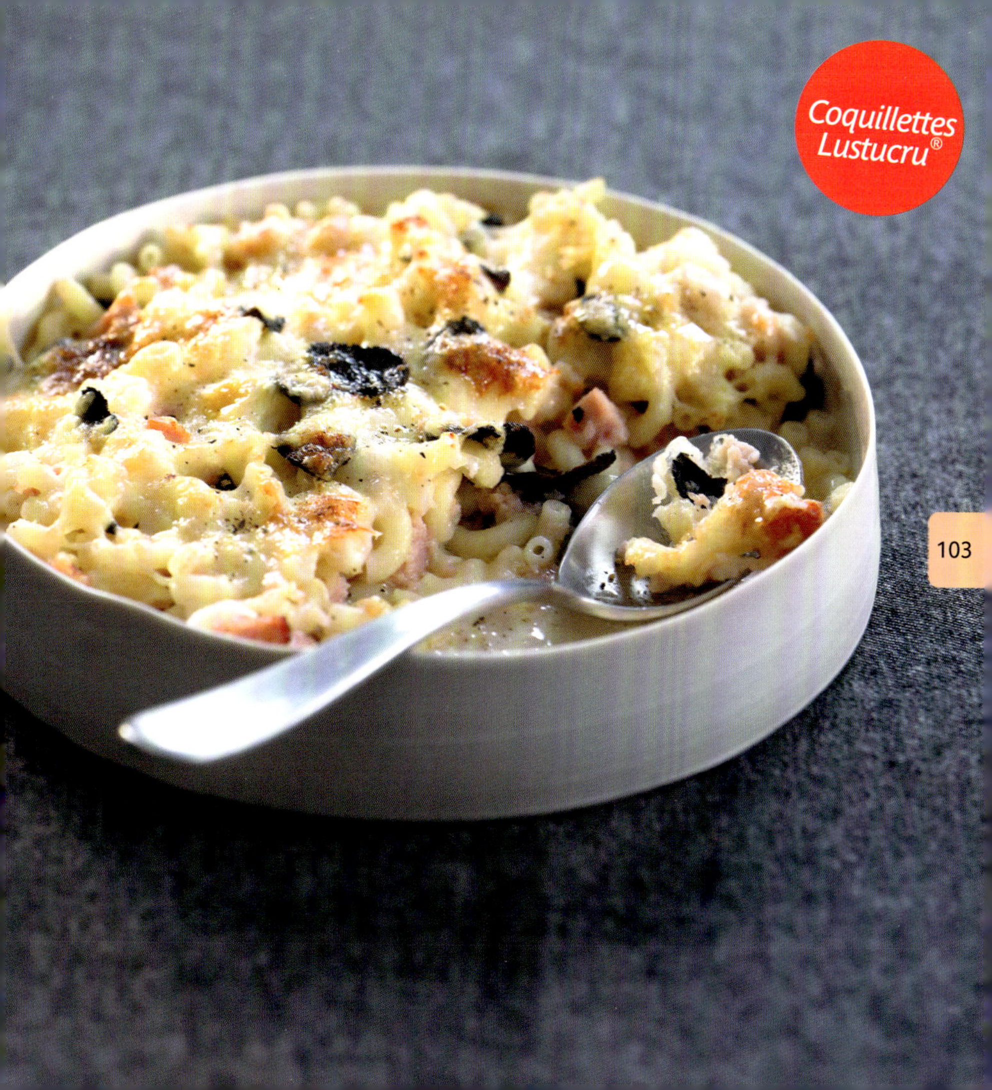
Coquillettes
Lustucru®

Salade de coquillettes poulet-fromage frais

Remplacez le jambon par 2 escalopes de poulet taillées en lamelles et revenues à la poêle avec 1 filet d'huile de tournesol. Mélangez 50 g de fromage frais avec 10 cl de crème liquide et 1 c. à c. de curry. Remplacez la vinaigrette par cette sauce.

Salade de coquillettes végétarienne

Remplacez le jambon blanc par 2 tomates pelées, épépinées et taillées en dés, 1 poivron rouge taillé en dés, et 1 oignon émincé et revenu à la poêle à l'huile d'olive.

Salade de coquillettes pastèque-mozzarella

Remplacez les melons par 600 g de pastèque, et le jambon par 200 g de mozzarella, le tout taillé en billes. Servez dans des bols.

Salade de coquillettes tomates-roquefort

Remplacez les melons par 2 barquettes de tomates cerises, et le jambon par 200 g de roquefort émietté. Servez dans des bols.

COQUILLETTES ET JAMBON EN COQUE DE MELON

Préparation : 10 min • **Cuisson** : 8 min • **Pour 4 personnes**

250 g de coquillettes Lustucru® • 3 c. à s. d'huile de tournesol
2 melons charentais • 4 tranches épaisses de jambon blanc
quelques feuilles de menthe • 1 c. à c. de vinaigre balsamique • sel

- Faites cuire les coquillettes Lustucru® al dente dans une grande casserole d'eau bouillante salée.
- Égouttez-les, arrosez-les de 1 c. à s. d'huile, puis laissez-les refroidir complètement.
- Pendant ce temps, coupez les melons en deux et prélevez des billes de chair à l'aide d'une cuillère parisienne. Mettez-les dans un saladier. Réservez les demi-melons évidés.
- Taillez le jambon blanc en allumettes et ajoutez-les dans le saladier.
- Rincez la menthe, essuyez-la avec du papier absorbant et hachez-la finement. Mettez-la dans le saladier.
- Salez, ajoutez le vinaigre balsamique, puis le reste d'huile, et mélangez bien.
- Versez les coquillettes Lustucru® refroidies dans le saladier et mélangez bien.
- Répartissez la préparation dans les demi-melons et servez frais.

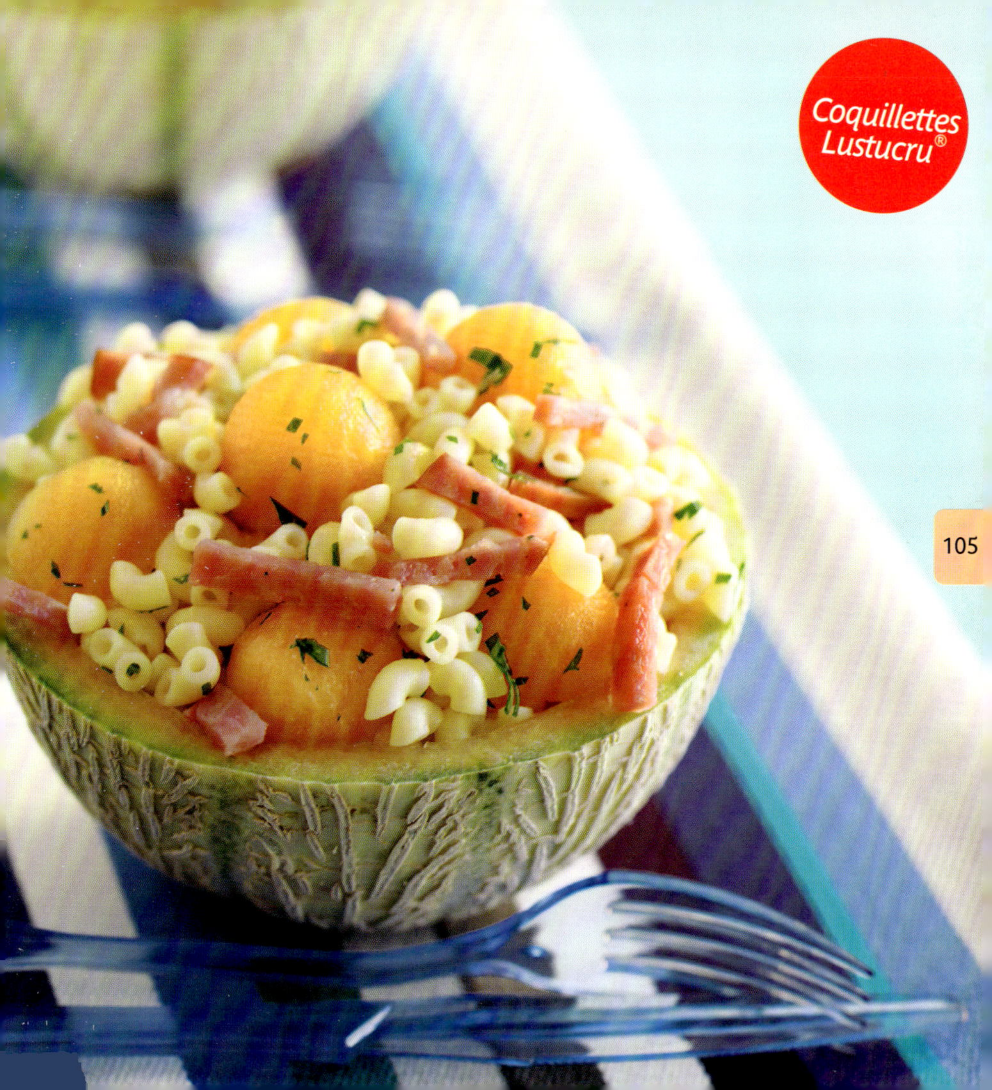

105

Coquillettes Lustucru®

RISOTTO DE COQUILLETTES AUX COQUES

Préparation : 20 min • **Cuisson** : 15 min • **Pour 4 personnes**

1 cube de bouillon de volaille • 1 gousse d'ail • 50 g de beurre
300 g de coquillettes Lustucru® • 1 oignon • 1 c. à s. d'huile d'olive
1 litre de coques • 10 cl de vin blanc sec • 10 brins de persil
25 cl de crème liquide • 100 g de parmesan râpé

- Portez 80 cl d'eau à ébullition et dissolvez-y le cube de bouillon. Épluchez l'ail et hachez-le finement.
- Faites fondre le beurre dans une casserole, puis ajoutez-y l'ail et les coquillettes Lustucru® et laissez prendre pendant 2 min en remuant.
- Versez 1 louche de bouillon dans la casserole, et faites chauffer à feu très doux, en remuant régulièrement, jusqu'à l'absorption complète du bouillon. Versez le reste de bouillon petit à petit, en laissant les coquillettes Lustucru® l'absorber complètement, avant d'en ajouter de nouveau, et en remuant souvent.
- Pendant ce temps, épluchez l'oignon et émincez-le finement. Faites-le revenir dans une cocotte avec l'huile d'olive jusqu'à ce qu'il soit translucide, puis ajoutez les coques et le vin blanc. Couvrez et faites chauffer à feu doux jusqu'à ce que les coques soient ouvertes.
- Rincez le persil, essuyez-le sur du papier absorbant, puis hachez-le.
- Lorsque les coquillettes Lustucru® ont absorbé tout le bouillon, ajoutez la crème liquide et le parmesan râpé. Remuez bien, couvrez et laissez reposer pendant 2 min.
- Juste avant de servir, ajoutez les coques et parsemez de persil.

Risotto de coquillettes aux poireaux
Ajoutez 2 blancs de poireaux taillés en rondelles dans la casserole en même temps que les coquillettes.

Risotto de coquillettes à l'artichaut
Ajoutez 8 cœurs d'artichaut à l'huile d'olive égouttés dans la casserole en même temps que la dernière louche de bouillon.

Risotto de coquillettes aux gambas et au curcuma
Remplacez les coques et le vin blanc par 500 g de gambas décortiquées, que vous ferez revenir à la poêle avec de l'huile d'olive. Parsemez-les de 1 c. à c. de curcuma avant de les ajouter au risotto.

Risotto de coquillettes à la pancetta et à la sauge
Remplacez les coques et le vin blanc par 150 g de pancetta taillée en carrés, que vous ferez revenir à la poêle avec de l'huile d'olive. Ajoutez 6 feuilles de sauge ciselées en même temps que la première louche de bouillon. Supprimez le persil.

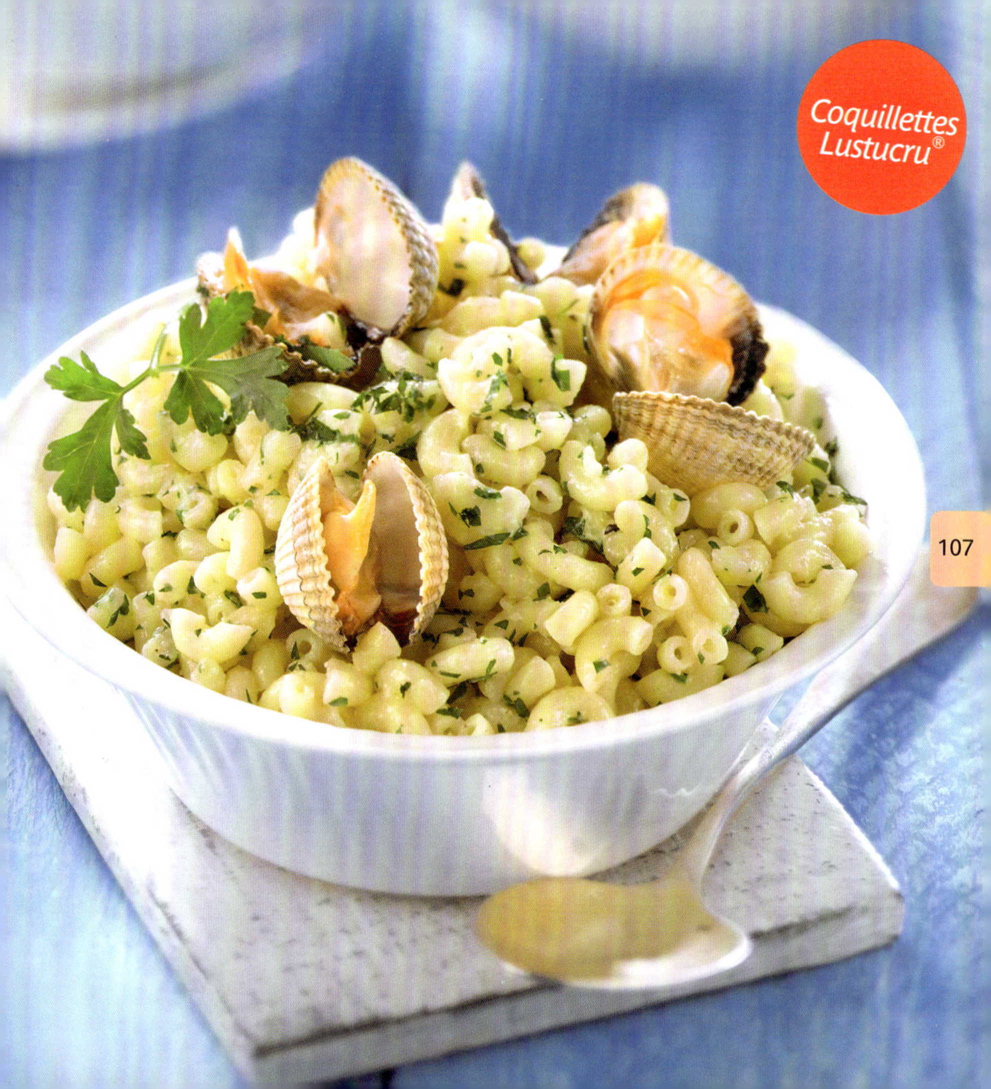
Coquillettes
Lustucru®

SALADE DE COQUILLETTES AUX POUSSES DE BETTERAVE

Préparation : 15 min • **Cuisson** : 8 min • **Pour 4 personnes**

250 g de coquillettes Lustucru® • 1 c. à s. d'huile de tournesol
1 boîte de thon au naturel • 10 cl de coulis de tomates • 1 c. à c. d'origan
1 poignée de jeunes pousses de betterave • 1 poignée de mesclun
50 g de copeaux de parmesan • 16 olives noires
1 c. à s. de vinaigre de vin rouge • 3 c. à s. d'huile d'argan • sel

- Faites cuire les coquillettes Lustucru® al dente dans une grande casserole d'eau bouillante salée.
- Égouttez-les, arrosez-les d'huile de tournesol, puis laissez-les refroidir complètement.
- Mettez-les dans un saladier. Ajoutez le thon grossièrement émietté et le coulis de tomates. Parsemez d'origan et mélangez bien. Répartissez le mélange dans 4 assiettes.
- Rincez les pousses de betterave et le mesclun, puis essorez-les bien. Répartissez-les sur les coquillettes. Ajoutez les copeaux de parmesan et les olives noires.
- Dans un bol, mélangez le vinaigre avec 1 pincée de sel et l'huile d'argan.
- Arrosez la salade de vinaigrette et servez.

Salade de coquillettes roses

Pressez 1 petite betterave cuite dans un linge au-dessus des coquillettes cuites, pour que le jus les colore et laissez refroidir. Ajoutez 1 betterave cuite taillée en dés dans la salade.

Salade de coquillettes à la grecque

Remplacez le thon par 2 tranches d'aubergine grillée taillées en dés, et le parmesan par de la feta.

Salade de coquillettes aux fraises et au chèvre

Remplacez le thon par 200 g de fraises lavées, équeutées et coupées en deux, et le parmesan par 1 crottin de Chavignol taillé en copeaux.

Salade de coquillettes à l'orange et aux carottes

Remplacez le thon par les quartiers pelés de 1 orange, et le parmesan par 1 carotte pelée et râpée. Parsemez de pignons de pin grillés.

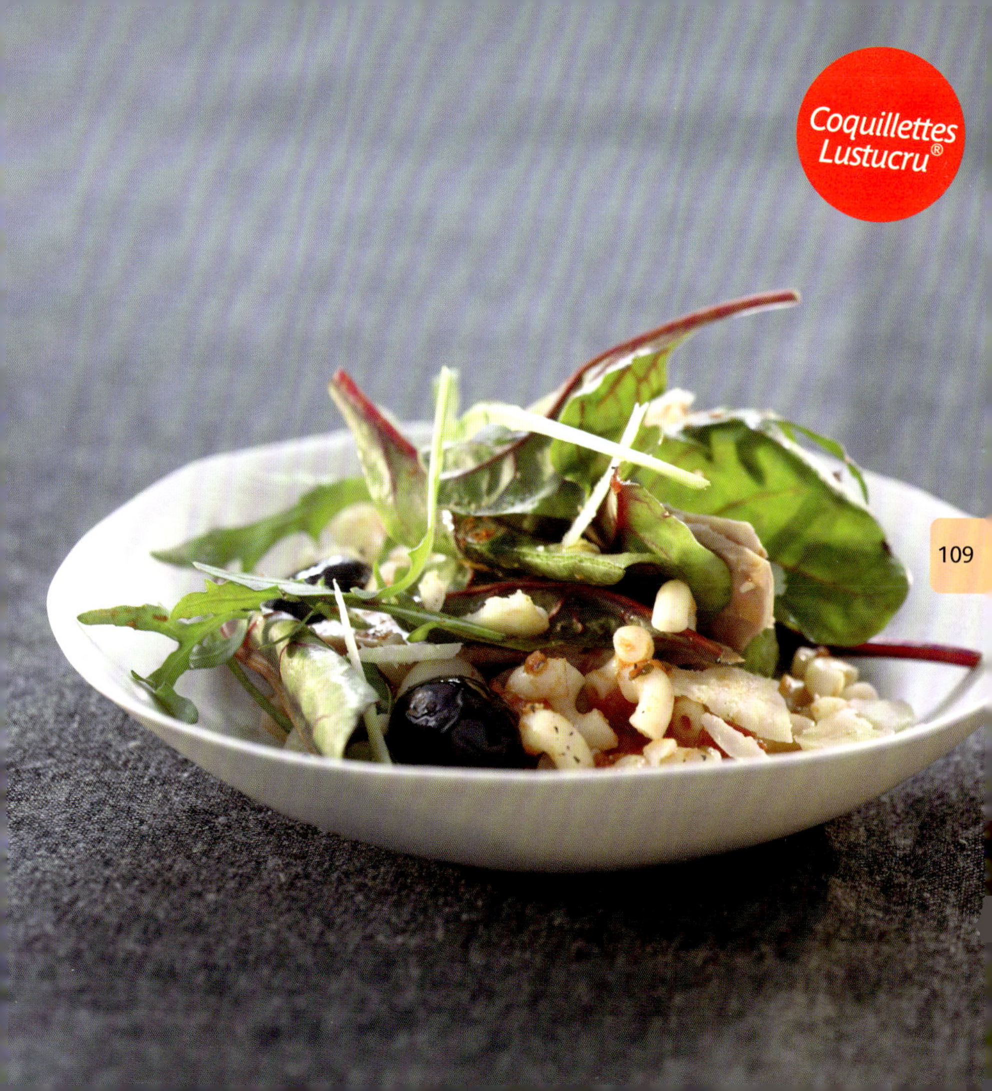
Coquillettes
Lustucru®

TABOULÉ AUX COQUILLETTES

Préparation : 20 min • **Cuisson :** 11 min • **Réfrigération :** 1 h
Pour 4 personnes

100 g de coquillettes Lustucru® • 2 c. à s. d'huile d'olive
1 botte de persil plat • quelques brins de menthe • 3 tomates
le jus de 1 citron • sel

- Portez à ébullition une casserole d'eau salée et faites-y cuire les coquillettes Lustucru® pendant 8 min.
- Égouttez-les, puis mettez-les dans un plat creux. Arrosez-les de 1 c. à s. d'huile d'olive. Mélangez, puis laissez refroidir.
- Lavez le persil et la menthe, et essuyez-les avec du papier absorbant. À l'aide d'une paire de ciseaux, coupez-les pour ne conserver que les feuilles. Versez celles-ci dans un saladier.
- Faites bouillir de l'eau dans une petite casserole et plongez-y les tomates pour 30 s. Passez-les ensuite sous l'eau froide pour arrêter la cuisson.
- Pelez les tomates, épépinez-les et coupez-les en cubes les plus petits possible.
- Ajoutez-les dans le saladier avec les coquillettes refroidies.
- Versez l'huile d'olive restante dans le saladier avec le jus de citron. Salez et mélangez.
- Réservez au réfrigérateur pendant au moins 1 h. Servez très frais, en entrée.

Taboulé au concombre et aux poivrons

Remplacez le persil par 1 concombre pelé, épépiné et taillé en dés, et par 1 poivron rouge et 1 poivron vert taillés en dés.

Taboulé au crabe et à l'avocat

Remplacez le persil par la chair de 2 avocats bien mûrs, taillés en dés, et par 125 g de chair de crabe émiettée.

Taboulé aux raisins secs et aux pignons de pin

Ajoutez 75 g de raisins de Corinthe mis à tremper dans de l'eau et 40 g de pignons de pin grillés à sec au mélange.

Tomates farcies au taboulé aux coquillettes

Coupez les chapeaux de 8 petites tomates, puis évidez-les à l'aide d'une petite cuillère. Garnissez-les de taboulé. Servez bien frais.

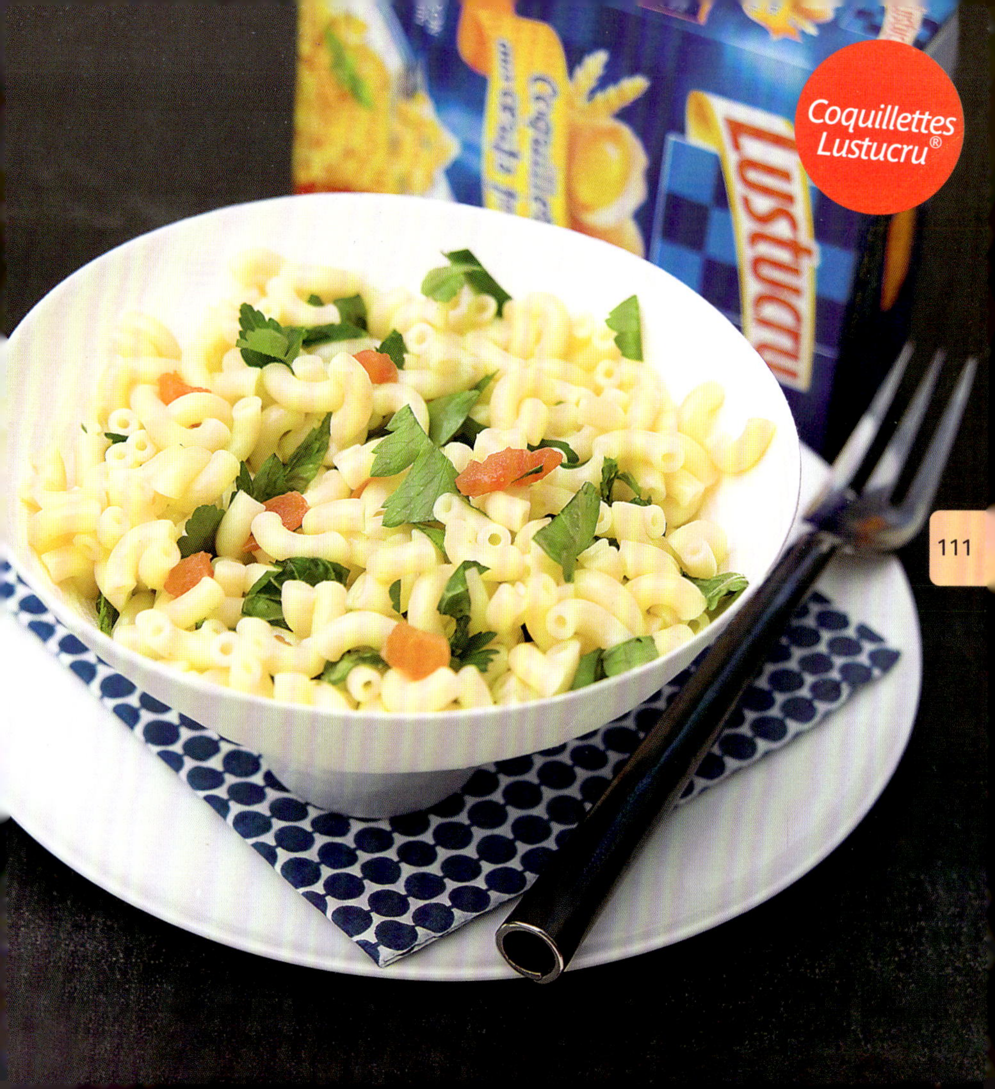
Coquillettes
Lustucru®

Faux macarons express aux marrons

Accolez des petites meringues deux par deux en mettant 1 c. à c. de crème aux marrons entre eux.

Macarons tout simples aux marrons

Mélangez 125 g de poudre d'amandes et 200 g de sucre glace. Incorporez-y 4 blancs d'œufs montés en neige. Formez des petits tas sur une plaque. Laissez reposer pendant 30 min, puis faites cuire au four préchauffé à 180 °C pendant 12 min. Accolez les macarons deux par deux en mettant 1 c. à c. de crème de marrons entre eux.

Whoopie pies au chocolat et aux marrons

Faites fondre 100 g de beurre et 60 g de chocolat noir au bain-marie. Ajoutez 3 œufs, 75 g de sucre, 150 g de farine et 1 sachet de levure. Mélangez, puis formez des tas de pâte sur une plaque. Faites cuire au four préchauffé à 180 °C pendant 10 min. Laissez refroidir, puis accolez les whoopies deux par deux en mettant 1 c. à c. de crème de marrons entre eux.

Crème de marrons Faugier®

MACARONS AUX MARRONS GLACÉS

Préparation: 40 min • **Cuisson**: 12 min • **Repos**: 1 h • **Pour 15 macarons**

160 g de sucre glace • 80 g de poudre d'amandes • 2 blancs d'œufs
1 c. à c. de jus de citron • 20 g de sucre en poudre
2 gouttes de colorant alimentaire rouge • marrons glacés • 30 g de beurre
150 g de crème de marrons Faugier® • sel

- Mixez finement le sucre glace et la poudre d'amandes. Battez les blancs d'œufs en neige ferme avec 1 pincée de sel et le jus de citron. Ajoutez le sucre en poudre et continuez de battre jusqu'à ce que la meringue soit brillante. À l'aide d'une maryse, incorporez délicatement le mélange sucre-amande à la meringue. Ajoutez le colorant et macaronez les blancs : avec une corne, soulevez délicatement la préparation de bas en haut pour faire légèrement tomber les blancs.

- À l'aide d'une poche à douille, formez 30 petits macarons sur une plaque à pâtisserie recouverte de papier sulfurisé, en les espaçant bien. Laissez reposer pendant 1 h à température ambiante.

- Préchauffez le four à 160 °C. Faites cuire de 12 à 15 min.

- Pendant ce temps, faites fondre le beurre dans une casserole, puis mélangez-le avec la crème de marrons Faugier®.

- Laissez refroidir pendant quelques minutes, puis accolez les macarons deux par deux en mettant 1 c. à c. de crème aux marrons entre eux.

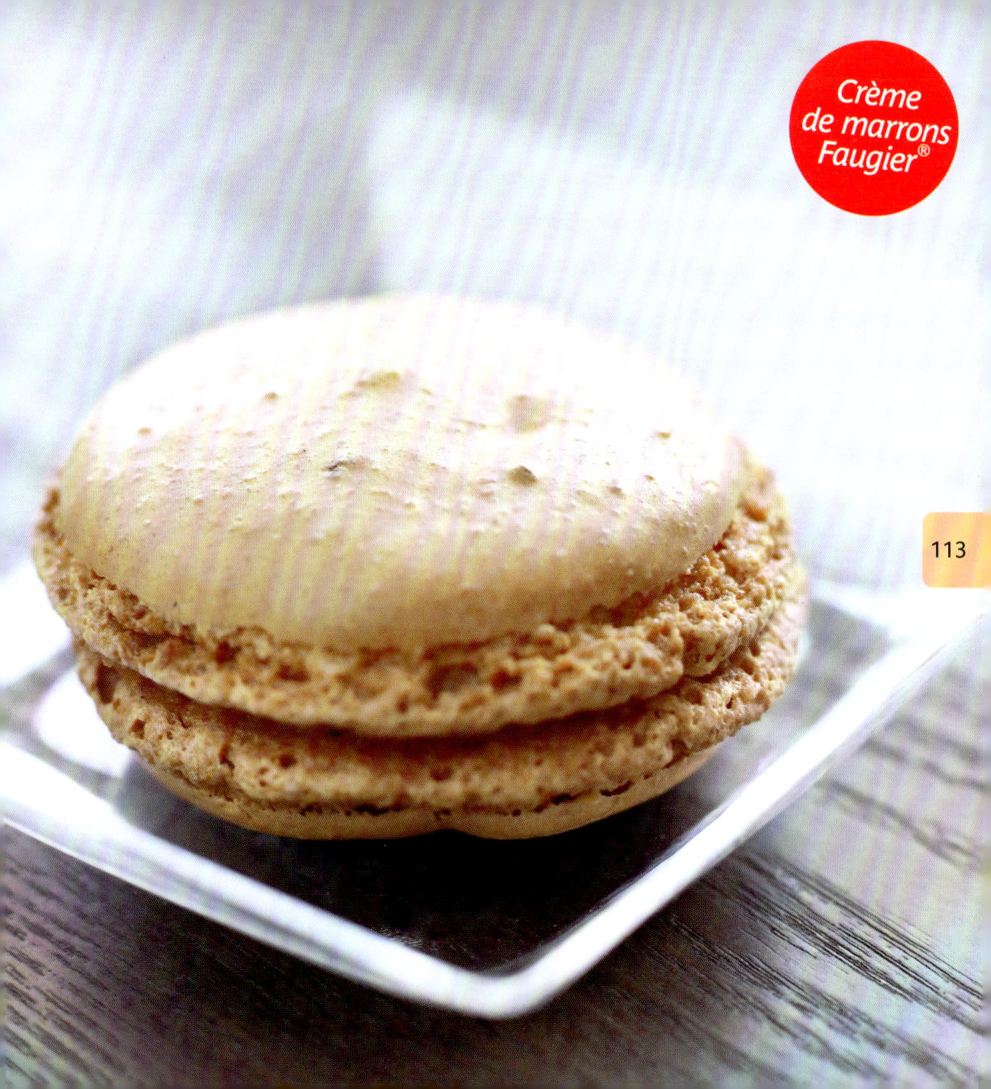

Crème de marrons Faugier®

Minimoelleux aux marrons glacés
Ajoutez 60 g de marrons confits grossièrement émiettés à la préparation.

Minimoelleux aux marrons et au chocolat blanc
Faites fondre 50 g de chocolat blanc avec 2 c. à s. de lait. Remplacez la chantilly par cette préparation.

Glace à la vanille
Préparez 1 l de crème anglaise, laissez refroidir et faites turbiner en sorbetière. Servez avec les minimoelleux.

Glace à la crème de marrons
Mélangez 250 g de crème de marrons avec 1 c. à c. de rhum et 2 c. à s. de crème fraîche. Battez 3 jaunes d'œufs avec 100 g de sucre. Ajoutez 40 cl de lait bouillant agrémenté des graines de 1 gousse de vanille. Faites épaissir en remuant sur feu moyen. Laissez refroidir, puis incorporez la crème de marrons au fouet. Faites turbiner en sorbetière. Servez avec le fondant.

Crème de marrons Faugier®

MINIMOELLEUX AUX MARRONS

Préparation : 15 min • **Cuisson :** 40 min • **Pour 6 minimoelleux**

100 g de chocolat noir à pâtisserie • 75 g de beurre + un peu pour les moules • 280 g de crème de marrons Faugier® • 2 œufs farine, pour les moules • 50 cl de crème liquide entière bien froide

- Préchauffez le four à 180 °C.
- Cassez le chocolat en morceaux. Mettez-les dans une jatte supportant la chaleur et ajoutez le beurre détaillé en parcelles. Faites chauffer au bain-marie en remuant jusqu'à ce que le mélange soit fondu et parfaitement lisse.
- Hors du feu, incorporez 250 g de crème de marrons Faugier®, puis les œufs entiers. Mélangez bien.
- Beurrez et farinez 6 petits ramequins. Garnissez-les de préparation en les remplissant aux 3/4.
- Faites cuire au four de 25 min à 30 min. Les moelleux doivent se démouler facilement. Laissez-les refroidir sur une plaque. Un petit cratère va se former à la surface.
- Pendant ce temps, fouettez la crème liquide en chantilly. Quand elle commence à monter, incorporez très délicatement le reste de crème de marrons Faugier®. Continuez à battre jusqu'à l'obtention d'une texture onctueuse.
- Garnissez le cratère à la surface des minimoelleux de chantilly à la crème de marrons. Servez sans attendre.

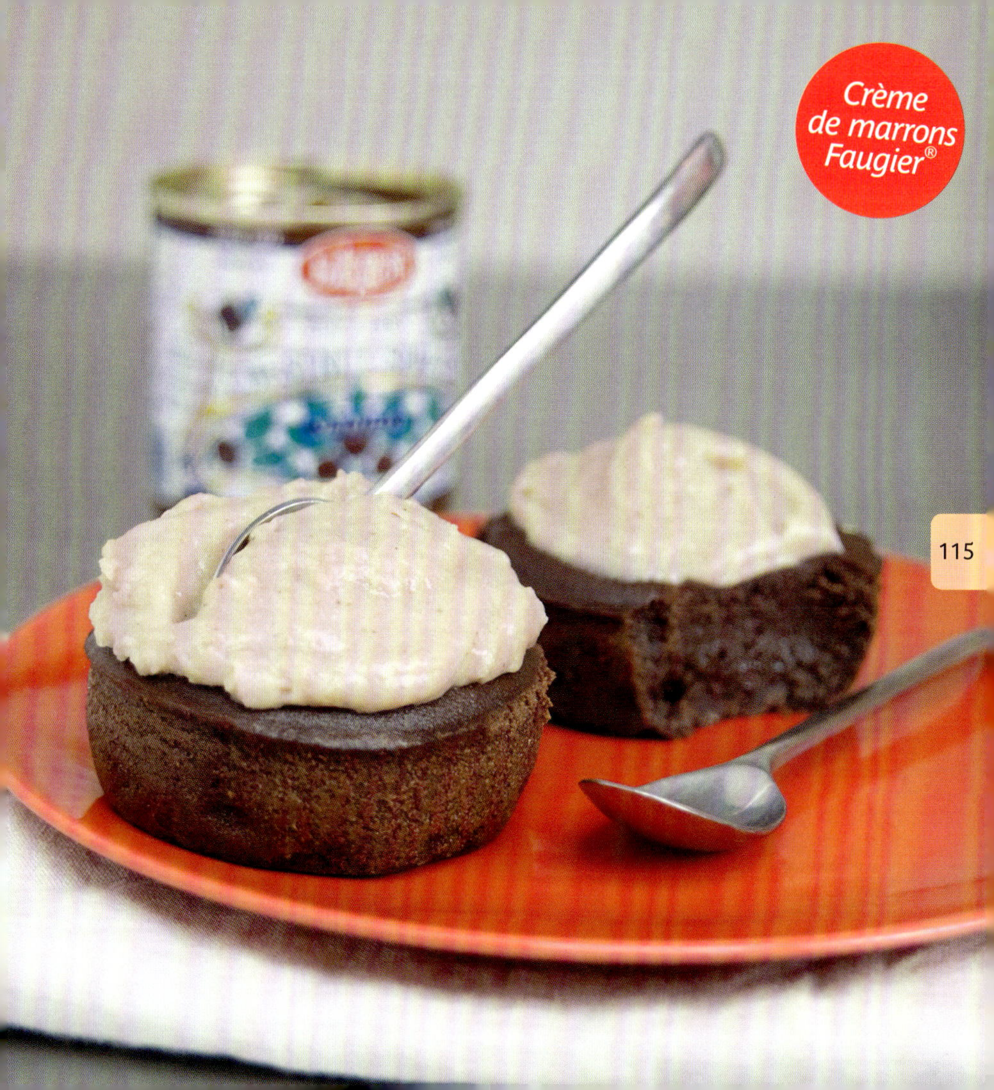
Crème
de marrons
Faugier®

Pain d'épice au pavot et au lin
Ajoutez 1 c. à s. de graines de pavot et 1 c. à s. de graines de lin à la préparation.

Pain d'épice aux deux farines et au son d'avoine
Utilisez seulement 100 g de farine de blé. Complétez avec 100 g de farine semi-complète et 50 g de son d'avoine.

Minisandwiches de pain d'épice à l'orange
Taillez les minicakes en tranches et accolez-les deux par deux en mettant 1 c. à s. de marmelade d'oranges entre eux.

Crumble aux pommes et au pain d'épice
Mettez 4 pommes pelées et taillées en cubes dans un moule beurré. Travaillez du bout des doigts 60 g de pain d'épice à la crème de marrons mixé avec 60 g de farine, 40 g de sucre et 60 g de beurre froid. Versez sur les pommes. Faites cuire au four préchauffé à 200 °C pendant 25 min.

Crème de marrons Faugier®

PAIN D'ÉPICE À LA CRÈME DE MARRONS

Préparation : 10 min • **Cuisson** : 30 min • **Pour 6 personnes**

125 g de crème de marrons Faugier® • 125 g de miel
1 c. à c. de quatre-épices • 1 c. à c. de cannelle • 250 g de farine de blé
1/2 sachet de levure chimique • le zeste de 1 orange • 1 pincée de sel

- Préchauffez le four à 180 °C.
- Versez 15 cl d'eau chaude dans un bol. Ajoutez la crème de marrons Faugier®, le miel et les épices. Délayez le tout en remuant.
- Mélangez la farine, la levure chimique, le zeste d'orange et 1 pincée de sel dans un saladier. Formez un puits au centre.
- Versez-y la préparation à la crème de marrons Faugier®. Battez au fouet jusqu'à l'obtention d'une pâte homogène.
- Répartissez la pâte dans 6 petits moules à cake tapissés de papier sulfurisé.
- Faites cuire au four de 25 à 30 min. Vérifiez la cuisson en piquant la pointe d'un couteau au centre des pains d'épice. Elle doit ressortir sèche.
- Laissez refroidir avant de servir.

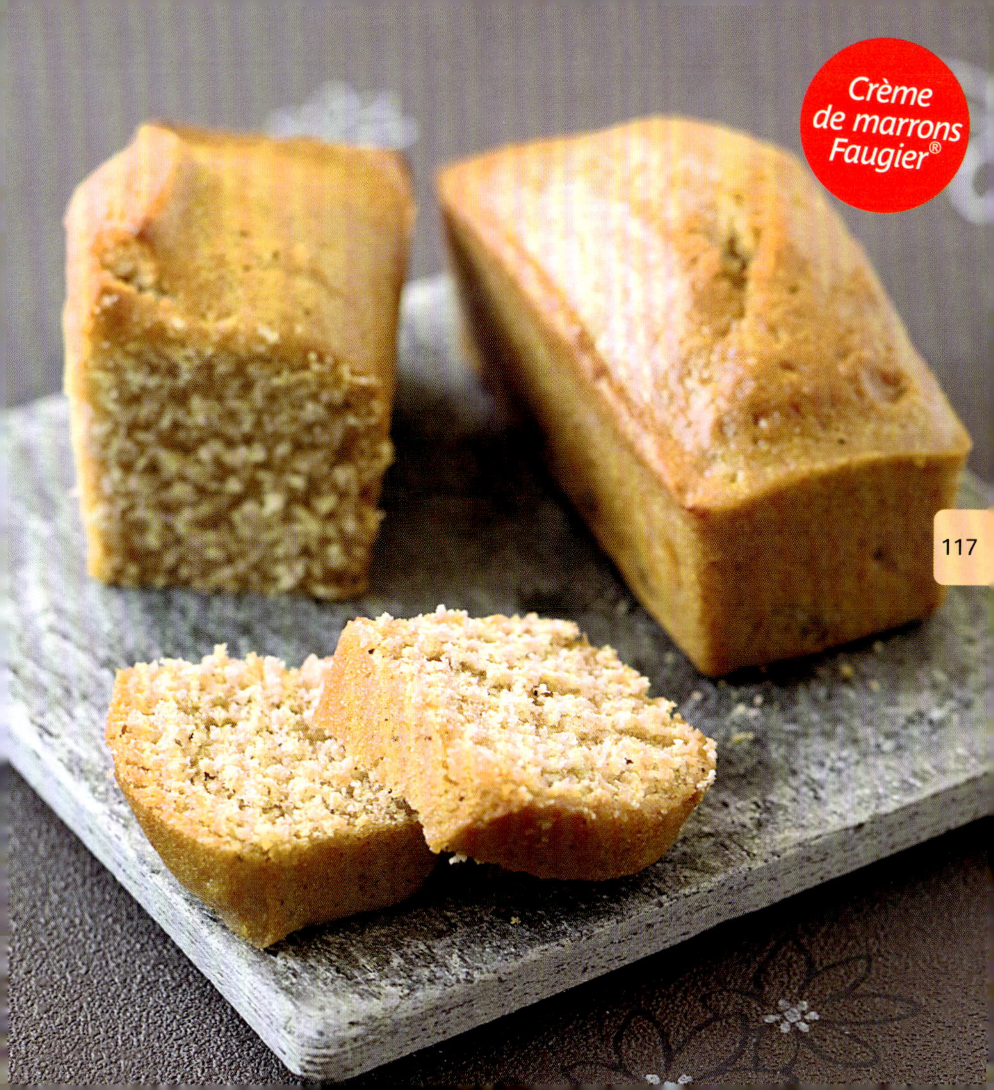
Crème
de marrons
Faugier®

RAVIOLES À LA CRÈME DE MARRONS

Préparation : 30 min • **Cuisson** : 5 min • **Pour 4 personnes**

400 g de farine + un peu pour le plan de travail • 5 jaunes d'œufs
100 g de crème de marrons Faugier® • 10 cl de crème liquide
15 g de beurre • sel

- Dans un saladier, mélangez la farine et 1 pincée de sel. Ajoutez 4 jaunes d'œufs un à un, puis pétrissez la pâte en ajoutant un peu d'eau, jusqu'à l'obtention d'une pâte assez compacte. Formez une boule et réservez.
- Dans une jatte, mélangez la crème de marrons Faugier® avec la crème liquide, le beurre et le jaune d'œuf restant. Battez énergiquement au fouet.
- Séparez la pâte en deux morceaux et étalez chacun au rouleau pour former 2 carrés de 2 mm d'épaisseur sur le plan de travail fariné.
- Sur le premier carré de pâte, déposez 1 c. à c. de la préparation à la crème de marrons Faugier® tous les 2 cm. Recouvrez du deuxième carré, puis découpez de petits carrés, à l'aide d'un appareil à roulette crantée.
- Faites cuire les ravioles dans de l'eau bouillante, jusqu'à ce qu'elles remontent à la surface.
- Égouttez-les et servez-les sans attendre.

Pâte à ravioles au cacao
Ajoutez 1 c. à s. de cacao amer à la farine pour la préparation de la pâte.

Ravioles aux marrons et au rhum
Ajoutez 5 cl de rhum à la préparation à la crème de marrons.

Chantilly à l'orange
Battez 300 g de crème fleurette très froide au fouet électrique. Quand elle commence à monter, incorporez 2 c. à s. de confiture d'oranges et 1 c. à s. de sucre glace. Servez avec les ravioles.

Ravioles de brick à la crème de marrons
Découpez 8 feuilles de brick en deux, puis pliez les demi-feuilles en deux. Déposez 1 c. à c. bombée de préparation aux marrons dans un angle, puis repliez le coin en un triangle, en enfermant la farce. Rabattez le triangle plusieurs fois sur lui-même. Faites dorer à la poêle avec un peu d'huile pendant 5 min.

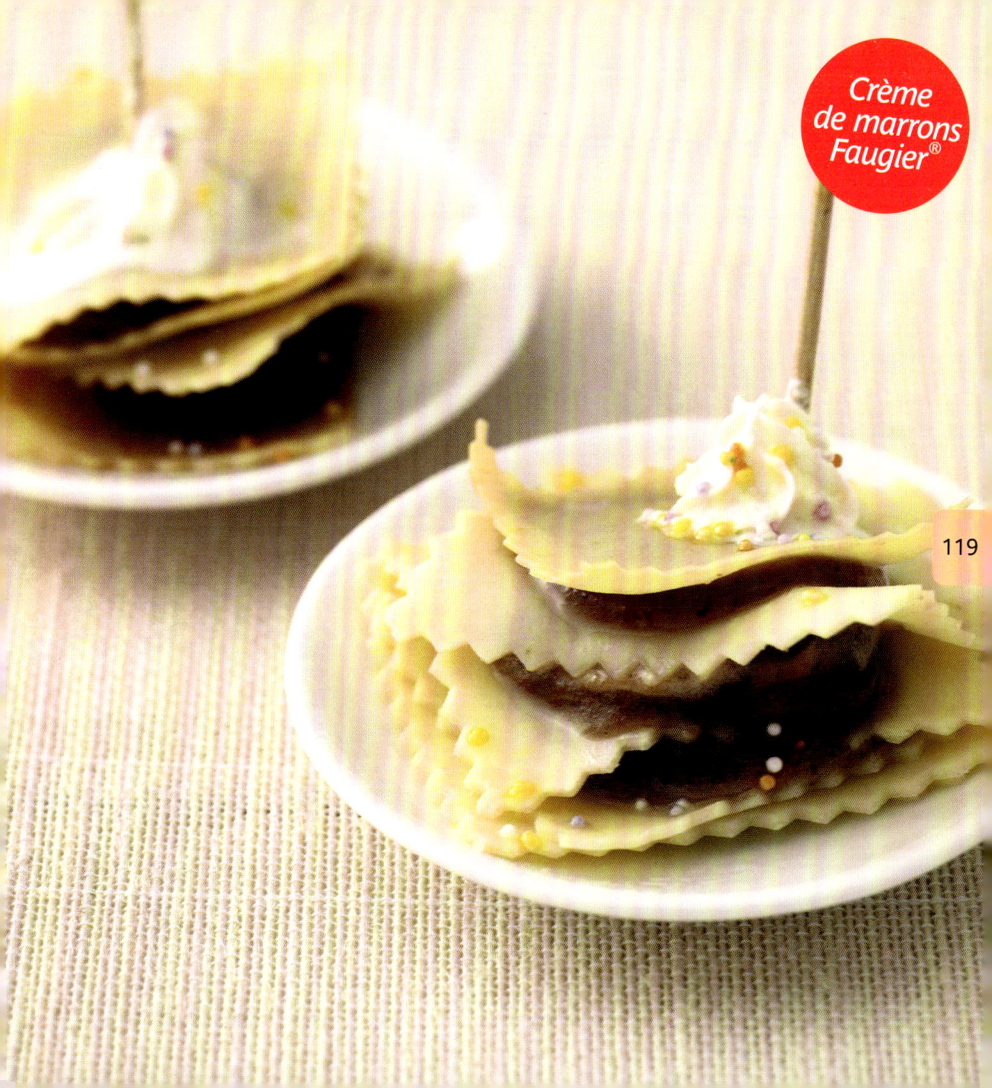
Crème
de marrons
Faugier®

TARTE AUX MARRONS ET AU CHOCOLAT

Préparation : 30 min • **Cuisson** : 30 min • **Pour 6 personnes**

2 œufs • 250 g de ricotta • 50 g de sucre en poudre
300 g de crème de marrons Faugier® • 40 g de chocolat noir
10 cl de crème liquide • 1 rouleau de pâte sablée

- Préchauffez le four à 180 °C.
- Dans un saladier, battez au fouet les œufs, la ricotta, le sucre et la crème de marrons Faugier®.
- Coupez le chocolat en carrés et faites-les fondre au bain-marie avec la crème liquide. Incorporez-le au mélange à la crème de marrons Faugier®.
- Déroulez la pâte et garnissez-en un moule à tarte tapissé de papier sulfurisé. Répartissez le mélange aux marrons par-dessus.
- Faites cuire au four pendant 30 min environ.
- Laissez refroidir avant de déguster.

Tarte aux marrons et aux noisettes

Ajoutez 40 g de noisettes grossièrement concassées à la préparation.

Tarte aux marrons et au caramel

Faites chauffer 300 g de sucre et 15 cl d'eau dans une casserole en remuant jusqu'à l'obtention d'un caramel clair. Laissez refroidir légèrement, puis ajoutez 10 cl de crème fleurette et 80 g de beurre demi-sel. Mélangez. Nappez la tarte de caramel avant d'enfourner.

Lait de poule

Versez 15 cl de lait bouillant dans un shaker. Ajoutez 4 cl de rhum ambré, 2 cl d'extrait de vanille liquide, 1 jaune d'œuf et 1 c. à s. de sucre en poudre, puis secouez. Servez parsemé de noix muscade râpée, avec la tarte.

Lait aux amandes

Mixez 50 g d'amandes entières avec 30 cl de lait très froid et 30 g de sucre en poudre. Servez aussitôt, avec la tarte.

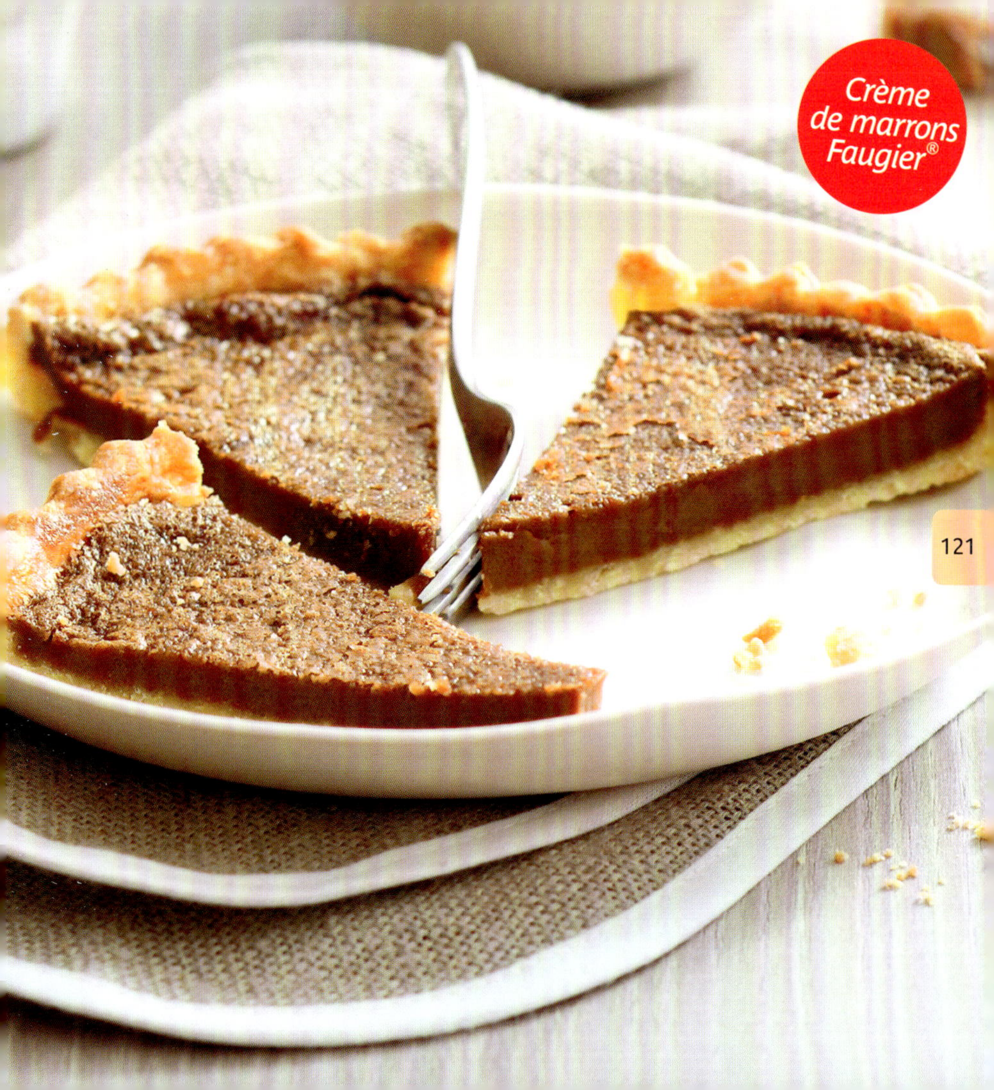
Crème
de marrons
Faugier®

Crème de marrons Faugier®

TARTE AUX POMMES ET À LA CRÈME DE MARRONS

Préparation : 20 min • **Cuisson** : 30 min • **Pour 6 personnes**

1 rouleau de pâte brisée • 200 g de crème de marrons Faugier®
4 pommes Golden • 10 g de sucre en poudre

- Préchauffez le four à 180 °C.
- Déroulez la pâte brisée dans un moule à tarte et piquez-la avec une fourchette. Recouvrez le fond de crème de marrons Faugier®.
- Épluchez les pommes, évidez-les, puis coupez-les en deux. Détaillez-les en lamelles, puis disposez-les en rosace, en les serrant bien. La crème de marrons doit être complètement recouverte.
- Saupoudrez légèrement de sucre et faites cuire au four pendant 30 min.
- Dégustez la tarte tiède.

Tarte aux poires et à la crème de marrons
Remplacez les pommes par 4 poires Comice. Vous pouvez également utiliser 2 pommes et 2 poires.

Tarte normande à la crème de marrons
Utilisez seulement 100 g de crème de marrons Faugier®. Mélangez-la avec 2 œufs battus, 60 g de sucre en poudre, 50 g d'amandes en poudre et 10 cl de crème liquide.

Tarte aux pommes, aux marrons et au calvados
Ajoutez 10 cl de calvados à la crème de marrons Faugier®.

Gâteau aux pommes et à la crème de marrons
Mélangez 2 pommes épluchées et taillées en dés avec 150 g de farine de châtaigne, 50 g de farine de blé, 1 sachet de levure chimique, 100 g de sucre, 6 c. à s. de crème de marrons Faugier® et 10 cl de lait. Faites cuire au four préchauffé à 180 °C pendant 25 min.

Crème de marrons Faugier®

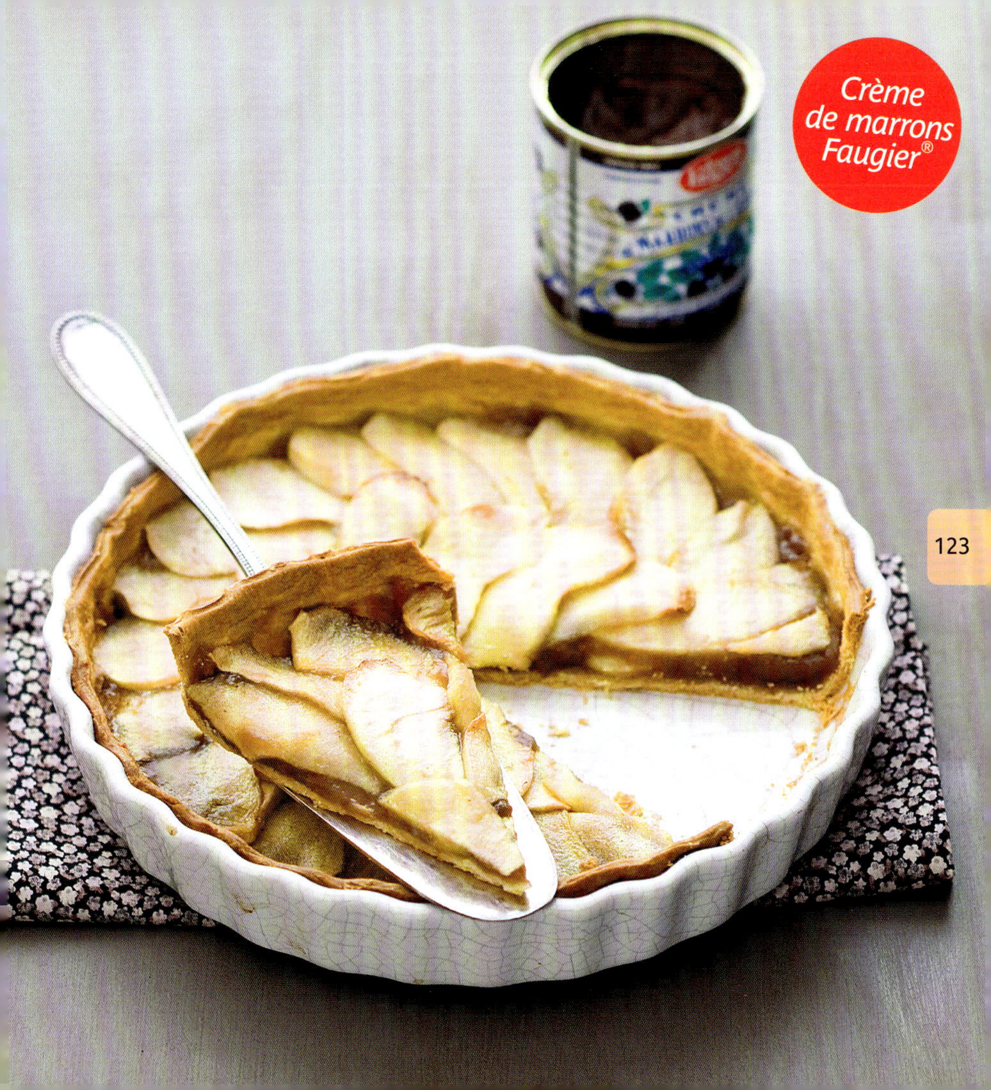

VERRINES AUX MARRONS ET TUILES CROUSTILLANTES

Préparation : 30 min • **Cuisson** : 10 min • **Pour 4 personnes**

pour les tuiles : *40 g de beurre • 50 g de sucre en poudre*
4 cl de crème liquide entière • 50 g d'amandes effilées
pour les verrines : *20 g de crème liquide entière très froide*
100 g de crème de marrons Faugier® • 400 g de fromage blanc
cacao amer en poudre, pour la décoration

- Pour les tuiles, préchauffez le four à 150 °C.
- Dans une casserole, faites fondre doucement le beurre, sans le laisser colorer. Hors du feu, ajoutez le sucre, la crème liquide et les amandes. Mélangez le tout avec une cuillère en bois.
- Avec le dos d'une cuillère à soupe, étalez une douzaine de petits cercles de pâte sur une plaque à pâtisserie recouverte de papier sulfurisé. Espacez-les suffisamment pour éviter qu'ils ne se collent entre eux.
- Faites cuire au four pendant 10 min, jusqu'à ce que les tuiles soient caramélisées. Laissez-les reposer pendant 2 minutes à la sortie du four, puis décollez-les délicatement avec une spatule.
- Pour les verrines, montez la crème liquide en chantilly au fouet. Mélangez 60 g de crème de marrons Faugier® et le fromage blanc, puis incorporez-y la chantilly très délicatement. Répartissez la préparation dans des verrines.
- Avant le service, parsemez de cacao en poudre et déposez 1 petite c. à c. de crème de marrons Faugier®. Servez très frais, accompagné d'une tuile aux amandes.

Verrines à la crème de marrons et au mascarpone

Remplacez le fromage blanc par du mascarpone. Vous pouvez également utiliser de la ricotta. Remplacez la chantilly par 2 blancs d'œufs battus en neige.

Verrines à l'abricot et à la crème de marrons

Ajoutez 8 oreillons d'abricot frais ou au sirop, coupés en dés, à la préparation à base de crème de marrons.

Tuiles à la crème de marrons

Déposez des petits tas de crème de marrons Faugier® bien espacés sur une plaque à pâtisserie recouverte de papier sulfurisé. Faites cuire au four préchauffé à 180 °C pendant 20 min, puis laissez refroidir.

Tuiles à la crème de marrons et au sésame

Reprenez la recette ci-dessus en ajoutant 1 ou 2 c. à s. de graines de sésame à la crème de marrons Faugier®.

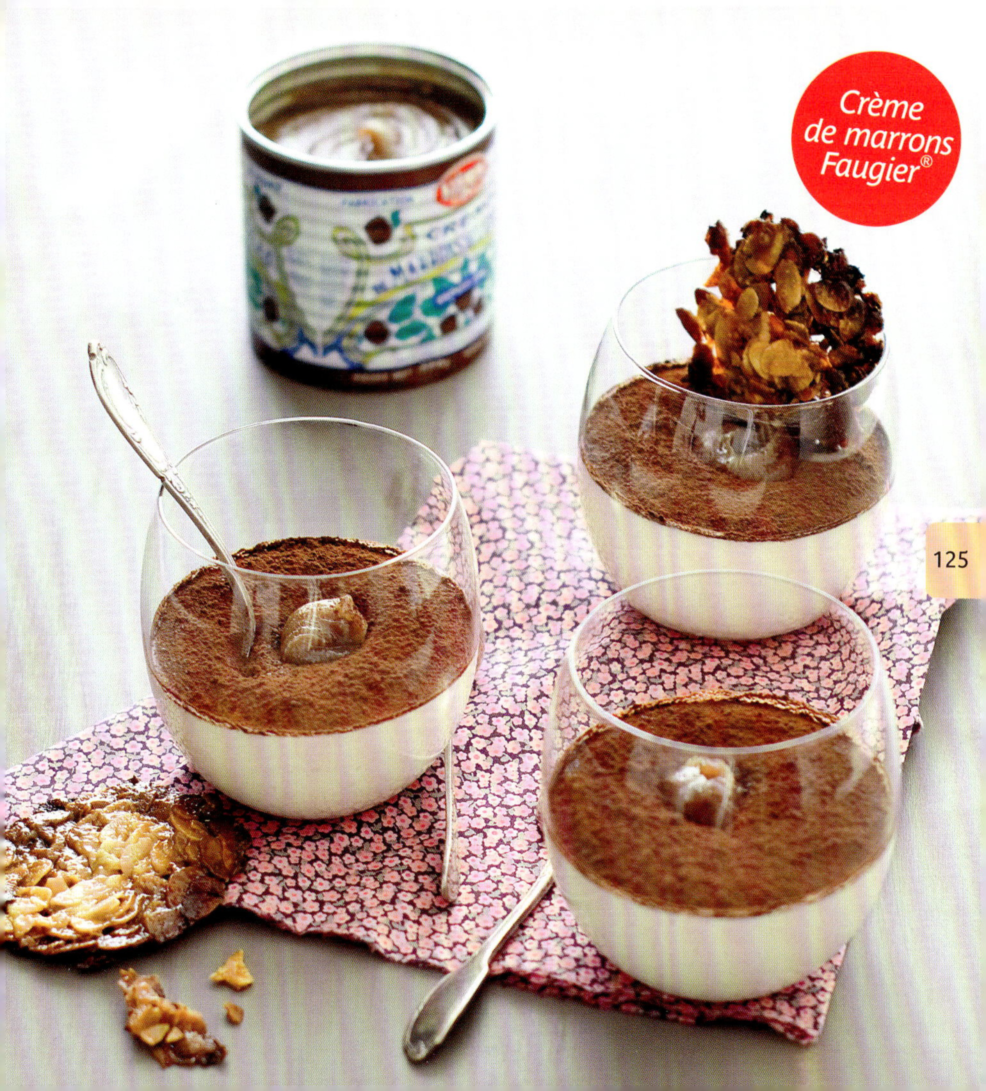

Crème
de marrons
Faugier®

CHARLOTTE AUX POIRES ET AU CHOCOLAT

Préparation : 10 min • **Cuisson** : aucune • **Réfrigération** : 2 h
Pour 4 personnes

1 boîte de poires au sirop • 125 g de noix de coco râpée
1 boîte de crème dessert Mont Blanc® au chocolat de 570 g
30 boudoirs

- Égouttez les poires, puis coupez-les en dés (conservez le sirop).
- Mélangez la noix de coco râpée et la crème Mont Blanc® au chocolat.
- Trempez les boudoirs dans le sirop des poires, puis disposez-les sur les bords et dans le fond du moule à charlotte.
- Répartissez les dés de poire dans le fond et recouvrez-les de crème Mont Blanc® au chocolat.
- Recouvrez la charlotte avec le reste des boudoirs.
- Placez au réfrigérateur pendant 2 h avant de servir.

Charlotte aux poires au Grand Marnier

Ajoutez 2 c. à s. de Grand Marnier dans le sirop des poires. Vous pouvez également utiliser de la crème Mont Blanc® au Grand Marnier.

Charlotte aux poires et à la cardamome

Préparez un sirop en faisant frémir pendant 15 min 50 cl d'eau, 150 g de sucre en poudre, les graines de 1 gousse de vanille et 2 capsules de cardamome écrasées. Faites-y cuire 6 poires pelées, épépinées et taillées en dés pendant 20 min. Utilisez à la place des poires au sirop en boîte.

Charlotte aux poires et à l'orange

Remplacez la crème Mont Blanc® au chocolat par de la crème Mont Blanc® à la vanille, et la noix de coco râpée par le zeste râpé de 2 oranges.

Charlotte aux pêches et au praliné

Remplacez la crème Mont Blanc® au chocolat par de la crème Mont Blanc® au praliné, et les poires par des pêches au sirop.

Crème Mont Blanc®

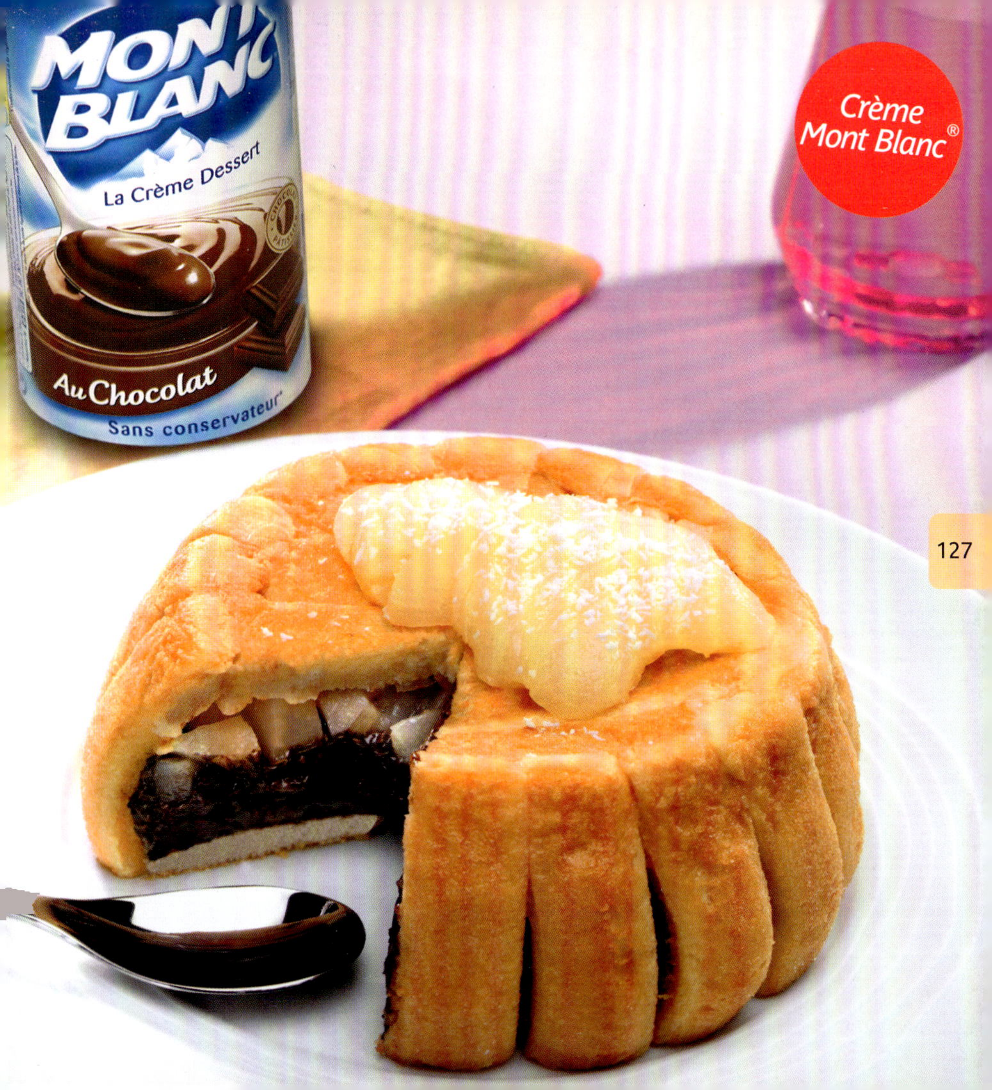

Sablés à la vanille et au citron
Ajoutez le zeste râpé de 1 petit citron aux ingrédients de la pâte sablée.

Sablés à la vanille et au tilleul
Réduisez en poudre 2 grosses poignées de feuilles de tilleul séchées et ajoutez-les aux ingrédients de la pâte sablée.

Shortbreads à l'espuma à la vanille
Versez la préparation à la crème Mont Blanc® dans un siphon muni de 2 cartouches de gaz. Réservez au frais, puis servez sur des shortbreads.

Café caramel
Versez 3 cl de sirop de caramel dans un grand verre réchauffé sous l'eau chaude. Superposez délicatement par-dessus 15 cl de lait bouillant, 1 trait de sirop de cannelle, puis 1 tasse d'expresso. Servez avec les sablés.

Crème Mont Blanc®

SABLÉS À LA VANILLE ET AU CARAMEL

Préparation : 25 min • **Cuisson :** 15 min • **Réfrigération :** 4 h
Pour 6 personnes

pour la crème à la vanille : *2 feuilles de gélatine*
1 boîte de crème Mont Blanc® à la vanille • 6 c. à s. de crème liquide
pour la pâte sablée : *125 g de beurre • 75 g de sucre en poudre*
275 g de farine + un peu pour le plan de travail • 1 œuf • sel
pour le caramel : *250 g de sucre en poudre*

- Pour la crème, faites ramollir la gélatine dans de l'eau froide. Mettez 5 c. à s. de crème Mont Blanc® dans une casserole avec la crème liquide et faites tiédir. Ajoutez les feuilles de gélatine égouttées en fouettant vivement. Versez le tout dans un saladier et ajoutez le reste de crème Mont Blanc®. Mélangez bien, puis réservez au frais pendant 4 h.

- Pour la pâte, mettez le beurre et le sucre dans le bol du mixeur et mixez, jusqu'à l'obtention d'un mélange mousseux. Ajoutez la farine, l'œuf et 1 pincée de sel, et mixez de nouveau. Étalez la pâte au rouleau sur le plan de travail fariné. Découpez-y de petits disques à l'aide d'un emporte-pièce ou, à défaut, d'un verre. Garnissez-en de petits moules à revêtement antiadhésif. Faites cuire au four de 8 à 10 min. Laissez refroidir complètement.

- Pour le caramel, faites chauffer 10 cl d'eau avec le sucre sans remuer, à feu vif. Portez à frémissements, puis baissez le feu. Dès que le caramel épaissit, retirez du feu et mettez la casserole dans un saladier rempli d'eau glacée. Mélangez rapidement, puis formez plusieurs petites décorations en versant le caramel en filet sur une feuille de papier sulfurisé en formant des zigzags. Laissez prendre. Garnissez les fonds de tarte de crème à la vanille, puis décorez avec le caramel.

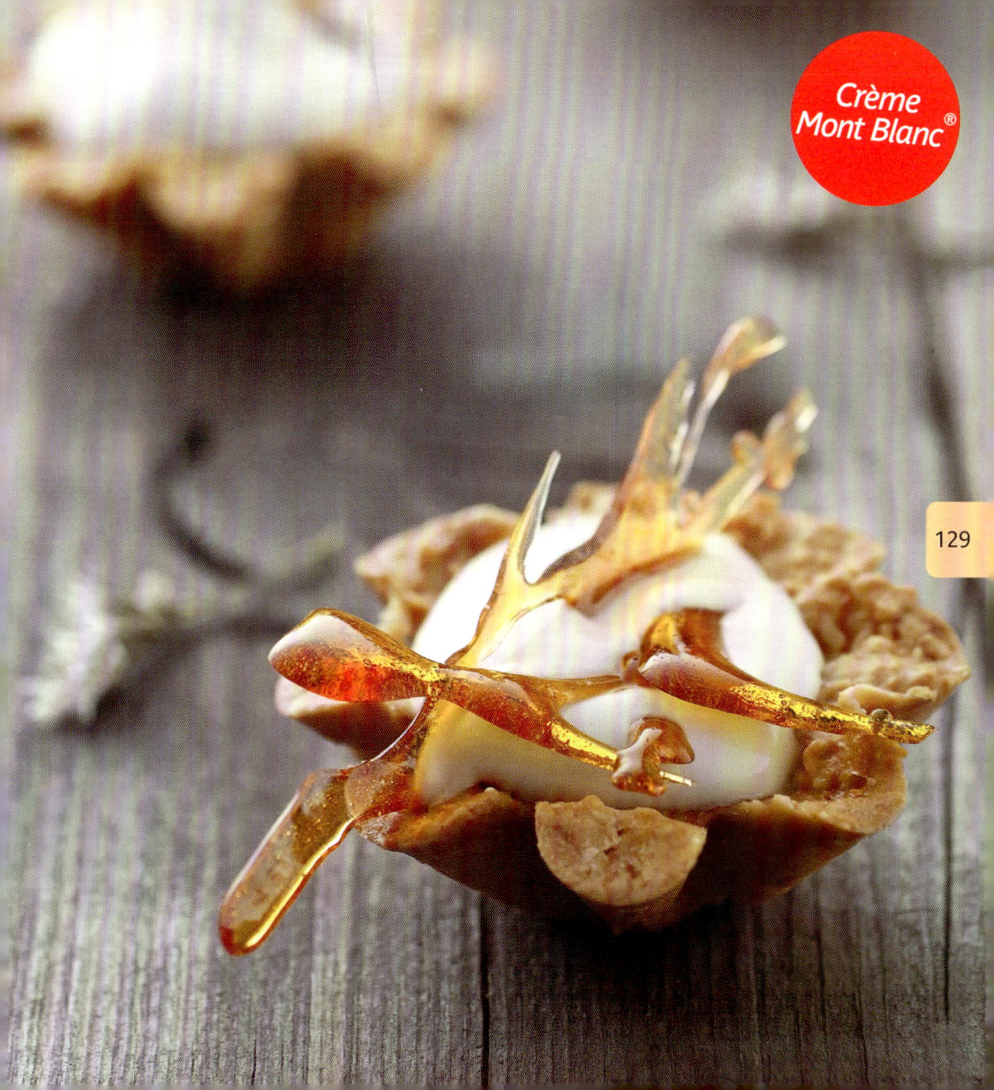
Crème
Mont Blanc®

VERRINES À LA VANILLE ET À LA PÊCHE

Préparation : 10 min • **Cuisson** : aucune • **Réfrigération** : 1 h
Pour 8 personnes

500 g de cake aux fruits confits • 420 g de pêches au sirop en quartiers • 100 g de crème Mont Blanc® à la vanille • 6 cl de cognac • 60 g de crème fraîche épaisse • 50 g de copeaux de chocolat noir

- Coupez le cake en tranches, puis coupez celles-ci en deux. Répartissez-les au fond de 8 verrines.
- Ajoutez les quartiers de pêches.
- Mélangez la crème Mont Blanc® à la vanille et le cognac. Versez le mélange sur les pêches.
- Battez rapidement la crème fraîche épaisse au fouet, puis ajoutez-la dans les verrines.
- Parsemez de copeaux de chocolat noir, puis servez sans attendre.

Verrines à l'orange

Pelez 4 oranges, puis prélevez les quartiers et retirez délicatement la fine membrane qui les entoure. Remplacez les pêches par les morceaux d'orange.

Verrines à l'abricot et à la lavande

Remplacez les pêches par 12 abricots frais dénoyautés. Mettez 3 demi-abricots dans chaque verrine. Remplacez les copeaux de chocolat par 1 ou 2 c. à s. de fleurs de lavande séchées.

Verrines estivales

Remplacez les pêches au sirop par 4 nectarines fraîches pelées, dénoyautées et coupées en quartiers. Remplacez les copeaux de chocolat par des framboises ou des groseilles.

Verrines exotiques

Remplacez les pêches par 2 mangues pelées, débarrassées de la partie dure au centre et taillées en petits dés. Remplacez les copeaux de chocolat par la pulpe de 2 fruits de la Passion.

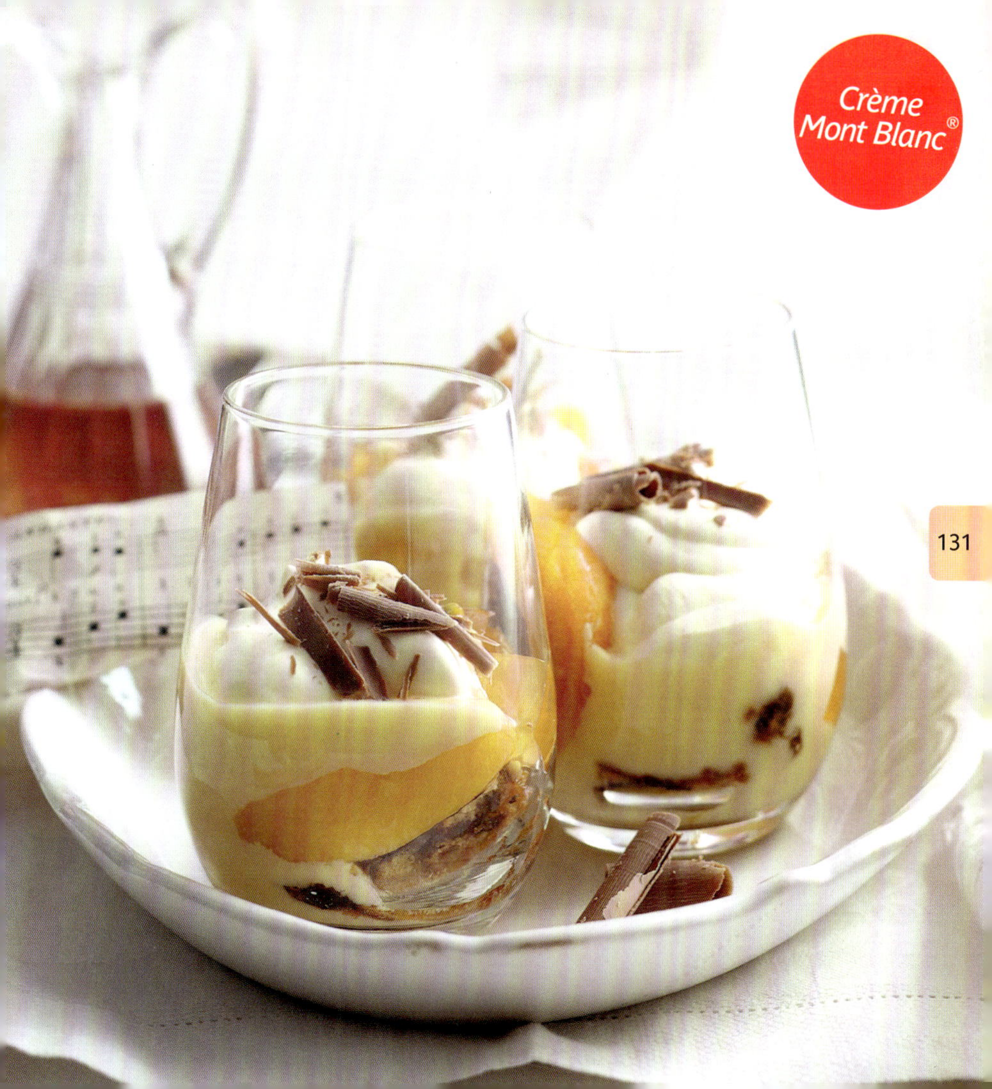
Crème
Mont Blanc®

CORNETS À LA VANILLE

Préparation: 10 min • **Cuisson**: 25 min • **Pour 12 feuilletés**

pour les cornets : 300 g de pâte feuilletée
farine, pour le plan de travail • 1 œuf
pour la crème : 250 g de Danette® à la vanille • 10 cl de crème liquide
le zeste de 1/2 citron

- Préchauffez le four à 220 °C.
- Déroulez la pâte feuilletée sur le plan de travail légèrement fariné et étalez-la au rouleau à pâtisserie pour obtenir une épaisseur de 5 cm.
- À l'aide d'un couteau bien aiguisé, découpez des bandes de pâte de 5 cm de longueur. Enroulez-les en petits cornets. Badigeonnez-les de l'œuf battu.
- Disposez-les sur une plaque à pâtisserie tapissée de papier sulfurisé, et faites cuire au four de 10 à 15 min.
- Pour la crème, mélangez la Danette®, la crème liquide et le zeste de citron dans une casserole, et laissez mijoter à feu moyen pendant 10 min environ.
- Répartissez la crème dans les cornets feuilletés. Servez sans attendre.

Feuilletés à la vanille et aux dattes

Remplacez le zeste de citron par 50 g de dattes coupées en dés.

Feuilletés à la vanille et aux pépites de chocolat

Supprimez le zeste de citron. Préparez la crème à la Danette® à l'avance, puis ajoutez-y 60 g de pépites de chocolat noir une fois qu'elle a refroidi. Garnissez-en les cornets chauds.

Feuilletés à la vanille et aux cerises confites

Reprenez la recette ci-dessus en remplaçant les pépites de chocolat noir par 50 g de cerises confites taillées en dés.

Café royal

Préparez l'café et versez-le dans une chope. Imbibez 1 morceau de sucre de cognac et faites-le flamber avant de le mettre dans le café. Mélangez, puis servez les cornets.

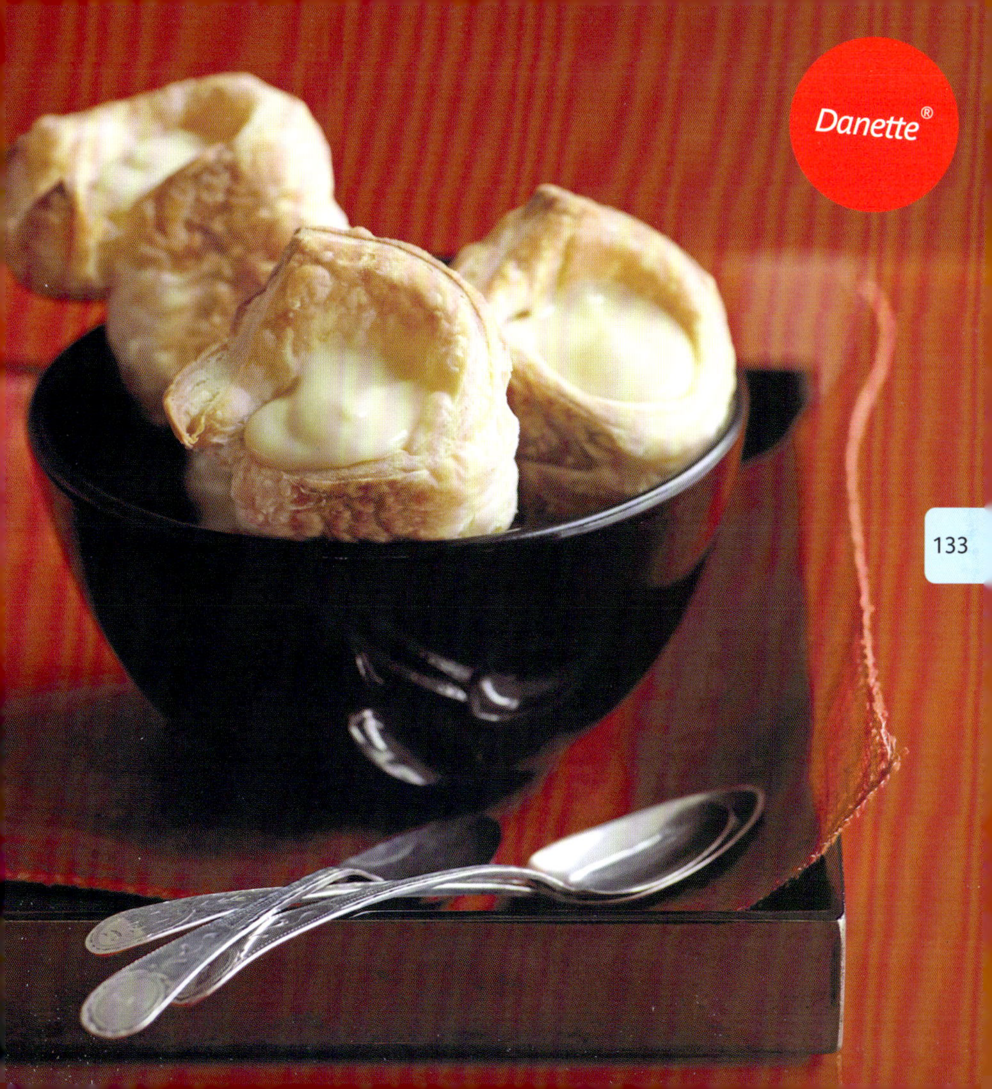
Danette®

Danette®

GLACE AU CHOCOLAT ET À LA MENTHE

Préparation : 10 min • **Cuisson** : 10 min • **Turbine** : 20 min
Pour 4 personnes

150 g de sucre en poudre • 2 c. à s. de liqueur de menthe
250 g de Danette® au chocolat

- Faites chauffer 40 cl d'eau dans une casserole, puis ajoutez le sucre et la liqueur de menthe.
- Portez à ébullition et laissez frémir pendant 5 min, puis retirez du feu. Laissez refroidir.
- Ajoutez la Danette®, puis battez au fouet.
- Versez le mélange dans une sorbetière et laissez turbiner.
- Conservez au congélateur.

Glace au chocolat et à l'orange confite

Supprimez la liqueur de menthe. Coupez 75 g d'écorces d'orange confites en tout petits dés, puis ajoutez-les à la préparation refroidie.

Glace au chocolat et au pralin

Supprimez la liqueur de menthe. Ajoutez 50 g de pralin à la préparation refroidie.

Glace au chocolat et au sirop d'érable

Supprimez la liqueur de menthe. Remplacez le sucre par 4 c. à s. de sirop d'érable. Ajoutez 50 g de noix de pécan à la préparation refroidie.

Coulis de caramel

Faites chauffer 120 g de sucre avec 30 cl d'eau, en remuant régulièrement, jusqu'à l'obtention d'un caramel à peine roux. Ajoutez 1 c. à s. d'eau, couvrez et faites cuire à feu doux jusqu'à ce que le caramel soit homogène. Ajoutez 10 cl de crème liquide. Servez avec la glace.

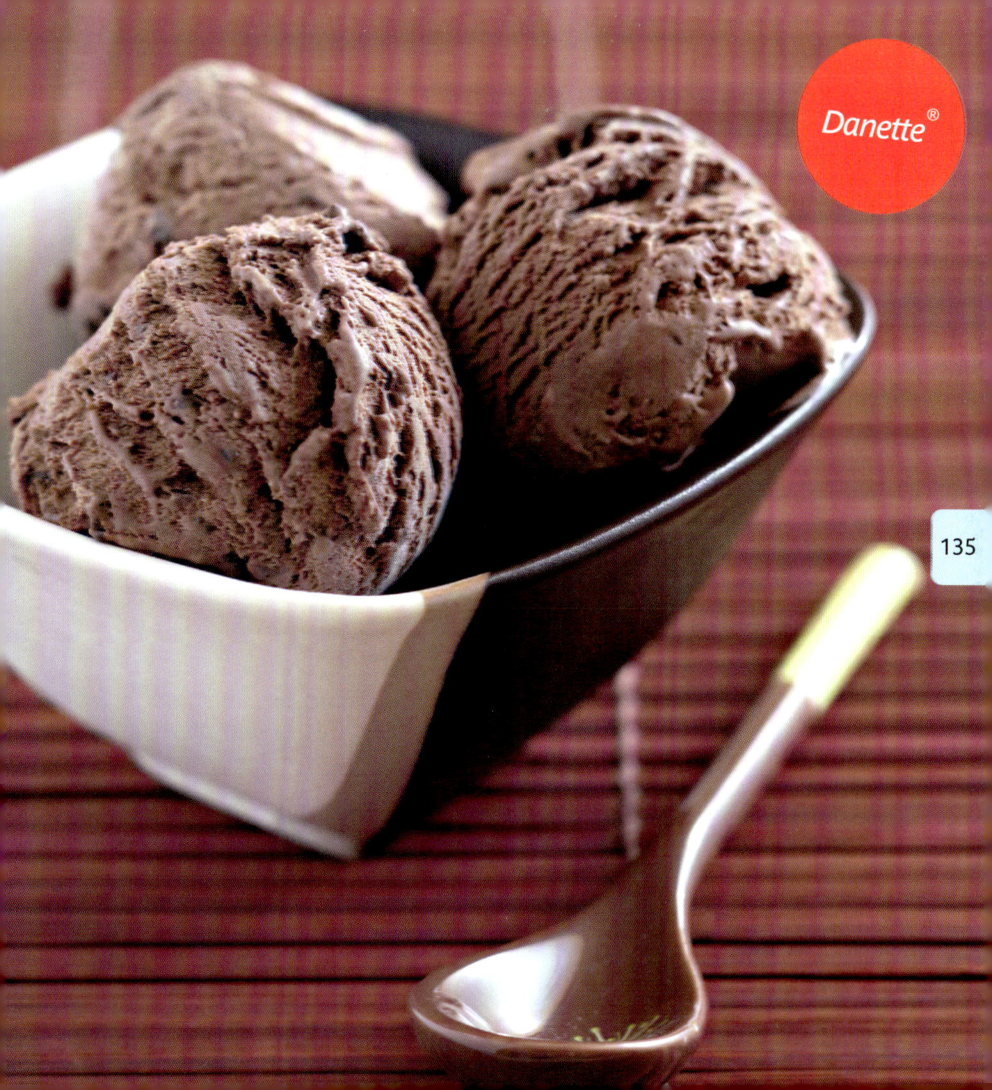
Danette®

MOELLEUX À LA PISTACHE ET AUX CERISES

Préparation : 15 min • **Cuisson :** 35 min • **Pour 6 personnes**

250 g de cerises • 4 œufs • 200 g de sucre en poudre • 125 g de farine
125 g de poudre de pistaches • 2 petits pots de Danette® à la pistache
15 cl d'huile de tournesol

- Préchauffez le four à 180 °C.
- Rincez les cerises, équeutez-les et dénoyautez-les.
- Séparez les blancs des jaunes d'œufs. Battez les jaunes avec le sucre jusqu'à l'obtention d'un mélange mousseux.
- Ajoutez la farine et la poudre de pistaches. Formez un puits au centre, puis incorporez les Danette® à la pistache et l'huile.
- Battez les blancs d'œufs en neige ferme au fouet électrique, puis incorporez-les à la préparation. Ajoutez enfin les cerises.
- Versez dans un moule carré tapissé de papier sulfurisé.
- Faites cuire au four de 30 à 35 min. Vérifiez la cuisson en piquant la pointe d'un couteau au centre du gâteau : elle doit ressortir sèche.

Moelleux à la pistache et aux abricots

Remplacez les cerises par 250 g d'abricots dénoyautés et coupés en quatre.

Moelleux au caramel et à la banane

Remplacez les Danette® à la pistache par des Danette® au caramel, et les cerises par 3 bananes pelées et coupées en rondelles.

Moelleux au chocolat et aux noisettes

Remplacez les Danette® à la pistache par des Danette® au chocolat, et les cerises par 1 poignée de noisettes concassées.

Moelleux au chocolat blanc et aux poires

Remplacez les Danette® à la pistache par des Danette® au chocolat blanc, et les cerises par 3 poires pelées, épépinées et taillées en dés.

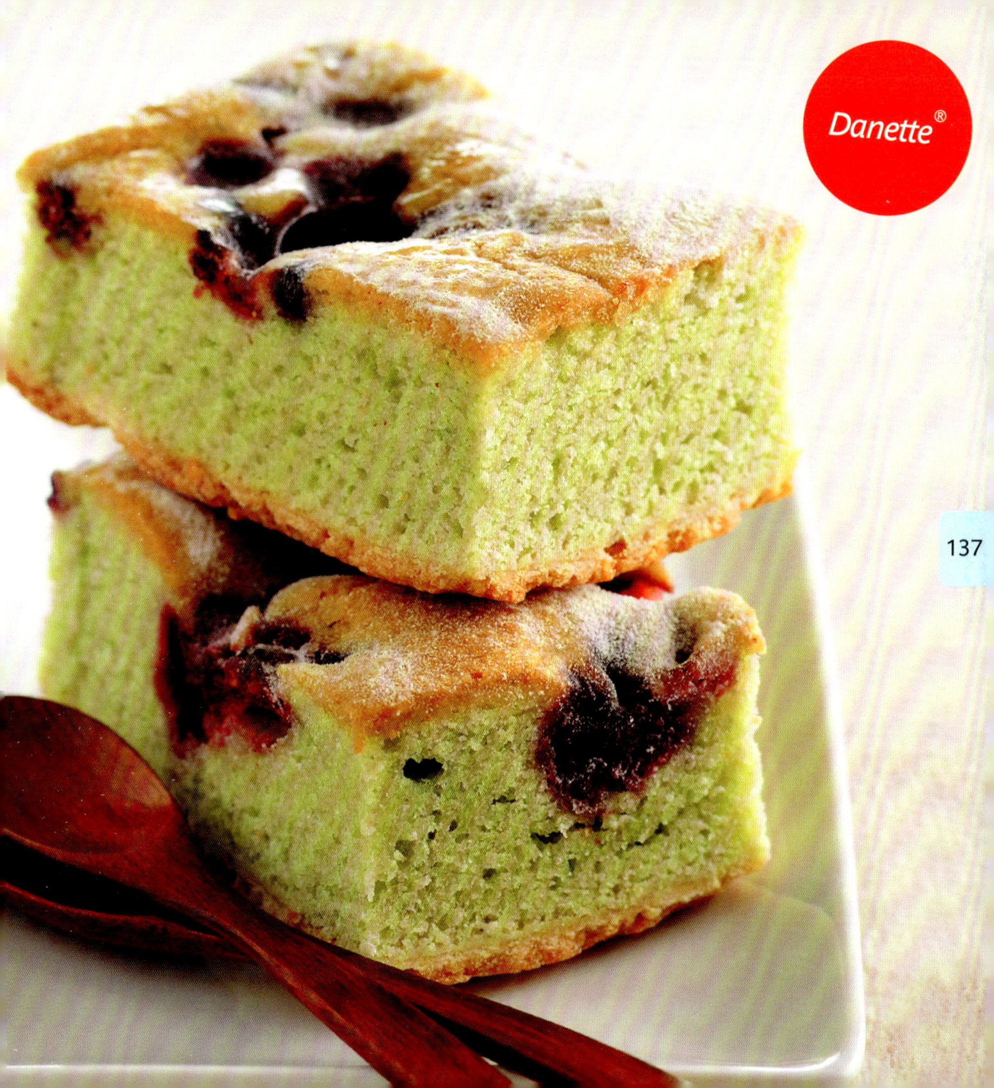
Danette®

PALMIERS AU CARAMEL

Préparation : 15 min • **Cuisson :** 25 min • **Congélation :** 30 min
Pour 25 palmiers

20 g de fécule de pomme de terre • 25 g de sucre en poudre • 1 œuf + 1 jaune • 2 pots de Danette® au caramel • 1 rouleau de pâte feuilletée

- Préchauffez le four à 180 °C.
- Mélangez la fécule de pomme de terre et le sucre en poudre dans une jatte supportant la chaleur. Incorporez l'œuf et mélangez bien, jusqu'à l'obtention d'un mélange lisse et homogène. Ajoutez ensuite le contenu des pots de Danette®.
- Faites chauffer la préparation au bain-marie. Poursuivez la cuisson en remuant pendant 2 min après l'ébullition. Retirez la jatte du feu et laissez refroidir.
- Déroulez la pâte feuilletée, puis nappez-la généreusement du mélange à la Danette®. Roulez la pâte sur elle-même jusqu'à la moitié, puis roulez l'autre moitié de même, de façon à obtenir deux boudins se rejoignant au centre de la pâte.
- Enveloppez les boudins accolés dans du film alimentaire et placez au congélateur pendant 30 min, de façon qu'ils soient suffisamment durs pour qu'on puisse les découper facilement.
- Détaillez les boudins en tranches de 2 cm d'épaisseur. Battez le jaune d'œuf avec un peu d'eau, puis badigeonnez-en les palmiers.
- Répartissez-les sur une plaque à pâtisserie recouverte de papier sulfurisé, puis faites-les cuire au four pendant 20 min. Dégustez chaud.

Palmiers au caramel et au pavot
Parsemez les palmiers de graines de pavot juste avant d'enfourner.

Palmiers au caramel et au chocolat
Faites fondre 150 g de chocolat avec 15 cl de crème liquide au bain-marie. Trempez les palmiers refroidis dans le chocolat fondu, puis laissez prendre sur une plaque recouverte de papier sulfurisé.

Croissants aux abricots secs et au caramel
Taillez la pâte feuilletée en 16 triangles. Déposez 1 abricot sec à la base de chacun, et nappez de crème au caramel, avant de rouler en croissant et de faire cuire au four.

Croissants aux figues et au caramel
Reprenez la recette ci-dessus en remplaçant les abricots secs par des morceaux de figue fraîche.

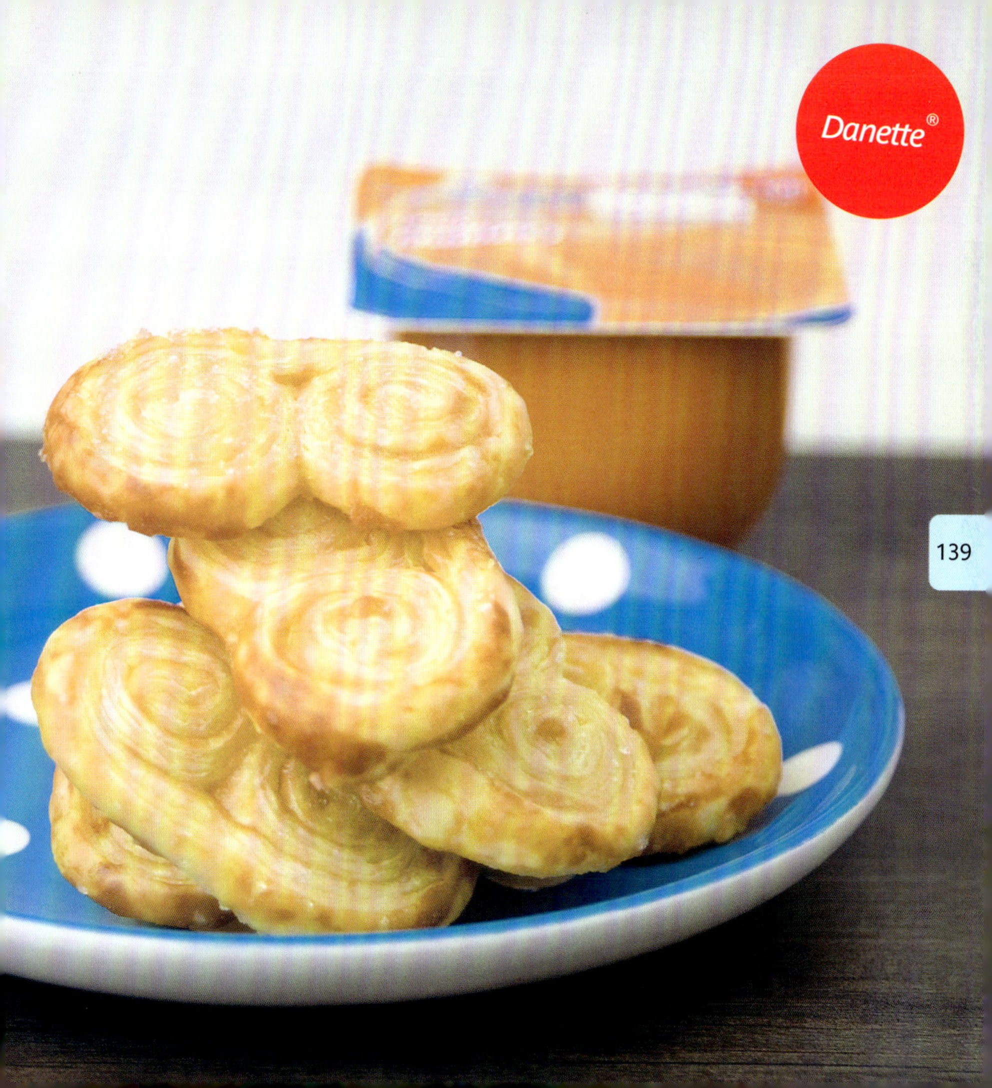
Danette®

BÂTONNETS GLACÉS AUX FRAISES TAGADA®

Préparation : 5 min • **Cuisson :** aucune • **Congélation :** 4 h
Pour 6 esquimaux

20 fraises Tagada® • 4 yaourts brassés nature • 20 cl de lait
2 c. à s. de sirop de grenadine • 125 g de sucre en poudre • sucre rose

- Mettez tous les ingrédients dans le bol du mixeur, et mixez jusqu'à l'obtention d'une préparation homogène.
- Répartissez le mélange dans 6 moules à esquimau. Mettez les couvercles et enfoncez les bâtonnets.
- Placez au congélateur pour 4 h.
- Sortez les esquimaux du congélateur 5 min avant de servir, retirez-les des moules et passez-les dans le sucre rose.
- Dégustez sans attendre.

Bâtonnets glacés vodka-Tagada®
Ajoutez 10 cl de vodka nature ou au citron à la préparation.

Bâtonnets glacés aux deux fraises
Ajoutez 50 g de fraises séchées à la préparation. Vous pouvez aussi utiliser des fraises fraîches coupées en morceaux.

Bâtonnets glacés soja-Tagada®
Utilisez des yaourts au soja et du lait de soja. Remplacez le sucre en poudre par de la cassonade.

Bâtonnets glacés au basilic et aux fraises Tagada®
Ajoutez 1 petite poignée de feuilles de basilic hachées à la préparation.

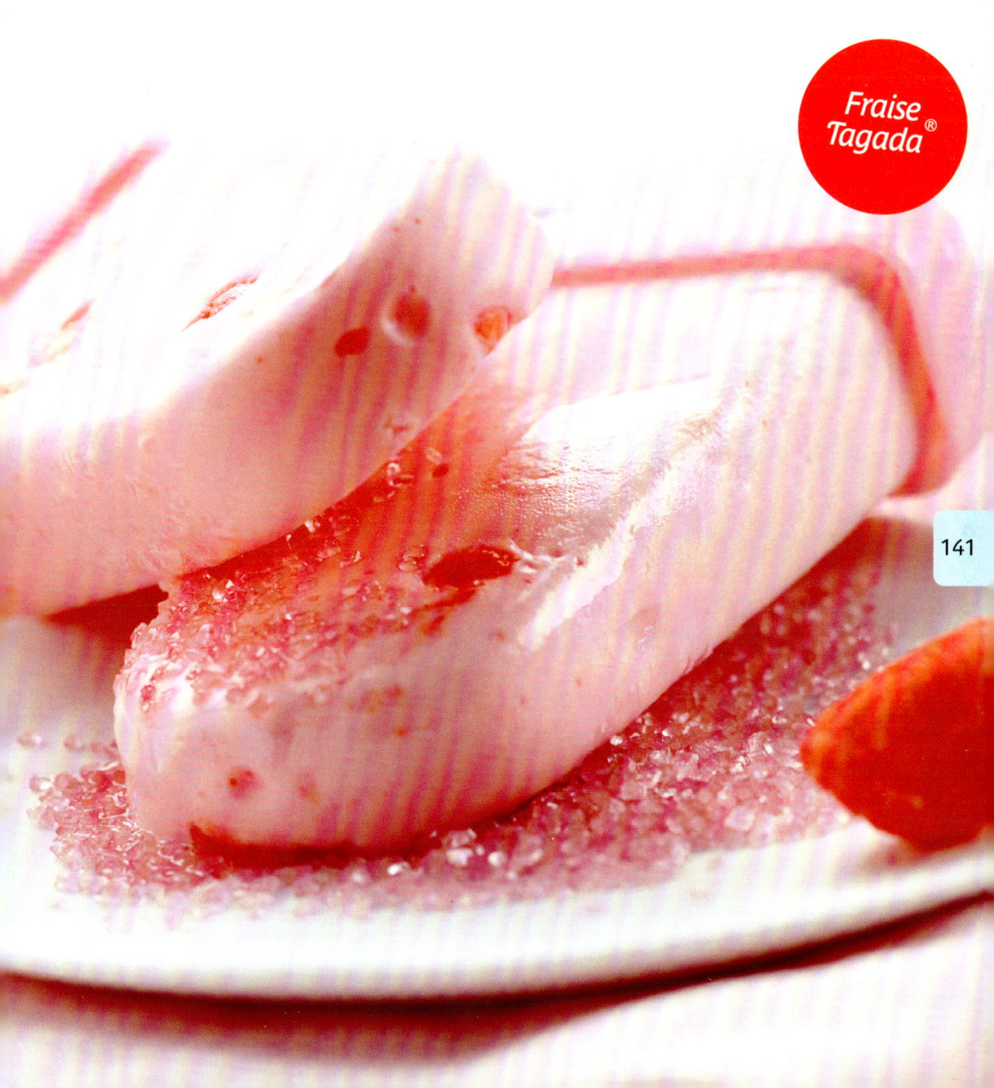

Fraise Tagada®

LAIT FRAPPÉ À LA FRAISE TAGADA®

Préparation : 5 min • **Cuisson** : 5 min • **Repos** : 45 min • **Pour 4 personnes**

80 cl de lait • 250 g de fraises Tagada® • 4 boules de glace à la vanille
8 glaçons

- Faites chauffer le lait dans une casserole sans laisser bouillir.
- Hors du feu, ajoutez les fraises Tagada® et laissez infuser pendant 30 min.
- Mixez le mélange, puis réservez au congélateur pendant 15 min.
- Ajoutez la glace et mixez de nouveau, puis versez dans un shaker avec les glaçons.
- Frappez, puis versez dans des verres hauts.
- Servez sans attendre.

Lait frappé framboises-Tagada®
Utilisez la moitié des fraises Tagada®. Ajoutez 150 g de framboises fraîches dans le mixeur avec la glace.

Lait frappé gingembre-Tagada®
Ajoutez 1 c. à c. de gingembre en poudre ou 1 morceau de 1 cm de gingembre frais râpé à la préparation.

Chantilly aux fraises Tagada®
Faites fondre 100 g de fraises Tagada® avec 50 g de sucre en poudre et 10 cl de crème liquide sur feu moyen. Hors du feu, incorporez 15 cl de crème liquide et mélangez. Laissez refroidir. Mettez dans un siphon et nappez-en le lait frappé.

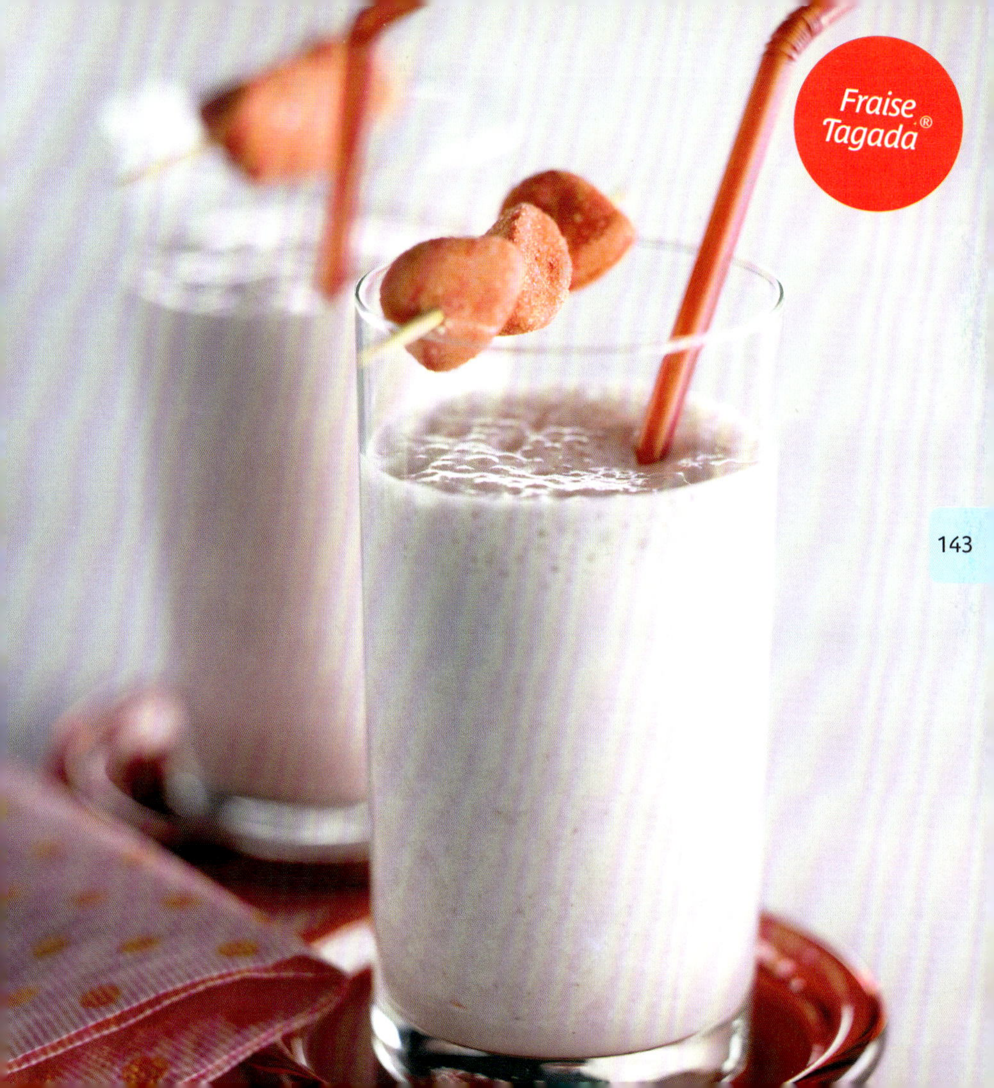
Fraise Tagada®

RIZ AU LAIT AUX FRAISES TAGADA®

Préparation : 10 min • **Cuisson** : 30 min • **Pour 4 personnes**

1 l de lait • 50 g de sucre en poudre • 200 g de riz rond
15 fraises Tagada® • 1 c. à s. de sirop de grenadine

- Mettez le lait et le sucre dans une casserole et portez à ébullition.
- Rincez le riz, puis ajoutez-le au lait, et faites cuire pendant 20 min à feu doux en remuant régulièrement pour éviter que le mélange n'attache.
- Coupez les fraises Tagada® en quatre, ajoutez-les à la préparation et poursuivez la cuisson pendant encore 10 min.
- Hors du feu, ajoutez le sirop de grenadine.
- Laissez refroidir avant de servir.

Riz au lait de chèvre
Remplacez le lait par du lait de chèvre (on en trouve dans les épiceries bios).

Semoule au lait Tagada®
Remplacez le riz par 80 g de semoule fine. Faites cuire pendant 5 min.

Verrines Tagada® surprises
Répartissez 10 palets bretons émiettés dans 6 verrines. Nappez de riz au lait aux fraises Tagada®, couvrez de fraises fraîches, puis de chantilly.

Nectarines au riz au lait
Lavez soigneusement 4 nectarines. Coupez-les en deux et dénoyautez-les. Garnissez chaque moitié de 2 c. à s. de riz au lait aux fraises Tagada®.

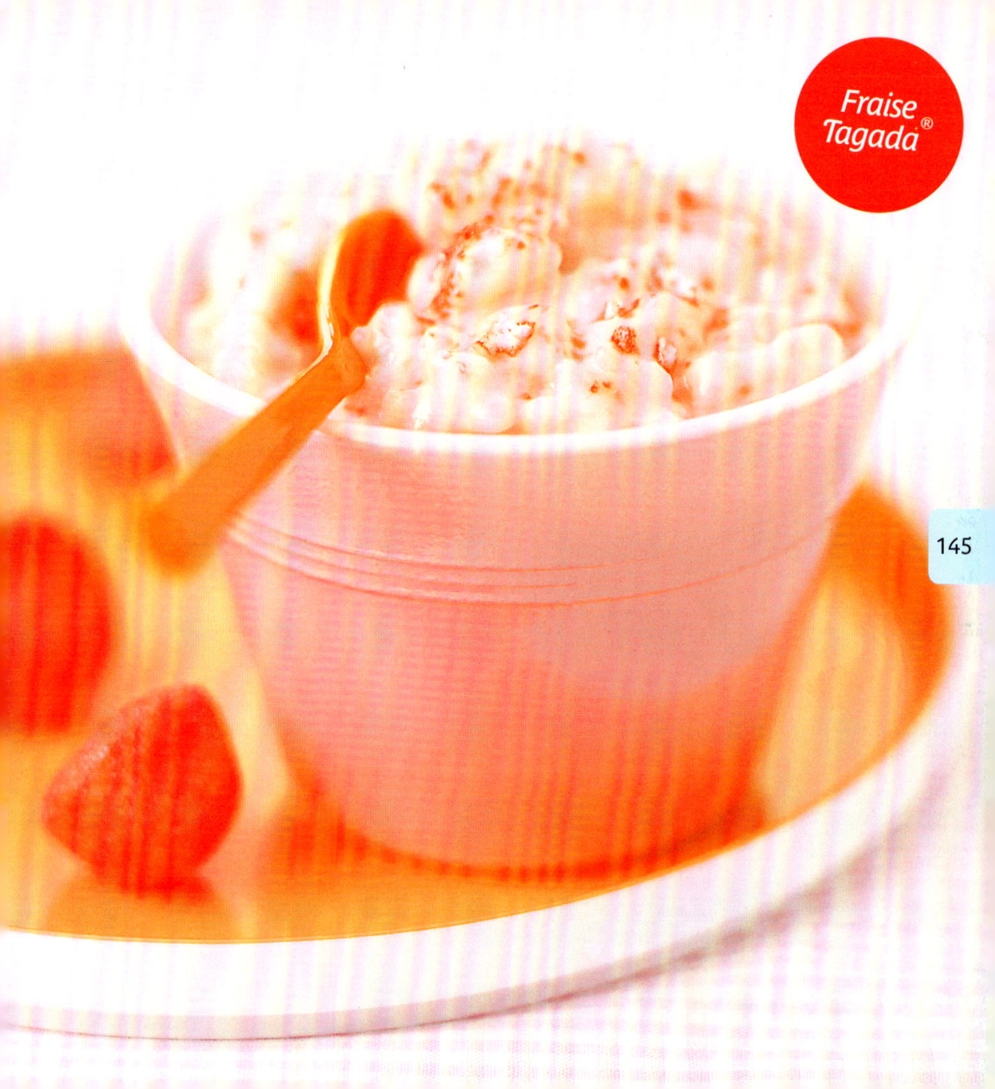

Fraise Tagada®

VERRINES À LA CRÈME TAGADA®

Préparation : 10 min • **Cuisson** : 10 min • **Réfrigération** : 4 h
Pour 4 personnes

pour la crème : *20 cl de crème liquide entière • 20 cl de lait*
20 fraises Tagada® • 2 feuilles de gélatine
pour les verrines : *1 paquet de fraises Tagada® • chantilly*
vermicelle de sucre coloré

- Versez la crème liquide et le lait dans une casserole. Ajoutez-y les fraises Tagada®, portez à frémissements et laissez cuire en remuant régulièrement jusqu'à ce que les fraises Tagada® soient fondues.
- Mettez la gélatine à ramollir dans un bol d'eau froide.
- Lorsque les fraises Tagada® sont fondues, ajoutez-y la gélatine essorée et mélangez bien.
- Répartissez le mélange dans 4 grandes verrines.
- Laissez refroidir, puis réservez au réfrigérateur pendant 4 h.
- Sortez les verrines du réfrigérateur. Déposez de 8 à 10 fraises Tagada® dans chacune et surmontez-les de chantilly. Parsemez de vermicelle de sucre coloré.
- Servez sans attendre.

Verrines Tagada® à la rhubarbe

Remplacez les fraises Tagada® des verrines par de la compote de rhubarbe.

Verrines Tagada® à la confiture

Remplacez les fraises Tagada® des verrines par de la confiture de fraises ou de mûres.

Verrines à la gelée de grenadine

Portez à ébullition 70 cl d'eau, 5 c. à s. de sirop de grenadine, 4 c. à s. de sucre et 2 g d'agar-agar. Mélangez, puis laissez prendre au réfrigérateur pendant 3 h. Surmontez la mousse de cette gelée.

Verrines aux tuiles Tagada®

Disposez 12 fraises Tagada® sur une plaque recouverte de papier sulfurisé et faites cuire au four préchauffé de 6 à 7 min, jusqu'à ce qu'elles commencent à se craqueler. Retirez du four et laissez refroidir sur une surface froide. Répartissez-les dans les verrines à la place des fraises Tagada®.

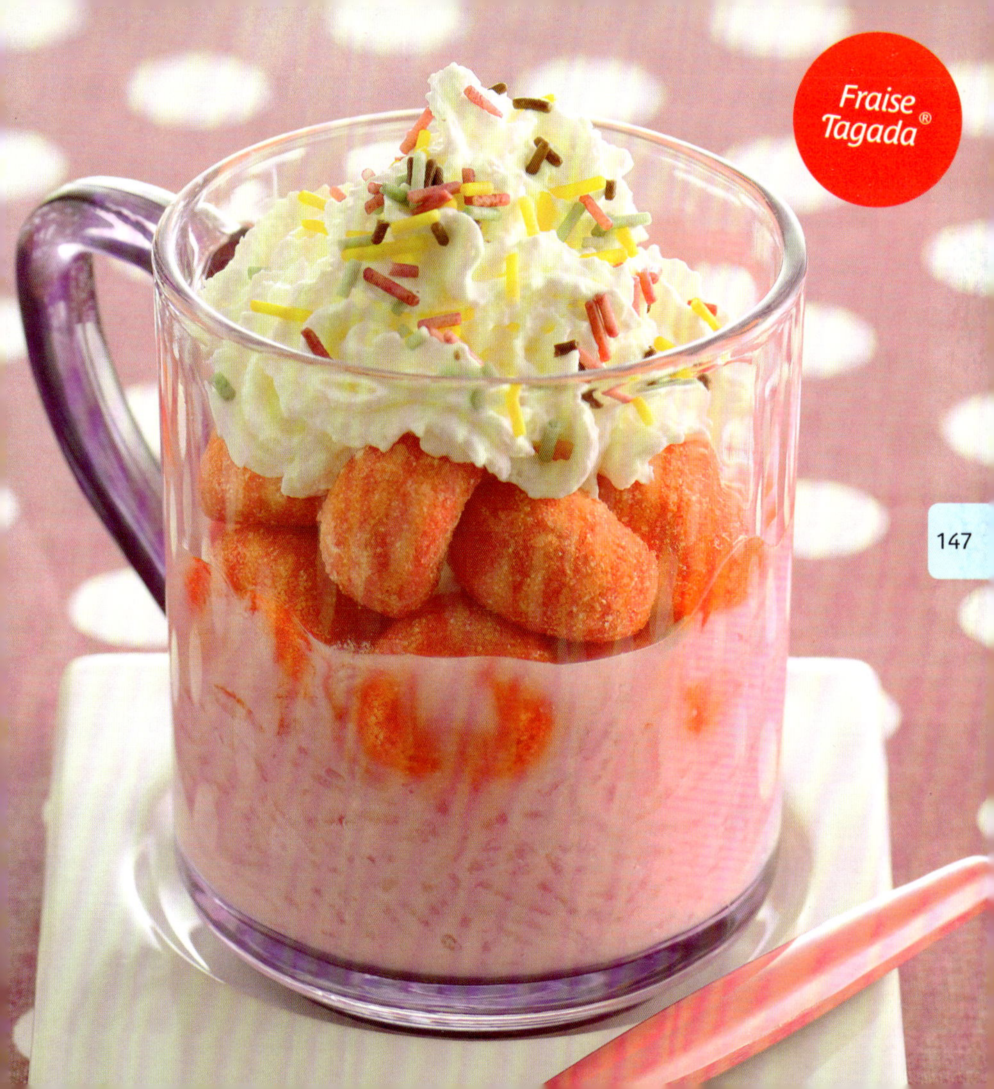
Fraise Tagada®

BIGOUDENS AUX FRAMBOISES

Préparation : 5 min • **Cuisson** : aucune • **Pour 4 bigoudens**

2 barquettes de framboises • 40 cl de crème liquide entière
16 galettes St Michel®

- Rincez les framboises et essuyez-les avec du papier absorbant.
- Fouettez rapidement la crème liquide.
- Déposez 4 framboises sur 1 galette St Michel®, puis surmontez-les de 1 c. à c. de crème fouettée. Déposez 1 galette St Michel® par-dessus, puis renouvelez l'opération 2 fois, en terminant par 1 galette St Michel®.
- Recommencez pour les 3 autres pyramides.
- Servez sans attendre.

Bigoudens à la rose et aux litchis

Aromatisez la crème avec 1 c. à s. d'eau de rose. Remplacez les framboises par des litchis pelés et dénoyautés.

Bigoudens aux pommes et à la cannelle

Aromatisez la crème avec 1 c. à c. de cannelle en poudre. Remplacez les framboises par des dés de pomme caramélisés à la poêle.

Bigoudens aux fraises et au lemon curd

Remplacez les framboises par des demi-fraises, et la crème fouettée par du lemon curd.

Bigoudens aux mûres et au mascarpone

Fouettez 120 g de mascarpone avec 60 g de sucre glace et le jus de 1 citron. Remplacez la crème fouettée par ce mélange, et les framboises par des mûres.

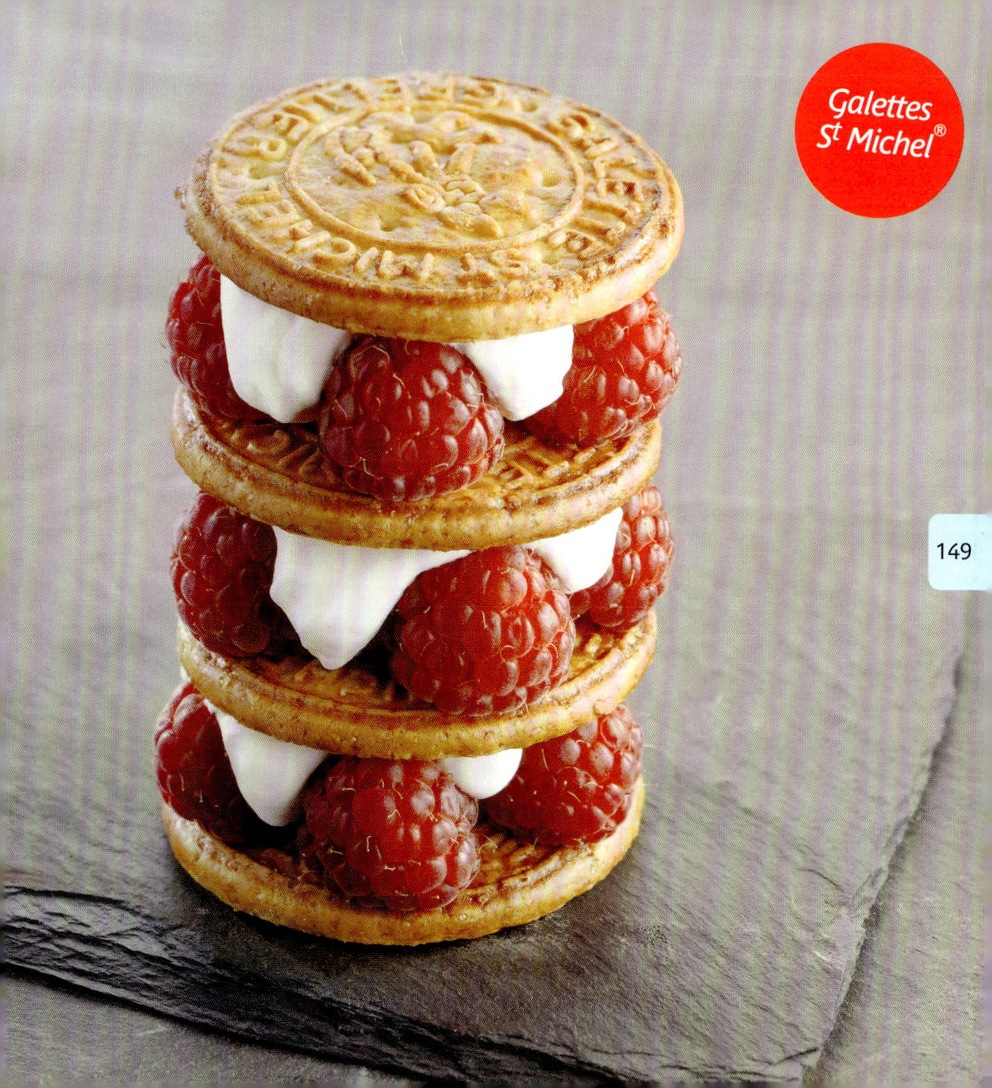
Galettes
St Michel®

CHEESECAKE AUX FRAMBOISES

Préparation : 30 min • **Cuisson** : 35 min • **Réfrigération** : 1 h
Pour 6 personnes

180 g de galettes St Michel® • 80 g de beurre • 500 g de ricotta
2 œufs • 100 g de sucre en poudre • 200 g de framboises

- Préchauffez le four à 180 °C.
- Écrasez grossièrement les galettes St Michel® puis mixez-les avec le beurre.
- Tapissez le fond d'un moule à charnière de cette préparation.
- Mixez la ricotta avec les œufs, le sucre et les framboises.
- Versez dans le moule, sur le fond de pâte.
- Faites cuire au four de 30 à 35 min.
- Laissez refroidir et réservez au réfrigérateur pendant au moins 1 h avant de servir.

Cheesecake au citron

Remplacez les framboises par le zeste râpé de 2 citrons. Faites chauffer 1/2 pot de marmelade de citron, à feu doux. Nappez le cheesecake encore chaud de marmelade. Laissez prendre au réfrigérateur pendant 4 h.

Cheesecake au coquelicot

Remplacez les framboises par 125 g de confit de coquelicot.

Cheesecake au chocolat blanc

Supprimez les framboises. Faites fondre 100 g de chocolat blanc, puis incorporez-le à la préparation à base de ricotta.

Cheesecake au chocolat blanc et à la lavande

Reprenez la recette ci-dessus en ajoutant 1 c. à s. de sirop de lavande à la préparation à base de ricotta.

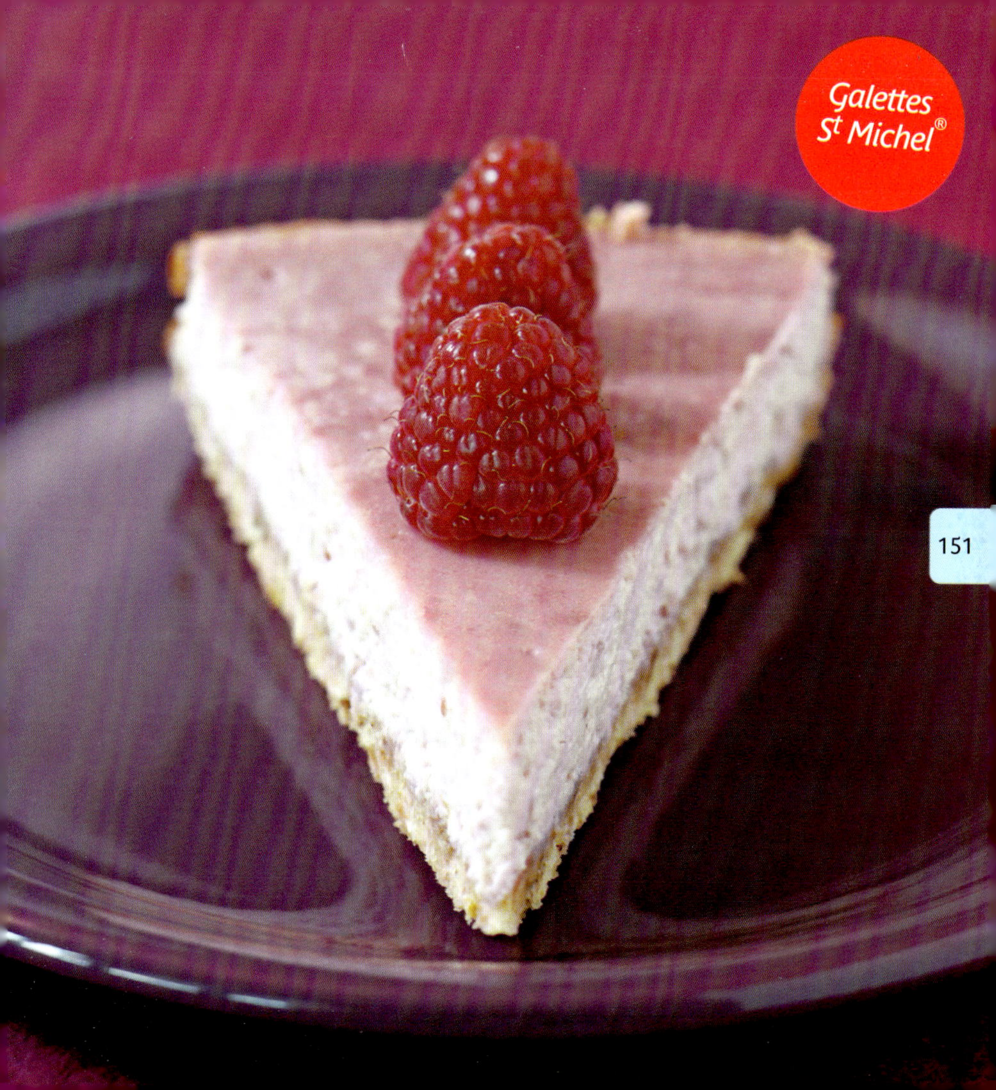
Galettes St Michel®

STREUSEL AUX POMMES ET AUX GALETTES ST MICHEL®

Préparation : 20 min • **Cuisson** : 35 min • **Pour 8 personnes**

pour le gâteau : *100 g de beurre demi-sel ramolli + un peu pour le moule 100 g de sucre en poudre • 3 œufs • le jus de 1/2 citron • 240 g de farine + un peu pour le moule • 1/2 sachet de levure chimique 1 c. à c. de bicarbonate de soude • 10 cl de crème liquide • 4 pommes*
pour le streusel *: 100 g de galettes St Michel® • 40 g de beurre ramolli 150 g de cassonade • 30 g de farine • 1 pincée de cannelle en poudre*

- Pour le gâteau, battez le beurre et le sucre au fouet. Ajoutez les œufs et le jus de citron, et mélangez.
- Mélangez la farine, la levure et le bicarbonate de soude dans un saladier. Incorporez petit à petit à la préparation précédente, en fouettant, puis versez la crème liquide, sans cesser de fouetter.
- Pelez les pommes et coupez-les en cubes. Ajoutez-les à la pâte et mélangez. Versez la pâte dans un moule à manqué beurré et fariné.
- Préchauffez le four à 180 °C.
- Pour le streusel, écrasez grossièrement les galettes St Michel® et taillez le beurre en parcelles. Mettez-les dans un saladier avec tous les autres ingrédients, et travaillez du bout des doigts jusqu'à l'obtention d'une pâte sableuse.
- Répartissez ce mélange sur le gâteau, puis faites cuire au four de 30 à 35 min.
- Servez tiède.

Streusel aux pommes et aux canneberges
Supprimez 1 pomme et remplacez-la par 100 g de canneberges. Si vous n'en trouvez pas de fraîches, prenez des séchées, que vous ferez ramollir dans de l'eau froide.

Streusel aux pommes et à la rhubarbe
Remplacez 2 pommes par 200 g de rhubarbe coupée en dés. Ajoutez 50 g de raisins secs.

Streusel aux prunes et à la vanille
Remplacez les pommes par 500 g de prunes lavées, dénoyautées et coupées en quatre. Remplacez la cannelle par 1 c. à c. d'extrait de vanille liquide.

Sauce au sirop d'érable
Faites fondre 25 cl de sirop d'érable avec 12,5 cl de crème liquide et 15 g de beurre. Laissez mijoter pendant 10 min. Servez chaud, avec le streusel.

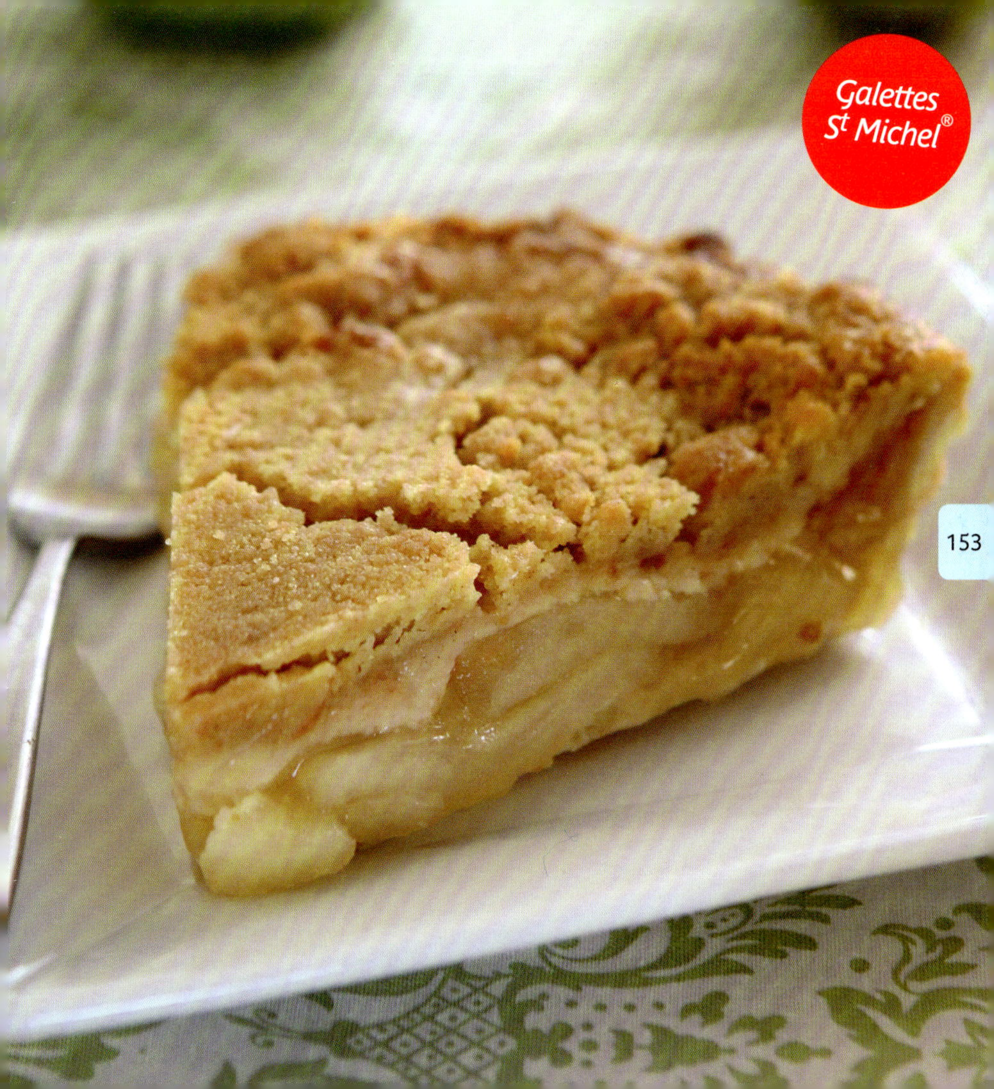
Galettes
St Michel®

TERRINE DE CHOCOLAT AUX GALETTES ST MICHEL®

Préparation : 10 min • **Cuisson** : 10 min • **Réfrigération** : 6 h
Pour 1 terrine

1 paquet de galettes St Michel® • 90 g de beurre + un peu pour le moule
20 cl de crème liquide • 400 g de chocolat noir à pâtisserie

- Cassez les galettes St Michel® en gros morceaux.
- Coupez le beurre en parcelles et mettez-le dans une jatte supportant la chaleur. Ajoutez la crème liquide et faites fondre au bain-marie.
- Coupez le chocolat en morceaux et ajoutez-les dans la jatte. Faites fondre sur feu doux, en remuant régulièrement.
- Laissez refroidir légèrement, puis versez la préparation dans un saladier. Ajoutez les morceaux de galettes St Michel®. Mélangez.
- Versez la préparation dans un moule à cake préalablement beurré.
- Laissez prendre au réfrigérateur pendant 6 h.
- Découpez en tranches, puis servez.

Terrine de chocolat aux fruits secs

Utilisez seulement 1/2 paquet de galettes St Michel®. Ajoutez 40 g de pistaches non salées, 40 g de noix de pécan et 40 g de noisettes.

Terrine de chocolat aux canneberges

Ajoutez 75 g de canneberges séchées à la préparation.

Terrine de chocolat blanc aux framboises

Remplacez le chocolat noir par du chocolat blanc.
Remplacez la moitié des galettes St Michel® par 150 g de framboises.

Sauce butterscotch

Faites fondre 125 g de beurre avec 100 g de sucre en poudre.
Laissez bouillir pendant 3 min, puis ajoutez 2 c. à s. de mélasse et 12,5 cl de crème fraîche.
Laissez mijoter pendant 10 min.
Hors du feu, ajoutez 1 c. à c. d'extrait de vanille liquide.
Servez tiède avec la terrine.

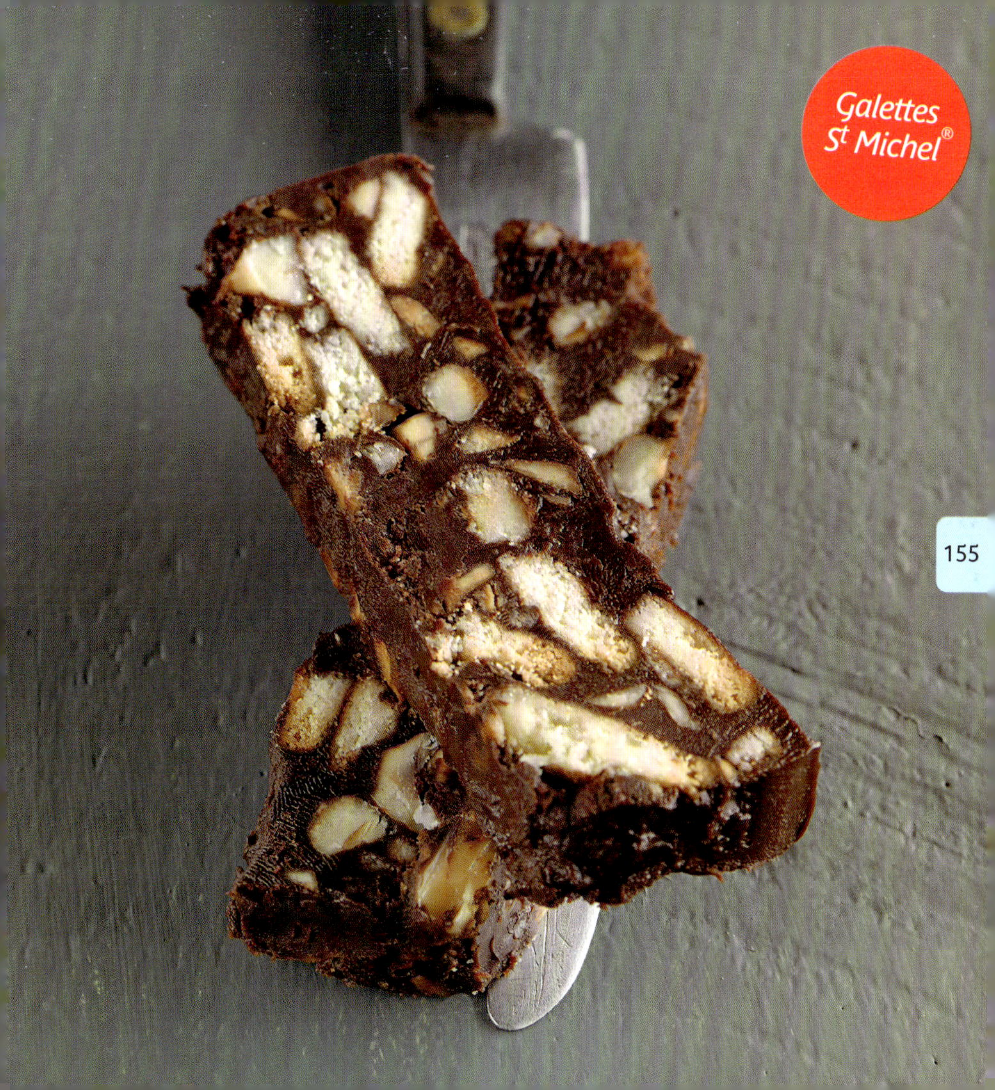
Galettes
St Michel®

TRUFFES AUX GALETTES ST MICHEL®

Préparation : 15 min • **Cuisson :** 10 min • **Réfrigération :** 2 h
Pour 20 truffes

200 g de chocolat blanc à pâtisserie • 20 g de beurre demi-sel
2 c. à s. de crème liquide • 6 galettes St Michel® • 2 c. à s. de cacao amer

- Cassez le chocolat en morceaux et mettez-les dans une jatte supportant la chaleur avec le beurre et la crème liquide. Faites fondre au bain-marie.
- Laissez refroidir pendant quelques minutes, puis placez la préparation au réfrigérateur, et laissez durcir pendant 2 h.
- Placez les galettes St Michel® dans un sac à congélation et fermez-le. Réduisez les galettes en poudre en les écrasant au rouleau à pâtisserie.
- Mélangez la poudre de biscuit et le cacao amer dans une assiette creuse.
- Modelez des boules de chocolat, puis roulez-les dans le mélange aux galettes St Michel® et au cacao.
- Conservez les truffes au réfrigérateur.

Truffes aux épices
Ajoutez à la préparation 1/2 c. à c. de cannelle en poudre et 1/2 c. à c. de gingembre moulu.

Truffes de pâte d'amandes
Remplacez la préparation pour les truffes par 200 g de pâte d'amandes blanche taillée en morceaux roulés en petites boules. Trempez-les dans du chocolat noir fondu, avant de les passer dans la chapelure de galettes.

Truffes de patate douce
Remplacez la préparation pour les truffes par 2 patates douces pelées, cuites à l'eau et écrasées en purée. Ajoutez 20 g d'écorces d'orange taillées en tout petits dés.

Vin chaud
Mettez 15 cl de vin rouge corsé, 2 cl de cognac, 1 c. à c. de sucre en poudre, 1 tranche de citron, 1 clou de girofle et 1 pincée de cannelle dans une casserole, et portez à frémissements. Servez avec les truffes.

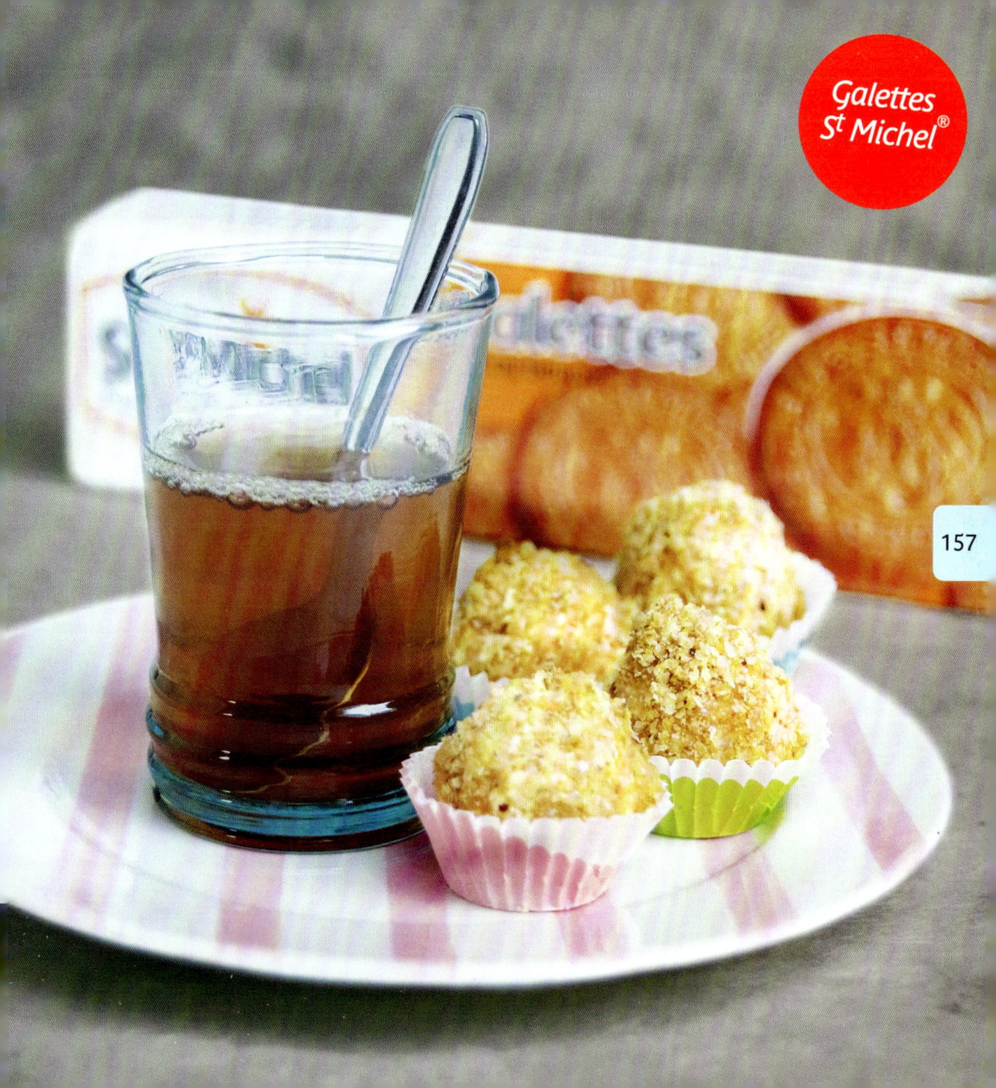

Galettes St Michel®

Croquants à l'amaretto
Aromatisez les croquants avec 2 c. à c. d'amaretto.

Croquants à l'anis vert
Remplacez la noix de coco râpée par de la farine complète, et les raisins secs par 2 c. à s. de graines d'anis vert.

Croquants à l'amande et à l'orange
Remplacez la noix de coco râpée par de la poudre d'amandes, et les raisins secs par 100 g d'écorces d'orange taillées en dés.

Croquants au chocolat et sirop de maïs
Remplacez la noix de coco râpée par 150 g de chocolat noir fondu, et le sucre par 5 c. à s. de sirop de maïs. Supprimez les raisins secs.

CROQUANTS AUX RAISINS SECS ET AUX CORN FLAKES

Préparation: 10 min • **Cuisson**: 12 min • **Pour 35 biscuits**

150 g de beurre • 2 œufs • 225 g de Kellogg's® corn flakes • 160 g de farine
1/2 sachet de levure chimique • 160 g de noix de coco râpée
120 g de raisins secs • 160 g de sucre • 80 g d'amandes effilées

- Préchauffez le four à 180 °C.
- Coupez le beurre en parcelles, puis faites-le fondre. Cassez les œufs et battez-les rapidement.
- Mettez les Kellogg's® corn flakes, la farine, la levure, la noix de coco, les raisins secs, le sucre et les amandes dans un saladier.
- Incorporez le beurre fondu et les œufs, et mélangez bien.
- Formez de petites boules de pâte et déposez-les sur une plaque à pâtisserie recouverte de papier sulfurisé, en les espaçant de 3 cm les unes des autres et en les aplatissant légèrement.
- Faites cuire au four de 10 à 12 min, jusqu'à ce que les biscuits soient bien dorés.
- Laissez refroidir sur une grille.

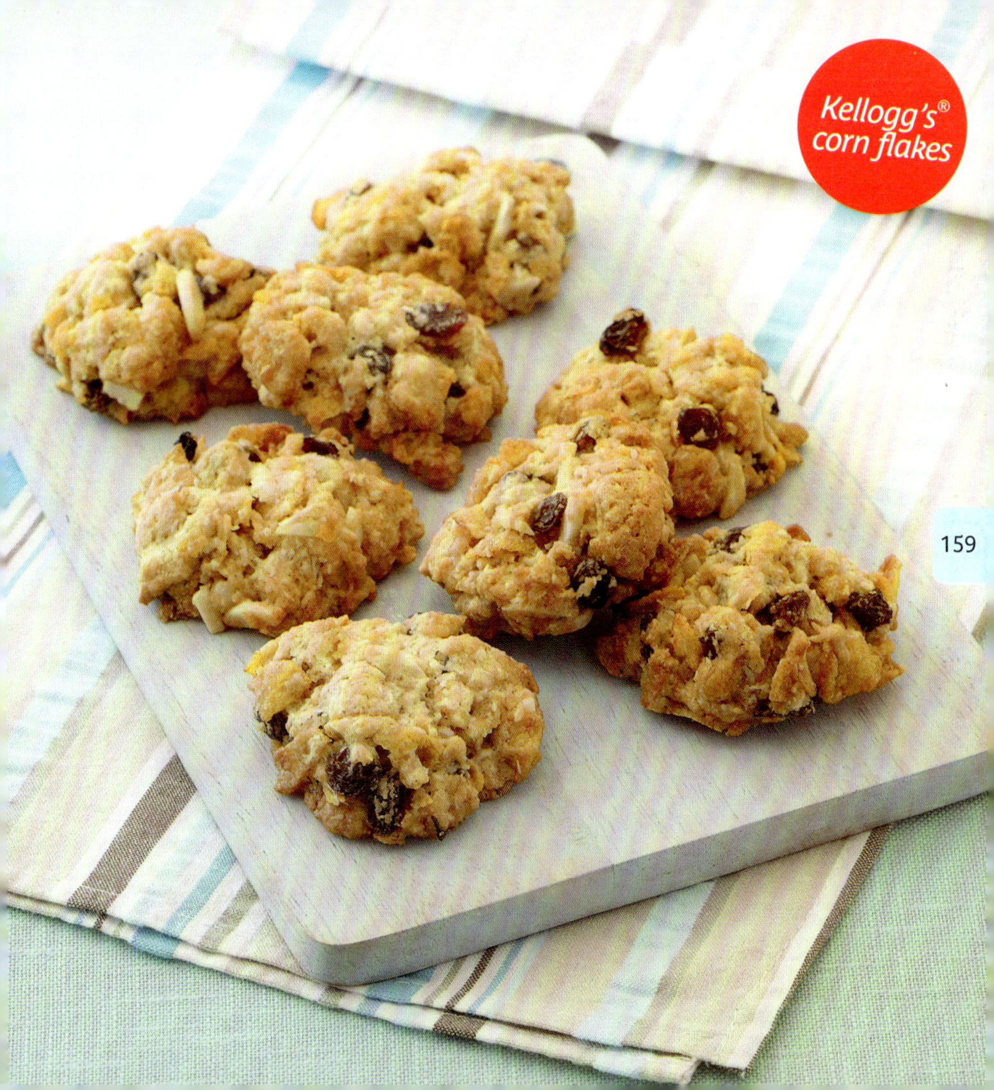
Kellogg's®
corn flakes

FLAPJACKS AUX CORN FLAKES

Préparation : 15 min • **Cuisson** : 25 min • **Pour 4 personnes**

75 g de Kellogg's® corn flakes • 100 g de beurre + un peu pour la plaque
1 c. à s. de golden syrup (à défaut, de sirop de canne)
100 g de sucre en poudre • 50 g de flocons d'avoine • 50 g de farine

- Préchauffez le four à 150 °C.
- Mettez les Kellogg's® corn flakes dans un sac à congélation, fermez-le, puis écrasez grossièrement les Kellogg's® corn flakes à l'aide d'un rouleau à pâtisserie.
- Mettez le beurre et le *golden syrup* dans une casserole et faites-les fondre à feu doux.
- Mettez les corn flakes écrasés, le sucre, les flocons d'avoine et la farine dans un saladier, puis mélangez.
- Ajoutez le beurre fondu et remuez bien.
- Étalez la préparation sur une plaque à pâtisserie préalablement beurrée. Pressez bien la pâte.
- Faites cuire au four pendant 20 min environ, jusqu'à ce que la pâte soit légèrement dorée.
- Laissez refroidir pendant quelques minutes, puis découpez les flapjacks en triangles.

Flapjacks à la banane et aux raisins secs

Ajoutez 2 bananes pelées et écrasées, ainsi que 30 g de raisins secs, à la préparation.

Flapjacks aux dattes et au miel

Ajoutez 12 dattes coupées en morceaux à la préparation, et remplacez le golden syrup par du miel.

Flapjacks aux myrtilles et aux noix

Ajoutez 50 g de myrtilles et 30 g de noix concassées à la préparation.

Flapjacks au chocolat au lait

Faites fondre 100 g de chocolat au lait au bain-marie. Nappez-en la surface des flapjacks cuits, découpés et refroidis.

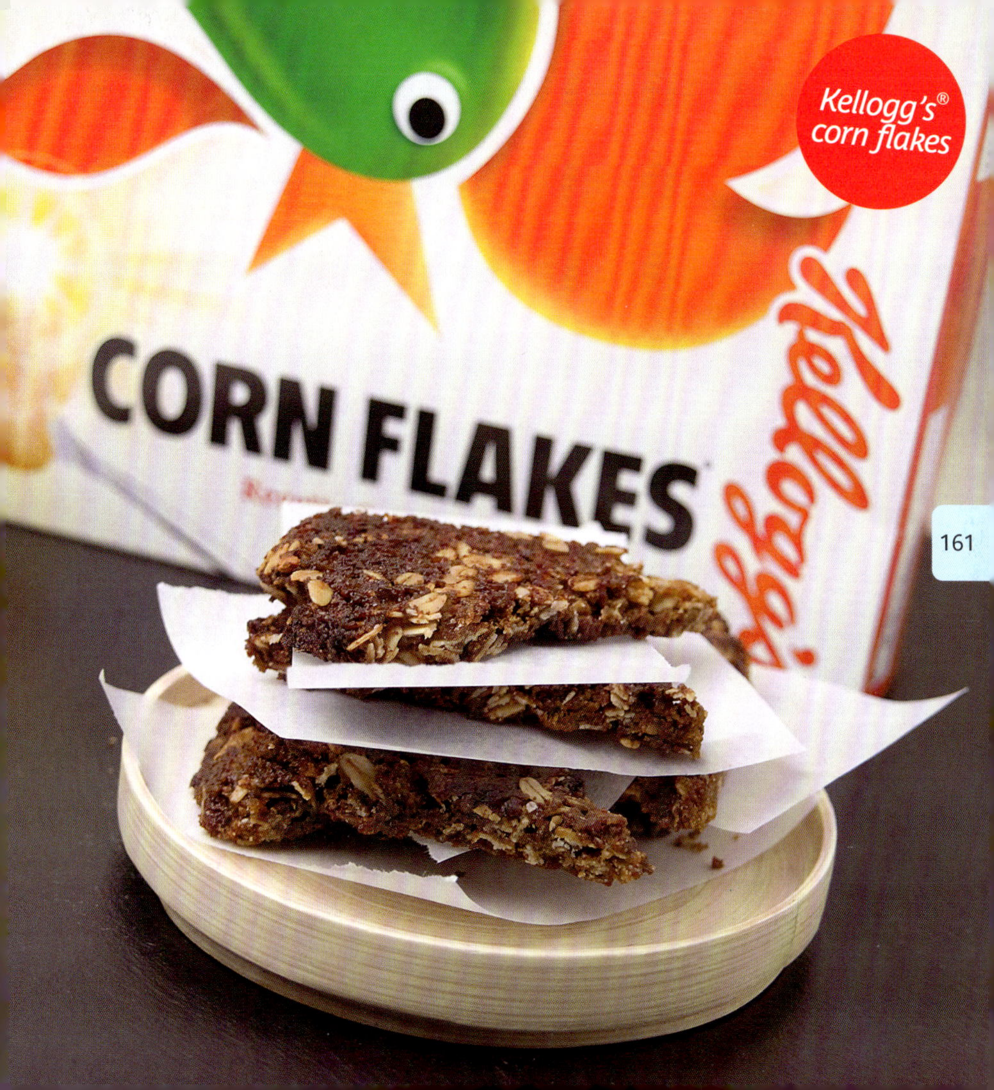
CORN FLAKES
Kellogg's

Roses des sables à la noix de coco
Ajoutez 40 g de noix de coco râpée à la préparation.

Roses des sables aux amandes
Ajoutez 60 g d'amandes effilées à la préparation.

Roses des sables blanches au citron vert
Remplacez le chocolat noir par du chocolat blanc, et ajoutez le zeste de 1 citron vert râpé à la préparation.

Roses des sables au chocolat au lait et aux fraises séchées
Remplacez le chocolat noir par du chocolat au lait, et ajoutez 60 g de fraises séchées à la préparation.

ROSES DES SABLES

Préparation : 15 min • **Cuisson :** aucune • **Réfrigération :** 1 h
Pour 30 roses des sables

*200 g de chocolat noir à pâtisserie • 100 g de beurre • 70 g de sucre glace
150 g de Kellogg's® corn flakes*

- Cassez le chocolat en morceaux, puis mettez-le dans une casserole avec le beurre, et faites fondre à feu doux, en remuant régulièrement.
- Hors du feu, incorporez le sucre glace.
- Versez le tout dans un saladier et incorporez les Kelloggs® corn flakes.
- Formez des petits tas et déposez-les sur une plaque à pâtisserie recouverte de papier sulfurisé.
- Laissez prendre au réfrigérateur pendant 1 h.

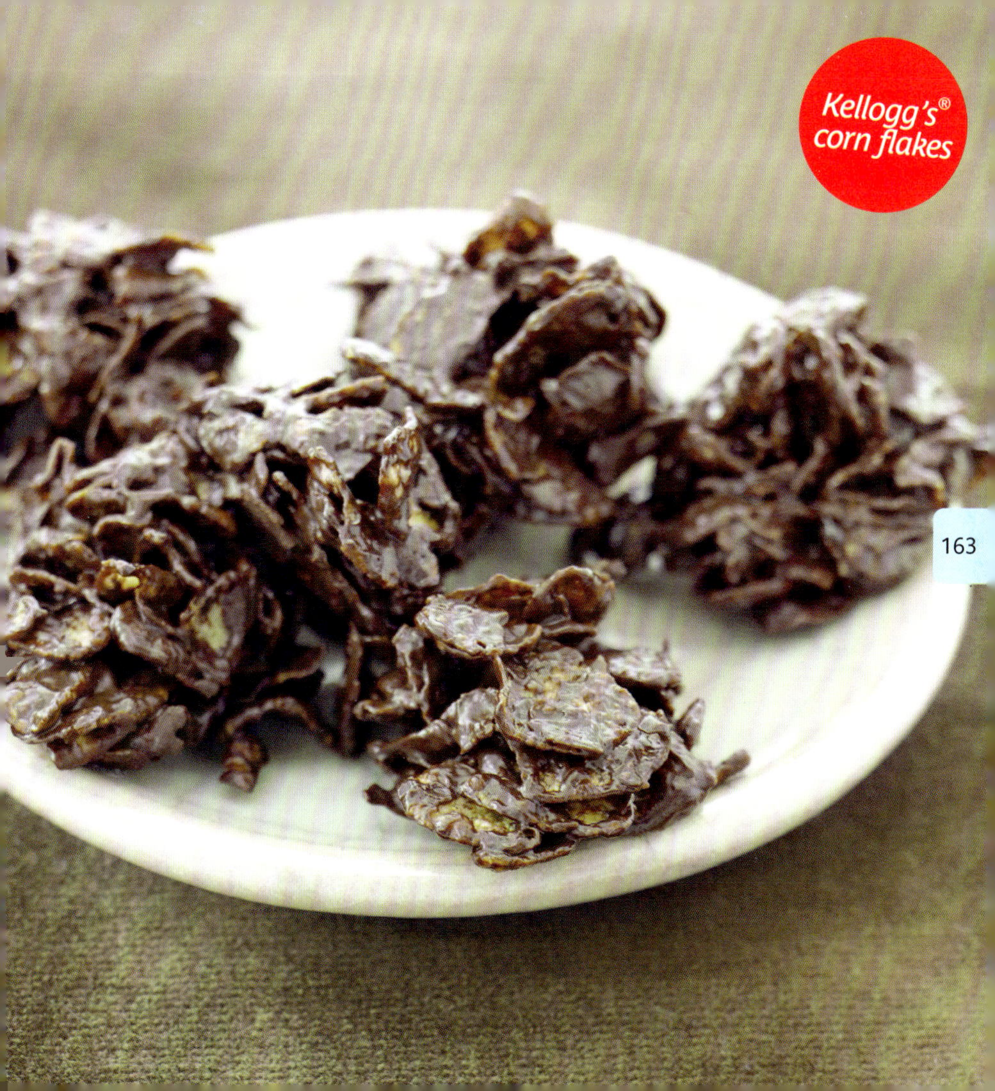
Kellogg's®
corn flakes

Brochettes de porc mariné aux épices

Ajoutez 1 pincée de piment de Cayenne, 1 pincée de cannelle, 2 pincées de gingembre, 1 pincée de cumin et 1 pincée de paprika à la marinade.

Brochettes de porc marinées à la moutarde

Remplacez la sauce soja par du vinaigre, et ajoutez 4 c. à s. de moutarde forte à la préparation.

Travers de porc marinés

Remplacez les brochettes de filet mignon par 600 g de travers de porc coupés en quatre. Faites cuire au four préchauffé à 180 °C pendant 45 min, en arrosant régulièrement de marinade.

Pommes de terre au barbecue

Enveloppez 4 grosses pommes de terre grattées chacune dans 1 feuille de papier d'aluminium. Déposez-les sur les braises et faites cuire de 25 à 35 min, en les retournant de temps à autre. Elles sont cuites lorsqu'une brochette piquée dans la chair s'enfonce facilement. Servez avec les brochettes.

Ketchup Heinz®

BROCHETTES DE PORC MARINÉES AU KETCHUP

Préparation : 20 min • **Cuisson :** 15 min • **Réfrigération :** 6 h
Pour 4 personnes

pour la marinade : *1 gousse d'ail • 4 c. à s. de ketchup Heinz® le jus de 1 citron • 2 c. à s. d'huile d'olive • 2 c. à s. de sauce soja 4 c. à s. de miel • poivre*
pour les brochettes : *600 g de filet mignon de porc • 8 petits oignons*

- Pour la marinade, épluchez l'ail et hachez-le finement. Mettez-le dans un bol.
- Ajoutez tous les autres ingrédients de la marinade, et mélangez.
- Coupez le filet mignon de porc en gros cubes et mettez-les dans un plat creux.
- Arrosez de marinade et mélangez pour bien enrober tous les morceaux.
- Laissez mariner au réfrigérateur pendant 6 h.
- Préparez les braises pour le barbecue ou préchauffez une poêle gril.
- Épluchez les petits oignons et coupez-les en deux.
- Sur des brochettes en bois préalablement trempées dans de l'eau, enfilez les morceaux de porc marinés et d'oignon en les alternant.
- Faites cuire au barbecue ou à la poêle gril pendant 15 min environ. La viande doit être bien cuite.

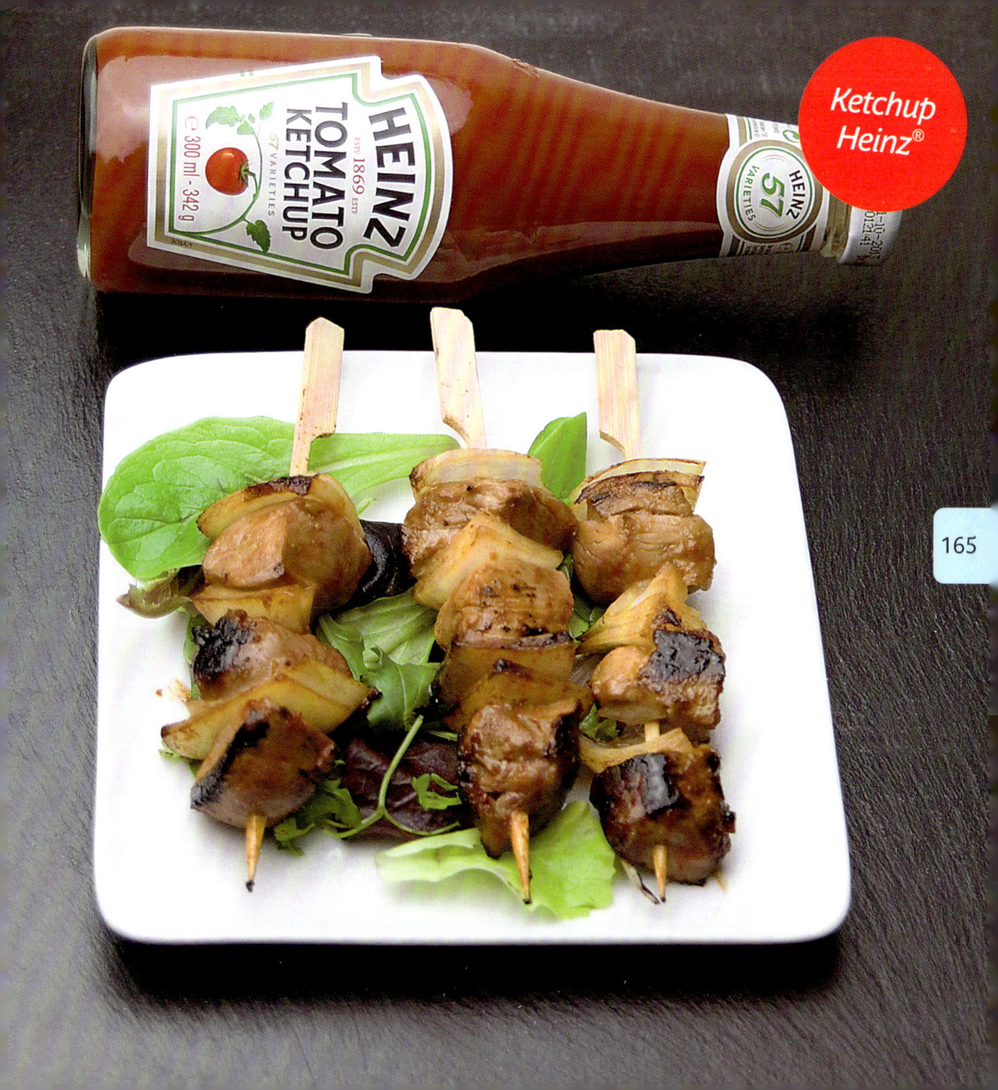

Ketchup Heinz®

Ketchup Heinz®

PETITES TOURTES AU BŒUF ET AUX LÉGUMES

Préparation : 20 min • **Cuisson :** 40 min • **Pour 6 personnes**

1 oignon • 1 poivron • 125 g de haricots rouges en conserve
125 g de maïs en conserve • 1 c. à s. d'huile végétale
500 g de viande de bœuf hachée • 2 c. à s. de concentré de tomate
1 c. à s. de farine • 1 c. à c. de piment en poudre
12 cl de bouillon de bœuf • 4 c. à s. de ketchup Heinz®
beurre, pour les moules • 2 rouleaux de pâte feuilletée
125 g de gruyère râpé • lait • crème fraîche, pour accompagner

- Épluchez l'oignon et émincez-le. Lavez le poivron, retirez les graines et la membrane blanche, et coupez-le en lamelles. Égouttez les haricots rouges et le maïs, puis rincez-les.

- Faites chauffer l'huile dans une sauteuse à feu moyen et faites-y revenir l'oignon et le poivron de 7 à 8 min. Ajoutez le bœuf haché et faites cuire de 4 à 5 min, jusqu'à ce qu'il soit bien doré. Incorporez le concentré de tomate, la farine et le piment. Faites cuire en remuant pendant 1 min. Ajoutez les haricots, le maïs, le bouillon et le ketchup Heinz®. Portez à ébullition, mélangez, puis baissez le feu et laissez mijoter pendant 5 min.

- Préchauffez le four à 200 °C et graissez 6 moules à tartelette.

- Coupez 12 cercles de pâte feuilletée et chemisez les moules avec 6 d'entre eux. Répartissez la garniture dans les moules. Parsemez de fromage râpé, puis couvrez des cercles de pâte restants, en soudant bien les bords.

- Badigeonnez de lait, puis faites cuire au four de 20 à 25 min, jusqu'à ce que les tourtes soient bien dorées. Servez chaud, avec de la crème fraîche et du ketchup Heinz®.

Tourtes au bœuf et au chorizo
Remplacez 150 g de bœuf haché par 1 chorizo fort pelé et taillé en cubes.

Tourtes au bœuf et aux carottes
Remplacez le poivron et les haricots rouges par 3 carottes pelées et taillées en cubes. Ajoutez 1 pincée de ras-el-hanout à la préparation.

Tourtes au bœuf et aux légumes d'été
Remplacez les haricots rouges par 1 courgette, et le maïs par 1 petite aubergine. Ajoutez 2 tomates épépinées et taillées en dés.

Tourtes au canard et aux cèpes
Remplacez le bœuf haché par du confit de canard, et le poivron, les haricots rouges et le maïs par 500 g de cèpes.

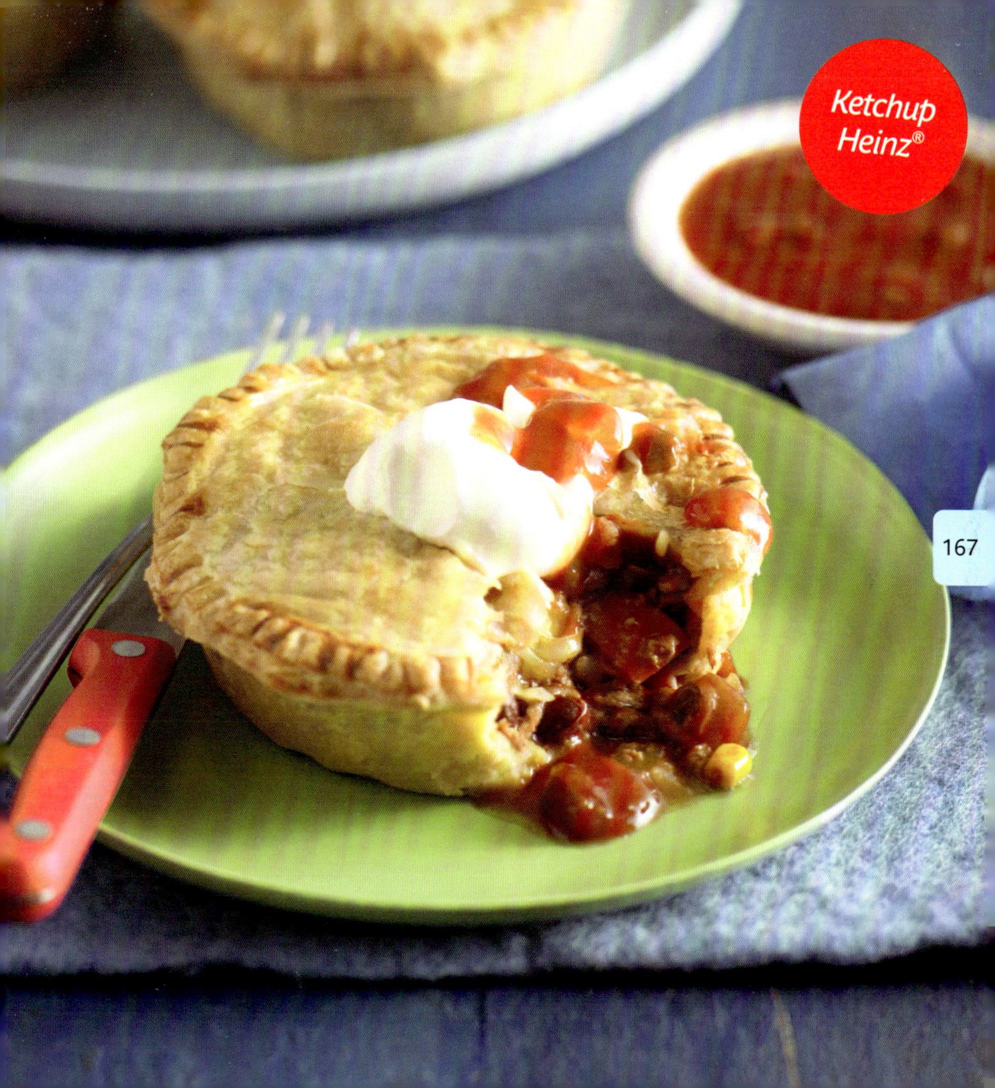
Ketchup
Heinz®

POULET À L'ANANAS

Préparation : 10 min • **Cuisson :** 20 min • **Pour 4 personnes**

1 oignon • 2 c. à s. d'huile de tournesol • 4 blancs de poulet
4 c. à c. de nuoc-mâm • 40 cl de bouillon de volaille
4 c. à s. de ketchup Heinz® • 2 boîtes d'ananas en morceaux au sirop
4 c. à c. de fécule de pomme de terre • riz, pour accompagner • sel

- Épluchez l'oignon, puis émincez-le grossièrement. Mettez-le dans une sauteuse avec l'huile et faites-le revenir jusqu'à ce qu'il soit translucide.
- Taillez le poulet en cubes, puis ajoutez-le dans la sauteuse.
- Ajoutez la sauce nuoc-mâm et laissez cuire pendant quelques minutes.
- Déglacez avec le bouillon, puis ajoutez le ketchup Heinz®, un peu de sirop des boîtes d'ananas, puis la fécule de pomme de terre délayée dans de l'eau. Laissez la sauce épaissir à feu doux.
- Ajoutez les morceaux d'ananas dans la sauteuse et laissez mijoter pendant quelques minutes. Salez.
- Servez chaud, avec du riz.

Poulet à l'ananas, au poivron et aux noix de cajou

Ajoutez 1 poivron rouge taillé en lanières en même temps que l'oignon. Ajoutez 50 g de noix de cajou en toute fin de cuisson.

Poulet à l'ananas au lait de coco

Remplacez le bouillon de volaille par du lait de coco. Ajoutez 1 c. à c. de curcuma à la préparation.

Poulet à l'ananas et au citron vert

Remplacez le nuoc-mâm par le jus de 2 citrons verts. Parsemez des zestes des citrons en toute fin de cuisson.

Poulet à l'ananas pimenté

Ajoutez 1 petit piment oiseau haché ou 1 c. à c. de purée de piments à la préparation.

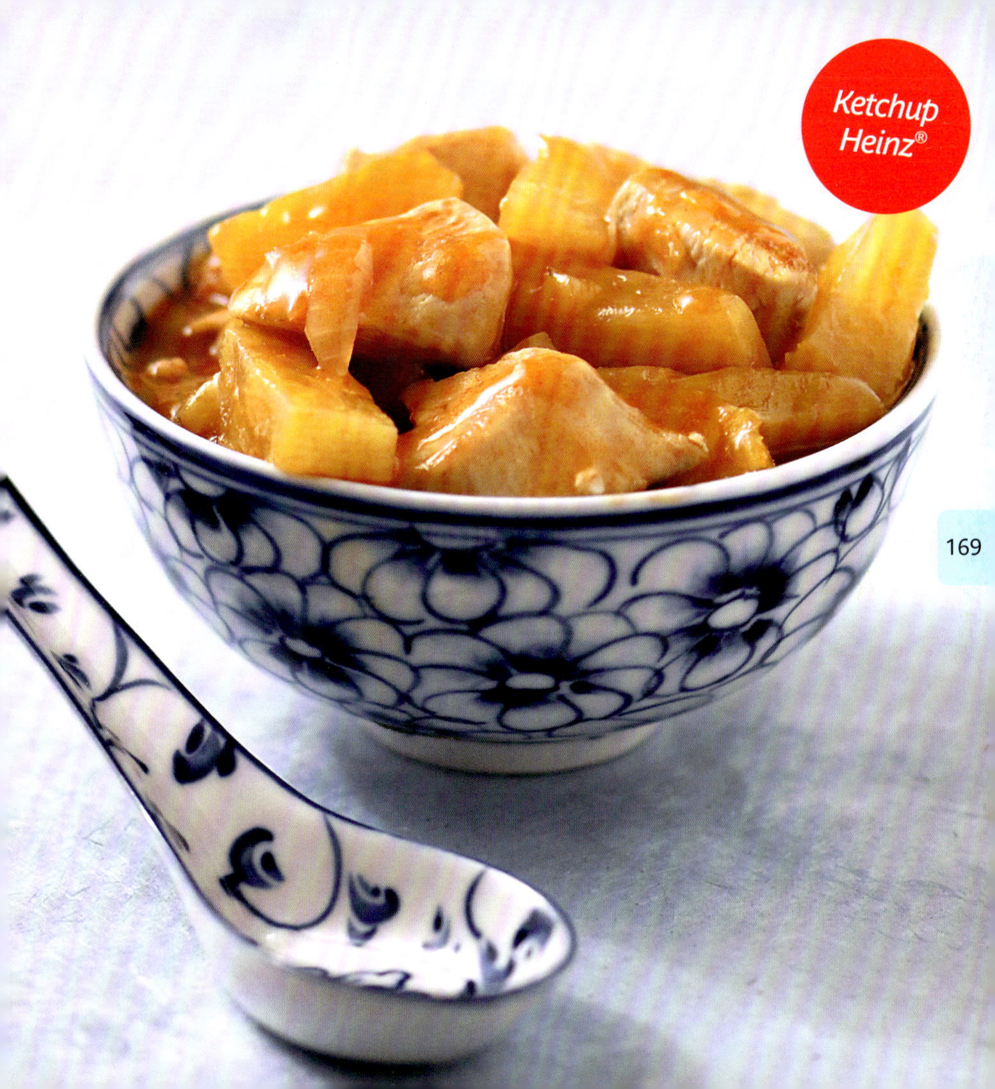
Ketchup
Heinz®

Ketchup Heinz®

QUENELLES GRATINÉES, BÉCHAMEL AU KETCHUP

Préparation : 15 min • **Cuisson** : 20 min • **Pour 4 personnes**

pour le gratin : *12 quenelles de brochet • 10 olives vertes dénoyautées*
75 g d'emmental râpé • sel
pour la béchamel au ketchup : *40 g de beurre • 4 c. à s. de farine*
50 cl de lait • 20 g d'emmental râpé • 3 c. à s. de ketchup Heinz®
sel et poivre

- Préchauffez le four à 180 °C.
- Faites pocher les quenelles dans une grande quantité d'eau bouillante salée de 4 à 5 min, jusqu'à ce qu'elles remontent à la surface.
- Pendant ce temps, préparez la béchamel : faites fondre le beurre dans une casserole, puis ajoutez-y la farine pour former un roux.
- Portez le lait à ébullition. Versez-le petit à petit sur le roux, en fouettant sans cesse, jusqu'à ce que la sauce soit bien épaisse.
- Salez, poivrez, ajoutez le fromage râpé et le ketchup Heinz®. Mélangez bien.
- Égouttez les quenelles, puis mettez-les dans un plat à gratin. Nappez-les de béchamel au ketchup Heinz®.
- Coupez les olives en rondelles et ajoutez-les dans le plat. Parsemez d'emmental râpé.
- Faites cuire au four de 8 à 10 min.
- Servez chaud.

Quenelles au jambon
Enveloppez chaque quenelle cuite dans 1 tranche de jambon sec avant de mettre au four.

Quenelles aux champignons
Taillez 300 g de champignons de Paris frais en lamelles et faites-les revenir à la poêle avec un peu d'huile de 10 à 15 min. Ajoutez-les à la béchamel.

Quenelles aux échalotes
Faites revenir 6 échalotes épluchées et hachées à la poêle avec un peu de beurre. Ajoutez-les à la béchamel.

Quenelles panées
Passez les quenelles dans de l'œuf battu, puis dans de la chapelure, avant de les faire cuire à la poêle avec un peu d'huile d'olive. Servez-les avec la béchamel chaude, à part.

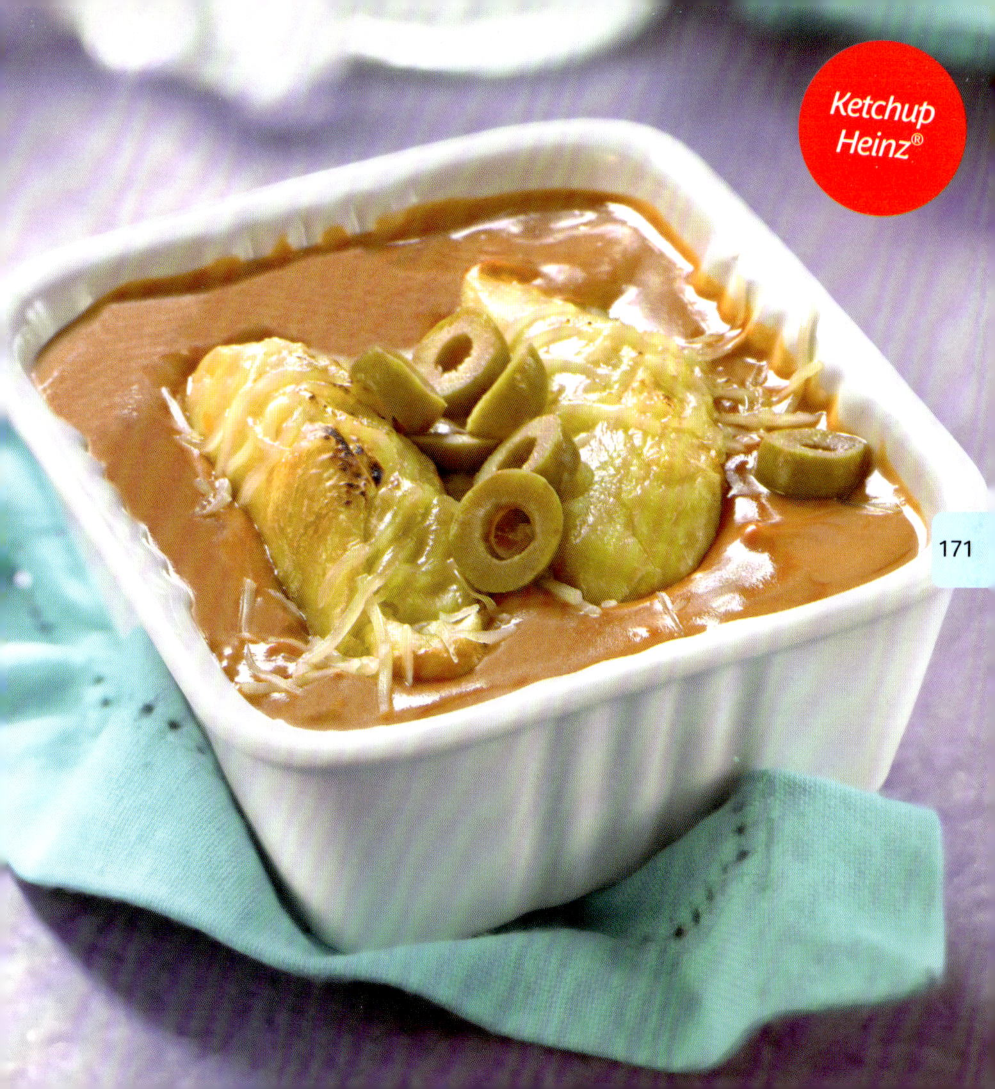
Ketchup
Heinz®

BRICKS DE KIRI® AUX HERBES FRAÎCHES

Préparation : 10 min • **Cuisson :** 5 min • **Pour 12 bricks**

8 Kiri® • 50 g de gruyère râpé • quelques brins de basilic quelques brins de coriandre • quelques brins de menthe 6 feuilles de brick • 1 blanc d'œuf • 1 c. à s. d'huile de tournesol • sel

- Écrasez les Kiri® dans un bol. Ajoutez le fromage râpé et mélangez.
- Nettoyez soigneusement les herbes fraîches, égouttez-les sur du papier absorbant, puis hachez-les.
- Ajoutez-les dans le bol, salez et mélangez.
- Coupez 1 feuille de brick en deux, puis pliez la demi-feuille de nouveau. Déposez 1 bonne c. à c. de farce dans un angle, puis repliez le coin en un triangle, en enfermant la farce. Rabattez le triangle plusieurs fois sur lui-même. Pour fermer le brick, enduisez-le de blanc d'œuf battu.
- Renouvelez l'opération pour réaliser les autres bricks.
- Faites chauffer l'huile dans une poêle. Déposez-y les bricks et faites-les cuire pendant 5 min environ, à feu moyen, en les retournant plusieurs fois, jusqu'à ce qu'ils soient bien dorés.
- Servez chaud, à l'apéritif ou en entrée.

Bricks de Kiri® à la marocaine

Faites revenir 2 oignons épluchés et émincés à la poêle avec un peu d'huile d'olive. Ajoutez-les à la préparation avec 2 c. à c. de ras-el-hanout. Remplacez les herbes par 10 brins de persil hachés. Utilisez 6 Kiri®.

Bricks de légumes au Kiri® et au safran

Faites revenir 200 g de carottes et 200 g de courgettes hachées à la poêle avec un peu d'huile d'olive. Ajoutez 2 c. à c. de safran. Supprimez les herbes et utilisez seulement 4 Kiri®.

Bricks de Kiri® au saumon

Remplacez les herbes par 200 g de saumon fumé taillé en dés et par quelques brins d'aneth. Ajoutez 30 g de pignons de pin. Utilisez 4 Kiri®.

Bricks de poivron au Kiri®

Remplacez les herbes par 1 poivron rouge taillé en dés et 1 oignon émincé et revenu à la poêle avec de l'huile d'olive. Utilisez 4 Kiri®.

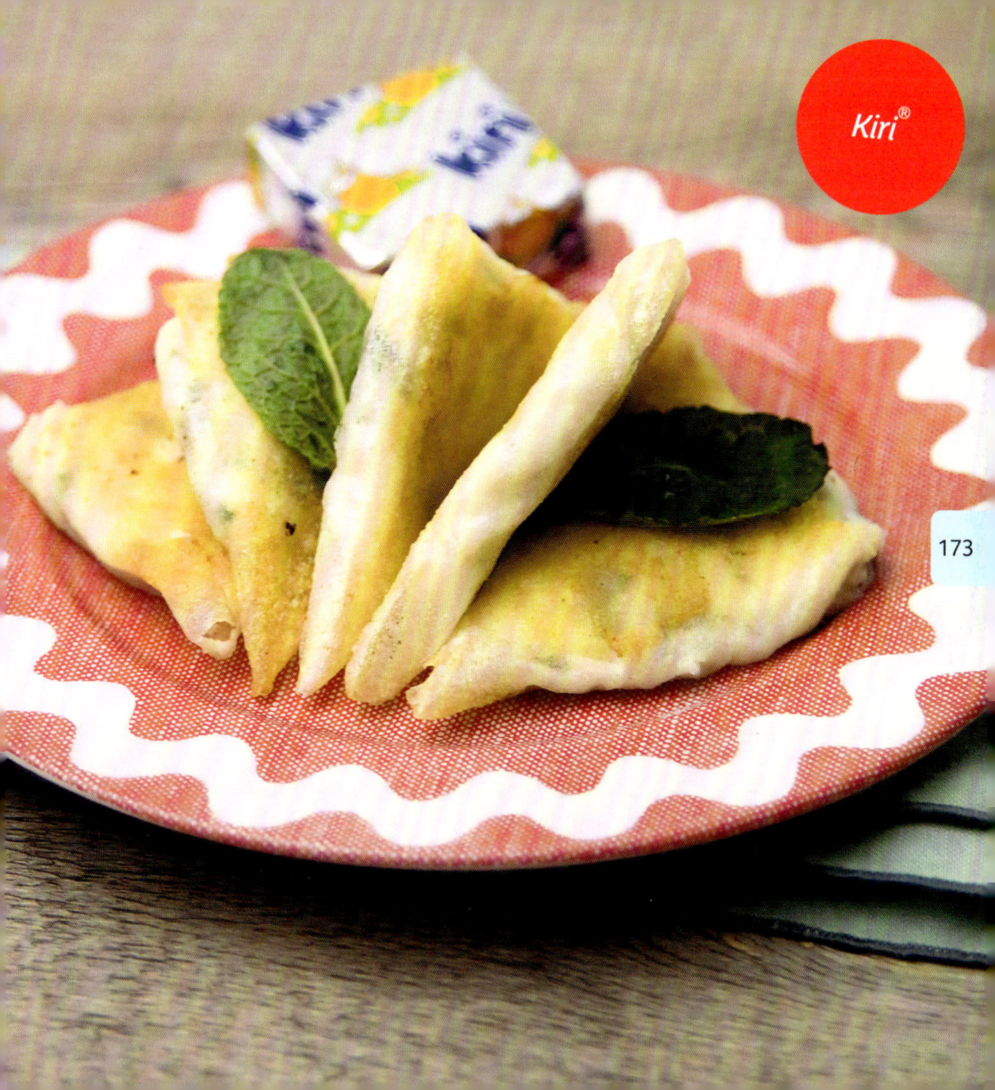
Kiri®

CRÉMEUX À LA CAROTTE ET À L'ORANGE

Préparation : 15 min • **Cuisson** : 40 min • **Pour 6 personnes**

2 oignons • 1 kg de carottes • 1 c. à s. d'huile d'olive
2 oranges • 3 Kiri® • sel et poivre

- Épluchez les oignons, puis émincez-les finement.
- Pelez les carottes, puis coupez-les en rondelles.
- Faites revenir le tout dans une grande cocotte avec l'huile d'olive. Salez et poivrez.
- Pelez les oranges et séparez les quartiers. Ajoutez-les dans la cocotte et versez 75 cl d'eau. Couvrez.
- Faites cuire pendant au moins 30 min.
- Ajoutez les Kiri®, puis mixez à l'aide d'un mixeur girafe ou au blender.
- Rectifiez l'assaisonnement et servez.

Crémeux à la carotte au miel
Ajoutez 2 c. à s. de miel d'acacia à la préparation.

Crémeux glacé à la carotte et à la coriandre
Remplacez les oranges par 1/2 bouquet de coriandre fraîche ciselée. Laissez refroidir complètement le crémeux, réservez-le au réfrigérateur et servez très frais.

Crémeux à la carotte, au potiron et au cumin
Remplacez la moitié des carottes par 500 g de potiron taillé en dés. Remplacez les oranges par 1 c. à c. de cumin.

Crémeux au panais et au gingembre
Remplacez les carottes par 1 kg de panais épluchés et taillés en rondelles. Remplacez les oranges par 1/2 cm de gingembre frais râpé.

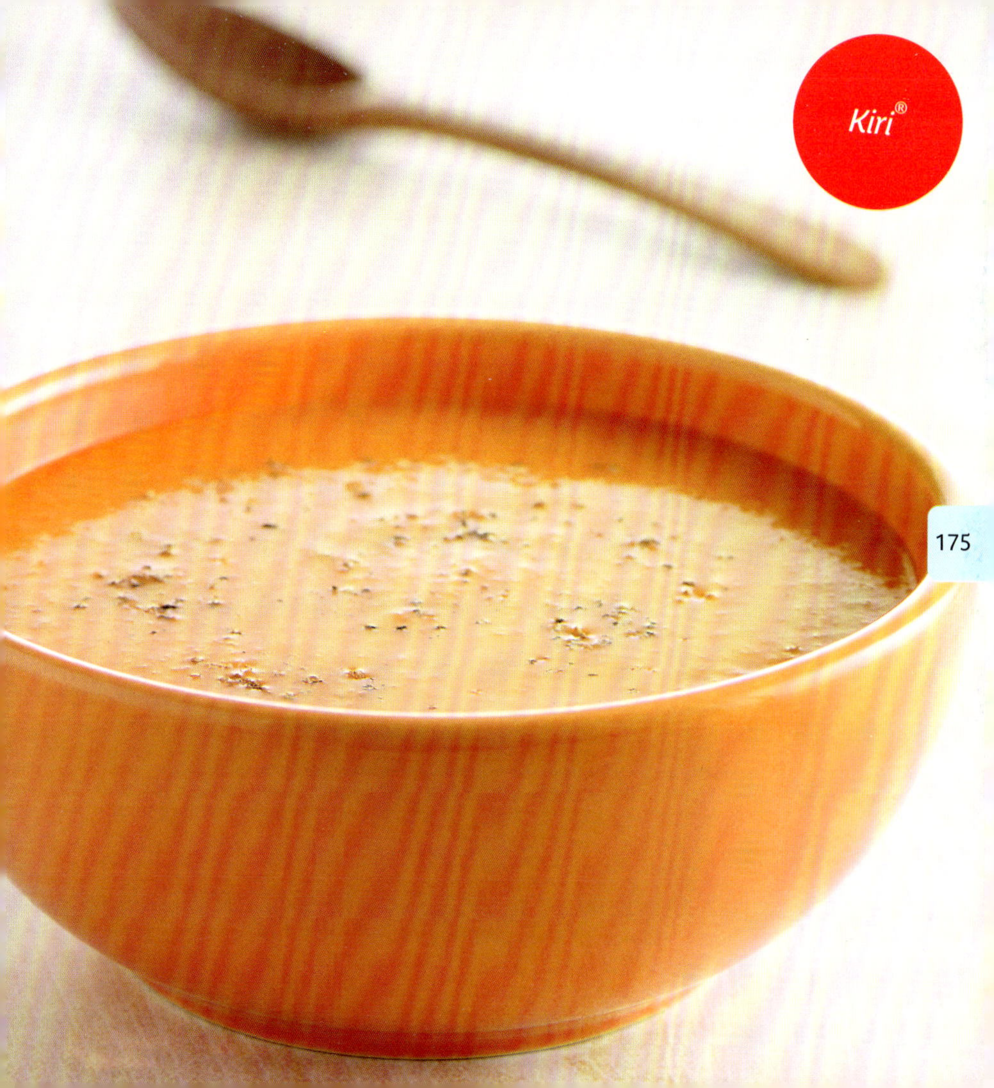
Kiri®

CRUMBLE DE COURGETTES AU KIRI®

Préparation : 15 min • **Cuisson :** 20 min • **Pour 4 personnes**

pour la garniture : 800 g de courgettes • 200 g de dés de jambon blanc 5 Kiri® • 3 c. à s. d'huile d'argan
pour la pâte à crumble : 100 g de farine • 100 g de beurre demi-sel sel et poivre

- Préchauffez le four à 200 °C.
- Lavez les courgettes, sans les peler, puis râpez-les finement.
- Mélangez-les avec les dés de jambon blanc et les Kiri®.
- Répartissez la préparation dans des ramequins supportant la chaleur.
- Arrosez d'huile d'argan.
- Préparez la pâte à crumble : mélangez la farine, le beurre coupé en parcelles, du sel et du poivre. Travaillez le mélange du bout des doigts jusqu'à ce qu'il forme des miettes.
- Répartissez la pâte à crumble sur les courgettes.
- Faites cuire au four pendant 20 min.

Crumble aux courgettes et aux noix

Ajoutez 30 g de cerneaux de noix concassés. Vous pouvez également utiliser des pignons de pin.

Crumble de courgettes à la menthe

Ajoutez les feuilles de 1/2 bouquet de menthe aux courgettes.

Crumble de ratatouille au romarin

Préparez une ratatouille en faisant revenir 1 oignon, 1 poivron rouge, 2 petites courgettes et 4 tomates. Ajoutez-y les feuilles de quelques brins de romarin.

Crumble d'aubergines aux lardons

Remplacez les courgettes par des aubergines taillées en dés, que vous ferez revenir pendant quelques minutes à la poêle avec un peu d'huile d'olive. Remplacez le jambon par des lardons fumés revenus à la poêle sans matière grasse.

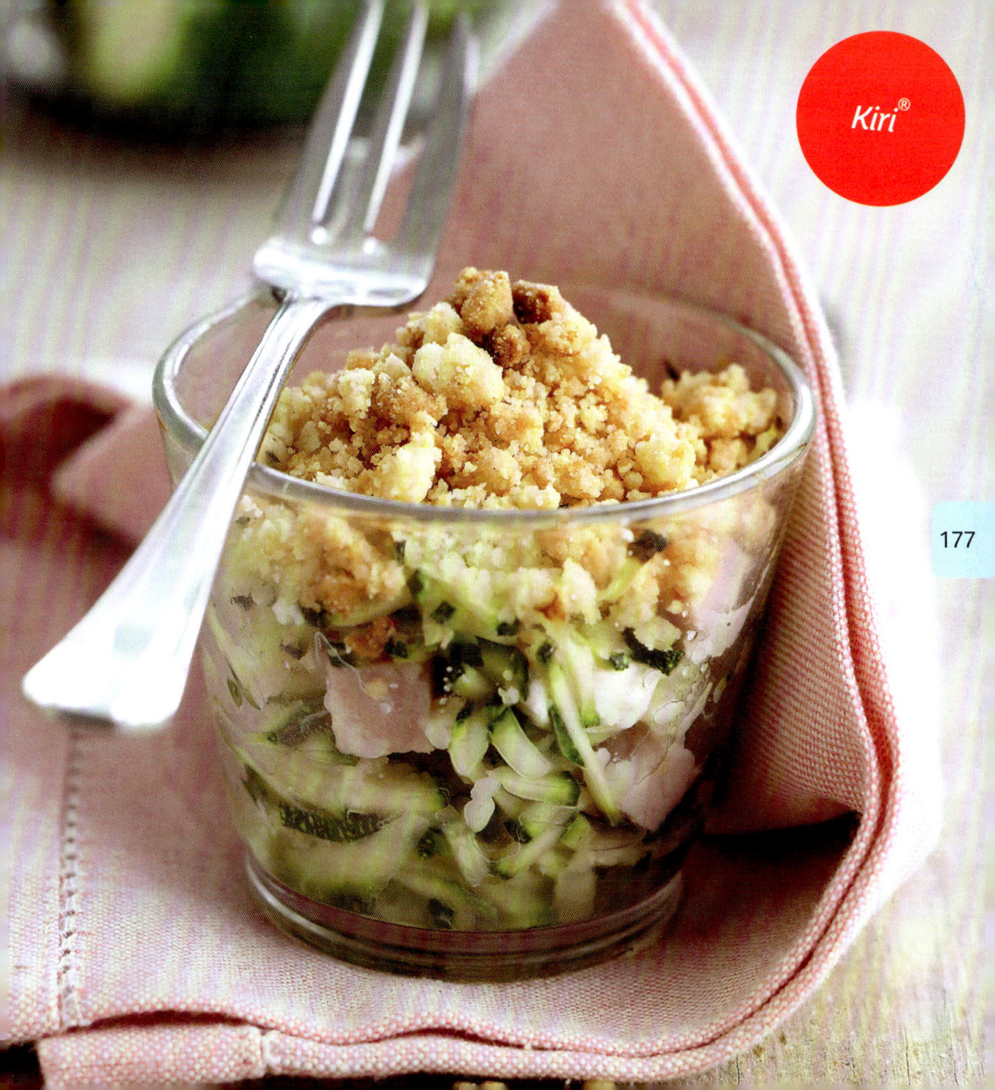

Kiri®

OMELETTE AU KIRI® ET AUX JEUNES POUSSES D'ÉPINARDS

Préparation : 10 min • **Cuisson** : 5 min • **Pour 4 personnes**

50 g de jeunes pousses d'épinards • 2 tomates • 1 gousse d'ail
5 Kiri® • 4 c. à s. d'huile d'olive • 6 œufs • sel et poivre

- Lavez les pousses d'épinards, puis essorez-les.
- Lavez les tomates, retirez la pulpe, et taillez-les en lamelles.
- Épluchez l'ail et écrasez-le.
- Mélangez les Kiri®, l'ail, 2 c. à s. d'huile d'olive, du sel et du poivre.
- Battez les œufs en omelette, salez et poivrez.
- Mettez le reste d'huile dans une poêle et faites chauffer à feu moyen.
- Cassez les œufs, ajoutez-les dans la poêle et faites prendre à feu moyen pendant 1 min.
- Versez dessus le mélange au Kiri® et les épinards, et poursuivez la cuisson pendant 2 min, puis retournez et faites cuire sur l'autre face pendant 2 min.
- Servez sans attendre, avec les lamelles de tomate.

Omelette au Kiri® et aux orties

Remplacez les jeunes pousses d'épinards par des feuilles d'ortie bien lavées. Ajoutez 1 gousse d'ail hachée à la préparation.

Omelette au Kiri® et à la pancetta

Ajoutez 50 g de pancetta taillée en lamelles à la préparation. À défaut, utilisez du jambon de Parme.

Omelette au chorizo et aux petits pois

Remplacez les pousses d'épinards par 30 g de chorizo taillé en dés et 40 g de petits pois cuits. Remplacez les tomates par des lamelles de poivron grillé.

Omelette au Kiri® et au maïs

Remplacez les jeunes pousses d'épinards par 50 g de grains de maïs doux en boîte égouttés.

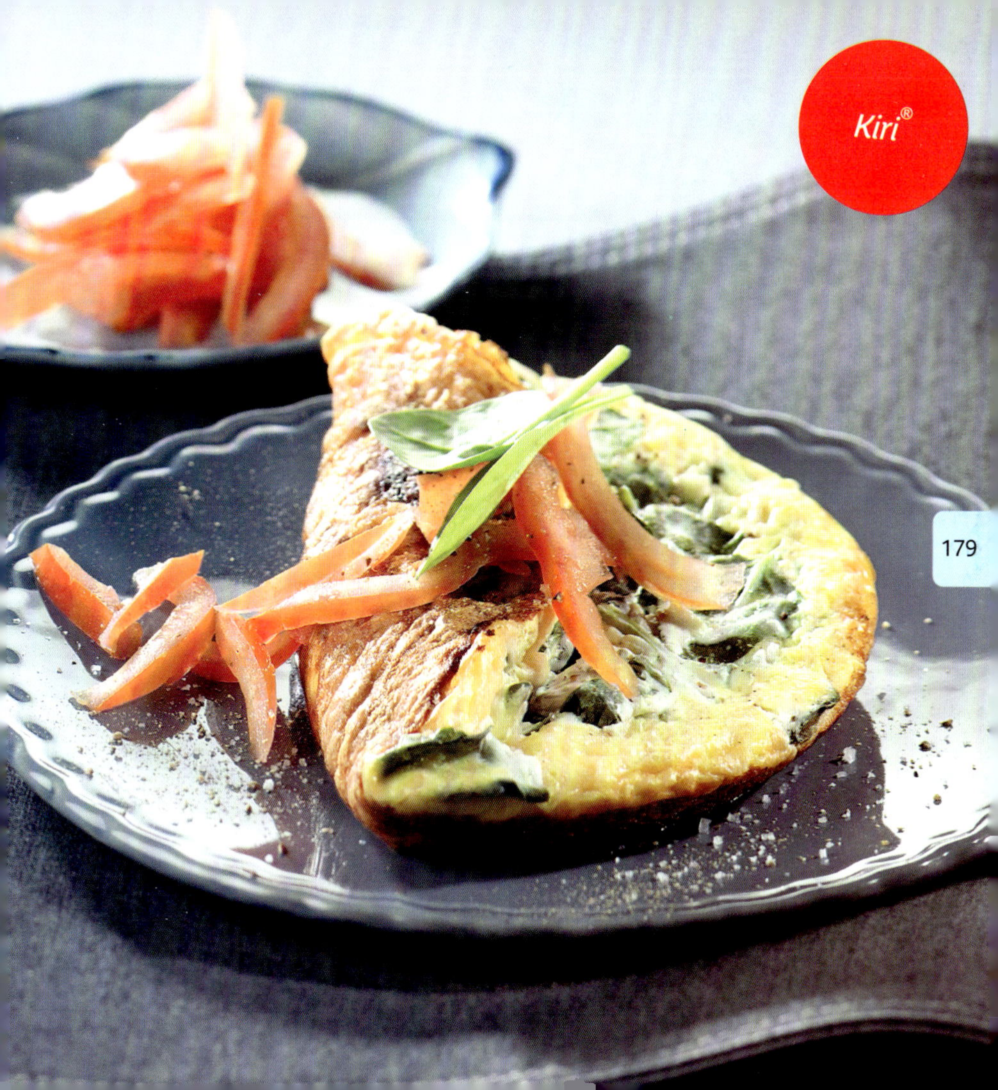
Kiri®

SOLE GRATINÉE AU KIRI®

Préparation : 5 min • **Cuisson** : 15 min • **Pour 2 personnes**

4 Kiri® • 2 c. à s. de crème fraîche épaisse • 4 filets de sole
4 c. à c. de chapelure • 4 noisettes de beurre • sel et poivre

- Préchauffez le four à 180 °C.
- Mélangez les Kiri® et la crème fraîche. Salez et poivrez.
- Tartinez les filets de sole de ce mélange, puis roulez-les. Maintenez-les à l'aide de piques en bois.
- Parsemez de chapelure. Déposez 1 noisette de beurre sur chaque roulé.
- Faites cuire au four pendant 15 min environ.
- Servez sans attendre.

Sole gratinée au lard
Déposez 1 tranche de lard fumé sur chaque filet de sole, avant de les napper de sauce au Kiri®.

Sole gratinée au saumon fumé
Déposez 1 tranche de saumon fumé et un peu de ciboulette ciselée sur chaque filet de sole, avant de les napper de sauce au Kiri®.

Sole gratinée à la crème
Faites revenir 6 champignons de Paris émincés à la poêle avec de l'huile, puis ajoutez 2 carottes râpées et faites cuire pendant 10 min. Arrosez de 20 cl de vin blanc sec et de 10 cl de fumet de poisson. Laissez mijoter pendant 15 min, puis ajoutez 200 g de crème fraîche. Servez avec la sole.

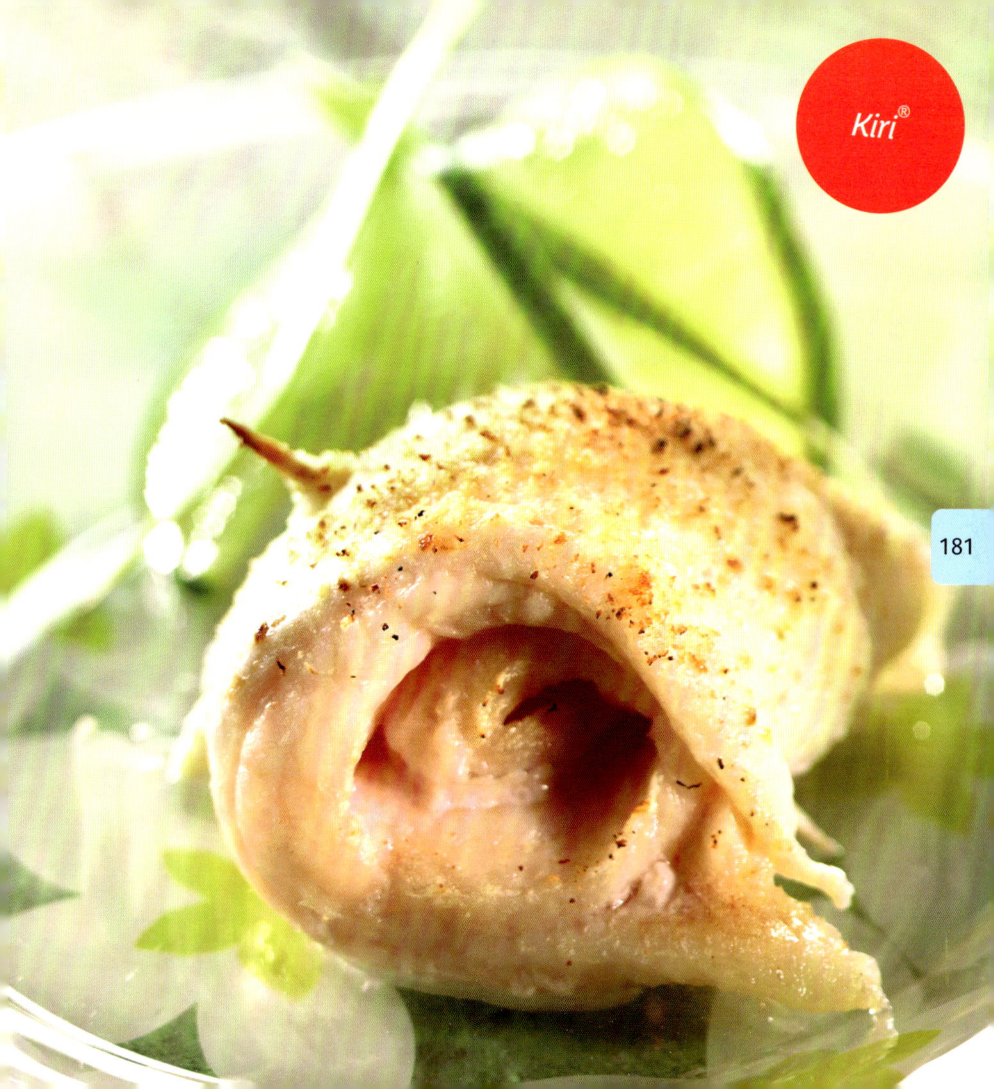
Kiri®

CRÈME À LA FRAMBOISE

Préparation : 15 min • **Cuisson** : aucune • **Réfrigération** : 4 h
Pour 4 personnes

2 sachets de gélatine à la framboise • 600 g de framboises
1 boîte de lait concentré sucré Nestlé®

- Faites ramollir la gélatine dans un bol d'eau froide.
- Réservez 8 framboises et mixez le reste avec le lait concentré sucré Nestlé®.
- Ajoutez la gélatine et mélangez, puis répartissez la préparation dans 4 verrines. Ajoutez 2 framboises entières dans chaque verrine.
- Couvrez de film alimentaire et laissez prendre au réfrigérateur pendant 4 h.

Crème à la framboise et au litchi

Remplacez la moitié des framboises par 300 g de litchis pelés et dénoyautés. Ajoutez 1 c. à s. de liqueur de litchi à la préparation.

Crème à la framboise et à la rose

Ajoutez 1 ou 2 c. à s. d'eau de rose à la préparation.

Crème à la poire et au chocolat

Remplacez les framboises par 3 belles poires pelées, épépinées et taillées en dés. Ajoutez 3 c. à s. de pépites de chocolat noir à la préparation une fois les poires mixées.

Verrines surprises aux framboises

Garnissez les verrines seulement à moitié. Une fois la crème prise, ajoutez dans chaque verrine 1/2 banane coupée en rondelles, 1 couche de crème fouettée à la vanille, et saupoudrez le tout de poudre de biscuit rose de Reims.

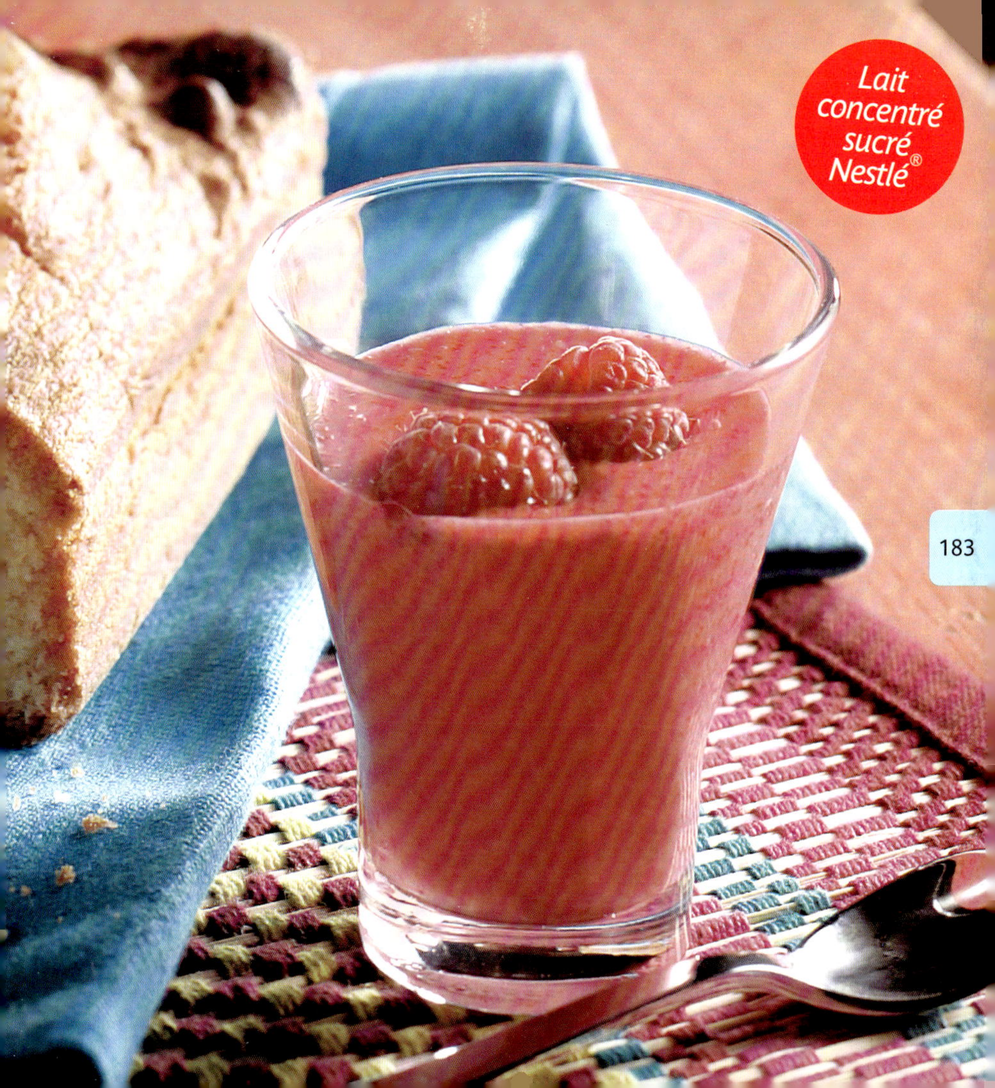
Lait
concentré
sucré
Nestlé®

Crème au caramel au gingembre
Ajoutez 15 g de gingembre frais râpé à la préparation.

Crème au caramel à l'orange
Remplacez le zeste et le jus de citron vert par le jus de 1 orange. Ajoutez 10 cl de Cointreau à la préparation.

Crème au caramel au café et au cognac
Remplacez le zeste et le jus de citron vert par 1 c. à s. d'extrait de café liquide et 2 c. à c. de cognac.

Crème au caramel aux raisins secs
Remplacez le zeste et le jus de citron vert par 1 petite poignée de raisins secs.

CRÈME AU CARAMEL

Préparation : 30 min • **Cuisson** : 1 h • **Infusion** : 30 min
Pour 4 personnes

25 cl de lait concentré sucré Nestlé® • 12,5 ml de lait
le zeste et le jus de 2 citrons verts non traités • 2 gousses de vanille
75 g de sucre de canne • 3 œufs

- Préchauffez le four à 120 °C.
- Versez le lait concentré sucré Nestlé® et le lait dans une casserole. Ajoutez le zeste de citron vert et les gousses de vanille fendues, dont vous aurez gratté les graines.
- Portez à ébullition, puis éteignez le feu et laissez infuser pendant 30 min.
- Mettez le sucre, 10 cl d'eau et 1 c. à c. de jus de citron vert dans une petite casserole. Portez à ébullition en remuant, jusqu'à l'obtention d'un caramel roux.
- Versez le caramel dans 4 moules en les inclinant pour bien recouvrir les parois.
- Battez les œufs dans une jatte, puis versez le lait infusé par-dessus à travers un tamis. Mélangez vivement, puis ajoutez le reste de jus de citron.
- Versez dans les moules et faites cuire au four, au bain-marie, pendant 1 h.
- Laissez refroidir complètement avant de déguster.

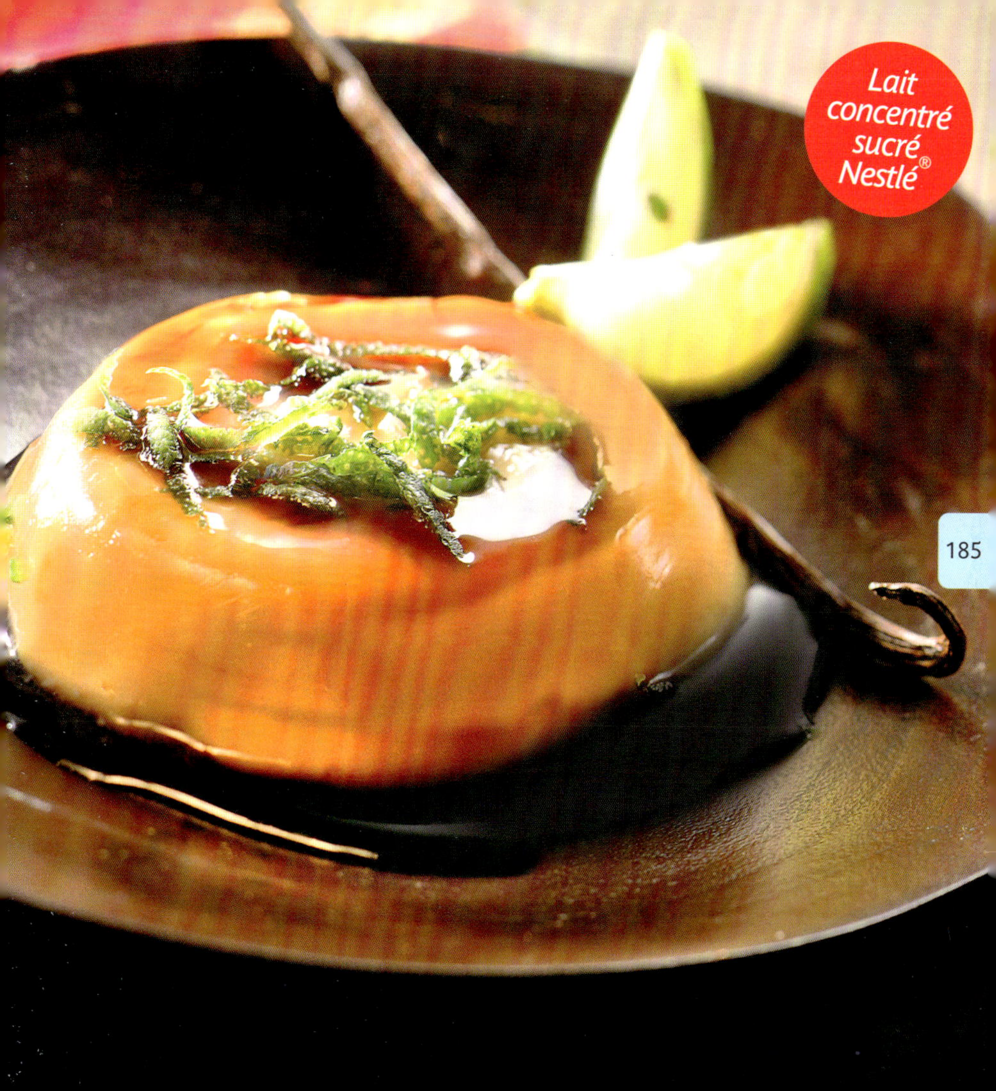
Lait
concentré
sucré
Nestlé®

FUDGES AU CHOCOLAT ET AUX NOISETTES

Préparation : 10 min • **Cuisson** : aucune • **Réfrigération** : 6 h
Pour 20 fudges

200 g de chocolat noir • 150 g de chocolat au lait • 75 g de noisettes
1 boîte de lait concentré sucré Nestlé® • sel

- Concassez grossièrement les chocolats et les noisettes, séparément.
- Mettez les chocolats dans une jatte supportant la chaleur, et faites-les fondre au bain-marie avec le lait concentré sucré Nestlé® et 2 pincées de sel, en remuant régulièrement. Ne laissez pas le mélange bouillir.
- Hors du feu, incorporez les noisettes concassées.
- Tapissez un grand plat rectangulaire de papier sulfurisé et versez-y la préparation. Lissez à la spatule.
- Réservez au réfrigérateur de 4 à 6 h.
- Coupez en cubes.
- Réservez au frais jusqu'au moment de déguster. Servez à l'heure du thé ou du café.

Fudges aux cacahuètes
Remplacez les noisettes par des cacahuètes non salées décortiquées.

Fudges au riz soufflé
Remplacez les noisettes par 75 g de riz soufflé.

Fudges au chocolat blanc et aux noix de pécan
Remplacez les chocolats par du chocolat blanc, et les noisettes par des noix de pécan. Aromatisez le tout avec 1 c. à s. d'extrait de vanille liquide.

Carrés croustillants aux fudges
Mélangez 220 g de flocons d'avoine, 180 g de farine, 150 g de cassonade et 200 g de beurre ramolli en parcelles. Étalez la moitié de la préparation dans le plat, avant d'ajouter le mélange pour les fudges, puis recouvrez du reste de préparation. Faites cuire au four préchauffé à 180 °C pendant 45 min.

Lait concentré sucré Nestlé®

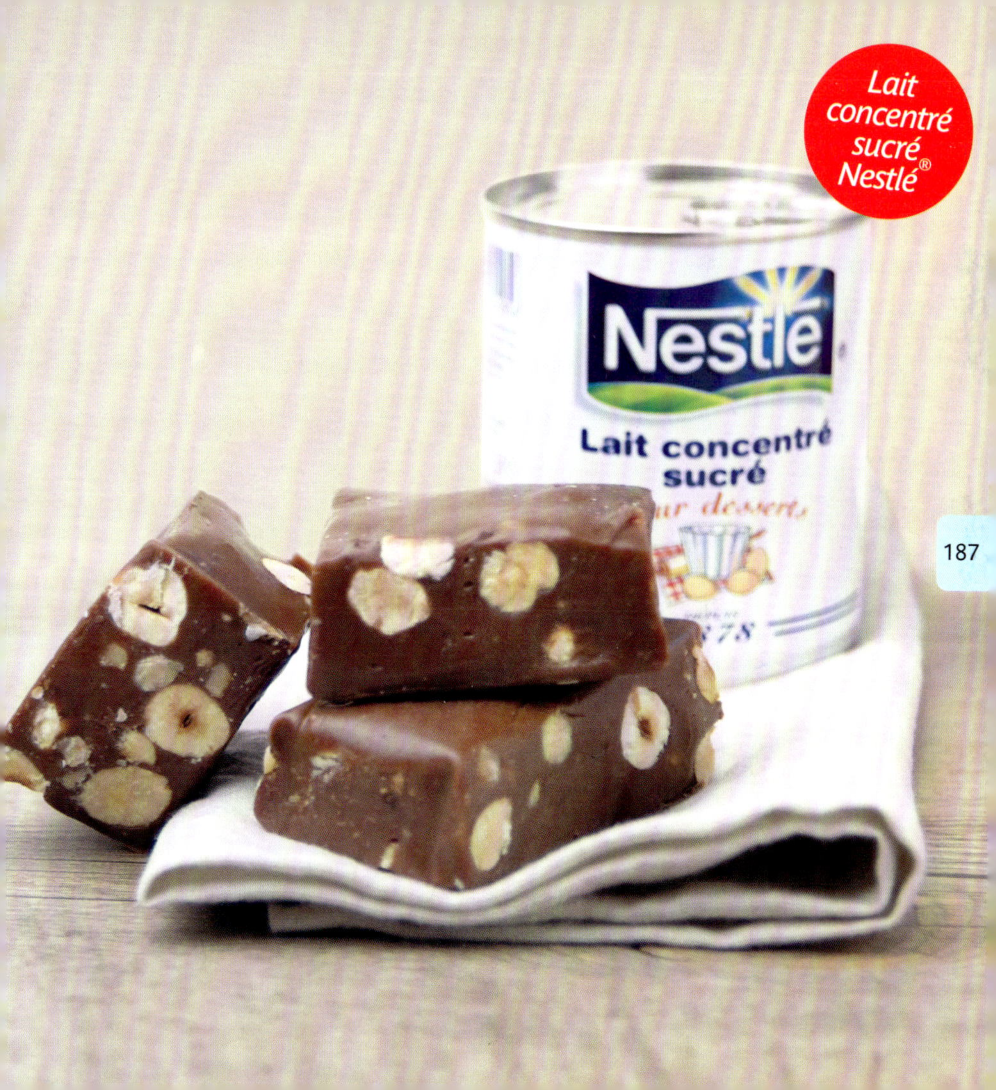

Lait concentré sucré Nestlé®

GÂTEAU AUX POMMES

Préparation: 20 min • **Cuisson**: 40 min • **Pour 6 à 8 personnes**

40 g de beurre • 120 g de sucre en poudre • 1 sachet de sucre vanillé
4 œufs • 100 g de lait concentré sucré Nestlé® • 200 g de farine
1 sachet de levure chimique • 5 pommes

- Sortez le beurre du réfrigérateur au moins 1 h avant de cuisiner pour qu'il se ramollisse.
- Préchauffez le four à 180 °C.
- Dans une jatte, mélangez le beurre avec le sucre en poudre et le sucre vanillé.
- Ajoutez les œufs légèrement battus et le lait concentré sucré Nestlé®, puis incorporez la farine et la levure tamisées.
- Pelez les pommes, retirez le cœur, puis coupez-les en cubes et mélangez-les à la préparation.
- Versez la préparation dans un moule à manqué beurré.
- Faites cuire au four de 30 à 40 min.
- Laissez refroidir complètement avant de déguster.

Gâteau aux pommes glacé à l'abricot

Faites tiédir 4 c. à s. de confiture d'abricots, puis badigeonnez-en le gâteau une fois refroidi.

Gâteau aux pommes et à la réglisse

Ajoutez 2 c. à s. de poudre de réglisse à la préparation. À défaut, utilisez des bonbons de type Zan, que vous ferez infuser dans 10 cl de lait. Ajoutez le lait aromatisé à la préparation.

Crème au calvados

Fouettez 25 cl de crème fleurette bien froide avec 1 sachet de sucre vanillé et 1 c. à s. de calvados. Servez avec le gâteau.

Cocktail pomme-canneberge au miel

Versez 12 cl de jus de pomme, 12 cl de jus de canneberge, 1 trait de jus de citron vert et 1/2 c. à c. de miel dans un shaker. Frappez, puis versez dans un verre rafraîchi. Servez avec le gâteau.

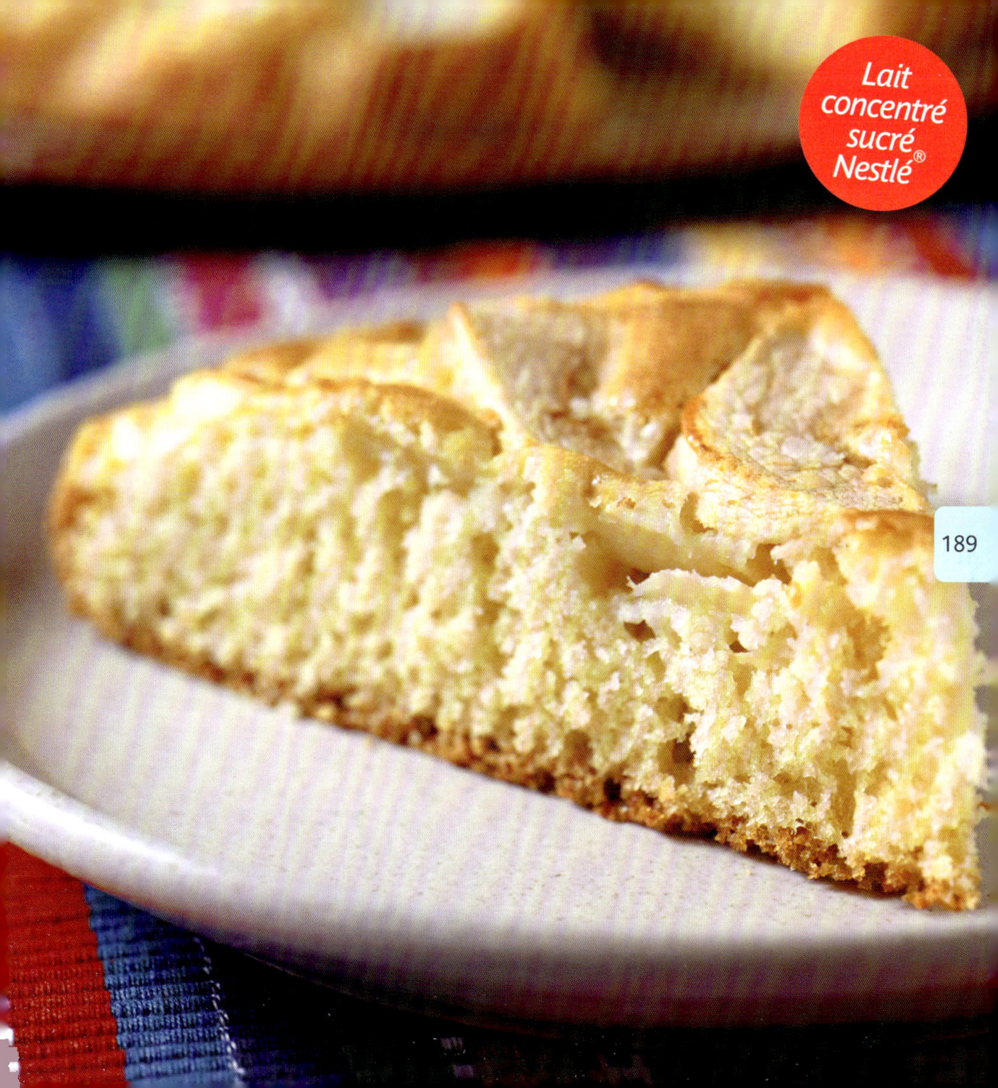
Lait
concentré
sucré
Nestlé®

Lardons Herta®

AUMÔNIÈRES DE POMMES AU CAMEMBERT ET AUX LARDONS

Préparation : 15 min • **Cuisson :** 12 min • **Pour 4 personnes**

2 pommes Golden • 200 g de lardons nature Herta®
1 camembert ferme • 50 g de beurre • 4 feuilles de brick
mesclun et cerneaux de noix, pour accompagner

- Préchauffez le four à 180 °C.
- Pelez les pommes, retirez le cœur et les pépins, puis coupez-les en petits dés.
- Faites dorer les lardons Herta® dans une poêle à revêtement antiadhésif, sans matière grasse.
- Retirez-les de la poêle et remplacez-les par les dés de pomme. Faites-les sauter rapidement en remuant sans cesse.
- Enlevez la croûte du camembert et détaillez-le en fines lamelles.
- Faites fondre le beurre.
- Étalez les feuilles de brick et badigeonnez-les de beurre fondu.
- Disposez au centre les lamelles de camembert, les lardons et les dés de pomme. Ramenez les bords des feuilles de brick en aumônière et nouez-les avec du fil alimentaire.
- Faites cuire au four pendant 10 min en surveillant la coloration.
- Servez chaud avec une salade de mesclun et des cerneaux de noix.

Aumônières de poires au brie

Remplacez les pommes par des poires, et le camembert par un morceau de brie de Meaux.

Aumônières de tomates au chèvre

Remplacez les pommes par 3 ou 4 tomates débarrassées de leur pulpe, et le camembert par du fromage de chèvre.

Aumônières de champignons aux lardons

Remplacez les pommes par 200 g de cèpes et 200 g de pleurotes taillés en dés et cuits à la poêle avec de l'huile, séparément, et avec de la persillade. Ajoutez 1 c. à s. de crème fraîche par aumônière.

Aumônières à la ratatouille et aux lardons

Préparez une ratatouille en faisant cuire dans une cocotte, avec de l'huile d'olive, 1 oignon émincé, 1 poivron rouge, 1/2 aubergine, 1 courgette et 4 tomates. Garnissez les feuilles de brick de ce mélange et ajoutez les lardons.

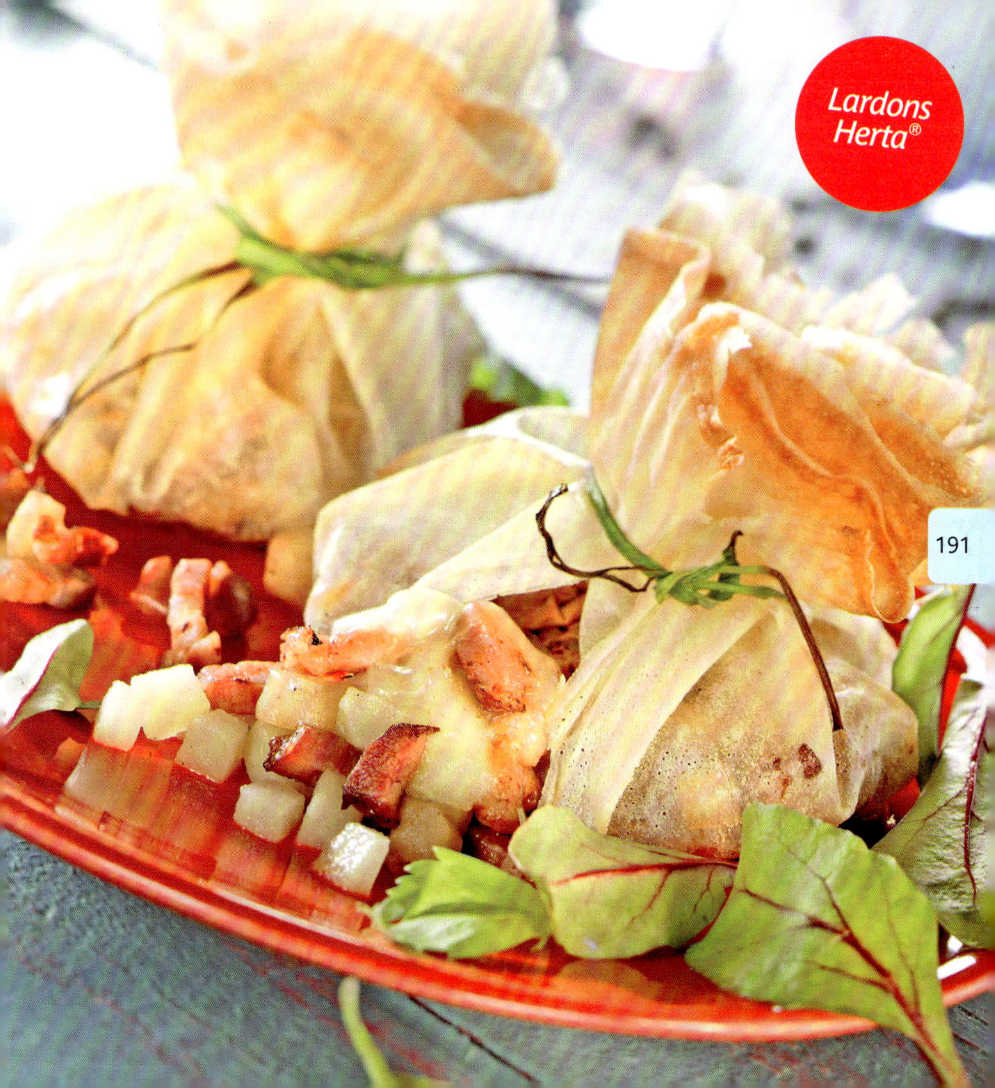
Lardons
Herta®

Lardons Herta®

BOUCHÉES AUX LARDONS ET AUX OIGNONS

Préparation : 2 min • **Cuisson** : 20 min • **Pour 24 bouchées**

2 gros oignons • 200 g de lardons nature Herta® • 4 gros œufs
25 cl de lait • 1 c. à c. de moutarde • poivre

- Préchauffez le four à 180 °C.
- Épluchez les oignons et émincez-les finement.
- Faites revenir les lardons Herta® dans une sauteuse à feu moyen, sans matière grasse, puis ajoutez l'oignon. Laissez réduire.
- Battez les œufs avec le lait dans une jatte. Ajoutez la moutarde et les lardons. Poivrez.
- Répartissez la préparation dans des moules à minimuffin.
- Faites cuire au four de 15 à 20 min.
- Servez chaud.

Bouchées aux lardons et aux épinards

Ajoutez 150 g d'épinards surgelés et décongelés dans la poêle avec les oignons.

Bouchées aux lardons et aux tomates

Remplacez les oignons par 12 tomates cerises coupées en quatre à la préparation. Ajoutez 100 g d'emmental râpé.

Bouchées aux lardons, aux courgettes et au chèvre

Remplacez les oignons par 2 belles courgettes râpées. Ajoutez 1 crottin de Chavignol émietté à la préparation. Ajoutez, éventuellement, quelques feuilles de basilic ou de menthe ciselées.

Bouchées aux lardons, aux asperges et au cumin

Ajoutez 150 g d'asperges en conserve égouttées et coupées en quatre à la préparation. Ajoutez 1 c. à c. de cumin.

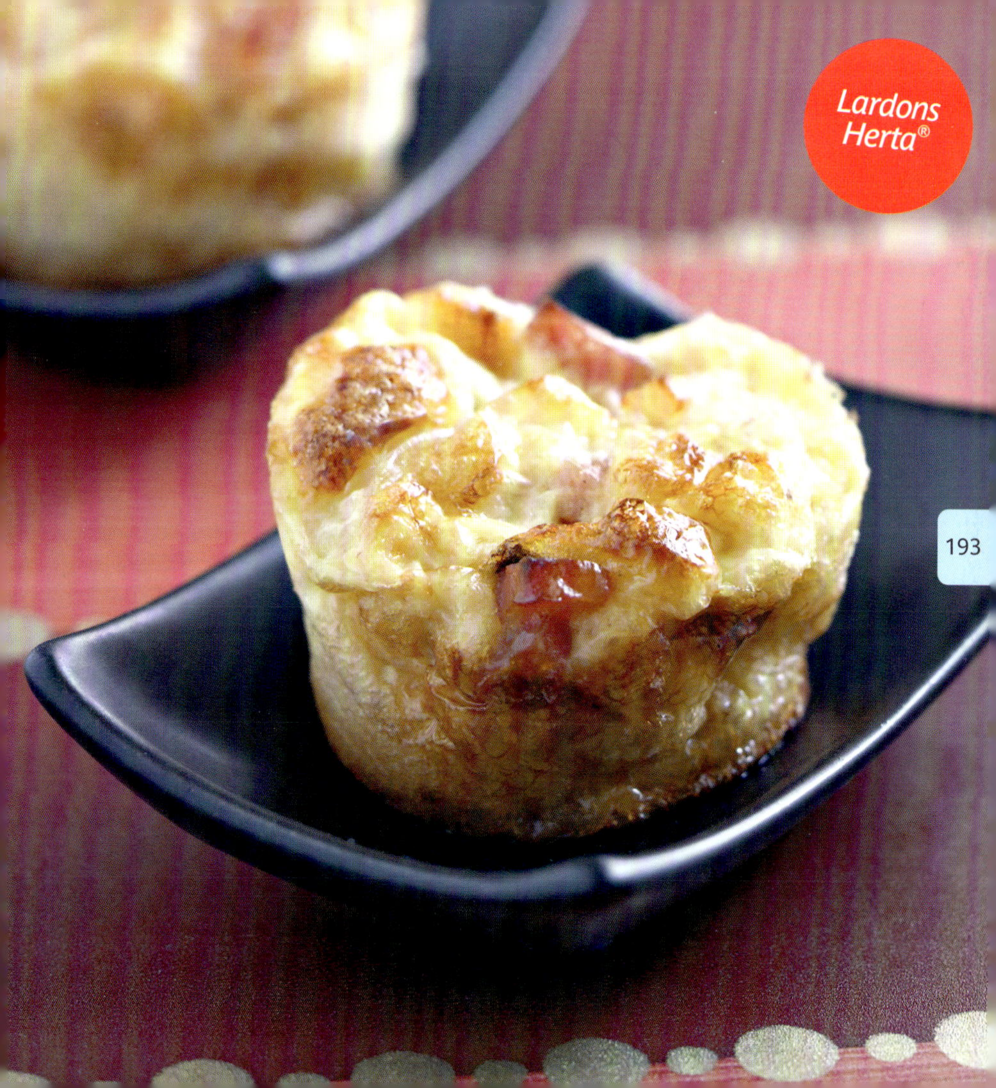
Lardons
Herta®

FLANS AUX BROCOLIS ET AUX LARDONS

Préparation : 15 min • **Cuisson** : 30 min • **Pour 6 personnes**

1 tête de brocoli (400 g) • 100 g de lardons fumés Herta® • 2 œufs 20 cl de lait • 50 g de parmesan • beurre, pour les moules • sel

- Préchauffez le four à 180 °C.
- Coupez la tête de brocoli pour séparer les bouquets, et rincez-les rapidement.
- Faites-les cuire pendant 10 min dans une grande casserole d'eau bouillante salée.
- Pendant ce temps, faites revenir les lardons Herta® dans une poêle sans matière grasse.
- Battez les œufs avec le lait dans un saladier.
- Ajoutez le parmesan, les lardons et les bouquets de brocoli.
- Répartissez la préparation dans 6 moules à muffin légèrement beurrés.
- Faites cuire au four de 15 à 20 min.
- Servez chaud.

Flans au chou romanesco et au lait de soja

Remplacez les brocolis par du chou romanesco, et le lait par du lait de soja.

Flans aux courgettes et au chèvre

Remplacez les brocolis par 400 g de courgettes coupées en rondelles et revenues à la poêle. Remplacez le parmesan par 2 crottins de Chavignol.

Flan aux carottes, à la ricotta et au curry

Remplacez les brocolis par des carottes taillées en rondelles cuites à la vapeur. Mixez-les avec le lait, 50 g de ricotta et 1 c. à c. de curry, avant d'incorporer les œufs et les lardons.

Coulis de tomates

Mélangez 250 g de pulpe de tomate avec 5 brins de basilic hachés, 1 gousse d'ail hachée et 3 c. à s. d'huile d'olive. Salez et poivrez. Servez avec les flans.

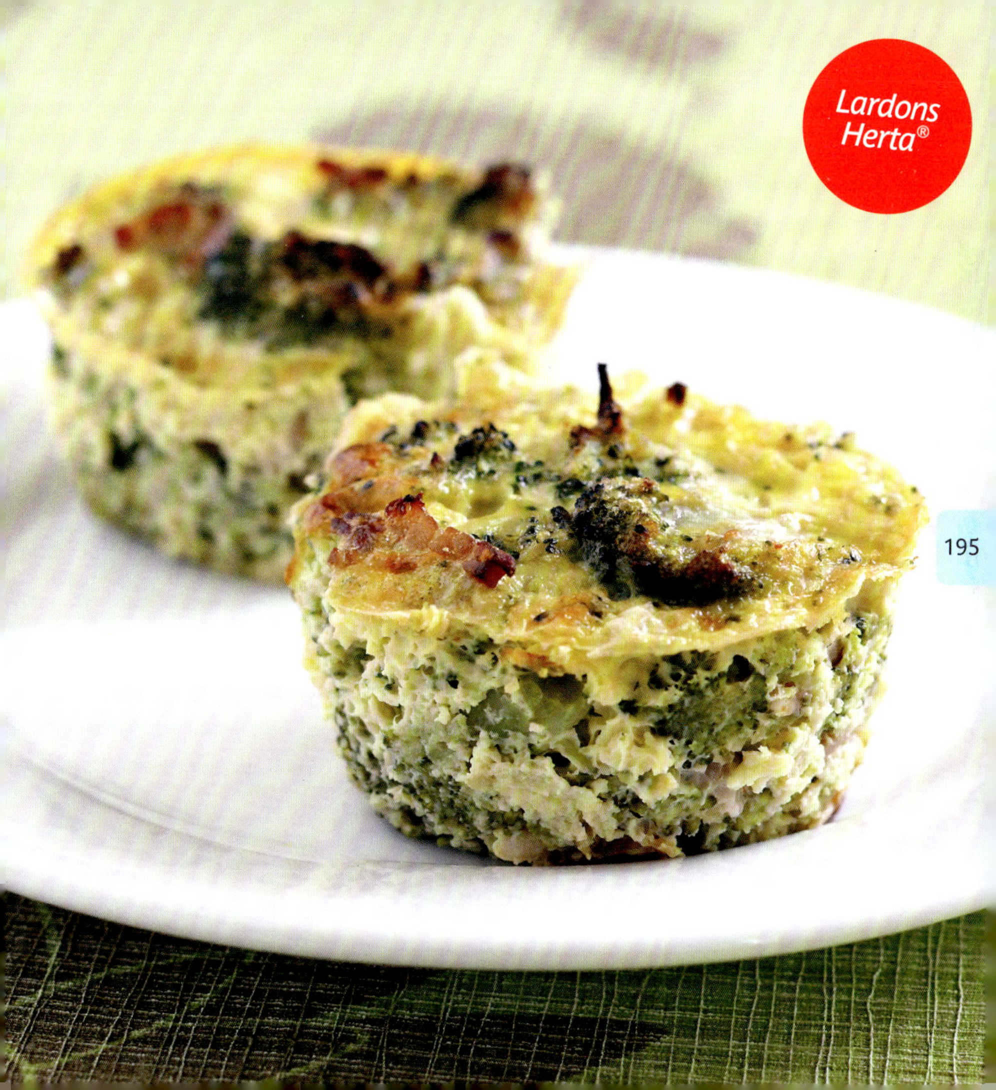

Lardons Herta®

Galettes aux lardons, aux champignons et au chèvre
Remplacez l'œuf par 1 grosse rondelle de bûche de chèvre.

Galettes aux lardons, aux champignons et à la tomate
Remplacez la crème fraîche par le contenu d'une petite boîte de concentré de tomate.

Galettes de sarrasin
Mélangez 330 g de farine de blé noir et 1 grosse pincée de sel. Incorporez progressivement 75 cl de mélange eau + lait en battant sans cesse au fouet. Ajoutez 1 œuf et mélangez. Laissez reposer pendant 1 h au frais. Versez 1 louche de pâte dans une crêpière chaude huilée. Faites cuire jusqu'à ce qu'elle se décolle, puis retournez-la et poursuivez la cuisson pendant 1 min. Renouvelez l'opération jusqu'à l'épuisement des ingrédients. Garnissez les galettes de préparation aux champignons.

Lardons Herta®

GALETTES AUX LARDONS ET AUX CHAMPIGNONS

Préparation: 10 min • **Cuisson**: 5 min par galette • **Pour 4 personnes**

300 g de champignons de Paris frais • 1 c. à s. d'huile de tournesol 10 brins de persil • 200 g de lardons fumés Herta® • 15 cl de crème fraîche • 4 galettes au sarrasin • 4 œufs • sel et poivre

- Rincez rapidement les champignons, puis coupez-les en lamelles.
- Faites-les revenir à la poêle avec l'huile jusqu'à ce qu'ils aient rendu toute leur eau.
- Rincez le persil, puis essuyez-le sur du papier absorbant. Ciselez-le.
- Ajoutez-le dans la poêle avec les lardons Herta®, puis faites cuire jusqu'à ce que les lardons soient bien dorés. Ajoutez la crème fraîche, mélangez et baissez le feu au minimum.
- Déposez 1 galette de sarrasin dans une crêpière chaude. Déposez par-dessus 1/4 de la préparation à base de champignons. Cassez un œuf au centre et repliez les bords de la galette. Salez et poivrez. Laissez chauffer de 1 à 2 min.
- Faites glisser la galette garnie sur une assiette chaude, et renouvelez l'opération avec les autres galettes.
- Servez sans attendre.

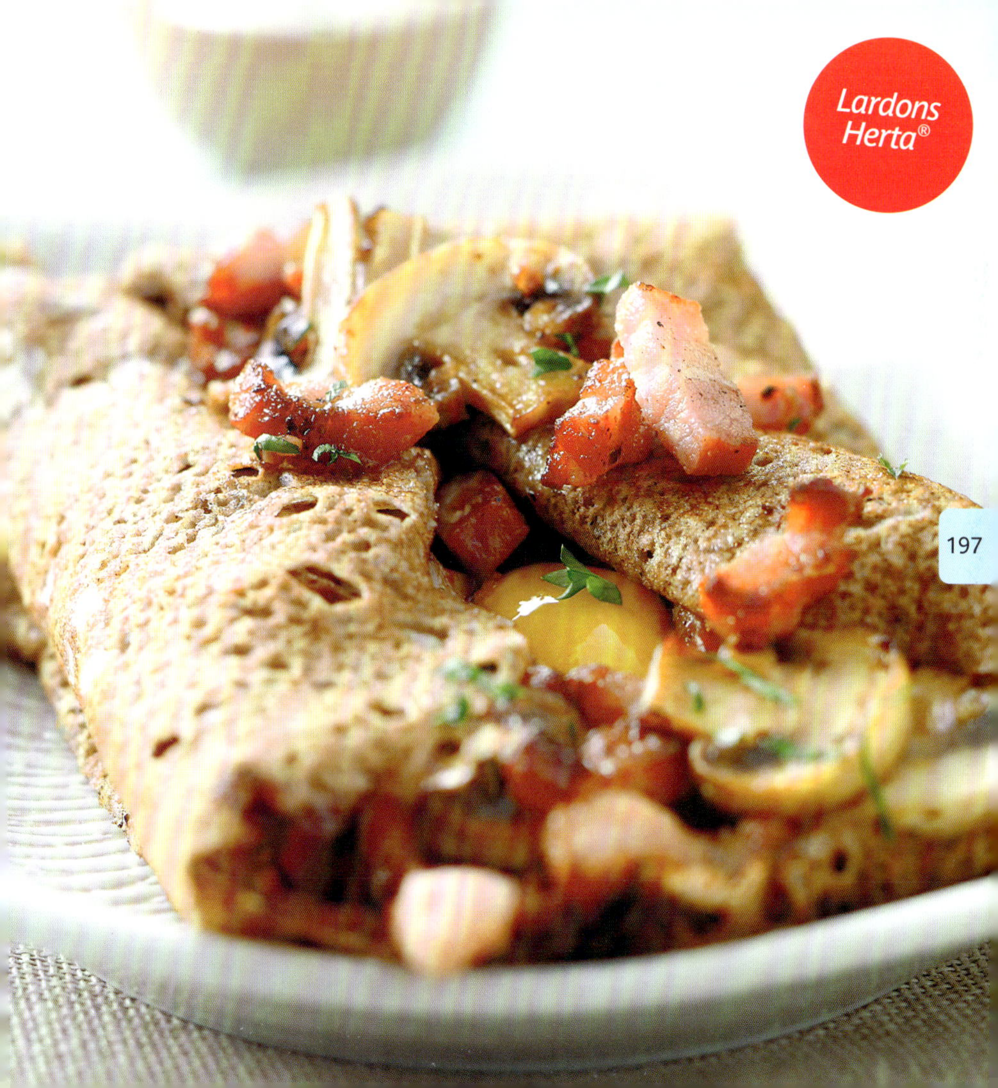
Lardons
Herta®

VELOUTÉ DE LENTILLES CORAIL AUX LARDONS

Préparation : 15 min • **Cuisson :** 30 min • **Pour 4 personnes**

1 oignon • 2 carottes • 2 tomates • 250 g de lentilles corail
20 cl de lait de coco • 1/2 c. à c. de curry en poudre
200 g de lardons Herta® • sel et poivre

- Épluchez l'oignon et émincez-le.
- Pelez les carottes et taillez-les en rondelles.
- Mettez-les dans une grande casserole.
- Ajoutez 1 l d'eau et portez à frémissements. Laissez cuire pendant 15 min.
- Concassez les tomates et ajoutez-les dans la casserole, avec les lentilles corail. Poursuivez la cuisson pendant 15 min.
- Mettez le lait de coco et le curry dans la casserole, puis mixez le tout à l'aide d'un mixeur girafe. Si le velouté est trop épais, ajoutez un peu d'eau chaude.
- Goûtez, salez et poivrez.
- Faites cuire les lardons Herta® dans une poêle, sans matière grasse, puis ajoutez-les au velouté.
- Servez bien chaud.

Velouté de lentilles vertes

Remplacez les lentilles corail par des lentilles vertes, que vous ferez cuire dans 4 fois leur volume d'eau pendant 45 min, avant de les ajouter dans la casserole. Remplacez le lait de coco par de la crème fraîche. Supprimez le curry.

Velouté de lentilles corail et patate douce

Remplacez les tomates par 1 grosse patate douce coupée en cubes, que vous ferez cuire avec les carottes. Remplacez le lait de coco par du lait.

Velouté de lentilles corail aux graines de courge

Ajoutez 2 c. à s. de graines de courge à la soupe en même temps que les lardons.

Velouté de potiron à la ricotta et aux lardons

Faites cuire 500 g de potiron coupé en cubes dans 1 l de bouillon de légumes jusqu'à ce qu'il soit tendre. Mixez, puis ajoutez 100 g de ricotta et 200 g de lardons revenus à la poêle.

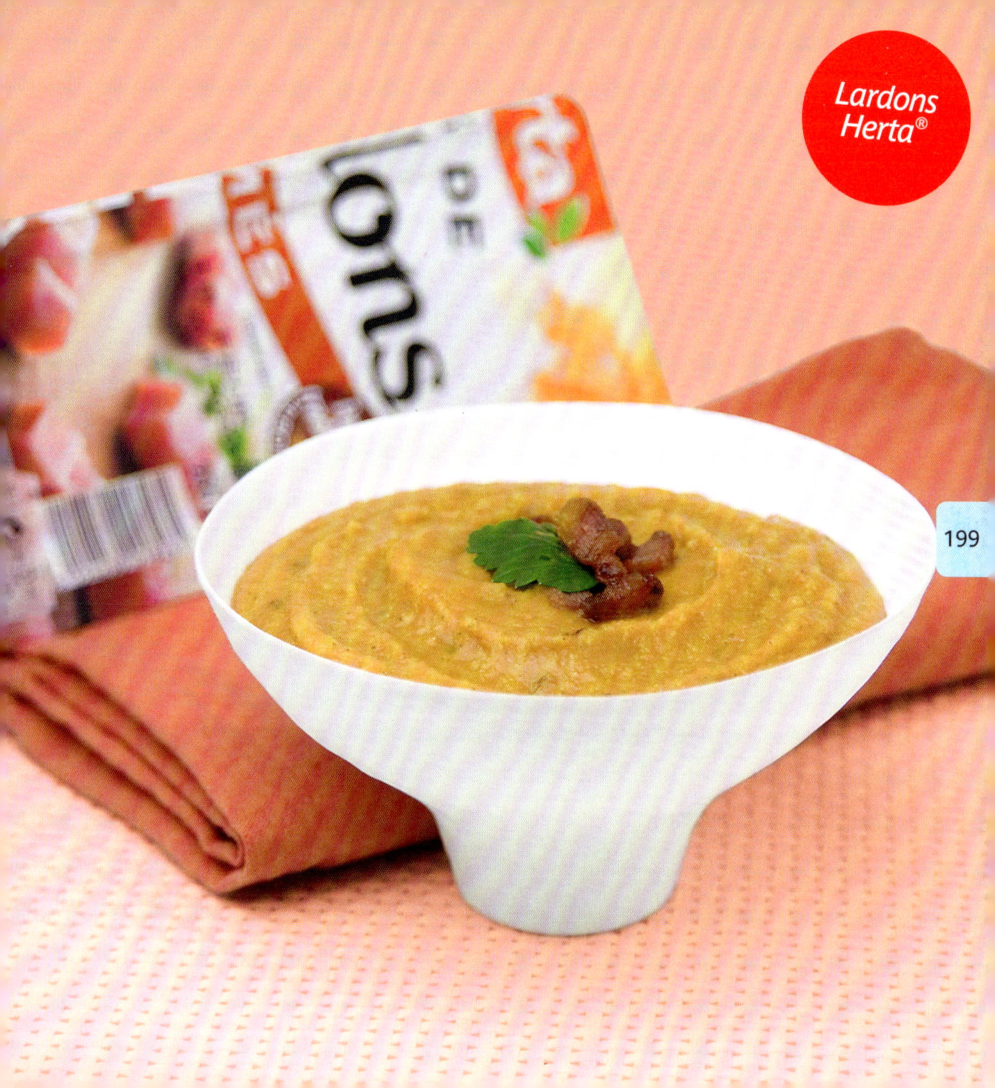
Lardons
Herta®

CHAMPIGNONS FARCIS AU JAMBON ET AUX NOIX

Préparation : 20 min • **Cuisson** : 30 min • **Pour 16 champignons**

16 petits champignons de Paris • 2 c. à s. d'huile d'olive • 2 échalotes
100 g de jambon sec • 1 petite poignée de noix décortiquées
1/2 botte de persil frais • 12 portions de Vache qui rit®

- Préchauffez le four à 180 °C. Coupez les pieds des champignons de Paris. Hachez-les et réservez-les pour la suite de la recette.
- Déposez les chapeaux des champignons sur une plaque à pâtisserie recouverte de papier sulfurisé, côté rond vers le haut. Badigeonnez-les de 1 c. à s. d'huile d'olive. Faites-les cuire au four pendant 20 min.
- Épluchez les échalotes et hachez-les finement. Faites-les revenir à la poêle avec le reste d'huile d'olive, jusqu'à ce qu'elles soient translucides. Ajoutez les pieds de champignons hachés, et faites revenir pendant 10 min.
- Pendant ce temps, hachez grossièrement le jambon. Ajoutez-le dans la poêle, et poursuivez la cuisson pendant 5 min.
- Versez la préparation dans une jatte et laissez refroidir.
- Concassez grossièrement les noix. Rincez le persil, essuyez-le avec du papier absorbant, puis ciselez-le. Ajoutez les noix, le persil et les Vache qui rit® dans la jatte. Mélangez bien.
- Sortez la plaque du four et retournez les champignons. Farcissez-les du mélange. Remettez au four et faites cuire pendant encore 10 min. Servez chaud ou tiède.

Champignons farcis aux lardons et à l'ail
Ajoutez 2 gousses d'ail hachées dans la poêle en même temps que les échalotes. Ajoutez 100 g de lardons fumés en même temps que les pieds de champignon. Supprimez le jambon.

Champignons farcis aux 2 fromages et au miel
Remplacez le jambon par 100 g de bûche de chèvre émiettée, et le persil par 2 c. à s. de miel.

Champignons à la courgette et au parmesan
Remplacez les noix et le persil par 1 courgette bien lavée et râpée, que vous ferez revenir en même temps que le jambon. Parsemez les champignons farcis de parmesan râpé avant d'enfourner.

Champignons farcis au curry
Ajoutez 1 c. à c. de curry en même temps que La Vache qui rit®. Pour relever le tout, vous pouvez aussi ajouter 1 pincée de paprika, 1 pincée de cumin et 1 pincée de piment d'Espelette.

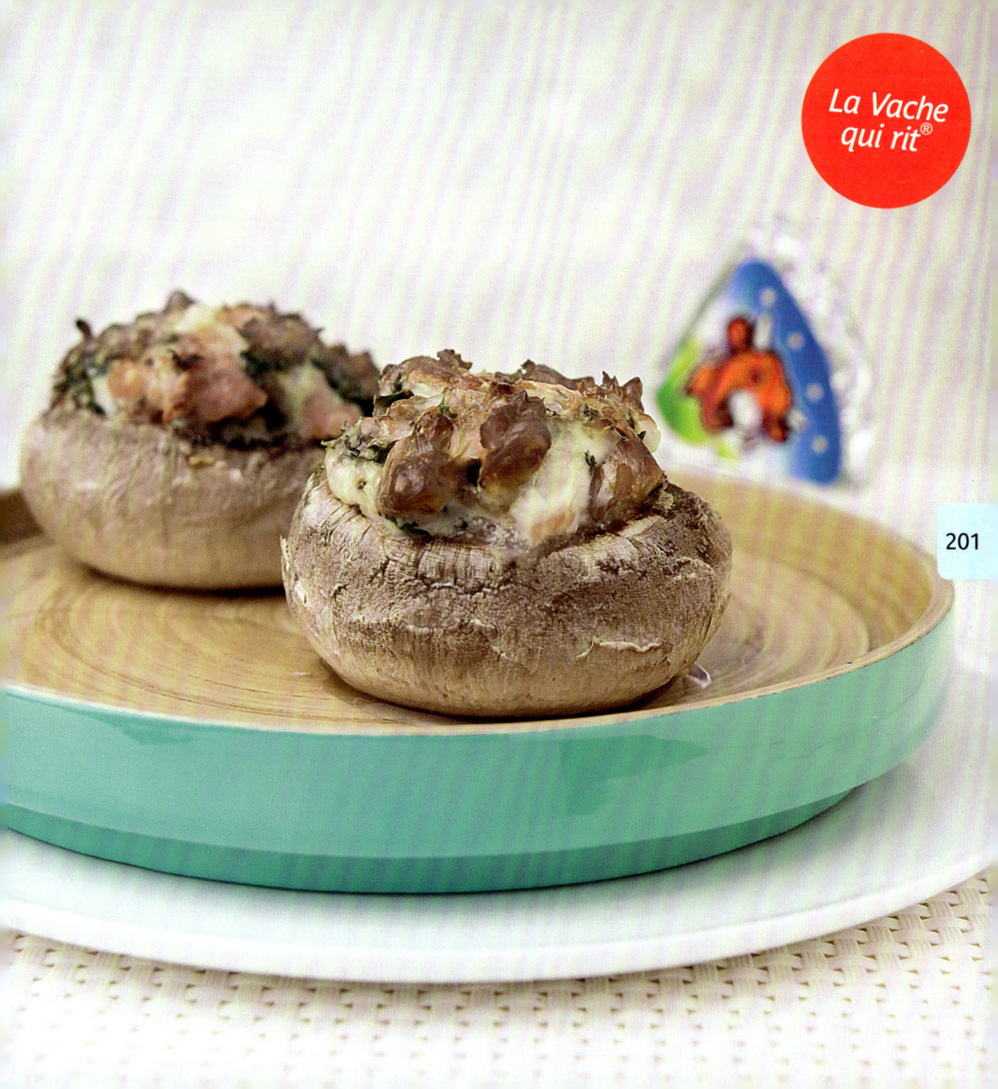
La Vache
qui rit®

CLAFOUTIS À LA VACHE QUI RIT® ET AUX TOMATES CERISES

Préparation : 15 min • **Cuisson** : 25 min • **Pour 4 ou 5 personnes**

16 tomates cerises • 8 feuilles de basilic • 4 œufs • 75 g de farine
40 cl de crème liquide • 4 portions de Vache qui rit® • 100 g de brousse
beurre, pour le moule • sel et poivre

- Préchauffez le four à 180 °C.
- Lavez rapidement les tomates cerises et essuyez-les avec du papier absorbant.
- Rincez les feuilles de basilic, épongez-les sur du papier absorbant, puis ciselez-les.
- Battez les œufs en omelette dans un saladier. Incorporez la farine, la crème liquide, les Vache qui rit®, la brousse, le basilic, du sel et du poivre. Mélangez bien.
- Versez la préparation dans un moule à manqué beurré, et répartissez les tomates cerises par-dessus.
- Faites cuire au four pendant 25 min environ.
- Servez chaud ou froid.

Clafoutis tomate-courgette-piment

Ajoutez 1 courgette râpée et 1 piment doux émincé à la préparation.

Clafoutis à la grecque

Ajoutez 60 g d'olives noires et 50 g de feta émiettée à la préparation.

Clafoutis aux asperges

Remplacez les tomates cerises et le basilic par 400 g d'asperges blanches taillées en morceaux. Ajoutez 1 pincée de noix muscade râpée et 30 g de parmesan râpé à l'appareil à clafoutis.

Clafoutis aux asperges et au saumon

Reprenez la recette ci-dessus en utilisant seulement 200 g d'asperges. Ajoutez 200 g de saumon cru taillé en lanières au mélange.

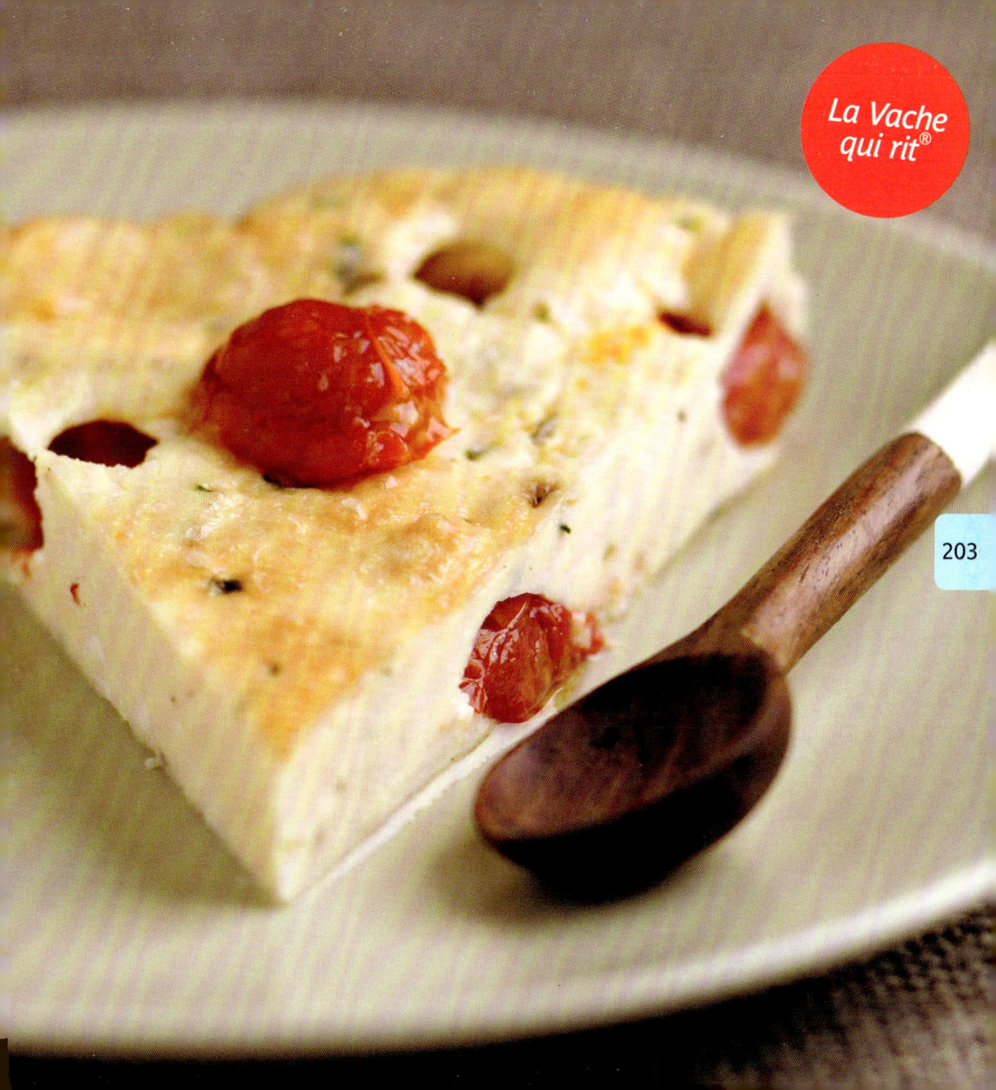
La Vache qui rit®

FRITTATAS À LA PATATE DOUCE ET À LA VACHE QUI RIT®

Préparation : 10 min • **Cuisson :** 30 min • **Pour 4 personnes**

1 patate douce de taille moyenne • 1 poivron rouge
500 g d'asperges blanches • 3 échalotes • 3 c. à s. d'huile d'olive
6 œufs légèrement battus • 1 c. à s. d'origan déshydraté
2 portions de Vache qui rit® • 4 tranches de pain de mie complet • poivre

- Pelez la patate douce et coupez-la en dés. Rincez le poivron, retirez les pépins et les membranes blanches, puis coupez-le en lamelles. Rincez les asperges et taillez-les en tronçons de 3 cm. Épluchez les échalotes et émincez-les finement.
- Faites chauffer 1 c. à s. d'huile d'olive dans une grande poêle sur feu moyen. Ajoutez les dés de patate douce et faites-les cuire de 10 à 15 min, en remuant, jusqu'à ce qu'ils soient bien tendres. Retirez-les de la poêle.
- Faites chauffer 1 autre c. à s. d'huile dans la poêle à feu vif. Faites cuire le poivron pendant 5 min, jusqu'à ce qu'il soit tendre. Retirez-le de la poêle. Faites ensuite revenir l'asperge à feu moyen pendant 3 min. Ajoutez 12 cl d'eau et faites cuire pendant 2 min. Retirez de la poêle et réservez.
- Mélangez les œufs, les échalotes, l'origan et les Vache qui rit® dans un saladier. Poivrez, incorporez les légumes, et mélangez.
- Mettez le reste d'huile dans la poêle et chauffez à feu moyen. Versez la préparation dans des cercles huilés posés dans la poêle, et faites cuire pendant 2 min environ sur chaque face, jusqu'à ce que les frittatas soient bien dorées.
- Faites griller le pain de mie et servez-le avec les frittatas.

Frittatas à la patate douce et aux épinards
Remplacez les asperges par 500 g de feuilles d'épinards fraîches, que vous ferez pocher très rapidement à l'eau bouillante et que vous ferez revenir à la poêle avec de l'huile d'olive pendant 2 min.

Frittatas d'hiver
Remplacez la patate douce par 2 petites pommes de terre, le poivron par 2 blancs de poireau et les asperges par 500 g de bouquets de chou-fleur.

Frittatas d'automne
Remplacez la patate douce par 400 g de potiron, le poivron par 120 g de cœurs d'artichaut, et les asperges par 500 g de cèpes.

Frittatas au poulet et aux brocolis
Remplacez la patate douce et le poivron par 400 g de filets de poulet taillés en lamelles, que vous ferez revenir à la poêle pendant 5 min. Remplacez les asperges par 500 g de brocolis cuits à la vapeur.

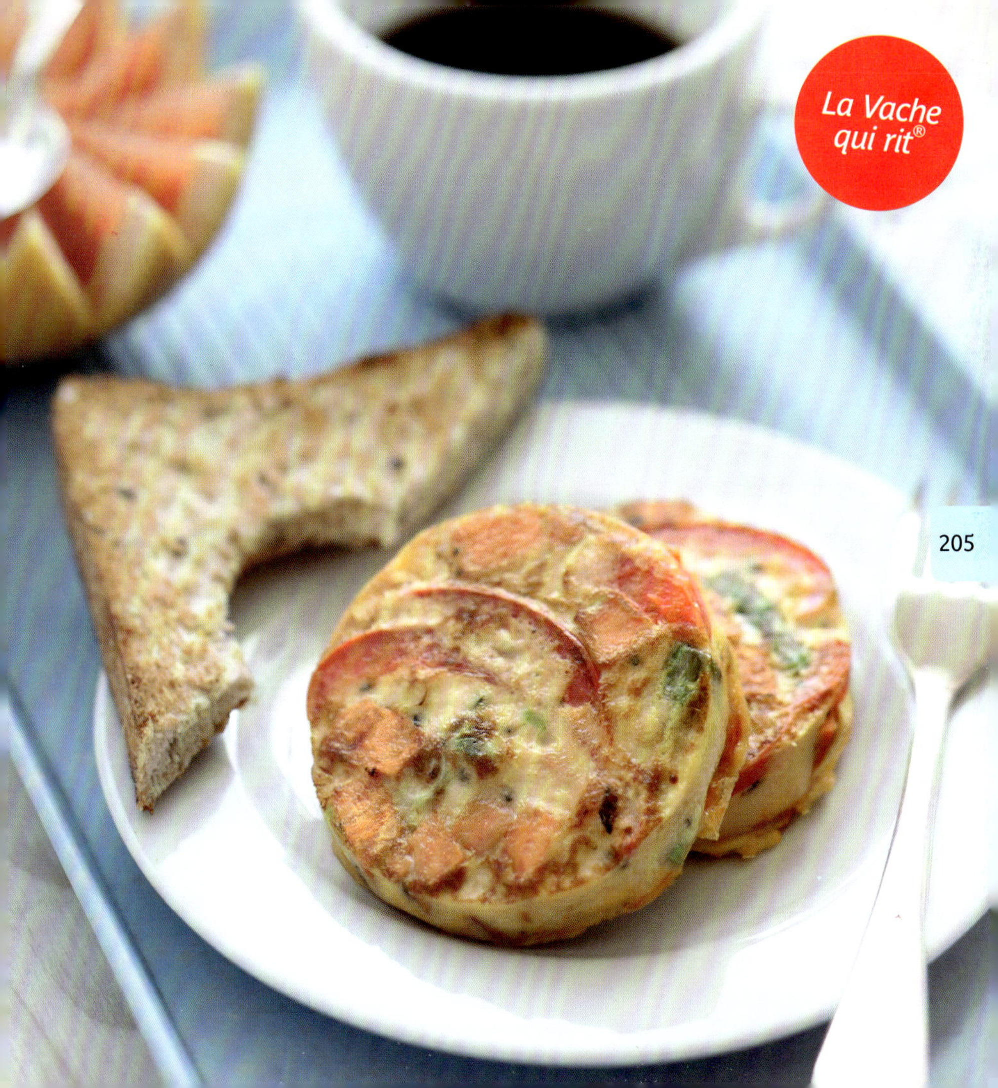
La Vache qui rit®

NAANS AU FROMAGE

Préparation : 10 min • **Cuisson** : 10 min • **Repos** : 1 h • **Pour 4 personnes**

200 g de farine • 1/3 de sachet de levure chimique • 1 c. à s. d'huile d'olive • 1/2 yaourt brassé nature • 8 portions de Vache qui rit® • sel

- Dans un saladier, mélangez la farine, 1 pincée de sel, la levure, l'huile et le yaourt.
- Pétrissez la pâte longuement, en ajoutant un peu d'eau si nécessaire, jusqu'à l'obtention d'une pâte molle et souple qui ne colle pas aux doigts. Laissez reposer pendant 1 h.
- Partagez la pâte en 4 portions et aplatissez-les pour former des galettes. Déposez 2 portions de Vache qui rit® sur une moitié de galette, puis repliez pour enfermer le fromage. Soudez bien les bords.
- Faites cuire dans une poêle à revêtement antiadhésif pendant 5 min sur chaque face, en retournant les naans à mi-cuisson.
- Servez chaud.

Naans au fromage et au cumin
Ajoutez 2 c. à s. de graines de cumin à la préparation.

Naans au fromage, à l'ail et à la coriandre
Ajoutez 2 gousses d'ail épluchées et écrasées, et 1/2 bouquet de coriandre ciselée à la préparation.

Naans au jambon et au fromage
Ajoutez 1 tranche de jambon blanc sur chaque naan avant de le replier et de souder les bords.

Naans au fromage et aux carottes au gingembre
Mélangez 2 carottes pelées et hachées avec 1 morceau de gingembre de 3 cm râpé ; salez et poivrez. Faites cuire à la poêle pendant 20 min. Garnissez les naans de 1 ou 2 c. à s. de ce mélange, en plus du fromage, avant de replier et de souder les bords.

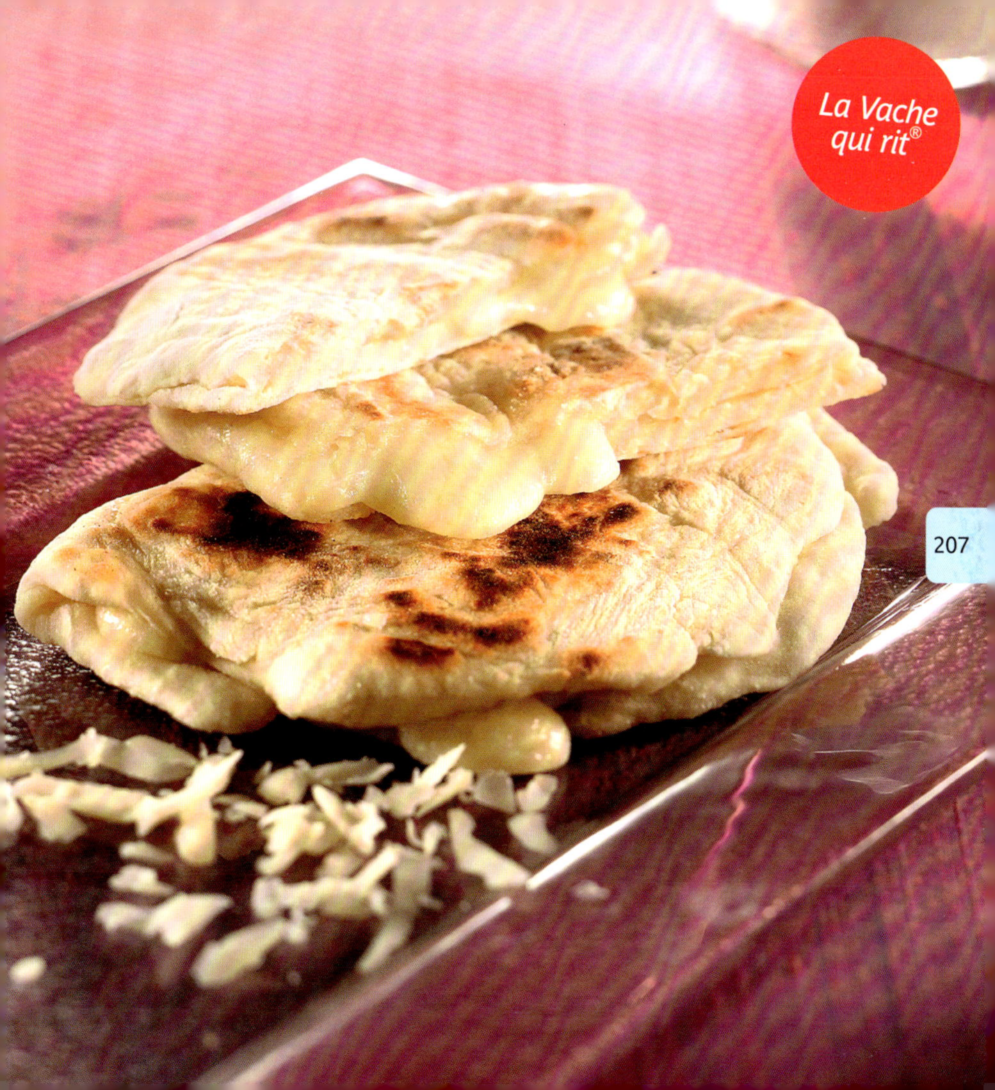
La Vache qui rit®

VELOUTÉ DE LÉGUMES À L'HUILE DE CORIANDRE

Préparation : 25 min • **Cuisson :** 25 min • **Pour 6 personnes**

pour le velouté : *2 oignons • 1 gros chou-fleur • 3 gros poireaux 2 branches de céleri • 2 pommes de terre • 2 c. à s. de beurre 1 c. à s. de graines de cumin • 1 cube de bouillon de légumes 75 cl de lait écrémé • 4 portions de Vache qui rit® • sel et poivre*
pour l'huile de coriandre : *2 gousses d'ail • 30 g de feuilles de coriandre le jus de 1/2 citron • 10 cl d'huile de lin*

- Épluchez les oignons et émincez-les. Séparez les bouquets du chou-fleur. Lavez les poireaux et le céleri, puis émincez-les. Épluchez les pommes de terre et coupez-les en dés.

- Faites chauffer le beurre dans une cocotte et faites-y suer les oignons, les poireaux et le céleri, jusqu'à ce qu'ils soient translucides. Ajoutez les graines de cumin et le cube de bouillon. Salez et poivrez. Ajoutez les bouquets de chou-fleur et les dés de pomme de terre, et faites-les revenir pendant 2 min. Couvrez de lait et laissez mijoter pendant 20 min.

- Ajoutez les Vache qui rit®, puis mixez au blender ou à l'aide d'un mixeur girafe. Ajoutez un peu d'eau si le mélange est trop épais.

- Préparez l'huile de lin à la coriandre : épluchez l'ail et hachez-le. Rincez la coriandre, épongez-la sur du papier absorbant, puis ciselez-la.

- Mettez-les dans le bol du mixeur avec le jus de citron, et mixez. Sans arrêter le mixeur, versez l'huile de lin, puis 2 c. à s. d'eau.

- Servez la soupe dans des bols et arrosez d'un filet d'huile de coriandre.

Velouté de légumes orange
Remplacez le chou-fleur par 1 gros morceau de potiron, les poireaux par 3 carottes, le céleri et les pommes de terre par 1 patate douce.

Velouté de légumes verts
Remplacez le chou-fleur par le même poids de brocolis ou de chou romanesco, le céleri par 200 g de haricots verts, et 1 pomme de terre par 100 g de fèves.

Velouté à la courgette
Mettez 1 kg de courgettes lavées et taillées en rondelles dans une cocotte avec 2 cubes de bouillon de légumes, 2 gousses d'ail écrasées, du sel et du poivre. Couvrez d'eau à hauteur et faites cuire de 15 à 20 min. Incorporez 6 Vache qui rit® et mixez.

Velouté à la courgette et à la menthe
Reprenez la recette ci-dessus en remplaçant l'ail par 1/2 bouquet de menthe fraîche.

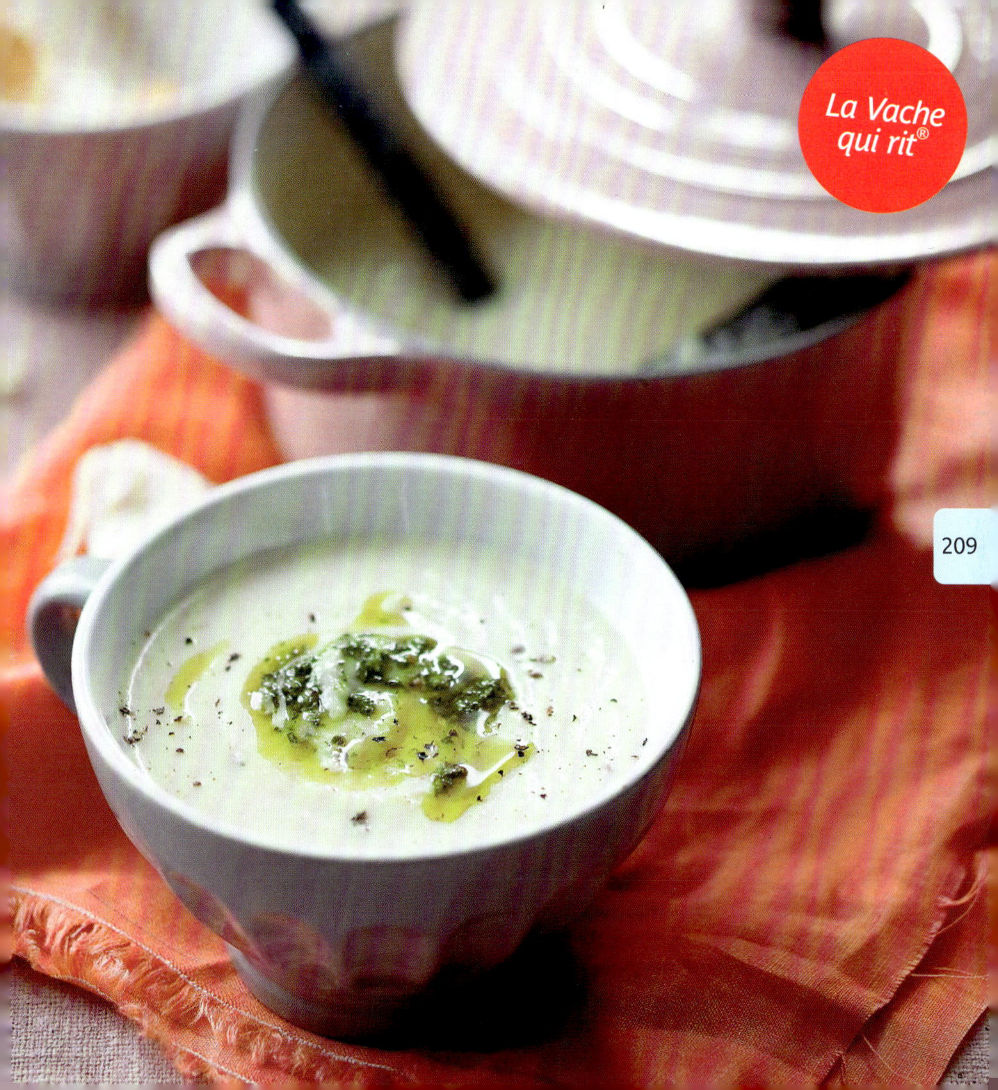
La Vache qui rit®

VERRINES DE CONCOMBRE À LA VACHE QUI RIT®

Préparation : 10 min • **Cuisson :** aucune • **Pour 6 verrines**

1/2 concombre • 1 c. à s. d'huile d'olive • quelques gouttes de Tabasco®
5 portions de Vache qui rit® • 2 c. à s. de lait • 6 c. à c. de tapenade
sel et poivre

- Lavez le concombre et mixez-le finement avec l'huile d'olive et 4 ou 5 gouttes de Tabasco®. Salez et poivrez. Réservez au frais.
- Mélangez les Vache qui rit® avec le lait dans une assiette creuse à l'aide d'une fourchette. Travaillez le mélange jusqu'à ce qu'il soit souple.
- Répartissez le mélange au concombre dans 6 petites verrines. Déposez une couche de fromage et 1 c. à c. de tapenade par-dessus.
- Servez frais.

Verrines version tzatziki

Mixez le concombre avec 1 gousse d'ail épluchée et ajoutez 1/2 bouquet de menthe au mélange à base de fromage.

Verrines express à la Vache qui rit®

Remplacez le velouté de concombre par du gaspacho, de la soupe fraîche de carotte à la coriandre ou de la soupe fraîche de courgette coco-curry en brique.

Glace au concombre et à la Vache qui rit®

Mixez le concombre avec l'huile d'olive, les Vache qui rit® et 2 c. à c. d'herbes de Provence. Faites turbiner en sorbetière. Servez dans des cuillères pour apéritif.

Tapenade maison

Mixez grossièrement 250 g d'olives noires dénoyautées, 6 filets d'anchois, 3 c. à c. de câpres et 1 gousse d'ail. Robot toujours en marche, incorporez 10 cl d'huile d'olive.

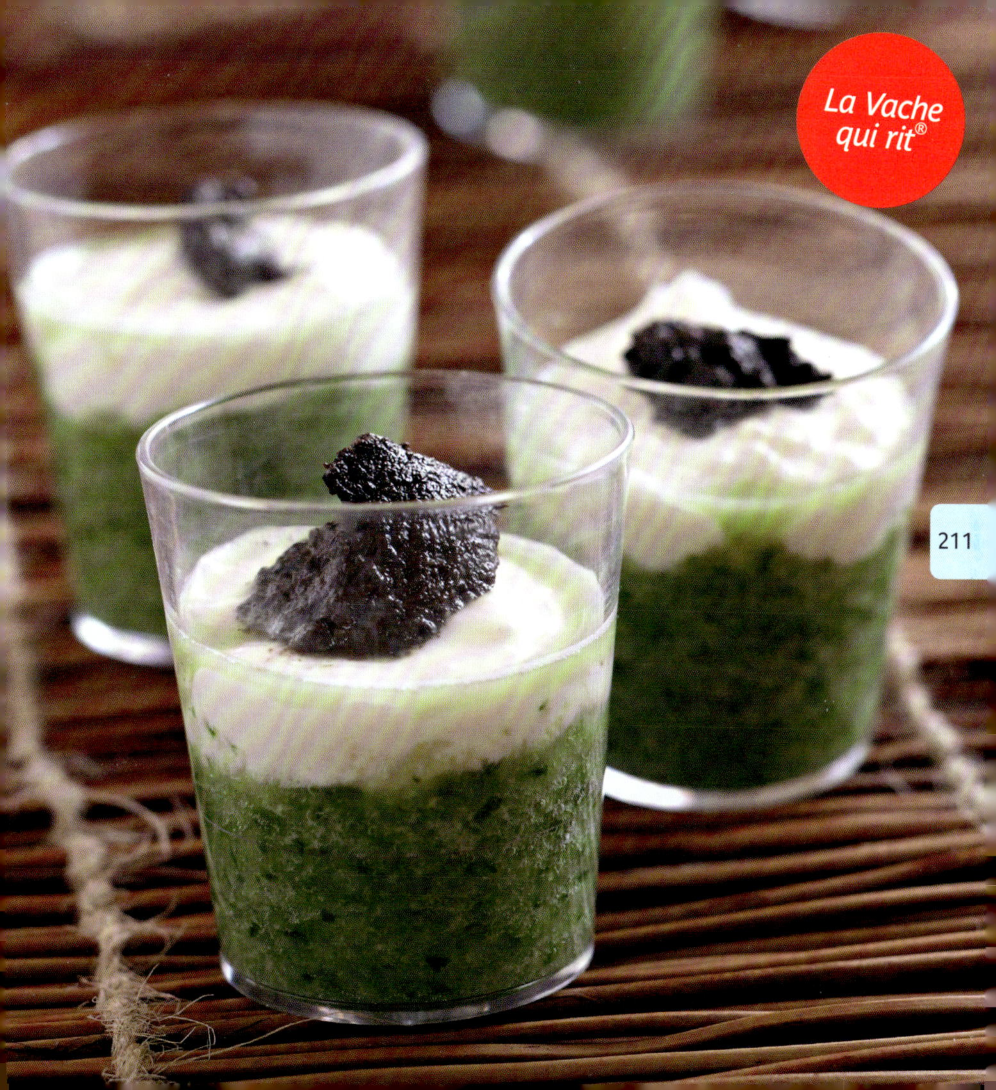
La Vache qui rit®

Bouchons aux M&M's® sans gluten
Remplacez la farine par de la farine de riz, ou augmentez la quantité de poudre d'amandes de 25 g. Supprimez la farine.

Bouchons aux M&M's® sans beurre
Remplacez le beurre par 50 g de compote de pommes.

Bouchons au miel et aux M&M's®
Remplacez la moitié du sucre par 2 c. à s. de miel d'acacia ou de miel des montagnes.

Bouchons au sirop d'érable et aux M&M's®
Remplacez le sucre par 5 c. à s. de sirop d'érable.

BOUCHONS AUX M&M'S®

Préparation : 10 min • **Cuisson** : 12 min • **Pour 20 bouchons**

75 g de sucre en poudre • 2 blancs d'œufs • 25 g de farine
25 g de poudre d'amandes • 40 g de beurre ramolli • 20 M&M's® peanut

- Préchauffez le four à 180 °C.
- Mettez le sucre et les blancs d'œufs dans un saladier, et battez au fouet jusqu'à l'obtention d'un mélange mousseux.
- Ajoutez la farine, la poudre d'amandes et le beurre détaillé en parcelles.
- Déposez 1 M&M's® au fond de petits moules en forme de pyramide.
- Recouvrez de pâte jusqu'aux 3/4 de la hauteur, puis enfournez.
- Faites cuire au four pendant 12 min.
- Laissez tiédir avant de démouler.

M&M's®

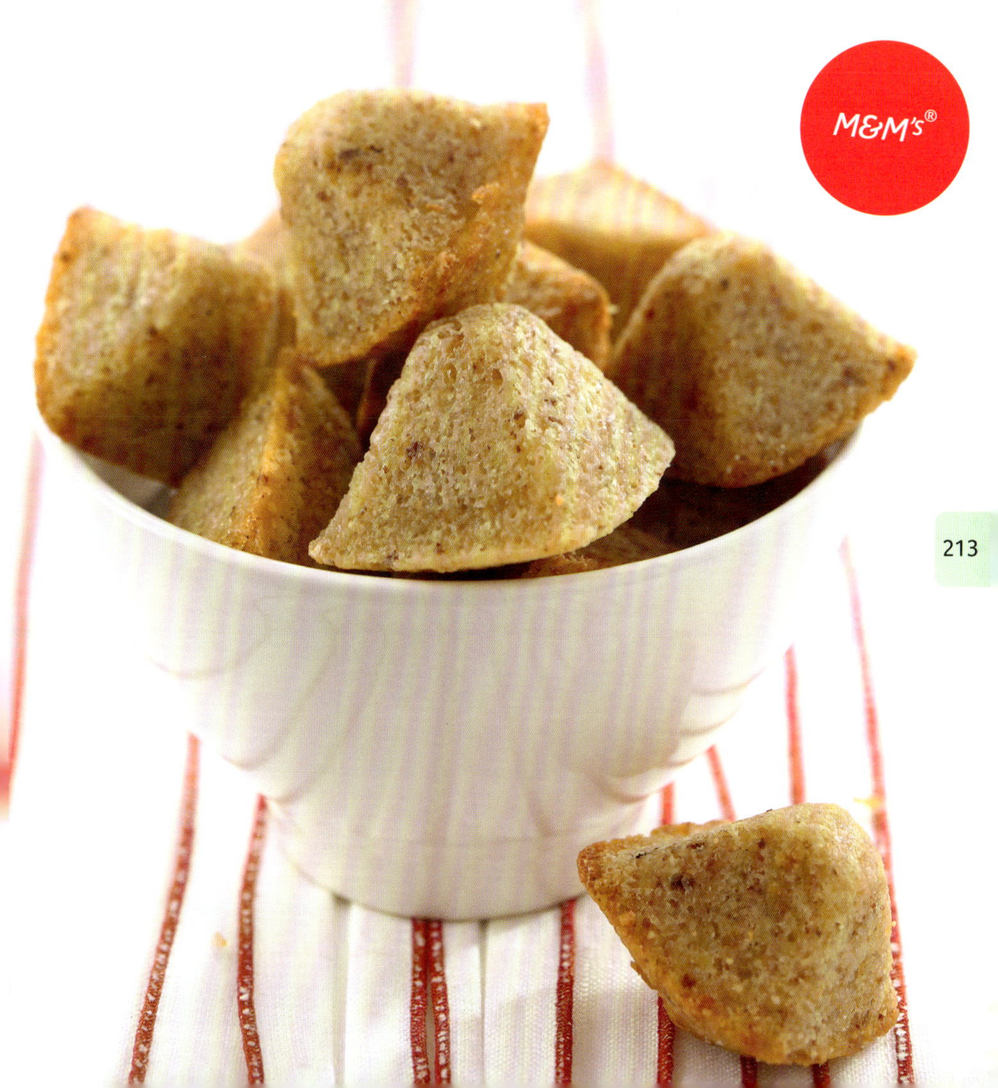

COOKIES AUX M&M'S®

Préparation : 15 min • **Cuisson :** 12 min • **Pour 10 cookies**

125 g de farine • 40 g de cassonade • 1/2 sachet de levure chimique
1 sachet de sucre vanillé • 50 g de beurre • 1 œuf
1 sachet de miniM&M's® chocolat

- Préchauffez le four à 200 °C.
- Dans un saladier, mélangez la farine, la cassonade, la levure et le sucre vanillé.
- Faites fondre le beurre dans une petite casserole. Versez-le dans un bol et ajoutez l'œuf. Battez au fouet. Incorporez ce mélange aux ingrédients secs.
- Façonnez de petites boules et déposez-les sur une plaque à pâtisserie recouverte de papier sulfurisé, en les espaçant de 5 cm.
- Répartissez les miniM&M's® sur les boules de pâte.
- Faites cuire au four de 10 à 12 min.
- Laissez refroidir quelques instants avant de déguster.

Cookies aux M&M's® et aux pépites de chocolat
Remplacez la moitié des miniM&M's® par 50 g de pépites de chocolat au lait.

Cookies aux M&M's® au beurre de cacahuète
Remplacez le beurre par du beurre de cacahuète. Utilisez des M&M's® peanut grossièrement écrasés à la place des miniM&M's®.

Cookies tout chocolat aux M&M's®
Incorporez 120 g de chocolat noir à pâtisserie fondu à la pâte.

Cookies aux M&M's® et aux flocons d'avoine
Ajoutez 75 g de flocons d'avoine à la préparation.

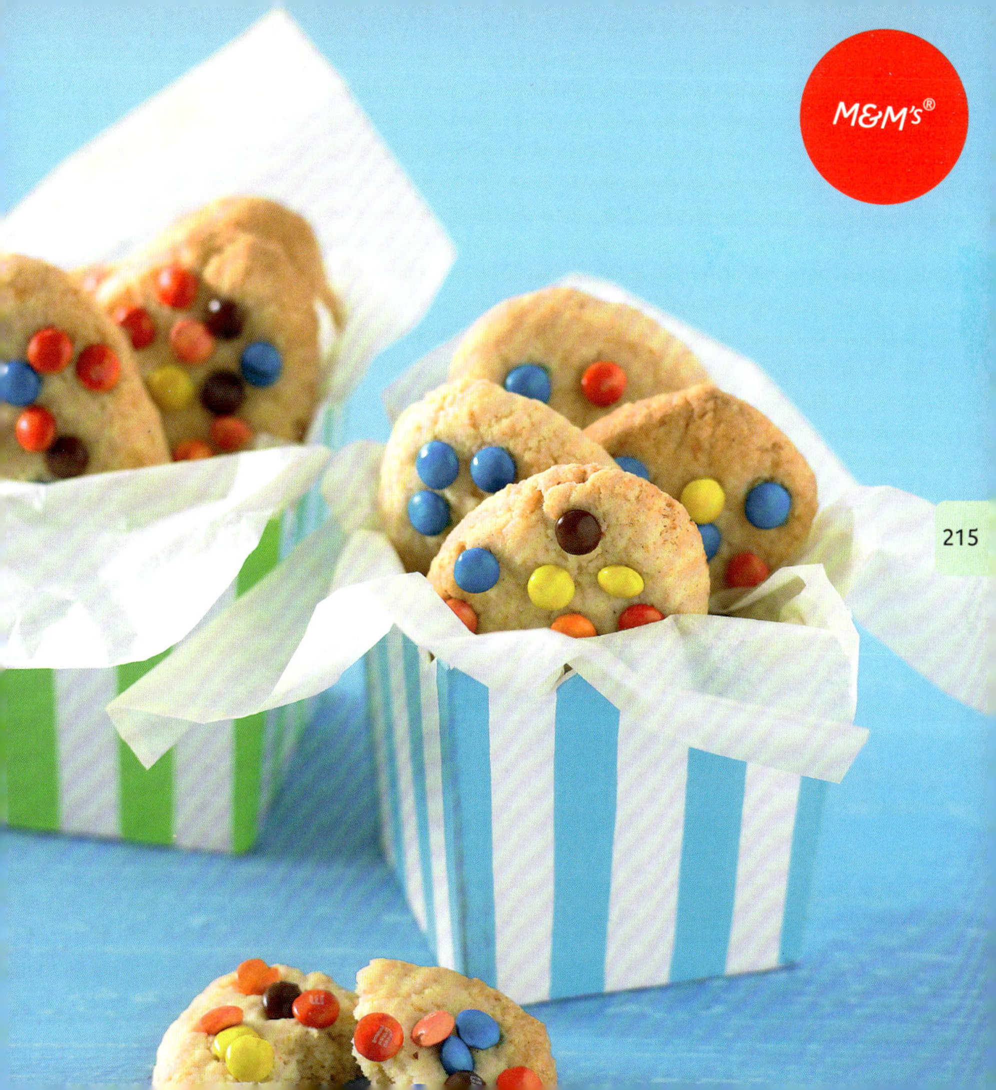
M&M's®

MENDIANTS AUX M&M'S®

Préparation : 10 min • **Cuisson :** aucune • **Pour 25 mendiants**

60 g de chocolat noir à pâtisserie • 60 g de chocolat blanc à pâtisserie
2 ou 3 sachets de M&M's peanut®

- Cassez les chocolats en morceaux et faites-les cuire séparément au bain-marie.
- Déposez 2 grandes feuilles de papier sulfurisé sur un marbre ou sur une surface froide et lisse.
- Sur la première feuille, formez rapidement de petits disques de chocolat noir (pour chaque mendiant, étalez 1 c. à c. de chocolat).
- Faites de même sur la seconde feuille de papier sulfurisé avec le chocolat blanc.
- Déposez 3 ou 4 M&M's® sur chaque disque de chocolat.
- Laissez refroidir complètement.

Mendiants aux pistaches et aux M&M's®

Remplacez la moitié des M&M's® par des pistaches non salées.

Mendiants aux M&M's® et à la noix de coco

Ajoutez 1 c. à s. de noix de coco râpée à chaque chocolat fondu. Parsemez les mendiants de noix de coco râpée après avoir ajouté les M&M's®.

Mendiants au chocolat au lait et à l'orange

Remplacez les chocolats par du chocolat au lait. Remplacez la moitié des M&M's® par des écorces d'orange confites taillées en dés.

Mendiants aux noix caramélisées

Faites chauffer à feu doux 100 g de cerneaux de noix avec 100 g de sucre et 10 cl d'eau, en remuant sans cesse. Laissez refroidir sur une plaque recouverte de papier sulfurisé. Remplacez la moitié des M&M's® par ces noix.

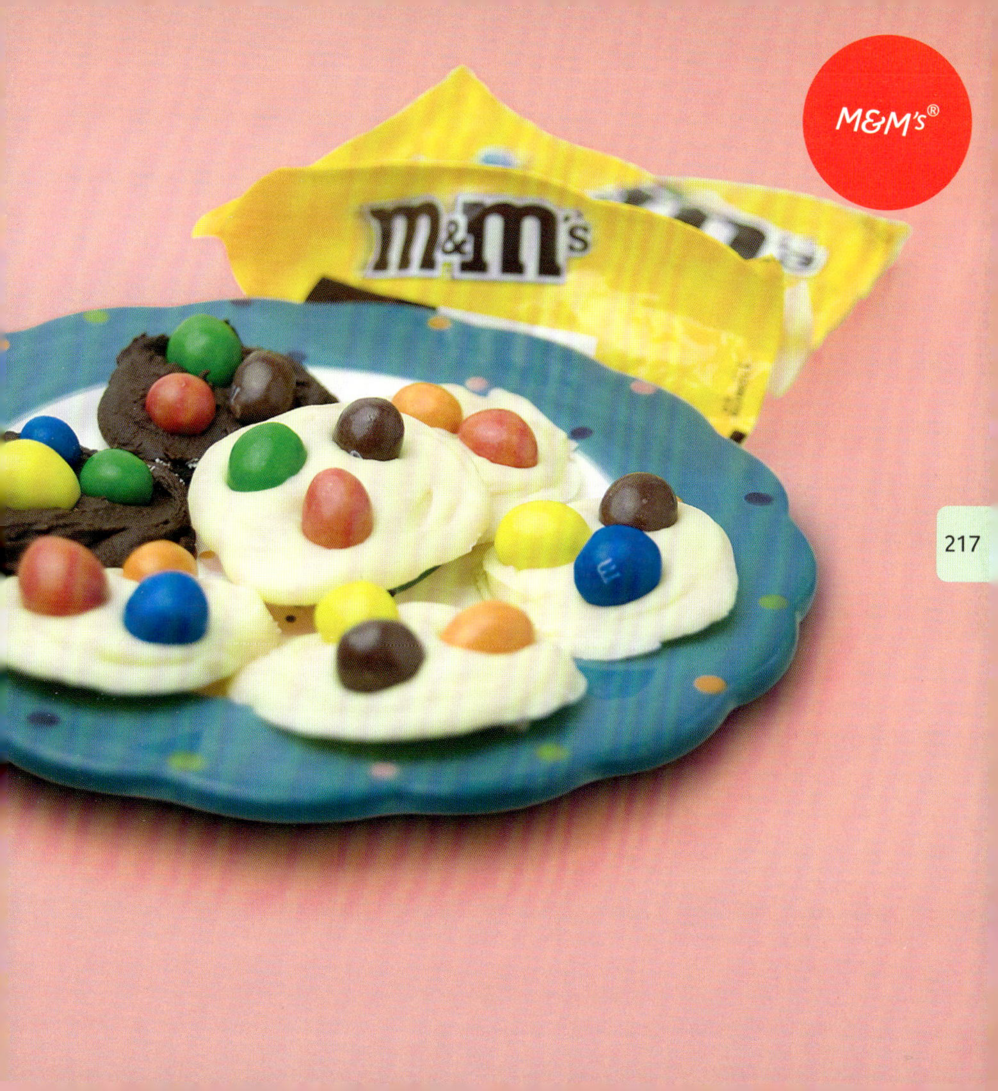
m&m's

COMPOTÉE DE POMMES À LA CRÈME DE MARS®

Préparation : 20 min • **Cuisson** : 15 min • **Réfrigération** : 2 h
Pour 6 personnes

pour la compotée de pommes : 1 kg de pommes golden
30 g de beurre demi-sel • 60 g de sucre en poudre
pour la crème de Mars® : 3 Mars® • 100 g de crème fleurette très froide
10 g de sucre glace

- Pour la compotée, pelez les pommes et évidez-les à l'aide d'un vide-pomme. Coupez-les en quartiers.
- Faites fondre le beurre dans une cocotte. Ajoutez les pommes et le sucre en poudre.
- Couvrez et laissez cuire pendant 15 min environ en remuant régulièrement.
- Laissez refroidir complètement.
- Pour la crème de Mars®, coupez les Mars® en morceaux et placez-les dans une jatte. Faites-les fondre au bain-marie en remuant régulièrement.
- Dans un saladier très froid, versez la crème fleurette et montez-la en chantilly au batteur électrique. Incorporez progressivement le sucre glace, puis les Mars® fondus.
- Répartissez la compotée de pommes dans des verrines et nappez-la de crème au Mars®.
- Réservez au frais pendant 2 h avant de servir.

Compotée de coings au Mars®

Remplacez 700 g de pommes par 700 g de coings pelés et coupés en morceaux, que vous ferez cuire à part, à la vapeur. Écrasez, puis mélangez les deux compotes.

Verrines croustifondantes au Mars®

Garnissez le fond de 6 verrines de biscuits à la cannelle émiettés. Recouvrez d'une couche de compotée de pomme, puis d'une couche de crème de Mars®. Renouvelez l'opération une fois.

Tartelettes aux pommes et au Mars®

Foncez 6 moules à tartelette de pâte sablée. Garnissez-les de compotée de pommes et nappez de crème au Mars®. Faites cuire au four préchauffé à 180 °C pendant 15 min environ.

Madeleines aux pommes et au Mars®

Coupez 12 madeleines en deux dans le sens de l'épaisseur. Garnissez chacune de 1 ou 2 c. à c. de compotée de pommes et nappez la surface de crème au Mars®.

Mars®

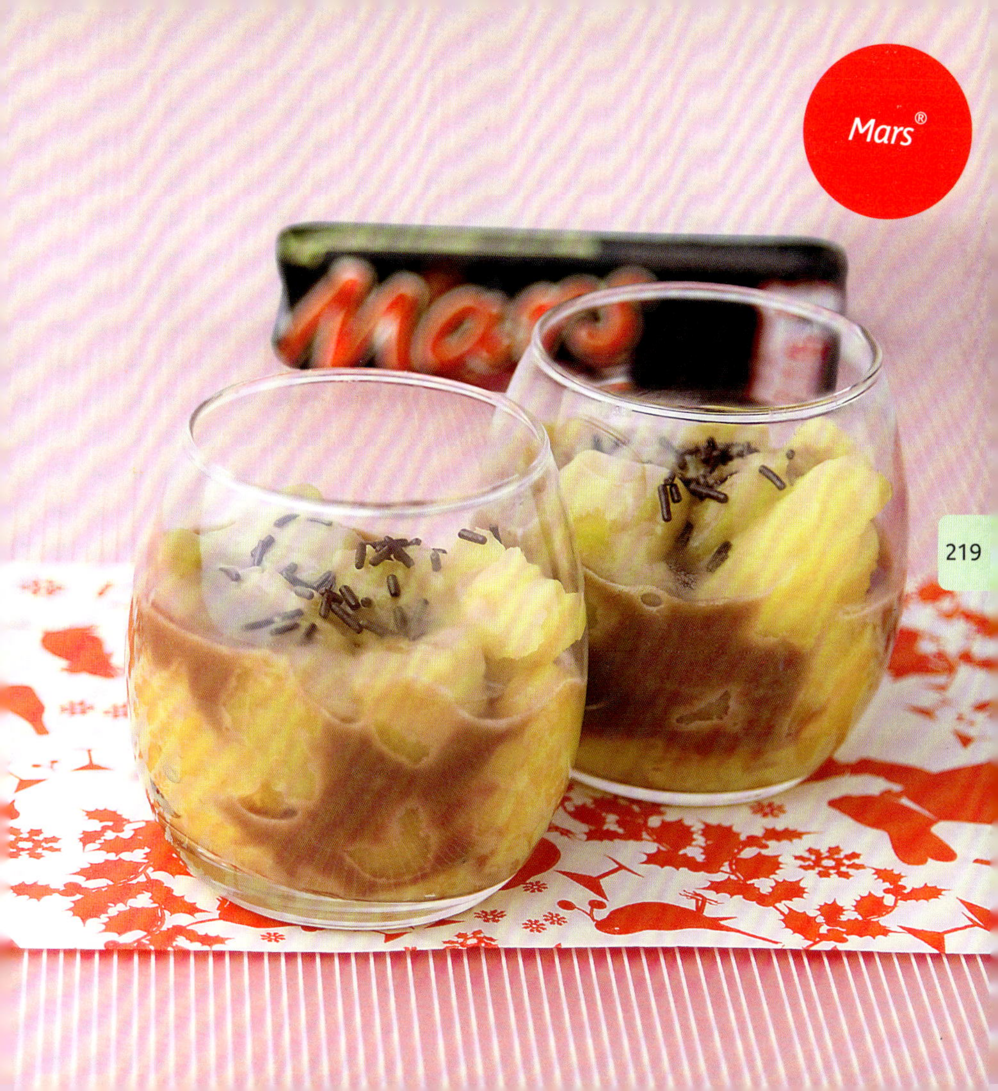

Pudding à la brioche et aux raisins secs
Remplacez les croissants par 4 grosses tranches de brioche rassise. Ajoutez 40 g de raisins secs préalablement mis à tremper dans de l'eau.

Pudding à la marmelade
Pour une version sans alcool, remplacez la liqueur d'orange par 5 c. à s. de marmelade d'oranges.

Pudding aux poires et à la cardamome
Supprimez la liqueur d'orange. Ajoutez 2 poires pelées et taillées en dés sur les croissants en même temps que les morceaux de Mars®. Remplacez l'extrait de vanille liquide par 2 capsules de cardamome écrasées.

PUDDING AU MARS®

Préparation : 20 min • **Cuisson :** 40 min • **Pour 4 à 6 personnes**

4 gros croissants rassis • beurre, pour le moule • 4 Mars®
3 c. à s. de liqueur d'orange • 30 cl de crème liquide
30 cl de lait • 1 c. à c. d'extrait de vanille liquide • 6 gros jaunes d'œufs
90 g de sucre en poudre • 30 g de cassonade
1 pincée de cannelle en poudre

- Préchauffez le four à 180 °C.
- Coupez les croissants en morceaux grossiers et disposez-en les 2/3 au fond d'un plat allant au four préalablement beurré.
- Coupez 2 Mars® en morceaux et répartissez-les sur les morceaux de croissant. Arrosez de liqueur d'orange.
- Versez la crème liquide, le lait et l'extrait de vanille dans une petite casserole et portez à ébullition. Réservez.
- Battez les jaunes d'œufs et le sucre au batteur électrique dans un saladier, puis incorporez un peu de préparation liquide et battez à nouveau. Ajoutez le reste du liquide et mélangez bien.
- Versez le tout dans le plat. Disposez les morceaux de croissant restants par-dessus et saupoudrez de cassonade et de cannelle.
- Faites cuire au four de 30 à 40 min.
- Pendant ce temps, faites fondre les Mars® restants dans une petite casserole, à feu doux, en remuant sans cesse.
- Arrosez le pudding de Mars® fondu, dès la sortie du four.

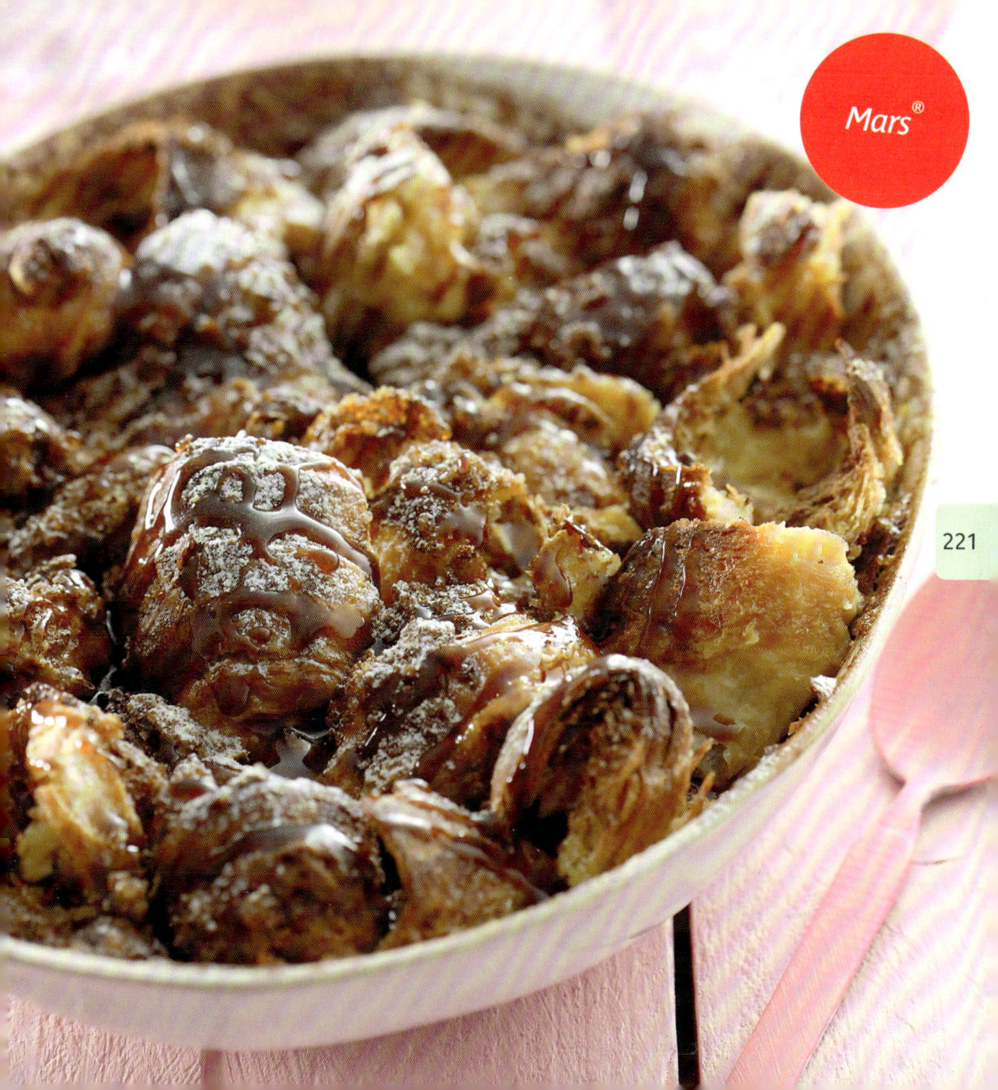

TARTE AU CARAMEL ET AU MARS®

Préparation : 30 min • **Cuisson** : 25 min • **Réfrigération** : 2 h
Pour 8 à 10 personnes

pour la pâte : *320 g de farine + un peu pour le plan de travail*
80 g de sucre glace • 125 g de beurre ramolli • 2 jaunes d'œufs
pour la garniture : *400 g de lait concentré sucré • 10 cl de caramel liquide*
100 g de beurre coupé en morceaux • 30 cl de crème liquide
4 Mars® • 160 g de noix de macadamia

- Pour la pâte, versez la farine et le sucre glace dans le saladier. Coupez le beurre en parcelles et ajoutez-le au mélange avec les jaunes d'œufs et 1 c. à s. d'eau. Travaillez du bout des doigts jusqu'à ce que des miettes se forment. Enveloppez la pâte dans du film alimentaire et réservez au réfrigérateur pendant 30 min.

- Étalez la pâte au rouleau sur le plan de travail fariné, puis chemisez-en un moule à tarte. Piquez le fond à la fourchette et réservez au congélateur pendant 30 min. Préchauffez le four à 180 °C. Faites cuire la pâte à blanc de 10 à 15 min, jusqu'à ce qu'elle soit bien dorée. Laissez refroidir.

- Pour la garniture, versez le lait concentré sucré, le caramel et le beurre dans une casserole. Faites chauffer à feu doux pendant 25 min en remuant. Laissez refroidir pendant 10 min avant d'ajouter 20 cl de crème liquide. Laissez refroidir complètement. Versez la garniture sur la pâte. Réservez au frais jusqu'à ce que la garniture au caramel soit bien ferme.

- Faites fondre les Mars® dans une casserole avec le reste de crème. Faites griller les noix de macadamia à sec. Versez les Mars® fondus sur la tarte puis parsemez de noix de macadamia. Laissez prendre pendant encore 30 min au réfrigérateur.

Tarte au citron et au Mars®

Ajoutez le jus de 1 citron à la préparation pour la garniture.

Tarte aux abricots et au Mars®

Remplacez la préparation au caramel par 8 à 10 abricots coupés en deux et dénoyautés. Parsemez de parcelles de beurre et faites cuire en même temps que la pâte pendant 30 min.

Tarte à la banane et au Mars®

Divisez par deux la quantité de lait concentré sucré pour la garniture. Remplacez-le par la chair de 2 bananes écrasées, que vous incorporerez en même temps que la crème liquide.

Tarte au Mars® et aux fraises

Remplacez les noix de macadamia par 200 g de fraises lavées, équeutées et coupées en deux.

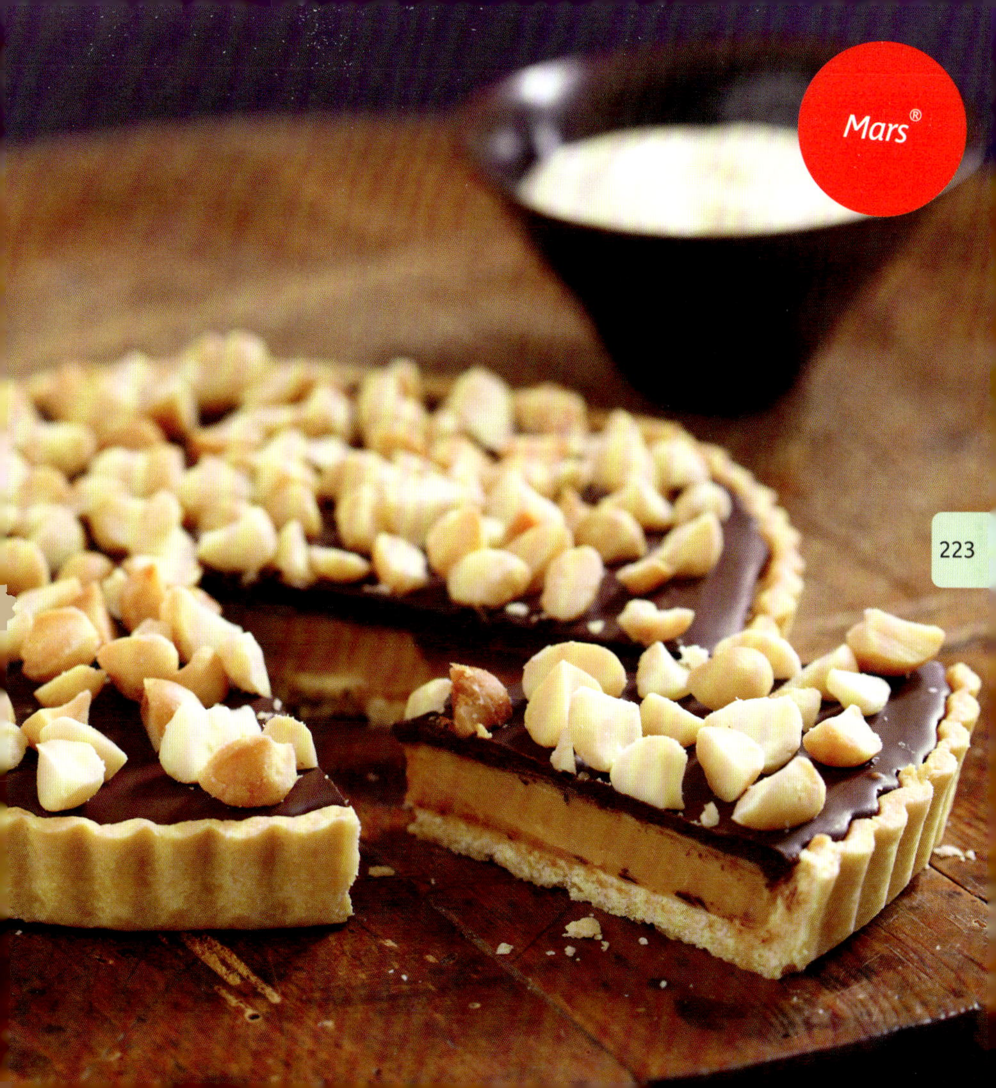
Mars®

DÔMES AU MI-CHO-KO®

Préparation : 20 min • **Cuisson** : 20 min • **Pour 4 à 6 personnes**

15 Mi-cho-ko® noirs • 50 g de beurre + un peu pour les ramequins 6 œufs • 115 g de sucre en poudre • 55 g de farine • 20 g de poudre d'amandes • crème glacée à la vanille, pour accompagner

- Préchauffez le four à 180 °C.
- Mettez les Mi-cho-ko® et le beurre dans une jatte, et faites-les fondre au bain-marie, à feu doux, en remuant régulièrement.
- Dans un saladier, battez les œufs et le sucre au fouet jusqu'à ce que le mélange soit clair et mousseux.
- Mettez la farine et la poudre d'amandes dans un autre saladier, puis ajoutez la préparation aux œufs et mélangez. Incorporez ensuite les Mi-cho-ko® fondus.
- Répartissez le mélange dans 6 ramequins préalablement beurrés.
- Faites cuire au four pendant 20 min environ.
- Laissez refroidir quelques minutes avant de démouler.
- Servez avec de la glace à la vanille.

Dômes au Mi-cho-ko® et aux noisettes

Ajoutez 75 g de noisettes concassées à la préparation. Remplacez la poudre d'amandes par de la poudre de noisettes.

Dômes au Mi-cho-ko® et aux griottes

Ajoutez 150 g de griottes dénoyautées à la préparation.

Dômes au Mi-cho-ko® et à l'orgeat

Remplacez 15 g de sucre par 2 c. à s. de sirop d'orgeat. À défaut, utilisez du sirop d'anis, voire de l'anisette.

Dômes au Mi-cho-ko® et au kirsch

Ajoutez 2 c. à c. de kirsch à la préparation. Vous pouvez également utiliser de la liqueur d'orange.

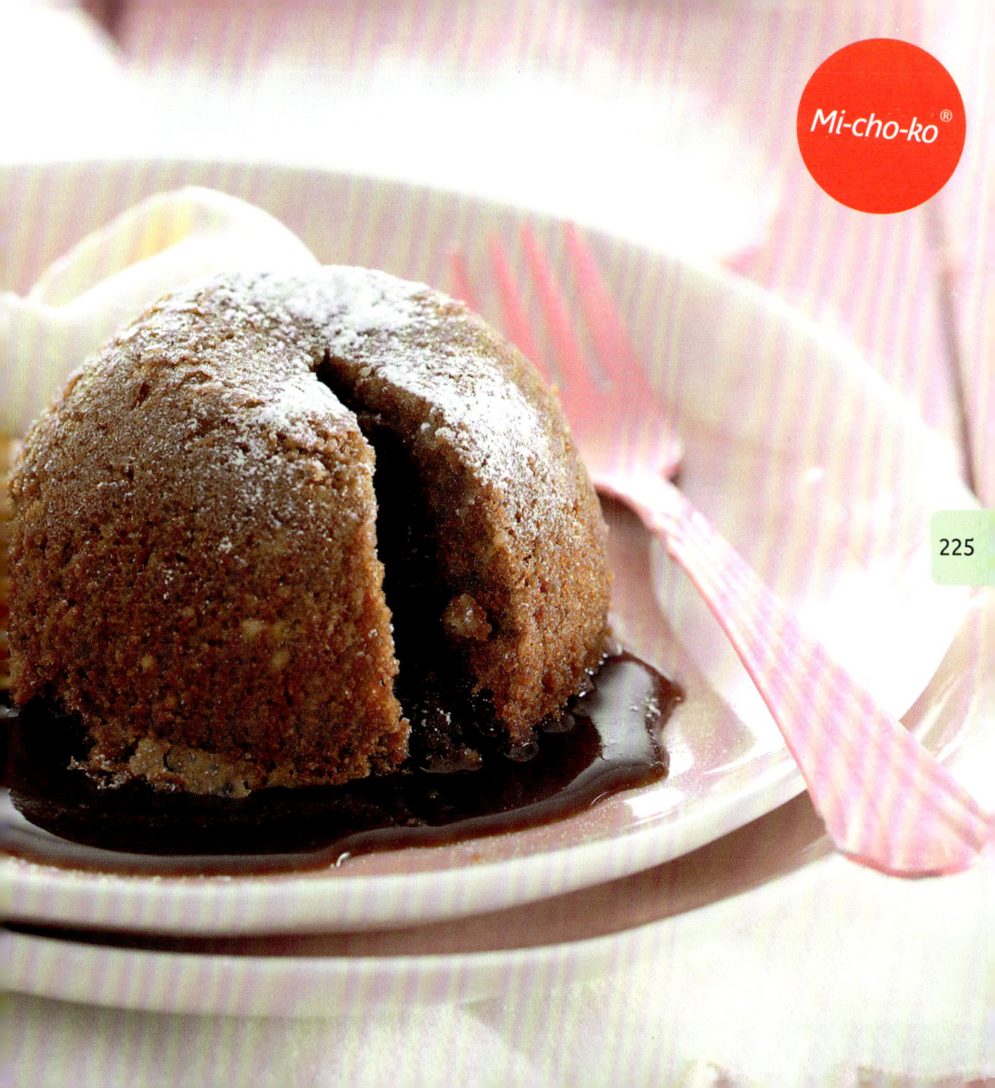
Mi-cho-ko®

FOIE GRAS POÊLÉ AU MI-CHO-KO®

Préparation : 10 min • **Cuisson** : 5 min • **Pour 4 personnes**

4 escalopes épaisses de foie gras d'oie • 6 Mi-cho-ko®
10 cl de fond de volaille • 4 c. à s. de vinaigre de xérès
4 c. à s. de Grand Marnier • fleur de sel

- Réservez les escalopes de foie gras au congélateur pendant 15 min.
- Pendant ce temps, préparez la sauce. Faites fondre les Mi-cho-ko® dans le fond de volaille, puis ajoutez le vinaigre et le Grand Marnier.
- Faites chauffer une poêle à revêtement antiadhésif, sans matière grasse, puis faites-y cuire les escalopes de foie gras à feu vif, de 30 s à 1 min sur chaque face.
- Retirez-les de la poêle et égouttez-les sur du papier absorbant. Saupoudrez de fleur de sel. Réservez au chaud.
- Retirez la graisse de la poêle et déglacez avec la sauce aux Mi-cho-ko®. Grattez les sucs, puis laissez réduire, jusqu'à ce que la sauce épaississe. Rectifiez l'assaisonnement.
- Dressez les escalopes de foie gras dans des assiettes. Arrosez d'un filet de sauce et servez sans attendre.

Foie gras aux Mi-cho-ko® et au vin rouge
Remplacez le vinaigre et le Grand Marnier par 8 c. à s. de vin rouge.

Foie gras aux Mi-cho-ko® au piment d'Espelette
Saupoudrez les escalopes poêlées de piment d'Espelette après les avoir égouttées.

Foie de veau aux Mi-cho-ko®
Remplacez le foie gras par du foie de veau, que vous ferez cuire de 3 à 4 min sur chaque face avec un filet d'huile de tournesol.

Escalopes de poulet aux Mi-cho-ko®
Pour une version moins festive, remplacez les escalopes de foie gras par des escalopes de poulet, que vous ferez cuire à la poêle pendant 5 min sur chaque face avec un filet d'huile de tournesol.

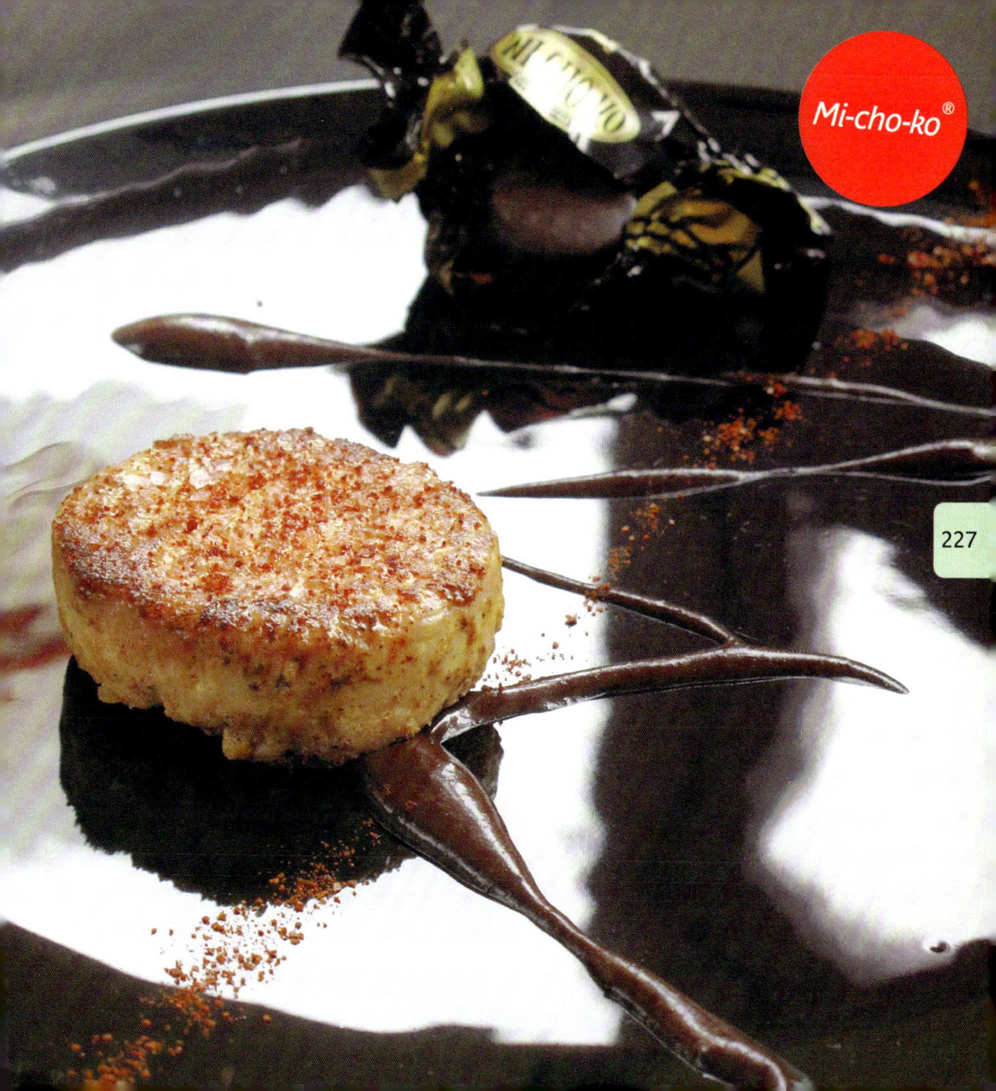

Mi-cho-ko®

MI-CUIT AUX MI-CHO-KO®

Préparation : 10 min • **Cuisson :** 25 min • **Pour 6 personnes**

200 g de chocolat noir à pâtisserie • 50 g de beurre demi-sel
3 œufs • 120 g de sucre en poudre • 80 g de farine • 6 Mi-cho-ko® noirs

- Préchauffez le four à 180 °C.
- Cassez le chocolat en morceaux. Mettez-les dans une jatte supportant la chaleur avec le beurre, et faites-les fondre au bain-marie, en remuant régulièrement. Versez dans un saladier et laissez tiédir.
- Cassez les œufs et mettez-les dans une autre jatte avec le sucre. Battez au fouet jusqu'à ce que le mélange soit clair et mousseux.
- Versez cette préparation dans le saladier et fouettez bien.
- Ajoutez la farine et mélangez.
- Répartissez la préparation dans des petits moules à revêtement antiadhésif. Plantez 1 Mi-cho-ko® dans chaque moule en l'enfonçant légèrement.
- Faites cuire au four de 15 à 20 min.
- Dégustez chaud ou tiède.

Mi-cuit aux Mi-cho-ko® sans beurre
Remplacez le beurre par 50 g de purée d'amandes. Vous pouvez aussi utiliser du fromage blanc ou de la compote de pommes.

Mi-cuit aux Mi-cho-ko® sans gluten
Remplacez la farine par de la farine de riz.

Mi-cuit aux Mi-cho-ko® et à la fève tonka
Remplacez le chocolat noir par du chocolat blanc, et ajoutez-y 1 fève tonka râpée.

Chantilly au chocolat blanc
Faites fondre 200 g de chocolat blanc à pâtisserie coupé en morceaux avec 40 cl de crème fleurette. Laissez refroidir au réfrigérateur pendant 3 h, puis montez en chantilly au fouet électrique. Servez avec les mi-cuits.

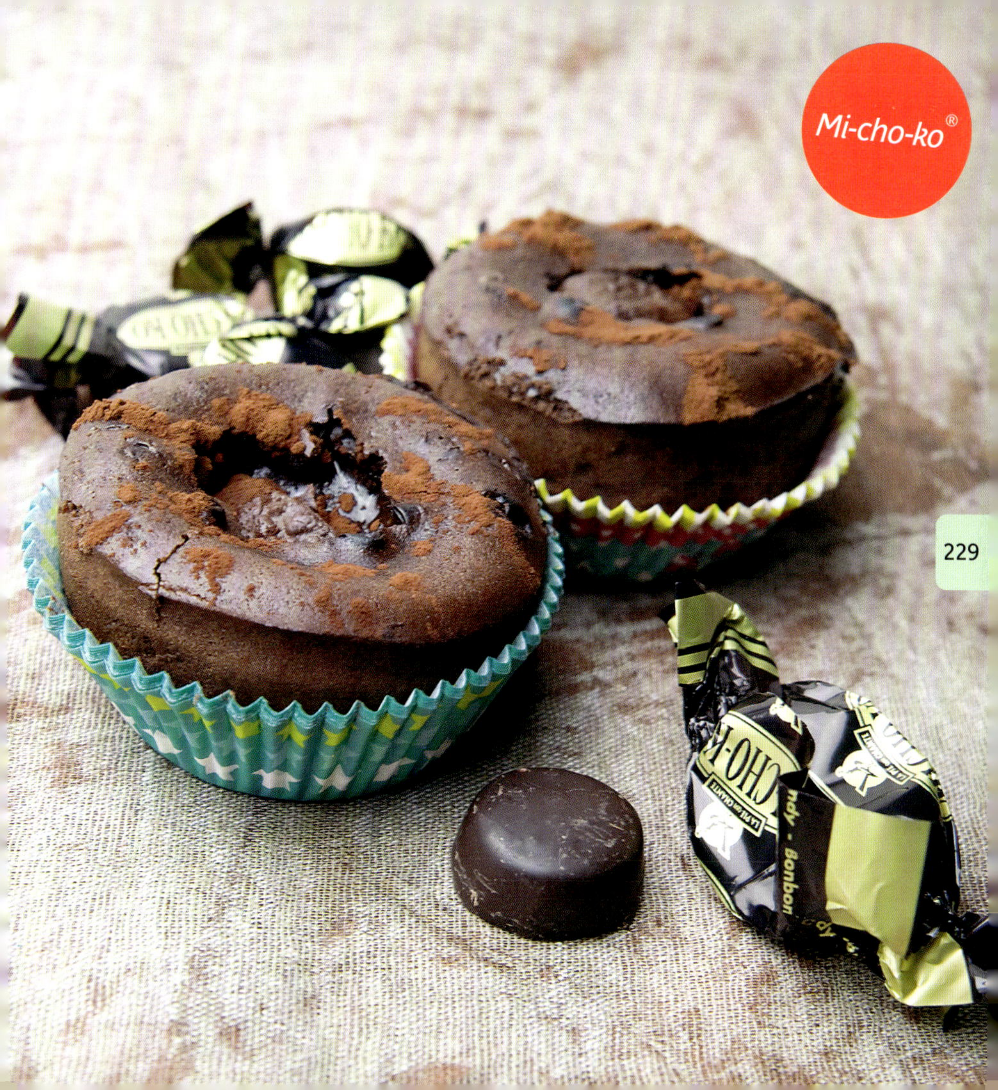

Mi-cho-ko®

PETITS MOELLEUX AUX MI-CHO-KO®

Préparation : 10 min • **Cuisson :** 17 min • **Pour 10 moelleux**

100 g de beurre • 2 œufs • 80 g de sucre en poudre • 100 g de farine 1/2 sachet de levure chimique • 15 Mi-cho-ko® au chocolat au lait 10 cl de crème liquide • 1 c. à c. de rhum • sel

- Coupez le beurre en parcelles, puis faites-le fondre dans une petite casserole.
- Mettez les œufs, le sucre et 1 pincée de sel dans un saladier, et battez au fouet jusqu'à ce que le mélange soit mousseux.
- Ajoutez la farine, la levure et le beurre fondu, puis mélangez.
- Préchauffez le four à 180 °C.
- Mettez les Mi-cho-ko® dans une casserole avec la crème liquide, et faites-les fondre à feux doux, en remuant régulièrement.
- Divisez la pâte en deux parties et ajoutez les Mi-cho-ko® fondus à l'une, le rhum à l'autre.
- Répartissez les deux pâtes dans 10 ramequins, en alternant les couches de l'une et de l'autre.
- Faites cuire au four pendant 15 min.
- Servez tiède.

Moelleux aux Mi-cho-ko® et au thé matcha

Remplacez le rhum par 2 c. à c. de thé vert matcha en poudre.

Moelleux aux Mi-cho-ko® et au pandan

Remplacez le rhum par 1 c. à c. d'extrait de pandan.

Moelleux aux Mi-cho-ko® et aux fraises séchées

Remplacez le rhum par 50 g de fraises séchées mixées. Ajoutez, éventuellement, 1 c. à s. de sirop de fraise.

Glaçage au gingembre

Mélangez le jus de 1 citron, 20 g de sucre en poudre et 2 c. à s. de sirop de gingembre. Nappez les moelleux de ce glaçage dès la sortie du four.

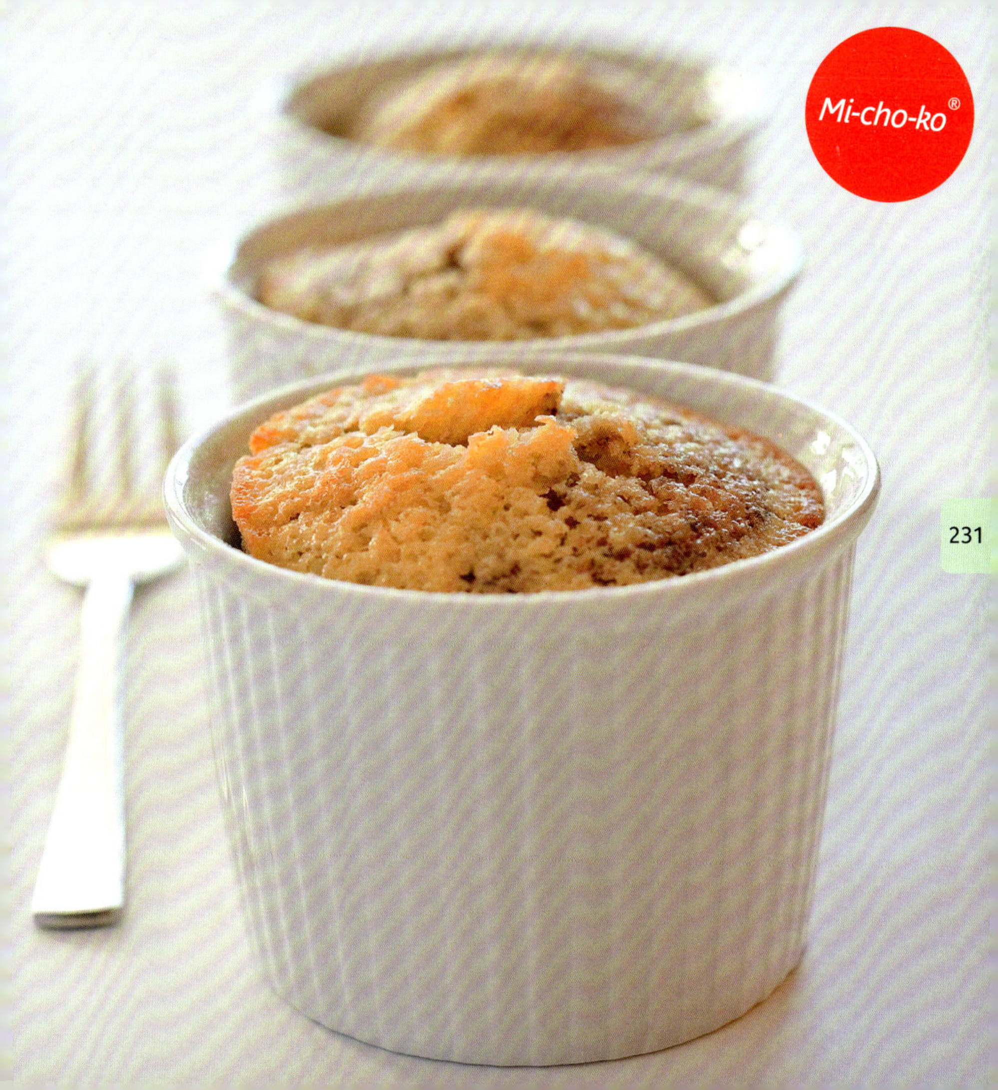
Mi-cho-ko®

Whoopie pies au piment d'Espelette
Ajoutez 1 pincée de piment d'Espelette à la pâte à biscuits.

Whoopie pies au nougat
Pour les biscuits, remplacez le cacao par 1/2 c. à c. d'arôme de nougat (en épicerie fine).

Whoopie pies à la patate douce
Préparez la pâte à biscuits en mélangeant 250 g de purée de patates douces, 160 g de farine, 60 g de sucre, 1/2 sachet de levure, 1 œuf battu et 80 g de beurre fondu.

Whoopie pies aux graines de nigelle
Ajoutez 1 c. à s. de graines de nigelle à la pâte à biscuits.

WHOOPIE PIES AUX MI-CHO-KO®

Préparation : 20 min • **Cuisson :** 15 min • **Réfrigération :** 15 min
Pour 25 whoopie pies

pour la garniture : *20 Mi-cho-ko® noirs • 5 cl de lait • 25 g de beurre*
pour les biscuits : *110 g de beurre ramolli • 120 g de sucre en poudre 10 g de cacao amer • 200 g de farine • 1 c. à c. de levure chimique 1 œuf • 50 g de chocolat noir à pâtisserie • 90 g de crème liquide*

- Préchauffez le four à 180 °C.
- Préparez la garniture : faites fondre les Mi-cho-ko® avec le lait dans une petite casserole. Hors du feu, incorporez le beurre et mélangez bien. Laissez refroidir complètement, puis réservez au réfrigérateur le temps de préparer les biscuits.
- Pour les biscuits, travaillez le beurre mou avec le sucre et le cacao. Ajoutez ensuite la farine, la levure et l'œuf. Mélangez bien.
- Cassez le chocolat en morceaux, puis faites-les fondre au bain-marie avec la crème liquide. Incorporez le mélange à la pâte.
- À l'aide d'une poche à douille, formez de petits disques de pâte de 3 cm de diamètre sur une plaque à pâtisserie tapissée de papier sulfurisé, en les espaçant légèrement.
- Faites cuire au four pendant 10 min environ. Laissez ensuite entièrement refroidir.
- Garnissez la moitié des whoopies de crème aux Mi-cho-ko® et refermez avec un deuxième petit gâteau.

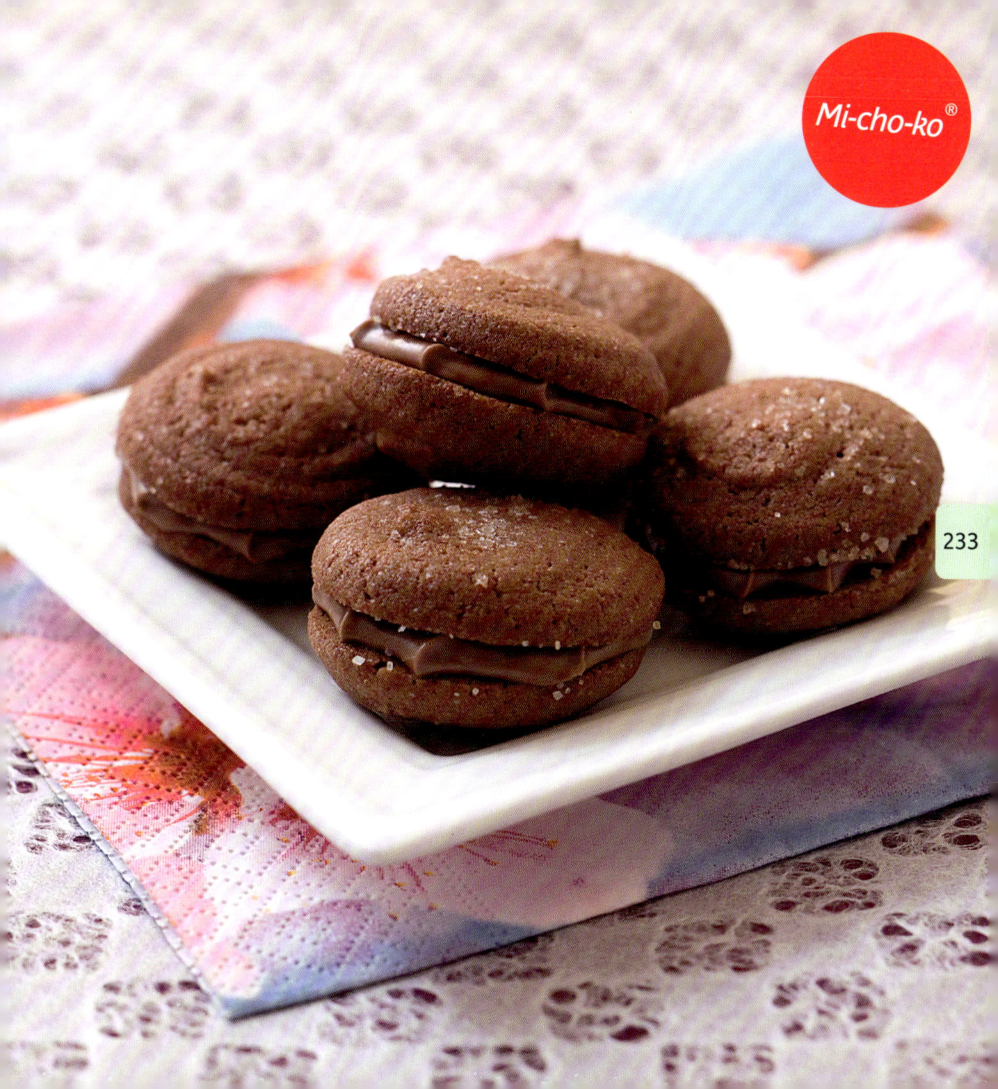
Mi-cho-ko®

POIRES BELLE-HÉLÈNE EN CROÛTE AUX MIKADO®

Préparation : 15 min • **Cuisson** : 50 min • **Pour 4 personnes**

*150 g de sucre en poudre • 1 étoile de badiane • 1 gousse de vanille
4 poires • le jus de 1/2 citron • 120 g de Mikado® + quelques-uns
pour la décoration • 80 g de beurre demi-sel • 40 g de farine
100 g de chocolat à pâtisserie • 15 cl de crème liquide*

- Portez à ébullition 50 cl d'eau avec le sucre en poudre, l'étoile de badiane, les graines grattées de la gousse de vanille ainsi que la gousse. Laissez frémir pendant 15 min.

- Pelez les poires, coupez-les en deux et retirez la partie dure au centre. Arrosez-les de jus de citron. Plongez-les dans le sirop et laissez cuire à feu doux pendant 20 min environ. Lorsque les poires sont tendres, laissez refroidir dans le jus.

- Préchauffez le four à 180 °C.

- Mixez grossièrement les Mikado®. Ajoutez le beurre coupé en morceaux et la farine, puis mixez de nouveau, rapidement : le mélange doit former des miettes. Disposez les poires côté creusé vers le haut dans un plat à four. Recouvrez-les du mélange aux Mikado®.

- Faites cuire au four pendant 15 min.

- Pendant ce temps, coupez le chocolat en morceaux et faites-le fondre au bain-marie avec la crème liquide.

- Dressez les poires dans des assiettes à dessert, et nappez de chocolat fondu. Servez sans attendre.

Pêches gratinées aux Mikado®

Remplacez les poires pochées par des pêches au sirop ou des pêches fraîches coupées en deux et dénoyautées.

Poires aux Mikado® et au sirop d'érable

Remplacez le chocolat fondu par du sirop d'érable tiède. Vous pouvez aussi utiliser du caramel au beurre salé.

Glace au miel

Fouettez 4 jaunes d'œufs avec 50 g de sucre. Ajoutez 40 cl de lait bouillant, puis faites chauffer à feu doux en remuant jusqu'à ce que le mélange épaississe. Ajoutez 60 g de miel, remuez, puis laissez refroidir. Incorporez 20 cl de crème fraîche au fouet. Faites turbiner en sorbetière. Servez avec les poires aux Mikado®.

Glace au miel et aux Mikado®

Reprenez la recette ci-dessus en ajoutant 100 g de Mikado® grossièrement broyés à la préparation.

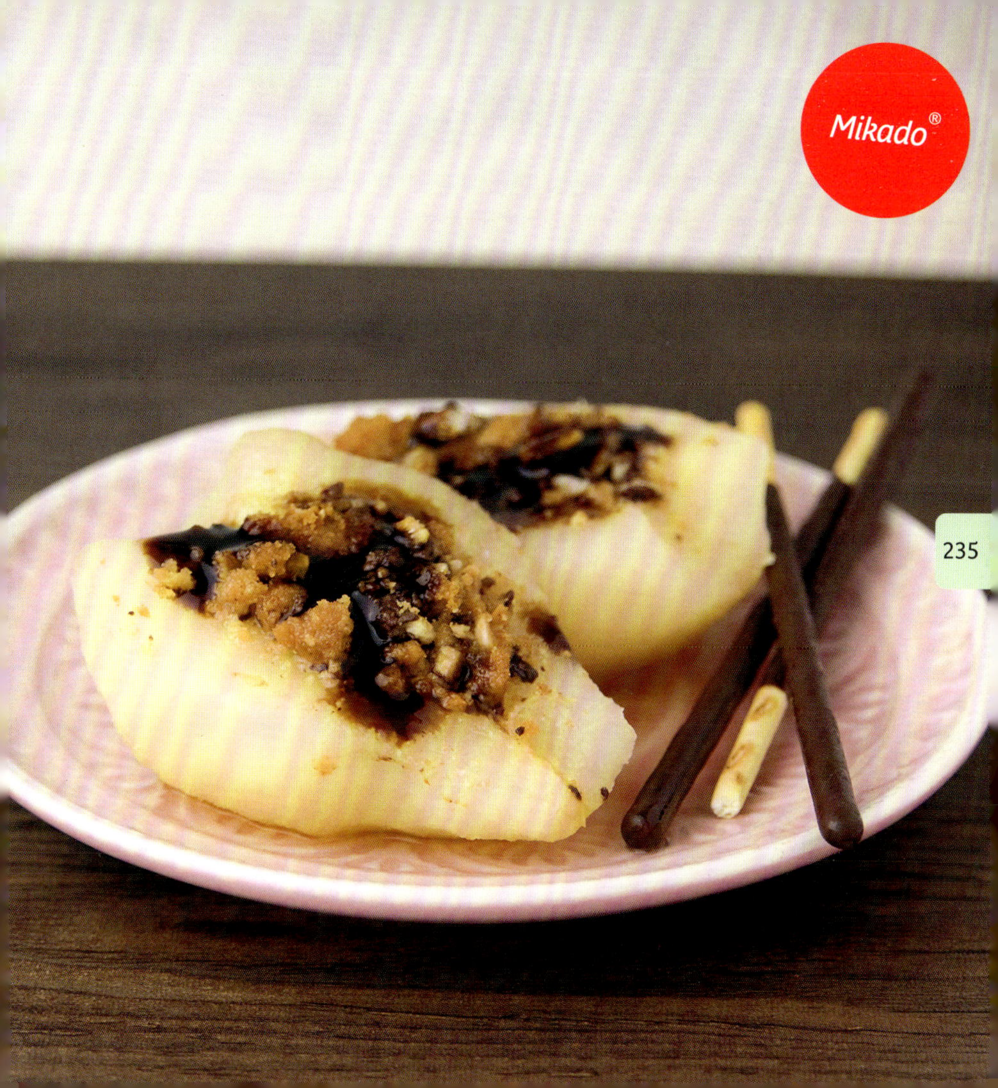
Mikado®

SUCETTES AU PRALINÉ

Préparation : 20 min • **Cuisson** : 5 min • **Réfrigération** : 3 h
Pour 40 sucettes

200 g de praliné • 150 g de chocolat noir à pâtisserie
20 cl de crème liquide • 55 Mikado® • sucre pétillant

- Cassez le praliné et le chocolat en morceaux, et mettez-les dans un saladier.
- Versez la crème liquide dans une casserole et portez à ébullition. Versez la crème sur les morceaux de chocolat et remuez à l'aide d'une cuillère en bois jusqu'à l'obtention d'une ganache homogène.
- Broyez grossièrement 15 Mikado® et ajoutez-les au mélange. Remuez bien. Réservez la préparation au frais pendant 3 h.
- Sortez la ganache du réfrigérateur 20 min avant de préparer les sucettes.
- Versez du sucre pétillant dans une assiette creuse.
- Prélevez 1 c. à c. de préparation et formez une boule. Roulez-la dans le sucre pétillant, puis posez-la sur une plaque à pâtisserie recouverte de papier sulfurisé.
- Piquez un Mikado® dans la boule.
- Renouvelez l'opération jusqu'à épuisement des ingrédients.
- Conservez les sucettes au réfrigérateur jusqu'au moment de déguster.

Sucettes au praliné à l'orange
Ajoutez 2 c. à s. de liqueur d'orange à la ganache.

Sucettes au praliné et aux raisins
Supprimez 75 g de praliné et ajoutez 100 g de grains de raisin blanc taillés en quatre à la ganache.

Sucettes au chocolat blanc
Remplacez le praliné et le chocolat noir par 350 g de chocolat blanc. Faites infuser 1 gousse de vanille et ses graines dans la crème liquide, avant de l'ajouter.

Sucettes à la noix de coco
Mélangez 250 g de noix de coco râpée, le contenu de 1 boîte de lait concentré sucré et les 15 Mikado® broyés. Formez des boulettes de pâte et posez-les sur une plaque. Laissez prendre au frais.